15th Conference of the Association for Machine Translation in the Americas (AMTA 2022)

Volume 2: MT Users & Providers Track and Government Track

Orlando, Florida, USA
12 – 16 September 2022

Editors:

Stephen Larocca
Janice Campbell
Jay Marciano
Stephen Richardson
Konstantin Savenkov
Alex Yanishevsky

ISBN: 978-1-7138-6758-6

Printed from e-media with permission by:

Curran Associates, Inc.
57 Morehouse Lane
Red Hook, NY 12571

Some format issues inherent in the e-media version may also appear in this print version.

Printed with permission by Curran Associates, Inc. (2023)

For permission requests, please contact the Association for Computational Linguistics at the address below.

Association for Computational Linguistics
209 N. Eighth Street
Stroudsburg, Pennsylvania 18360

Phone: 1-570-476-8006
Fax: 1-570-476-0860

acl@aclweb.org

Additional copies of this publication are available from:

Curran Associates, Inc.
57 Morehouse Lane
Red Hook, NY 12571 USA
Phone: 845-758-0400
Fax: 845-758-2633
Email: curran@proceedings.com
Web: www.proceedings.com

AMTA ORLANDO 2022

The 15th Conference of the Association for Machine Translation in the Americas

2022.amtaweb.org

PROCEEDINGS

Volume 2: MT Users & Providers Track and Government Track

Editors

Government Track Chair
Stephen Larocca

Users & Providers Track Co-chairs
Janice Campbell, Jay Marciano,
Konstantin Savenkov and
Alex Yanishevsky

General Conference Chair
Stephen Richardson

Welcome to the 15th biennial conference of the Association for Machine Translation in the Americas – AMTA 2022!

Dear MT Colleagues and Friends,

For this year's conference of the Association for Machine Translation in the Americas – AMTA 2022 – we are finally able to come together in person at the venue we had intended to enjoy two years ago, the spectacular Sheraton Orlando Lake Buena Vista Resort in Orlando, Florida! We are very grateful that the COVID pandemic is now sufficiently controlled (albeit still with us) that we can once again meet, network, and enjoy one another's company while expanding our knowledge of the ever-accelerating field of machine translation. At the same time, we will be joined by likely more than twice the number of remote attendees, as the last two years of virtual conferences and ongoing health concerns will forever more require us to adopt a hybrid conference format. While this format certainly creates complexity for organizers, and it can feel a little less personal as we interact with remote speakers and attendees, it nevertheless provides significantly greater accessibility and opportunities to learn from colleagues around the globe. We are grateful for their very positive contributions to our conference!

Since the MT Summit we hosted last year, we have continued to witness amazing progress in MT technology and tremendous growth in the adoption of this technology by individual translators, language services providers, small businesses, large enterprises, non-profits, governments, and NGOs. Indeed, a unique aspect of AMTA conferences is that it brings together users and practitioners from across the MT spectrum of academia, industry, and government so that R&D personnel can learn from those who are using the technology and vice versa.

We are pleased once again with the number of submissions to our conference. As MT has become more mainstream than ever, we have had to be more selective in the presentations included in our conference tracks. This is unfortunate on the one hand, but on the other, it demonstrates the growth of our field and the increasing quality and relevance of the work performed by so many people. Of special note this year is the emphasis on speech translation and dubbing, MT quality evaluation, and massively multilingual MT systems. These topics are reflected by the topics of our keynote speakers and panels in the conference schedule, and we trust you will find them most enlightening.

As with all our conferences, AMTA 2022 would simply not have been possible without the selfless work of so many people on the AMTA board and organizing committee, all of whom are volunteers. I express my deepest thanks, respect, and admiration to each one of them. They include:

Patti O'Neill-Brown, AMTA VP, Local Arrangements, Networking
Natalia Levitina, AMTA Secretary, Sponsorships
Jen Doyon, AMTA Treasurer, Local Arrangements
Kevin Duh, Research Track
Paco Guzman, Research Track
Janice Campbell, Users and Providers Track, Networking
Jay Marciano, Users and Providers Track, Workshops and Tutorials
Konstantin Savenkov, Users and Providers Track

Alex Yanishevsky, Users and Providers Track, Conference Online Platform
Steve La Rocca, Government Track
Kenton Murray, Student Mentoring,
Konstantin Dranch, Communications
Lara Daly, Marketing
Alon Lavie, AMTA Consultant
Elaine O'Curran, AMTA Counselor, Publications
Elliott Macklovitch, Publications
Derick Fajardo, Exhibitions

Finally, I express my gratitude to our amazing sponsors, whose tremendous financial support has enabled us to handle the added complexity and cost of the hybrid format. Once again, greatly discounted student registrations have been provided by Microsoft, our Visionary++ sponsor, as well as an included conference banquet for in-person attendees. Systran has also contributed significantly to our online platforms as a Visionary sponsor. Our Leader-level sponsors are Pangeanic, Meta, Acclaro, AppTek, and Intento, and our Patron-level sponsors are AWS, Google, RWS, Star, and Welocalize. Additional exhibitors are ModelFront and Unbabel, and our Media and Marketing sponsors are Slator, Multilingual, and Akorbi. Many of these sponsors and exhibitors will provide demonstrations of their systems and software during our Technology Exhibition sessions, and we hope that all our attendees will take advantage of this great opportunity to see the very latest commercial offerings and advancements in the world of MT.

Again, welcome to AMTA 2022! I look forward to finally being with many of you in person in Orlando and to interacting with many others online.

Steve Richardson
AMTA President and AMTA 2022 General Conference Chair

User/Provider Track: Introduction

The User/Provider Track at AMTA 2022 features twenty-six presentations by and for machine translation experts and practitioners, language service providers, technology service providers, universities, linguists, and commercial enterprises.

We are privileged to have Marco Trombetti, a renowned computer scientist, entrepreneur and investor as well as Co-Founder and CEO of Translated, one of the first companies to utilize AI in translation, as the keynote speaker for the track.

The latest State of Machine Translation report will present MT engine performance results across industries and language pairs and provide additional details about scoring methodologies.

New this year is a presentation on a machine translation non-profit organization whose goals are to provide access to open resources as well as build a community of contributors.

As would be expected in a commercial track, there are presentations which focus on making business cases showing the financial and market benefits of incorporating MT in the translation workflow. Case studies carried out jointly by a technology and/or language service provider and a client, showcase real world use cases.

Recurring themes at this conference continue to be data, engine training, AI applications, low resource languages and PEMT.

Quality of MT output is a matter of concernment in the industry and there are several presentations addressing it from various perspectives. A range of topics are presented, such as monitoring, assessing, predicting quality outcomes and applying risk modeling. Source-based Quality Estimation against TMs is offered as a new approach. Automatic Post Editing is improved by leveraging GPT-3 features. Setting customer quality expectations can be achieved by defining Business Critical Errors. Finally, commonly applied auto scores are compared to the ATA grading framework.

Translating speech is rapidly growing in importance. Presentations on this topic include methods to connect subtitles to the correct speakers; STT/TTS for audio visual translation using neural voices; voice synthesis for e-learning content; and real-time simultaneous interpreting with automatic dubbing and STS translation.

As far as engine training and model fine-tuning, presentation topics focus primarily on data used as input for training. Data augmentation, quality vs quantity, deep learning to achieve better segmentation and alignment, and advanced filtering techniques are discussed. Customizing NMT for limited support language pairs and regional language variants are also discussed. One presentation challenges the sustainability of the engine training process by promoting knowledge distillation to decrease power consumption.

Finally, there are presentations that focus on challenges in very specific domains: MT for video gaming, where in-domain data is quite limited; patent translations which must hold up to intense legal and scientific scrutiny.

We would like to thank the AMTA organizing committee for the intense planning that went into hosting a hybrid conference. We also thank the session and keynote speakers for their excellent presentations. We are especially grateful to the volunteer moderators for supporting the speakers, fielding the questions and keeping the presentations on schedule.

Sincerely,

Janice Campbell, Jay Marciano, Konstantin Savenkov, Alex Yanishevsky

The User/Provider Track Co-Chairs

Government Track: Introduction

The Government Track at AMTA 2022 features eleven presentations. North American government issues in machine translation figure prominently, with the Government of Canada's Translation Bureau and the United States' government efforts sharing eight of the eleven presentations.

Contributions from colleagues overseas are of course most welcome, including those from the Dalian University of Foreign Languages in the People's Republic of China and Singapore's Ministry of Communications and Information. Likewise, SYSTRAN, a multinational corporation with a very long history of providing translation technology to governments, is a welcome contribution to the government track program at AMTA 2022.

The government track is proud to be associated with Dr. Alex Waibel of Carnegie Mellon University and Karlsruhe Institute of Technology who is our Keynote Speaker. Dr. Waibel also anchors the special panel on Advances in Spoken Language MT, an area of translation technology in which Alex's contributions are unmatched and where interest by government entities is on the rise.

Cordially,

Steve LaRocca

Government Track Chair, "standing on the shoulders" of those who precede me

Contents

Users and Providers Track

Government Track

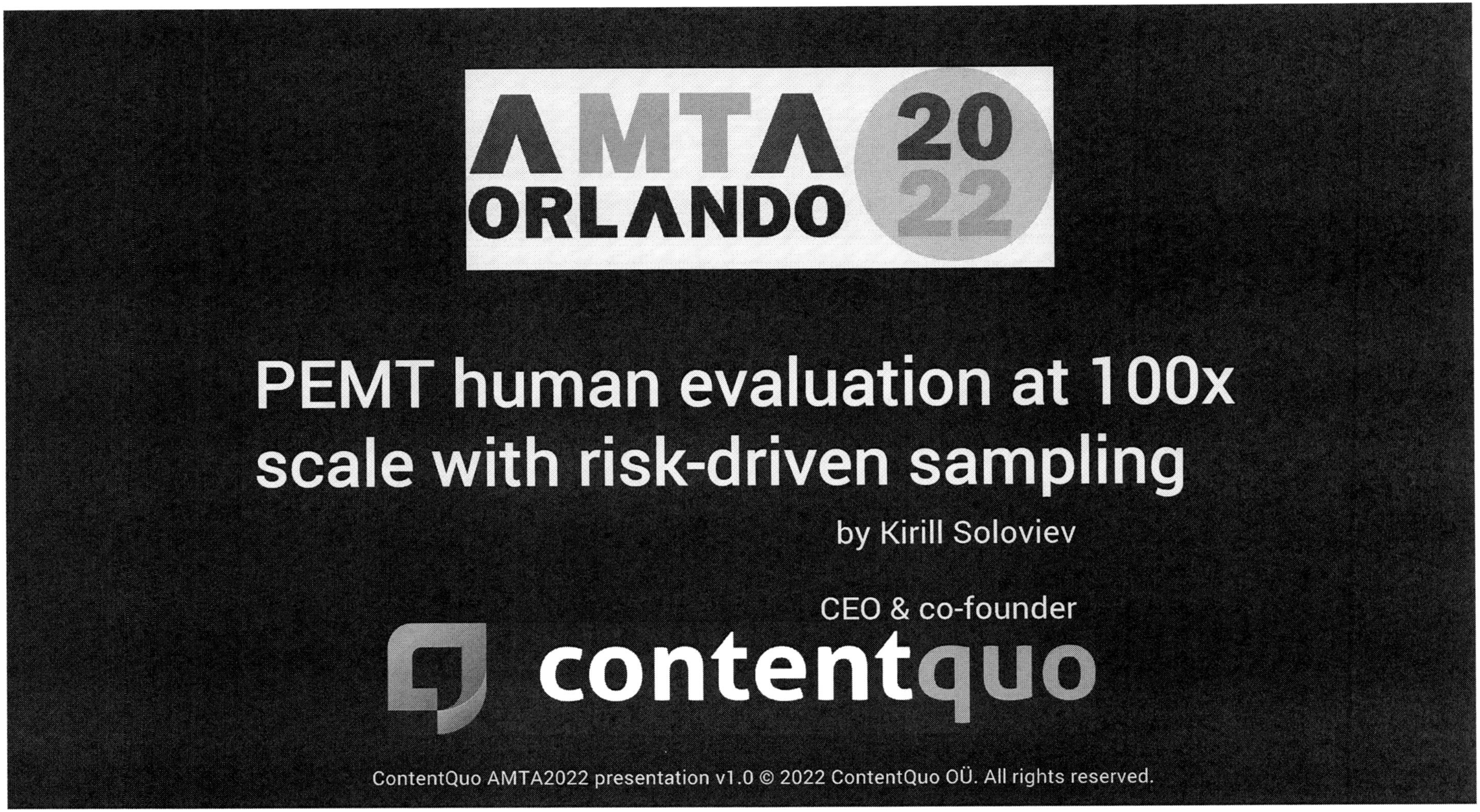
AMTA ORLANDO 2022
PEMT human evaluation at 100x
scale with risk-driven sampling
by Kirill Soloviev
CEO & co-founder
contentquo
ContentQuo AMTA2022 presentation v1.0 © 2022 ContentQuo OÜ. All rights reserved.

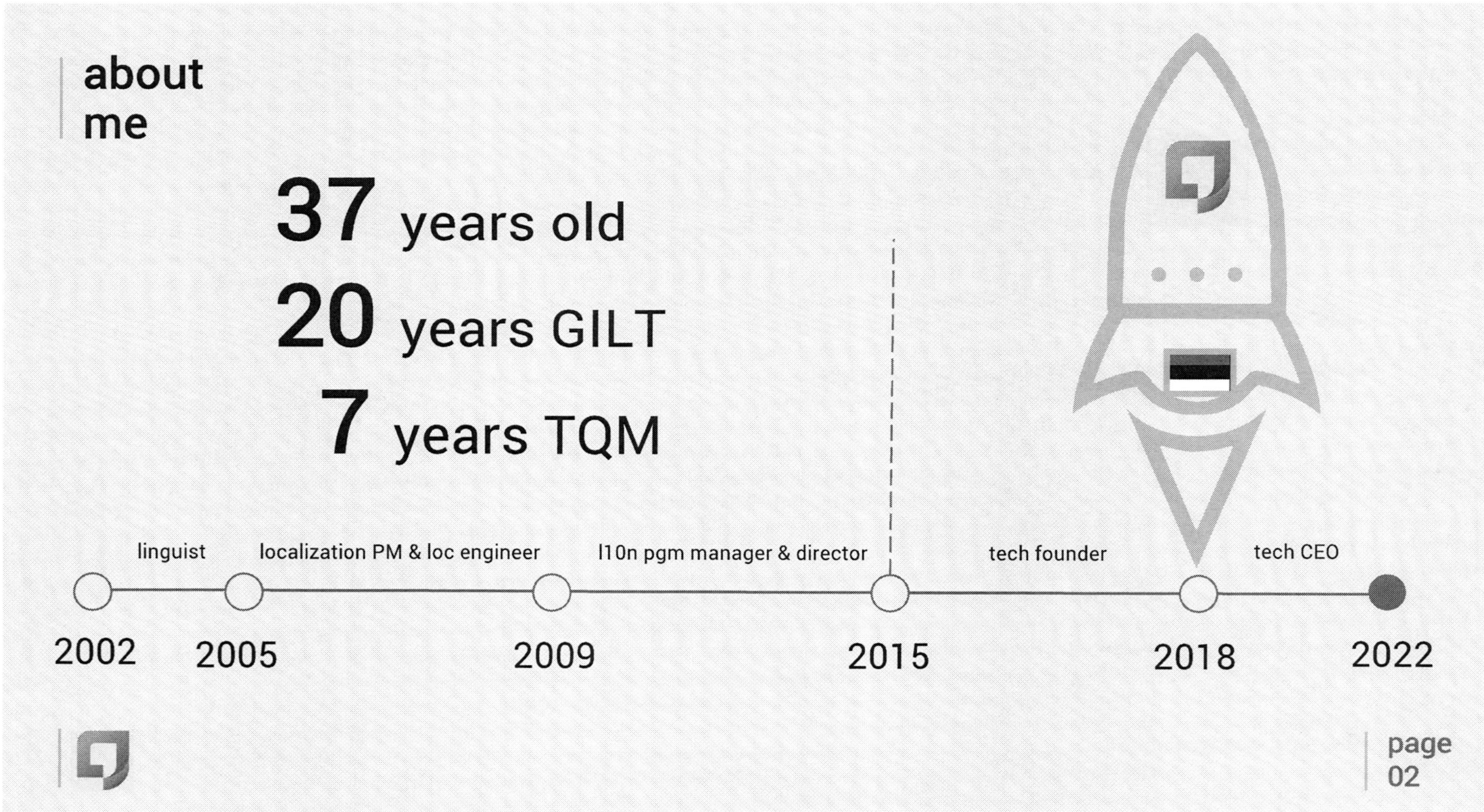
about
me
37 years old
20 years GILT
7 years TQM
linguist
localization PM & loc engineer
l10n pgm manager & director
tech founder
tech CEO
2002
2005
2009
2015
2018
2022
page
02

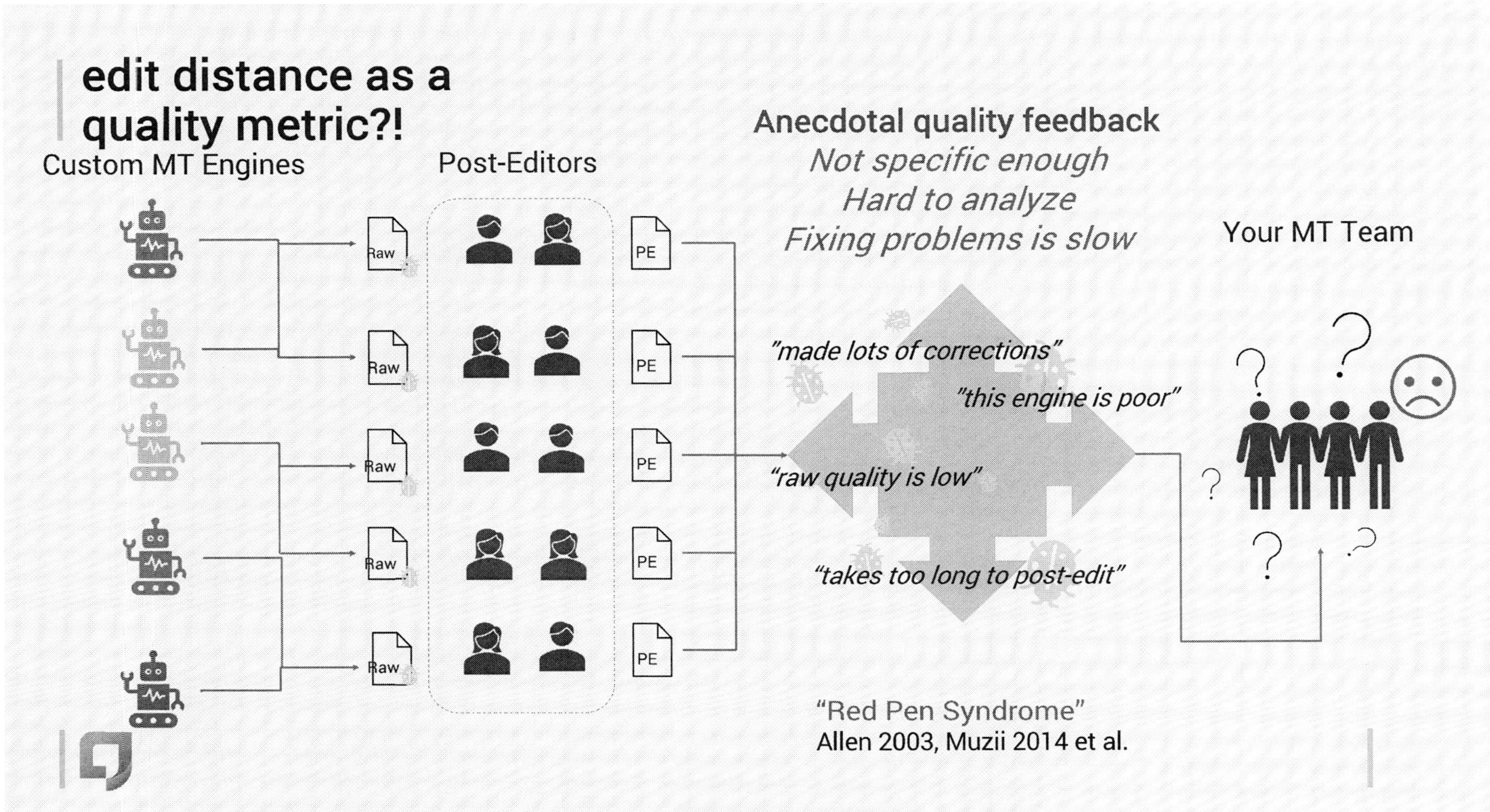
edit distance as a quality metric?!
Custom MT Engines
Post-Editors
Raw
Raw
Raw
Raw
Raw
PE
PE
PE
PE
PE
Anecdotal quality feedback
Not specific enough
Hard to analyze
Fixing problems is slow
"made lots of corrections"
"this engine is poor"
"raw quality is low"
"takes too long to post-edit"
Your MT Team
"Red Pen Syndrome"
Allen 2003, Muzii 2014 et al.

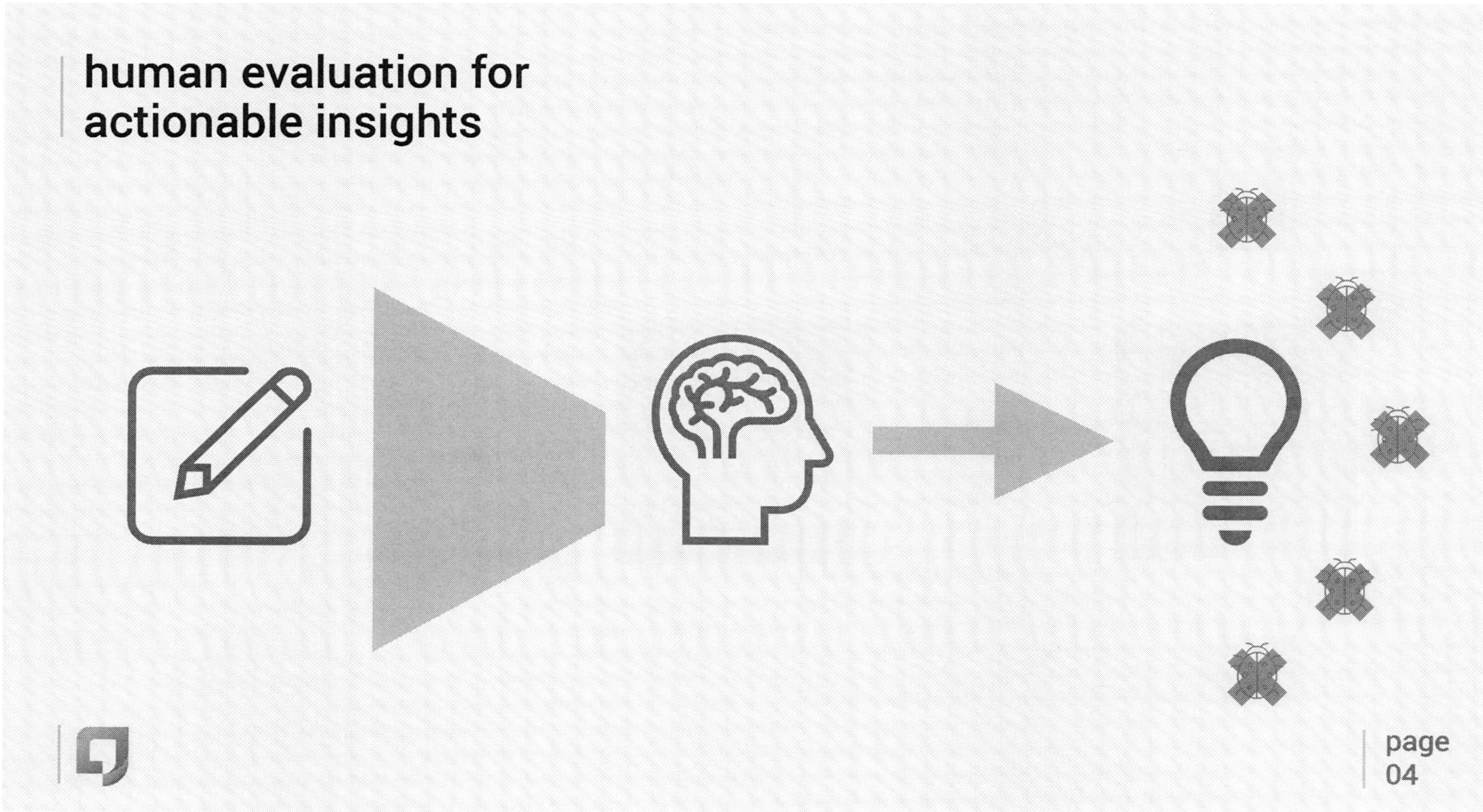
human evaluation for
actionable insights
page
04

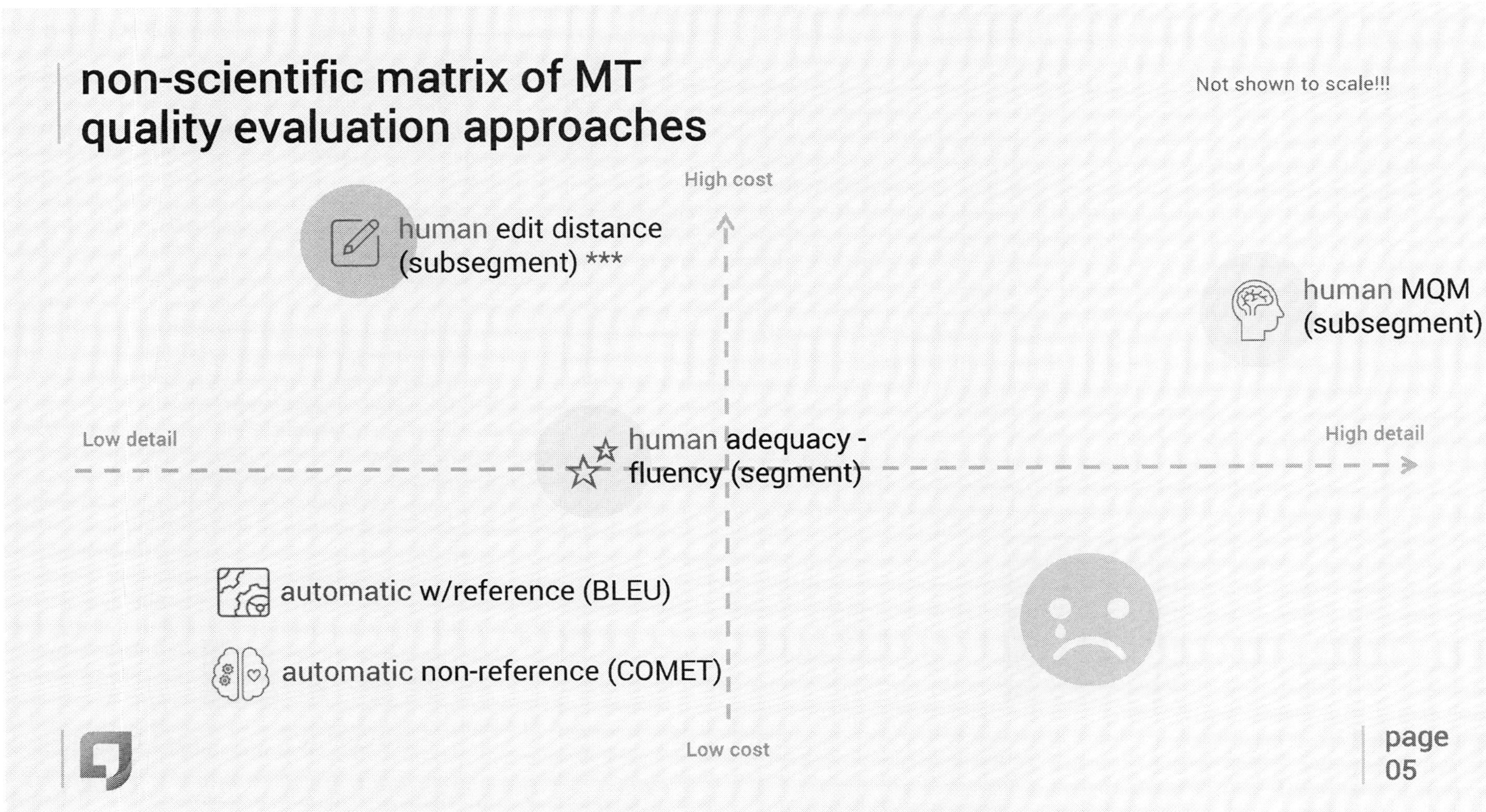
non-scientific matrix of MT
quality evaluation approaches
Not shown to scale!!!
High cost
human edit distance
(subsegment) ***
human MQM
(subsegment)
Low detail
human adequacy -
fluency (segment)
High detail
automatic w/reference (BLEU)
automatic non-reference (COMET)
Low cost
page
05

output of human quality evaluations

		Rating Scale		Error Annotation	
English (en-US)	**Estonian (et-EE)**	**Adequacy**	**Fluency**	**MQM Annotation**	**Edit Distance**
The quick brown fox jumps over the lazy dog	Kiire pruun rebane hüppab üle laisa ~~kaera~~koera	4 out of 4	4 out of 4	Accuracy / Major Spelling / Minor	5%

page 06

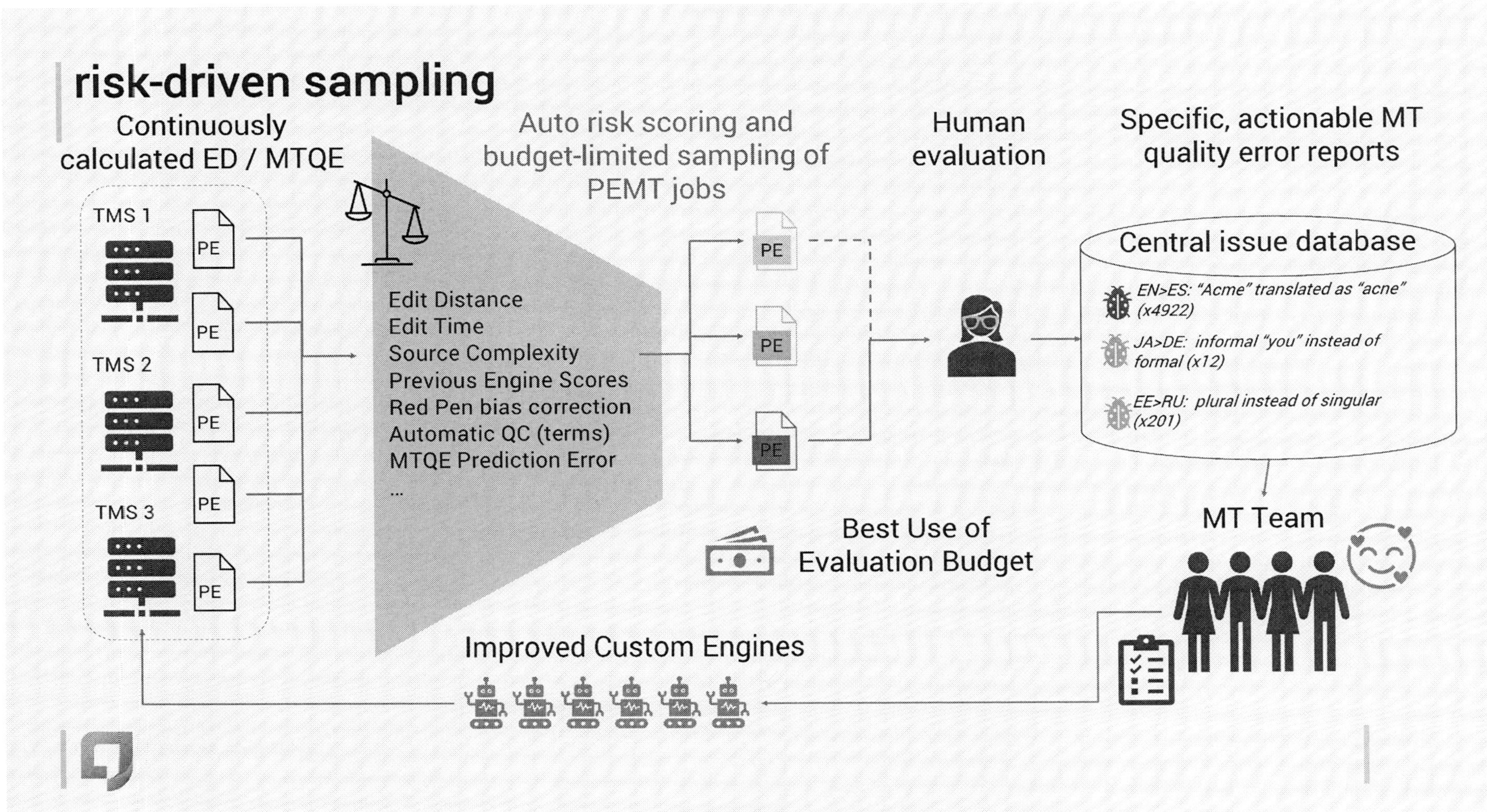
risk-driven sampling
Continuously calculated ED / MTQE
Auto risk scoring and budget-limited sampling of PEMT jobs
Human evaluation
Specific, actionable MT quality error reports
TMS 1
TMS 2
TMS 3
PE
Edit Distance
Edit Time
Source Complexity
Previous Engine Scores
Red Pen bias correction
Automatic QC (terms)
MTQE Prediction Error
...
Central issue database
EN>ES: "Acme" translated as "acne" (x4922)
JA>DE: informal "you" instead of formal (x12)
EE>RU: plural instead of singular (x201)
MT Team
Best Use of Evaluation Budget
Improved Custom Engines

example quality risk rules

PEMT jobs should be more likely to be picked for human quality evaluation when:

- [x4] Average Edit Distance for language X changed >10% over last 1 month
- [x2] Maximum Edit Distance for engine Y hit 60% twice over 10 translators
- [x0.5] Predicted Edit Distance for MTQE model Z differed >30% from ED
- [x1.5] Post-editor M's median Edit Distance is >30% different from average
- etc.

\+ Budget-guided cutoff point

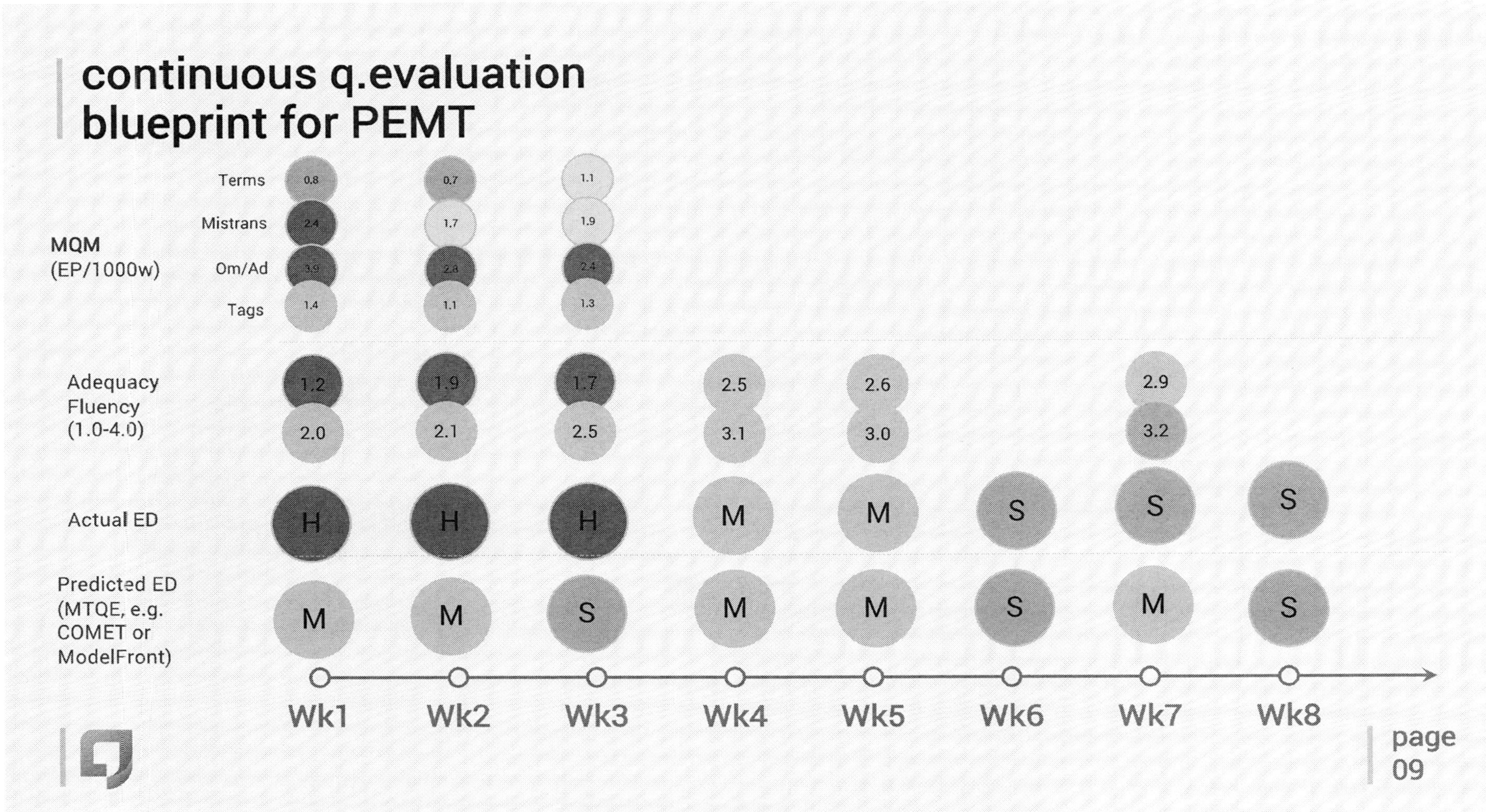
continuous q.evaluation
blueprint for PEMT
MQM
(EP/1000w)
Terms
Mistrans
Om/Ad
Tags
0.8
2.4
3.9
1.4
0.7
1.7
2.8
1.1
1.1
1.9
2.4
1.3
Adequacy
Fluency
(1.0-4.0)
1.2
2.0
1.9
2.1
1.7
2.5
2.5
3.1
2.6
3.0
2.9
3.2
Actual ED
H
H
H
M
M
S
S
S
Predicted ED
(MTQE, e.g.
COMET or
ModelFront)
M
M
S
M
M
S
M
S
Wk1
Wk2
Wk3
Wk4
Wk5
Wk6
Wk7
Wk8
page
09

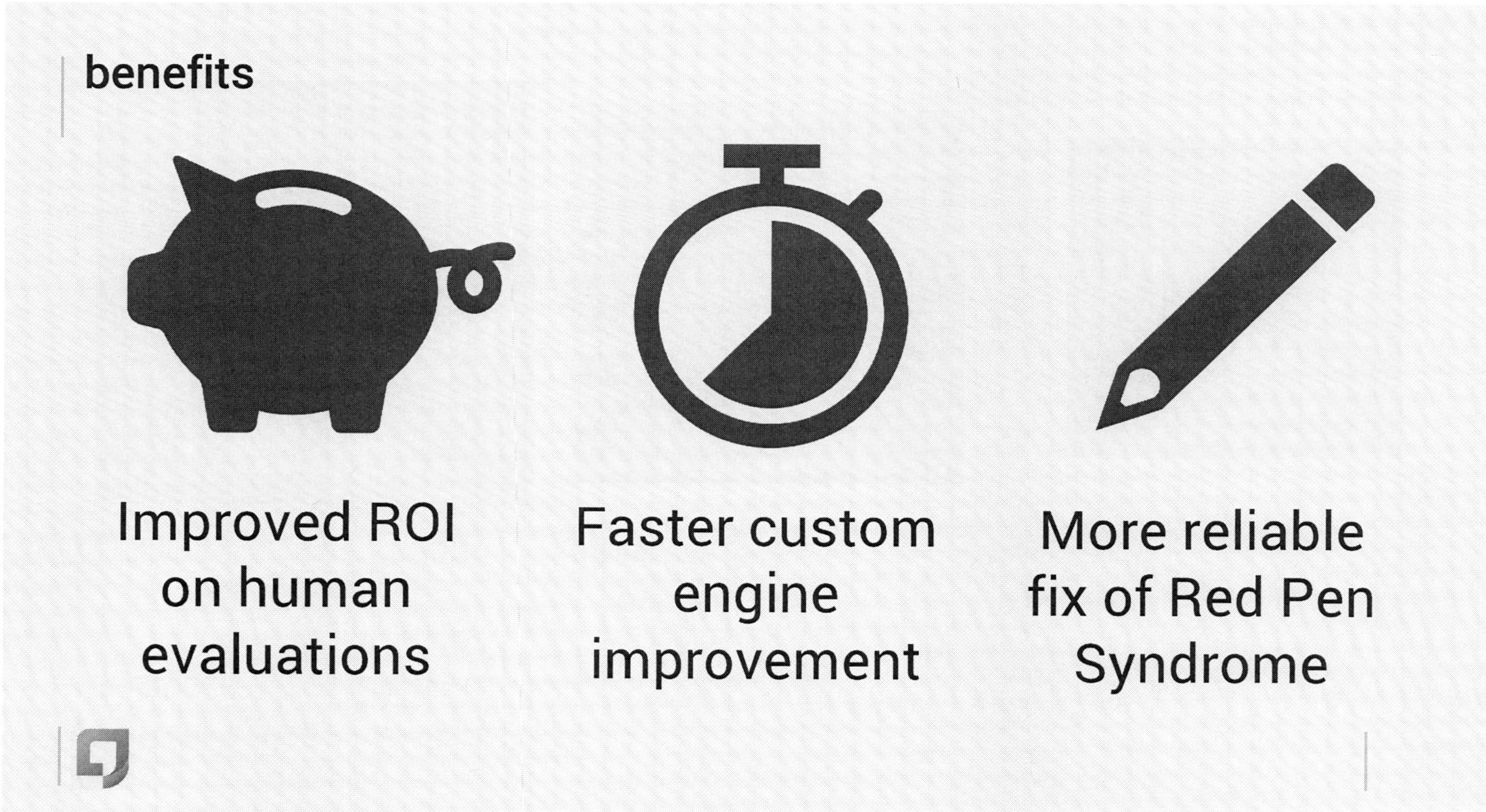
benefits
Improved ROI on human evaluations
Faster custom engine improvement
More reliable fix of Red Pen Syndrome

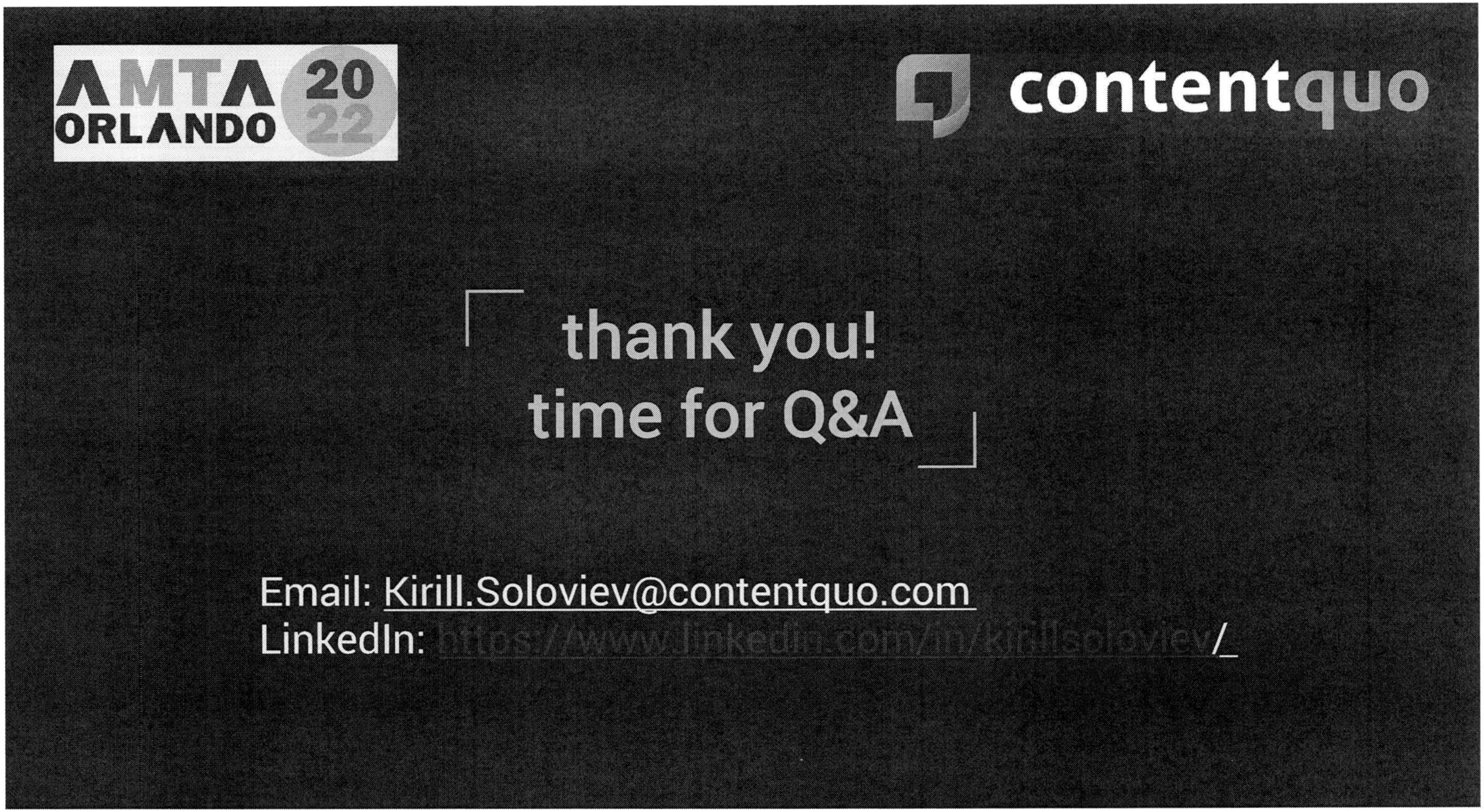
AMTA ORLANDO 2022
contentquo
thank you!
time for Q&A
Email: Kirill.Soloviev@contentquo.com
LinkedIn: https://www.linkedin.com/in/kirillsoloviev/

Picking Out the Best MT Model: On the Methodology of Human Evaluation

Stepan Korotaev s.korotaev@effectiff.com
CTO, Effectiff LLC., Walnut Creek, 94596, USA

Andrey Ryabchikov a.ryabchikov@effectiff.com
Lead NLP Specialist, Effectiff LLC., Lauderdale by the Sea, 33308, USA

Abstract

Human evaluation remains a critical step in selecting the best MT model for a job. The common approach is to have a reviewer analyze a number of segments translated by the compared models, assigning those segments categories and also post-editing some of them when needed. In other words, a reviewer is asked to make numerous decisions regarding very similar, out-of-context translations. It can easily result in arbitrary choices. We propose a new methodology centered around real-life post-editing of a set of cohesive translated texts coming from *homogeneous* source documents. The homogeneity is established using a number of metrics on a preselected corpus. The key assumption is that two or more identical in length translated texts coming from different but homogeneous source documents should take approximately the same *effort* when edited by the same editor. Hence, if one text requires more effort, it is an indication of a relatively lower quality of machine translation used for this text. We proceed to show how this new methodology can be applied in practice and share results of an experiment carried out for the English > Russian language combination. We also discuss other possible applications of the methodology and directions of future research.

1. Introduction

Today, machine translation (MT) is available in a multitude of forms and shapes. The market is saturated, with dozens of providers competing for the supremacy in different language combinations and domains (Intento, 2021). From a practical standpoint, it means any party faced with a task of applying MT in their processes needs to select the best option among the available alternatives. There are two main tools for that:

- automatic metrics;
- human evaluation.

Metrics (like BLEU, hLEPOR, BERTScore, etc.), which are normally used for primary selection and narrowing down options, are beyond the scope of this paper. We will focus on the next step, human evaluation. It normally takes place after several models are picked out based on their higher automatic metric scores. Then, as part of the common methodology, a human reviewer is asked to review and, in some cases, post-edit a number of automatically sampled segments translated by different engines. The results of such evaluation are used to determine a winner. We present our critique of this approach in the next subsection.

1.1. Critique of the Common Methodology of Human Evaluation

The methodology outlined in this subsection is widely used in the translation industry, with slight modifications (incl. in Intento, 2021).

Each reviewer is asked to perform two kinds of work: to evaluate a number of segments by assigning them *categories* (like types of errors found in those segments) and to *post-edit* a different set of segments, which allows to calculate a distance (i.e., represent an amount of changes made as a number). We will call these two types of work *categorizing* and *post-editing*, respectively. A reviewer, consequently, must be both a *categorizer* and a *post-editor*. Typically, a reviewer will have to deal with the output of several engines that they will need to categorize and post-edit. For extra reliability, larger studies usually seek to engage several reviewers working in parallel with the same task, and then average the results. There are several problems, however, that hinder this process and, consequently, the trustworthiness of the human evaluation step as a whole.

Qualification requirements: Not every translator or editor can be a categorizer. It is a separate qualification requiring a certain personal disposition and a number of skills that are not very easy to come by.

Long preparation and training: Even if a researcher has enough categorizers at their disposal, they still need to be trained to make sure they understand the instructions, which can be quite extensive and complex. A researcher will also have to spend time on creating instructions or adapting them given the exact nature of the experiment.

Loss of focus during the post-editing stage: For the post-editing stage of the evaluation, reviewers are asked to post-edit various translated versions of the same source segment provided by all engines in the running. Then an amount of changes in each post-edited translation is calculated, which allows to rank engines by how much work each of them required. A reviewer's task is worded along the following lines: *amend each and every translation* to a state that you would call satisfactory but *don't try to replicate changes*—each translation should be *changed individually* based on its unique structure and possible shortcomings, *without taking into account changes made to other versions*. The problems caused by this approach and its expectations are obvious. Machine outputs can be quite similar, and it is almost impossible to 1) post-edit all of them as if each of them was unique—the *fatigue bias* on the part of a reviewer, and 2) change them all to a more or less equivalent degree—again, the fatigue bias caused by the repetitive process. As a result, different post-edited versions might end up being either very similar (i.e., changed based on a once found formula) or, conversely, amended inconsistently (some subjected to a deeper editing process, others left half-baked).

Lack of context during the post-editing stage: Not only are reviewers asked to work with several similar translations, those translations are usually also out-of-context and presented as a series of standalone sentences. It further hinders meaningful post-editing and contributes to the arbitrariness of the process.

Summing it up, the common methodology as outlined above requires too much time for preparation and training and might yield unreliable results due to a very likely fatigue bias on the part of reviewers.

1.2. Alternative Methodology of Human Evaluation

To overcome the limitations outlined in the previous subsection, we came up with a different approach based on the following concepts:

- No categorization: the methodology *only relies on the results of post-editing.*

- Instead of a set of out-of-context translations of the same source text, each reviewer *works with the cohesive, non-repetitive document* where the output of different engines is combined with human translation for benchmarking.
- Translation quality can be represented as an amount of *effort* required to edit a text to a desired state—hence we measure each editor's productivity across several metrics (*time spent, edit distance, percentage of segments changed*) and use these metrics to rank engines. The lesser the effort spent on an engine output, the higher the quality is deemed to be.
- No special requirements to the post-editors: they must be qualified enough to be able to work with a translated text; however, their style of editing and level of domain expertise are mostly unimportant as we are only interested in the *relative* effort—how much work is spent on each part of a text as compared to other parts. We are looking for a consistent correlation and pay little attention to the actual changes made to a text.

Below, we will describe the methodology in greater detail, present the results of its practical application, and discuss some of the interesting topics for future research.

2. Methodology

2.1. Key Assumptions and Process

The methodology is based on several key assumptions:

- Asking a reviewer to post-edit a cohesive, non-repetitive translation should produce better results compared to post-editing several similar, out-of-context translations of the same source text.
- Different but close in length (word count) and *homogeneous* texts (see below on how to determine homogeneity) take a reviewer approximately the same time to complete.
- It is possible to reliably determine if any two or more texts are homogeneous.
- If one of the engines' output consistently takes less effort to be post-edited across different homogeneous texts than the other's, it is proof that the first engine provides better quality for this language combination and domain.

Based on these assumptions, the following process can be set up:

1. Given the language combination and the domain that we are interested in, find several homogeneous texts (together called a *translation kit*).
2. Have different engines translate the whole translation kit.
3. Prepare a good human translation of the translation kit for the benchmarking purposes.
4. Shuffle machine and human translations to create *review kits*, which consist of the same parts as the translation kit, but with the condition that each of those parts is translated by a different engine (or a human).
5. Assign different post-editors to work with the review kits. Each post-editor works with one review kit.
6. Measure post-editors' productivity across all parts of the review kit: time spent, edit distance, percentage of changed segments.
7. Compare data measured for all post-editors to determine if there is a meaningful correlation between productivity metrics and the output of different engines.

2.2. Homogeneity

To establish the homogeneity of two or more texts (we will be calling them *documents*), we used the following principles:

- Documents should be of the same domain and genre.
- Documents should have similar complexity and/or readability scores based on selected metrics.
- Documents should be close in the density (number of occurrences) of specialized terminology.
- Documents should not have (or have very few) overlapping specialized terms—otherwise, the first part of a translation kit might require disproportionately more work to check terminology when it first occurs, with other parts benefitting from this work.

The practical application of these principles as regards our experiment is described below (see *Selection of Homogeneous Texts*).

2.3. Effort

Effort is calculated for each of the three measured metrics: time spent, edit distance, percentage of changed segments. In each case, we are *only interested in relative values*. One editor might feel more comfortable rewriting the text; another will only touch it in several places. For our methodology, it is not important. What is important, however, is how different parts of a review kit are stacked up against each other: which one has received more effort, regardless of whether large or small in absolute values, from a given reviewer?

2.4. Human Benchmark

Adding human translations to a mix for benchmarking purposes is a common approach. We did it as well but slightly modified this idea. Usually, human translations are taken from a "trustworthy" source like a large translation memory or other corpus. It is implicitly presumed that this translation must be, by definition, at least on par with MT, and most likely better. However, human translations in large corpora 1) are unpredictable in quality and 2) *can easily be not human at all*. The latter is especially valid and, in our view, largely overlooked in similar research. The use of MT in the industry is widespread, incl. by the translators copy-pasting MT for their own convenience without even telling anybody. It leads to a significant contamination of translation memories, presumed to only contain human translation, by machine output. On top of that, the real quality of any given human translation in a large corpus cannot be guaranteed. To solve these problems and create a reliable benchmark, we made sure to translate our translation kit by a trusted translator and then edit this text by an equally trusted and experienced editor. We also double-checked the final version of the translation for traces of MT. Though still subjective in nature, these measures helped us achieve a substantial level of confidence that our benchmark was reliable and high-quality.

2.5. Hypotheses

We formulated two hypotheses that we hoped to prove during our experiment.

Hypothesis 1 (H1): The average distribution of effort among documents will prove their homogeneity established based on our metrics. In other words, on average, all documents will require roughly the same amount of work.

Hypothesis 2 (H2): The human benchmark will be consistently shown to require less effort than any of the competing engines.

3. Structure of the Experiment

3.1. General Parameters

The experiment was set up with the following general parameters:

Language Combination: English into Russian.

Domain: Information Technology, Big Data & Machine Learning.

Genre: Popular Science (book).

Volume: Three parts of approximately two pages (500 words) each, total of six pages (1500 words) for each review kit. The volume was determined so it could be processed by a post-editor in one go, without getting too tired and thus losing speed.

Engines: Google Translate, Amazon Translate, Human (for benchmarking). For each engine, a stock version was used (no additional training had been performed).

Post-editors: Six post-editors, each working with a unique review kit.

3.2. Selection of Homogeneous Texts

This section contains a high-level overview of the procedure. For a more detailed description and code (Python scripts), see GitHub (2022). At the time of writing, it is being updated and expected to be finalized soon, with all relevant materials available for reference and download.

To find homogenous documents, we first looked for a corpus consisting of coherent sentences, written in more or less plain language and not overloaded with specialized terminology. The text had to be publicly available, not protected from use in our purposes (scientific research) and also not known to be published in the target language (Russian). We ended up with a monograph on big data (Richterich, 2018). Only the main text of the monograph was taken; other parts like the introduction, the table of contents, the reference aids and the bibliography were left out. The text was then cleaned using regular expressions to remove references to endnotes, endnotes themselves, bracketed references to literary sources, etc.

The resulting cleaned text was divided into paragraphs, and then consecutive paragraphs were combined into pieces of approximately 500 words. This way, each piece contained related paragraphs and was expected to be internally cohesive and providing enough context to a post-editor. In total, about 70 pieces were obtained for further processing.

The selected pieces then underwent tokenization (using the BlingFire library[1]) and segmentation (division into sentences). Pieces with an average sentence length less than six words were removed from the dataset.

Then the readability metrics and general textual statistical metrics were calculated for each piece. We used the following metrics as features for further clustering: Flesch Reading Ease, LIX, Dale-Chall Index, Characters Per Word, and Type Token Ratio. The first three metrics are based on the average number of words in a sentence and also include the average number of syllables in a word (Flesch Reading Ease), the proportion of long words (LIX), or the proportion of "difficult" words (Dale-Chall Index). In addition, metrics related to the number of characters in a word (Characters Per Word) and the proportion of different words (Type Token Ratio) were also used.

Metric values were then normalized using the min-max method and grouped into clusters using the DBSCAN algorithm. The distance between the points was calculated as a Euclidean metric, and the minimum number of pieces in the cluster was set as three.

---

[1] https://github.com/microsoft/BlingFire

The obtained clusters of homogeneous pieces were then checked for properties related to terminology based on the two stated principles: 1) homogeneous texts should not have a (significant) number of shared terms and 2) homogeneous text should have approximately the same density of terminology. For term extraction, we used a combination of seven methods based on the identification of individual frequent words, collocations, terms based on part-of-speech properties, and all suitable bigrams. For more details see GitHub (2022).

Finally, three pieces were taken from one cluster for which further subdivision into subclusters and sub-subclusters with respect to terminology did not lead to additional fragmentation for most term extraction methods that we used.

The numerical values of the readability and statistical metrics used for the selection are summarized in Table 1 (selected pieces were named *Doc I*, *Doc II*, and *Doc III*).

Texts	Flesh Reading Ease	LIX	Dale Chall Index	Char Per Word	Type Token Ratio	Words Per Sentence	Total Words	Total Sentences	Total Paragraphs
Doc I	33.08	58.42	12.00	5.43	0.52	23.22	534	23	5
Doc II	33.04	57.88	12.08	5.44	0.53	21.58	518	24	7
Doc III	32.35	58.09	12.10	5.40	0.51	22.44	561	25	7

Table 1. Readability and Statistical Metrics Used for the Selection of Homogeneous Texts.

As a final step, the selected documents were checked by a trusted human expert to make sure they looked similar in complexity to a human eye.

3.3. Preparation of Review Kits

Once a translation kit of three documents was formed, we proceeded to translate it using the engines we intended to compare (Amazon and Google). We also had the kit translated by a trusted linguist. The human translation was then edited and double checked to ensure quality. Linguists involved in the translation and editing at this stage did not participate in the other stages of the experiment.

As we wanted to study the results of the experiment for various potential correlations, we opted for a combinatorial approach in preparing the review kits. Having six post-editors as participants, we had prepared six unique review kits (all possible permutations without repetitions).[2]

Each of these kits consisted of the same documents in the same order (Doc I, Doc II, and Doc III), with each document translated by a different translator, machine or human. The idea behind this arrangement of review kits was to facilitate the detection of correlations between effort spent and any given engine or document. If it turned out that the correlation with effort was stronger for a particular document (e.g., Doc I always required more work than other parts, regardless of the engine), it would indicate that we did not do a good enough job finding homogeneous documents (see our hypothesis H1). However, if the correlation were to be stronger for a particular engine (e.g., Google consistently required more effort regardless of the document it was used for), it would offer evidence that this engine's output was poorer in quality than the competitor's.

3.4. CAT Environment and Instructions

Translation and post-editing were carried out in Memsource, a cloud-based CAT environment. It provides useful statistics that we needed to measure the effort, incl. editing time for each

[2] They were as follows (*A* stands for Amazon, *G* for Google, *H* for Human; *DocI-A* means that Doc I was translated by Amazon): {DocI-A, DocII-G, DocIII-H}, {DocI-A, DocII-H, DocIII-G}, {DocI-G, DocII-A, DocIII-H}, {DocI-G, DocII-H, DocIII-A}, {DocI-H, DocII-A, DocIII-G}, {DocI-H, DocII-G, DocIII-A}.

segment.[3] All post-editors were asked specifically to try to complete the job in one go, without distractions, to make time measurement more reliable. They were also warned that the job consisted of three documents, not directly related to each other. No other specific instructions were given. Our goal was to make this job as similar to any other as possible. The post-editors were not notified that the job included parts translated by different translators or engines or that MT was used at all. No glossaries or translation memories were included as part of the translation package.

3.5. Calculation of Effort

Effort was to be calculated for each of the three metrics (time spent, edit distance, percentage of segments changed). All document-level and editor-level values were averaged across segment-level scores. For a broader comparison, we also used aggregated (summed) or averaged values derived as an average of the three individual metric-level values. As we were only interested in relative values (i.e., a distribution of effort for every given post-editor across different parts of a review kit), in all cases, we standardized values as a *ratio to mean*.[4] Though this method is not scientifically strict, on a small dataset like ours it provides results very similar to a T-score standardization and has an added benefit of only producing positive values. In addition, effort values for different metrics standardized as ratio to mean are, in most cases, quite comparable in their absolute size and thus lend themselves well to aggregating and averaging. For time spent, we also additionally standardized values as words edited per minute (rather than per document) to account for variations in word count among the documents.

4. Results

For total results of the experiment, see GitHub (2022). Below we present the main findings, with several key visualizations.

4.1. Homogeneity (H1)

As stated above, we were interested to see if our methodology was actually capable of determining homogeneous texts, i.e., texts consistently requiring similar relative effort. The visualizations below show that the three selected texts proved to be close enough, if not perfectly similar.

The aggregate effort was obtained by summing average effort values for each of the metrics. Each metric-level effort, in turn, was averaged across all post-editors' efforts in the respective category.

[3] The time is measured between the moment a post-editor clicks into the translation field for a segment and the moment when they click into another segment. If a segment receives several sessions of post-editing (as is often the case), all sessions' times are summed.

[4] E.g., for changed segments, if Editor X changed 45% of segments in Doc I, 32% of segments in Doc II, and 15% of segments in Doc III, the effort would be calculated as 1.467391304 for Doc I (45/[(45+32+15)/3)]), 1.043478261 for Doc II (32/[(45+32+15)/3)]), and 0.489130435 for Doc III (15/[(45+32+15)/3)]).

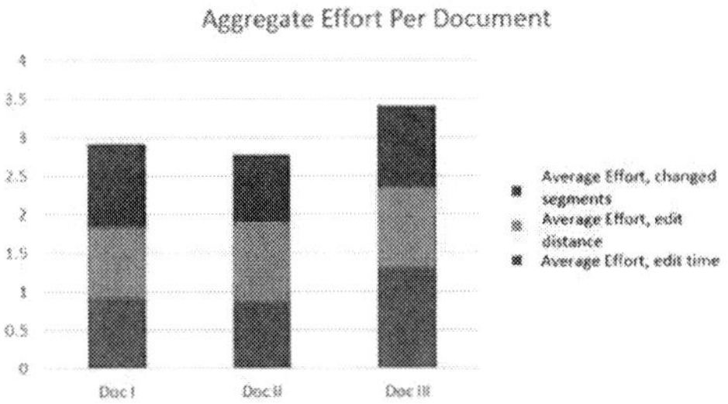

Figure 1. Aggregate Effort Across Documents.

As can be seen, Doc III required more effort than the other two, but it is not immediately clear how significant the margin is. Not only that but the difference is mostly connected to the time metric, which is inherently less reliable than the other two. In other metrics, Doc III was on par with the others as can be seen from the table below (used as the data source for Figure 1; selected are the largest values in each column):

	Time	Distance	Segments
Doc I	0.9143482	0.9199029	1.084156729
Doc II	0.8712726	1.038835	0.865417376
Doc III	1.3182554	1.0412621	1.050425894

Table 2. Metric-Level Efforts Averaged Across Documents (Ratios to Mean).

To make it more manageable, we averaged the metric-level efforts for each document and compared them using the confidence interval of 83% (recommended in Intento, 2021). Though somewhat arbitrary, this comparison shows that effort values are close enough:

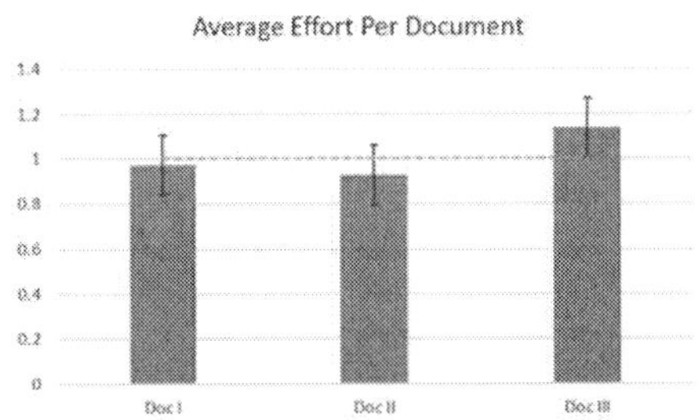

Figure 2. Average of Aggregate Effort Across Documents.

Based on the above, we cannot claim that H1 is proved. However, it cannot be rejected either, and, from a practical standpoint, the methodology seems to have yielded the results we had hoped for.

4.2. Human Benchmark (H2)

The human translation held its own against both engines and consistently required less effort from all post-editors.

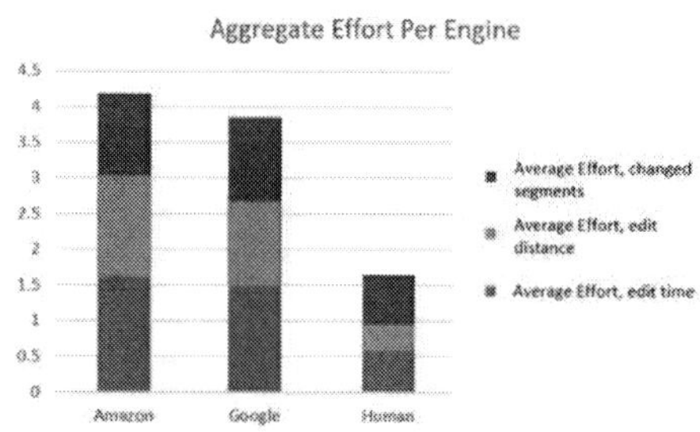

Figure 3. Aggregate Effort Across Engines.

Hence, H2 can be considered proved. It is important as it shows that the results, post-editor to post-editor, are not random, despite a significant variance in the absolute values. Some of the post-editors spent more time or made more changes on the whole than the others; however, all of them would consistently work less on a document translated by a human. It gives us more reason to believe that the relative distribution of effort between the engines was not random either and did reflect the quality.

4.3. Comparison of Engines

Amazon and Google, on the whole, performed very closely. It came as no surprise as major stock models, based on our experience, have become pretty similar in their output in recent years. However, in our case, we still could see consistent evidence in favor of Google. For practical purposes, it can be deemed enough to make a justifiable choice.

As shown in Figure 3 above, Amazon required more effort on aggregate. Below are the values for each metric:

	Time	Distance	Segments
Amazon	1.6108999	1.4126214	1.160136286
Google	1.4801239	1.2063107	1.162521295
Human	0.5869889	0.381068	0.677342419

Table 3. Metric-Level Efforts Averaged Across Engines (Ratios to Mean).

Drilling down to the post-editor-level, Figure 4 below shows how the aggregate effort varied across all participants of the experiment. Note that all values are relative. Long bars do not indicate that a given post-editor spent more absolute effort on a given document. It only shows that this particular document took this particular post-editor much more effort as compared to the other two documents in this post-editor's review kit.[5]

[5] In fact, the results are somewhat skewed in case of Editor 2 as she changed very little in *all* documents. The relative values turned out to be drastically different (and in favor of Amazon), but the absolute difference in effort behind this relative discrepancy was very small.

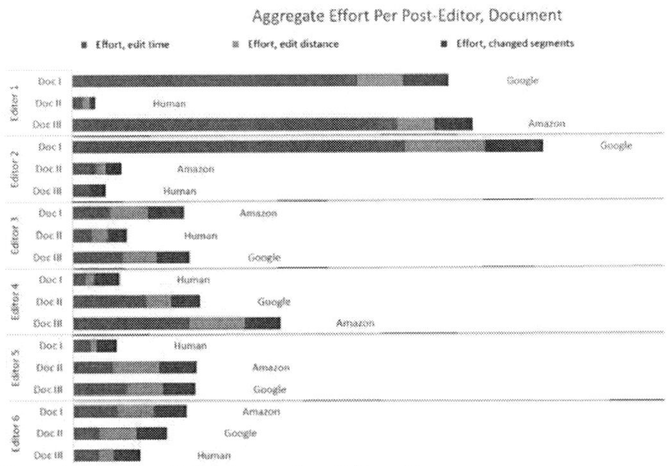

Figure 4. Aggregate Effort Across Post-Editors, Documents.

Another way to break down this data is to rank the engines based on their relative performance in each post-editor's set of documents. If a document required the least effort as compared to two others within a given post-editor's set of documents, we assigned the respective engine (or human) one point. Two points were given to the runner-up, and three points to the most effort-consuming engine. The greater the final score (summed across all post-editors), the poorer the performance.

Engine	Effort (from least to most, total for all post-editors and documents)			Score
	Least effort (1 point)	Middle effort (2)	Most effort (3)	
Amazon	0	2	4	16
Google	0	4	2	14
Human	6	0	0	6

Table 4. Aggregate Effort Ranking (Across All Post-Editors, Documents).

Again, the results are pretty close, yet Google scored slightly better.

5. Discussion

The main benefit of the proposed methodology lies in its relative simplicity and independence from unreliable human preferences and biases. Instead of creating a set of new requirements for the evaluation stage (which necessitates training and narrows the selection of candidates for the job), the methodology relies on parameters obtained through a typical editing process performed by regular (post-)editors. As was shown, the methodology provides interpretable, actionable results when applied to a real-life problem (selection of the best engine for a particular language combination and domain). The reliability of the results was corroborated by a consistent preference given to the benchmark (human) translation by all participants of the experiment.

In connection with the proposed methodology, we have also developed a separate methodology to establish homogeneity among different documents or parts of the same document. It can be used for various purposes, incl. outside the realm of MT (e.g., to quickly evaluate complexity of any given corpus or its part). It remains to be seen, however, if this methodology is reliable enough to ensure accurate selection of homogeneous documents.

5.1. Limitations

The methodology as described in this paper relies on a combinatorial approach where each post-editor is given a unique review kit. It works well enough as long as we compare two engines (plus a human benchmark): we only need 3! = 6 review kits and, consequently, post-editors. Even for three engines, the number goes up significantly (4! = 24), which renders the procedure unpractical.

One possible solution would be to do away with combinatorics and create identical review kits (e.g., Doc I is always translated by Engine I, Doc II by Engine II, etc.). It will work if all documents are reliably homogeneous, i.e., any difference in effort could be traced to the MT quality and not to the general complexity of a document.

Another limitation is that time, which serves as one of the three main metrics, cannot be measured 100% reliably. During our experiment, we tried to take special precautions to make sure the time measurement was done in a right way; however, it is not always possible to ensure that. A solution could be to either exclude time from the set of metrics (and focus on edit distance and number of changed segments only) or reduce the weight of this metric.

5.2. Future Research

Below are several possible directions of future research. Our hope is that other researchers will join in exploring at least some of them.

As the methodology is perfectly suited for a two-engine setup, it can be used to test a custom, trained version of a model against a previous or stock version. Currently, this evaluation is often based on automatic metrics and/or subjective opinions.

To further test the methodology for establishing homogeneity, it will be interesting to see if the distribution of effort can be shown to be consistent for non-homogeneous documents as well. In other words, will documents with a higher complexity score (based on our methodology) actually require more effort, on a consistent basis? An experiment could be set up along the lines of the one described in this paper.

The apparatus used to calculate effort could be enhanced to make it stricter, incl. possible normalization of all values.

The methodology seems to be useful in verifying human parity claims (i.e., claims that a certain engine is capable of outputting translations of the same quality as provided by a good human translator). As of now, such claims can only be taken at face value. Our methodology offers a way to prove or debunk them.

It would also be intriguing to see how our results might stack up against those of a more traditional evaluation process (akin to Intento, 2021) for the same set of parameters (languages, domain, etc.).

6. References

GitHub. (2022). *GitHub*. Available at: https://github.com/Effectiff-Tech/homogeneity-scripts. Effectiff LLC.

Intento. (2021). *The State of Machine Translation 2021*. Intento, Inc.

Richterich, A. (2018). *The Big Data Agenda: Data Ethics and Critical Data Studies*. University of Westminster Press, London.

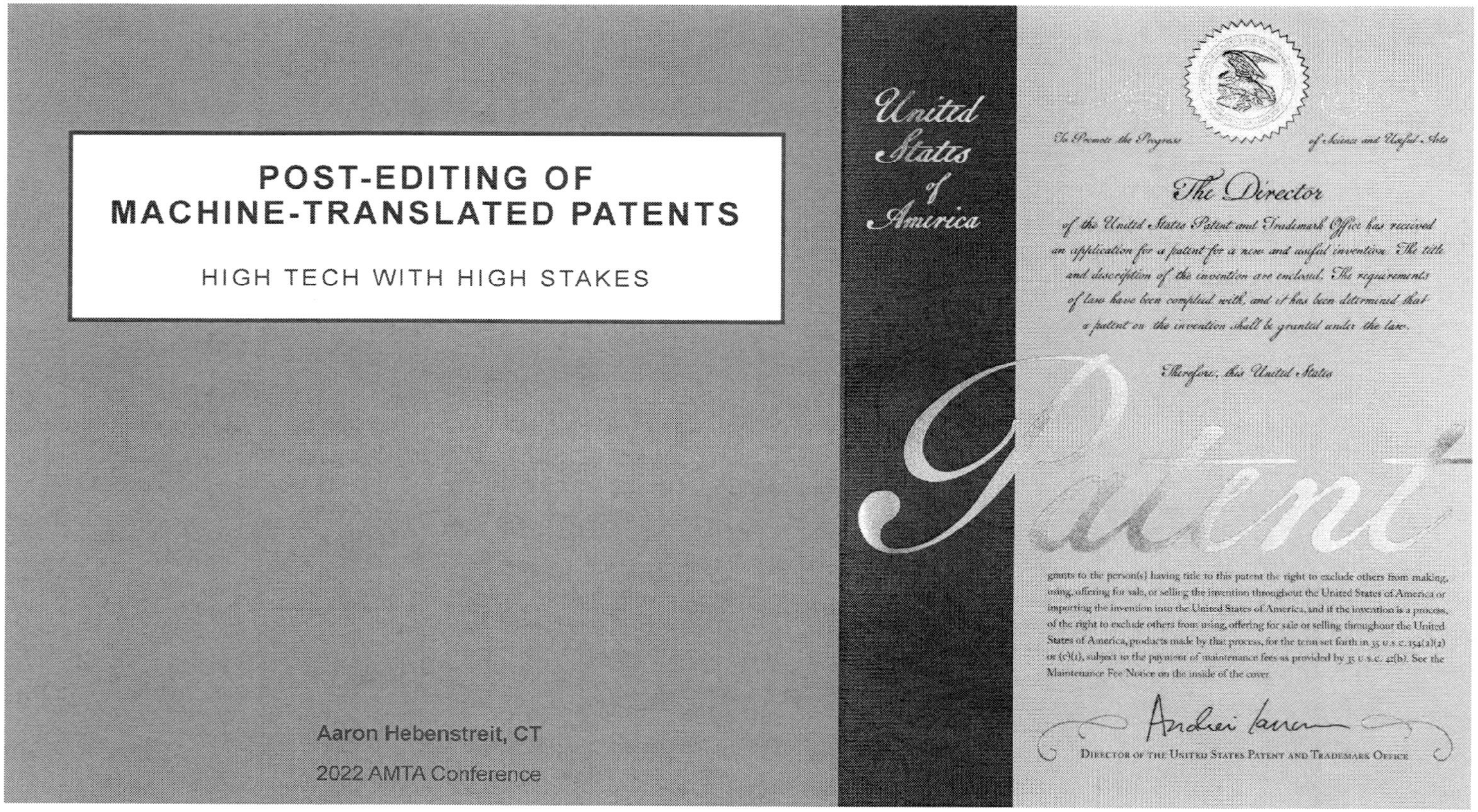
POST-EDITING OF
MACHINE-TRANSLATED PATENTS
HIGH TECH WITH HIGH STAKES
Aaron Hebenstreit, CT
2022 AMTA Conference
United States of America
To Promote the Progress of Science and Useful Arts
The Director
of the United States Patent and Trademark Office has received an application for a patent for a new and useful invention. The title and description of the invention are enclosed. The requirements of law have been complied with, and it has been determined that a patent on the invention shall be granted under the law.
Therefore, this United States
Patent
grants to the person(s) having title to this patent the right to exclude others from making, using, offering for sale, or selling the invention throughout the United States of America or importing the invention into the United States of America, and if the invention is a process, of the right to exclude others from using, offering for sale or selling throughout the United States of America, products made by that process, for the term set forth in 35 U.S.C. 154(a)(2) or (c)(1), subject to the payment of maintenance fees as provided by 35 U.S.C. 41(b). See the Maintenance Fee Notice on the inside of the cover.
Director of the United States Patent and Trademark Office

Identifying meaning errors in HT vs. MT

- 所述结合蛋白为左右对称的结构
- the binding protein has a **roughly** symmetrical structure
- the binding protein has a **left-right** symmetrical structure

Identifying meaning errors in HT vs. MT

- 对第一电子设备周围的一个或多个第二电子设备进行定位
- position one or more second electronic devices that **surround** a first electronic device
- position one or more second electronic devices **in the area surrounding** a first electronic device

Determining the principles, rules, and patterns underlying error types

- 则将初始化缺陷检测模型作为训练完成的缺陷检测模型。若大于，则将初始化缺陷检测模型作为训练完成的缺陷检测模型。
- determine whether the prediction accuracy is greater than the preset accuracy threshold, and if it is, the initialized defect detection model is used as the **completed** defect detection model **for training**
- determining whether the prediction accuracy is greater than a preset accuracy threshold, and, if greater, then using the initialized defect detection model as a **trained** defect detection model

Comparisons of raw MT output

- 在病人无法自助求救时启动救助程序，并告知周边的救助人员病人的体征信息和地理位置，为救助人员提供门禁开放，为救助人员提供基本的救助指导和任务分配，充分利用黄金救治时间
- initiate rescue procedures when the patient is unable to help himself, and inform the surrounding rescuers of the patient's physical information and geographic location, provide access opening for rescuers, provide basic rescue guidance and task assignment for rescuers, and make full use of the **golden rescue time**
- start the rescue procedure when the patient cannot help themselves, and inform the surrounding rescuers of the patient's physical information and geographic location, provide access control for the rescuers, provide basic rescue guidance and task assignments for the rescuers, and make full use of the **golden rescue time**

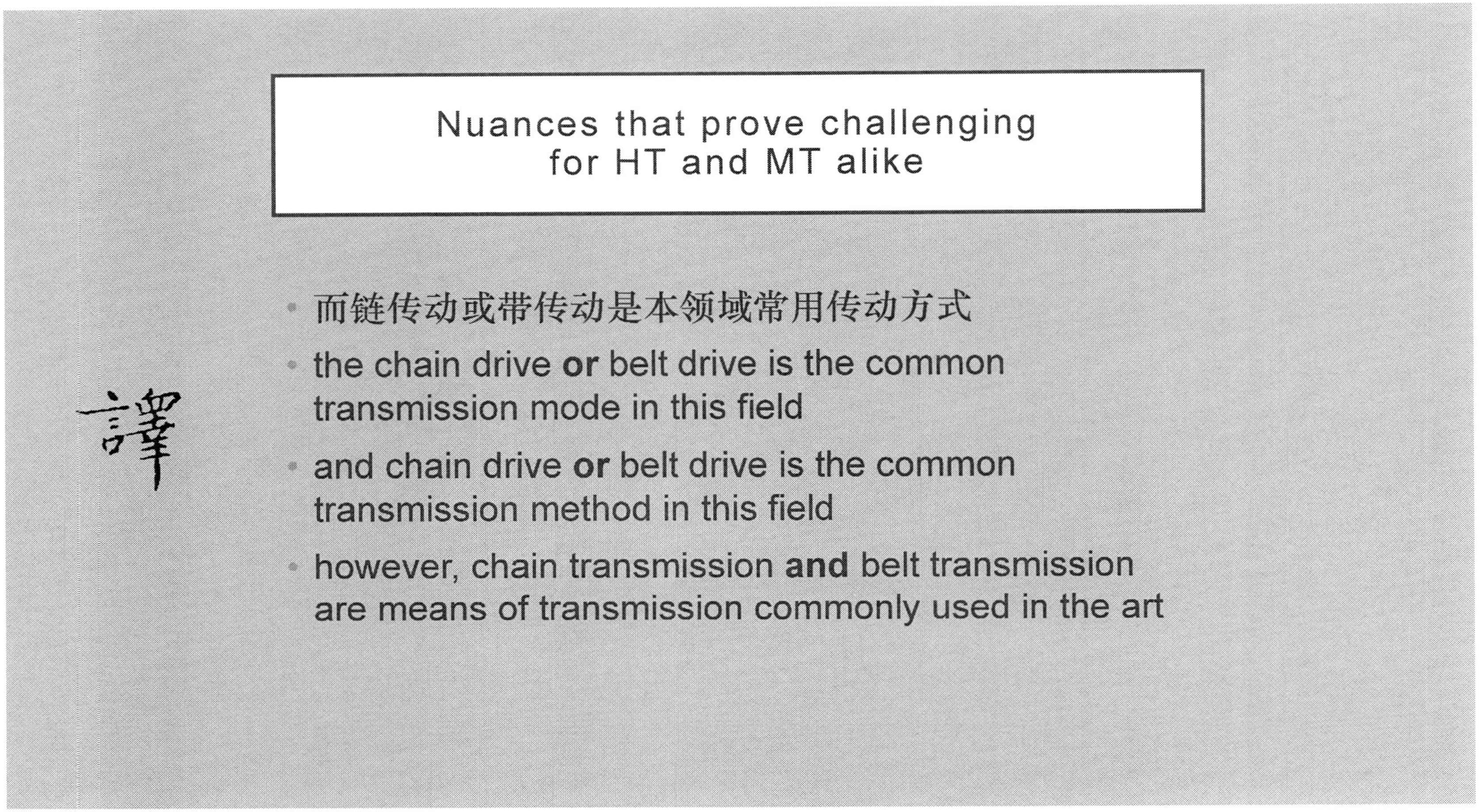
Nuances that prove challenging
for HT and MT alike
譯
而链传动或带传动是本领域常用传动方式
the chain drive or belt drive is the common transmission mode in this field
and chain drive or belt drive is the common transmission method in this field
however, chain transmission and belt transmission are means of transmission commonly used in the art

Nuances that prove challenging for HT and MT alike

- 所述空心转轴的旋转区间为初始位置双向旋转180度
- the rotation interval of the hollow shaft is a **bidirectional** rotation of 180 degrees from the initial position
- the rotation interval of said hollow shaft is 180 degrees of rotation **in both directions** of the initial position
- the range of rotation of the hollow rotary shaft is 180 degrees **in either direction** from an initial position

Can MT and HT achieve the same level of linguistic flexibility and quality for technical purposes?

- Accuracy
- Terminology
- Consistency
- Omission/addition
- Transcreation
- Compensation

- Clarity
- Logical links
- Syntactical adjustment
- Expansion
- Explicitation
- Source text errors

intento e2f

AMTA 2022 - Orlando

The State of Machine Translation 2022

An independent evaluation of MT engines

Konstantin Savenkov, CEO at Intento (speaker)
Michel Lopez, CEO at e2f

31 MT Engines

11 Language pairs

9 Industry sectors

Agenda

1. Datasets
2. Evaluation methodology
3. Evaluation results
4. Miscellaneous
5. Key conclusions

31 Machine Translation Engines

11 Language Pairs

9 Industry sectors

GET FULL REPORT AT
https://bit.ly/mt-2022

intento e2f

AMTA 2022, Orlando

About Intento

Gartner
COOL VENDOR 2021

Translate 20x more
on the same budget

Intento allows global enterprises to translate 20x more on the same budget. It helps evaluate, select, customize, and connect best-fit AI with existing software and vendors. With Intento, businesses can also monitor translation performance to continuously improve their entire machine translation program.

Trusted by Global Enterprise

SUBWAY · Government of Canada · Agilent · PROCORE · playrix · JOOM

About e2f

Established in 2004, e2f helps people and machines understand each other fluently, regardless of language, content, and culture. e2f solutions empower Fortune 50 brands to monitor, objectively assess, and improve communications on a global scale.

e2f delivers world-class translation and training data with its proprietary technology stack for translation, quality review, and AI services. e2f offers a global resource pool of skilled professionals in virtually all countries and languages.

To learn more, contact e2f or visit website.

e2f services

→ MT detection and MT quality evaluation services that enable organizations to monitor suppliers for compliance with brand standards for human and machine translation.

→ Creation of custom Lingosets™, or augmented multilingual datasets that represent real human conversational flow. Lingosets serve as benchmarks for conversational AI deployments.

→ Golden datasets and training datasets that enable leading MT providers to evaluate and fine-tune engine performance.

intento e2f

AMTA 2022, Orlando

Machine Translation Landscape

Generic stock models

- AISA
- Alibaba
- Amazon
- AppTek
- Baidu
- DeepL
- eBay
- Elia
- Fujitsu
- Globalese
- Google
- GTCom
- IBM
- iFlyTek
- Kakao
- Kingsoft
- Lesan
- Lindat
- LingvaNex
- Microsoft
- Mirai
- ModernMT
- Mondragon Lingua
- Naver
- NiuTrans
- Kawamura powered by NICT
- NTT
- Omniscien
- PangeaMT
- Process9
- Prompsit
- +12

Vertical Stock Models

- Alibaba
- Baidu
- CloudTranslation
- Microsoft
- NiuTrans
- Omniscien
- PROMT
- +5

Custom terminology support

- Amazon
- Baidu
- DeepL
- Google
- IBM
- Microsoft
- Rozetta
- +4

Auto domain adaptation

- Amazon
- Globalese
- Google
- IBM
- KantanAI
- Microsoft
- ModernMT
- +5

Manual domain adaptation

- Alibaba
- AppTek
- Baidu
- CloudTranslation
- Omniscien
- PangeaMT
- Prompsit
- +6

intento e2f

AMTA 2022, Orlando

Machine Translation Engines

Evaluated in the study

Customization options: ○ none ◒ TM ◓ glossary ● both

Engine	Product	Customization
AISA	Neural Machine Translation API	none
Alibaba	eCommerce MT	none
Alibaba Cloud	General	none
Amazon	Translate	both
Apptek	Neural Machine Translation	none
Baidu	Translate API	glossary
DeepL	API	glossary
Elia	Elhuyarren itzultzaile automatikoa	none
Globalese	Machine Translation	TM
Google Cloud	Advanced Translation	both
GTCom	YeeCloud MT	none
IBM Watson	eCommerce MT	both
Meta AI	NLLB	none
Microsoft	Language Translator	both
ModernMT	Realtime	TM
Naver	Papago NMT Commercial	none
NiuTrans	Translation Cloud Platform	none
Pangeanic	Machine Translation API	none
PROMT	Cloud API	none
RoyalFlush Finance	Translation	none
Rozetta T-400	Machine Translation API	both
SYSTRAN	PNMT	both
Tilde	Machine Translation API	none
Tencent Cloud	TMT API	none
Ubiqus	Translation API	both
Yandex	Translate API	TM
Youdao	Cloud Translation API	none
XL8	Machine Translation	none

intento e2f AMTA 2022, Orlando

Datasets — Preparation

Translation

→ Selected native translators with expert-level qualifications and positive feedback in each language and domain.
→ For reviews, selected native language experts in editing and proofreading across multiple domains, and positive customer feedback.
→ Proofread strings supplied by Intento for compliance with proper English grammar, spelling, and punctuation and supplied files to translators via e2f's Translation, Editing, and Proofreading (TEP) platform.

To mitigate the possibility that a supplier could gain an unfair advantage by training an engine against the same dataset used for evaluation, Intento commissioned e2f to build an original golden dataset for this year's study.

Quality Assurance

Provided via e2f's TEP portal

→ Human translations were compared with ones generated by the leading machine translation engines using e2f's MT Detection tool, and accessed the probability that they contained machine-translated and/or post-edited content (MTPE).
→ Strings whose MTPE probability exceeded e2f's threshold triggered expert review and was followed by re-translations, which were automatically reassessed. **The resulting golden dataset does not bear traces of MTPE.**
→ Quality assurance reports were run on capitalization, punctuation, spelling, numbers, spaces, and typos. Reviewers implemented necessary changes and proofread the dataset prior to final delivery.

intento e2f AMTA 2022, Orlando

Datasets — Preparation

- **9** industry sectors per language pair
- **500** segments in **11** language pairs per industry sector
- This year, we have identical segment coverage for all language pairs.

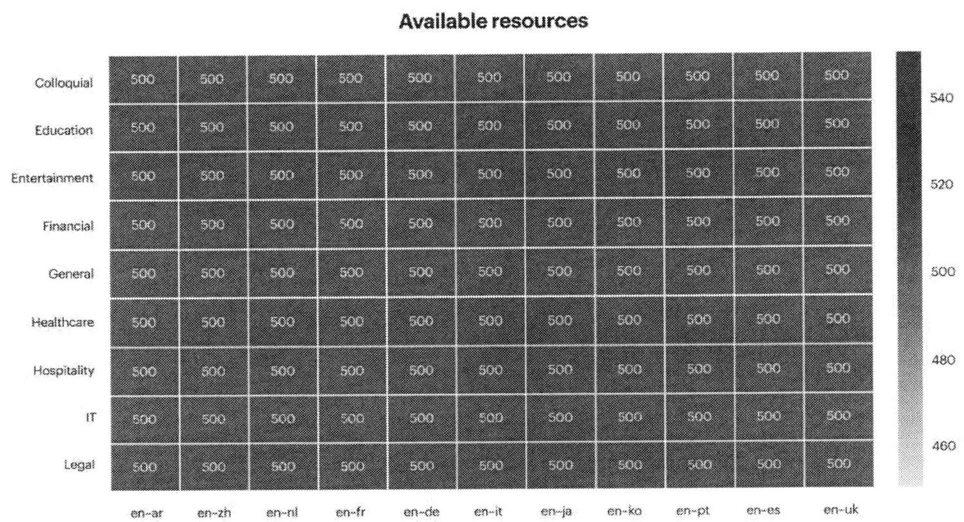

intento e2f

AMTA 2022, Orlando

Content Samples

Industry Sectors

General
"Walmart is also the largest grocery retailer in the United States."

Finance
"Both operating profit and net sales for the three-month period increased, respectively from €16m and €139m, as compared to the corresponding quarter in 2006."

Hospitality
"Very reasonably priced and the food is excellent, I had pasta which was delicious, and my friend had the Italian meats & cheeses."

Healthcare
"Leishmaniosis caused by Leishmania infantum is a parasitic disease of people and animals transmitted by sand fly vectors."

Legal
"Landlord and Tenant acknowledge and agree that the terms of this Amendment and the Existing Lease are confidential and constitute proprietary information of Landlord and Tenant."

Entertainment
"Further, they are aided by a magnificent cast of co-stars, most notably their secretary, played by Isabel Tuengerthal, who is a rare gem with great comic potential."

Education
"Find what straight lines are represented by the following equation and determine the angles between them."

IT
"Result shows that GPU based the stream processor architecture ate more applicable to some related applications about neural networks than CPU."

Colloquial
"and, in fact, there are two huge lenses that frame the figure on either side".

intento e2f

AMTA 2022, Orlando

Evaluation Approach

1. Rank MT engines based on a score showing distance from a reference human translation.

2. Identify a group of top-runners (**BEST**) within a confidence interval of the leader.

→ Using segment-level scores averaged across the corpus and an 83% confidence interval [1,2]

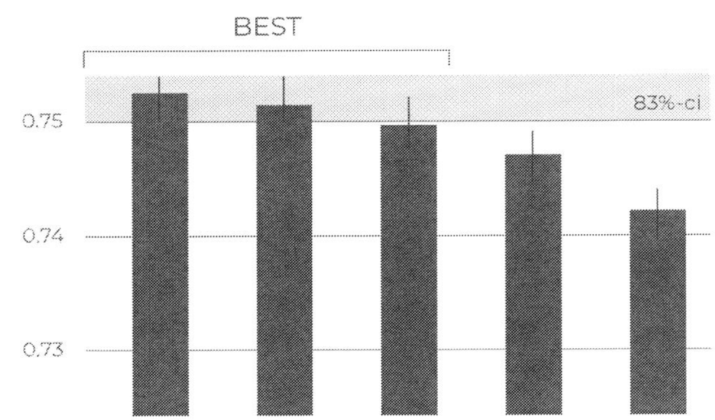

[1] Harvey Goldstein; Michael J. R. Healy. The Graphical Presentation of a Collection of Means, Journal of the Royal Statistical Society, Vol. 158, No. 1. (1995), p. 175-177.

[2] Payton ME, Greenstone MH, Schenker N. Overlapping confidence intervals or standard error intervals: what do they mean in terms of statistical significance?. J Insect Sci. 2003;3:34. doi:10.1093/jis/3.1.34

intento e2f AMTA 2022, Orlando

What Scores to Use?

Type	Score	Description
SYNTACTIC SIMILARITY	**hLEPOR** paper + code	Compares similarity of token-based ngrams. Penalizes both omissions and additions. Penalizes paraphrases / synonyms. Penalizes translations of different length.
SEMANTIC SIMILARITY	**BERTScore** paper + code	Analyzes cosine distances between BERT representations of machine translation and human reference **(semantic similarity)**. Does not penalize paraphrases / synonyms. May not detect factual errors (gender etc). May be unreliable for terminology and synonyms in domains and languages underrepresented in BERT model.
SYNTACTIC SIMILARITY	**TER** paper + code	Measures the number of edits (insertions, deletions, shifts, and substitutions) required to transform a machine translation into the reference translation. Penalizes paraphrases/synonyms. Penalizes translations of different length.
SEMANTIC SIMILARITY	**PRISM** paper + code	Evaluates machine translation as a paraphrase of a human reference translation. Penalizes both fluency and adequacy errors. Does not penalize paraphrases/synonyms. N/A for Korean.
SEMANTIC SIMILARITY	**COMET** paper + code	Predicts machine translation quality using information from both the source input and the reference translation. Achieves state-of-the-art levels of correlation with human judgement. May penalize paraphrases/synonyms.

intento e2f

AMTA 2022, Orlando

Best MT Engines per Industry Sector

- **16** MT engines are among the statistically significant leaders for **9** industry sectors and **11** language pairs.
- **6** MT engines provide minimal coverage for all language pairs and industries, **2-4** per industry sector.
- Many engines perform best with English to **Spanish**, and **Chinese**.
- **Legal**, **Financial**, **IT**, and **Healthcare** require a careful choice of MT vendor, as few perform at the top level.
- Despite of having several comparable MT engines per language pair, **Entertainment** and **Colloquial** shows relatively low scores, which may indicate the importance of customization in this domain.

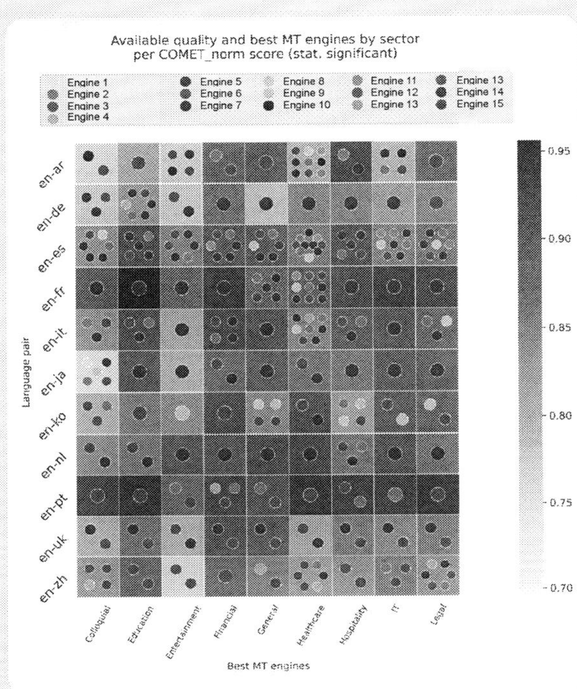

GET FULL REPORT AT https://bit.ly/mt-2022

intento e2f AMTA 2022, Orlando Intento

122,831 Language Pairs Across All MT engines*

From 99,760 in August'20 to 122,831 in August'21

Significant growth for Microsoft, ModernMT and Amazon

Added new niche MT providers with few languages.

● total language pairs ● unique language pairs

Unique language pairs — supported exclusively by one provider

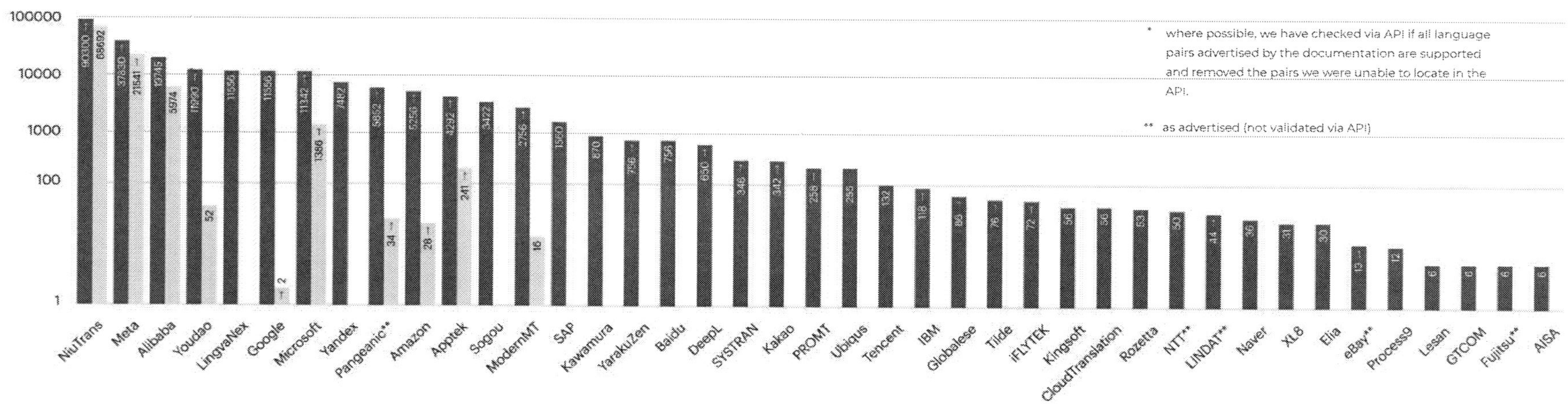

* where possible, we have checked via API if all language pairs advertised by the documentation are supported and removed the pairs we were unable to locate in the API.

** as advertised (not validated via API)

intento e2f AMTA 2022, Orlando

Independent Cloud MT Vendors with Stock Models

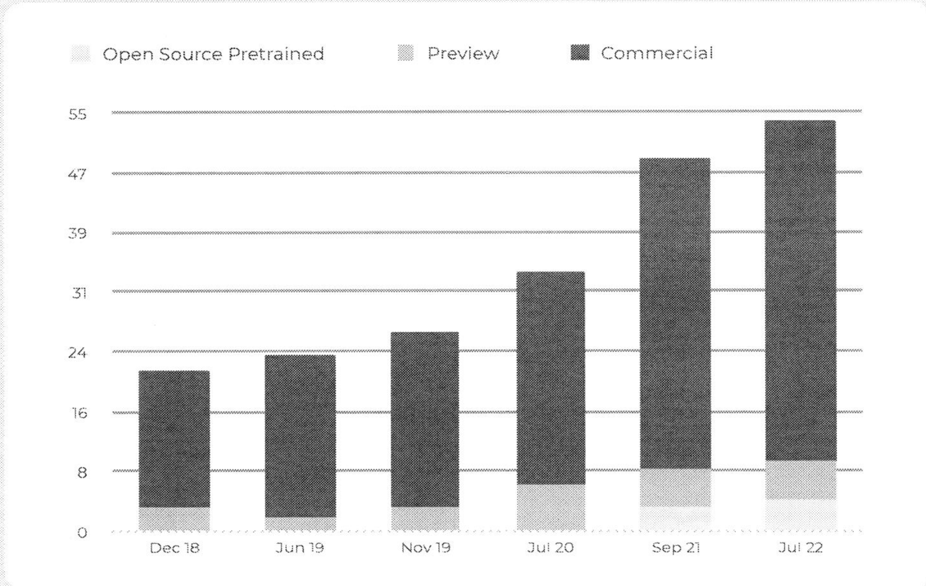

Commercial (45)

AISA, Alibaba, Amazon, Apptek, Baidu, CloudTranslation, DeepL, Elia, Fujitsu, Globalese, Google, GTCom, IBM, iFlyTec, HiThink RoyalFlush, Lesan, Lindat, Lingvanex, Kawamura / NICT, Kingsoft, Masakhane, Microsoft, Mirai, ModernMT, Naver, Niutrans, NTT, Omniscien, Pangeanic, Prompsit, PROMT, Process9, Rozetta, RWS, SAP, Sogou, Systran, Tencent, Tilde, Ubiqus, Viscomtec, XL8, Yandex, YarakuZen, Youdao

Preview / Limited (5)

eBay, Kakao, QCRI, Tarjama, Birch.AI

Open Source Pretrained (3)

M2M-100, mBART, NLLB by Meta, OPUS

intento e2f

AMTA 2022, Orlando

Open Source MT Performance (BERTScore)

- **NLLB** by Meta AI mostly show performance in the 2nd tier of commercial systems.
- For en-es, **NLLB** scores are on par with the best commercial systems
- For **en-zh** and **en-ja**, the scores are quite low.
- **NLLB** with 3.3B parameters leads for en-uk, en-ar, en-it, en-nl, en-de, en-ko, and en-fr.
- **NLLB** with 1.3B parameters (distilled) leads for en-pt and en-es.

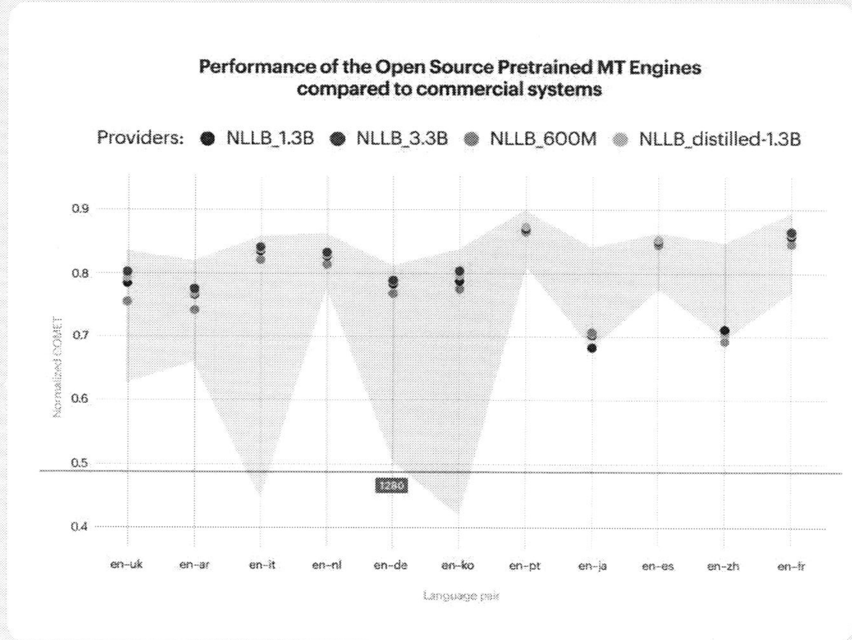

intento e2f AMTA 2022, Orlando

Key takeaways

The **MT market is growing. 4 more vendors** offer pre-trained MT models since August 2020, plus there are one new **open-source** pre-trained MT engine available (NLLB from Facebook). We have evaluated **31 MT engines - 2 more than a year ago.**

Unprecedented language coverage: **122,831 language pairs** across all MT engines. It was 99K a year ago. The main contributors are **Niutrans** with their 90K language pairs, **NLLB by Meta** with 38K, and **Alibaba** with 20K.

16 MT engines are among the statistically significant leaders for **9** industry sectors and **11** language pairs. **6** MT engines provide minimal coverage for all language pairs and industries, **2-4** per industry sector.

Many engines perform best with English to **Spanish** and **Chinese**. **Legal**, **Financial**, **IT**, and **Healthcare** require a careful choice of MT vendor, as relatively few perform at the top level. Despite having several comparable MT engines per language pair, **Entertainment** and **Colloquial** show relatively low scores, which may indicate the importance of customization in this domain.

Open-source engines perform in the 2nd tier of commercial systems, except for **en-es** (on par with top-tier systems) and **en-zh** & **en-ja** (much lower than commercial systems).

New scores on the block! This time, we have selected COMET as the main score based on the high correlation with human judgement in other evaluation projects.

GET FULL REPORT AT https://bit.ly/mt-2022

intento e2f AMTA 2022, Orlando

BONUS TRACK 1: Score correlation with human judgement (based on another research of Intento)

We have run a separate study on 15 language pairs and 21 unique MT models, where we compared several metrics with human reviewers' judgement.

We found that in 10 out 15 language pairs COMET has a better correlation with human ratings than other metrics, in 3 out of 15 language pairs BERTScore shows slightly better correlation, and in 2 language pairs based only on the data we currently posses both BERTScore and COMET show lower correlation results.

Please note that we have analyzed the post-editing case, and for other use cases, such as gisting or understanding MT, BERTScore may be better.

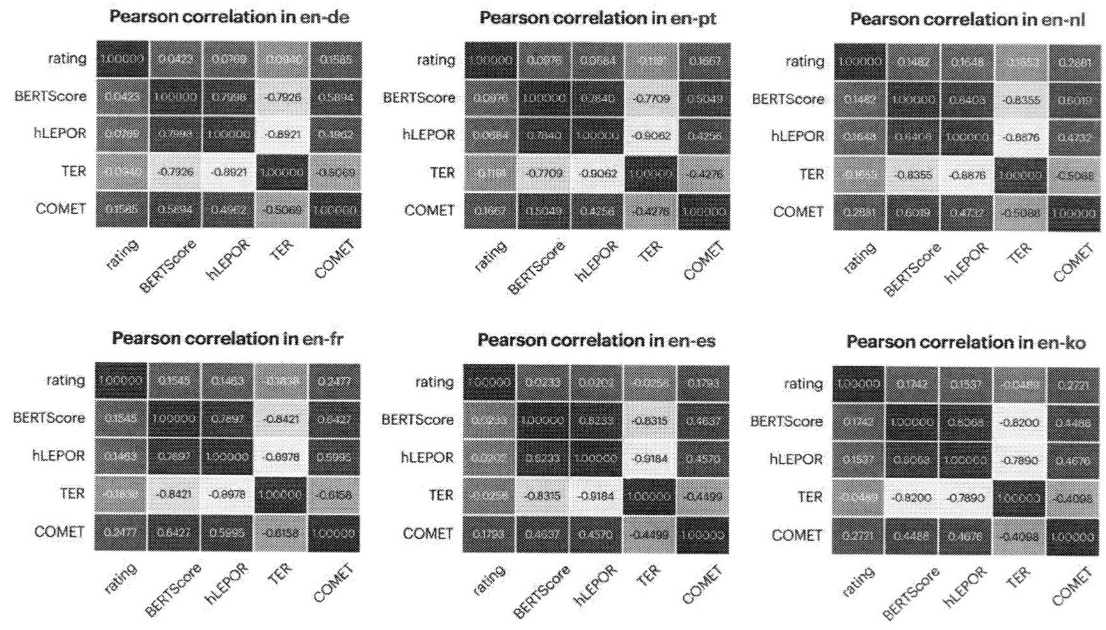

intento e2f

AMTA 2022, Orlando

BONUS TRACK 2: Classic BLEUs Hit

We present highest scores in each combination of sector and language pair.

The score here is solemnly corpus-based as BLEU does not provide segment scores due to its specifics.

Please keep in mind that BLEU, as a corpus-level score with a number of parameters, is not comparable not only across different languages but also across different datasets and different BLEU implementations.

Highest BLEU score for pair x domain

	en-ar	en-de	en-es	en-fr	en-it	en-ja	en-ko	en-nl	en-pt	en-uk	en-zh
Colloquial	21	29	45	67	36	27	18	50	69	26	56
Education	31	43	62	91	54	59	21	46	67	31	65
Entertainment	26	39	47	63	32	31	32	77	54	25	33
Financial	30	42	43	66	50	42	33	41	49	33	57
General	57	23	57	51	55	60	15	79	49	41	61
Healthcare	35	63	50	63	44	52	43	72	78	19	45
Hospitality	59	49	47	58	33	43	9	38	48	26	46
IT	34	40	54	89	59	59	41	77	72	39	67
Legal	51	63	44	73	40	59	33	50	72	31	56

intento e2f AMTA 2022, Orlando

translated. modernMT

The Translation Impact of Global CX

Creating Multilingual Content At Scale

Kirti Vashee
Translated, Srl
kirti@translated.com

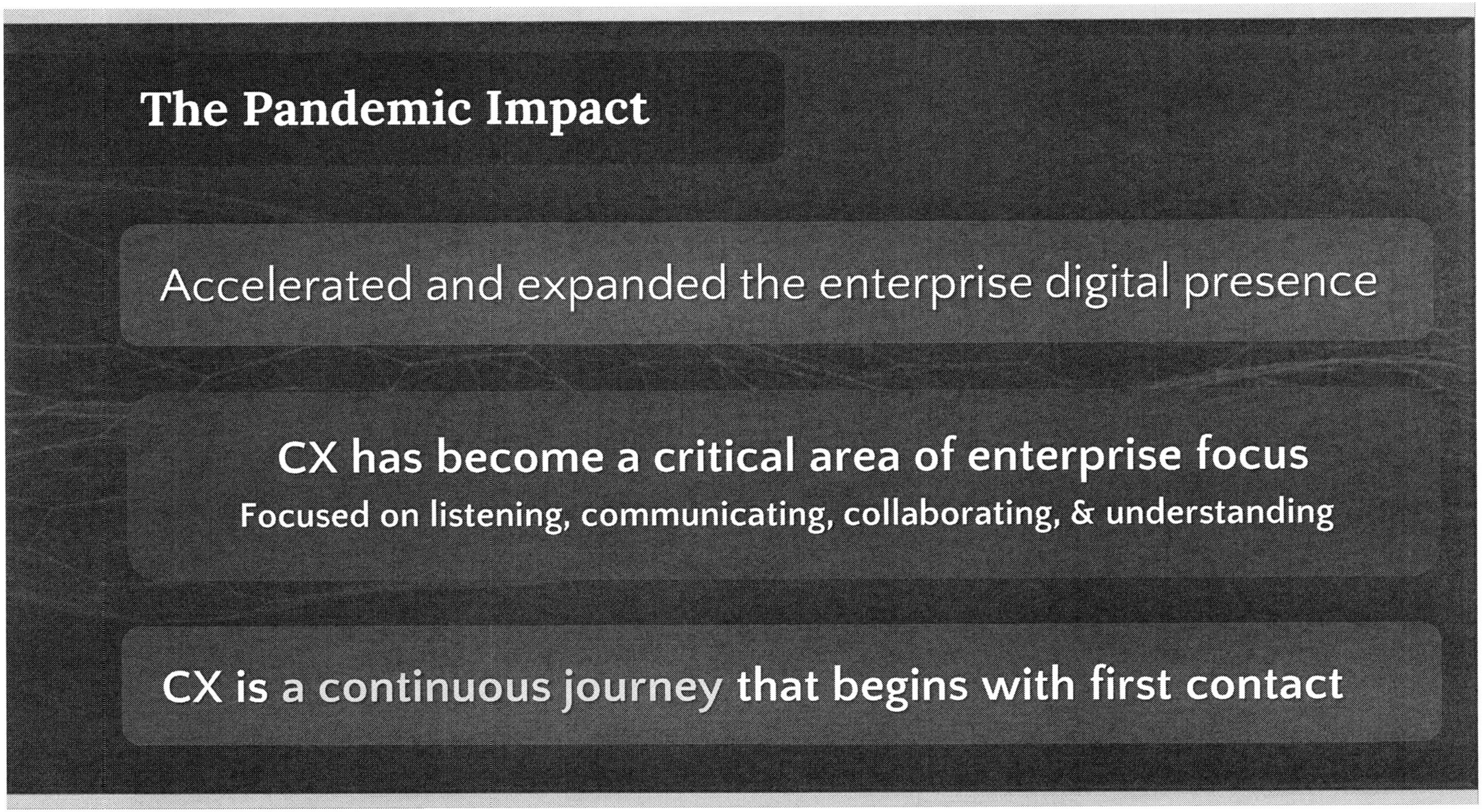
The Pandemic Impact
Accelerated and expanded the enterprise digital presence
CX has become a critical area of enterprise focus
Focused on listening, communicating, collaborating, & understanding
CX is a continuous journey that begins with first contact

translated.

The Modern Buyer & Customer Journey

Even for B2B the average number of digital interactions increased from 15 to 25

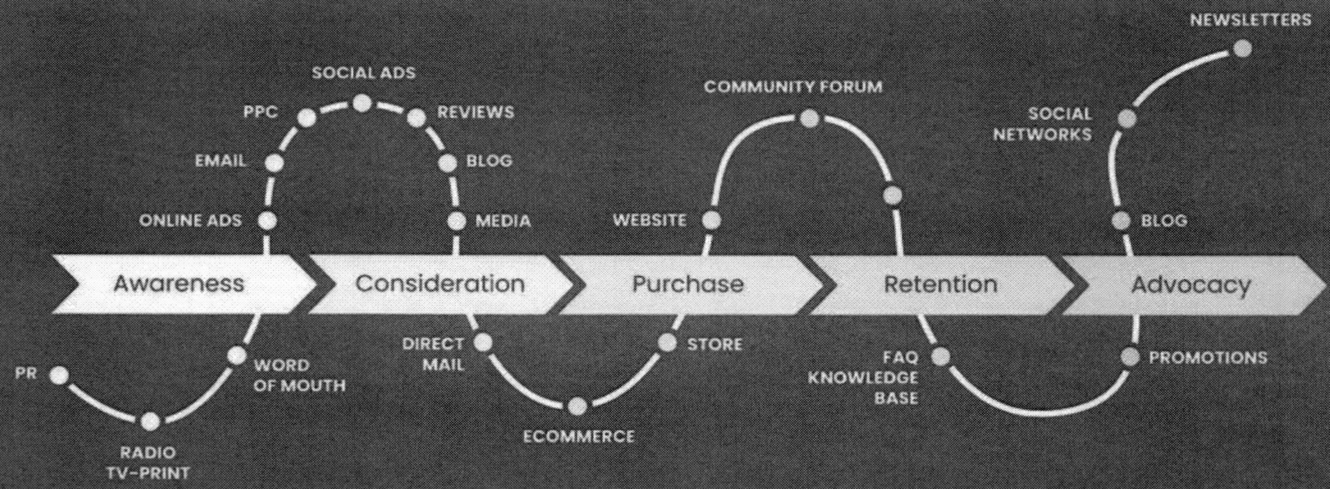

CX is the aggregate perception of the brand gathered over time through multiple interactions, both digital and physical

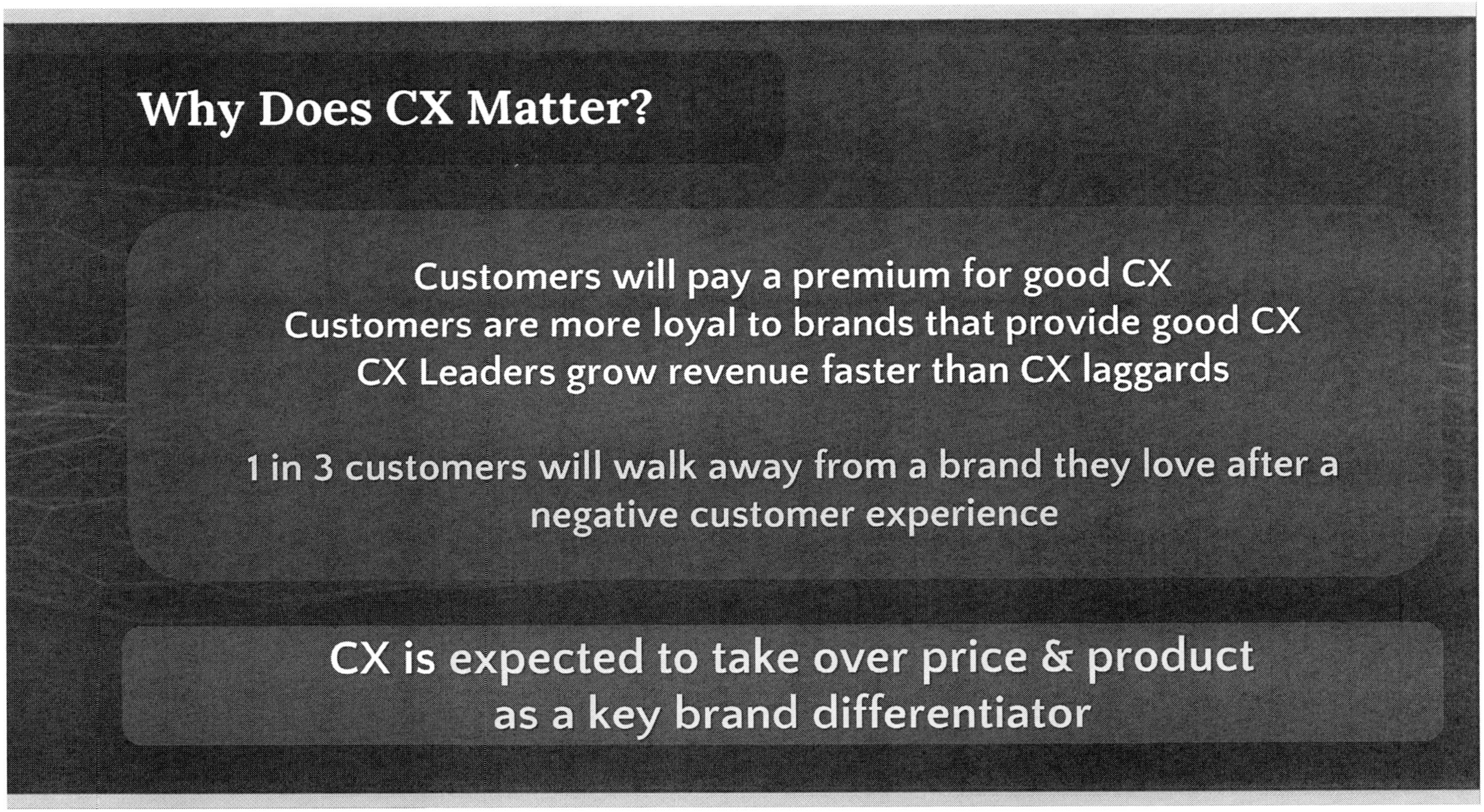
Why Does CX Matter?
Customers will pay a premium for good CX
Customers are more loyal to brands that provide good CX
CX Leaders grow revenue faster than CX laggards
1 in 3 customers will walk away from a brand they love after a negative customer experience
CX is expected to take over price & product as a key brand differentiator

translated.

An Expanded Digital Presence Requires More Content

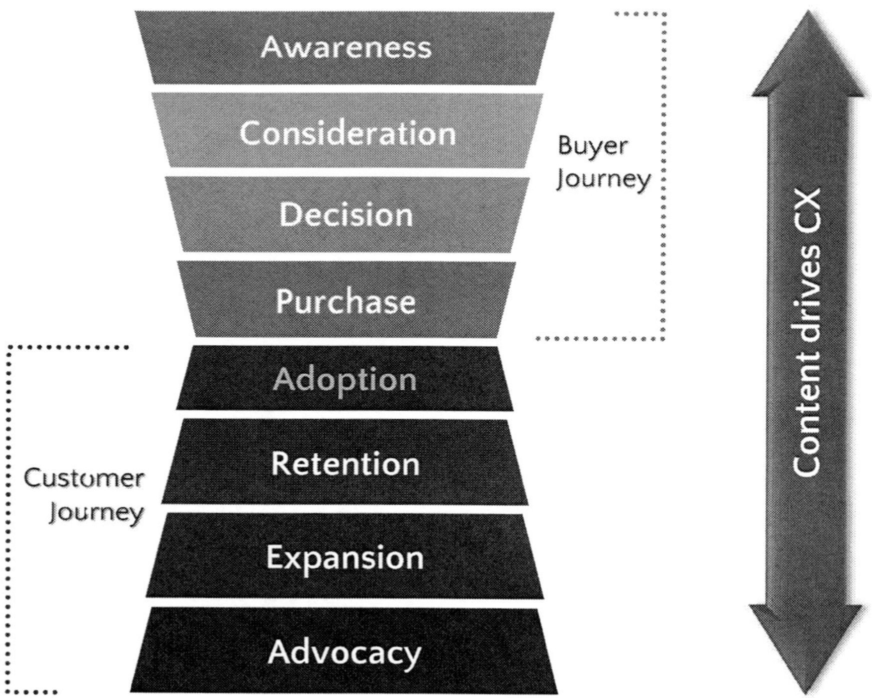

Customers expect large volumes of relevant data available across all digital channels 24/7

Content is the best salesperson for the active digitally savvy customer

Rapid response with the right information is a requirement to be digitally relevant

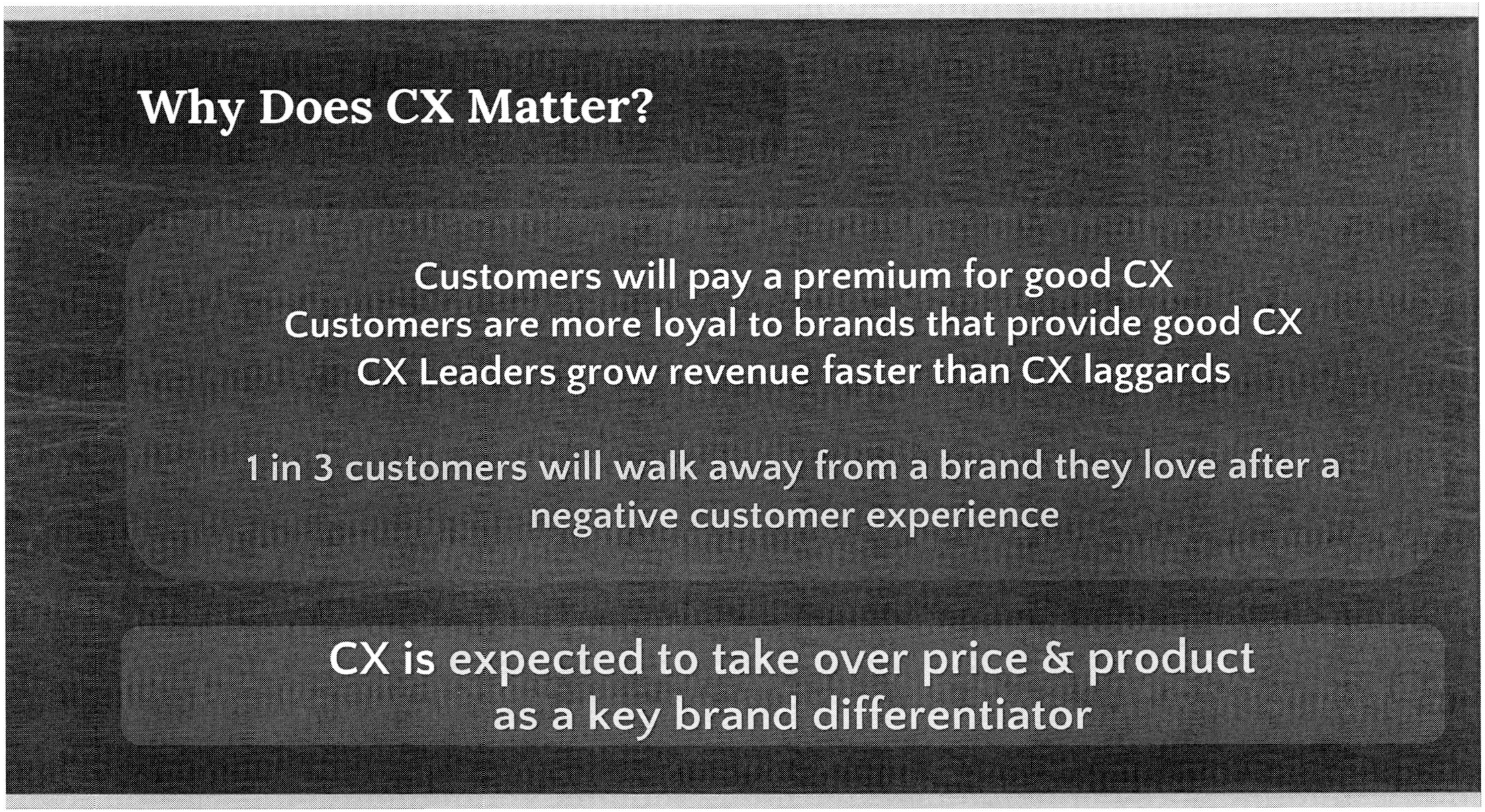
Why Does CX Matter?
Customers will pay a premium for good CX
Customers are more loyal to brands that provide good CX
CX Leaders grow revenue faster than CX laggards
1 in 3 customers will walk away from a brand they love after a negative customer experience
CX is expected to take over price & product as a key brand differentiator

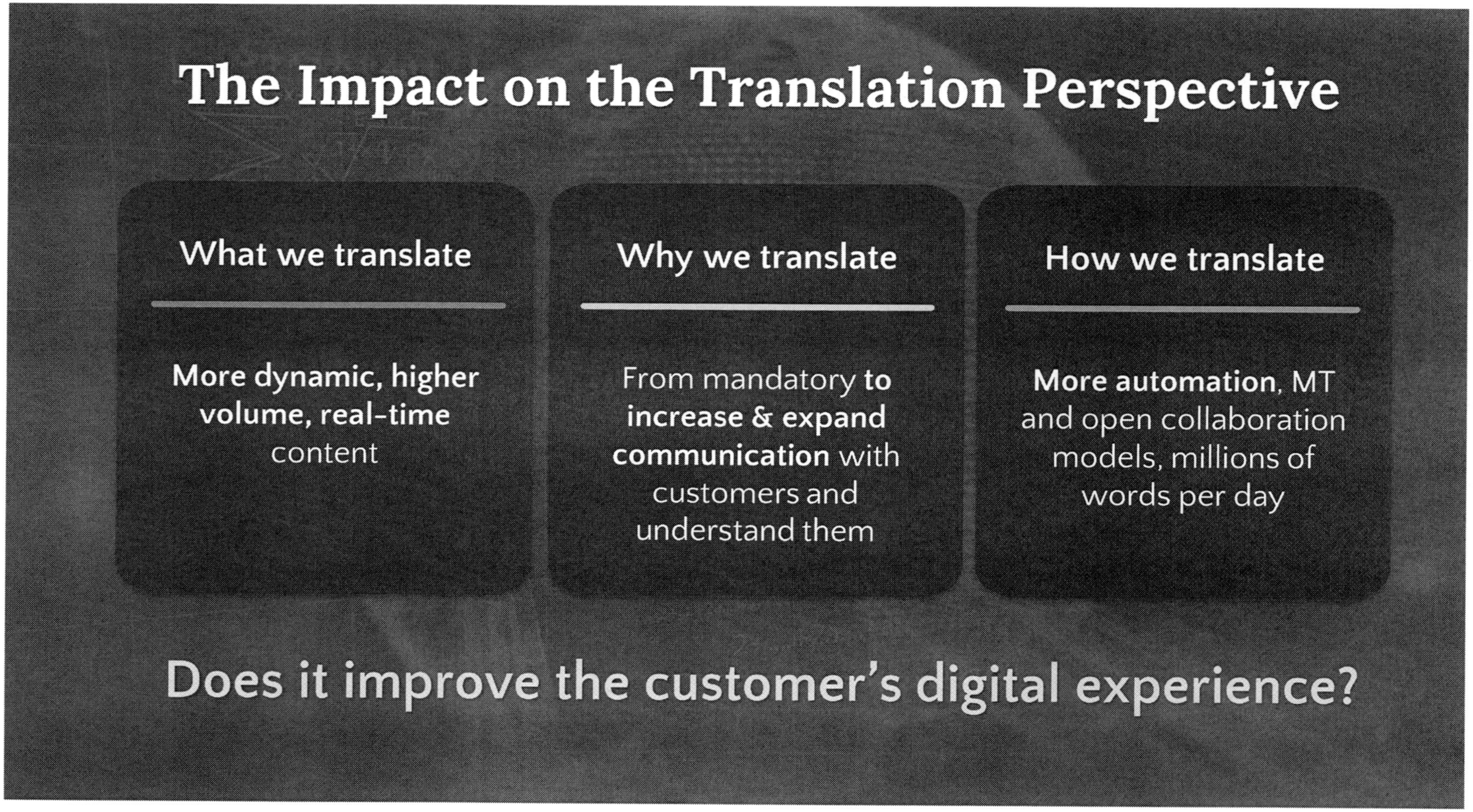
The Impact on the Translation Perspective
What we translate
More dynamic, higher volume, real-time content
Why we translate
From mandatory to increase & expand communication with customers and understand them
How we translate
More automation, MT and open collaboration models, millions of words per day
Does it improve the customer's digital experience?

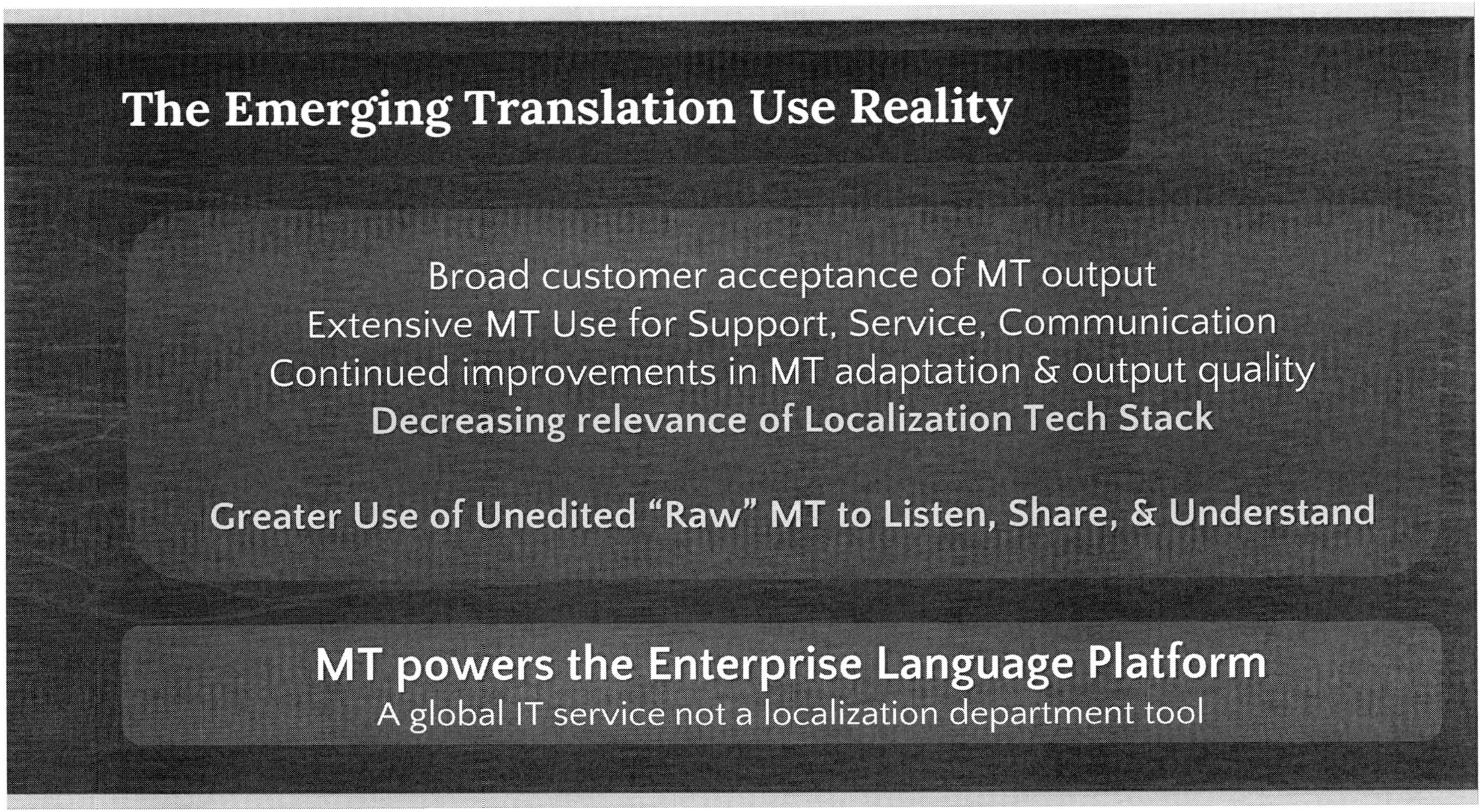
The Emerging Translation Use Reality
Broad customer acceptance of MT output
Extensive MT Use for Support, Service, Communication
Continued improvements in MT adaptation & output quality
Decreasing relevance of Localization Tech Stack
Greater Use of Unedited "Raw" MT to Listen, Share, & Understand
MT powers the Enterprise Language Platform
A global IT service not a localization department tool

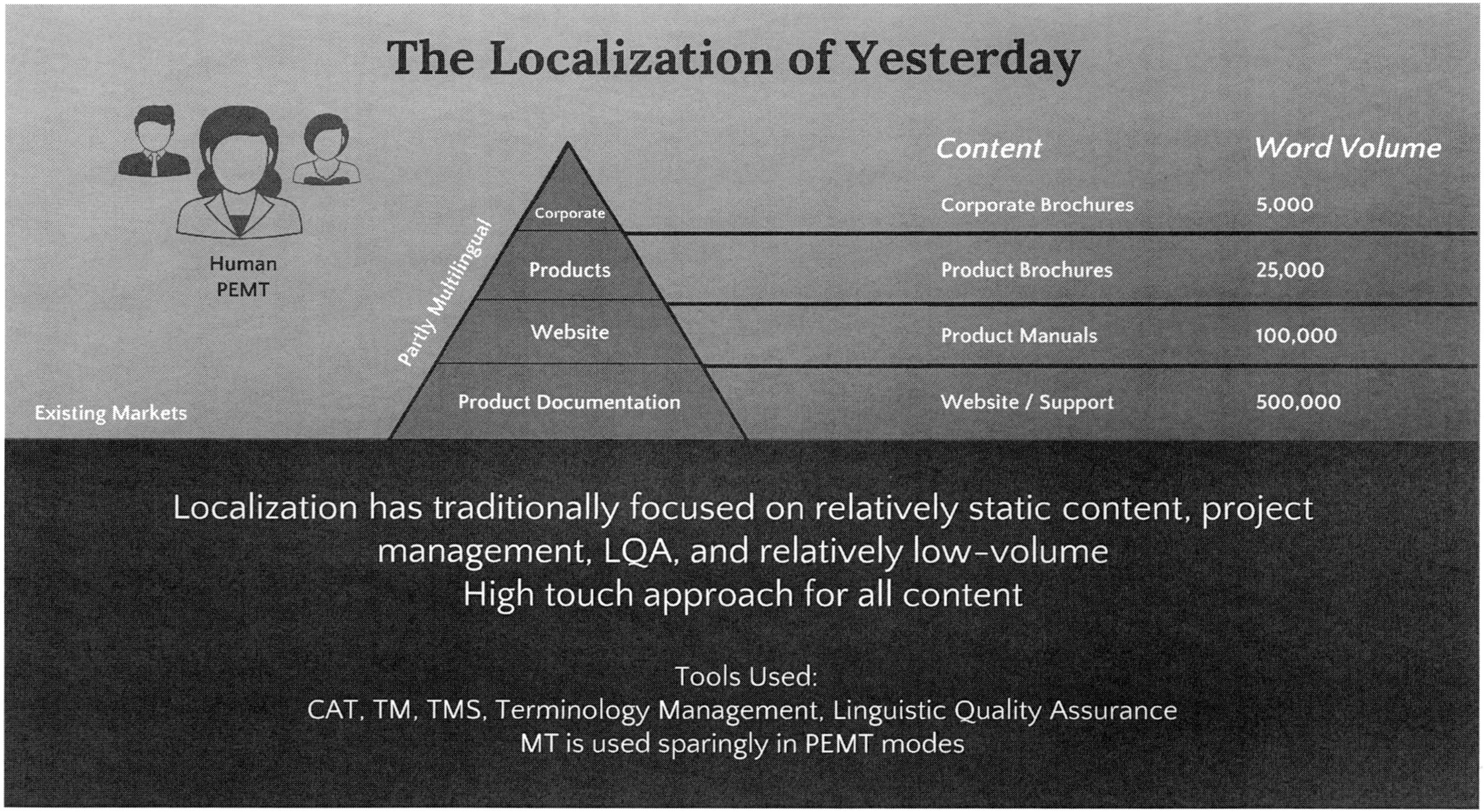
The Localization of Yesterday
Human
PEMT
Existing Markets
Partly Multilingual
Corporate
Products
Website
Product Documentation
Content
Word Volume
Corporate Brochures
5,000
Product Brochures
25,000
Product Manuals
100,000
Website / Support
500,000
Localization has traditionally focused on relatively static content, project management, LQA, and relatively low-volume
High touch approach for all content
Tools Used:
CAT, TM, TMS, Terminology Management, Linguistic Quality Assurance
MT is used sparingly in PEMT modes

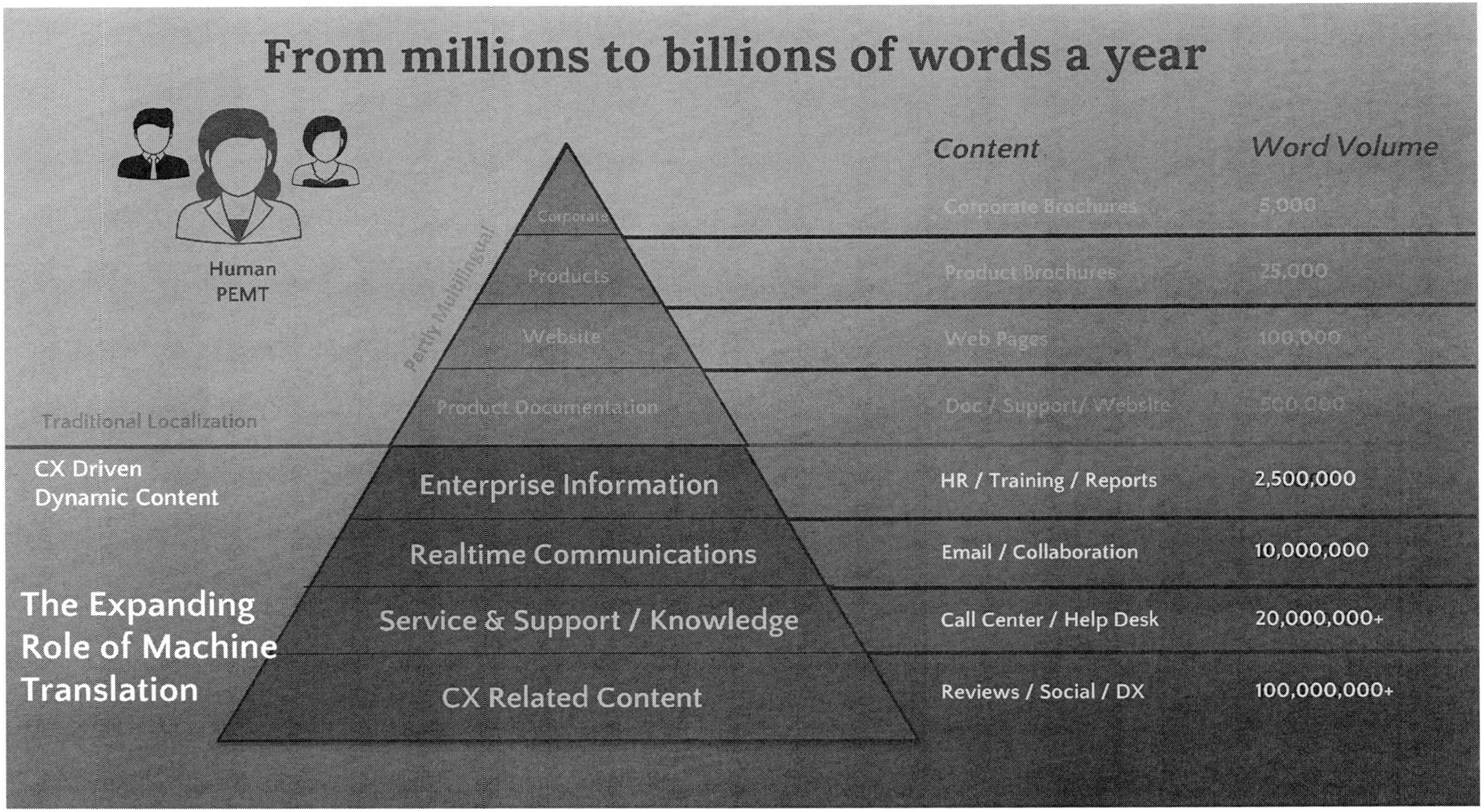
From millions to billions of words a year
Human
PEMT
Content
Word Volume
Corporate
Products
Website
Product Documentation
Partly Multilingual
Corporate Brochures
5,000
Product Brochures
25,000
Web Pages
100,000
Doc / Support/ Website
500,000
Traditional Localization
CX Driven
Dynamic Content
The Expanding
Role of Machine
Translation
Enterprise Information
Realtime Communications
Service & Support / Knowledge
CX Related Content
HR / Training / Reports
2,500,000
Email / Collaboration
10,000,000
Call Center / Help Desk
20,000,000+
Reviews / Social / DX
100,000,000+

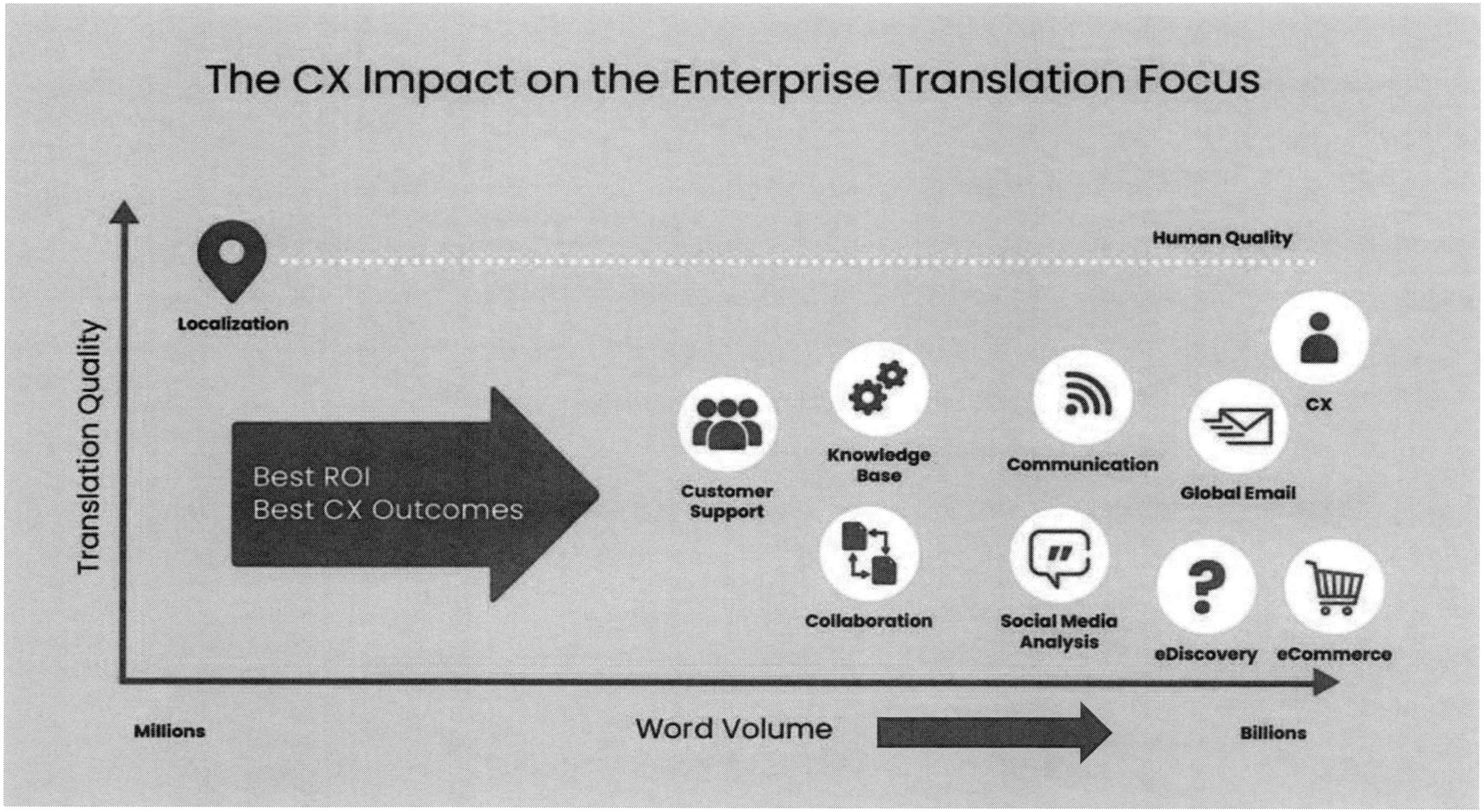
The CX Impact on the Enterprise Translation Focus
Translation Quality
Localization
Human Quality
Best ROI
Best CX Outcomes
Customer Support
Knowledge Base
Collaboration
Communication
Social Media Analysis
Global Email
CX
eDiscovery
eCommerce
Millions
Word Volume
Billions

Translation in the Age of CX is different

- Enterprise Pervasive
- Varied in Quality
- More Real-Time
- Able to handle unstructured and UGC with ease

- Scales from millions to billions of words a month
- Integrated into critical communication, collaboration, & customer data platform infrastructure
- Able to vary production modes for varying translation quality needs
- Enables pervasive but differently optimized translation capabilities across the enterprise

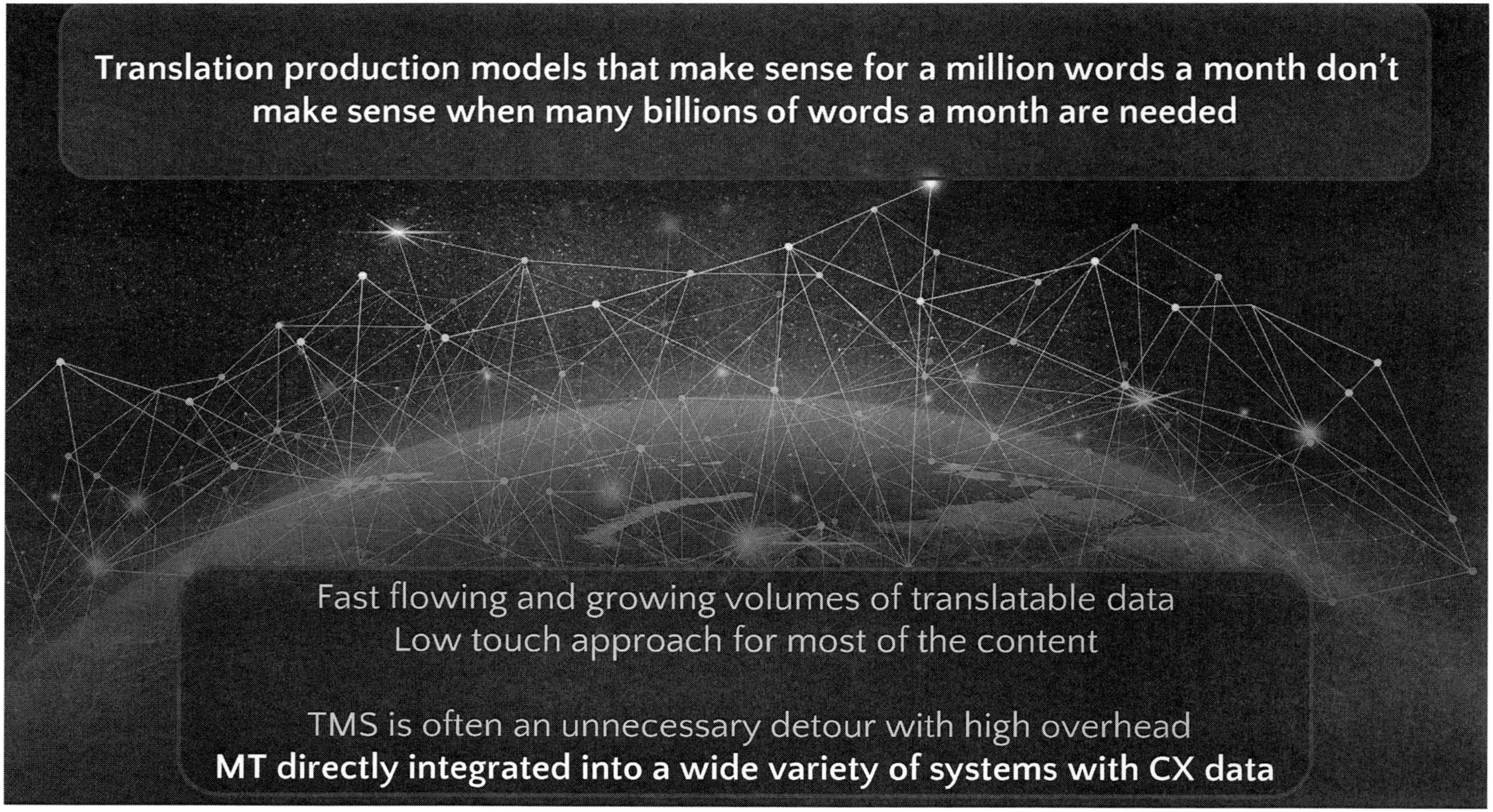
Translation production models that make sense for a million words a month don't make sense when many billions of words a month are needed
Fast flowing and growing volumes of translatable data
Low touch approach for most of the content
TMS is often an unnecessary detour with high overhead
MT directly integrated into a wide variety of systems with CX data

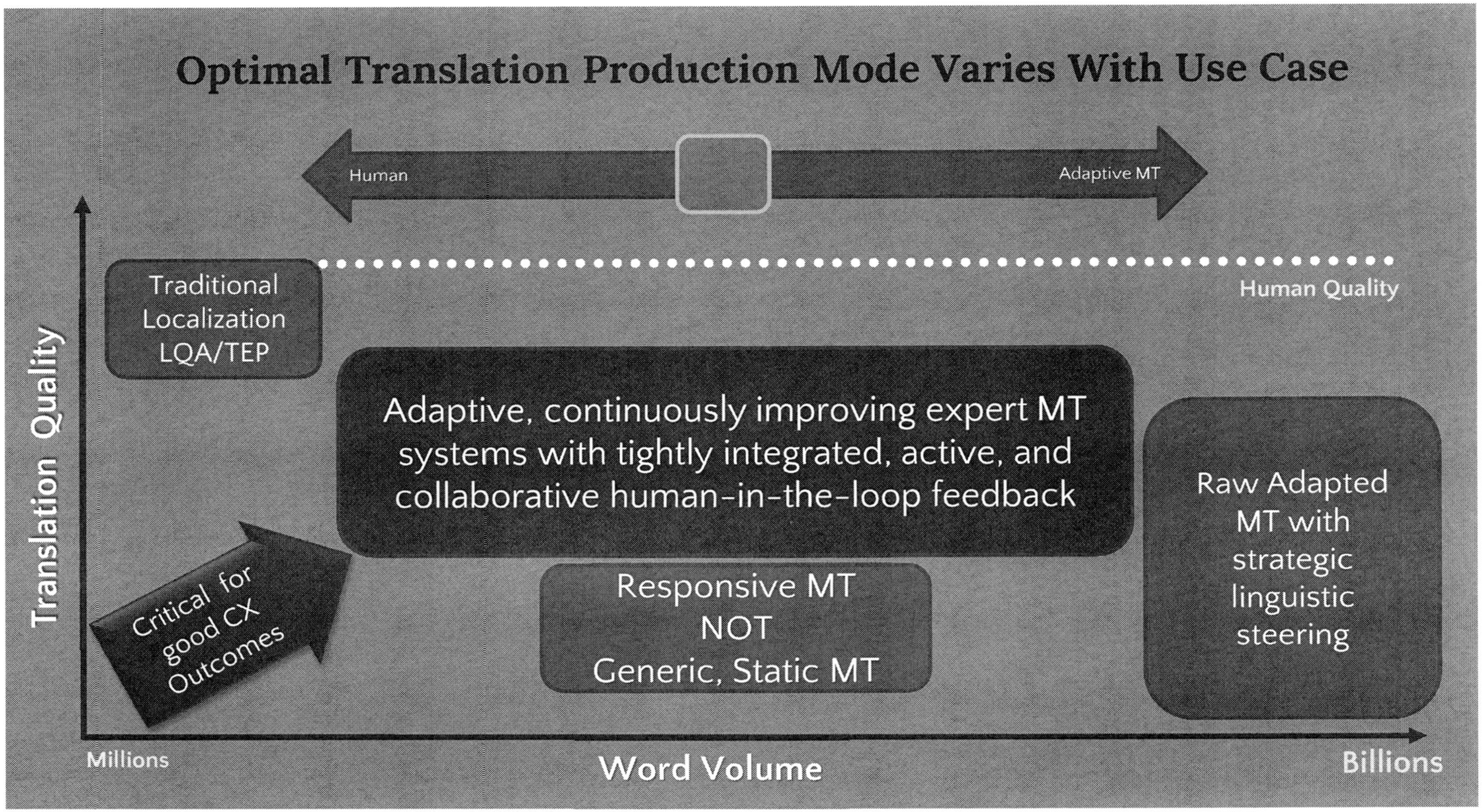
Optimal Translation Production Mode Varies With Use Case
Human
Adaptive MT
Human Quality
Traditional Localization LQA/TEP
Adaptive, continuously improving expert MT systems with tightly integrated, active, and collaborative human-in-the-loop feedback
Critical for good CX Outcomes
Responsive MT NOT Generic, Static MT
Raw Adapted MT with strategic linguistic steering
Translation Quality
Millions
Word Volume
Billions

The Optimal Translation Production Mode Varies with Use-case Specific Requirements

Human Translation Options

Human TEP	Human	Full MTPE FPE	Light MTPE LPE

Slider is moved to L or R based on content type, content volume, translation quality

Adaptive MT Options

Human In The Loop (HITL)		Batch

Higher Cost

Lower Cost

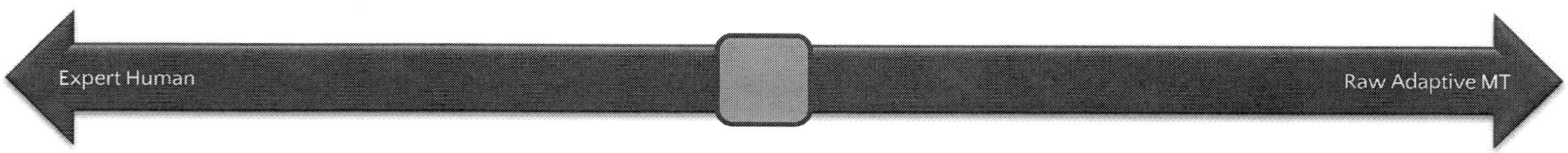

Lower Volume
Higher Quality
Slower Production
Revision & Review
Translator Selection

Higher Volume
Lower Quality
Fast Production
Limited Revision
Rapidly Adaptive MT

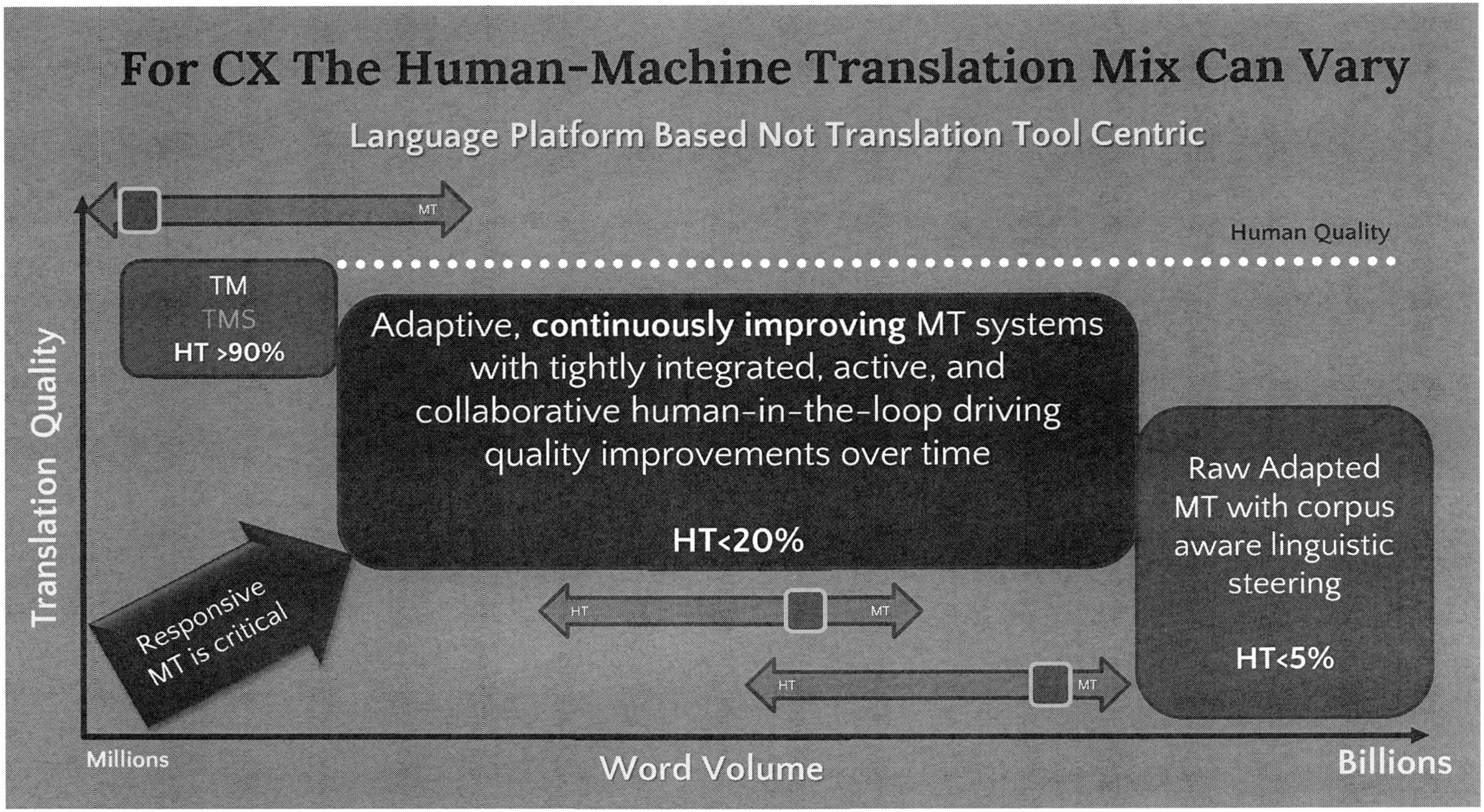
For CX The Human-Machine Translation Mix Can Vary
Language Platform Based Not Translation Tool Centric
MT
Human Quality
TM
TMS
HT >90%
Adaptive, continuously improving MT systems with tightly integrated, active, and collaborative human-in-the-loop driving quality improvements over time
HT<20%
Raw Adapted MT with corpus aware linguistic steering
HT<5%
Responsive MT is critical
HT
MT
HT
MT
Translation Quality
Millions
Word Volume
Billions

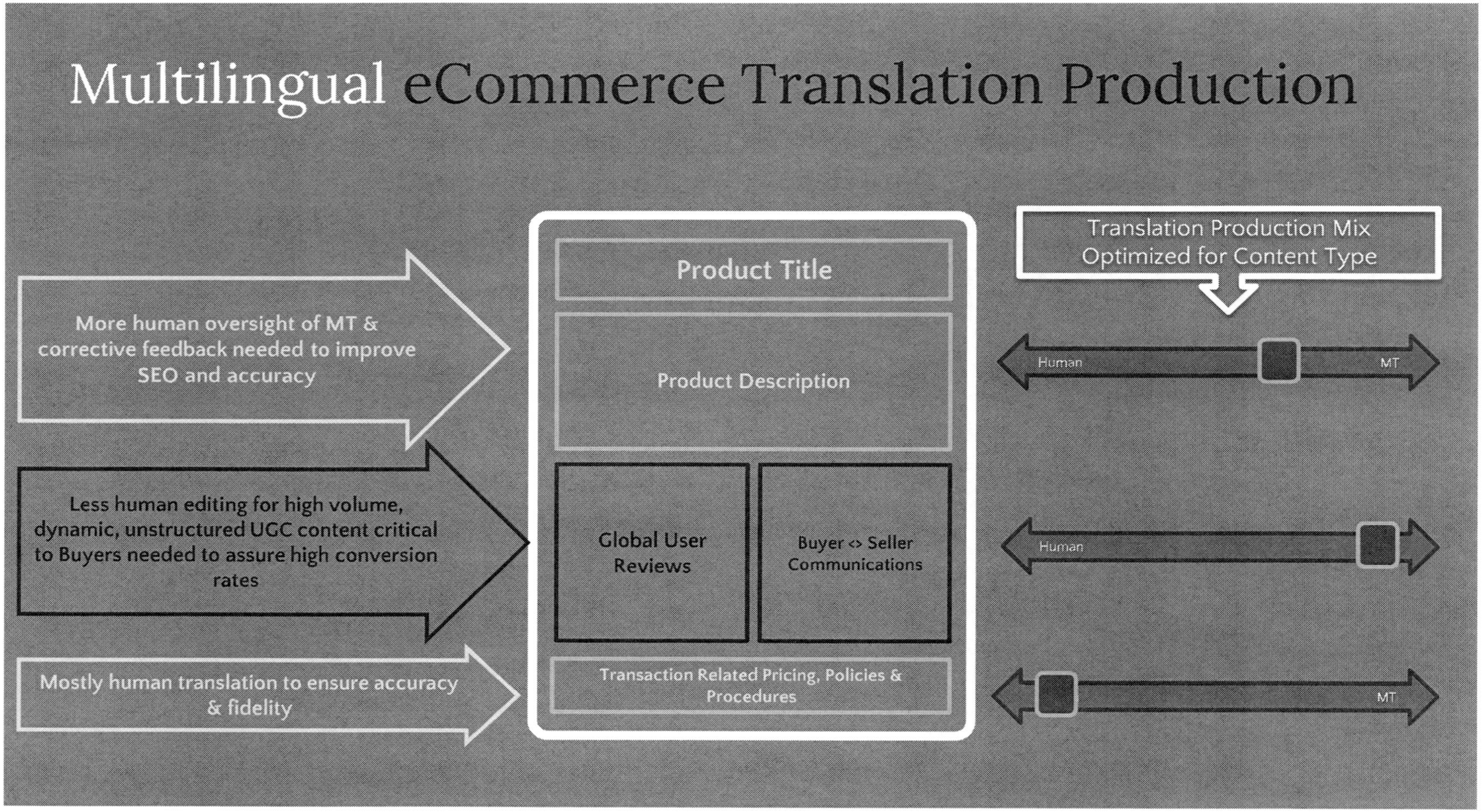
Multilingual eCommerce Translation Production
More human oversight of MT & corrective feedback needed to improve SEO and accuracy
Less human editing for high volume, dynamic, unstructured UGC content critical to Buyers needed to assure high conversion rates
Mostly human translation to ensure accuracy & fidelity
Product Title
Product Description
Global User Reviews
Buyer <> Seller Communications
Transaction Related Pricing, Policies & Procedures
Translation Production Mix Optimized for Content Type
Human
MT
Human
MT

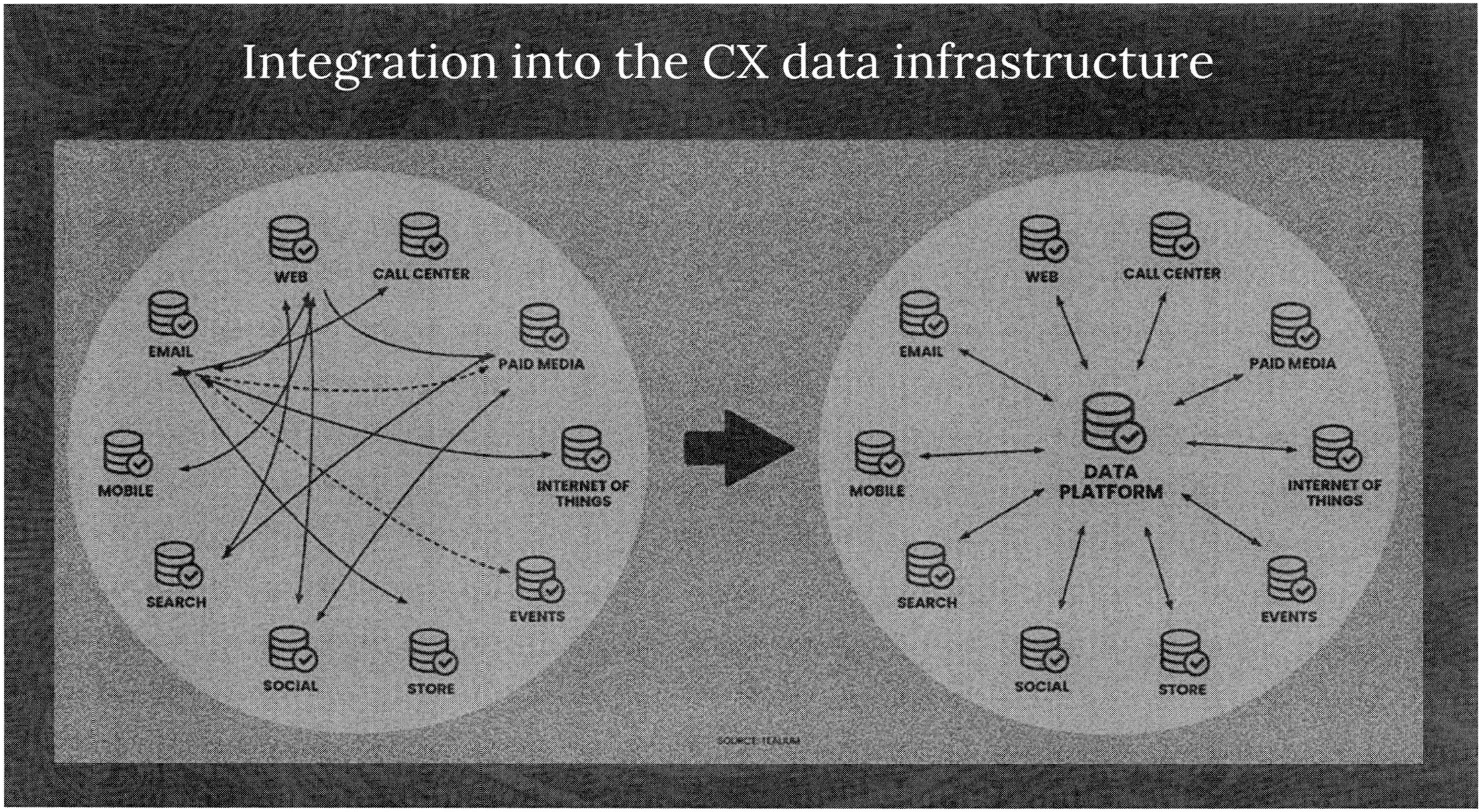
Integration into the CX data infrastructure
WEB
CALL CENTER
EMAIL
PAID MEDIA
MOBILE
INTERNET OF THINGS
SEARCH
EVENTS
SOCIAL
STORE
WEB
CALL CENTER
EMAIL
PAID MEDIA
DATA PLATFORM
MOBILE
INTERNET OF THINGS
SEARCH
EVENTS
SOCIAL
STORE

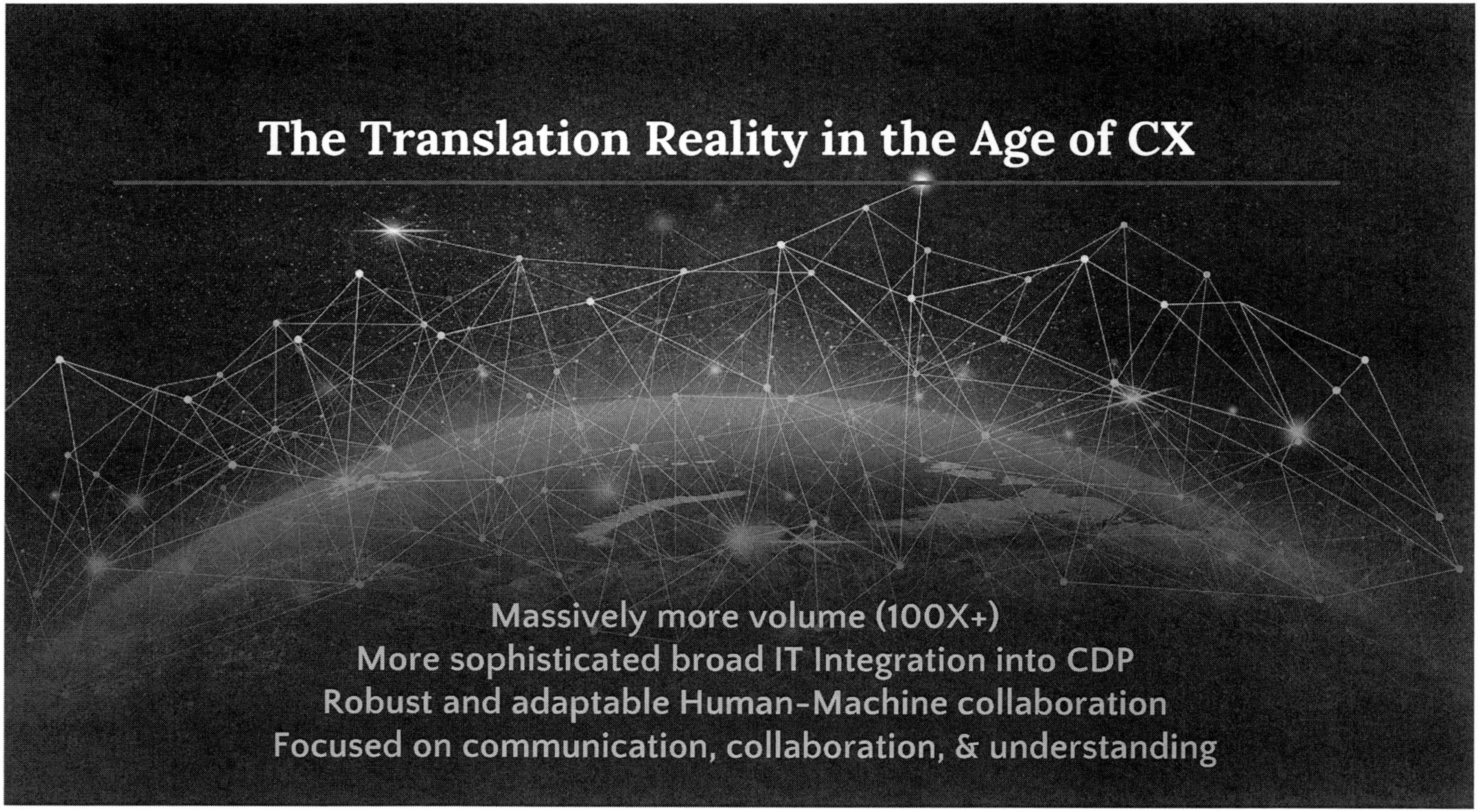
The Translation Reality in the Age of CX
Massively more volume (100X+)
More sophisticated broad IT Integration into CDP
Robust and adaptable Human-Machine collaboration
Focused on communication, collaboration, & understanding

translated.

This is covered in more detail at:
https://blog.modernmt.com/translation-in-the-age-of-cx/

Thanks!

Questions?

You can find me at:

@kvashee
kirti@translated.com

https://blog.modernmt.com/

modernMT

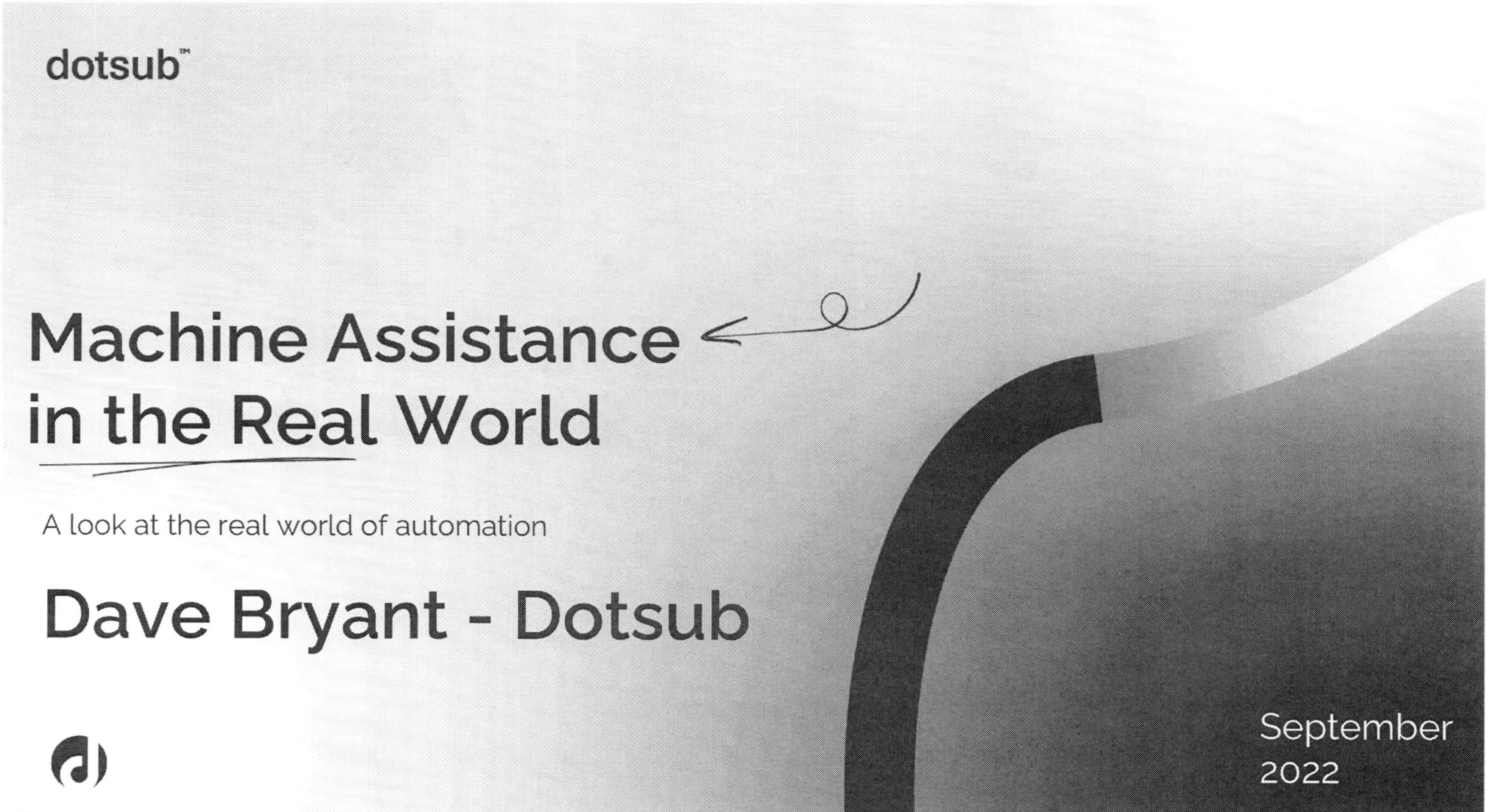
dotsub™
Machine Assistance
in the Real World
A look at the real world of automation
Dave Bryant - Dotsub
September
2022

The ideal world

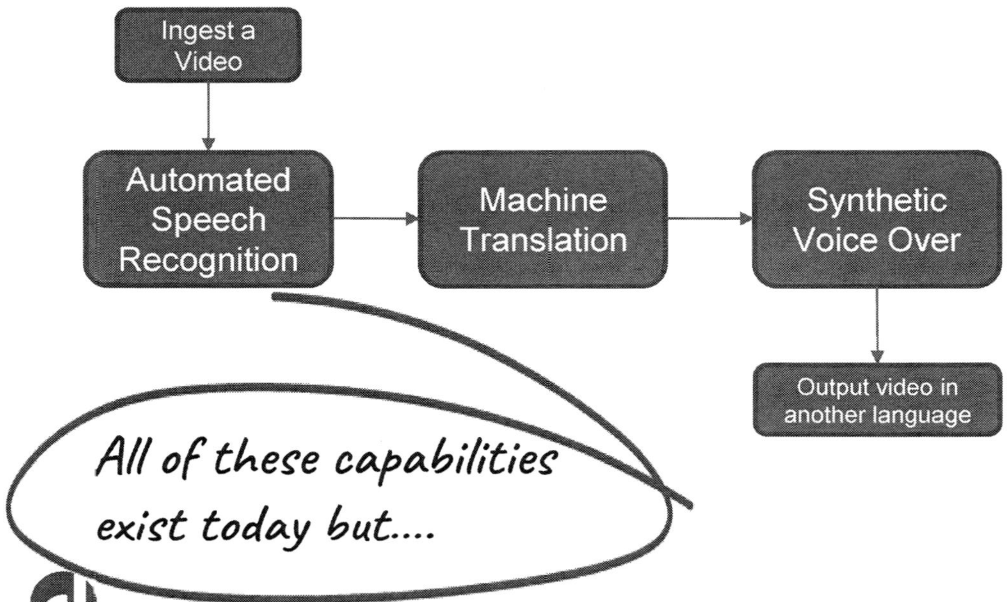

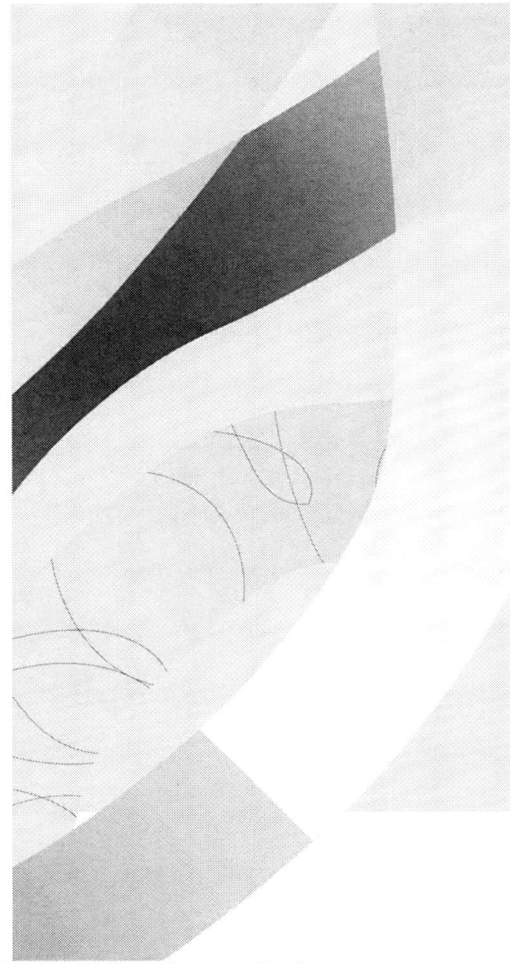

Lorem Ipsum

Lorem ipsum dolor sit amet consectetur adipiscing elit Lorem ipsum dolor..

02

Ideal Video for automation

01. Single Speaker

02. Good Audio Quality

03. No background or ambient noise

04. Little or no jargon

05. Relatively short sentences

06. Simple, clear Language

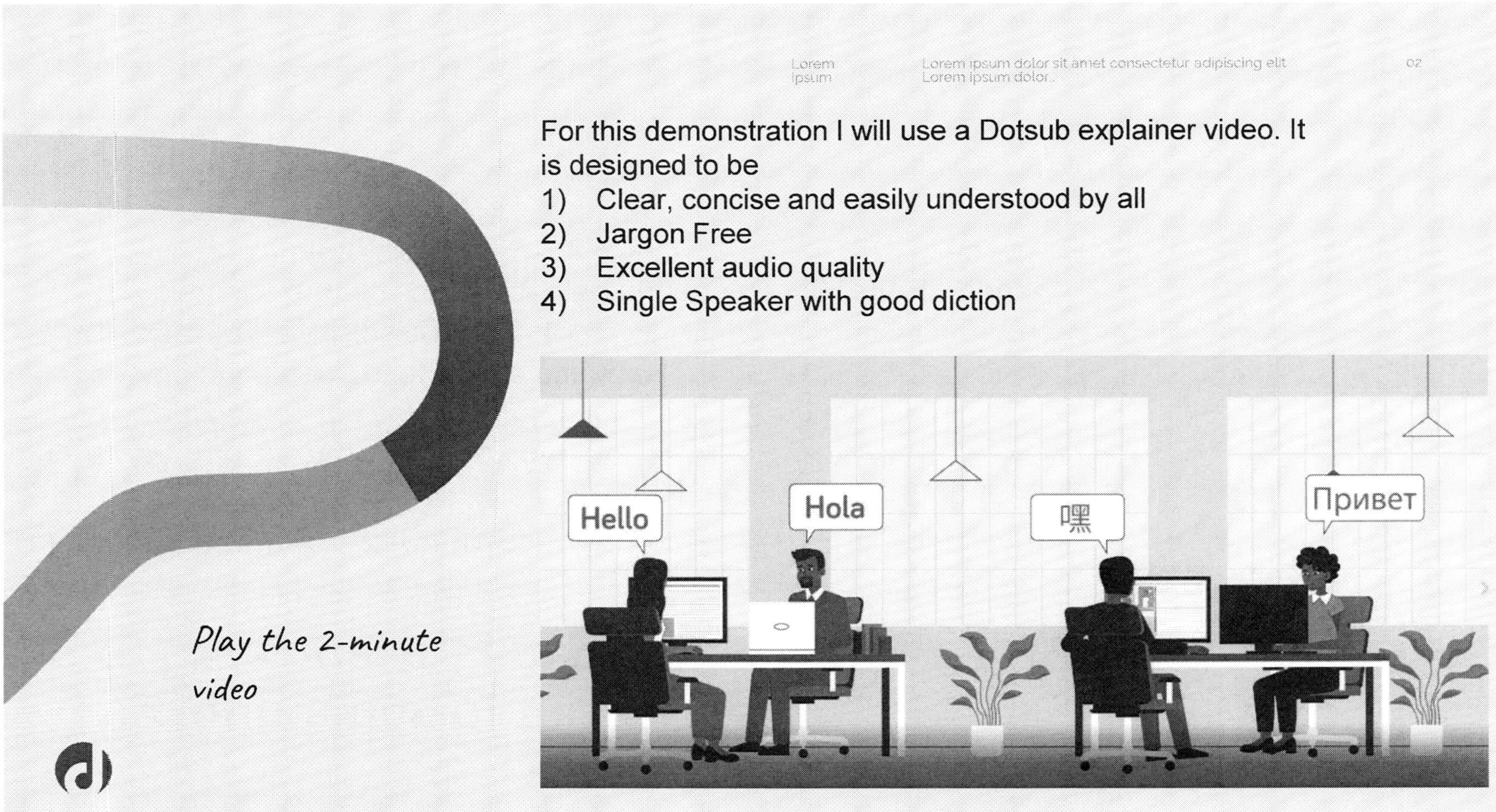
Lorem ipsum
Lorem ipsum dolor sit amet consectetur adipiscing elit
Lorem ipsum dolor.
02
For this demonstration I will use a Dotsub explainer video. It is designed to be
1) Clear, concise and easily understood by all
2) Jargon Free
3) Excellent audio quality
4) Single Speaker with good diction
Hello
Hola
嘿
Привет
Play the 2-minute video

The foundation of this process are the English Captions

- The captions need to be transcribed correctly.
  - The only errors should be with proper nouns and names
- They should be timed correctly
  - No captions on the screen for too long or not long enough
  - Should not extend over scene changes
- They should be well segmented
  - The captions that are on the screen need to be logically grouped
  - Should be comfortable to read

Let's run it through the ASR engine

The first line of the video's dialogue is "Your awesome video is in the can"

The ASR engine gives

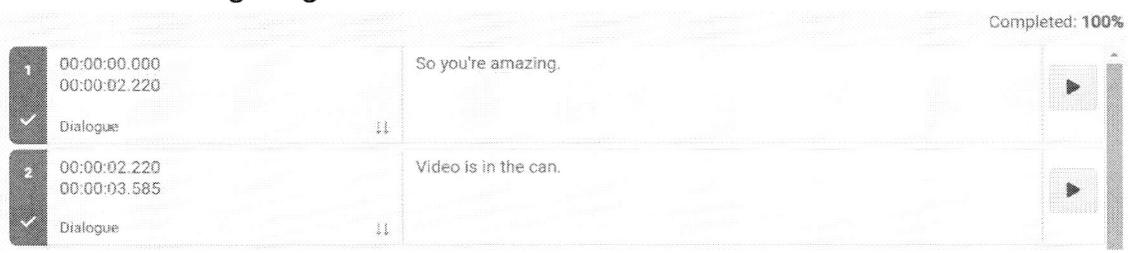

Not a great start.

Let's run it through the ASR engine (continued)

Other errors

Should be "Not so. Welcome to Any Video, Any Language from Dotsub."
ASR gave "Not so welcome to any video. Any language from dot sub."

Many examples of poor segmentation and therefore poor timing.

Comparing human captioner to ASR

Most cues are very different

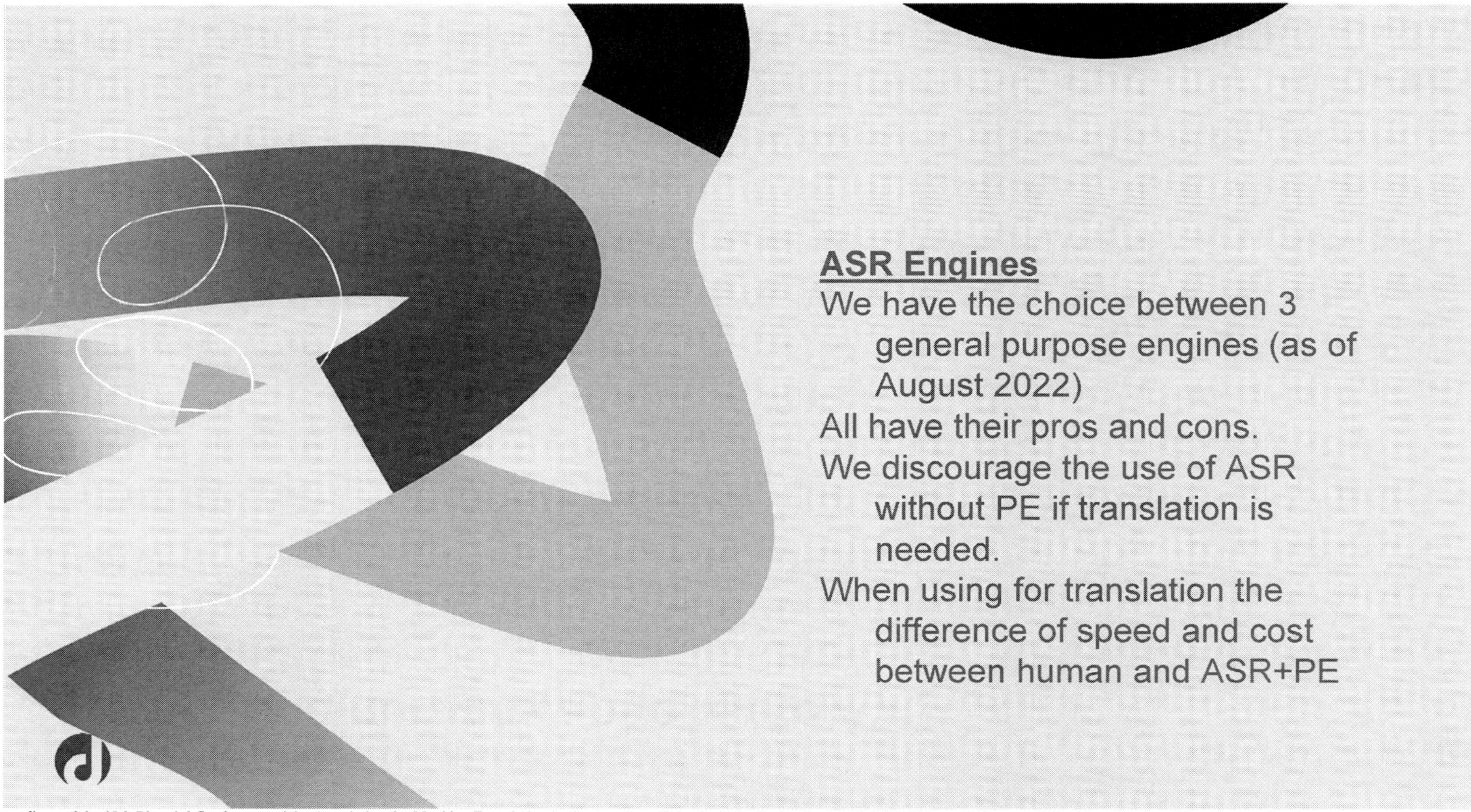
ASR Engines
We have the choice between 3 general purpose engines (as of August 2022)
All have their pros and cons.
We discourage the use of ASR without PE if translation is needed.
When using for translation the difference of speed and cost between human and ASR+PE

Machine Translation

MT for AVT is more difficult as a translation segment may be split across more than one cue

To maintain context you need to intelligently combine cues to make sure the correct concepts are translated

Once the translation is done then the timing and segmentation needs to be reapplied.

If used with excellent input (captions), then MT with light post editing works well

Synthetic Voice Overs – text to speech

This is the most exciting aspect of the whole scenario

Neural voices are generally very human like when used
to voice videos that do not have a lot of emotional range.
Good for explainer videos, how to videos, training videos
and less
useful for dramatic entertainment videos.

Demonstrate a few voices to show quality

Currently, Microsoft Azure Cognitive Services provides
87 languages, each language having at least a male and
female versión, more common languages have multiple
dialects and speakers

Synthetic Voice Overs (continued)

Functionality includes

1) Fully automated workflow
2) Speaker ID and multiple voice support
    1) User can designate different voices to different speakers in the original video
3) No limit to the length of a SVO video
    1) Overcome limits of vendors
4) Videos synced with videos using the timing of the captions
    1) Long and short languages dealt with.
5) Editor within the platform that allows the prosody, emphasis and pronunciation of the SVO to be modified
6) Voiceover burnin
    1) The ability to demux the audio track so that the voice track is replaced while keeping the background audio (music or ambient)
7) Ability to create custom voices

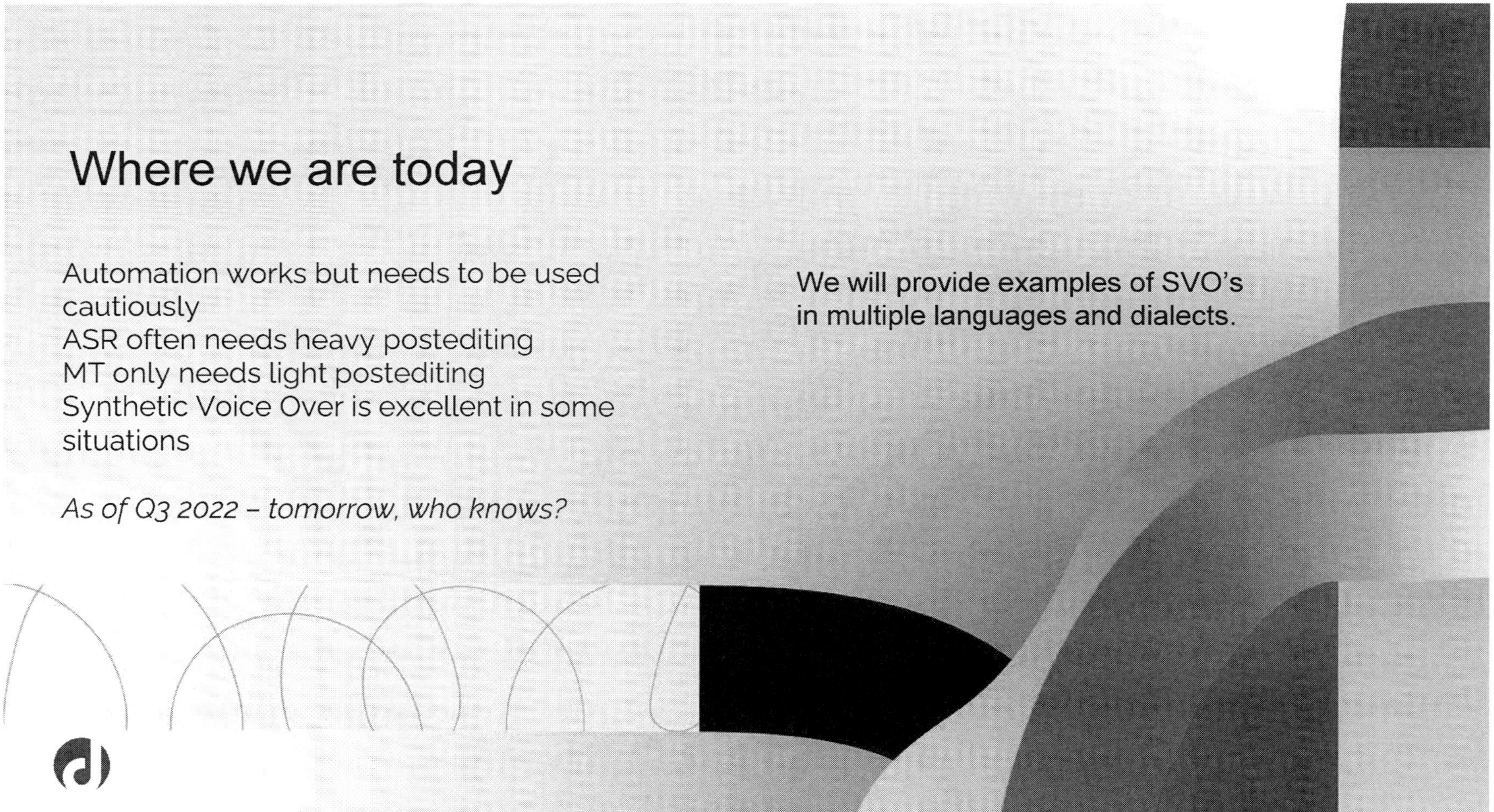
Where we are today
Automation works but needs to be used cautiously
ASR often needs heavy postediting
MT only needs light postediting
Synthetic Voice Over is excellent in some situations
As of Q3 2022 – tomorrow, who knows?
We will provide examples of SVO's in multiple languages and dialects.

Thanks!
Dave Bryant
CEO, Dotsub
dave.bryant@dotsub.com
https://dotsub.com

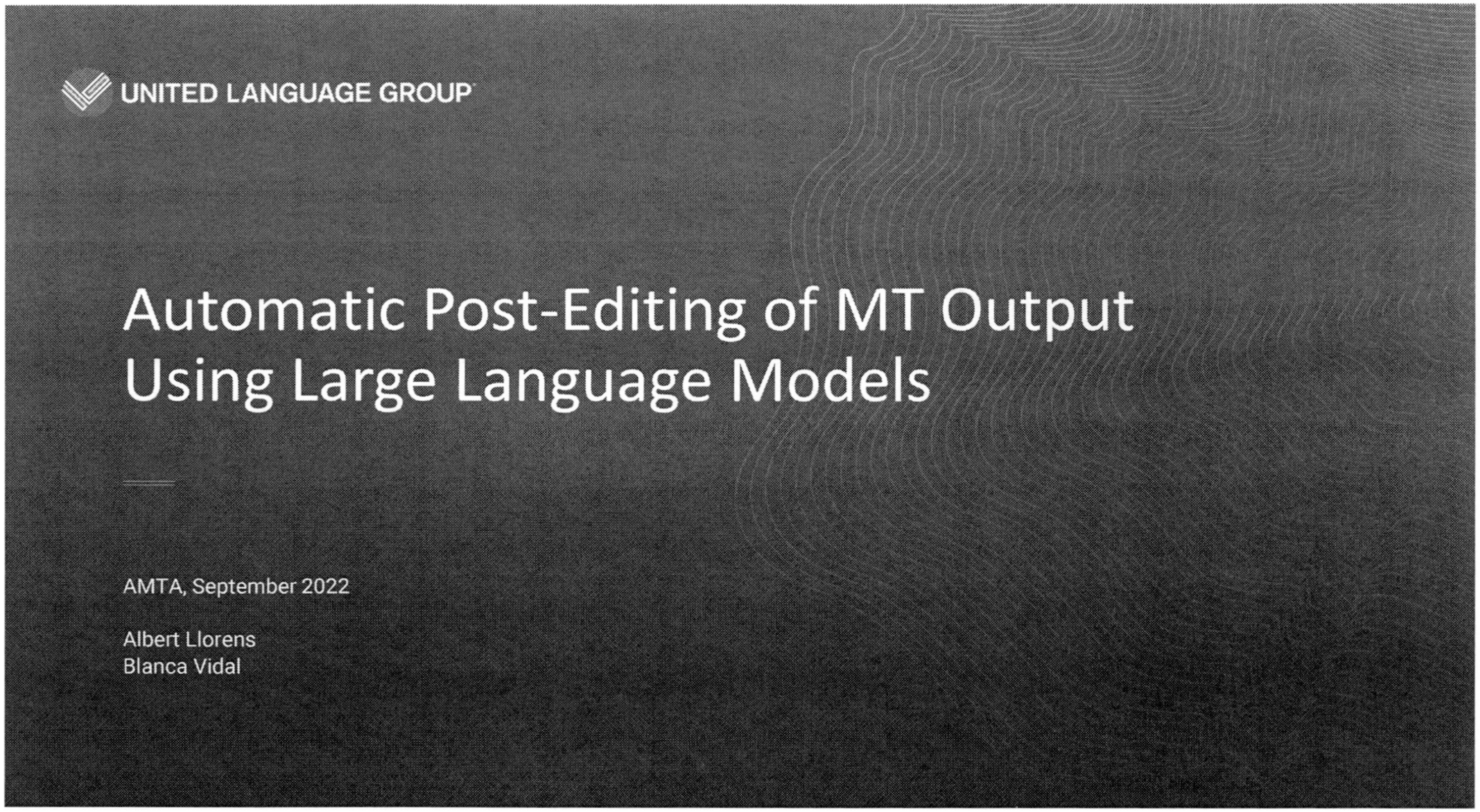
UNITED LANGUAGE GROUP
Automatic Post-Editing of MT Output
Using Large Language Models
AMTA, September 2022
Albert Llorens
Blanca Vidal

Why Glossaries Matter in the Translation Business

Accuracy of translation

- Not using the industry or company specific translation of a term may lead to inaccurate translations

Glossaries ensure the **consistency** of the translation of key terms, both within and across documents

Client glossaries typically include

- Product names
- Company names
- Ambiguous words
- Abbreviations
- Borrowed words
- Terminology (specialized industry/field terms)

UNITED LANGUAGE GROUP

Glossaries and Machine Translation

- Pre-translation with NMT is widely used in the Translation business
- NMT is a black box to users, developers, and researchers
- NMT models can be trained, but not forced
- Glossaries are more about "forcing" than "training"
- It is not straightforward to "force" a NMT system to translate terms according to a glossary

UNITED LANGUAGE GROUP

ULG Use Case

- ULG main NMT provider handles **glossaries** by doing a brute force find-and-replace operation
- This approach **guarantees close to 100% consistency** of machine translations with glossary translations
- But it has **negative side effects** in the translation quality, mostly in:
  - Grammatical agreement (gender, number, case)
  - Word order
- ULG Glossaries are used in MT in two different ways:
  - As bilingual dictionaries that can be referenced at request level with a category id
  - At runtime, by annotating the terms that require a specific translation with xml tags in the input string of the request

UNITED LANGUAGE GROUP

Proposed Solution

- Keep the current workflow: translation with **annotated input**
- Add **a post-processing step** where the grammar and word order errors are fixed
- Use a general-purpose large language model, like OpenAI GPT-3, **to do the post-editing** of the NMT output

UNITED LANGUAGE GROUP

About OpenAI API and GPT-3 Models

- The **OpenAI API** can be applied to virtually any task that involves understanding or generating natural language
- The API is **powered by GPT-3**, a set of models with different capabilities
- The API requests are headed by a **prompt** that describes the task to be done by the model
- The **prompts** used in the experiment are:
  - "Corregir la gramática en español"
  - "Corregir el orden de las palabras en español"
  - "Traducir al español con el glosario {}={}:\n\n{}."
- The **models** used in the experiment are:
  - text-davinci-edit-001
  - text-davinci-002
- The **endpoints** used in the experiment are
  - /completions: input text as a prompt, and get a text completion that matches the prompt instruction
  - /edits: change existing text via a prompt, instead of completing it

UNITED LANGUAGE GROUP

Experiment Objectives

The experiment we implemented wanted to check the following points:

1. Check if **GPT-3** can be used as **an MT engine**
2. Check if **GPT-3** can be used as an **Automated Post-Editor**
3. Check if **GPT-3** can **improve its own Post-Editing** by requesting **word order correction**
4. Check if **GPT-3** can be used as an **MT engine using Glossary annotations**

UNITED LANGUAGE GROUP

Test Data Selection

- Translation Memory and glossary of a ULG client
- Both TM and glossary must be big enough, and **TM** must be highly **consistent with the glossary**
- Choice of languages: English to German and to Spanish
- Data size: **~500k TM segments and ~600 glossary terms**

UNITED LANGUAGE GROUP

Test Data Preparation

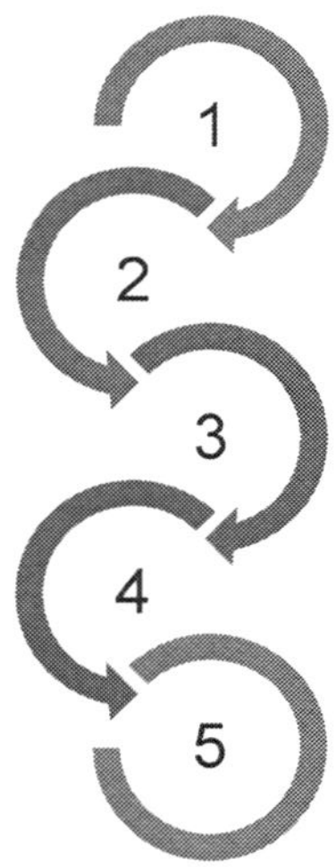

- Restricting the set to **English-Spanish**
- **Filtering** the data set by
  - Lemmatizing source and target segments
  - Removing all segments that don't match any pair in the glossary
- Data size after preparation: **~2,000 segments**
- **Annotating** source segments with glossary translations. Examples:
  - Side view <term trans=**disco de ruptura**>**rupture disk**</term>
  - Sensor < term trans =**procesador central extendido>extended core processor**</term>
- Selecting a **sample of 250 segments** from the test data

UNITED LANGUAGE GROUP

Experiment Requests and Outputs

#		Tasks, requests, prompts, outputs
1	ULG MT	Source file without annotation sent to ULG MT
2	ULG MT	Source file with Glossary annotation sent to ULG MT
3	GPT-3	Output of (2) sent to GPT-3 'edits' endpoint with prompt "Corregir la gramática en español" ["temperature": 0 , engine="text-davinci-edit-001"]
4	GPT-3	Output of 3 sent to GPT-3 'edits' endpoint with prompt "Corregir el orden de las palabras en español" ["temperature": 0, engine="text-davinci-edit-001"]
5	GPT-3	Source file without annotation sent to GPT-3 'completions' endpoint with prompt "Traducir al español" ["temperature": 0, engine="text-davinci-002"]
6	GPT-3	Source file with Glossary annotation sent to GPT-3 'completions' endopoint with prompt "Traducir al español con el glosario {source term}={target term}" ["temperature": 0, engine="text-davinci-002"]

UNITED LANGUAGE GROUP

Experiment Results

BLEU, TER and Terminology Consistency scores

		BLEU	TER	TC
1	ULG MT without glossary	57.6	26.0	87.12%
2	ULG MT with glossary	54.8	27.4	99.24%
3	GPT-3 PE grammar	54.8	30.5	98.11%
4	GPT-3 PE grammar and order	49.6	34.6	83.71%
5	GPT-3 MT without glossary	49.7	35.8	75.00%
6	GPT-3 MT with glossary	43.2	54.4	85.61%

UNITED LANGUAGE GROUP

Results: Output Scores

BLEU, TER and Terminology consistency scores

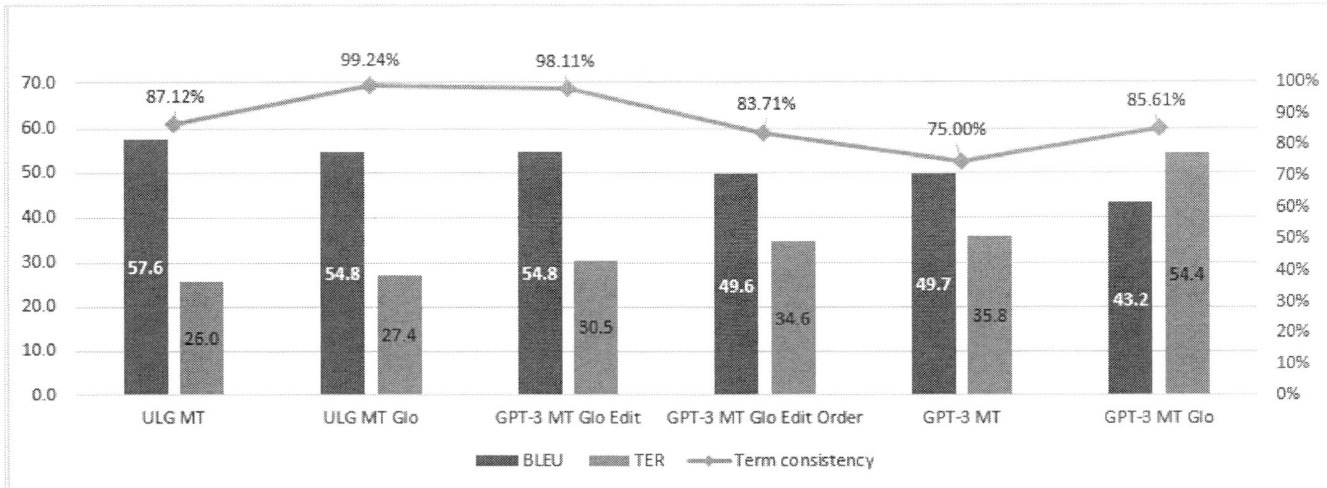

UNITED LANGUAGE GROUP

Results: Comparative Analysis

1 Check if **GPT-3** can be used as **an MT engine**

RESULTS
- Most outputs are either similar or identical to the ones of our current models.
- GPT-3 is less conservative in the preservation of the source.
- Makes changes that need to be contrasted with the input.
- Need to fix GPT-3's addition of extra dots (and blanks)

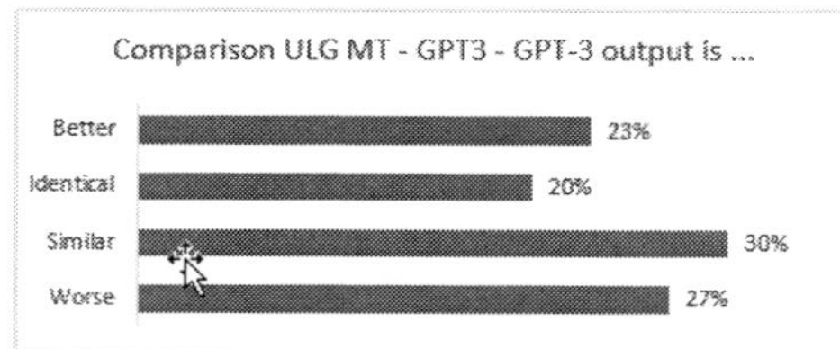

34	{for example, **argon**{***argón*** }}	34	{por ejemplo, argón}	<>	Por ejemplo, el argón.
35	**dry inert gas**{***gas inerte seco*** }	35	gas inerte seco	<>	Gas inerte y seco.
36	Simultaneously available 4-20 mA **active output**{***salida activa*** }, represents on-line density or temperature	36	Salida activa de 4-20 mA disponible simultáneamente, representa la densidad o la temperatura en línea	<>	Disponible simultáneamente 4-20 mA salida activa, representa en línea densidad o temperatura.

UNITED LANGUAGE GROUP

Results: Comparative Analysis

2 Check if **GPT-3** can be used as an **Automated Post-Editor**

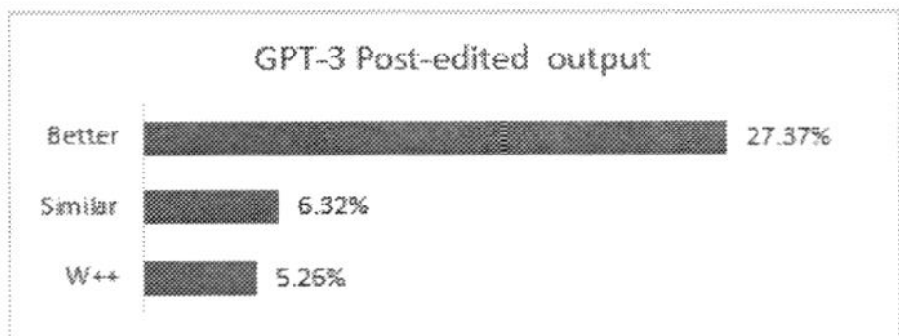

RESULTS
- GPT-3 managed to fix gender agreement problems
- It also fixed number agreement
- Addition of determiners and prepositions added fluency
- Addition of other terms also added fluency

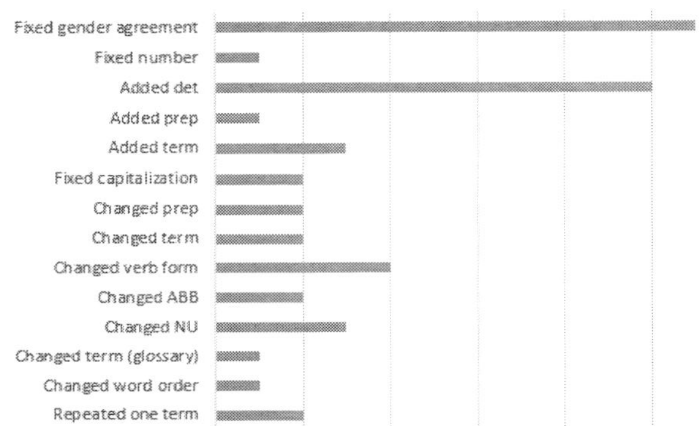

UNITED LANGUAGE GROUP

Results: Comparative Analysis

EXAMPLES OF IMPROVED OUTPUTS

Rating	ID	Source	Output 1		Output 2
★★★	78	Test points with **Product01**{*Product01*} tool	Puntos de prueba con Product01 herramienta	<>	Puntos de prueba con la herramienta Product01
★★★	19	For Model 1500, output voltage is +15 VDC ±3% with a 2,2 kohm internal **pull-up resistor**{*resistencia pull-up*}.	Para el modelo 1500, el voltaje de salida es de +15 VCC ±3% con un resistencia pull-up interno de 2,2 kohm.	<>	Para el modelo 1500, el voltaje de salida es de +15 VCC ±3% con una resistencia pull-up interna de 2,2 kohm.
★★☆	95	If you are installing a cable gland at the I.S. barrier, a standard cable gland with a sealing washer, **lock washer**{*arandela*}, and lock nut is required.	Si está instalando un prensaestopas en la barrera I.S., se requiere un prensaestopas estándar con una arandela de sellado, arandela y tuerca de bloqueo.	<>	Si está instalando un prensaestopas en la barrera I.S., se requiere un prensaestopas estándar con una arandela de sellado, una arandela y una tuerca de bloqueo.
★★☆	241	One exception is **nitric acid**{*ácido nítrico*}, for which 304 stainless steel has better corrosion resistance.	Una excepción es ácido nítrico, para el cual el acero inoxidable 304 tiene una mejor resistencia a la corrosión.	<>	Una excepción es el ácido nítrico, para el cual el acero inoxidable 304 tiene una mejor resistencia a la corrosión.
★★☆	104	**infrared port**{*puerto infrarrojo*} write-protection	puerto infrarrojo protección contra escritura	<>	puerto infrarrojo con protección contra escritura
★☆☆	66	To poll an **external temperature device**{*dispositivo de temperatura externo*}, configure polling for temperature as described in.	Para sondear un dispositivo de temperatura externo, configure el sondeo para la temperatura como se describe en.	<>	Para sondear un dispositivo de temperatura externo, configure el sondeo para la temperatura como se describe en la sección.
★☆☆	107	If you are using the **infrared port**{*puerto infrarrojo*}, position the infrared device for communication with the infrared port (see).	Si está utilizando el puerto infrarrojo, coloque el dispositivo infrarrojo para la comunicación con el puerto infrarrojo (consulte).	<>	Si está utilizando el puerto infrarrojo, coloque el dispositivo infrarrojo para la comunicación con el puerto infrarrojo (consulte la figura).

UNITED LANGUAGE GROUP

Results: Comparative Analysis

EXAMPLES OF WRONG CORRECTIONS

Changed glossary term

238	**config I/O custom**{***E/S configurables personalizadas*** }	E/S configurables personalizadas	<>	E/S personalizadas configurables
239	**config I/O default**{***E/S configurables predeterminadas*** }	E/S configurables predeterminadas	<>	E/S configurables por defecto

Acceptable worsening

133	Maximum distance between remote **booster amplifier**{***amplificador booster*** } and sensor is 18m.	La distancia máxima entre el amplificador booster remoto y el sensor es de 18 m.	<>	La distancia máxima entre el amplificador booster remoto y el sensor es de 18 metros.
76	External means that an external **pull-up resistor**{***resistencia pull-up*** } and source are required.	Externo significa que se requieren resistencia pull-up y una fuente externas.	<>	Externo significa que se requieren resistencia pull-up y una fuente externa.
18	**engineering unit of measurement**{***unidad de ingeniería de medición, unidad de ingeniería de medida*** }	unidad de ingeniería de medición, unidad de ingeniería de medida	<>	unidad de ingeniería de medición, unidad de ingeniería de medida, unidad de ingeniería de mediciones

CORRECTION NOT SUPPORTED

63	For F-Series sensors with a junction box or an **extended core processor**{***procesador central extendido*** }, the maximum ambient temperature is 60°C (140°F).	Para los sensores de la serie F con una caja de conexiones o un procesador central extendido, la temperatura ambiente máxima es de 60 ° C (140 ° F).	<>	Para los sensores de la serie F con una caja de conexiones o un procesador central extendido, la temperatura ambiente máxima es de 60 ° C (140 ° F).

UNITED LANGUAGE GROUP

Results: Comparative Analysis

3 Check if **GPT-3** can **improve its own Post-Editing** by requesting **word order correction**

RESULTS

ORDER CHANGES

- Improve: apposition of proper names
- Similar: order of exchangeable noun modifiers
- Worsening: change order in glossary terms, change in term meaning, change of the translation of a glossary term

REST OF CHANGES

- Improve: added fluency (adding determiners)
- Worsening: adds a duplicated term

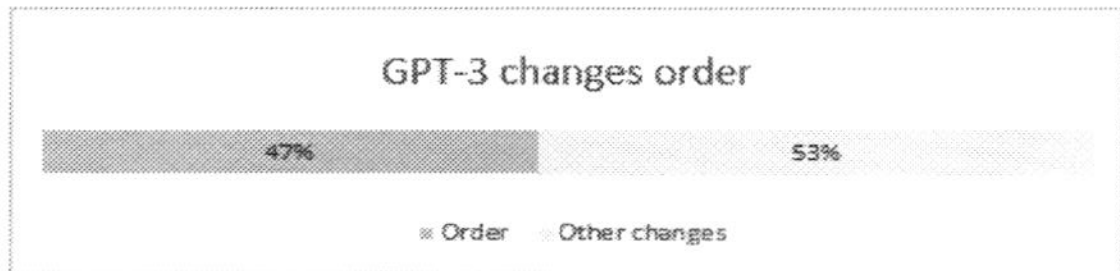

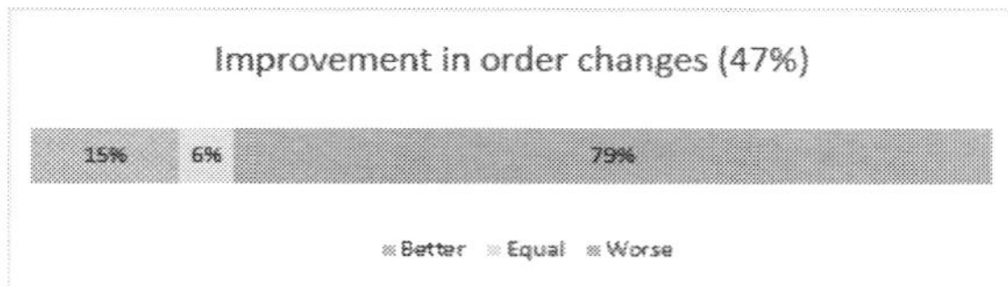

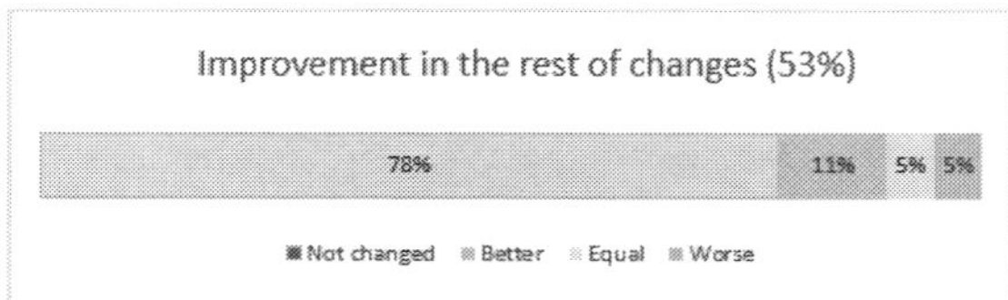

UNITED LANGUAGE GROUP

Results: Comparative Analysis

EXAMPLES OF IMPROVED OUTPUTS

★★☆

249	**Product01{Product01} 5-pin Product02 connector in M20 housing**	Product01 conector Product02 de 5 pines en carcasa M20.	<>	Conector Product01 Product02 de 5 pines en carcasa M20.

EXAMPLES OF WRONG CORRECTIONS

!

236	(or pin 2-3 of Product02™ Product01{Product01}™ connector)	(o pin 2-3 del conector Product02™ Product01 ™).	<>	(o pin 2-3 del conector Product01 ™ Product02™).

!

2	Using a **DeviceNet**{***DeviceNet***} tool, three methods are available for totalizer and inventory control:	Utilizando una herramienta de DeviceNet, hay tres métodos disponibles para el totalizador y el control de inventario.	<>	Utilizando una herramienta de DeviceNet, hay tres métodos disponibles para el control de inventario y el totalizador.

!

13	**DIN rail enclosure**{***cubierta de carril DIN***}	cubierta de carril DIN.	<>	cubierta de DIN carril.
14	**core processor entity parameter**{***parámetro de entidad del procesador central***}	parámetro de la entidad del procesador central	<>	parámetro de la entidad central del procesador
15	**Construction Identification Code**{***código de identificación de construcción***}	código de identificación de construcción.	<>	código de construcción de identificación.
16	Side view with **rupture disk**{***disco de ruptura***}	Vista lateral con disco de ruptura.	<>	Vista lateral con ruptura de disco.
18	**engineering unit of measurement**{***unidad de ingeniería de medición, unidad de ingeniería de medida***}	unidad de ingeniería de medición, unidad de ingeniería de medida, unidad de ingeniería de mediciones	<>	unidad de medición de ingeniería, unidad de medida de ingeniería, unidad de mediciones de ingeniería

UNITED LANGUAGE GROUP

Results: Comparative Analysis

4 Check if **GPT-3** can be used as an **MT engine using Glossary annotations**

RESULTS

- ULG MT Glossary gets applied in all segments (100%)
- GPT-3 is only applied in 76% of the segments due to different reasons
- In both cases there are side effects already found in previous tests

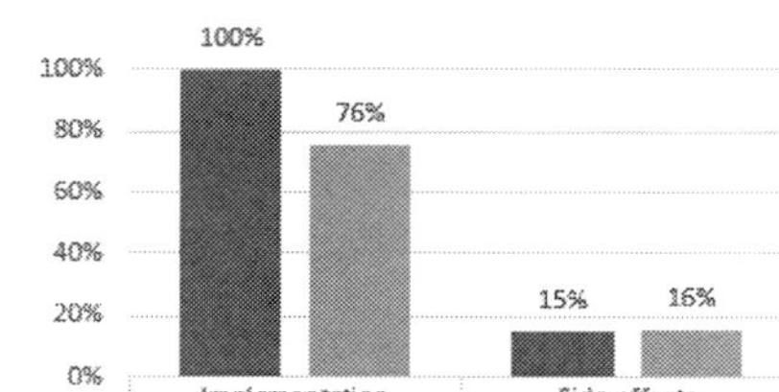

	Implementation	Side-effects
ULG MT GLO	100%	15%
GPT-3 MT GLO	76%	16%

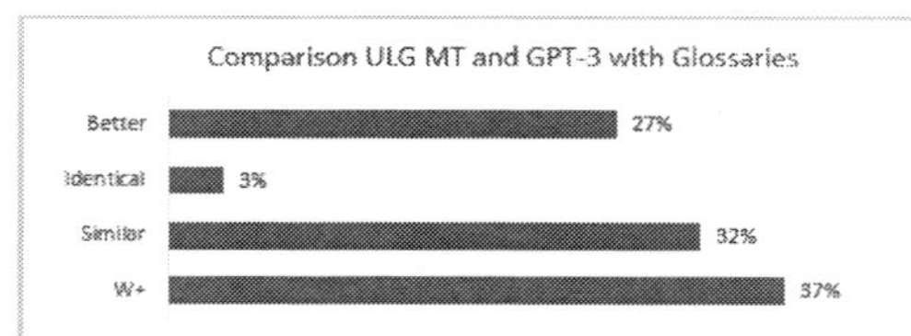

UNITED LANGUAGE GROUP

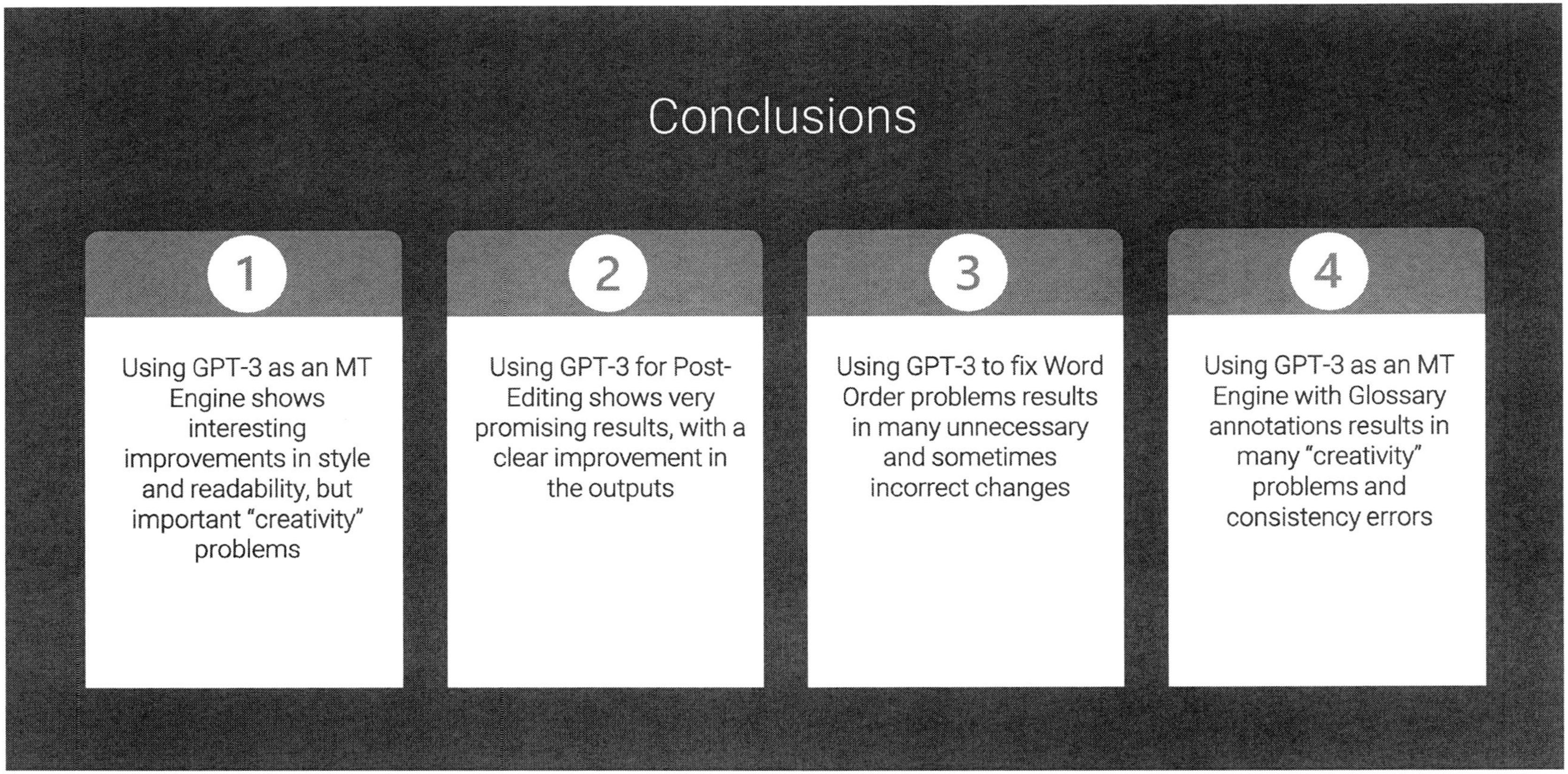

UNITED LANGUAGE GROUP

Future Work

Prompt engineering
- Prompt language makes a difference
- Adding examples, find the most appropriate wording of the instructions

Adjusting request parameters
- temperature: lower temperature, less risks
- top_p: select tokens with top probability mass

Fine-tuning the GPT-3 models with ULG data

Using logprobs and beam search with higher temperature to filter undesired responses

UNITED LANGUAGE GROUP

Credits

Alonso, Juan Alberto
juan.alonso@ulgroup.com

Llorens, Albert
albert.llorens@ulgroup.com

Madan, Mehul
mehul.madan@ulgroup.com

Vidal, Blanca
blanca.vidal@ulgroup.com

UNITED LANGUAGE GROUP

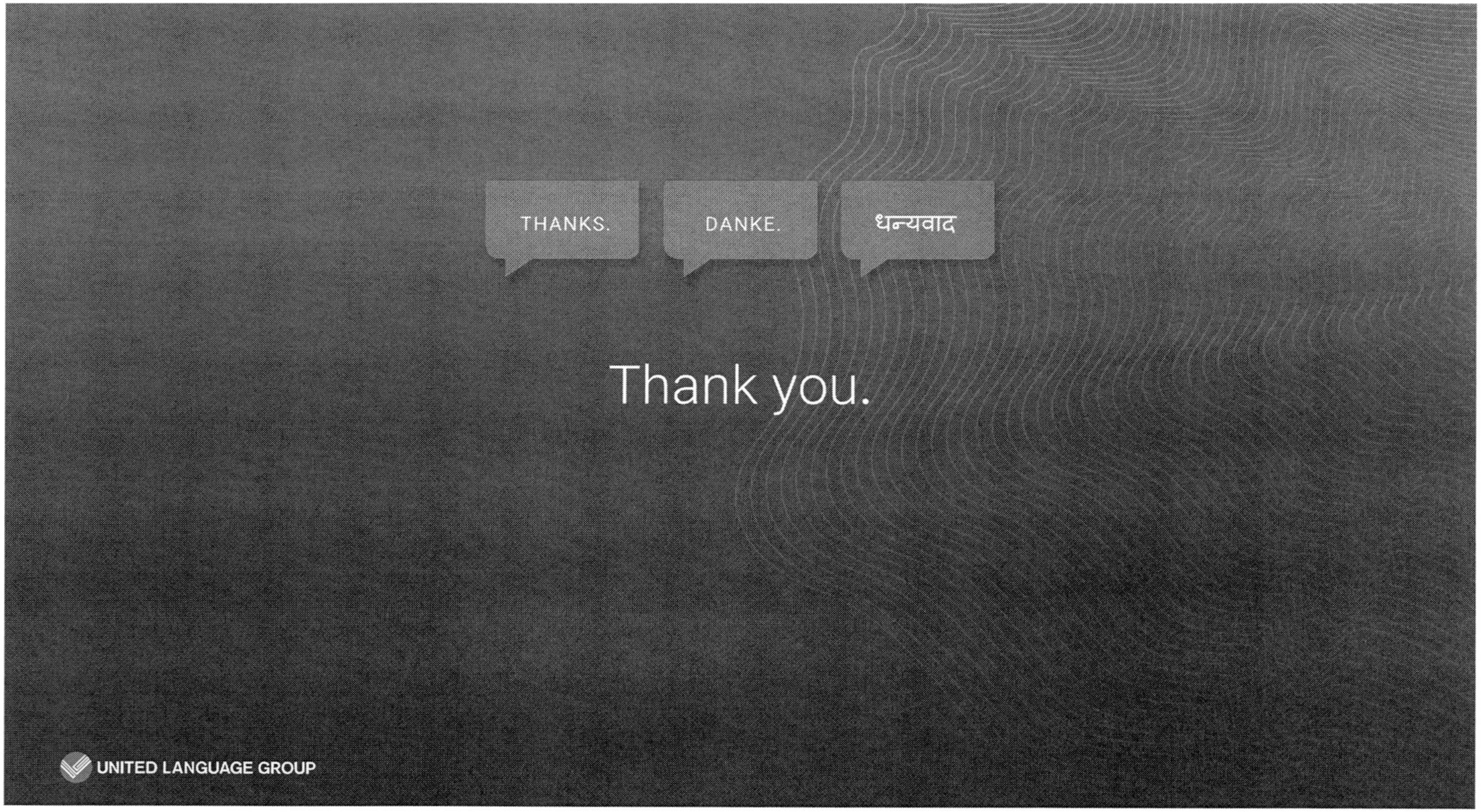
THANKS.
DANKE.
धन्यवाद
Thank you.
UNITED LANGUAGE GROUP

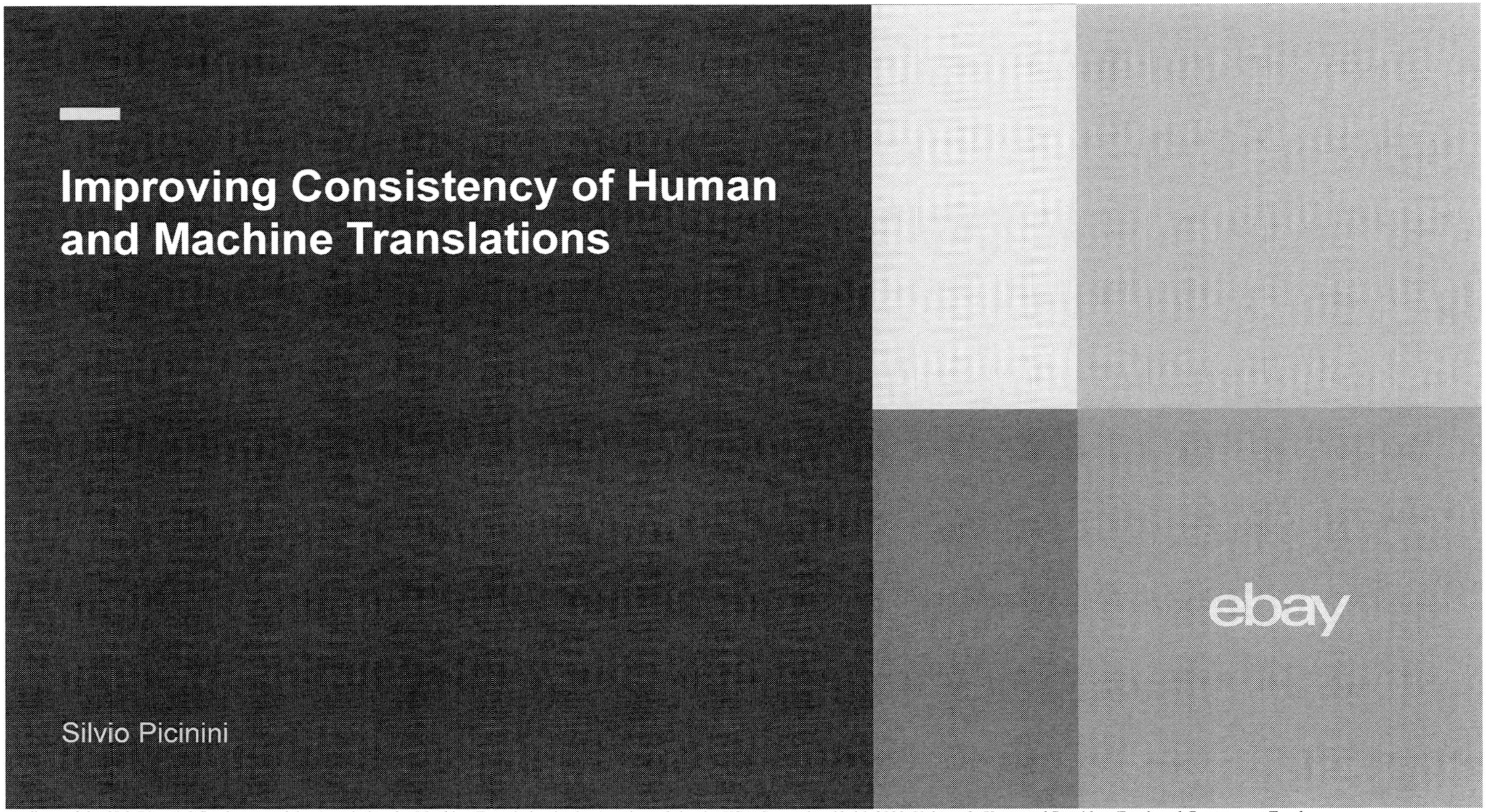
Improving Consistency of Human and Machine Translations
Silvio Picinini
ebay

Topics

- Intro
- Method
- Sense of quality
- Results
- MT and glossary creation
- Measuring MT Consistency

Intro

Objective

- Increase consistency in the postediting of large volumes of data

How

Hey, data, can show me where you are wrong?

- Find inconsistency candidates and correct the errors
  - Idea: Terms can be translated or untranslated
  - If they are both, this could indicate inconsistency

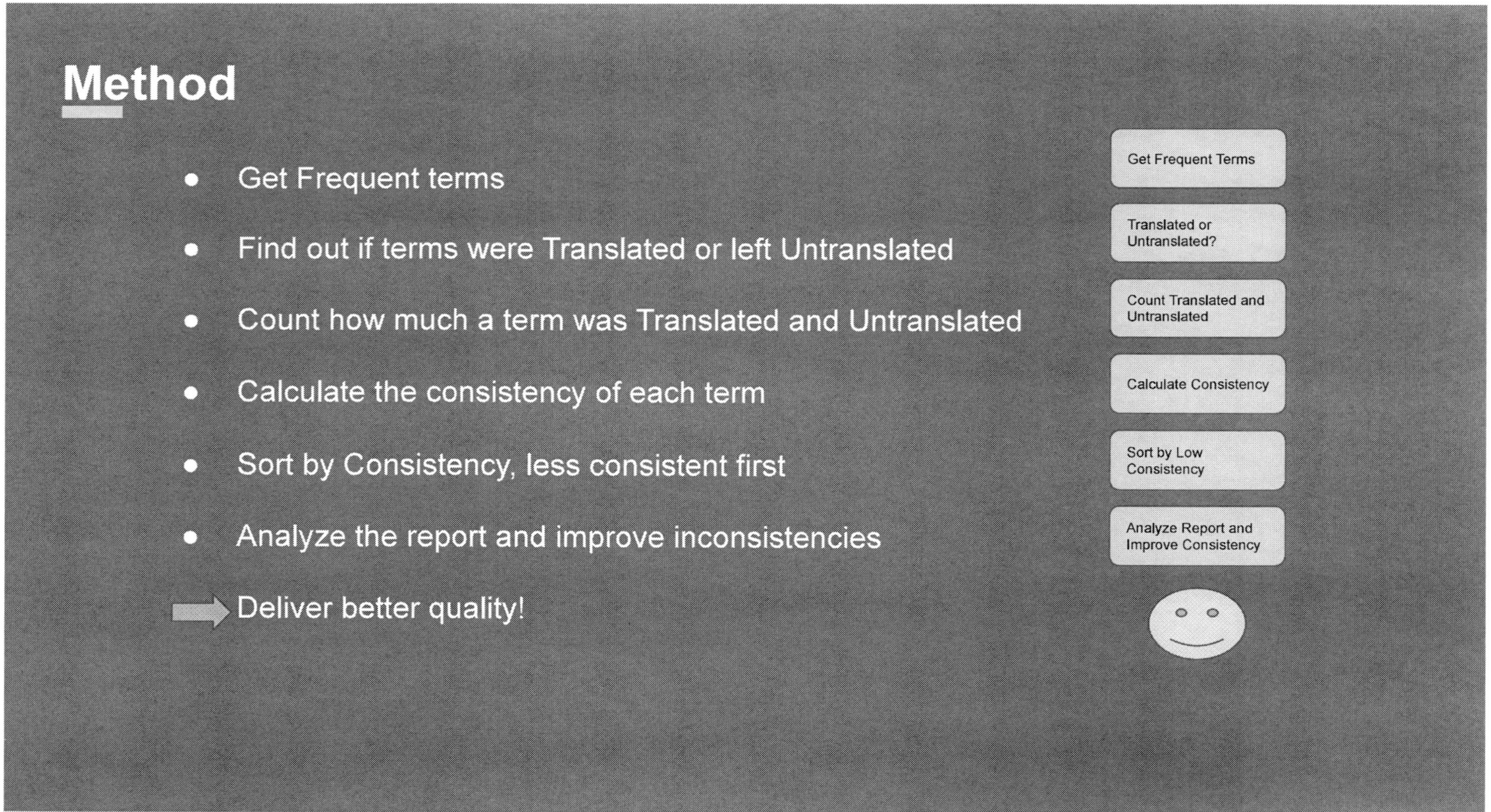
Method
Get Frequent terms
Find out if terms were Translated or left Untranslated
Count how much a term was Translated and Untranslated
Calculate the consistency of each term
Sort by Consistency, less consistent first
Analyze the report and improve inconsistencies
Deliver better quality!
Get Frequent Terms
Translated or Untranslated?
Count Translated and Untranslated
Calculate Consistency
Sort by Low Consistency
Analyze Report and Improve Consistency

Method

- Get Frequent terms

A short Python script extracts the most frequent 1000 source terms, sorted in order of frequency.

Method

- Find out if terms were Translated or left Untranslated
- Count how much a term was Translated and Untranslated

The Python script:

- takes each source term
- finds a segment that contains it in the source
- checks if the target segment contains that term:
  - if yes, it counts as untranslated for that term
  - if no, it it counts as translated for that term

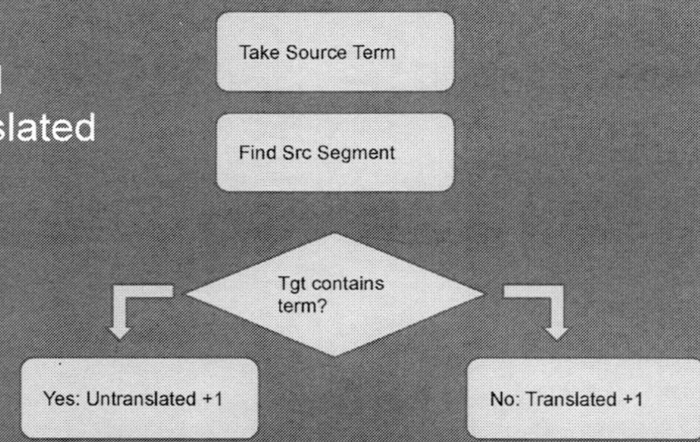

The result looks like this:

Word	Untranslated	Translated
fuchs	11	11
one	15	16
jersey	10	9
shopper	28	22
italy	11	15
sport	15	21

Method

- Calculate the consistency of each term

The Python script:

- calculates the consistency score
  - If a term is translated 12 times and untranslated 8 times:
  - the 8 times (lower number) are “inconsistent” with the majority of 12
  - the total instances is 20 (12 + 8)
  - the Consistency score is 8 out of 20
    - this is 40% inconsistent **- so it is 60% consistent**

The result looks like this:

Word	Untranslated	Translated	Consistency score
fuchs	11	11	50.0
one	15	16	51.6
jersey	10	9	52.6
shopper	28	22	56.0
italy	11	15	57.7
sport	15	21	58.3

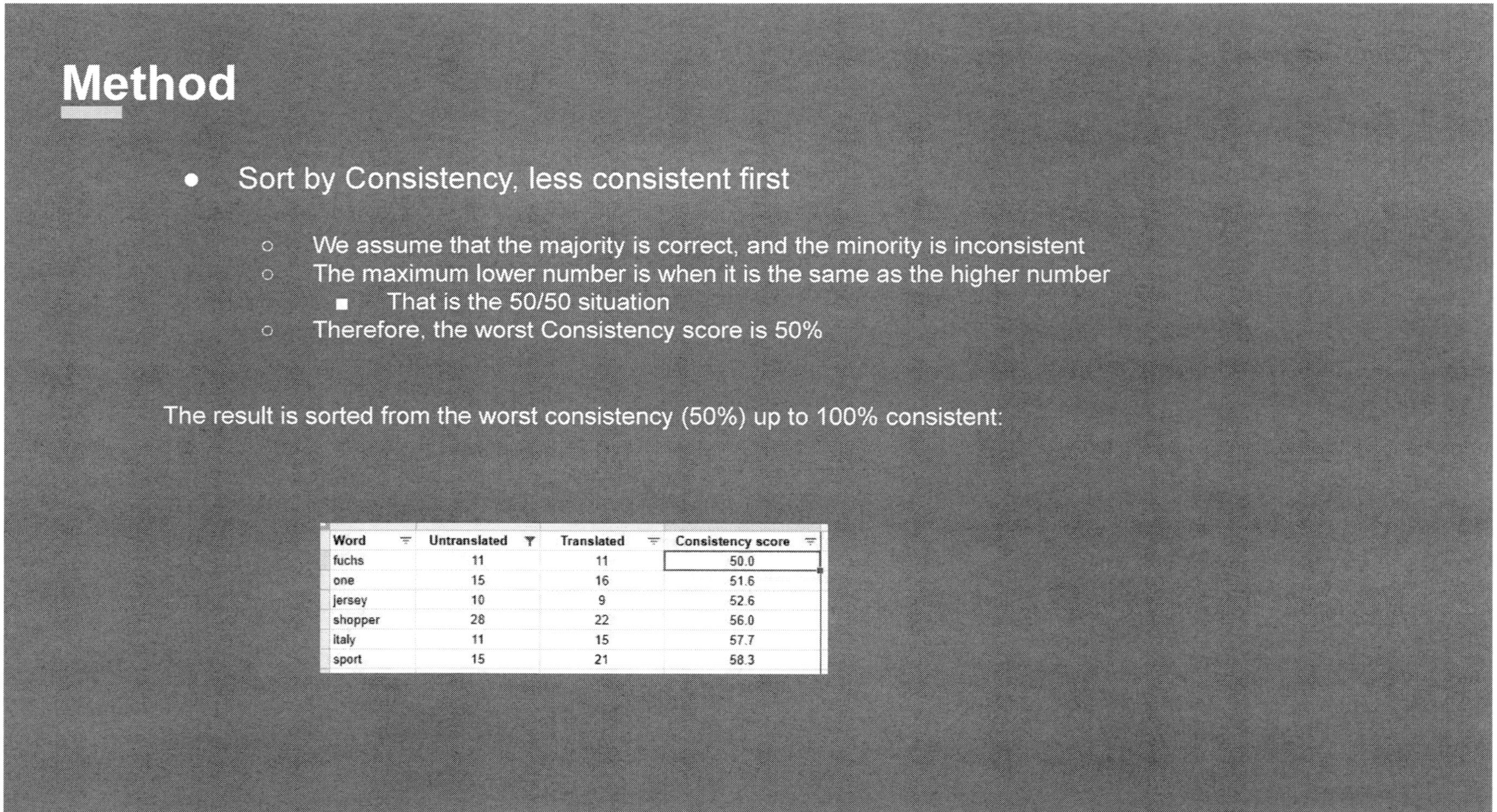

Word	Untranslated	Translated	Consistency score
fuchs	11	11	50.0
one	15	16	51.6
jersey	10	9	52.6
shopper	28	22	56.0
italy	11	15	57.7
sport	15	21	58.3

Method

- Analyze the report and improve inconsistencies

Word	Untranslated	Translated	Consistency score
fuchs	11	11	50.0
one	15	16	51.6
jersey	10	9	52.6
shopper	28	22	56.0

The Python script:

- creates a list of segments containing the term
- marks the segments as translated or untranslated

This facilitates the analysis.

- Translated shows nákupni often

Word	Transl/Untra	Source segment	Target Segment
shopper	translated:	mcm wende shopper tasche liz.med. org. rech.neu 625 €.ovp. neu.ungetr.ohne pouch	mcm wende nákupní taška liz. medium, nové 625 €.ovp. nové, bez sáčku
shopper	translated:	tasche! campomaggi! shopper! cognac! so schön! groß! klassiker!��	taška. campomaggi! nakupní! koňak barva! tak krásná! velká! klasika!��
shopper	translated:	bree fantastic 4leder-shopper tasche hobo-bag leder red rot neu np:299€	bree fantastic 4 kožené bag hobo-bag taška kůže červená nové cena: 299 €
shopper	translated:	geniale xxl echt leder tasche/shopper braun stabil robust neuwertig np215,44 eur	důmyslná xxl pravá kožená taška / nákupní hnědá stabilní robustní jako nové cena 215,44 eur
shopper	translated:	ledertasche echtes fell, cognac, braun, shopper - italy tasche	kožená taška pravá kožešina, koňak, hnědá, nákupní taška - itálie taška
shopper	translated:	campomaggi shopper bag,groß, grün und pflegeset für leder, neu	campomaggi nákupní taška,velká, zelená a kožená sada na péči, nové
shopper	translated:	massimo palomba tasche, edel, handgeflochtenes leder, großer shopper, wie neu	taška massimo palomba, ušlechtilá, ručně tkaná kůže, velká nákupní taška, jako nové
shopper	translated:	neu handtasche leder handmade rehard unikat shopper elegant tasche neu	nové kožená kabelka rehard unikátní nákupní elegantní taška nové
shopper	translated:	tasche shopper gift vip chanel	nákupní taška dárek vip chanel

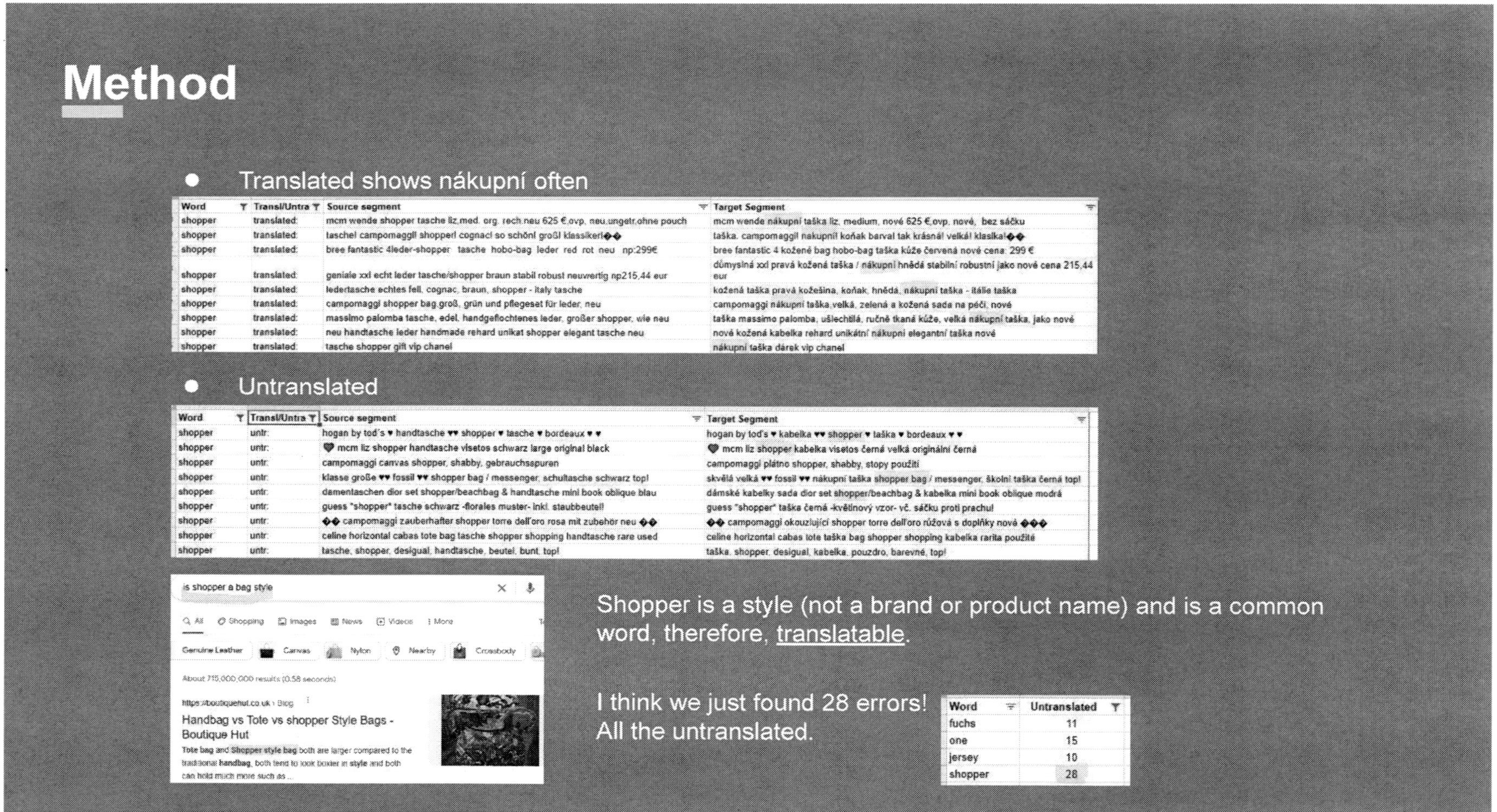
Method
Translated shows nákupní often
Word | Transl/Untra | Source segment | Target Segment
shopper | translated: | mcm wende shopper tasche liz,med. org. rech.neu 625 €,ovp, neu,ungetr,ohne pouch | mcm wende nákupní taška liz, medium, nové 625 €,ovp, nové, bez sáčku
shopper | translated: | taschel campomaggil shopperl cognacl so schönl großl klassikerl | taška. campomaggil nákupnil koňak barval tak krásnál velkál klasikal
shopper | translated: | bree fantastic 4leder-shopper tasche hobo-bag leder red rot neu np:299€ | bree fantastic 4 kožené bag hobo-bag taška kůže červená nové cena: 299 €
shopper | translated: | geniale xxl echt leder tasche/shopper braun stabil robust neuwertig np215,44 eur | důmyslná xxl pravá kožená taška / nákupní hnědá stabilní robustní jako nové cena 215,44 eur
shopper | translated: | ledertasche echtes fell, cognac, braun, shopper - italy tasche | kožená taška pravá kožešina, koňak, hnědá, nákupní taška - itálie taška
shopper | translated: | campomaggi shopper bag groß, grün und pflegeset für leder, neu | campomaggi nákupní taška velká, zelená a kožená sada na péči, nové
shopper | translated: | massimo palomba tasche, edel, handgeflochtenes leder, großer shopper, wie neu | taška massimo palomba, ušlechtilá, ručně tkaná kůže, velká nákupní taška, jako nové
shopper | translated: | neu handtasche leder handmade rehard unikat shopper elegant tasche neu | nové kožená kabelka rehard unikátní nákupní elegantní taška nové
shopper | translated: | tasche shopper gift vip chanel | nákupní taška dárek vip chanel
Untranslated
Word | Transl/Untra | Source segment | Target Segment
shopper | untr: | hogan by tod's handtasche shopper tasche bordeaux | hogan by tod's kabelka shopper taška bordeaux
shopper | untr: | mcm liz shopper handtasche visetos schwarz large original black | mcm liz shopper kabelka visetos černá velká originální černá
shopper | untr: | campomaggi canvas shopper, shabby, gebrauchsspuren | campomaggi plátno shopper, shabby, stopy použití
shopper | untr: | klasse große fossil shopper bag / messenger, schultasche schwarz top! | skvělá velká fossil nákupní taška shopper bag / messenger, školní taška černá top!
shopper | untr: | damentaschen dior set shopper/beachbag & handtasche mini book oblique blau | dámské kabelky sada dior set shopper/beachbag & kabelka mini book oblique modrá
shopper | untr: | guess "shopper" tasche schwarz -florales muster- inkl. staubbeutel! | guess "shopper" taška černá -květinový vzor- vč. sáčku proti prachu!
shopper | untr: | campomaggi zauberhafter shopper torre dell'oro rosa mit zubehör neu | campomaggi okouzlující shopper torre dell'oro růžová s doplňky nové
shopper | untr: | celine horizontal cabas tote bag tasche shopper shopping handtasche rare used | celine horizontal cabas tote taška bag shopper shopping kabelka rarita použité
shopper | untr: | tasche, shopper, desigual, handtasche, beutel, bunt, top! | taška, shopper, desigual, kabelka, pouzdro, barevné, top!
is shopper a bag style
All
Shopping
Images
News
Videos
More
Genuine Leather
Canvas
Nylon
Nearby
Crossbody
About 715,000,000 results (0.58 seconds)
https://boutiquehut.co.uk › Blog
Handbag vs Tote vs shopper Style Bags - Boutique Hut
Tote bag and Shopper style bag both are larger compared to the traditional handbag, both tend to look boxier in style and both can hold much more such as ...
Shopper is a style (not a brand or product name) and is a common word, therefore, translatable.
I think we just found 28 errors!
All the untranslated.
Word | Untranslated
fuchs | 11
one | 15
jersey | 10
shopper | 28

Sense of quality

- A non-speaker can get a sense of quality
  - You just did!
- You can also see how some terms could need to be inconsistent
  - If you think of “golf”, can you think of two meanings for it?

The sport (translatable)

Word	Transl/Untra	Source segment	Target Segment
golf	translated:	golf polo shirts	koszulki golfowe polo
golf	translated:	golf left-handed clubs	kije golfowe leworęczne
golf	translated:	taylor made burner golf clubs	kije golfowe taylormade burner
golf	translated:	golf tees	nóżki pod piłki golfowe

The VW car (untranslatable)

Word	Transl/Untra	Source segment	Target Segment
golf	untr:	mk4 golf 312mm brakes	hamulce mk4 golf 312mm
golf	untr:	henry cotton golf	henry bawełniany golf
golf	untr:	mazel golf	mazel golf
golf	untr:	golf grd	golf grd
golf	untr:	vw citi golf	vw citi golf
golf	untr:	long drive golf	długi golf
golf	untr:	j lindenberg golf	j lindenberg golf
golf	untr:	vessell golf	golf vessell
golf	untr:	jb4 golf r	jb4 golf r
golf	untr:	mk1 golf -plus	mk1 golf -plus

“Golf” is supposed to have some inconsistency. If you are looking at the list of candidates, you could consider skipping golf because the term can be both translated and untranslated. And move on to more obvious errors.

Method

- It is nice that someone could get some sense of quality
- But the **primary goal of this report is to help the posteditor improve the quality**
  - Once we facilitated finding 28 errors, they will fix them.

Results

These results are net improvements from the use of this method:

Project	Same:	Changed:	Total:	Impact %
82-3-6	20870	26	20896	0.1%
74-2-4	35400	69	35469	0.2%
90-1-3	38103	69	38172	0.2%
68-3-1	35277	196	35473	**0.6%**

- The content had already been improved by postediting. These are improvements to the postediting.
- This method seems to be a good contribution to existing QA checks
- This method was appreciated as helpful by posteditors and reviewers in actual projects

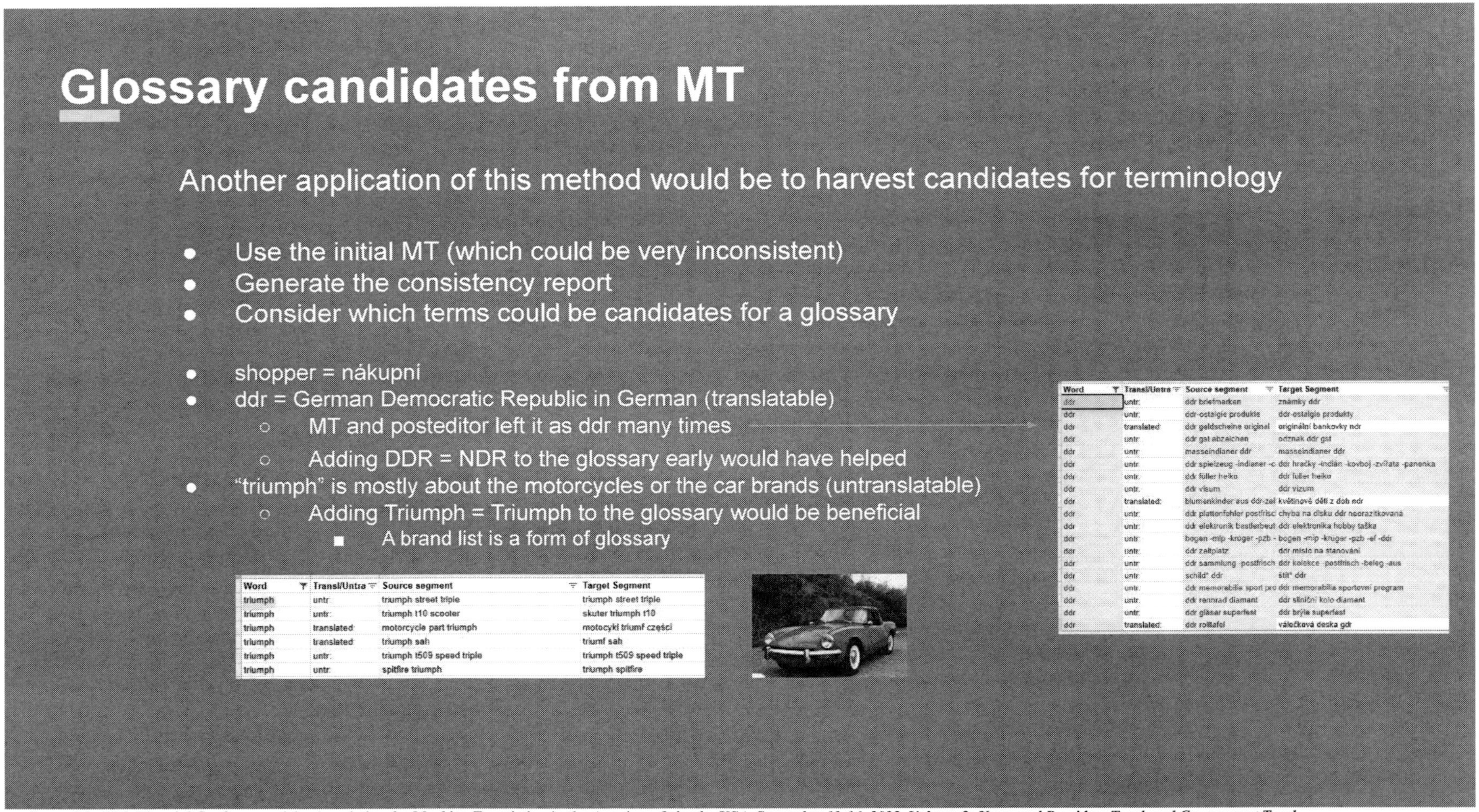
Glossary candidates from MT
Another application of this method would be to harvest candidates for terminology
Use the initial MT (which could be very inconsistent)
Generate the consistency report
Consider which terms could be candidates for a glossary
shopper = nákupní
ddr = German Democratic Republic in German (translatable)
MT and posteditor left it as ddr many times
Adding DDR = NDR to the glossary early would have helped
"triumph" is mostly about the motorcycles or the car brands (untranslatable)
Adding Triumph = Triumph to the glossary would be beneficial
A brand list is a form of glossary
Word Transl/Untra Source segment Target Segment
triumph untr: triumph street triple triumph street triple
triumph untr: triumph t10 scooter skuter triumph t10
triumph translated: motorcycle part triumph motocykl triumf części
triumph translated: triumph sah triumf sah
triumph untr: triumph t509 speed triple triumph t509 speed triple
triumph untr: spitfire triumph triumph spitfire
Word Transl/Untra Source segment Target Segment
ddr untr: ddr briefmarken známky ddr
ddr untr: ddr-ostalgie produkte ddr-ostalgie produkty
ddr translated: ddr geldscheine original originální bankovky ndr
ddr untr: ddr gst abzeichen odznak ddr gst
ddr untr: masseindianer ddr masseindianer ddr
ddr untr: ddr spielzeug -indianer -c ddr hračky -indián -kovboj -zvířata -panenka
ddr untr: ddr füller heiko ddr füller heiko
ddr untr: ddr visum ddr vizum
ddr translated: blumenkinder aus ddr-zei květinové děti z dob ndr
ddr untr: ddr plattenfehler postfrisc chyba na disku ddr neorazítkovaná
ddr untr: ddr elektronik bastlerbeut ddr elektronika hobby taška
ddr untr: bogen -mip -krüger -pzb - bogen -mip -krüger -pzb -ef -ddr
ddr untr: ddr zeltplatz ddr místo na stanování
ddr untr: ddr sammlung -postfrisch ddr kolekce -postfrisch -beleg -aus
ddr untr: schild* ddr štít* ddr
ddr untr: ddr memorabilia sport pro ddr memorabilia sportovní program
ddr untr: ddr rennrad diamant ddr silniční kolo diamant
ddr untr: ddr gläser superfest ddr brýle superfest
ddr translated: ddr rolltafel válečková deska gdr

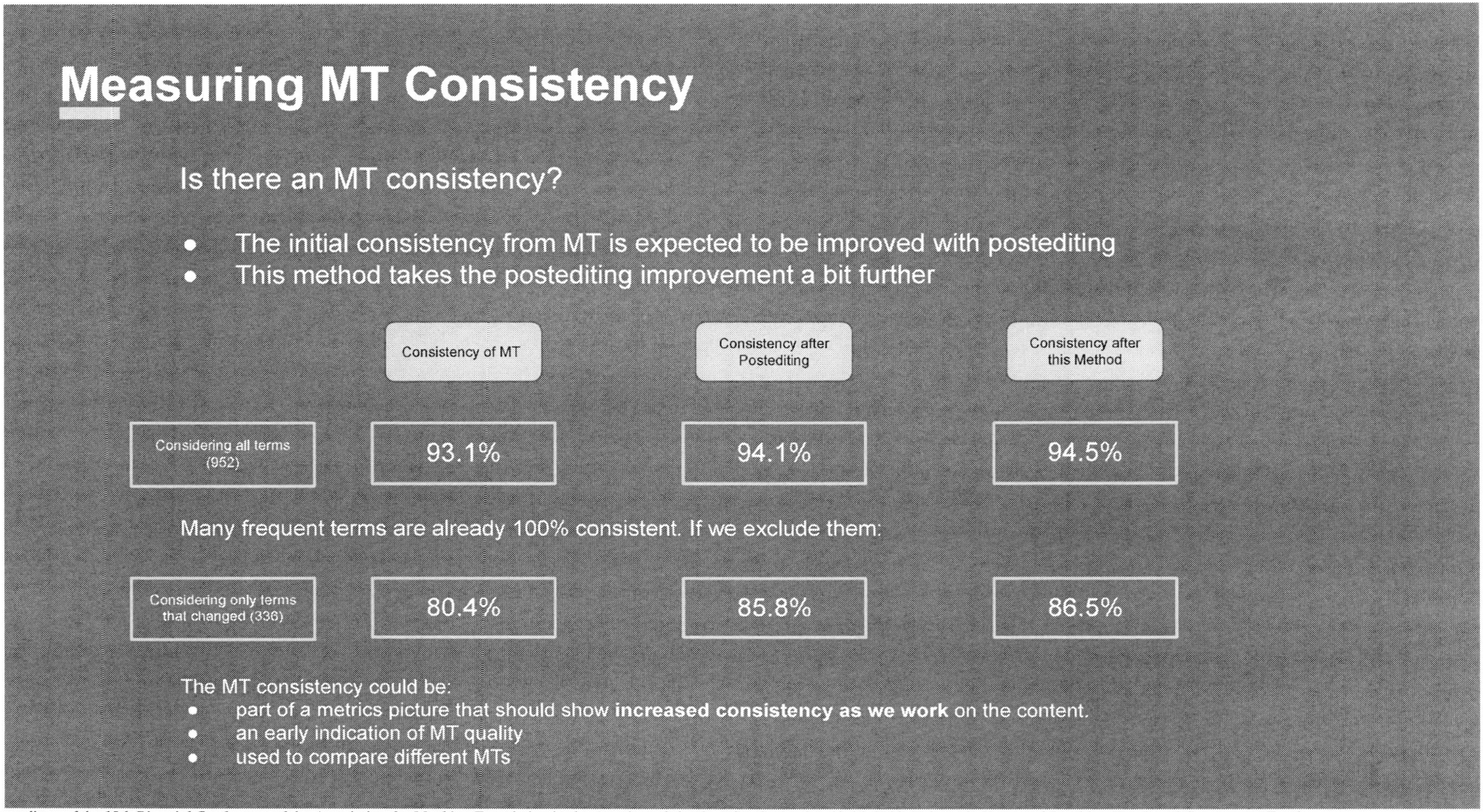
Measuring MT Consistency
Is there an MT consistency?
The initial consistency from MT is expected to be improved with postediting
This method takes the postediting improvement a bit further
Consistency of MT
Consistency after Postediting
Consistency after this Method
Considering all terms (952)
93.1%
94.1%
94.5%
Many frequent terms are already 100% consistent. If we exclude them:
Considering only terms that changed (336)
80.4%
85.8%
86.5%
The MT consistency could be:
part of a metrics picture that should show increased consistency as we work on the content.
an early indication of MT quality
used to compare different MTs

Takeaways

- It helps posteditors improve quality by facilitating finding errors
- It was appreciated by posteditors in real projects
- It is an efficient QA check that finds many errors quickly
- A non-speaker (such as a project manager) can get quality insights
- It can be used as a tool to propose glossary terms
- MT consistency could be part of metrics
- *Everything* done here for Post-editing can be done for Human Translations

Thank you!

Improve MT for Search with selected Translation Memory using Search Signals

Bryan Zhang bryzhang@amazon.com
Amazon.com

Abstract

Multilingual search is indispensable for a seamless e-commerce experience. E-commerce search engines typically support multilingual search by cascading a machine translation step before searching the index in its primary language. In practice, search query translation usually involves a translation memory matching step before machine translation. A translation memory (TM) can reduce the computation footprint in production, enforce certain terminology translation and enable us to fix translation issues quickly. In this study, we propose (1) a method of improving MT query translation using such TM entries when the TM entries are only substrings of a customer search query, and (2) an approach to selecting TM entries using search signals that can contribute to better search results.

1 Introduction

Localization of e-commerce sites has led users to expect search engines to handle multilingual queries and return product information in customers' preferred language. Multilingual product search capability is essential for modern e-commerce product discovery (Lowndes and Vasudevan, 2021). Recent proposals of cross-lingual information retrieval that handle multilingual queries and language-agnostic cross-border product indexing have gained traction with neural search engines (Hui et al., 2017; McDonald et al., 2018; Nigam et al., 2019a; Lu et al., 2021; Li et al., 2021), but legacy e-commerce search indices are still built on monolingual product information and support for multilingual search is bridged using machine translation (*Search MT*) (Nie, 2010; Rücklé et al., 2019; Saleh and Pecina, 2020; Bi et al., 2020; Jiang et al., 2020). In practice, a translation memory matching step is usually arranged before machine translation systems for search query translation.

A translation memory (TM) is a database which stores the source text and its corresponding translation in language pairs that have been previously translated. For example, *rasierwasser* → *aftershave*, *kinder schokolade* → *kinder chocolate* are entries for German-English translation memory. The translation memory is usually activated when a run-time query exactly matches an entry in the memory. Therefore, a translation memory can (i) reduce the computation footprint and latency for synchronous translation (ii) effectively enforce terminologies for specific brands or products. Although such issues can be mitigated through terminology constraint mechanism in the machine translation model (Dinu et al. (2019); Post and Vilar (2018); Susanto et al. (2020); Wang et al. (2021); Ailem et al. (2021)), the turnover time to fix the translation would be unacceptable to the users and companies that expect an instant fix and, (iii) fix machine translation issues that cannot be resolved easily or quickly without retraining/tuning the machine translation engine in production (Kanavos and Kartsaklis (2010); Caskey and Maskey (2013); Luo et al. (2022); Tan (2022)).

We have also observed that many translation memory (TM) entries can partially match a large percentage of queries at run-time. It is necessary to integrate translation memory (TM) to the machine translation systems and enable a run-time query to partially match an entry in the memory, that way one query translation can come from both translation memory and machine translation systems. Unlike exact string matching, one TM entry can only impact one run-time query, partial matching can allow one TM entry to impact a large number of queries, so it is crucial only to select TM entries that can bring a positive impact to the customers' shopping experience. Therefore, in this paper we propose:

- a method of exploiting the placeholder features of modern industrial machine translation, and implementing a sub-string partial matching feature that enables the NMT models at run-time to recognize the longest TM entry as sub-string, then use the sub-string TM translation to replace the MT output of that sub-string.
- an approach to selecting an optimal translation memory (TM) subset for partial matching using search signals. The selected TM subset can have contribute to better query translation quality and have larger positive impact on the search results

The rest of the paper is organized as following: we will propose the method of integrating translation memory to machine translation systems enabling sub-string matching in section 2; In section 3 we will propose an approach to selecting an optimal translation memory subset using search signal; Section 4 is the experiment setup and section 5 is result and analysis. We draw the conclusion in section 6.

2 Machine translation with selected translation memory in production

This approach includes a sub-string partial matching feature that enables neural machine translation (NMT) models at run-time to recognize the longest TM entry as a sub-string, then use the sub-string TM translation to replace the MT output of that sub-string. Figure 1.illustrates this approach using a query translation example from German to English:

- STEP 1-2: Given a query *rasierwasser tabak*, if there is an entry (or entries) matched to the query as sub-string (s) (e.g. *rasierwasser - aftershave*)[1], the matched sub-string in the source query is replaced with a placeholder. (e.g. *[placeholder_1] tabak*)
- STEP 3: The query with the placeholder will be passed to the machine translation model. The machine translation model returns the query translation with placeholder (e.g. *[placeholder_1] tobacco*)
- STEP 4: The placeholder will be replaced by the translation from the matched entry (e.g. *aftershave tobacco*).

2.1 Sub-string matching

We propose to use a back-off n-gram matching algorithm that will match the translation memory entries in the source language to queries as sub-strings: given a query, the query is first converted into n-grams, then we try to match the n-grams to the entries in the translation memory. We start the value of n as the number of the tokens in the query and then decrease the value of n for the n-grams until $n = 1$ or until we find a match in the memory. This way, we can aim at finding the longest match.

[1]For cases where a term (s) in the source needs to preserved in the translation, the same entry (in the source language) is stored on both source and translation sides

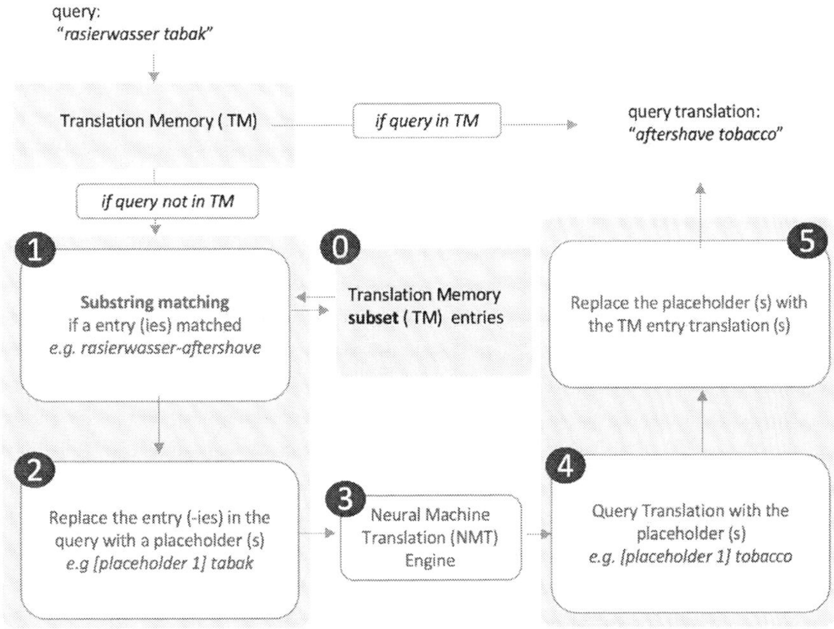

Figure 1: The method of MT with selected TM entry substitution in production

2.2 Augmenting NMT with placeholders

We augment the neural machine translation (NMT) models with placeholder data during the training, so the NMT models can translate queries with placeholders and keep those placeholders intact during the translation process. Those placeholders are also serialized tokens e.g. *placeholder_1, placeholder_2* which are part of the vocabulary used at inference time.

3 Translation memory (TM) subset selection using search signal

Partial matching enables one TM entry to impact a larger number of queries, so it is crucial only to select TM entries that can bring a positive impact to the customers' shopping experience. The search results matter from the customer's perspective and MT query translations are used as intermediate artifacts for search. We rely on customer purchasing behavior as a signal for relevance judgments to automatically estimate the search performance of MT query translations, and a TM entry is selected if the MT query translation with the TM sub-string substitution has better search performance than the default MT query translation.

Figure 2 illustrates our proposed translation memory subset selection workflow. For a given TM entry e, we first sample queries in the source language Q_{src} from the historical traffic data that can partially match to the entry. We then also sample hundreds of thousands of the purchased product IDs P and their frequencies F associated with each source query. We will use the top two most frequent source queries $q_{src}(q_{src} \in Q_{src})$ for selection: for each source query q_{src}, we will use MT to generate two versions of query translation, one t_{mt} is returned from the MT and other t_{mt+tm} is returned from MT with translation memory (TM). We will retrieve two sets of search results R_{mt} and R_{mt+tm} for these two versions of query translations

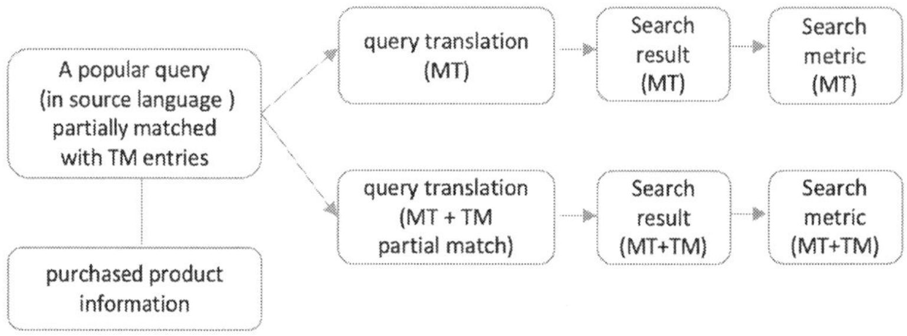

Figure 2: The translation memory entry selection approach

t_{mt} and t_{mt+tm} respectively; then we will use the purchased product IDs P_q associated the source query q_{src} as a proxy to the relevant products and logarithm of their frequencies F_q as the scaled relevance for the search rank-based metrics S computation of these two sets of search results S_{mt} and S_{mt+tm}. The TM entry is selected if the search rank-based metric of the MT query translation with TM S_{mt+tm} is higher than the search rank-based metric of default query MT translation S_{mt} for both source queries.

We also observe some TM entries are terminologies such as brands, and they also overlap with the common vocabulary of the source language that usually needs to be translated. For example, take the entry *kinder*. This word is both a brand and a common word in German meaning *children*; when it refers to the brand it is expected to be preserved in the German-to-English translation. Therefore, if such entries exist in the TM, we suggest creating a frequent collocation *kinder schokolade* alone based on the query log and adding the new entry pair *kinder schokolade - kinder chocolate* to the translation memory before the subset selection.

4 Experiment

We conduct both offline and online experiments for the proposed approaches for Portuguese queries on *Amazon.es*, German queries on *Amazon.com (US)*, and Dutch queries on *Amazon.de*.

Machine Translation models: For each language pair we train a transformer-based ((Vaswani et al., 2017)) MT system that is encoder-heavy (20 encoder and 2 decoder layers) (Domhan et al. (2020)) using the Sockeye MT toolkit. We use a vocabulary of 32K BPE (Sennrich et al. (2016)) tokens. We optimise using ADAM (Kingma and Ba (2015)) and perform early-stopping based on perplexity on a held-out dev set. We train on internal general out-domain news data and fine-tune on human translated search queries and synthetically generated query translations through back-translation.

Selected translation memory: Based on the proposed translation memory subset selection workflow from section 3, we have used search rank-based metric *nDCG* (normalized Discounted Cumulative Gain) on the top 16 product search result (*nDCG@16*) as search signal. We have selected approximate 30 thousands translation memory entries for each one of the following language pairs: *nlnl-dede, ptpt-eses* and *dede-enus*.

Test sets: For each language pair, we have sampled 2500 test cases from the query data which has been previously sampled for the translation memory selection. Each test case includes (1) a query in the source language and (2) purchased product IDs and (3) respective frequencies, and is not used in the TM subset selection. And the source query in each test case can partially match a unique entry from the selected TM.

Metric hyper-parameters for evaluation: We set K to 16 for the top-k search results, using the top-16 products in the search results to compute *nDCG* (normalized discounted cumulative gain), *MAP* (mean average precision) and *MRR* (mean reciprocal rank) (Järvelin and Kekäläinen, 2002; Wu et al., 2018; Nigam et al., 2019b).

5 Results and analysis

Table 1 presents the offline evaluation metrics *nDCG, MAP* and *MRR*. All the search metrics have been scaled from 0-1 to 0-100 for convenience. Based on the results, query translations from MT using selected TM have much bigger improvement than the original query translation from MT consistently cross the three language pairs. It suggests the matched sub-strings in the query are translated better with the translation from selected translation memory, and brand-like terms in query translation are also handled properly. For example, with the German-English TM entry *haus laboratories - haus laboratories* in the selected TM, the brand in the source query *haus laboratories lippenstift* is preserved in the query translation *haus laboratories lip stick* whereas the original MT query translation is *house laboratories lip stick*. Table 2 shows more examples of improved query translations using our proposed approaches. It shows both of our proposed approaches are effective, and the query machine translation as a component has much bigger positive impact on the search ecosystems.

		MAP@16	MRR	nDCG@16
German-English	MT	44.2	50.3	51.0
	MT + TM	63.7	75.3	67.5
Dutch-German	MT	47.7	54.1	53.7
	MT + TM	68.7	79.8	70.5
Portuguese-Spanish	MT	15.6	18.2	23.5
	MT + TM	37.7	45.3	49.7

Table 1: Search metrics of two versions of query translations for 3 language pairs

Query (German)	Query Translation (English) Default MT	Query Translation (English) MT with selected TM subset	Translation Memory (TM)
happy hippos kinder schokolade	happy hippos kids chocolate	happy hippos kinder chocolate	kinder schokolade → kinder chocolate
uhren herren patek philippe	watches for men patek philip	watches for men luxury patek philippe	patek philippe → patek philippe
haus laboratories lippenstift	house laboratories lip stick	haus laboratories lip stick	haus laboratories → haus laboratories
game of thrones staffel 8	game of thrones relay 8	game of thrones series 8	game of thrones staffel → game of thrones series
rasierwasser tabak	shaving water tobacco	aftershave tobacco	rasierwasser → aftershave
morgenmantel damen japanisch	morning coat women japanese	dressing gown womens japanese	morgenmantel damen → dressing gown womens
leinwände set	linen set	canvases set	leinwände → canvases
würfelbecher leder	cube cup leader	dice cup leather	würfelbecher → dice cup

Table 2: Examples of MT query translation with and without selected translation memory subset

A/B testing: We have also conducted parallel online A/B testing for the three language pairs. For each language pair, we have deployed a baseline MT and an improved MT model with selected translation memory (TM). Both are integrated into the search pipeline for the designated store. The A/B testing lasted for 4 weeks on average for all the experiments. The improved MT with TM of three language pairs impacted 3-5% of query traffic, and have seen large increases in business metrics, such as, Order Product Sales (OPS), composite contribution profit (CCP), compared to the baseline MT models. Moreover, they all have much larger positive impact on the search result quality, which indicates that our approach has the overall user's multilingual search experiences have received larger improvements.

6 Conclusion

In this paper, we have proposed a method of improving MT query translation using such translation memory (TM) entries when the TM entries are only sub-strings of a customer search query, and an approach to selecting TM entries using search signals that can contribute to better search results. We have conducted both offline and online experiments for improving MT with the selected TM subset using the search signal for Portuguese queries on Amazon.es, German queries on Amazon.com (US), and Dutch queries on Amazon.de. Both off-line and on-line results have shown our approach can improve search query translation and have seen increased order product sales and improved user experience in the multilingual e-commerce search.

References

Ailem, M., Liu, J., and Qader, R. (2021). Encouraging neural machine translation to satisfy terminology constraints. In *Findings of the Association for Computational Linguistics: ACL-IJCNLP 2021*, pages 1450–1455, Online. Association for Computational Linguistics.

Bi, T., Yao, L., Yang, B., Zhang, H., Luo, W., and Chen, B. (2020). Constraint translation candidates: A bridge between neural query translation and cross-lingual information retrieval.

Caskey, S. P. and Maskey, S. (2013). Translation cache prediction.

Dinu, G., Mathur, P., Federico, M., and Al-Onaizan, Y. (2019). Training neural machine translation to apply terminology constraints. In *Proceedings of the 57th Annual Meeting of the Association for Computational Linguistics*, pages 3063–3068, Florence, Italy. Association for Computational Linguistics.

Domhan, T., Denkowski, M., Vilar, D., Niu, X., Hieber, F., and Heafield, K. (2020). The sockeye 2 neural machine translation toolkit at AMTA 2020. In *Proceedings of the 14th Conference of the Association for Machine Translation in the Americas (Volume 1: Research Track)*, pages 110–115, Virtual. Association for Machine Translation in the Americas.

Hui, K., Yates, A., Berberich, K., and de Melo, G. (2017). PACRR: A position-aware neural IR model for relevance matching. In *Proceedings of the 2017 Conference on Empirical Methods in Natural Language Processing*, pages 1049–1058, Copenhagen, Denmark. Association for Computational Linguistics.

Järvelin, K. and Kekäläinen, J. (2002). Cumulated gain-based evaluation of ir techniques. *ACM Transactions on Information Systems (TOIS)*, 20(4):422–446.

Jiang, Z., El-Jaroudi, A., Hartmann, W., Karakos, D., and Zhao, L. (2020). Cross-lingual information retrieval with BERT. In *Proceedings of the workshop on Cross-Language Search and Summarization of Text and Speech (CLSSTS2020)*, pages 26–31, Marseille, France. European Language Resources Association.

Kanavos, P. and Kartsaklis, D. (2010). Integrating machine translation with translation memory: A practical approach. In *Proceedings of the Second Joint EM+/CNGL Workshop: Bringing MT to the User: Research on Integrating MT in the Translation Industry*, pages 11–20, Denver, Colorado, USA. Association for Machine Translation in the Americas.

Kingma, D. P. and Ba, J. (2015). Adam: A method for stochastic optimization. volume abs/1412.6980.

Li, S., Lv, F., Jin, T., Lin, G., Yang, K., Zeng, X., Wu, X.-M., and Ma, Q. (2021). Embedding-based product retrieval in taobao search. In *Proceedings of the 27th ACM SIGKDD Conference on Knowledge Discovery & Data Mining*, pages 3181–3189.

Lowndes, M. and Vasudevan, A. (2021). Market guide for digital commerce search.

Lu, H., Hu, Y., Zhao, T., Wu, T., Song, Y., and Yin, B. (2021). Graph-based multilingual product retrieval in E-commerce search. In *Proceedings of the 2021 Conference of the North American Chapter of the Association for Computational Linguistics: Human Language Technologies: Industry Papers*, pages 146–153, Online. Association for Computational Linguistics.

Luo, C., Lakshman, V., Shrivastava, A., Cao, T., Nag, S., Goutam, R., Lu, H., Song, Y., and Yin, B. (2022). Rose: Robust caches for amazon product search. In *The Web Conference 2022*.

McDonald, R., Brokos, G., and Androutsopoulos, I. (2018). Deep relevance ranking using enhanced document-query interactions. In *Proceedings of the 2018 Conference on Empirical Methods in Natural Language Processing*, pages 1849–1860, Brussels, Belgium. Association for Computational Linguistics.

Nie, J.-Y. (2010). Cross-language information retrieval. *Synthesis Lectures on Human Language Technologies*, 3(1):1–125.

Nigam, P., Song, Y., Mohan, V., Lakshman, V., Ding, W. A., Shingavi, A., Teo, C. H., Gu, H., and Yin, B. (2019a). Semantic product search. In *Proceedings of the 25th ACM SIGKDD International Conference on Knowledge Discovery Data Mining*, KDD '19, page 2876–2885, New York, NY, USA. Association for Computing Machinery.

Nigam, P., Song, Y., Mohan, V., Lakshman, V., Weitian, Ding, Shingavi, A., Teo, C. H., Gu, H., and Yin, B. (2019b). Semantic product search.

Post, M. and Vilar, D. (2018). Fast lexically constrained decoding with dynamic beam allocation for neural machine translation. In *Proceedings of the 2018 Conference of the North American Chapter of the Association for Computational Linguistics: Human Language Technologies, Volume 1 (Long Papers)*, pages 1314–1324, New Orleans, Louisiana. Association for Computational Linguistics.

Rücklé, A., Swarnkar, K., and Gurevych, I. (2019). Improved cross-lingual question retrieval for community question answering. In *The World Wide Web Conference*, WWW '19, page 3179–3186, New York, NY, USA. Association for Computing Machinery.

Saleh, S. and Pecina, P. (2020). Document translation vs. query translation for cross-lingual information retrieval in the medical domain. In *Proceedings of the 58th Annual Meeting of the Association for Computational Linguistics*, pages 6849–6860, Online. Association for Computational Linguistics.

Sennrich, R., Haddow, B., and Birch, A. (2016). Neural machine translation of rare words with subword units. In *Proceedings of the 54th Annual Meeting of the Association for Computational Linguistics (Volume 1: Long Papers)*, pages 1715–1725, Berlin, Germany. Association for Computational Linguistics.

Susanto, R. H., Chollampatt, S., and Tan, L. (2020). Lexically constrained neural machine translation with Levenshtein transformer. In *Proceedings of the 58th Annual Meeting of the Association for Computational Linguistics*, pages 3536–3543, Online. Association for Computational Linguistics.

Tan, L. (2022). Tmnt:translation memory and neural translation.

Vaswani, A., Shazeer, N., Parmar, N., Uszkoreit, J., Jones, L., Gomez, A. N., Kaiser, Ł., and Polosukhin, I. (2017). Attention is all you need. *Advances in neural information processing systems*, 30.

Wang, K., Gu, S., Chen, B., Zhao, Y., Luo, W., and Zhang, Y. (2021). TermMind: Alibaba's WMT21 machine translation using terminologies task submission. In *Proceedings of the Sixth Conference on Machine Translation*, pages 851–856, Online. Association for Computational Linguistics.

Wu, L., Hu, D., Hong, L., and Liu, H. (2018). Turning clicks into purchases: Revenue optimization for product search in e-commerce. SIGIR '18, page 365–374, New York, NY, USA. Association for Computing Machinery.

A Multimodal Simultaneous Interpretation Prototype : Who Said What

Xiaolin Wang xiaolin.wang@nict.go.jp
Masao Utiyama mutiyama@nict.go.jp
Eiichiro Sumita eiichiro.sumita@nict.go.jp
Advanced Translation Research and Development Promotion Center
National Institute of Information and Communications Technology, Japan

Abstract

"Who said what" is essential for human users to understand video streams that have more than one speaker, but conventional simultaneous interpretation (SI) systems merely present "what was said" in the form of subtitles. Because translations unavoidably have delays and errors, users often find it difficult to trace the subtitles back to speakers. Therefore, we propose a multimodal SI system that explicitly presents users "who said what" – translation annotated with the textual tags and face icons of speakers.

Speaker recognition requires heavy computation which poses a big challenge to implementing our proposed system especially given the real-time characteristics of SI. We integrate multimodal speaker recognition with online sentence-based SI to meet this challenge as follows. First, our system employs automated speech recognition and online sentence segmenter to segment video streams into video clips each of which contains one sentence. Next, our system recognizes the speaker in each video clip using active speaker detection, voice embeddings and face embeddings; in the meantime, it translates the sentence into target language in the meantime. In the end, our system presents users both the translation and the speaker of each sentence.

Our method has two major merits. First, speaker recognition is performed per video clip, so GPUs can have enough input data to produce large batches and run efficiently. Second, speaker recognition is synchronized with machine translation, so no extra latency is introduced. As a result, our demo system is capable of interpreting video streams in real-time on a single desktop equipped with two Quadro RTX 4000 GPUs.

In addition, we full respect the privacy of users. Our system aims at distinguishing different speakers appearing in a video stream rather than figuring out the real name or identity of speakers in the physical world. As a side merit, our system requires no prior knowledge of speakers.

1 Introduction

Automated simultaneous interpretation (SI) is promising for facilitating real-time cross-lingual communication. Video streams have become a most popular form of communication nowadays because of the blossom of smart phones, video sites, chat apps and so on. Therefore, there is an increasing trend towards applying SI to video streams.

Figure 1: User Interface of Multimodal Simultaneous Interpretation

Spoken language such as conversations, discussions and debates are common in video streams where two or more speakers are involved. Working out "who said what" is a natural path for people to understand these video streams. However, when applying conventional SI, users are merely presented "what was said", that is, the translation of the transcripts from speech recognition. Therefore, users must guess who the speaker of the source utterance of each translation was. Given the following facts between the source utterances and translations,

- uncertain delays in the timeline;
- mismatch in length due to different languages;
- speech recognition errors;
- translation errors;
- speaking too fast;
- ...

users often become exhausted or even desperate in working out the speaker of each translation.

To address this problem, this paper presents a novel multimodal SI system that presents users "who said what" from video streams. As illustrated by Figure 1, in the graphic user interface of our system, each record consists of the translation of an utterance which indicates "what was said"; a speaker tag, e.g., *spk 0*, *spk 1*, and a face icon which indicates "who said". Users will be able to understand the video streams easily through reading these records.

The main challenges for us to build the proposed multimodal SI system are

1. How to recognize speakers from video streams?
2. How to maintain low latency for interpretation?

To solve the first challenge, we develop a speaker predictor (SP). SP creatively adapts a multimodal speaker recognition approach that combines voice embedding (Li et al., 2017), face

I work well under pressure
wonderful
and what would you say are some of your weaknesses
one of my biggest weaknesses is asking for help when I need it .
I 'd like to do better at that
I appreciate your honesty mister wang
what can you tell me about some of your goals over the next few years
my primary goal is to gain more work experience
so a position like this would help me meet that goal
I 'd also like to learn more about the different aspects of banking
I think those goals are very smart

(a) Plain Translations

spk0 :	I work well under pressure
spk1 :	wonderful
spk1 :	and what would you say are some of your weaknesses
spk0 :	one of my biggest weaknesses is asking for help when I need it .
spk0 :	I 'd like to do better at that
spk1 :	I appreciate your honesty mister wang
spk1 :	what can you tell me about some of your goals over the next few years
spk0 :	my primary goal is to gain more work experience
spk0 :	so a position like this would help me meet that goal
spk0 :	I 'd also like to learn more about the different aspects of banking
spk1 :	I think those goals are very smart

(b) Translations annotated with speakers

Figure 2: Comparison of Readability of Translations with and without Speaker Annotations

embedding (Schroff et al., 2015) and active speaker detection (Roth et al., 2019). To solve the second efficiency challenge, we synchronize all the heavy multimodal computation with the sentence-based interpretation (Wang et al., 2019) so that neural networks can run efficiently on GPUs through processing large batches as input.

The rest of this paper is organized as follows. First, Section 2 describes the user interface of our system. Then, Section 3 presents the architectures of sentence-based multimodal SI and multimodal speaker recognition. Next, Section 4 describes the implementation of each module in detail. After that, Section 5 briefly analyzes the real-time capability of our system. Furthermore, Section 6 compares our system with related works on multimodal machine translation. Finally, Section 7 concludes this paper with a description on future works.

2 User Interface

The user interface of our system is split into two parts as illustrated by Figure 1. The input video stream is displayed in the left part of the window, below which translations are presented in the conventional way as subtitles. The main output of our SI system is displayed in the right part of the window which consists of speaker tags, face icons and translations.

Speaker Tags are texts that follow the pattern of *spk n*, such as *spk 0* and *spk 1*, where n is a number assigned to each physical speaker based on the order of his or her appearance in video streams. Because these tags are plain texts, in addition to being shown in the graphic user interface, they can also be used to generate textual transcripts for review or post-editing. Speaker annotations can greatly improve the readability of the transcripts as illustrated by Figure 2.

Face Icons are the face shots of the speakers when they are saying the corresponding utterances. These face icons have two merits. First, they allow users to double check whether

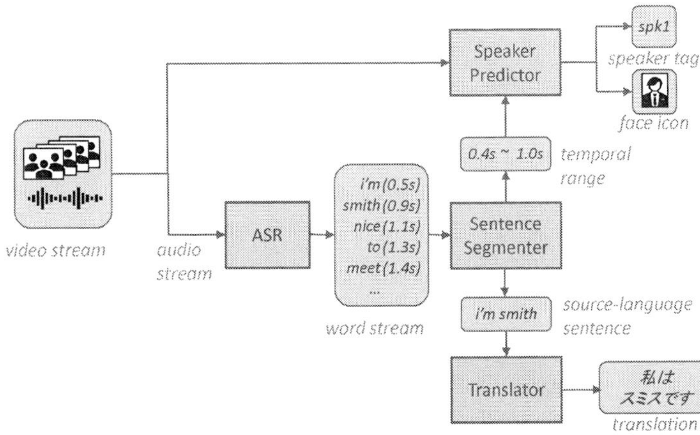

Figure 3: System Architecture

the speaker tags are correct or not. Second, they allow users to predict the sentiments of the utterances from the facial expressions of the speakers.

Translations are translated sentences. Our system performs sentence-based simultaneous interpretation. Instead of waiting for a speaker to finish speaking, it detects the event that the speaker has finished a sentence (Wang et al., 2016b). Then our system translates that sentence and displays it to users.

3 System Architecture

Our system consists of an automatic speech recognition (ASR) engine, a sentence segmenter, a speaker predictor and a translator as illustrated by Figure 3). Blue rectangles represent modules and red rounded rectangles represent data examples. Arrows show the direction of data flow.

The system takes a video stream as input, and generates the speaker tags, face icons and translations in an online manner. The system accomplishes this multimodal simultaneous interpretation task in four steps as follows.

1. The ASR engine receives audio signals from the video stream and convert it a word stream. The word stream consists of words and their time stamps. For example, "i'm (0.5s)" means that the word "i'm" appears at the 0.5 seconds of the video stream.

2. The sentence segmenter splits the word stream into source-language sentences. Each sentence consists of a text and a temporal range. For example, the first sentence is "i'm smith" with a temporal range of 0.4 seconds to 1.0 seconds.

3. The speaker predictor first extracts a clip from the video stream following the temporal range of each sentence, and then recognizes the active speaker, that is, the person who is speaking in the clip. The active speaker is assumed to say the corresponding sentence. Each active speaker is presented by a textual tag and a face icon.

4. The translator translates the text of each sentence into target-language, which is a standard machine translation task. For example, "i'm smith" is translated into a Japanese one.

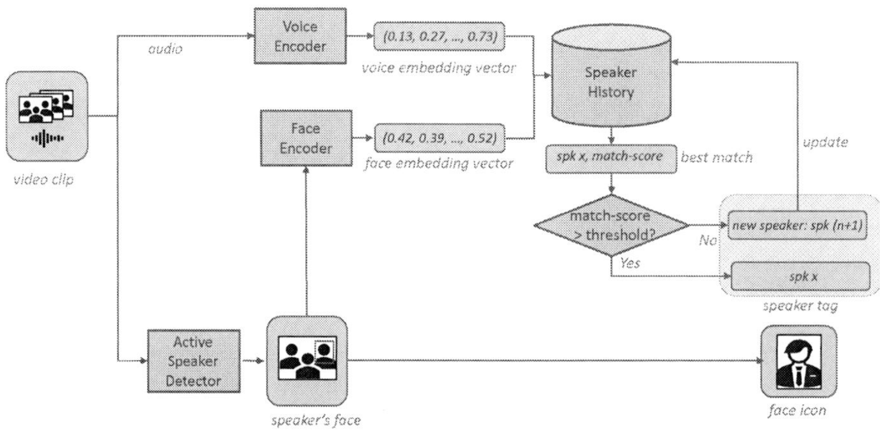

Figure 4: Speaker Predictor Architecture

3.1 Speaker Predictor

The speaker predictor is more complicated than the other three modules, which further consists of an active speaker detector, a face encoder, and a voice encoder (Figure 4). In addition, an ad-hoc database named speaker history contains the face embedding vectors and voice embedding vectors of the speakers who have appeared in the current video stream.

The speaker predictor takes a video clip as input and generates the speaker tags and face icons as output. The speaker prediction task is accomplished as follows,

1. The active speaker detector recognizes the person who is speaking in the video clip. A face icon of the active speaker is extracted to represent the prediction result.

2. The face encoder converts the face icon into a face embedding vector, noted as v_f.

3. The voice encoder converts the audio of the video clip into a voice embedding vector, noted as v_a.

4. The database of speaker history is searched for the speaker that best matches the face and voice embedding vectors, noted as spk x, with a matching score, formulated as,

$$\begin{aligned} x &= \underset{x}{argmax}\, cos(v_f, v_f^x) \\ &\quad + cos(v_a, v_a^x) \end{aligned} \tag{1}$$

   where v_f^x and v_a^x is the face and voice embedding vectors of the speaker x, cos means cosine similarity.

5. The matching score is compared with a predefined threshold. If the matching score exceeds the threshold, the current speaker will be predicted as spk x.

6. If the matching score is lower than the threshold, the current speaker will be treated as a new speaker. A new tag spk (n+1) will be assigned, where n is the number of appeared speakers. In addition, the new tag together with the face and voice embedding vectors will be added into the database of speaker history

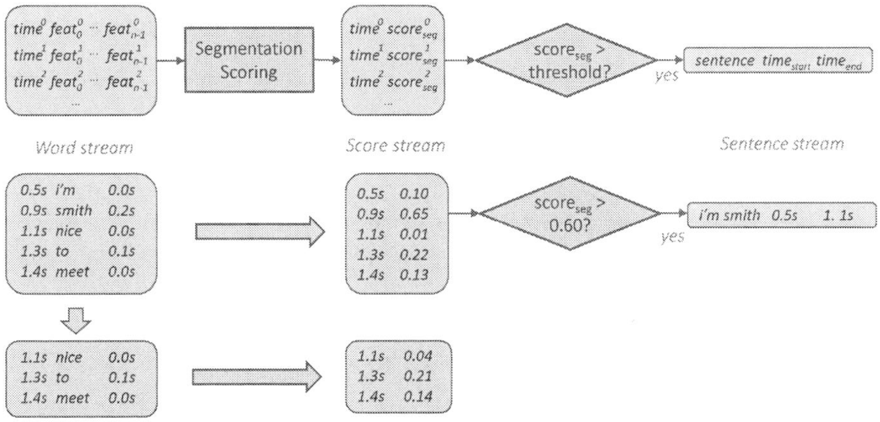

Figure 5: Senentence Segmenter

3.2 Sentence Segmenter

The sentence segmenter adopts a sequence labelling architecture (Figure 5). The input of word stream is viewed as a sequence of time stamps $time^k$ and features $feat_0^k \dots feat_{n-1}^k$ which represent the k-th word.

The sentence segmenter calculates a segmentation confidence score as,

$$score_{seg}(k) = F_{seg}(feat_0^0, \cdots, feat_{n-1}^0, \\ \cdots, feat_0^{k+K}, \cdots, feat_{n-1}^{k+K}) \quad (2)$$

where $score_{seg}(k)$ means the confidence of segmenting after the k-th word, F_{seg} represents a scoring model, and K is the size of right context,

Our system employs two features to represent a word as illustrated by Figure 5. One is the surface text of the word, and the other is the duration of the speaker pause after the word. The implementation of the scoring model is presented in Section 4.2.

The segmentation scores are compared with a predefined threshold. If $score_{seg}(k)$ exceeds the threshold, a segment will be produced from $time_0$ to $time_{k+1}$. After that, the segmenter module will be reset to process the remaining words that start from $time_{k+1}$.

4 System Implement

4.1 Automated Speech Recognition

The ASR module is required to be not only accurate but also low-latency due to the real-time characteristic of the simultaneous interpretation task (Wang et al., 2016b; Novitasari et al., 2019; Nguyen et al., 2020). Our current solution is the streaming convolution model proposed by Pratap et al. (2020) [1]. We are aware that state-of-the-art speech recognition models are transformers (Likhomanenko et al., 2021) and conformers (Gulati et al., 2020). They are more accurate than convolution models, but they typically operate on audio segments instead of audio streams. Adapting transformers and conformers to the input of audio streams is a trending topic (Moritz et al., 2020; Tsunoo et al., 2020; Chen et al., 2021). We are paying close attention

[1] https://github.com/flashlight/wav2letter/tree/main/recipes/streaming_convnets

to this field, and plan to upgrade our system when matured streaming transformer or conformers are available.

4.2 Sentence Segmenter

The sentence segmenter module segments word stream into sentences in an online manner (Stolcke et al., 1998; Sridhar et al., 2013; Wang et al., 2016a, 2019; Iranzo-Sánchez et al., 2020; Li et al., 2021; Wicks and Post, 2021; Gravellier et al., 2021).

Because large-scale supervised training corpora for the sequence labelling problem of sentence segmentation (Section 3.2) are not publicly available, we manually craft the scoring model for sentence segmentation as

$$\begin{aligned} score_{seg}(k) &= score_{RNN}(w_0, \cdots, w_{k+K}) \\ &\quad + \alpha\, pause(k) \end{aligned} \tag{3}$$

where $score_{RNN}$ is the segmentation score from the RNN-based model proposed by Wang et al. (2019) [2], $pause(k)$ is the duration of speaker pause after the word w measured in seconds, and α is a manually tuned weight.

4.3 Translator

The translator module translates one source-language sentence into one target-language sentence, which is a standard machine translation task (Brown et al., 1993; Zens et al., 2002; Chiang, 2005; Bahdanau et al., 2014). We employ our in-house machine translation system as the translator module. The machine translation system is publicly accessible through a Web API [3].

4.4 Active Speaker Detector

The active speaker detector module recognizes who is speaking in a visual scene from one or more candidates (Roth et al., 2019; Kim et al., 2021). Active speaker detection is an emerging research topic (Chakravarty et al., 2016; Chung, 2019; Zhang et al., 2021; Tao et al., 2021; Köpüklü et al., 2021; León-Alcázar et al., 2021). Our system adopts the end-to-end multimodal (video and audio) active speaker detection framework proposed by Roth et al. (2019) because of the trade-off between accuracy and efficiency. The framework first employs 3-D convolutional neural networks to convert visual and audio into embedding vectors, and then concatenates the embedding vectors to make predictions.

4.5 Face Encoder

The face encoder module converts face images into embedding vectors, the similarity of which directly corresponds to a measure of face similarity (Schroff et al., 2015). For our application, the face encoder is highly demanding on efficiency as simultaneous interpretation is a real-time task, while less demanding on accuracy as the encoder only needs to distinguish a small number of people that appear in a same video stream. Therefore, our face encoder is a middle-sized model of Resnet50 (He et al., 2016) which is trained on the dataset of labeled faces in the wild (LFW) (Huang et al., 2008) using the triplet loss proposed by Schroff et al. (2015).

4.6 Voice Encoder

The voice encoder module converts audio utterances into embedding vectors, the similarity of which corresponds to a measure of voice similarity. Voice encoder is related to the task of speaker verification which aims at verifying the identity of a person from the characteristics of

[2] `https://github.com/arthurxlw/cytonNss`

[3] `https://mt-auto-minhon-mlt.ucri.jgn-x.jp/`

Module	Workload
ASR	45.0%
Sentence Segmenter	0.2%
Translator	2.2%
Speaker Predictor	10.4%

Table 1: Workload Percentage of Each Module. The lower the better.

his or her voice (Li et al., 2017; Chung et al., 2018; Wan et al., 2018; Nagrani et al., 2020). Our voice encoder is a pretrained Resnet34 model released in (Chung et al., 2020; Heo et al., 2020)[4].

5 Real-time Capability

Our SI system employs a parallel pipeline to integrate the main modules to meet the real-time requirement. We estimate the real-time capability of each module using workload percentage, which is calculated as,

$$\frac{T_{running}}{T_{running} + T_{idle}} \times 100\%, \tag{4}$$

where $T_{running}$ and T_{idle} are running and idle durations respectively.

Table 1 shows that the workload percentages of all the modules are below 100% thus our system is fully capable of interpreting video streams in real-time.

6 Related Works

Multimodal machine translation – the task of doing machine translation with multiple data sources – is a trending topic (Specia et al., 2016; Di Gangi et al., 2019; Sanabria et al., 2018). A large volume of research effort has been dedicated to improving the translation quality through drawing information from modalities other than text (Sulubacak et al., 2019; Hirasawa et al., 2019; Lin et al., 2020; Yao and Wan, 2020; Mitzalis et al., 2021).

Our interpretation system approaches the task of multimodal machine translation from a different angle. Imaging when interpretating a video stream, the visual contents of the video stream will mainly fall into two categories,

1. the speakers;

2. the subjects of the speeches.

Our interpretation system focuses on the first category. It recognizes the speaker of each utterance, and then annotates the translation with the speaker, so that users can better understand the video stream despite translation latencies and errors. In contrast, the related works focus on the second category of contents so that users can get better translations.

Nevertheless, our interpretation system and the related works on multimodal machine translation are complement with each other. Integrating our system with the related works will lead to very effective interpretation systems which can generate both well-annotated and high-quality translations from video streams.

[4]https://github.com/clovaai/voxceleb_trainer

7 Conclusion

In this paper, we propose an automated multimodal simultaneous interpretation system to improve the user experience on interpreting video streams, and build an efficient implementation based on the sentence-based interpretation.

Our system has been tested on various video streams. The system works very well on some of the video streams and produces high-quality translations which are correctly annotated with the tags and face icons of speakers.

However, our system performs poorly on some video streams which have difficult speeches. When the speech is not clear enough for the ASR module to generate decent transcripts, the sentence segmenter will fail to produce sensible sentences, and then the whole system will perform poorly. Therefore, in the future, we plan to address this problem through adding more audio and visual features into the sentence segmenter and the translator to improve the robustness of our system.

Ethic

Our proposed simultaneous interpretation system fully respects users' privacy. The system is designed not to figure out the real name or identity of speaker in the physical world. Instead, speakers are only given plain tags such as $spk\,0$ and $spk\,1$ to distinguish from each other.

As a result, our simultaneous interpretation system requires no prior knowledge of speakers. It only collects the necessary information to distinguish speakers when performing interpretation tasks. The collected information will be erased when the tasks finish.

Acknowledgement

A part of this work was conducted under the commissioned research program "Research and Development of Advanced Multilingual Translation Technology" in the "R&D Project for Information and Communications Technology (JPMI00316)" of the Ministry of Internal Affairs and Communications (MIC), Japan.

References

Bahdanau, D., Cho, K., and Bengio, Y. (2014). Neural machine translation by jointly learning to align and translate. *Proceedings of the 3rd International Conference on Learning Representations.*, pages 1–15.

Brown, P. F., Pietra, V. J. D., Pietra, S. A. D., and Mercer, R. L. (1993). The mathematics of statistical machine translation: parameter estimation. *Computational linguistics*, 19(2):263–311.

Chakravarty, P., Zegers, J., Tuytelaars, T., and Van hamme, H. (2016). Active speaker detection with audio-visual co-training. In *Proceedings of the 18th ACM International Conference on Multimodal Interaction*, pages 312–316.

Chen, X., Wu, Y., Wang, Z., Liu, S., and Li, J. (2021). Developing real-time streaming transformer transducer for speech recognition on large-scale dataset.

Chiang, D. (2005). A hierarchical phrase-based model for statistical machine translation. In *Proceedings of the 43rd annual meeting of the association for computational linguistics (acl'05)*, pages 263–270.

Chung, J. S. (2019). Naver at activitynet challenge 2019–task b active speaker detection (ava). *arXiv preprint arXiv:1906.10555.*

Chung, J. S., Huh, J., Mun, S., Lee, M., Heo, H. S., Choe, S., Ham, C., Jung, S., Lee, B.-J., and Han, I. (2020). In defence of metric learning for speaker recognition. In *Interspeech*.

Chung, J. S., Nagrani, A., and Zisserman, A. (2018). Voxceleb2: Deep speaker recognition. *arXiv preprint arXiv:1806.05622*.

Di Gangi, M. A., Cattoni, R., Bentivogli, L., Negri, M., and Turchi, M. (2019). MuST-C: a Multilingual Speech Translation Corpus. In *Proceedings of the 2019 Conference of the North American Chapter of the Association for Computational Linguistics: Human Language Technologies, Volume 1 (Long and Short Papers)*, pages 2012–2017, Minneapolis, Minnesota. Association for Computational Linguistics.

Gravellier, L., Hunter, J., Muller, P., Pellegrini, T., and Ferrané, I. (2021). Weakly supervised discourse segmentation for multiparty oral conversations. In *Proceedings of the 2021 Conference on Empirical Methods in Natural Language Processing*, pages 1381–1392.

Gulati, A., Qin, J., Chiu, C.-C., Parmar, N., Zhang, Y., Yu, J., Han, W., Wang, S., Zhang, Z., Wu, Y., and Pang, R. (2020). Conformer: Convolution-augmented transformer for speech recognition.

He, K., Zhang, X., Ren, S., and Sun, J. (2016). Deep residual learning for image recognition. In *Proceedings of the IEEE conference on computer vision and pattern recognition*, pages 770–778.

Heo, H. S., Lee, B.-J., Huh, J., and Chung, J. S. (2020). Clova baseline system for the voxceleb speaker recognition challenge 2020. *arXiv preprint arXiv:2009.14153*.

Hirasawa, T., Yamagishi, H., Matsumura, Y., and Komachi, M. (2019). Multimodal machine translation with embedding prediction. *arXiv preprint arXiv:1904.00639*.

Huang, G. B., Mattar, M., Berg, T., and Learned-Miller, E. (2008). Labeled faces in the wild: A database forstudying face recognition in unconstrained environments. In *Workshop onfaces in'Real-Life'Images: detection, alignment, and recognition*.

Iranzo-Sánchez, J., Pastor, A. G., Silvestre-Cerda, J. A., Baquero-Arnal, P., Saiz, J. C., and Juan, A. (2020). Direct segmentation models for streaming speech translation. In *Proceedings of the 2020 Conference on Empirical Methods in Natural Language Processing (EMNLP)*, pages 2599–2611.

Kim, Y. J., Heo, H.-S., Choe, S., Chung, S.-W., Kwon, Y., Lee, B.-J., Kwon, Y., and Chung, J. S. (2021). Look who's talking: Active speaker detection in the wild.

Köpüklü, O., Taseska, M., and Rigoll, G. (2021). How to design a three-stage architecture for audio-visual active speaker detection in the wild.

León-Alcázar, J., Heilbron, F. C., Thabet, A., and Ghanem, B. (2021). Maas: Multi-modal assignation for active speaker detection.

Li, C., Ma, X., Jiang, B., Li, X., Zhang, X., Liu, X., Cao, Y., Kannan, A., and Zhu, Z. (2017). Deep speaker: an end-to-end neural speaker embedding system.

Li, D., Te, I., Arivazhagan, N., Cherry, C., and Padfield, D. (2021). Sentence boundary augmentation for neural machine translation robustness. In *ICASSP 2021-2021 IEEE International Conference on Acoustics, Speech and Signal Processing (ICASSP)*, pages 7553–7557. IEEE.

Likhomanenko, T., Xu, Q., Pratap, V., Tomasello, P., Kahn, J., Avidov, G., Collobert, R., and Synnaeve, G. (2021). Rethinking evaluation in asr: Are our models robust enough?

Lin, H., Meng, F., Su, J., Yin, Y., Yang, Z., Ge, Y., Zhou, J., and Luo, J. (2020). Dynamic context-guided capsule network for multimodal machine translation. In *Proceedings of the 28th ACM International Conference on Multimedia*, pages 1320–1329.

Mitzalis, F., Caglayan, O., Madhyastha, P., and Specia, L. (2021). Bertgen: Multi-task generation through bert.

Moritz, N., Hori, T., and Roux, J. L. (2020). Streaming automatic speech recognition with the transformer model.

Nagrani, A., Chung, J. S., Xie, W., and Zisserman, A. (2020). Voxceleb: Large-scale speaker verification in the wild. *Computer Speech & Language*, 60:101027.

Nguyen, T. S., Niehues, J., Cho, E., Ha, T.-L., Kilgour, K., Muller, M., Sperber, M., Stueker, S., and Waibel, A. (2020). Low latency asr for simultaneous speech translation.

Novitasari, S., Tjandra, A., Sakti, S., and Nakamura, S. (2019). Sequence-to-sequence learning via attention transfer for incremental speech recognition. *Proceedings of Interspeech*, pages 3835–3839.

Pratap, V., Xu, Q., Kahn, J., Avidov, G., Likhomanenko, T., Hannun, A., Liptchinsky, V., Synnaeve, G., and Collobert, R. (2020). Scaling up online speech recognition using convnets.

Roth, J., Chaudhuri, S., Klejch, O., Marvin, R., Gallagher, A., Kaver, L., Ramaswamy, S., Stopczynski, A., Schmid, C., Xi, Z., and Pantofaru, C. (2019). Ava-activespeaker: An audio-visual dataset for active speaker detection.

Sanabria, R., Caglayan, O., Palaskar, S., Elliott, D., Barrault, L., Specia, L., and Metze, F. (2018). How2: A large-scale dataset for multimodal language understanding.

Schroff, F., Kalenichenko, D., and Philbin, J. (2015). Facenet: A unified embedding for face recognition and clustering. *2015 IEEE Conference on Computer Vision and Pattern Recognition (CVPR)*.

Specia, L., Frank, S., Sima'An, K., and Elliott, D. (2016). A shared task on multimodal machine translation and crosslingual image description. In *Proceedings of the First Conference on Machine Translation: Volume 2, Shared Task Papers*, pages 543–553.

Sridhar, V. K. R., Chen, J., Bangalore, S., Ljolje, A., and Chengalvarayan, R. (2013). Segmentation strategies for streaming speech translation. In *Proceedings of the 2013 Conference of the North American Chapter of the Association for Computational Linguistics: Human Language Technologies*, pages 230–238.

Stolcke, A., Shriberg, E., Bates, R. A., Ostendorf, M., Hakkani, D., Plauche, M., Tür, G., and Lu, Y. (1998). Automatic detection of sentence boundaries and disfluencies based on recognized words. In *Proceedings of 5th International Conference on Spoken Language Processing*, pages 2247–2250.

Sulubacak, U., Caglayan, O., Grönroos, S.-A., Rouhe, A., Elliott, D., Specia, L., and Tiedemann, J. (2019). Multimodal machine translation through visuals and speech.

Tao, R., Pan, Z., Das, R. K., Qian, X., Shou, M. Z., and Li, H. (2021). Is someone speaking? exploring long-term temporal features for audio-visual active speaker detection. *Proceedings of the 29th ACM International Conference on Multimedia*.

Tsunoo, E., Kashiwagi, Y., and Watanabe, S. (2020). Streaming transformer asr with blockwise synchronous beam search.

Wan, L., Wang, Q., Papir, A., and Moreno, I. L. (2018). Generalized end-to-end loss for speaker verification. In *2018 IEEE International Conference on Acoustics, Speech and Signal Processing (ICASSP)*, pages 4879–4883. IEEE.

Wang, X., Finch, A., Utiyama, M., and Sumita, E. (2016a). An efficient and effective online sentence segmenter for simultaneous interpretation. In *Proceedings of the 3rd Workshop on Asian Translation (WAT2016)*, pages 139–148, Osaka, Japan. The COLING 2016 Organizing Committee.

Wang, X., Finch, A., Utiyama, M., and Sumita, E. (2016b). A prototype automatic simultaneous interpretation system. In *Proceedings of COLING 2016, the 26th International Conference on Computational Linguistics: System Demonstrations*, pages 30–34.

Wang, X., Utiyama, M., and Sumita, E. (2019). Online sentence segmentation for simultaneous interpretation using multi-shifted recurrent neural network. In *Proceedings of Machine Translation Summit XVII Volume 1: Research Track*, pages 1–11.

Wicks, R. and Post, M. (2021). A unified approach to sentence segmentation of punctuated text in many languages. In *Proceedings of the 59th Annual Meeting of the Association for Computational Linguistics and the 11th International Joint Conference on Natural Language Processing (Volume 1: Long Papers)*, pages 3995–4007, Online. Association for Computational Linguistics.

Yao, S. and Wan, X. (2020). Multimodal transformer for multimodal machine translation. In *Proceedings of the 58th Annual Meeting of the Association for Computational Linguistics*, pages 4346–4350.

Zens, R., Och, F. J., and Ney, H. (2002). Phrase-based statistical machine translation. In *Advances in Artificial Intelligence*, pages 18–32. Springer.

Zhang, Y., Liang, S., Yang, S., Liu, X., Wu, Z., Shan, S., and Chen, X. (2021). Unicon: Unified context network for robust active speaker detection. In *Proceedings of the 29th ACM International Conference on Multimedia*, pages 3964–3972.

AMTA ORLANDO 2022

Data Analytics Meet Machine Translation

Allen Che and Martin Xiao

2022 Sep

Proceedings of the 15th Biennial Conference of the Association for Machine Translation in the Americas, Orlando, USA, September 12-16, 2022. Volume 2: Users and Providers Track and Government Track vmware

$12.85B in revenue (USD) in FY2022

VMware is the leading provider of multi-cloud services for all apps, enabling digital innovation with enterprise control.

37,500+ employees

Allen Che
Senior Technical Localization Program Manager

Martin Xiao
Senior Technical Localization Program Manager

AMTA ORLANDO 2022

Objective

Business Manager

Localization PM

Technical Lead

Data is the key

Discovery	Insight	Predict
Discovery the data to uncover the pattern and trends.	Gain an Insight of the data to acquire the new value/new knowledge/new story.	Predict what could happen and make better and more scientific decisions.

Our Study – MT Quality

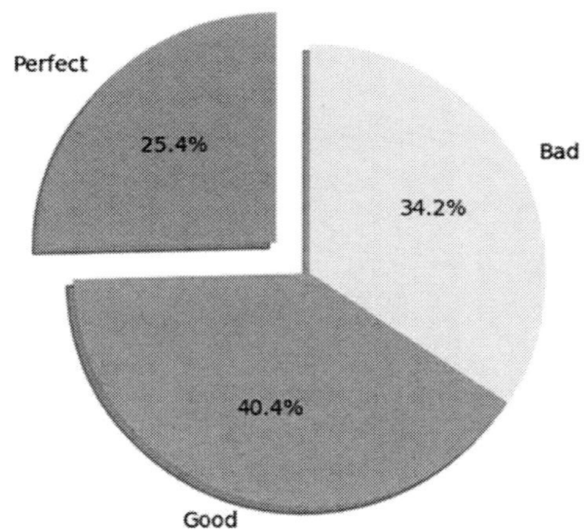

Perfect: PE% = 0 Good: 0 < PE% < 20% Bad: PE% > 20%

MT Solution – ML aided

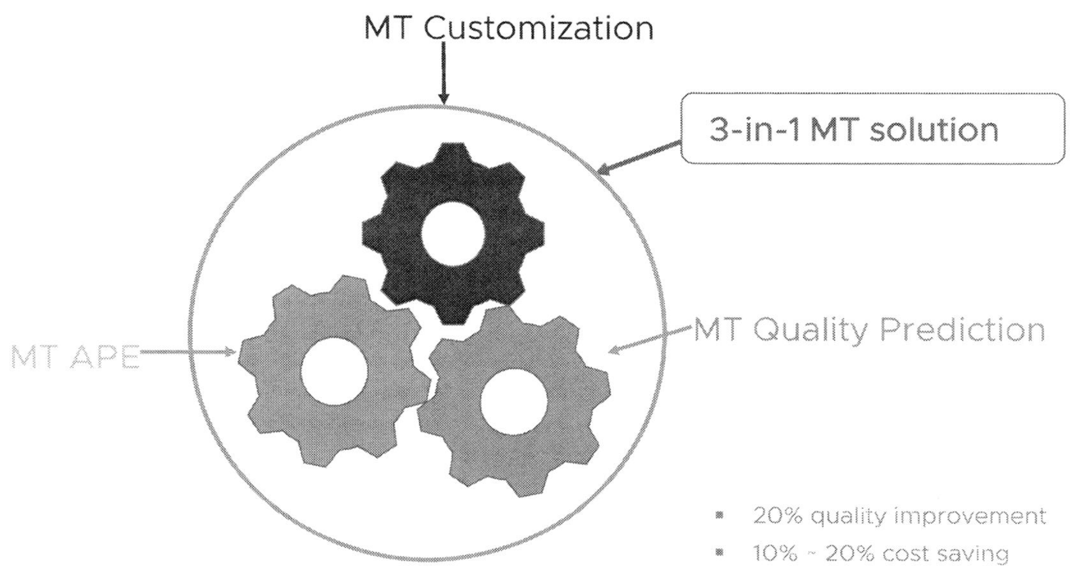

- 20% quality improvement
- 10% ~ 20% cost saving

How the MT solution works

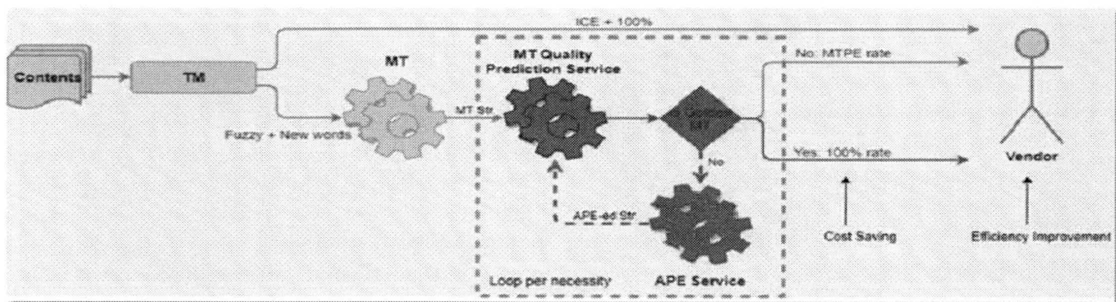

ML-Aided workflow

- MT Quality Prediction: auto quantify MT quality, ML based;
- MT Quality Prediction: Perfect MT use-case
- APE Service: auto post editing to improve MT quality, ML based

Challenge

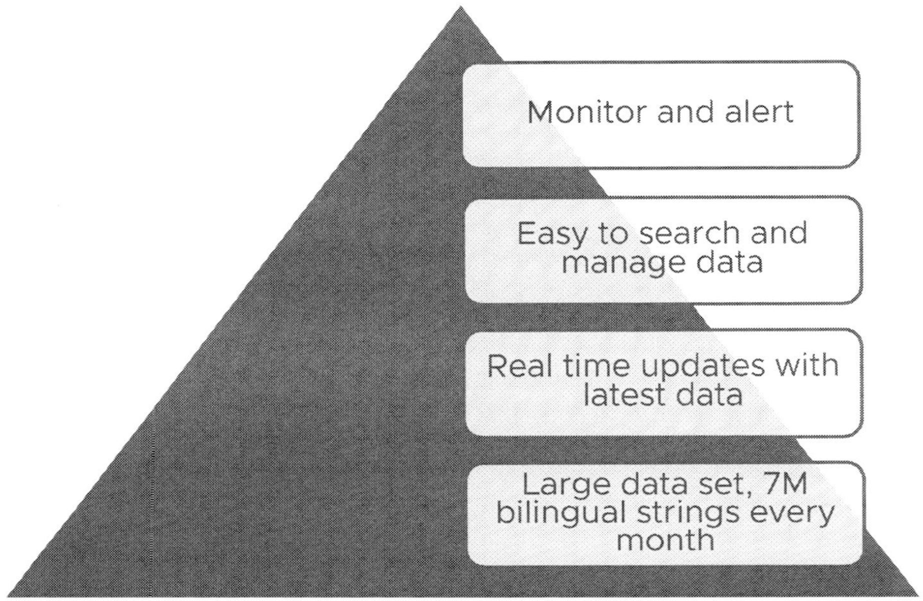
Monitor and alert
Easy to search and manage data
Real time updates with latest data
Large data set, 7M bilingual strings every month

Solution – Elasticstack

Automate, Monior and Visualize

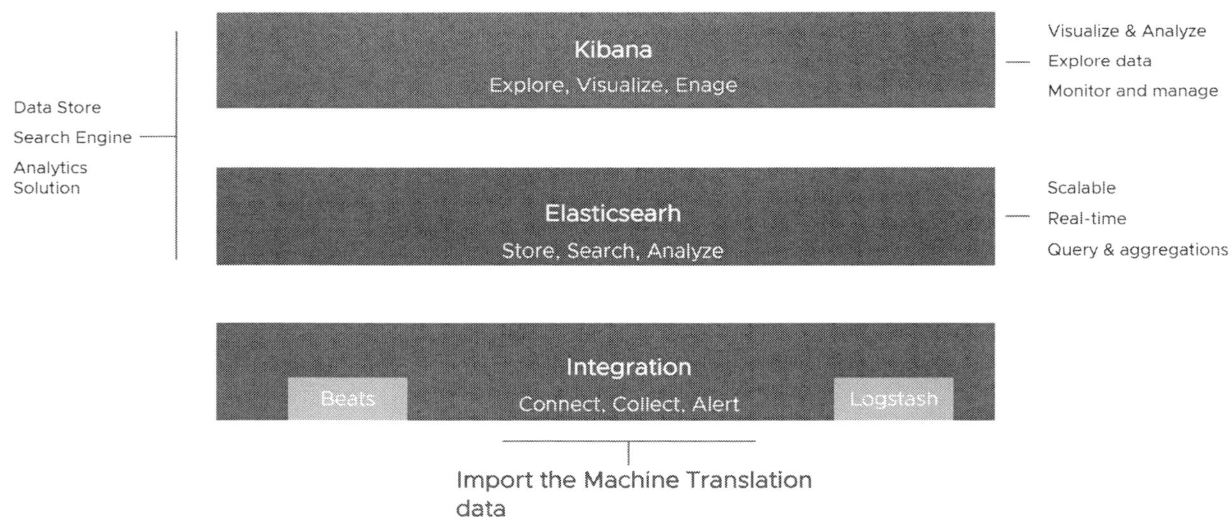

Automate Data Collection

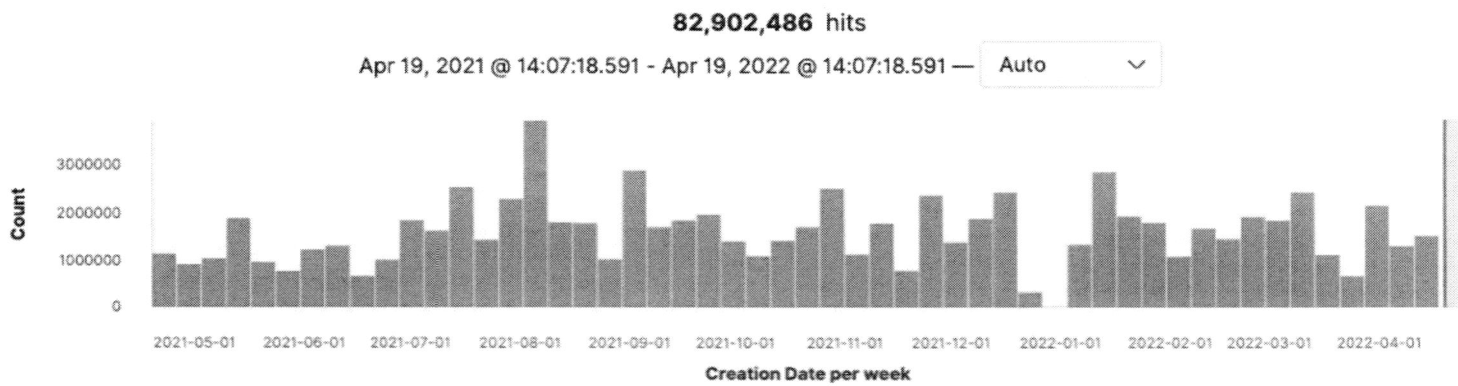

Monitor

Post-edit disance

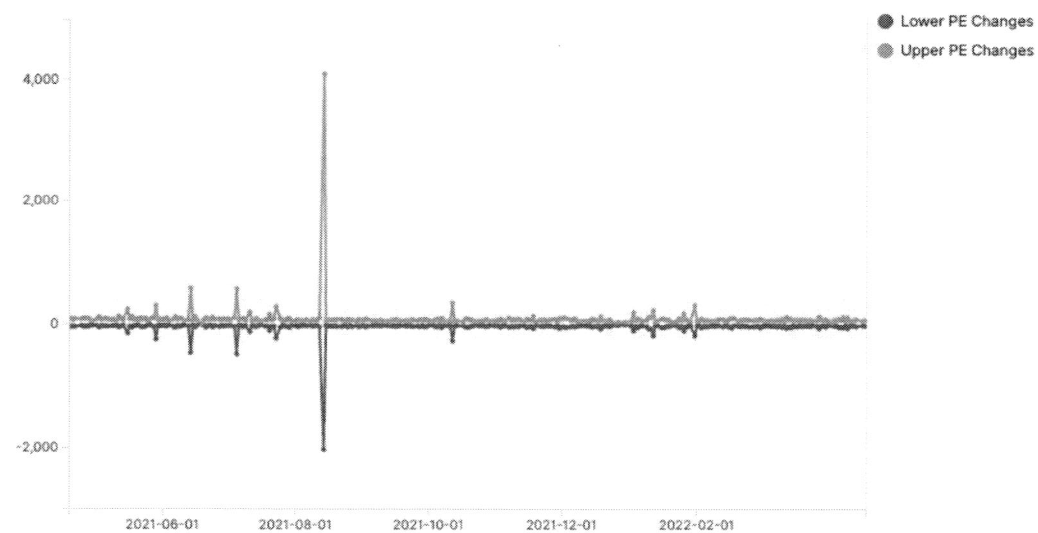

Visualize the data

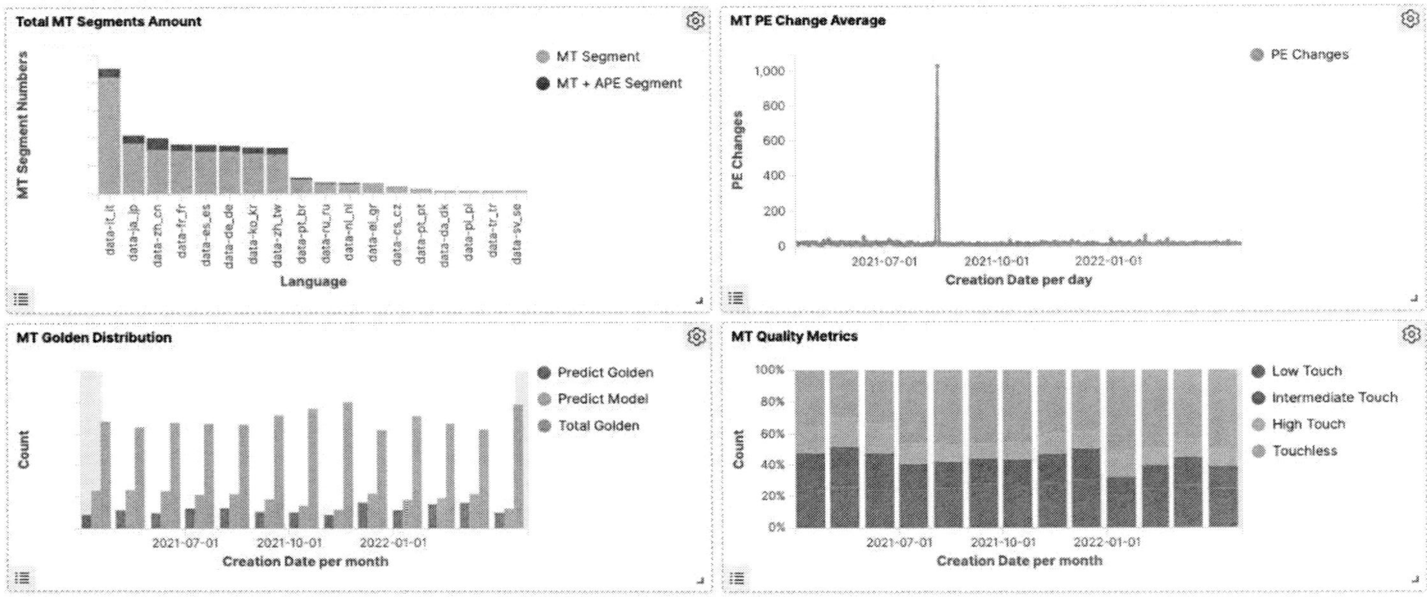

What's Next

Intelligent Data Platform

- Automate the process
- API integration
- NLP layer on top of automation

What's Next

Architect

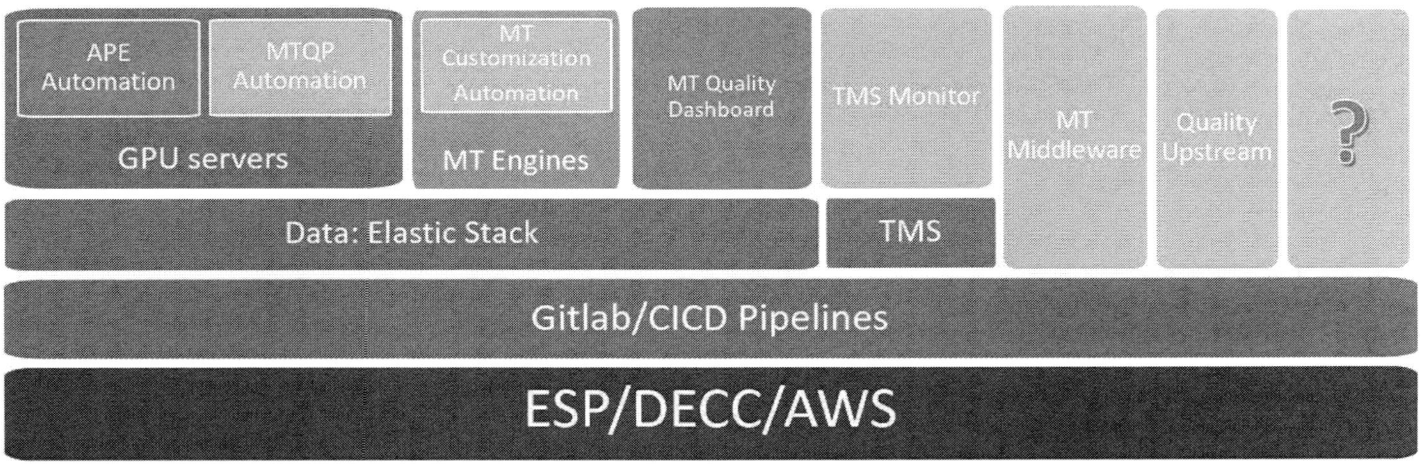

AMTA ORLANDO 2022

Live Q & A

vmware Confidential | © VMware, Inc.

Quality prediction

Use good machine translations like 100% translation memory matches

Adam Bittlingmayer

CEO

ModelFront

Artur Aleksanyan

CTO

ModelFront

Boris Zubarev

ML LEAD

ModelFront

MISSION

Make quality translation faster and cheaper

HOW TO MAKE QUALITY TRANSLATION FASTER AND CHEAPER

Beyond better machine translation

POST-EDITING

You send 100% to humans, humans edit __% of segments.

POST-EDITING

Humans **don’t edit** __% of segments.

POST-EDITING

Humans **don’t edit** __% of segments.

Can we predict which?

HOW IT WORKS

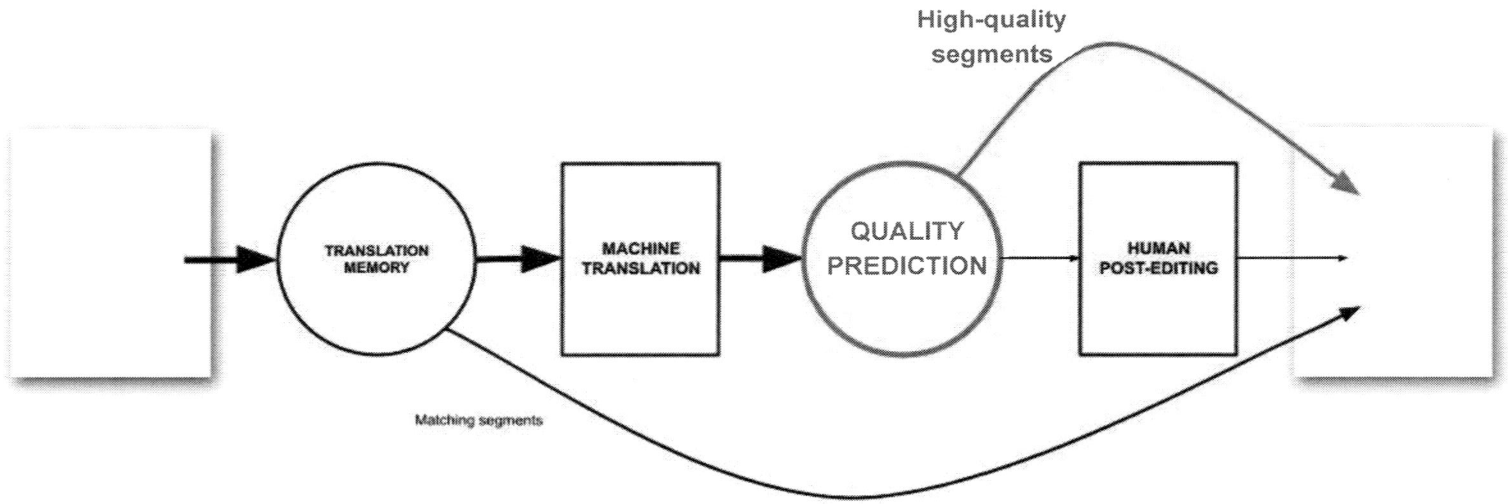

machinetranslate.org/hybrid-translation

“QUALITY ESTIMATION”

No human reference translation

source segment, target segment → score

USE CASES

POST-EDITING WORKFLOW

RAW MACHINE TRANSLATION

USE CASES

POST-EDITING WORKFLOW

Same quality,

faster and cheaper

RAW MACHINE TRANSLATION

USE CASES

POST-EDITING WORKFLOW

Same quality,

faster and cheaper

RAW MACHINE TRANSLATION

Better quality

(no “catastrophes”)

USE CASES

POST-EDITING WORKFLOW

Same quality,

faster and cheaper

90% QUALITY THRESHOLD

42% SKIP HUMANS

RAW MACHINE TRANSLATION

Better quality

(no "catastrophes")

USE CASES

POST-EDITING WORKFLOW

Same quality,

faster and cheaper

90% QUALITY THRESHOLD

42% SKIP HUMANS

RAW MACHINE TRANSLATION

Better quality

(no "catastrophes")

1% QUALITY THRESHOLD

99% SKIP HUMANS

RoI?

ROI

Skip humans for most of the good machine translations

Adoption

EVOLUTION

1. In-house
2. API providers
3. TMS integrations

ADOPTION

Customer support

Technical documentation

Product titles and descriptions

PROVIDERS

	ENGINES	CUSTOMIZATION	ACCESS
KantantQES	only KantanMT	✔	only KantanStream
Omniscien CS/QE	only Omniscien	✔	✔ API
Memsource QE	**all**		only Memsource
ModelFront	**all**	✔	✔ API, TMS integrations

TMS INTEGRATION

	UNILATERAL	OFFICIAL	
Memsource	✔	✔	Memsource QE
KantanStream		✔	KantanQES
Translate5	✔	✔	ModelFront
Crowdin	✔	✔	ModelFront
XTM	✔		
Lokalise	✔		
SDL Worldserver	✔		
SDL TMS			
MemoQ			

Questions?

Comparison Between ATA Grading Framework Scores and Auto Scores

Evelyn Yang Garland
Acta Chinese Language Services LLC, egarland@actalanguage.com
Carola F Berger
CFB Scientific Translations LLC, info@cfbtranslations.com
Jon Ritzdorf
Procore, jon@ritzdorfacademy.com

Question

- How much **agreement** is there between **human evaluation scores** and **auto evaluation scores** when they are used to evaluate human translations and MTs?

Methodology

- Exploratory study
  - Data from a previous study
  - Not specifically designed to test the hypothesis question
- 2 source passages, English-into-Chinese, general

- Passage A: 263 words
  - 8 human translations (HTAs)
    - No use of MT
    - 6 professional translators and 2 students
  - 2 reference translations (for auto scoring)
    - RefA1: plain, error-free reference
    - RefA2: fancy, few errors

- Passage B: 264 words
  - 8 human translations (HTBs)
    - One MT provided for reference
    - Free to use other MTs
    - Same 6 professional translators and 2 students
  - 3 MTs (including the reference MT)
  - 2 reference translations (for auto scoring)
    - RefA1: plain, error-free reference
    - RefA2: fancy, few errors

Methodology (cont'd)

- Human evaluation
  - ATA Grading Framework
  - Graded by 2 ATA certified translators
  - Average of the 2 graders' scores
- Auto evaluation
  - BLEU
  - TER
  - COMET (wmt20-da)
  - COMET no reference (wmt20-da, wmt20-da v2, wmt21-mqm)

Result 1

- Auto scores that rely on reference translations depend heavily on which reference is used

Result 1 – Passage A, BLEU, TER

RefA1: "plain"

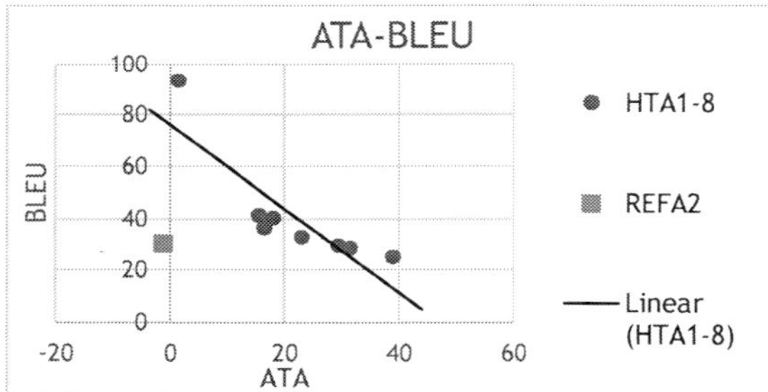

Pearson: -0.857, p: 0.006

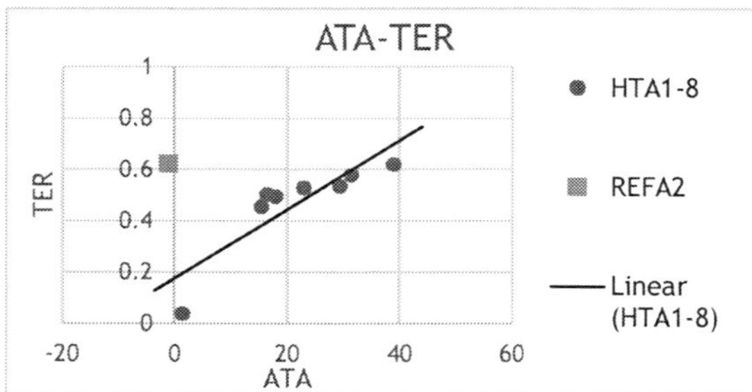

Pearson: 0.866, p: 0.005

RefA2: "fancy"

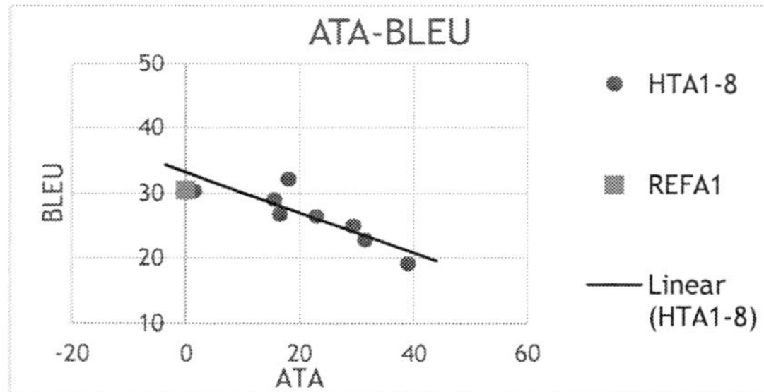

Pearson: -0.853, p: 0.007

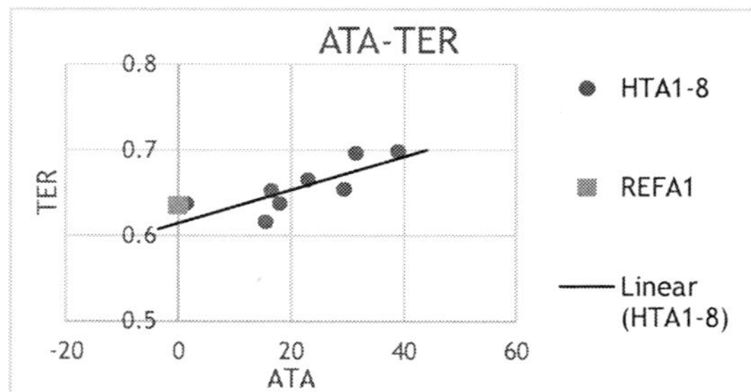

Pearson: 0.786, p: 0.021

- ATA, TER: higher quality = lower score; BLEU: higher quality = higher score
- Trendline based on HTA1-8

Result 1 – Passage A, COMET

RefA1: similar to HTA1-8

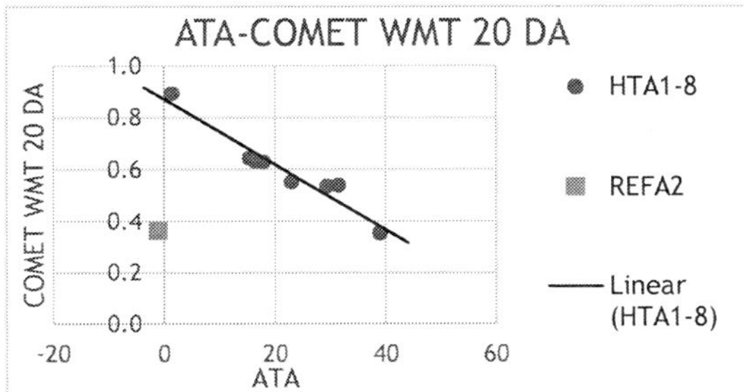

Pearson: -0.965, p: 0.0001

RefA2: independent

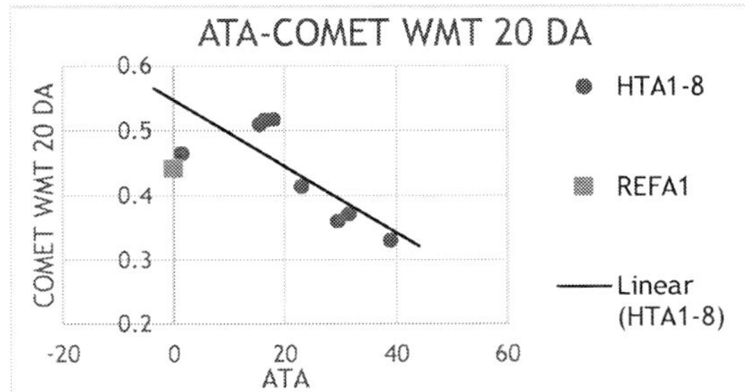

Pearson: -0.777, p: 0.0023

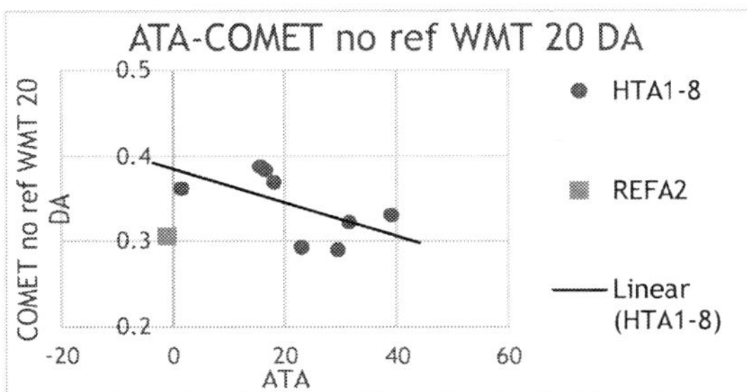

Pearson: -0.588, p: 0.126

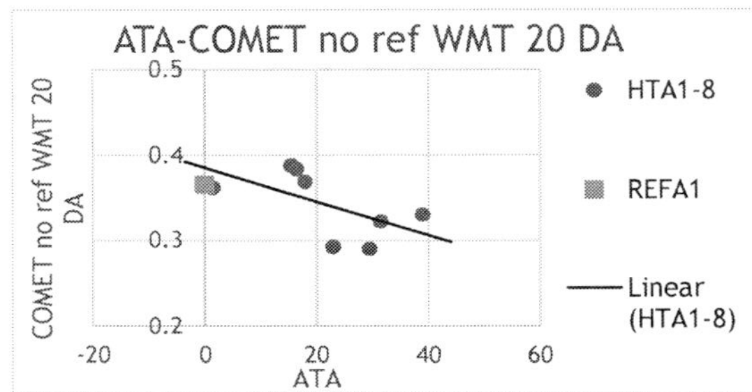

Pearson: -0.588, p: 0.126

- ATA: higher quality = lower score; COMET: higher quality = higher score
- Trendline based on HTA1-8

Result 1 – Passage A, COMET(cont'd)

RefA1: "plain"

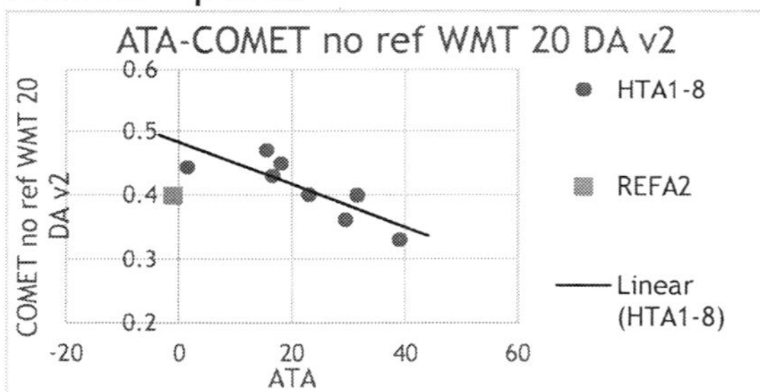

Pearson: -0.824, p: 0.012

RefA2: "fancy"

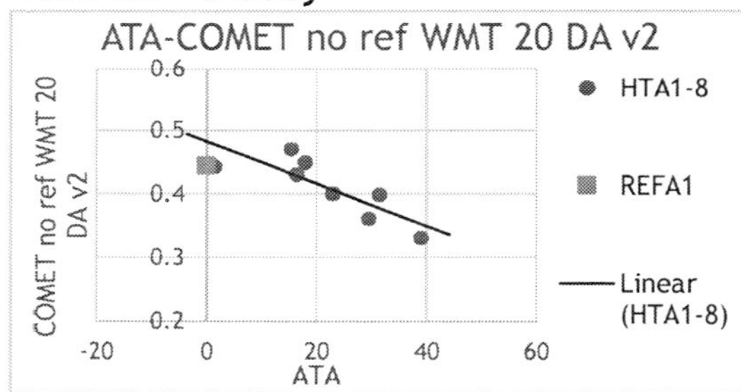

Pearson: -0.824, p: 0.012

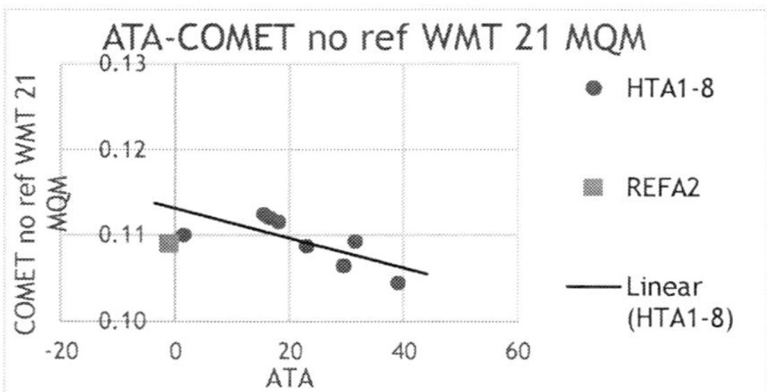

Pearson: -0.722, p: 0.043

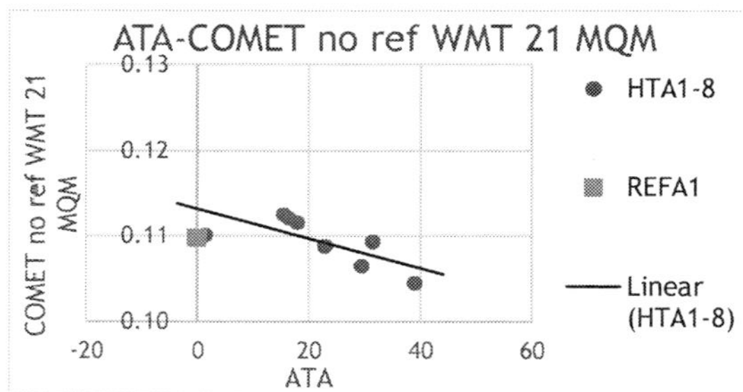

Pearson: -0.722, p: 0.043

- ATA: higher quality = lower score; COMET: higher quality = higher score
- Trendline based on HTA1-8

Result 1 – Passage B, COMET

RefB1: "plain"

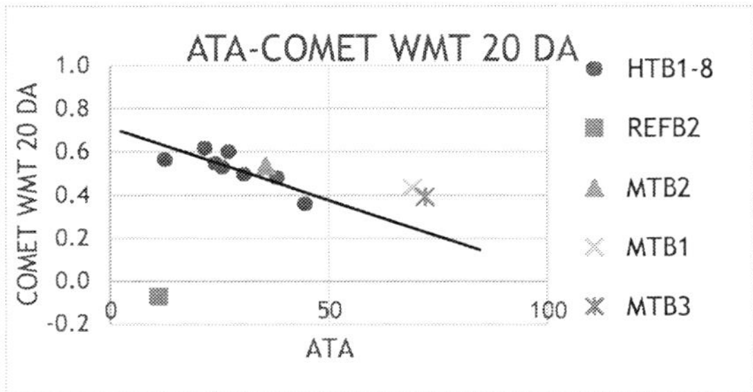

Pearson: -0.819, p: 0.013

RefB2: "fancy"

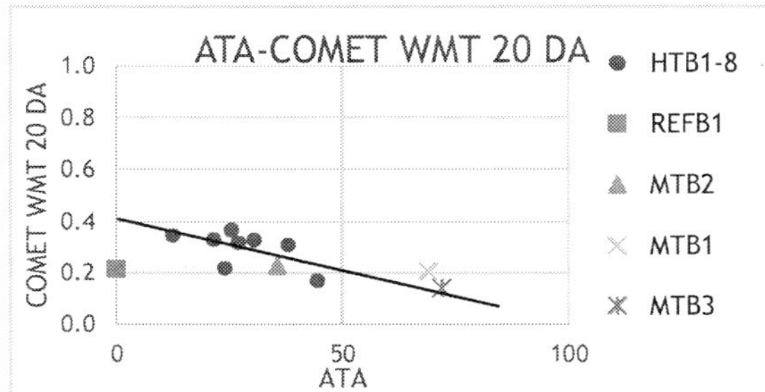

Pearson: -0.588, p: 0.125

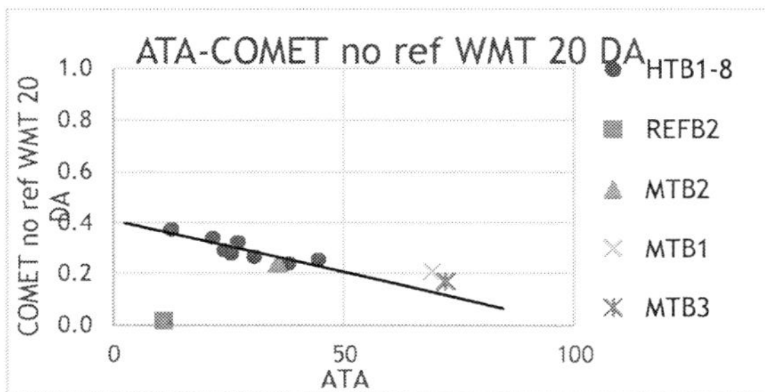

Pearson: -0.873, p: 0.005

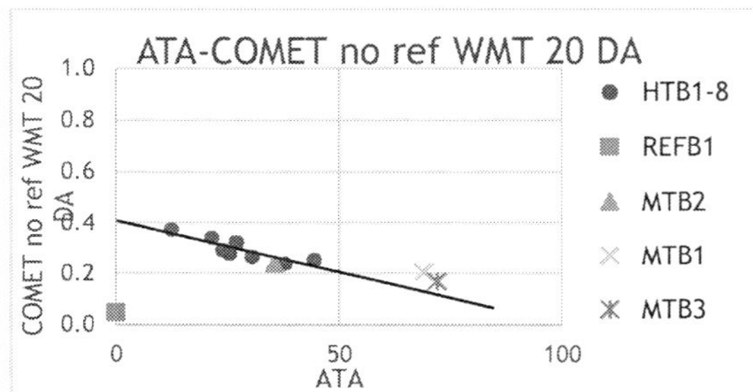

Pearson: -0.873, p: 0.005

- ATA: higher quality = lower score; COMET: higher quality = higher score
- Trendline based on HTB1-8
- BLEU, TER, and COMET no ref WMT 21 MQM: no significant agreement;
- COMET no ref WMT 20 DA v2: did not obtain

Proceedings of the 15th Biennial Conference of the Association for Machine Translation in the Americas, Orlando, USA, September 12-16, 2022. Volume 2: Users and Providers Track and Government Track

Result 2

- Referenceless COMET seems promising when it is used to evaluate translations of short passages (~250 English words)

Result 2 – Passage A, COMET no ref

RefA1: "plain"

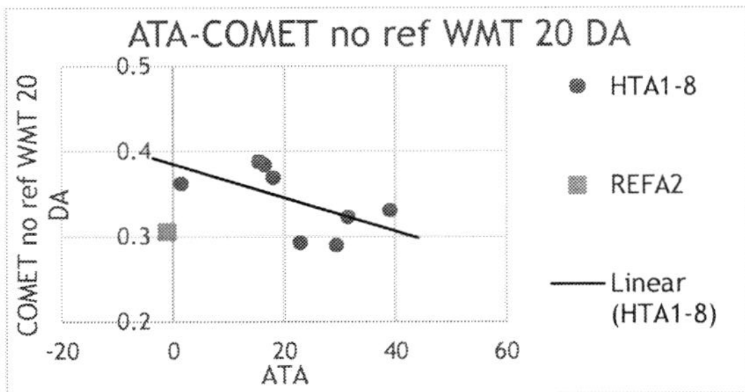

Pearson: -0.588, p: 0.126

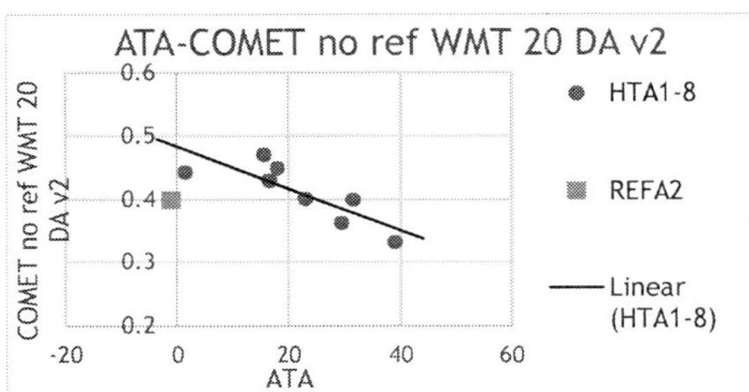

Pearson: -0.824, p: 0.012

RefA2: "fancy"

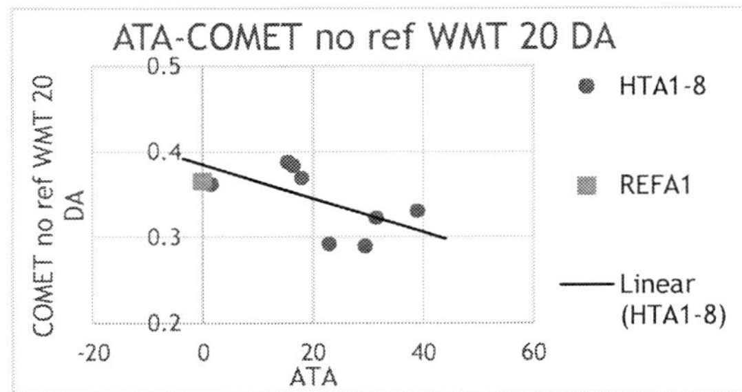

Pearson: -0.588, p: 0.126

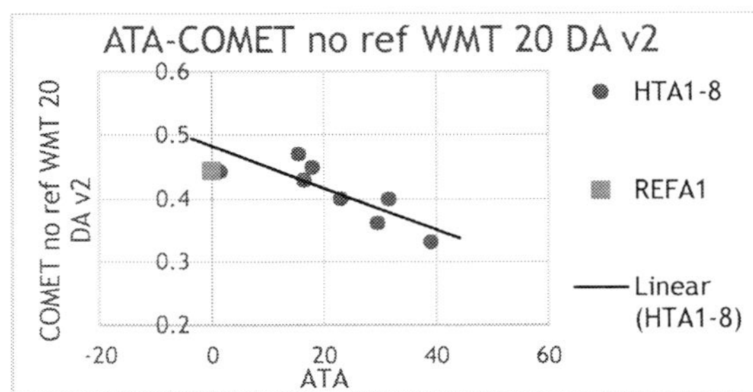

Pearson: -0.824, p: 0.012

- ATA: higher quality = lower score; COMET: higher quality = higher score
- Trendline based on HTA1-8

Result 2 – Passage A, COMET no ref (cont'd)

RefA1: "plain"

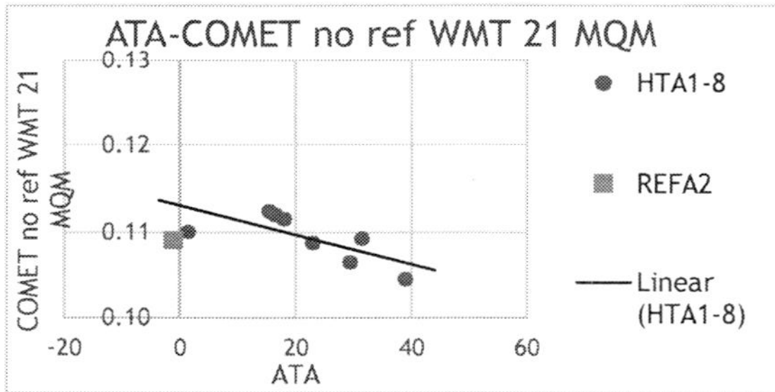

Pearson: -0.722, p: 0.043

RefA2: "fancy"

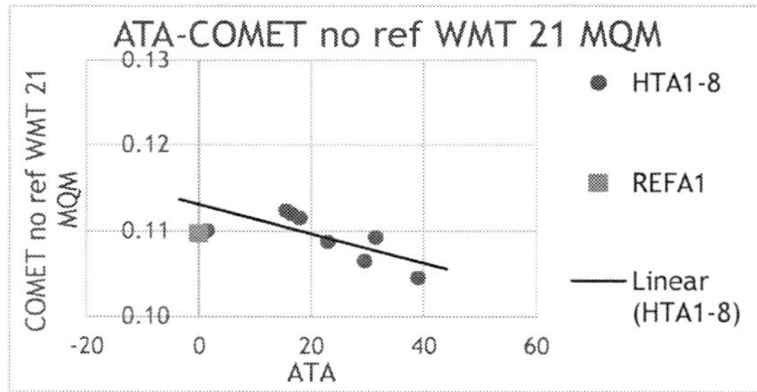

Pearson: -0.722, p: 0.043

- ATA: higher quality = lower score; COMET: higher quality = higher score
- Trendline based on HTA1-8

Result 2 – Passage B, COMET no ref

RefB1: "plain"

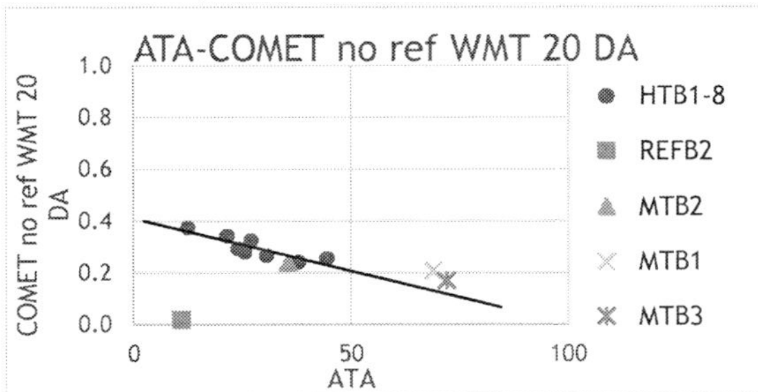

Pearson: -0.873, p: 0.005

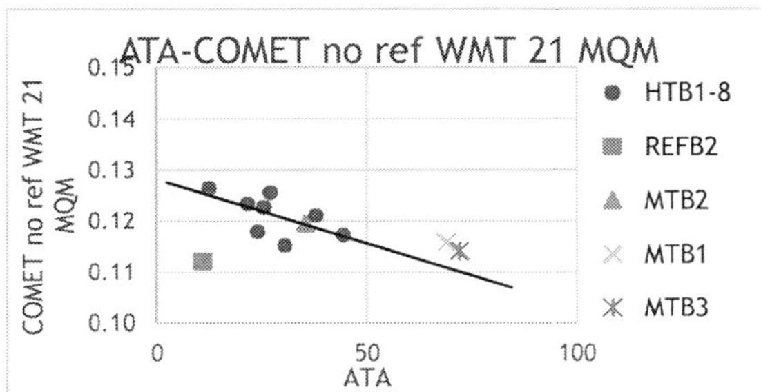

Pearson: -0.610, p: 0.108

RefB2: "fancy"

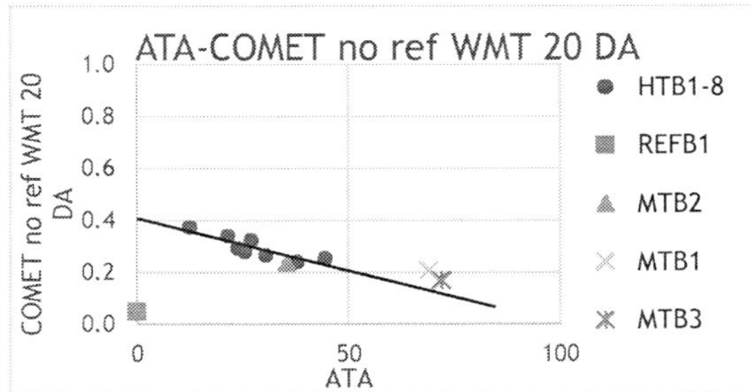

Pearson: -0.873, p: 0.005

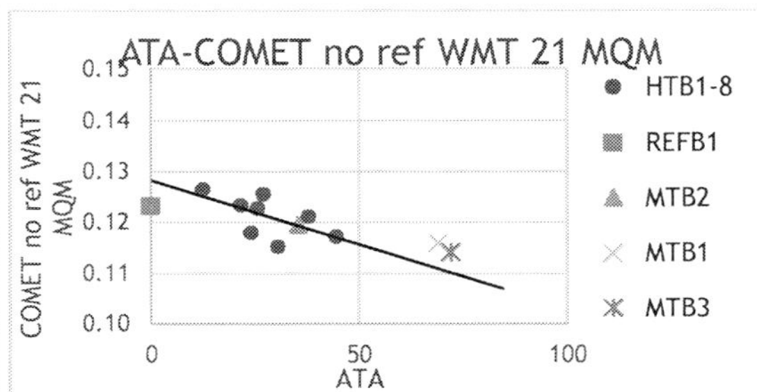

Pearson: -0.610, p: 0.108

- ATA: higher quality = lower score; COMET: higher quality = higher score
- Trendline based on HTB1-8
- COMET no ref WMT 20 DA v2: did not obtain

Result 3

- Good agreement between the ATA-Framework score and auto scores within a middle range, but the relationship becomes non-monotonic beyond the middle range

Result 3 – Passage A, ref = RefA1 (“plain”)

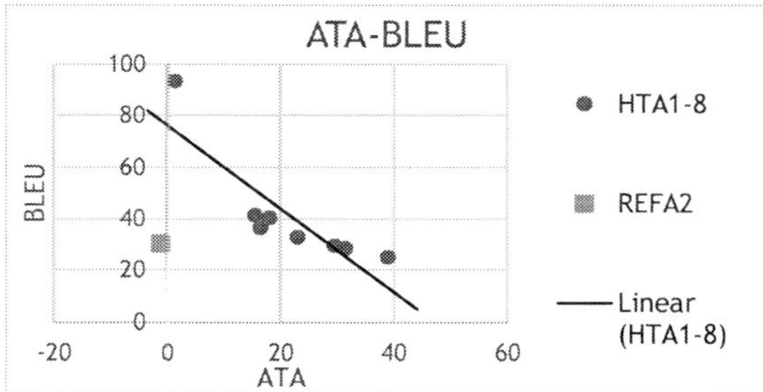

Pearson: -0.857, p: 0.006

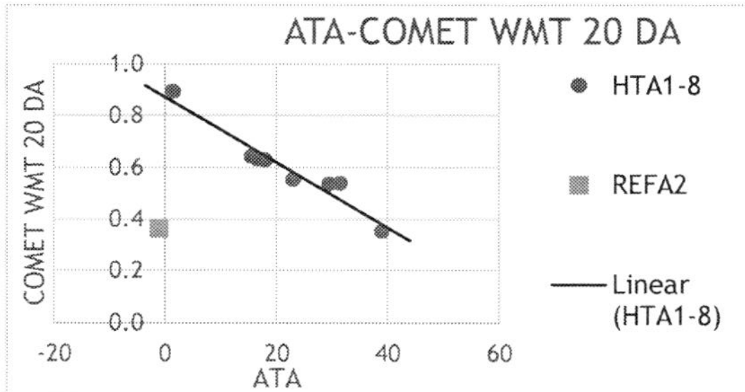

Pearson: -0.965, p: 0.0001

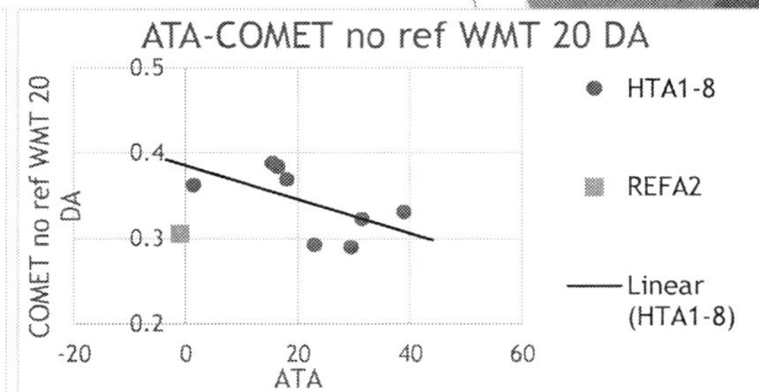

Pearson: -0.588, p: 0.126

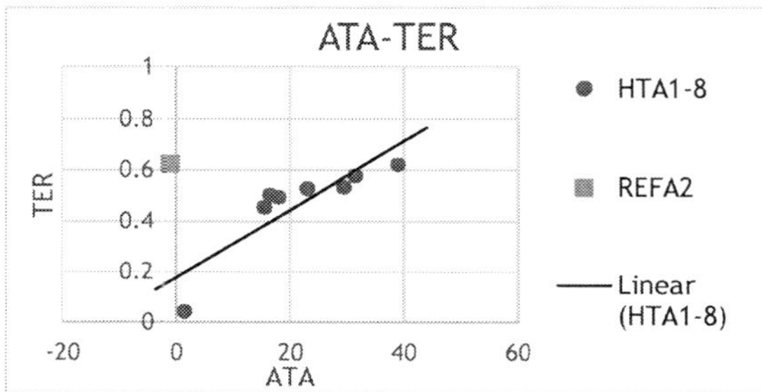

Pearson: 0.866, p: 0.005

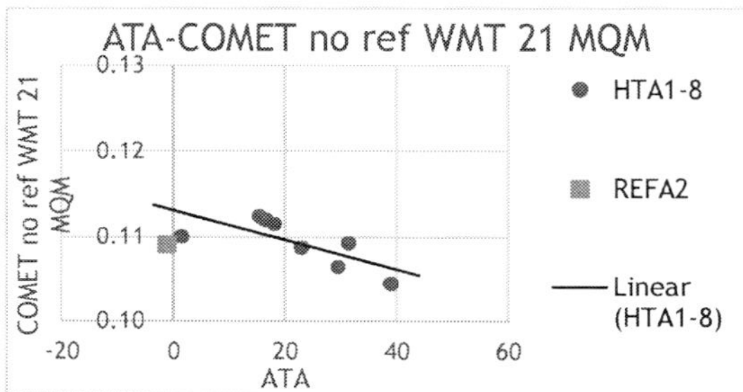

Pearson: -0.722, p: 0.043

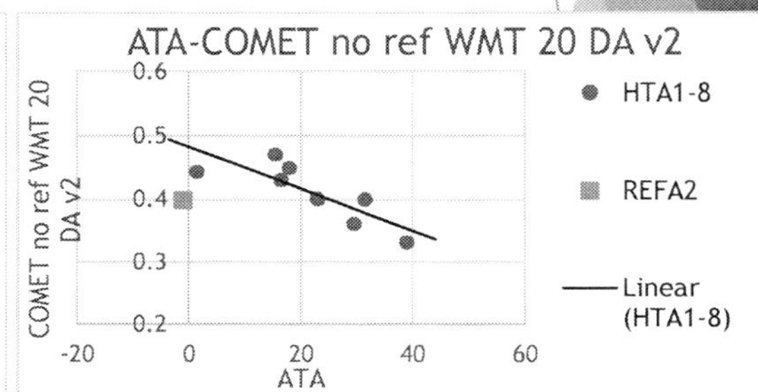

Pearson: -0.824, p: 0.012

- ATA, TER: higher quality = lower score; BLEU, COMET: higher quality = higher score
- Trendline based on HTA1-8

Result 3 – Passage A, ref = RefA2 (“fancy”)

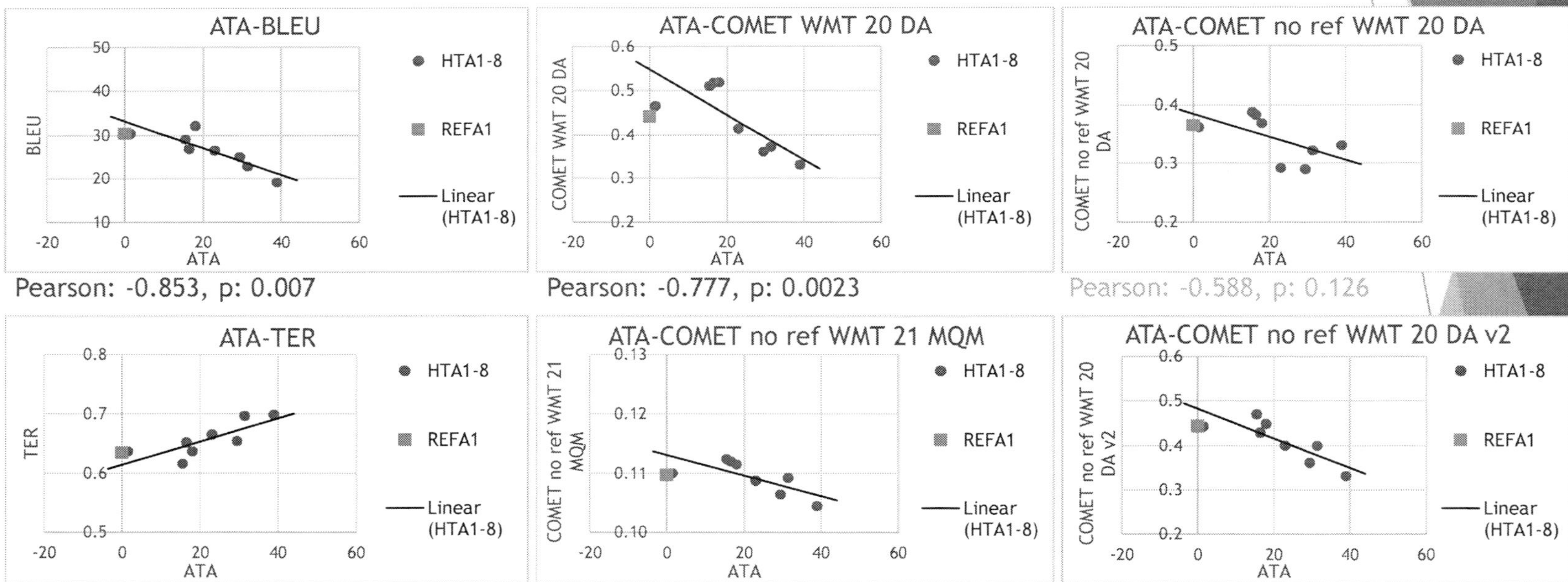

Pearson: -0.853, p: 0.007

Pearson: -0.777, p: 0.0023

Pearson: -0.588, p: 0.126

Pearson: 0.786, p: 0.021

Pearson: -0.722, p: 0.043

Pearson: -0.824, p: 0.012

- ATA, TER: higher quality = lower score; BLEU, COMET: higher quality = higher score
- Trendline based on HTA1-8

Result 3 – Passage B, ref = RefB1 (“plain”)

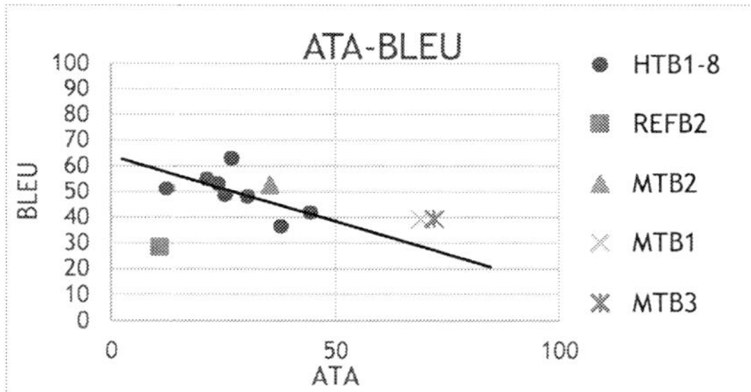

Pearson: -0.623, p: 0.099

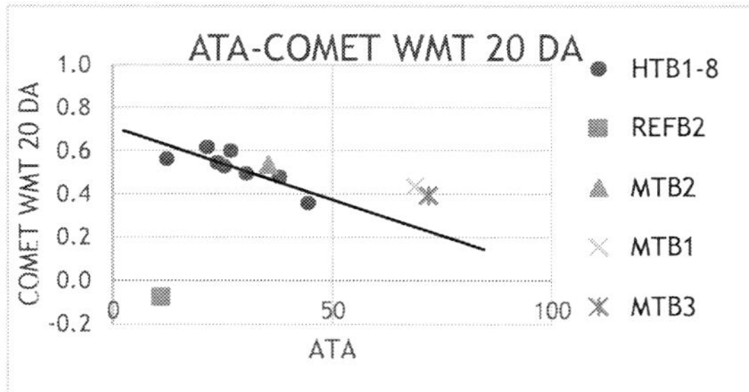

Pearson: -0.819, p: 0.013

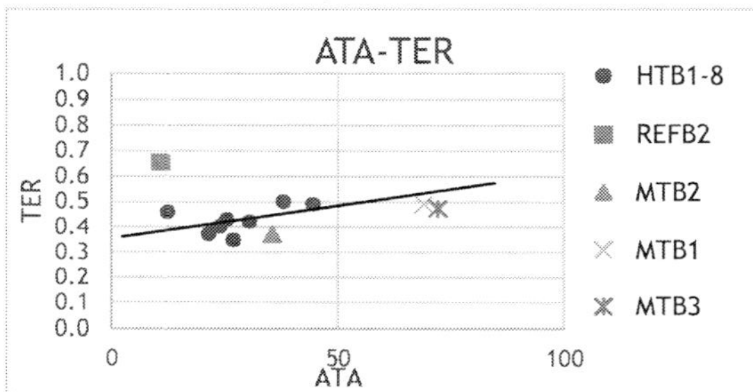

Pearson: 0.479, p: 0.230

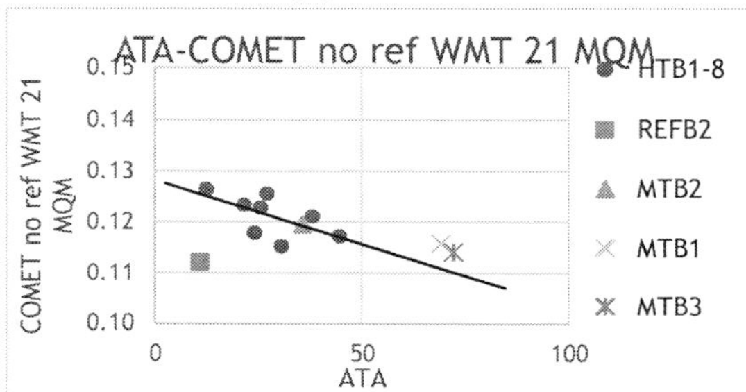

Pearson: -0.610, p: 0.108

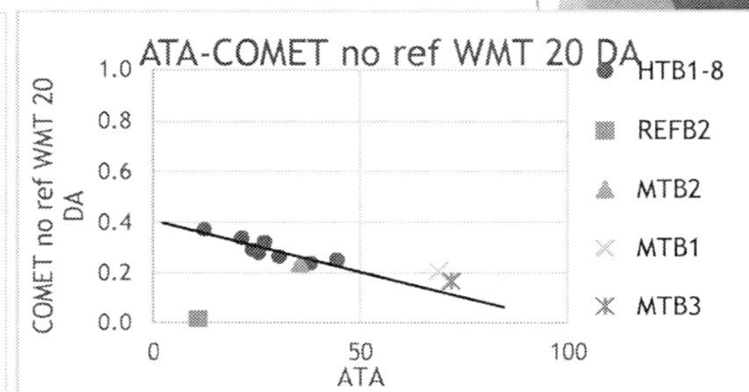

Pearson: -0.873, p: 0.005

- ATA, TER: higher quality = lower score; BLEU, COMET: higher quality = higher score
- Trendline based on HTB1-8

Result – Passage B, ref = RefB2 (“fancy”)

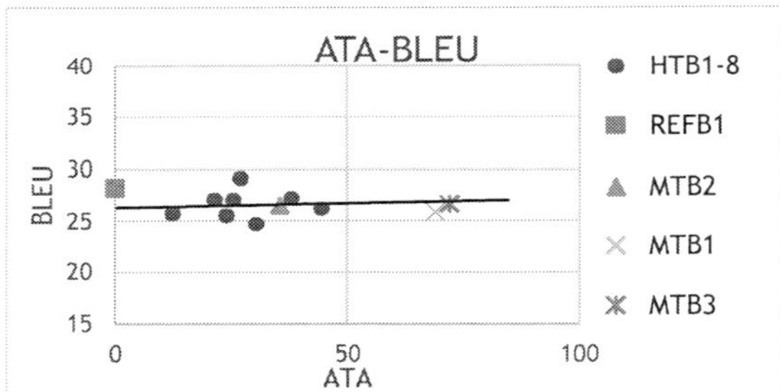

Pearson: 0.064, p: 0.881

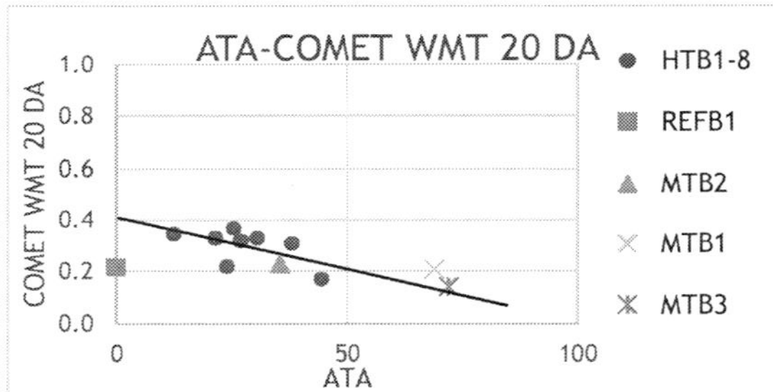

Pearson: -0.588, p: 0.125

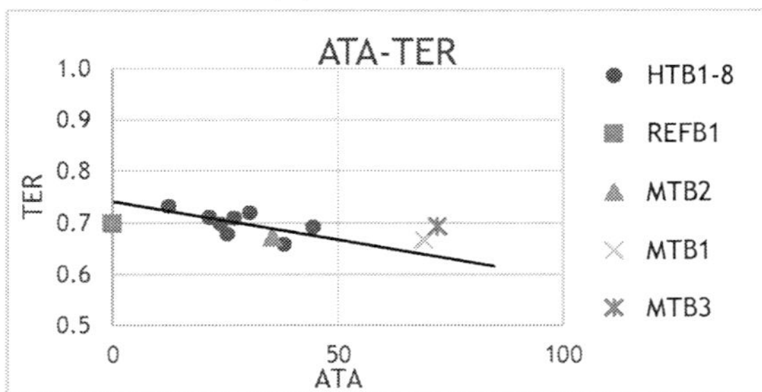

Pearson: -0.621, p: 0.100

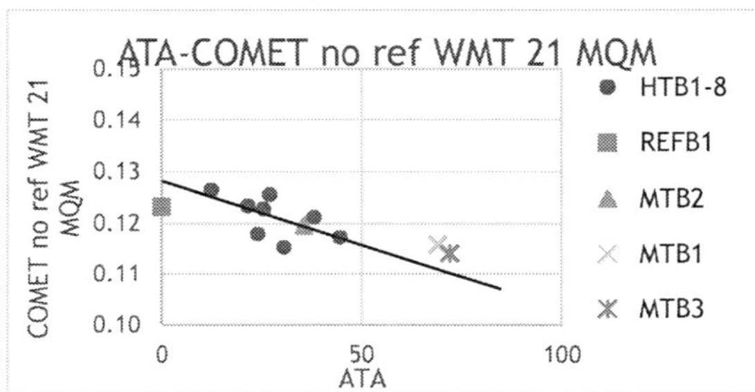

Pearson: -0.610, p: 0.108

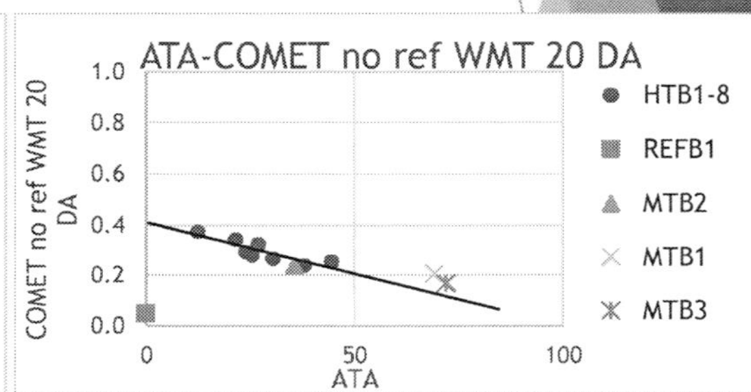

Pearson: -0.873, p: 0.005

- ATA, TER: higher quality = lower score; BLEU, COMET: higher quality = higher score
- Trendline based on HTB1-8

Results & Conclusions

1. Auto scores that rely on reference translations depend heavily on which reference is used
   - ➢ Reference translation must be selected with care
2. Referenceless COMET seems promising when it is used to evaluate translations of short passages (~250 English words)
   - ➢ Potential of referenceless COMET as a QE tool (subject to limitation below)?
3. Good agreement between the ATA-Framework score and auto scores within a middle range, but the relationship becomes non-monotonic beyond the middle range
   - ➢ Auto scores do not work well beyond a middle range

Limitations

- Small sample size
- Exploratory study
- Only one evaluation criterion: quality score under the ATA grading framework
  - Time, productivity, or cost not measured

Acknowledgment

- Ji Chen, Achim Ruopp, Rony Gao, Jessie Lu & Tianlu Redmon
- Translators and graders who generously donated their time and expertise

Lingua: Addressing Scenarios for Live Interpretation and Automatic Dubbing

Nathan J. Anderson njanders@cs.cmu.edu
Language Technologies Institute, Carnegie Mellon University

Caleb Wilson caleb.wilson@byu.net
Shift Technology

Stephen D. Richardson srichardson@cs.byu.edu
Department of Computer Science, Brigham Young University

Abstract

Lingua is an application that can perform near-real-time interpretation of video recordings and live speeches as well as synchronized automatic video dubbing. It has been developed and is being piloted at the Church of Jesus Christ of Latter-day Saints. The system pipeline includes customized automatic speech recognition (ASR) and machine translation (MT) components. A script may be uploaded in advance to improve the translation accuracy and decrease the lag behind the speaker, while flexibly handling instances when the speaker goes off script. The speed of the text-to-speech (TTS) outputs are dynamically adjusted to match the rate of speech. Lingua is currently capable of interpreting English to 38 other languages.

1 Introduction

Lingua is an automatic speech-to-speech (STS) interpreter and video dubber that is being developed and piloted at the Church of Jesus Christ of Latter-day Saints. This application is suitable for interpreting live speeches and video recordings on-the-fly from English to 38 other languages. It can also assist in creating exactly synchronized audio tracks for the professional dubbing of video recordings.

A common pitfall of STS systems built on a cascaded architecture is the propagation of errors from one component of the pipeline to the later components (Sperber et al., 2019). For instance, if the ASR module registers "ice cream" as "I scream", the MT module is typically incapable of rectifying the mistake, and it will indiscriminately translate the incorrect transcription. Lingua affords the possibility of course corrections by allowing the user to upload a script of the speech in advance. It then uses a dynamic programming algorithm to align the ASR transcription with the official script on the phonemic level and override the ASR when a likely match is found. Not only does this feature improve the accuracy of downstream outputs, it can also reduce the *décalage* or lag between the original speaker and the live interpretation (Riccardi, 2005). Rather than waiting for the speaker to finish their sentence, Lingua can detect which sentence is being uttered early on and get a head start on producing the appropriate outputs.

Lingua is intended to facilitate the distribution of multimedia content into languages for which it would otherwise be cost-inefficient to provide manual interpretation and dubbing. It is of special interest for improving the accessibility of live events and undubbed video recordings for speakers of underserved languages when interpreters are not readily available. It can also accelerate the process of dubbing previously recorded content, including not only speeches but also short films and other multimedia presentations.

2 Related Work

There has been significant research over the past few years in the field of automatic speech-to-speech translation and more specifically in its application to automatic video dubbing (AVD). For example, improvements detailed by Amazon researchers include the use of human-like, customizable neural voices, integration with Neural MT, adjustments to the duration and prosody of translated utterances, and the handling of background noise and reverberation (Federico et al., 2020; Lakew et al., 2021).

Several companies are now joining the fray with their own research and product development. AppTek recently announced plans to release an AVD tool that includes speaker diarization, limited prosody transfer, and basic utterance length control, with planned improvements in transfer of emotion, utterance length adjustment, and simulated lip movement (Di Gangi et al., 2022). Other companies are already providing self-serve dubbing services on the internet. For example, both Maestra Video Dubber (Maestra, 2021) and Aloud (Google, 2022) provide capabilities for users to upload video files and corresponding text files. If the latter are not uploaded, the systems can transcribe the videos to produce text. Users can then edit the transcriptions and their corresponding, MT-produced translations, selecting from available synthetic voices, and making needed modifications to ensure acceptable video dubbing quality.

3 Speech-to-Speech Pipeline

Lingua is similar to these systems in that it can also perform automatic dubbing given video files and, optionally, corresponding text files in either SRT or a proprietary XML format. It currently uses Microsoft's Cognitive Services APIs in a traditional ASR – MT – TTS pipeline. The ASR component has been customized with 50+ hours of audio from Church speeches and their aligned human transcriptions, resulting in a reduction in word error rate from 7.2% to 3.3%. The MT systems have also been customized using hundreds of thousands to millions of sentence pairs from the Church's extensive translation memories, resulting in an increase of BLEU scores over generic MT baselines between 6 and 22 points, with an average increase of 13 points. The TTS component has not been customized, but the switch to neural voices for all languages in early 2021 was a significant, albeit subjectively evaluated, improvement.

3.1 Real-Time Interpretation

Lingua's unique contribution is that it can operate in near-real-time with a slight delay of a few seconds on average to perform ASR, MT, and TTS of live speeches and videos, while also providing additional processing to produce synchronized automatic video dubbing. If no source-language script is provided, the spoken translations are exactly as recognized by ASR and translated by MT. However, if a script is provided, Lingua uses a fuzzy matching algorithm to align the recognized ASR segments with the corresponding script segments and then passes the latter to the MT component for translation and subsequent TTS. If a human translation is also provided, it passes that translation directly to TTS.

An important feature of Lingua is that it can switch between these three modes dynamically, as illustrated in Figure 1. Thus, if a script is provided but the speaker makes off-script comments, the unmatched ASR segments are translated by MT and the spoken translations are generated. As soon as the speaker comes back on script, matching continues, and the script's sentences are passed to MT. This results in more accurate MT output based on the well-formed sentences in the script while providing reasonable translations of interjected comments. If human translations are provided for some languages and not for others, the result is high-quality

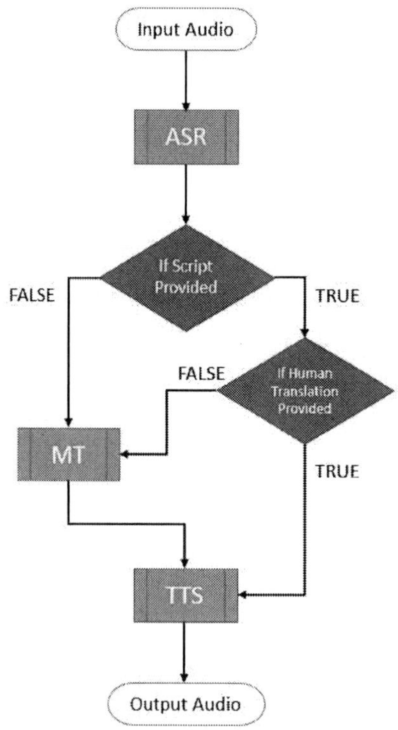

Figure 1: Flowchart of Lingua's modes

human translations for the former languages and good quality machine translations for the latter ones.

3.2 Automatic Dubbing

As Lingua processes incoming audio, translating it directly, using a monolingual script, or using a multilingual script with aligned translations, it records the times at which utterances started as supplied by the ASR. These timestamps can be exported into an SRT file along with the source language transcriptions of the speech. When generating a synchronized dub, the speech timestamps and machine or human translations are passed to an audio export thread, which generates an audio file containing spoken translations occurring exactly in sync with the corresponding spoken English. For each timestamped utterance, the audio file is filled (with silence) up to the time at which it was uttered, then Lingua uses TTS to obtain audio in the target language to write to the audio file. If the target audio speech is too long to fit in the same time as the source utterance, its speed is increased before it is written to the file. While generating this audio file, the translated speech and its timestamps are exported as another SRT file, which may also be used to add subtitles to the dubbed video. The audio file can then be mixed with the original video to provide fully synchronized dubbing.

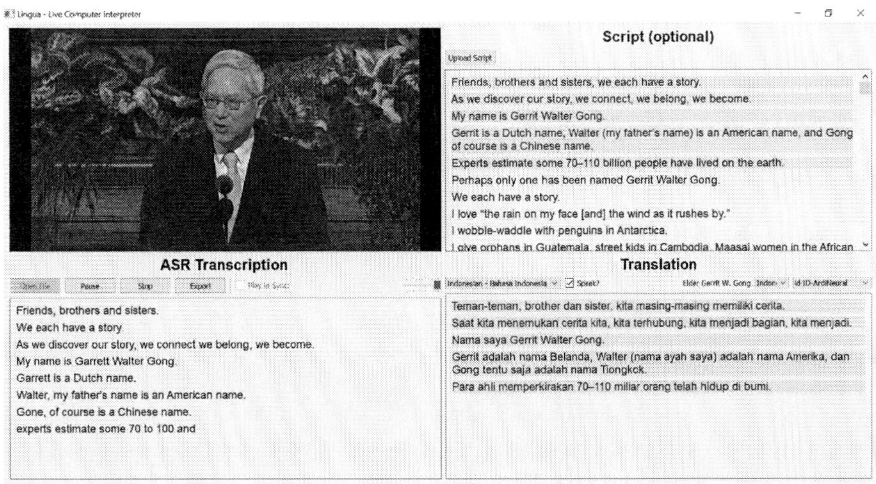

Figure 2: Screenshot of the Lingua interface in action. As the ASR transcription updates in the bottom left quadrant, Lingua uses the fuzzy matcher to align it with the script in the top right quadrant. The translations are displayed in the bottom right.

4 Fuzzy Matching Classifier

4.1 Algorithm

The fuzzy-matching algorithm continuously compares the incoming ASR partial transcriptions with a window of the next n utterances in the speech. It converts both the transcriptions and the official script to phonemic representations and uses a dynamic programming algorithm to compute the Levenshtein edit distance between the current utterance and each of the candidate sentences. To avoid penalizing longer sentences, the initial pass truncates the candidate transcriptions to the same length as the partial transcription. This truncation does not necessarily occur in the optimal location, as the ASR transcription may contain more or fewer phonemes than the correct match. Therefore, whenever the algorithm determines that the final phoneme in the alignment is an insertion or a deletion, it iteratively shifts the truncation location until the final phoneme is a match or a substitution. See Figure 3 for a simplified demonstration of this alignment algorithm.

Each alignment with a candidate sentence is rated according to a cost formula:

$$cost = Lev/Phon \tag{1}$$

where Lev is the Levenshtein distance and $Phon$ is the number of phonemes in the ASR transcription. A predefined threshold determines the maximum cost that qualifies as a match.

4.2 Evaluation

We developed a test set to evaluate the performance of the fuzzy matching classifier. This set contains 62 minutes of speech that has been hand-annotated with time stamps and gold-standard labels. It includes 6 different speakers, representing multiple age ranges, genders, and nationalities. These speakers rarely went off script, so we artificially increased the difficulty of the test set by randomly deleting, adding, and shuffling approximately 10% of the lines in the scripts.

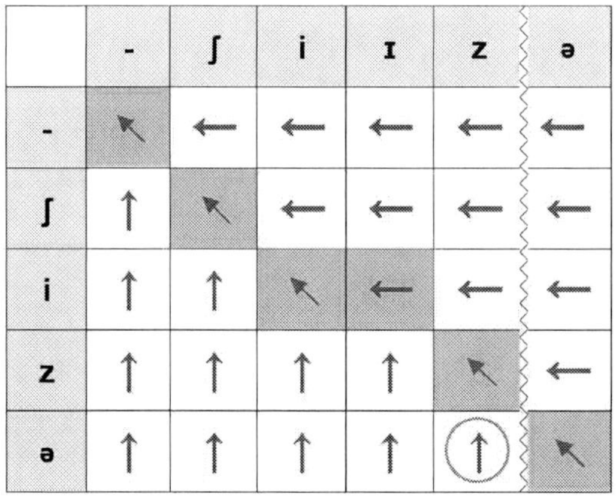

Figure 3: Toy example of fuzzy matching dynamic algorithm. The partial ASR transcription ("She's a...") is displayed on the first column, and the candidate sentence from the script ("She is a good person.") is on the top row. The candidate sentence was originally truncated to 4 phonemes to match the ASR transcription, along the jagged line. However, the final backtrace (circled) was not a match/substitution, so the window was expanded an additional column. As the new column ends in a match, this matrix is considered the optimal alignment for these sentences.

The relevant performance metrics are:

1. F1 Score: Harmonic mean of precision and recall. To calculate these measures, we defined "true positives" as utterances that are correctly matched to the script, "false positives" as utterances that were assigned to an incorrect sentence in the script, and "false negatives" as utterances that were incorrectly not matched to any sentence in the script.

2. Average Lag: The time (in seconds) that it takes to identify the correct sentence from the script. We count the time from the start of the utterance to the moment the decisive phoneme is uttered, disregarding the time subsequently spent computing the answers, because calculation speeds are largely dependent on the hardware.

See Table 1 for the baseline metrics.

Metric	Score
Precision	0.9529
Recall	0.9701
F1	0.9614
Avg. Lag	0.72 s

Table 1: Fuzzy matching classifier baseline performance metrics

4.3 Hyperparameters

The fuzzy matching classifier relies on three hyperparameters: 1) **Beamwidth**: the number of candidate sentences considered at a time, 2) **Phoneme threshold**: the minimum number of

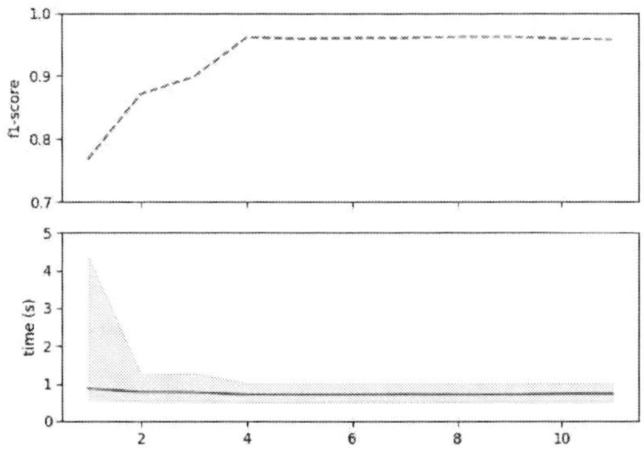

Figure 4: Beamwidth

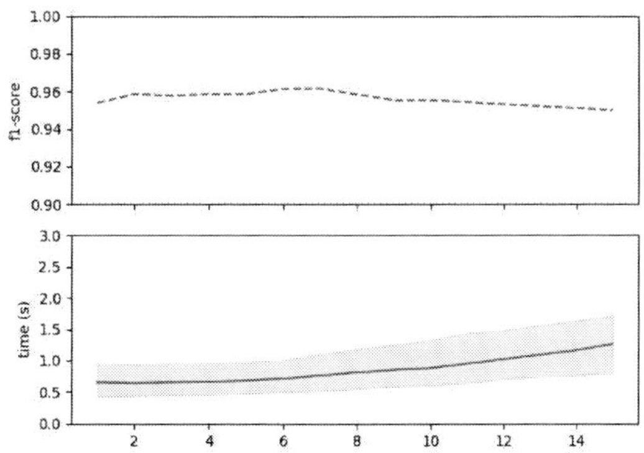

Figure 5: Minimum phoneme count threshold

phonemes required to make a decision, and 3) **Cost threshold**: the maximum allowable cost for a match.

We tuned these parameters to maximize the F1 score and minimize the décalage. Figures 4 - 6 show the effect of manipulating each parameter while holding the others constant. Within each figure, the x-axis represents values for the relevant parameter. The top plot tracks the F1 score, and the bottom plot displays the average lag time and shades the interquartile range.

Increasing the beamwidth increases the time and space requirements to complete the computation. It could theoretically increase the likelihood of false positive matches from later in the speech, although this error did not occur frequently in our tests. On the other hand, it is also possible for the window to be too small so that if the speaker skips a portion of the planned speech, the fuzzy matcher won't be able to identify the current location and it will have to default to MT.

As expected, increasing the phoneme threshold results in a greater lag behind the speaker. We had hypothesized that it would also improve the overall accuracy, as the model would gather

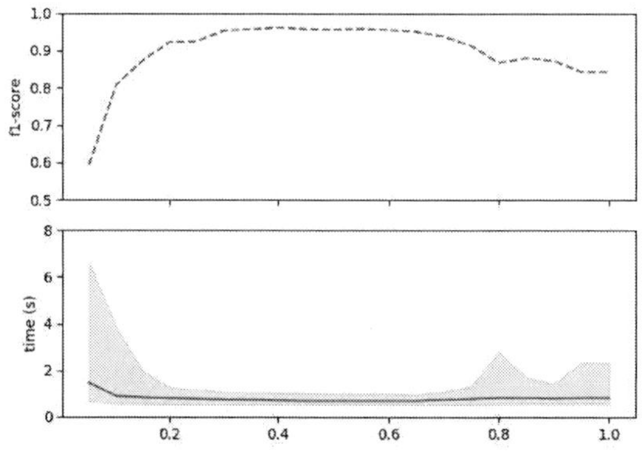

Figure 6: Maximum cost threshold

additional information before making an informed conclusion. However, our empirical tests revealed that this is only true to a certain point, after which the F1 score gradually decreases. Apparently, the model sometimes loses confidence in a correct decision as errors crop up in additional ASR partial transcriptions.

Extreme cost threshold values result in lower performance for opposite reasons. High values are cause the model to become too stringent, rejecting true matches due to noisy transcriptions or slight changes in the speaker's wording. Low values are too accepting, so the model requires very little evidence before making a decision.

The hyperparameters we selected based on these results are shown in Table 2.

Param	Value
Beamwidth	4
Phoneme Thresh	6
Cost Thresh	0.4

Table 2: Selected hyperparameters

5 Future Work

The dynamic speed adjustment for the TTS sometimes results in dubbing that is unnaturally fast. Additional hyperparameter tuning may help to distribute the dubbing more evenly. However, this strategy is unlikely to resolve the problem entirely, as translations are generally longer than the source (Frankenberg-Garcia, 2009). Manual dubbings often intentionally abbreviate the translations to improve the alignment with the original. Methods similar to those described in Federico et al. (2020) and Lakew et al. (2021) may be implemented to optimize the MT to generate outputs that are roughly equivalent in length to the input.

To prepare Lingua for deployment in real-world settings, we will need to run additional user studies. These experiments will be essential to assess the subjective acceptability of the outputs across all of the target languages.

6 Conclusion

In this paper, we described Lingua, an application that is capable of interpreting live speeches and creating synchronized dubbings for videos. It mitigates the shortcomings of cascaded STS systems by following an optional uploaded script, although it can revert to the default cascade if the speaker goes off script. We assessed the performance of the fuzzy matching classifier, and we found that it achieves F1 scores > 0.95 on a difficult test set. We discussed the primary hyperparameters and demonstrated how they affect the performance of the fuzzy matching algorithm. Finally, we proposed future avenues of research to improve the TTS component and prepare Lingua for deployment.

We anticipate that Lingua will increase accessibility to church multimedia content for underserved linguistic communities. It will decrease the time, cost, and expertise required to perform live interpretation and produce professional dubbings.

References

Di Gangi, M., Rossenbach, N., Pérez, A., Bahar, P., Beck, E., Wilken, P., and Matusov, E. (2022). Automatic video dubbing at AppTek. In *Proceedings of the 23rd Annual Conference of the European Association for Machine Translation*, pages 349–350.

Federico, M., Enyedi, R., Barra-Chicote, R., Giri, R., Isik, U., Krishnaswamy, A., and Sawaf, H. (2020). From speech-to-speech translation to automatic dubbing. In *Proceedings of the 17th International Conference on Spoken Language Translation*, pages 257–264.

Frankenberg-Garcia, A. (2009). Are translations longer than source texts. *A corpus-based study of explicitation In: Beeby, A., Rodríguez P., & Sánchez-Gijón, P.(eds.) Corpus use and learning to translate (CULT): An Introduction. Amsterdam & Philadelphia: John Benjamins*, pages 47–58.

Google (2022). Aloud. `https://aloud.area120.google.com/`, Accessed 07/25/2022.

Lakew, S. M., Federico, M., Wang, Y., Hoang, C., Virkar, Y., Barra-Chicote, R., and Enyedi, R. (2021). Machine translation verbosity control for automatic dubbing. In *ICASSP 2021-2021 IEEE International Conference on Acoustics, Speech and Signal Processing (ICASSP)*, pages 7538–7542. IEEE.

Maestra (2021). Maestra Video Dubber. `https://maestrasuite.com/video-dubber`, Accessed 07/25/2022.

Riccardi, A. (2005). On the evolution of interpreting strategies in simultaneous interpreting. *Meta: Journal des traducteurs/Meta: Translators' Journal*, 50(2):753–767.

Sperber, M., Neubig, G., Niehues, J., and Waibel, A. (2019). Attention-passing models for robust and data-efficient end-to-end speech translation. *Transactions of the Association for Computational Linguistics*, 7:313–325.

All You Need is Source!
A Study on Source-based Quality Estimation for Neural Machine Translation

Jon Cambra Guinea
Welocalize Inc
Frederick, MD, United States
jon.cambra@welocalize.com

Mara Nunziatini
Welocalize Inc
Frederick, MD, United States
mara.nunziatini@welocalize.com

Abstract

Segment-level Quality Estimation (QE) is an increasingly sought-after task in the Machine Translation (MT) industry. In recent years, it has experienced an impressive evolution not only thanks to the implementation of supervised models using source and hypothesis information, but also through the usage of MT probabilities. This work presents a different approach to QE where only the source segment and the Neural MT (NMT) training data is needed, making possible an approximation to translation quality before inference. Our work is based on the idea that NMT quality at a segment level depends on the similarity degree between the source segment to be translated and the engine's training data. The features proposed measuring this aspect of data achieve competitive correlations with MT metrics and human judgment and prove to be advantageous for post-editing (PE) prioritization task with domain adapted engines.

1 Introduction

Quality of Neural Machine Translation (NMT) systems keeps improving and gives humans the ability to translate enormous amounts of segments in a short time. However, raw machine translation is seldom perfect. Therefore, MT in standard localization processes is most of the times followed by some level of human or automated editing aimed at fixing issues in the MT output.

In the translation industry we are witnessing a surge in demand for translation services, as well as increased requests for raw MT (without human review). Often, clients are very concerned about their translation spend, or they do not have time to translate all the content they would like to see translated, therefore more and more of them look for raw machine translation services to get savings and quicker turnaround time. However, depending on the language pairs, use cases and content types involved, raw machine translation for direct consumption (without PE) might not be a good solution.

In an ideal scenario, the quality of the output delivered by MT engines is measured before they are used in production. This exercise is aimed to understand if MT will be helpful for the linguist, or even just to understand if a MT engine training was successful or not.

Typically, the quality of MT translations is measured by comparing how different the MT output is from its reference translation. But how do we measure the quality of MT if we do not have a reference translation? It happens very frequently: imagine that you need to translate a new content type or into a new language pair for which you do not have any reference translation. This conflict led to the recent emergence of Quality Estimation (QE) techniques that try to estimate the quality of a translation when the reference information is not available. In WMT20 QE shared task, state-of-the-art (SOTA) QE models were supervised models trained exclusively on labeled data composed of source segments, the corresponding translations, and human Direct Assessment (DA) (WMT20 QE findings, 2020). The same year, an unsupervised method was proposed to estimate translations (Fomicheva et al., 2020). The paper introduced the idea of using NMT as a glass-box to estimate translation quality by using token level probabilities. From that breakthrough, WMT21 SOTA QE models combined the supervised and unsupervised approaches (WMT21 QE findings, 2021).

Despite the outstanding results of these QE models, we observed that they cannot easily be implemented in production environments for different reasons. Firstly, because a substantial amount of human-labeled data is needed to fine-tune such architectures for a specific language pair and domain. In many cases, it can be problematic to find or generate this type of data without creating some domain shift between the QE training data and the data that has to be estimated in production. This can lead to catastrophic results. Secondly, these models rely on large language models that are expensive to train, store and run. Thirdly, depending on how the adapted NMT models are put in production, they can deprive the owner of NMT probabilities used as features which can also be computationally expensive to extract.

This work tries to elude these challenges by proposing a more "data-centric" direction to estimate NMT quality. Indeed, the importance of data in NMT has been extensively studied in different fields such as domain shift (Wang and Sennrich, 2020), catastrophical forgetting (Goodfellow et al., 2015; Gu and Feng, 2020) and domain robustness (Müller et al., 2020). Hence, it is well known that adapted models will have higher performance on segments from the same domain, or similar to the ones contained in the training data in some aspect. In this perspective, we think that there could be a way to estimate the NMT performance on a segment by checking the source segment and comparing it to the source segments contained in the training data. This work presents two simple techniques to perform this task: a) by measuring the similarity between the segment to be translated and the source segments found in the training data and b) by counting the number of words in the source segment that do not appear in the engine training data (unknown words for the engine).

We evaluate our approach in two steps. Firstly, we create generic engines in three language pairs, and then we adapt each one of them with client-specific data. With these six engines, we translate a set of segments for which the reference is known, score at a segment level those translations using BLEU, chrF3 and COMET, and compute our new source-similarity features. After that, we study and discuss the correlation between these new features and the segment-level MT metrics and human evaluations. Secondly, we focus on the in-domain scenarios to evaluate the impact of using this simple approach as QE metrics to prioritize the segments to be post-edited.

Our main contributions at the end of this study are: (a) a simple, unsupervised and effective approach to estimate the MT quality without checking the reference translation or before producing the translation; (b) an evaluation of how these features correlate with several MT scores and human judgement, both in generic and adapted NMT systems, similarly to previous QE methods; (c) an evaluation of how these features can be used as competitive indicators to prioritize segments to be post-edited. While the study focuses on an unsupervised segment level usage, it opens the door to explain quality changes at a project level and can inspire future architectures for QE models where the source side similarity information could be included.

2 Related work

QE QE aims to address the problem of evaluating the translation quality of a NMT model when a reference is not available. In recent years, the explosion of multilingual language models like M-BERT (Devlin et al., 2018) or XLM Roberta (Conneau et al., 2019), giving the ability to represent into a single space text from different languages, gave birth to new QE models reaching SOTA results in WMT competitions. In WMT19, a model was presented using cross-lingual sentence embedding information from both source and hypothesis (Zhang and van Genabith, 2019) to learn how to score a translation without a reference. In WMT20, quality estimators like Transquest (Ranasinghe et al., 2020) and COMET as QE (Rei et al., 2020), based on an architecture composed of a multilingual model encoding the source and the hypothesis trained on human-labeled data, outperformed older techniques. In parallel, an unsupervised technique was proposed for QE (Fomicheva et al., 2020). The paper proposed the usage of NMT as a glass-box, which means using the internal states and token level probabilities to reflect the uncertainty of the NMT at inference. This uncertainty revealed consistent correlations with human Direct Assessment (DA).

Therefore, these features are good indicators for QE. A year later, the WMT21 shared task on QE made available data composed of source, translation, and human DA, as well as the resulting glass-box features produced by the NMT model for each translation. As a consequence, the best performing models combined the WMT20 winning architectures with the uncertainty features extracted from the token-level probabilities such as QEMind's (Wang et al., 2021) and Unbabel models (Zerva et al., 2021).

Domain shift in NMT The MT field went from Statistical MT (SMT) to the current NMT models leading to state-of-the-art results in most cases (Stahlberg, 2020). The best performing MT models rely on neural architectures that are trained in two steps. Firstly, the model is trained on large amounts of generic parallel data to get a generic understanding about how to go from the source language to the target language. Secondly, this generic model is fine-tuned with bilingual data from the expected domain before it is used in production. This is what we call domain adaptation.

During this process, due to its neural architecture, NMT suffers from catastrophic forgetting (Goodfellow et al., 2015; Gu and Feng, 2020) which is the process of progressively "forgetting" previous data while strongly fitting to the new in-domain data. The performance on out-of-domain data decreases, while it improves on in-domain data. Therefore, when translating with an adapted model a text different to the in-domain data, the model could fail or produce hallucinations (Müller et al., 2020; Wang and Sennrich, 2020).

3 Source QE for NMT

In this work, we try to extract information that can describe how familiar a segment is to a given engine by comparing each source segment that needs to be translated against all the source segments included in the training data. The two following subsections propose features by transforming the segments into vectors and getting some statistical measurements of the vectors' similarity. These vector similarities are computed with the cosine similarity defined as follows for vectors A and B:

$$\mathrm{sim}(\mathrm{A},\mathrm{B}) = \frac{A.B}{\|A\|\,\|B\|}$$

With this score we can capture how similar the vectors are. In absolute terms, the values returned are contained in [0,1]: values approaching 1 represent high similarity, while values closer to 0 represent low similarity. For explanatory purposes, we denote S_{train} the set of n_{train} source segments composing the training data and S_{test} the set of n_{test} source segments to translate.

3.1 Bag of words similarity

We create a bag of words (BOW) model for each language pair to transform all segments in $\mathrm{S_{train}}$ and $\mathrm{S_{test}}$ into vectors. These vectors are a simplified representation of segments where the features are a bag of words appearing in the document. Hence, the vectors describe how many times a word appears in the encoded segment. For a segment $\mathrm{s_{train}}$ in $\mathrm{S_{train}}$ and a segment $\mathrm{s_{test}}$ in $\mathrm{S_{test}}$, we denote the corresponding vector representations as $\mathrm{s\vec{train}_{bow}}$ and $\mathrm{s\vec{test}_{bow}}$. With this information, we compute for every segment in $\mathrm{S_{test}}$ the following features.

Average BOW similarity This is the arithmetic mean of the cosine similarity between the segment to be translated and all the source segments contained in the training data.

$$\mathrm{avg_{bow}(s_{test})} = \frac{1}{n_{\mathrm{train}}} \sum_{s \in S_{\mathrm{train}}} \mathrm{sim}(\mathrm{s\vec{test}_{bow}}, \mathrm{s\vec{_{bow}}})$$

With this feature, we try to determine globally how similar the segment is to the full training set. However, this might not be as relevant as we think. Let's picture a scenario where all the segments in $\mathrm{S_{train}}$ are completely different from the segment to translate except one. If the exception segment is almost identical, we expect that the model probably retained that information and will produce a decent translation by reproducing some similar example.

Maximum BOW similarity Given the previous argument, we hypothesize that we do not need the distance of all the segments since at inference time the NMT model will appeal to the most similar instances of the segment to translate. As a consequence, we will capture the information related to the most similar segment in $\mathrm{S_{train}}$ by capturing the similarity to it. The feature is defined as follows:

$$\mathrm{max_{bow}(s_{test})} = \max_{s \in S_{\mathrm{train}}} \mathrm{sim}(\mathrm{s\vec{test}_{bow}}, \mathrm{s\vec{_{bow}}})$$

A limitation of this first group of features is the fact that they rely on a rudimentary transformation as it is BOW modelling. In fact, by definition, this representation can capture quite well the string or word similarity between two segments. However, this does not constitute an accurate semantic representation.

3.2 Semantic similarity

To describe the semantic relationship between our segments we make use of SOTA models in the semantic textual similarity field, such as sentence transformer models (Reimers, Gurevych, 2019; Reimers, Gurevych, 2020). Thanks to those architectures we transform all segments in $\mathrm{S_{train}}$ and $\mathrm{S_{test}}$ into sentence embeddings with the 'all-mpnet-base-v2' model which is the mpnet-base model (Song et al., 2020) fine-tuned on a SNLI dataset with more than 1 Billion segment pairs. As a result, the vector representations produced by the model seem to capture the semantic information of the text into a unique space where the distance between two pieces of text is correlated to the semantic similarity. Hence, similar texts are closely represented while different texts have distant representations. As before, we denote $\vec{\mathrm{s_{train}}}_{\mathrm{sem}}$ and $\vec{\mathrm{s_{test}}}_{\mathrm{sem}}$ the semantic embedding representation of a segment in $\mathrm{S_{train}}$ and $\mathrm{S_{test}}$, and compute the same features as we did with BOW representations:

Average semantic similarity The arithmetic mean of the cosine similarity between $\mathrm{s_{test}}$ and every segment in $\mathrm{S_{train}}$

$$\mathrm{avg_{sem}}(\mathrm{s_{test}}) = \frac{1}{n_{\mathrm{train}}} \sum_{s \in S_{\mathrm{train}}} \mathrm{sim}(\vec{\mathrm{s_{test}}}_{\mathrm{sem}}, \vec{\mathrm{s_{sem}}})$$

Maximum semantic similarity The maximum cosine similarity of $\mathrm{s_{test}}$ over all segments in $\mathrm{S_{train}}$

$$\mathrm{max_{sem}}(\mathrm{s_{test}}) = \max_{s \in S_{\mathrm{train}}} \mathrm{sim}(\vec{\mathrm{s_{test}}}_{\mathrm{sem}}, \vec{\mathrm{s_{sem}}})$$

3.3 Unknown words

A problem exists with the previous similarity approaches. A segment to be translated can be highly similar to a segment in the training set but with a crucial difference. We illustrate the statement in Table 1. This example presents a segment to be translated which is highly similar to a segment used for engine adaptation. The cosine similarity is 0.95, which is only 0.05 below the score for identical segments (1.00). Both segments share the same structure and same words except for the city name. The city name is responsible for that small difference with a score representing identical segments.

source	The best museums are in **London**.
hyp	Los mejores museos están en London.
ref	Los mejores museos están en Londres.
source	The best museums are in Madrid.
ref	Los mejores museos están en Madrid.

Table 1: Example on NMT errors due to unknown words. The first example describes the translation produced by a NMT system. We highlight **in bold the unseen word** in training and in red the translation error. The second example corresponds to the most similar segment found in training with a cosine similarity of 0.95

This light difference can be a problem for the NMT model. If the word "London" is not contained in the source side of the training data, the engine will not know how to translate it into Spanish as "Londres" and will certainly produce the untranslated term since it saw that "Madrid" remained untranslated.

Therefore, we create an unk variable to capture the information. For each segment in $\mathrm{S_{test}}$, the unk feature counts the number of unknown words in the segment but not in $\mathrm{S_{train}}$. To do that, we produce from $\mathrm{S_{train}}$ the set of words occurring in the dataset which we call $\mathrm{D_{S_{train}}}$ and $\mathrm{w_{s_{test}}}$ the set of words in a segment $\mathrm{s_{test}}$. The formula below defines how the score is computed.

$$\mathrm{unk}(\mathrm{s_{test}}) = \mathrm{n}(\mathrm{w_{s_{test}}}) - \mathrm{n}(\mathrm{w_{s_{test}}} \cap \mathrm{D_{S_{train}}})$$

where n is the operator to count the number of elements, or words in this case, contained in a particular set.

4 Datasets setup

NMT data We call generic data the parallel bilingual pairs used to train the generic engines. All data was extracted from OPUS (Tiedemann, 2012) and contains different domains such as medical, political, scientific or religious among many others. The language pairs involved, and the amount of segment pairs used to train our NMT systems are described in Table 2. The test data used for experiments in Section 5 is obtained from newstest2019 for En-De and News Commentary for En-It. The En-Ko test set was made of segments from multiple domains found in OPUS (Tiedemann, 2012). In-domain data is composed of data provided by an IT security company. More specifically, the content types included in the data are User Interface (UI) and User Assistance (UA). The amount of training data used for

	Generic	In-domain
En-De	11,568,049	181,061
En-It	32,187,643	89,835
En-Ko	17,299,009	173,662

Table 2: Summary table counting the amount of segment pairs used to train NMT systems

the adapted NMT systems can be seen in Table 2. The test data is obtained from documents that were translated and reviewed in the past by human translators, which are not contained in the training data.

NMT systems We built MT engines for three language pairs (En-De, En-It and En-Ko) with OpenNMT-tf toolkit (Klein et al., 2020) by training the Transformer architecture (Vaswani et al., 2017) with the generic data described above. Additionally, we adapted those engines with the in-domain data by fine-tuning the final generic model exclusively with in-domain data (Chu et al., 2018).

MT scores In the presence of reference translations or post-edited segments, we automatically score the translations with three different segment-level metrics to have a first view of how our approach correlates with the most commonly-referenced MT metrics in the industry. At a token level, we compute the BLEU score (Papineni et al., 2002) which is extensively used across the industry despite its weakness. At a character level, we use the chrF3 score, which showed high correlations in WMT14 evaluation task (Popovic, 2015). Finally, we also rely on the SOTA metric COMET (Rei et al., 2020) with its last version 'wmt21-comet-mqm'. This metric has been described as the automatic metric which shows the highest correlation with human DA in recent years (Kocmi et al., 2021; Nunziatini, Alfieri, 2021).

Direct Assessment As for Direct Assessment, due to budget constraints, we decided to narrow the experiment to two language pairs which are particularly relevant for us for business reasons: English into Italian and English into German. Three linguists for each language pair performed Direct Assessment on 1,000 machine translated segments. We decided to involve three linguists per language because we believe it is a good compromise between budget restrictions and relevance of the exercise from a statistical point of view. The source segments were randomly selected from projects which were previously translated and reviewed. All segments in this dataset were never seen during training by the domain adapted engines. However, the content type of this dataset is very similar to the domain adapted engine training material content type.

Linguists were provided with detailed evaluation criteria and asked to score Adequacy and Fluency for each segment. For both Adequacy and Fluency, they were asked to provide a score from 1 (lowest) to 5 (highest). In order to get robust scores, fluency and adequacy scores from each annotator were standardized by transforming them into z-scores and averaged across the three linguists.

The linguists involved in this experiment were very familiar with the content type evaluated, as they are the preferred translators for this content type and client. Therefore, close attention was paid to client and domain-specific terminology and segments with little or no context were evaluated considering the context in which those segments would normally appear. Each one of them was allowed plenty of time to complete the exercise, since we understand that scoring the Adequacy and Fluency of 1,000 segments can be tiring and confusing in the long run. In order to make sure that the linguists understood the task correctly, we asked them to start with a small sample and deliver the evaluation, then wait for feedback before proceeding with the biggest sample.

5 First experiment and results

In the following experiment, we describe correlations between the proposed features and the previous MT metrics for generic and domain-adapted systems trained as explained in Section 4. Additionally, we compute the correlations with DA for the in-domain translations with data described in the same Section. Note that, to compute the indicators for the adapted engine, only the in-domain training data is considered to compare the source segments.

5.1 Settings

Benchmarks We use baseline features extracted from previous works in the field to compare the performance of our approach to QE indicators which do not need any training. On the one hand, we make use of **Comet as QE** (Rei et al., 2020), representing a supervised model trained on data from previous WMT competitions. On the other hand, we compute the **sequence-level translation probability normalized by length** (Fomicheva et al., 2020) defined as **TP**, representing the simplest feature to extract from the NMT model at inference.

5.2 Results

Correlations with MT metrics Table 3 describes Pearson correlation between the proposed MT metrics and the source QE features for generic engine translations. On the one hand, if we compare against the baseline features (TP and $\mathrm{COMET_{QE}}$), we observe competitive performance in punctual correlations. Indeed, $\mathrm{max_{sem}}$ provides the best information to estimate COMET above all our proposed approaches for En-It and En-De. For its part, $\mathrm{max_{bow}}$ correlates with BLEU in En-It but also with COMET in En-De. Additionally, unk can provide information for COMET only in En-De since for the other languages it rarely found segments with unknown word(s). Within this experiment with generic engines, we observe the absence of correlations for $\mathrm{avg_{bow}}$, $\mathrm{avg_{sem}}$ and unk when string MT metrics (chrF3, BLEU) are involved. In other words, this table shows that our features strongly correlate with semantic similarity, but not with string similarity between hypothesis and reference. This observation highlights a well-known problem for metrics like BLEU or chrF3: they fail to correctly evaluate the quality of flawless translations which use different terminology or style compared to the reference. It is particularly true in this scenario: because the engine and the test set are generic, we notice that the reference strays away from the source, whereas the model produces more literal translations.

This problem is overcome in the in-domain experiments presented in Table 4. Indeed, correlations are present to some degree for both string and semantic MT metrics since domain-adapted engines reproduce the style and terminology seen in the training material. Besides, for obvious reasons, the content type itself is not characterized by stylistic flourishes or use of synonyms. In this analysis, $\mathrm{max_{sem}}$ provides consistent correlations with all the MT metrics for all the language pairs. This indicator computes leading results for string metrics in En-It and En-De, while $\mathrm{max_{bow}}$ is uncorrelated. Nevertheless, for En-Ko, $\mathrm{max_{bow}}$ also competes with $\mathrm{max_{sem}}$. It is also the case for unk, which shows moderate correlations with almost all the metrics for En-It and En-De.

Average features Contrary to our intuition, we notice that $\mathrm{avg_{bow}}$ and $\mathrm{avg_{sem}}$ compute low negative correlations with some MT metrics. This means that high-quality translations correspond to source segments with low average similarity to the training set. The assumption is difficult to believe, because it would mean that completely out-of-domain segments are most likely to get high-quality translations than in-domain segments. As a consequence, we decide to drop these features from Table 4.

Correlations with Direct Assessment In Table 4, we also analyze the correlations with Fluency (Fcy) and Adequacy (Adcy) for En-It and En-De. For the first language pair, TP seems to contain the best information to estimate both Adcy and Fcy with medium-high Pearson correlations. This indicator is followed closely by $\mathrm{COMET_{QE}}$ and our approaches $\mathrm{max_{sem}}$ and unk, which provide medium-low correlations with these human-labeled metrics. The unk feature outperforms all our proposed approaches for Fcy, while for Adcy $\mathrm{max_{sem}}$ leads the board. Similarly, for En-De, TP continues to obtain the highest correlations with DA metrics. The second place is shared by $\mathrm{COMET_{QE}}$ and $\mathrm{max_{sem}}$, with similar results for both indicators. Furthermore, $\mathrm{max_{bow}}$ can be ranked after them with low correlations, and unk is only informative for Fcy estimation. Finally, for both language pairs the difference to TP for Fcy is moderate, but we see a larger difference to Adcy, meaning that our approaches are more competitive when measuring Fcy.

We have seen how $\mathrm{max_{sem}}$ contains competitive information to estimate segment-level quality, even if it does not outperform TP globally in terms of Pearson correlation. However, we observe that our semantic similarity approach has an advantage over features using NMT probabilities in short segments. This type of segments often lack context: this causes uncertainty in NMT as it tends to return low probabilities independently of the accuracy of the translation, while $\mathrm{max_{sem}}$ is able to indicate better quality if it detects that this segment can be somehow similar to some training instance.

As a final observation, we are aware that the probabilities returned by NMT systems depend on the training and inference data. We could think that our $\mathrm{max_{sem}}$ and $\mathrm{max_{bow}}$ indicators are

	En-It			En-De			En-Ko		
	BLEU	chrF3	COMET	BLEU	chrF3	COMET	BLEU	chrF3	COMET
TP	**0.191**	**0.376**	0.389	**0.200**	**0.297**	0.423	**0.492**	**0.662**	0.440
COMET$_{QE}$	0.191	0.166	**0.821***	0.053	0.048	**0.824***	0.048	0.004	**0.622***
avg$_{bow}$	-0.077	0.094	-0.099	-0.029	-0.063	-0.002	-0.021	-0.067	0.037
max$_{bow}$	**0.123**	0.093	0.042	0.006	0.020	0.168	0.030	0.041	0.015
avg$_{sem}$	0.048	**-0.133**	-0.152	-0.129	**-0.124**	0.148	0.053	0.043	**-0.198**
max$_{sem}$	0.027	-0.063	**0.196**	**0.132**	0.032	**0.324**	-0.009	-0.050	0.021
unk	-0.015	-0.044	0.099	-0.010	-0.001	-0.131	-	-	-

Table 3: Pearson correlation table between features and different automatic MT metrics for generic NMT settings. Highest and relevant correlations from all the proposed approaches are in bold; find also in bold the best result between the two baselines. *The correlation is high because COMET and COMET$_{QE}$ were trained on similar data

	En-It					En-De					En-Ko		
	BLEU	chrF3	COMET	Fcy	Adcy	BLEU	chrF3	COMET	Fcy	Adcy	BLEU	chrF3	COMET
TP	**0.230**	**0.379**	0.349	**0.374**	**0.456**	**0.131**	**0.336**	0.339	**0.217**	**0.343**	**0.344**	**0.531**	0.379
COMET$_{QE}$	0.199	0.119	**0.646***	0.326	0.312	0.102	0.192	**0.604***	0.193	0.177	0.011	0.026	**0.553***
max$_{bow}$	0.073	0.055	0.056	0.109	0.127	0.070	0.071	0.170	0.174	0.146	**0.282**	**0.271**	0.163
max$_{sem}$	**0.241**	**0.161**	0.269	0.246	**0.253**	**0.264**	**0.285**	**0.355**	**0.189**	**0.175**	0.237	0.224	**0.174**
unk(-)	0.138	0.078	**0.374**	**0.282**	0.237	0.139	0.160	0.333	0.156	0.072	0.057	0.065	0.046

Table 4: Pearson correlation between features and different automatic MT metrics and DA scores for domain adapted NMT settings. Highest correlations with all the proposed approaches are in bold; find also in bold the best result between the two baselines.

highly correlated with the averaged probabilities. If we check the Pearson correlation for the domain adapted examples, we observe correlations with TP around 0.3 for $\mathrm{max}_{\mathrm{sem}}$ and 0.4 for $\mathrm{max}_{\mathrm{bow}}$. Our interpretation of this observation is that the dependence exists. However, this does not imply that the information to estimate quality contained in each indicator is redundant, as it can be seen in the performance difference between $\mathrm{max}_{\mathrm{sem}}$ and $\mathrm{max}_{\mathrm{bow}}$.

6 Second experiment and results: Post-Editing segment prioritization

Given the previous results showing that $\mathrm{max}_{\mathrm{sem}}$ and unk can be considered consistent source QE indicators for domain-adapted engines, we decide to evaluate the impact in a production context where the goal is to maximize the document-level MT quality improvement by performing PE on a small subset of segments only. The following experiment uses both the indicators mentioned above to prioritize the segments to be post-edited, and compares the BLEU performance with other features.

6.1 Settings

We conduct the experiment on En-It and En-De in-domain sets where we have at our disposal, for each source segment, the corresponding hypothesis and reference as well as all the features from the previous experiment along with MT metrics and human annotations. For each QE indicator, we plot the BLEU score after simulating PE on a selected number of segments according to the corresponding indicator. The K percentage of selected segments corresponds to those with the K percent "worse" scores. As an example, if we selected 10% of all segments with $\mathrm{max}_{\mathrm{sem}}$, we would post-edit the top 10% segments with lowest similarity scores. On the other hand, if we selected 20% of the segments with unk, we would post-edit the top 20% segments with highest number of unknown words on the source side.

Tested features We test $\mathrm{max}_{\mathrm{sem}}$ and unk along with the features used as benchmark in the first experiment: (TP and $\mathrm{COMET}_{\mathrm{QE}}$). Additionally, we implement a selection method which combines our two source approaches defined as unk+$\mathrm{max}_{\mathrm{sem}}$ which first selects segments based on unk, and once all segments with at least one unknown word have been selected for PE, it uses

$\mathrm{max}_{\mathrm{sem}}$ as the indicator for selection.

Benchmarks In order to understand the performance of the different approaches, we create two benchmarks. On the one hand, a lower benchmark defined as the theoretical random selection where the segments are randomly selected for PE. The values computed for that benchmark are an average approximation of multiple random selections. On the other hand, an upper benchmark described as BLEU selection, where we know beforehand which segments have the worse translations based on BLEU scores. We then use this information to choose the subset of segments to be post-edited. Note that, although this benchmark sets a high standard for the experiment, it can be outperformed when you observe the resulting corpus level BLEU score. This benchmark does not consider segments length which are essential to compute the corpus BLEU as the weighted average of segment BLEU scores.

6.2 Results and discussion

The results from this experiment can be seen in Figure 1. Below we comment the results by focusing on the indicators proposed in this paper. The $\mathbf{unk}$ indicator brings benefit when selecting less than 30% of the segments. In other words, this indicator can help to prioritize segments to post-edit while there are segments with at least one unknown word. When all this type of segments has been post-edited, the remaining ones, with 0 unknown words, can only be selected randomly since the indicator scores them equally. Despite this weakness, we observe that, in the range of interest, the BLEU gain provided by unk surpasses any other indicator except $\mathrm{COMET}_{\mathrm{QE}}$ for En-It. We can therefore assert that unk is an important feature to select segments to post-edit in the first stages, while segments with unknown words are present.

The performance of $\mathbf{max}_{\mathbf{sem}}$ can be described in two ranges: [0%,40%] and [40%,100%]. In the first range, $\mathrm{max}_{\mathrm{sem}}$ is between the two worst indicators. In fact, in En-De it only outperforms TP, while for En-It our proposed feature provides the lowest improvement closely behind TP. Additionally, there is a common trend in this range for both language pairs where the gain provided over the baseline monotonously increases. In the second range, the BLEU gain provided by the indicator remains globally constant at the maximum value reached in the first range and has a competitive performance compared to other indicators using hypothesis information: for En-De it outperforms $\mathrm{COMET}_{\mathrm{QE}}$ and competes with TP, while for En-It it is better than $\mathrm{COMET}_{\mathrm{QE}}$, but behind TP. Finally, the heuristic indicator $\mathbf{unk{+}max}_{\mathbf{sem}}$ can be seen as the best technique to approach the upper benchmark. For En-De, the method consistently outperforms all the other indicators for every selected amount. For En-It, the BLEU gain provided by this method is only outperformed by $\mathrm{COMET}_{\mathrm{QE}}$ for the first 40% segments. Above that threshold, our combined approach outperforms any other indicator. These results are not a surprise given the previous observations made on each source QE indicator. In the first range, the poor performance of $\mathrm{max}_{\mathrm{sem}}$ is compensated with the benefits from unk. While in the second range, our approach wins thanks to the advantages given by $\mathrm{max}_{\mathrm{sem}}$, leading to high and constant BLEU gain.

7 Business Implementations

There are many scenarios in which this feature could be useful in production, for a Language Service Provider. While we briefly mentioned quite a few ideas in this paper, we would now like to focus on the implementation that we believe would bring the biggest benefit to the client. If we used $\mathrm{unk{+}max}_{\mathrm{sem}}$ to identify a fixed amount of mostly challenging segments, by looking at the source only, and decided to post-edit only this sample of potentially incorrect segments, the client could get a dramatic improvement in the quality of the content translated with a little effort. By knowing the budget of the client for translating a document, we could estimate the number of words that can be post-edited with that budget and the extent of the improvement we could get. Let's assume that the client has budget (or time) only to post-edit the 10% of the document. In a traditional scenario, the client would probably rather have raw MT on everything, prioritize post-editing only on those part of the content (if any) that get more visibility, or even worse, post-edit only some randomly selected chunks of text. Conversely, by using these indicators, we could aim at performing post-editing only on the top 10% segments that we know have a higher probability of containing issues. Similarly, if the client has no fixed budget or turnaround time, but is trying anyway to save as much money and

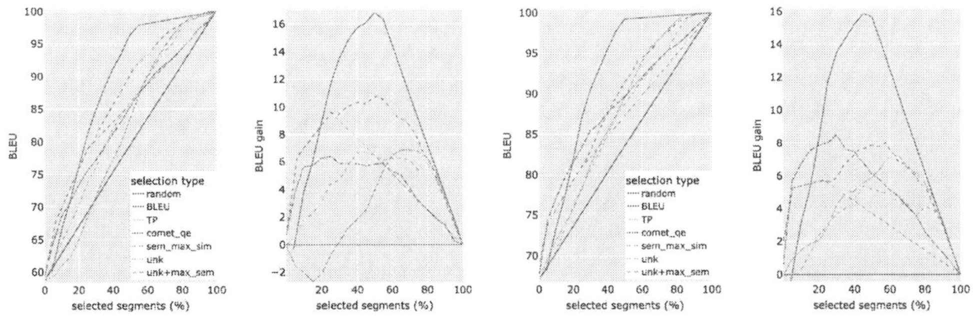

(a) En-De BLEU evolution (b) En-De BLEU gain over random selection (c) En-It BLEU evolution (d) En-It BLEU gain over random selection

Figure 1: PE selection strategy comparison showing: competitive results for unk on the first 30-40% of selected segments for PE, and $\max_{\text{sem}}$ for larger selections; superiority of unk+$\max_{\text{sem}}$ for En-De and competitive results for En-It.

time as possible, we could recommend that they do PE only on that percentage of segments which could increase BLEU. This estimation would help them publish their content more quickly, because part of it would not need any human intervention and would enable linguists to focus only on what really needs to be fixed. Also, while there might of course still be errors in the MT output that do not get reviewed, this approach gives clients with budgetary constraints a focused way to spend and some certainty that the worst segments will not reach the reader.

8 Conclusions

In this paper, we offered a new approach to unsupervised segment-level QE for NMT systems by only evaluating the source segment with the help of NMT training data. By using sentence transformers and bag of words methods, we transformed all the segments into vectors and computed the maximum semantic and string similarity. These scores, along with a feature counting the number of unknown words for the NMT system, seem to contain relevant information for estimating the translation quality at a character, token, semantic, fluency and adequacy levels before producing the translation. The results were comparable to other QE techniques using NMT hypothesis or probabilities.

Moreover, we analyzed how the different indicators can heuristically help prioritize segments for PE. On the one hand, the unknown words count is an insightful indicator to select the very first segments to prioritize by choosing segments with one or more unknown words. On the other hand, the maximum semantic similarity is advantageous when the PE task can be applied to more than 40% of the segments. As a result, the combination of both indicators to select segments for PE led to the highest BLEU gains above all the QE indicators in most data selection settings.

Our work opens the door to new perspectives in QE. Firstly, we know that the source QE features presented are just a small sample of many other indicators that could be computed to compare a source segment to the NMT training data. Nevertheless, this paper highlights the importance of looking back to the training data to evaluate how easily and accurately a segment can be translated by a NMT system. Consequently, as it happened with glass-box features in the last WMT QE task, we think that future research on QE supervised models should incorporate these features or any other information that compares the data to be translated against the engine training data.

References

Chaojun Wang and Rico Sennrich. 2020. On Exposure Bias, Hallucination and Domain Shift in Neural Machine Translation. *Proceedings of the 58th Annual Meeting of the Association for Computational Linguistics*, Online.

Chu, Chenhui and Wang, Rui. 2018. A survey of domain adaptation for neural machine translation. *arXiv preprint arXiv:1806.00258*

Conneau, Alexis and Khandelwal, Kartikay and Goyal, Naman and Chaudhary, Vishrav and Wenzek, Guillaume and Guzmán, Francisco and Grave, Edouard and Ott, Myle and Zettlemoyer, Luke and Stoyanov, Veselin. 2019. Unsupervised cross-lingual representation learning at scale. *arXiv preprint arXiv:1911.02116*

Devlin, Jacob and Chang, Ming-Wei and Lee, Kenton and Toutanova, Kristina 2018. Bert: Pre-training of deep bidirectional transformers for language understanding. *arXiv preprint arXiv:1810.04805*

Fomicheva, Marina and Sun, Shuo and Yankovskaya, Lisa and Blain, Frédéric and Guzmán, Francisco and Fishel, Mark and Aletras, Nikolaos and Chaudhary, Vishrav and Specia, Lucia. 2020. Unsupervised quality estimation for neural machine translation. *Transactions of the Association for Computational Linguistics* 8, 539-555, MIT Press

Ian J. Goodfellow, Mehdi Mirza, Da Xiao, Aaron Courville and Yoshua Bengio. 2015 An Empirical Investigation of Catastrophic Forgetting in Gradient-Based Neural Networks. *arXiv preprint arXiv:1312.6211.*

Jörg Tiedemann. 2012. Parallel Data, Tools and Interfaces in OPUS. *Proceedings of the Eight International Conference on Language Resources and Evaluation (LREC'12)* Istanbul, Turkey. European Language Resources Association (ELRA).

Klein, Guillaume and Hernandez, François and Nguyen, Vincent and Senellart, Jean. 2020. The OpenNMT neural machine translation toolkit: 2020 edition. *Proceedings of the 14th Conference of the Association for Machine Translation in the Americas (Volume 1: Research Track)*, 102-109

Kocmi, Tom and Federmann, Christian and Grundkiewicz, Roman and Junczys-Dowmunt, Marcin and Matsushita, Hitokazu and Menezes, Arul. 2021. To ship or not to ship: An extensive evaluation of automatic metrics for machine translation. *arXiv preprint arXiv:2107.10821*

Libovickỳ, Jindřich and Rosa, Rudolf and Fraser, Alexander. 2019. How language-neutral is multilingual BERT? *arXiv preprint arXiv:1911.03310*

Mathias Müller, Annette Rios and Rico Sennrich. 2020. Domain Robustness in Neural Machine Translation. *arXiv preprint arXiv:1911.03109.*

Nunziatini, Mara and Alfieri, Andrea. 2021 A Synthesis of Human and Machine: Correlating "New" Automatic Evaluation Metrics with Human Assessments. *Proceedings of Machine Translation Summit XVIII: Users and Providers Track*, "440-465" Virtual, *Association for Machine Translation in the Americas, https://aclanthology.org/2021.mtsummit-up.29".*

Papineni, Kishore and Roukos, Salim and Ward, Todd and Zhu, Wei-Jing 2002. BLEU: a method for automatic evaluation of machine translation. *Proceedings of the 40th annual meeting of the Association for Computational Linguistics*, 311-318.

Popović, Maja 2015. chrF: character n-gram F-score for automatic MT evaluation *Proceedings of the Tenth Workshop on Statistical Machine Translation*, 392-395.

Ranasinghe, Tharindu and Orasan, Constantin and Mitkov, Ruslan. 2020. TransQuest: Translation quality estimation with cross-lingual transformers. *arXiv preprint arXiv:2011.01536*

Rei, Ricardo and Stewart, Craig and Farinha, Ana C and Lavie, Alon. 2020. COMET: A neural framework for MT evaluation *arXiv preprint arXiv:2009.09025*

Reimers, Nils and Gurevych, Iryna. 2019. Sentence-BERT: Sentence Embeddings using Siamese BERT-Networks *Proceedings of the 2019 Conference on Empirical Methods in Natural Language Processing Association for Computational Linguistics https://arxiv.org/abs/1908.10084*

Reimers, Nils and Gurevych, Iryna. 2020 Making Monolingual Sentence Embeddings Multilingual using Knowledge Distillation", *Proceedings of the 2020 Conference on Empirical Methods in Natural Language Processing, Association for Computational Linguistics.*

Shuhao Gu and Yang Feng. 2020. Investigating Catastrophic Forgetting During Continual Training for Neural Machine Translation. *arXiv preprint arXiv:2011.00678.*

Song, Kaitao and Tan, Xu and Qin, Tao and Lu, Jianfeng and Liu, Tie-Yan. 2020. Mpnet: Masked and permuted pre-training for language understanding *Advances in Neural Information Processing Systems* 16857-16867

Specia, Lucia and Blain, Frédéric and Fomicheva, Marina and Fonseca, Erick and Chaudhary, Vishrav and Guzmán, Francisco and Martins, André FT. 2020. Findings of the WMT 2020 shared task on quality estimation. *Association for Computational Linguistics*

Specia, Lucia and Blain, Frédéric and Fomicheva, Marina and Zerva, Chrysoula and Li, Zhenhao and Chaudhary, Vishrav and Martins, André 2021. Findings of the WMT 2021 shared task on quality estimation *Association for Computational Linguistics*

Stahlberg, Felix. 2020. Neural Machine Translation: A Review and Survey.

Vaswani, Ashish and Shazeer, Noam and Parmar, Niki and Uszkoreit, Jakob and Jones, Llion and Gomez, Aidan N and Kaiser, Łukasz and Polosukhin, Illia. 2017. Attention is all you need. *Advances in neural information processing systems*, volume 30

Wang, Jiayi and Wang, Ke and Chen, Boxing and Zhao, Yu and Luo, Weihua and Zhang, Yuqi. 2021. QEMind: Alibaba's Submission to the WMT21 Quality Estimation Shared Task. *arXiv preprint arXiv:2112.14890*

Zerva, Chrysoula and van Stigt, Daan and Rei, Ricardo and Farinha, Ana C and Ramos, Pedro and de Souza, José GC and Glushkova, Taisiya and Vera, Miguel and Kepler, Fabio and Martins, André FT. 2021. Istunbabel 2021 submission for the quality estimation shared task. *Proceedings of the Sixth Conference on Machine Translation*, 961-972.

Zhang, Jingyi and van Genabith, Josef. 2020. Translation Quality Estimation by Jointly Learning to Score and Rank. *Proceedings of the 2020 Conference on Empirical Methods in Natural Language Processing (EMNLP)*, 2592-2598.

Knowledge Distillation for Sustainable Neural Machine Translation

Wandri Jooste wandri.jooste@adaptcentre.ie
Andy Way andy.way@adaptcentre.ie
ADAPT Centre, Dublin City University, Dublin, Ireland

Rejwanul Haque rejwanul.haque@ncirl.ie
National College of Ireland, Dublin, Ireland

Riccardo Superbo riccardos@kantanai.io
KantanAI, DCU Alpha, Dublin, Ireland

Abstract

Knowledge distillation (KD) can be used to reduce model size and training time, without significant loss in performance; in some instances, it even leads to performance gains. These smaller models, also known as student models, are much more efficient in terms of time and energy costs, and they emit far less CO_2. However, the process of distilling knowledge requires translation of sizeable data sets, and the translation is usually performed using large cumbersome models, also known as teacher models. The intuition is to produce smaller student models that can mimic well the large teacher models which are usually good in quality. Nevertheless, producing translations of sizeable data sets by large-scale teacher models for KD is expensive in terms of both time and cost, which is a significant concern for translation service providers (TSPs). On top of that, the use of cumbersome models for translating large-scale data sets can be the cause of higher carbon footprints. In this work, we tested different variants of a teacher model in order to produce translations of a large-scale data set, tracked the power consumption of the graphic processing units (GPUs) used during translation, recorded overall translation time, estimated translation cost, and measured the accuracy of the student models. The findings of our investigation demonstrate to the translation industry a cost-effective, high-quality alternative to the standard KD training methods which are highly time-consuming and computationally expensive. More importantly still, we show that our proposed solutions are the most environmentally friendly training methods to distil knowledge from a teacher to a student model, while maintaining an insignificant drop in accuracy.

1 Introduction

Deep neural networks (DNNs) underpin state-of-the-art applications of artificial intelligence in almost all fields, such as image (Voulodimos et al., 2018), speech (Park et al., 2019) and natural language processing (NLP) (Wolf et al., 2019). However, DNN architectures (LeCun et al., 2015) are often data-, compute-, space-, power- and energy-hungry, typically requiring powerful GPUs or large-scale clusters to train and deploy, which has been viewed as a "non-green" technology (Strubell et al., 2019). Furthermore, often the best-performing models are ensembles of hundreds or thousands of base-level models, which require large amounts of space and time for storage and execution (Singh et al., 2016; Wen et al., 2017; Fedus et al., 2021).

Neural MT (NMT) (Cho et al., 2014; Sutskever et al., 2014; Bahdanau et al., 2014) systems have greatly improved MT compared to statistical MT (SMT) (Koehn, 2009) systems. These state-of-the-art NMT systems, however, require much more computing power and data than SMT systems (Östling and Tiedemann, 2017; Dowling et al., 2020), and if the effects of climate change are to be controlled they are unsustainable in the long run. These systems are also largely unsuitable for training engines for low-resource languages and scenarios, where the data simply does not exist in the amounts required for high quality results to be achieved. To some extent, model compression, more specifically knowledge distillation techniques, can remedy this.

Knowledge distillation (Buciluă et al., 2006) can be used to transfer the knowledge from a teacher network (a large model) to a student network (a smaller model). This is generally done by using a smaller, fast model to approximate the function learned by a much larger and slower model with better performance (Buciluă et al., 2006; Hinton et al., 2015).

The methods described by Buciluă et al. (2006) and Hinton et al. (2015) can be used for word-level knowledge distillation, since NMT models make use of multi-class prediction at the word-level. These models, however, need to predict complete sequences that are dependent on previous predictions as well.

Kim and Rush (2016) propose sequence-level KD wherein a new training set is generated by translating a data set with the teacher model using beam search. The newly generated training set is then used to train a smaller student model. The data sets often contain millions of sentences and thus translating the training set by a large-scale teacher model for KD training (Bapna et al., 2022) can be a cumbersome task and computationally expensive process. Thus, KD training in MT is responsible for a considerable amount of CO_2 emissions. This is a concerning matter for the environment. Besides, this is also a concern for TSPs who want to increase their margins in translation productivity by offering translations by smaller student models to their clients. More specifically, the standard and computationally expensive KD training process can negatively impact the translation productivity gain in industry.

The standard KD training methods use large-scale teacher models. We tested a number of variants of a teacher model for translating the source sentences of our training data. For example, we investigated the effects of changing the beam size and using quantisation (Polino et al., 2018; Prato et al., 2020) while translating the training data. More specifically, we tested the approaches of both Bogoychev et al. (2020) and Behnke et al. (2021), who focused on quantisation during inference to reduce the size of their student models and increase the speed at which these models translate sentences. The quality of translations by a quantised teacher model would naturally be worse than that of the translations by non-quantized teacher model. The same is true when one uses a very small batch size (e.g. 1) at decoding. As a result, the translations by these fast decoders would naturally impact the quality the resultant student model. In other words, you are likely to obtain a worse student model when you use a quantised teacher model to distil knowledge. Our investigation focused on examining the magnitude of quality drop of the student models when using the different variants of the teacher models for KD, and in return how faster, cheaper and environmental friendly the KD training process would be.

We considered English-to-German for our investigation, and recorded a number of parameters (i.e. CO_2 emissions, translation time, accuracy) including power consumption of the GPUs used for translation. We empirically demonstrated that our proposed KD training methods are computationally less expensive in comparison to the standard KD methods, and more importantly, they do not deteriorate the accuracy of the student models much. As far as we are aware, related work on model efficiency and knowledge distillation (Kim and Rush, 2016; Bhandare et al., 2019; Bogoychev et al., 2020; Prato et al., 2020; Heafield et al., 2021) focus on performance during inference whereas in this paper we focus on the effects of quantisation for

KD training, in order to make the process as a whole more efficient rather than just reducing the size and increasing the speed of the student models.

2 Experimental Setup

In this section we describe the various aspects of our experiments. We first discuss the data and how it was preprocessed and then move on to describe how our MT systems are trained. Lastly, we describe how we evaluate the quality of these MT systems.

2.1 Data

We use the Europarl [1] (Koehn, 2005) corpus with parallel sentences in German and English for the language direction German to English. The corpus is randomly divided into three subsets, namely the training set, validation set and test set. The training set consists of roughly two million sentences and the validation and test sets of 3,000 sentences, respectively.

The Moses toolkit (Koehn et al., 2007) was used to tokenize and clean the three datasets by removing all sentences with a length greater than 100. The toolkit was also used to decase all sentences before training and after training, we used a pretrained truecaser to recase all translated sentences. Furthermore, SubwordNMT[2] (Sennrich et al., 2016) was used to segment the sentences in the corpus into subword units. More specifically, the Byte Pair Encoding (BPE) vocabularies were set to $32k$ words. Jooste et al. (2022) experimented with limiting the vocabulary sizes during training and the models with smaller vocabularies (16k and 8k) trained faster on average, albeit with lower quality in terms of runtime performance. Since this work aims at investigating how sustainable the KD training process would be, we kept this hyperparametr constant across our all experiments.

2.2 MT Systems

We use the MarianNMT[3] toolkit (Junczys-Dowmunt et al., 2018) and Transformer (Vaswani et al., 2017) architecture to train the models for our experiments. All models were trained for a maximum of 20 epochs, since that was the lowest number of epochs needed to finish training for one of our models. We used NVIDIA RTX 2080ti GPUs to train our models as well as during decoding when distilling knowledge.

We used the same setup for training as described in the work of Jooste et al. (2022), who investigated how sustainable today's neural MT systems are on industrial setups. The student models and baseline models have an encoder and decoder depth of 3, whereas the teacher models have an encoder and decoder depth of 6. Other than the difference in encoder and decoder layers, the training parameters are the same but the student models are trained on the knowledge-distilled data set instead of the original training set.

Setup	Beam Size	Mini/Maxi Batch	Quantisation
Original	12	10/100	fp32
Beam	1	10/100	fp32
Quantisation	12	10/100	fp16
Combined	1	128/256	fp16

Table 1: Comparison of decoding experiments.

Table 1 shows the various setups we used for decoding. Originally we used a beam size of 12 without quantisation when distilling knowledge. We then investigated the effects of changing

[1] https://opus.nlpl.eu/Europarl-v3.php
[2] https://github.com/rsennrich/subword-nmt
[3] https://github.com/marian-nmt/marian

the beam size to one and using quantisation to use 16 bit floating point numbers (fp16) rather than 32 bit floating point numbers (fp32). Since using smaller floating point numbers requires less memory, we are also able to use a better combination of the mini- and maxi-batch sizes.

In Jooste et al. (2022), they showed that the student models outperform the teacher models when training them on the original training set combined with the knowledge distilled training set (KD-set). In this work, however, we will only focus on the effects when using only the KD-set for training student models.

2.3 Evaluation

The accuracy of all our models was measured with three automatic evaluation metrics, namely BLEU (Papineni et al., 2002), TER (Snover et al., 2006) and chrF[4] (Popović, 2015), using the MultEval toolkit[5] (Clark et al., 2011). We decided to use three metrics instead of one to better represent the accuracy of the models.

In order to gain more insight into the efficiency of distilling knowledge from our teacher models, we tracked the power usage during inference. The NVIDIA System Management Interface (nvidia-smi) was used to report the power draw of the GPUs being used, which was then used to approximate the CO_2 emitted during inference.

CO_2 can be computed using the Power Usage Effectiveness (PUE) of the data centre, kilowatt per hour (kWh) and the CO_2 intensity (I^{CO_2}) as in equation (1) (Strubell et al., 2019; Henderson et al., 2020):

$$CO_2 Emissions = \frac{PUE * kWh * I^{CO_2}}{1000} \tag{1}$$

Sherionov and Vanmassenhove (2022) pointed out that the values of PUE and I^{CO_2} are dependent on various factors and also constantly changing. In this paper we will use the same values as reported by Sherionov and Vanmassenhove (2022) ($PUE = 1.59$ and $I^{CO_2} = 229.8718 \pm 77.4026$). The kWh is calculated by dividing the total kW measured per second by 360 in order to get the kW per hour rather than seconds.

The translation time was also tracked in order to estimate the cost of using the various decoding methods. To estimate the cost we used the AWS Pricing Calculator[6] for EC2 instances, on demand and located in Ireland. The cost of an instance varies on the number of GPUs needed and is then multiplied by the number of hours it is used for. For each scenario the cost of adding 30 GiB of memory is a flat of of 3.30 US Dollars (USD) per month and since it is constant, it was left out of our estimated cost calculations.

3 Results and Discussion

Table 2 compares different setups that we described in Section 2.2 in terms of the translation time, power draw, approximate CO_2 emissions and estimated cost in US Dollars (USD). As can be seen from the table, the combined methods ('Combined' in Table 2) are the most efficient way of distilling knowledge. We illustrate the performance of the student models that correspond to the KD training setups of Table 2 in Table 3. We can clearly see from both tables that the difference in translation time has been improved by 7 hours on average, while the quality of the student models drops by less than 1 BLEU point. The same trends are observed with the other MT evaluation metrics too. Such a small drop in quality is unlikely to be spotted by a human, even an expert translator.

[4]https://github.com/m-popovic/chrF
[5]https://github.com/jhclark/multeval
[6]https://calculator.aws/#/createCalculator/EC2

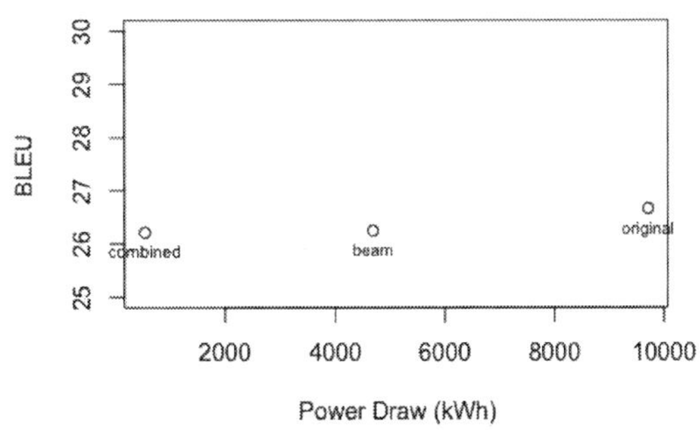

Figure 1: BLEU score of student models compared to the corresponding power draw of the distillation methods mentioned when using 1 GPU

In Figure 1 we show the BLEU scores of the student models and the power draw (required to create the training sets) of the various distillation methods proposed. In the figure we only show the distillation method when using 1 GPU since that is the most power-efficient option in most cases. When taking the power draw, and especially the CO_2 missions shown in Table 2, into account, the loss in BLEU score is very insignificant if we assume that all our AI models need to become much more sustainable.

Setup	# of GPUs	Time	Power (kW)	CO_2 (kg)	Cost in (USD)
	1	13:35:28	9,705.34	9.85 ± 3.32	8.21
Original	2	10:34:02	11,531.92	11.71 ± 3.94	20.46
	4	11:21:34	10,467.93	10.63 ± 3.58	31.90
	1	11:07:05	4,685.21	4.76 ± 1.60	6.72
Beam	2	07:26:50	4,337.43	4.40 ± 1.48	14.42
	4	08:31:21	5,893.63	5.98 ± 2.01	23.93
	1	11:10:30	6,146.91	6.24 ± 2.10	6.75
Quantisation	2	06:59:42	8,207.46	8.33 ± 2.80	13.54
	4	10:31:47	8,779.62	8.91 ± 3.00	29.57
	1	00:47:36	560.59	0.57 ± 0.19	0.48
Combined	2	00:30:26	618.17	0.63 ± 0.21	0.98
	4	00:42:58	646.55	0.66 ± 0.22	2.01

Table 2: Comparison of the translation time, power draw and approximate CO_2 emissions of various decoding setups.

When using only a smaller beam size or quantisation, respectively, the translation times are only marginally improved, i.e. two or three hours compared to six when using the combined method. Interestingly, quantisation alone leads to a minimal speedup, and it is experimenting with mini- and maxi-batch size that has the most significant impact. When trying to use the same batch sizes without quantisation however, the GPUs would run out of memory after translating only a few sentences. We therefore draw attention to utilising the GPU specifications when considering mini- and maxi-batch size when using quantisation for speeding up the distillation

Setup	# of GPUs	Training time	BLEU	TER	chrF
Original	1	07:17:39	26.66	49.5	59.37
	2	04:22:14	26.49	49.3	59.51
	4	04:05:28	26.22	50.1	59.11
Beam	1	06:42:33	26.25	48.6	60.51
	2	04:23:33	26.38	48.5	60.52
	4	04:38:00	26.49	50.3	59.44
Combined	1	06:18:08	26.21	48.7	60.32
	2	04:25:53	26.53	48.7	60.49
	4	04:38:00	26.21	49.5	60.02

Table 3: Comparison of the performance of the student models using the various decoding setups.

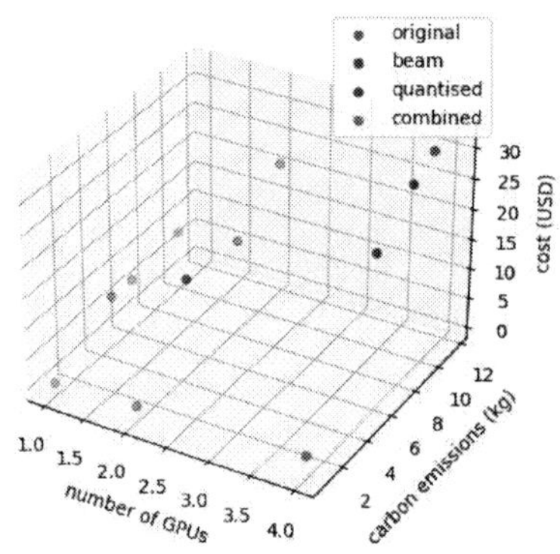

Figure 2: The CO_2 emissions and cost in USD of translation when using 1,2 or 4 GPUs during the distillation process.

process.

Taking the power draw and CO_2 emissions into account, Table 2 shows that using a beam size of 1 decreases the power draw by almost half and in turn the carbon emissions, even though the translation time is only marginally shorter. When using quantisation without optimal batch sizes however, the power draw is more than that of the beam setup while the translation time remains similar. Quantisation is therefore only an optimisation method for inference when the correct batch sizes are taking into account, depending on the GPU specifications.

The effects that these methods of speeding up decoding have on the accuracy of the student models are shown in Table 3. When taking the carbon emissions, decoding time and accuracy into account, it is clear that using the combined method is the most efficient setup to use when distilling knowledge from a teacher to a student model, since the accuracy decreased by less than 1 BLEU point while translation time decreased by 10 or more hours.

When considering the cost for TSPs, as seen in Table 2, using only 1 GPU is the most cost-effective for all methods of decoding. Interestingly, while using 2 GPUs speeds up the translation time for all methods, the estimated cost is double that of using only 1 GPU.

Figure 2 provides a summary of the most notable results in Table 2. It is clear that as the number of GPUs in the translation process increases, the CO_2 emissions go up in most cases and the cost of using an AWS EC2 instance rises in all scenarios. The increase in CO_2 emissions and cost is not linear as the number of GPUs is increased, nor is the translation time shown in Table 3 due to the performance overheads of using multiple GPUs (Xu et al., 2021).

4 Conclusions and Future Work

We described various methods in which the distillation of knowledge can be made more efficient and in turn more sustainable. Most significantly, the impact of batch sizes when using quantisation and a smaller beam size result in a less than 1 BLEU point drop in accuracy, while at the same time reducing decoding time hby at least 10 hours compared to the original method.

In terms of efficiency, the combined setup is found to be the best method for distilling knowledge from the teacher to student models. The CO_2 emissions of our combined setup is on average 10kg less than the original setup while accuracy decreases only slightly. The environmental impact of distilling knowledge from a teacher model to a student model are encouraging, and we contend that more importance should be given to this issue since inefficient methods emit on average 10 times more CO_2 than optimised methods, yet the cost in accuracy of the student models is minimal. Taking only the end result (student model) into account is not sustainable and more consideration needs to be put into the whole process.

We have shown that during the process of distilling knowledge from a teacher model to a student model, using just 2 GPUs can result in the fastest translation time while using 1 GPU is the most cost-effective and in most cases the most environmentally friendly as well. Interestingly, from our results it is clear that when taking CO_2 emissions and cost into account, using 4 GPUs is much less efficient compared to using only 1 GPU.

In future we will investigate the efficiency of using CPUs during the distillation process as well as during inference when the student models are deployed. We also aim to develop a composite metric that takes carbon emissions, accuracy and access to resources into account in order to rate the performance of MT Systems. Furthermore, we aim to investigate to what extent these decoding methods work on different language pairs, especially their effect on low-resource languages where access to data is considerably more problematic.

5 Acknowledgements

This publication has emanated from research conducted with the financial support of Science Foundation Ireland under Grant number 18/CRT/6183. The ADAPT Centre for Digital Content Technology (`https://www.adaptcentre.ie/`) is funded under the Science Foundation Ireland Research Centres Programme (Grant number 13/RC/2106) and is co-funded under the European Regional Development Fund. We also wish to thank KantanAI (`https://www.kantanai.io/`) for hosting the first-named author on her ML-Labs (`https://www.ml-labs.ie/`) placement, and for permission to use the statistics quoted in this paper.

References

Bahdanau, D., Cho, K., and Bengio, Y. (2014). Neural machine translation by jointly learning to align and translate.

Bapna, A., Caswell, I., Kreutzer, J., Firat, O., van Esch, D., Siddhant, A., Niu, M., Baljekar, P., Garcia, X., Macherey, W., Breiner, T., Axelrod, V., Riesa, J., Cao, Y., Chen, M. X., Macherey, K., Krikun, M., Wang, P., Gutkin, A., Shah, A., Huang, Y., Chen, Z., Wu, Y., and Hughes, M. (2022). Building machine translation systems for the next thousand languages.

Behnke, M., Bogoychev, N., Aji, A. F., Heafield, K., Nail, G., Zhu, Q., Tchistiakova, S., van der Linde, J., Chen, P., Kashyap, S., and Grundkiewicz, R. (2021). Efficient machine translation with model pruning and quantization. In *Proceedings of the Sixth Conference on Machine Translation*, pages 775–780, Online. Association for Computational Linguistics.

Bhandare, A., Sripathi, V., Karkada, D., Menon, V., Choi, S., Datta, K., and Saletore, V. (2019). Efficient 8-Bit Quantization of Transformer Neural Machine Language Translation Model. *arXiv:1906.00532 [cs]*. arXiv: 1906.00532.

Bogoychev, N., Grundkiewicz, R., Aji, A. F., Behnke, M., Heafield, K., Kashyap, S., Farsarakis, E.-I., and Chudyk, M. (2020). Edinburgh's submissions to the 2020 machine translation efficiency task. In *Proceedings of the Fourth Workshop on Neural Generation and Translation*, pages 218–224, Online. Association for Computational Linguistics.

Buciluǎ, C., Caruana, R., and Niculescu-Mizil, A. (2006). Model compression. In *KDD '06: Proceedings of the Twelfth ACM SIGKDD International Conference on Knowledge Discovery and Data Mining*, pages 535–541, Philadelphia, PA, USA. ACM.

Cho, K., Van Merriënboer, B., Bahdanau, D., and Bengio, Y. (2014). On the properties of neural machine translation: Encoder-decoder approaches. *arXiv preprint arXiv:1409.1259.*

Clark, J. H., Dyer, C., Lavie, A., and Smith, N. A. (2011). Better hypothesis testing for statistical machine translation: Controlling for optimizer instability. In *Proceedings of the 49th Annual Meeting of the Association for Computational Linguistics: Human Language Technologies*, pages 176–181, Portland, Oregon, USA. ACL.

Dowling, M., Castilho, S., Moorkens, J., Lynn, T., and Way, A. (2020). A human evaluation of English-Irish statistical and neural machine translation. In *Proceedings of the 22nd Annual Conference of the European Association for Machine Translation*, pages 431–440, Lisboa, Portugal. European Association for Machine Translation.

Fedus, W., Zoph, B., and Shazeer, N. (2021). Switch transformers: Scaling to trillion parameter models with simple and efficient sparsity.

Heafield, K., Zhu, Q., and Grundkiewicz, R. (2021). Findings of the WMT 2021 shared task on efficient translation. In *Proceedings of the Sixth Conference on Machine Translation*, pages 639–651, Online. Association for Computational Linguistics.

Henderson, P., Hu, J., Romoff, J., Brunskill, E., Jurafsky, D., and Pineau, J. (2020). Towards the systematic reporting of the energy and carbon footprints of machine learning. *Journal of Machine Learning Research*, 248:1–43.

Hinton, G., Vinyals, O., and Dean, J. (2015). Distilling the knowledge in a neural network.

Jooste, W., Haque, R., and Way, A. (2022). Knowledge distillation: A method for making neural machine translation more efficient. *Information*, 13(2).

Junczys-Dowmunt, M., Grundkiewicz, R., Dwojak, T., Hoang, H., Heafield, K., Neckermann, T., Seide, F., Germann, U., Aji, A. F., Bogoychev, N., Martins, A. F. T., and Birch, A. (2018). Marian: Fast Neural Machine Translation in C++. In *Proceedings of ACL 2018, System Demonstrations*, pages 116–121, Melbourne, Australia. ACL.

Kim, Y. and Rush, A. M. (2016). Sequence-Level Knowledge Distillation. In *Proceedings of the 2016 Conference on Empirical Methods in Natural Language Processing*, pages 1317–1327, Austin, Texas. ACL.

Koehn, P. (2005). Europarl: A parallel corpus for statistical machine translation. In *Proceedings of Machine Translation Summit X: Papers*, pages 79–86, Phuket, Thailand.

Koehn, P. (2009). *Statistical machine translation*. Cambridge University Press.

Koehn, P., Hoang, H., Birch, A., Callison-Burch, C., Federico, M., Bertoldi, N., Cowan, B., Shen, W., Moran, C., Zens, R., Dyer, C., Bojar, O., Constantin, A., and Herbst, E. (2007). Moses: Open source toolkit for statistical machine translation. In *Proceedings of the 45th Annual Meeting of the Association for Computational Linguistics Companion Volume Proceedings of the Demo and Poster Sessions*, pages 177–180, Prague, Czech Republic. ACL.

LeCun, Y., Bengio, Y., and Hinton, G. (2015). Deep learning. *Nature*, 521(7553):436–444.

Östling, R. and Tiedemann, J. (2017). Neural machine translation for low-resource languages. *arXiv preprint arXiv:1708.05729*.

Papineni, K., Roukos, S., Ward, T., and Zhu, W. J. (2002). Bleu: a method for automatic evaluation of machine translation. In *Proceedings of the 40th Annual Meeting on Association for Computational Linguistics*, page 311–318, Philadelphia, Pennsylvania, USA. ACL.

Park, D. S., Chan, W., Zhang, Y., Chiu, C.-C., Zoph, B., Cubuk, E. D., and Le, Q. V. (2019). Specaugment: A simple data augmentation method for automatic speech recognition. *arXiv preprint arXiv:1904.08779*.

Polino, A., Pascanu, R., and Alistarh, D. (2018). Model compression via distillation and quantization. Number: arXiv:1802.05668 arXiv:1802.05668 [cs].

Popović, M. (2015). chrF: character n-gram F-score for automatic MT evaluation. In *Proceedings of the Tenth Workshop on Statistical Machine Translation*, pages 392–395, Lisbon, Portugal. ACL.

Prato, G., Charlaix, E., and Rezagholizadeh, M. (2020). Fully Quantized Transformer for Machine Translation. In *Findings of the Association for Computational Linguistics: EMNLP 2020*, pages 1–14, Online. Association for Computational Linguistics.

Sennrich, R., Haddow, B., and Birch, A. (2016). Neural machine translation of rare words with subword units. In *Proceedings of the 54th Annual Meeting of the Association for Computational Linguistics (Volume 1: Long Papers)*, pages 1715–1725, Berlin, Germany. ACL.

Sherionov, D. and Vanmassenhove, E. (2022). The ecological footprint of neural machine translation systems. *arXiv preprint arXiv:2202.02170*.

Singh, S., Hoiem, D., and Forsyth, D. (2016). Swapout: Learning an ensemble of deep architectures. *arXiv preprint arXiv:1605.06465*.

Snover, M., Dorr, B., Schwartz, R., Micciulla, L., and Makhoul, J. (2006). A study of translation edit rate with targeted human annotation. In *Proceedings of the 7th Conference of the Association for Machine Translation in the Americas: Technical Papers*, page 223–231, Cambridge, Massachusetts, USA. AMTA.

Strubell, E., Ganesh, A., and McCallum, A. (2019). Energy and policy considerations for deep learning in NLP. In *Proceedings of the 57th Annual Meeting of the Association for Computational Linguistics*, pages 3645–3650, Florence, Italy. ACL.

Sutskever, I., Vinyals, O., and Le, Q. V. (2014). Sequence to sequence learning with neural networks. *arXiv preprint arXiv:1409.3215*.

Vaswani, A., Shazeer, N., Parmar, N., Uszkoreit, J., Jones, L., Gomez, A. N., Kaiser, L., and Polosukhin, I. (2017). Attention is all you need. In *Advances in Neural Information Processing Systems 30: Annual Conference on Neural Information Processing Systems 2017*, pages 5998–6008, Long Beach, CA, USA. NIPS.

Voulodimos, A., Doulamis, N., Doulamis, A., and Protopapadakis, E. (2018). Deep learning for computer vision: A brief review. *Computational intelligence and neuroscience*, 2018.

Wen, G., Hou, Z., Li, H., Li, D., Jiang, L., and Xun, E. (2017). Ensemble of deep neural networks with probability-based fusion for facial expression recognition. *Cognitive Computation*, 9(5):597–610.

Wolf, T., Debut, L., Sanh, V., Chaumond, J., Delangue, C., Moi, A., Cistac, P., Rault, T., Louf, R., Funtowicz, M., et al. (2019). Huggingface's transformers: State-of-the-art natural language processing. *arXiv preprint arXiv:1910.03771*.

Xu, W., Zhang, Y., and Tang, X. (2021). Parallelizing dnn training on gpus: Challenges and opportunities. In *Companion Proceedings of the Web Conference 2021*, WWW '21, page 174–178, New York, NY, USA. Association for Computing Machinery.

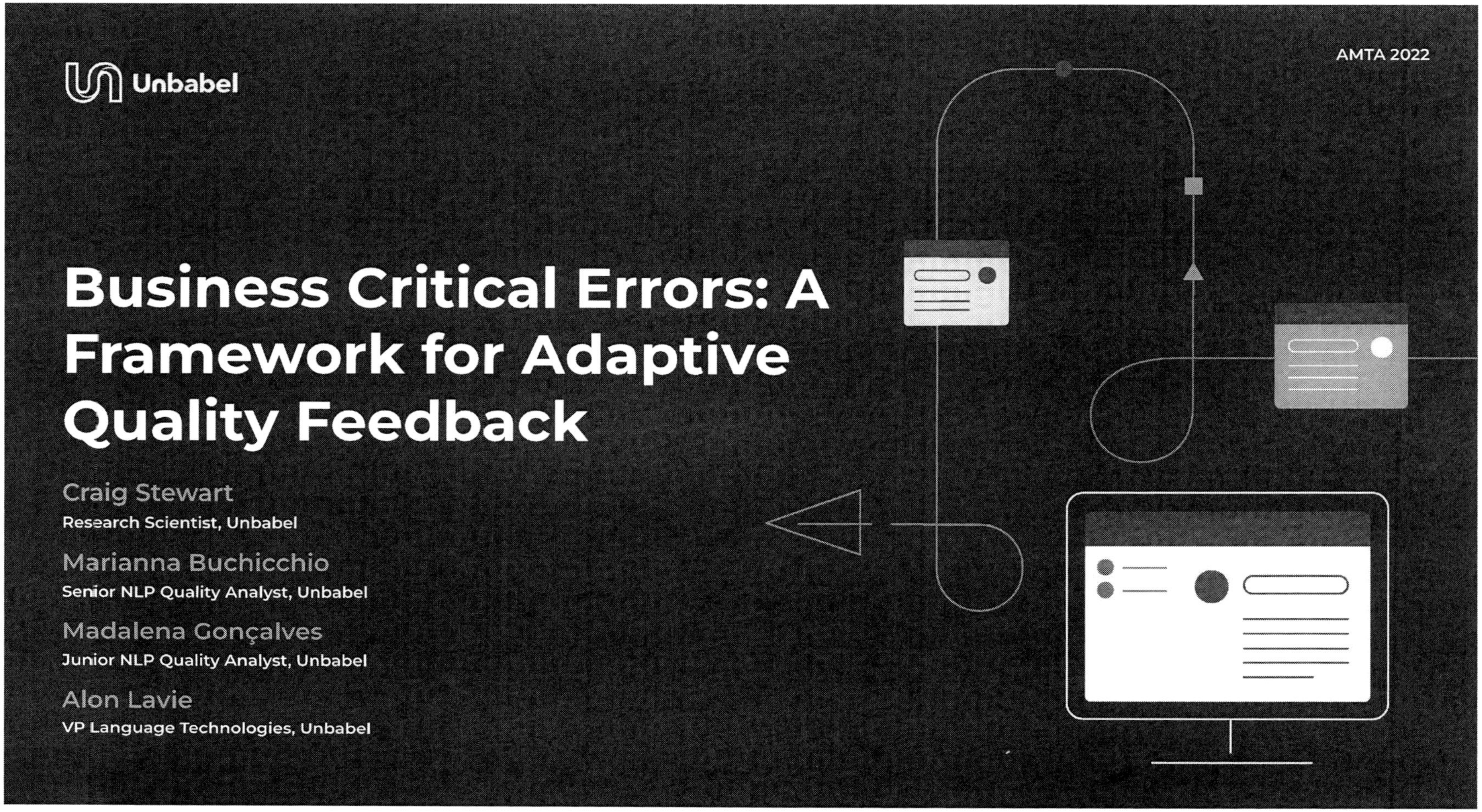
Unbabel
AMTA 2022
Business Critical Errors: A Framework for Adaptive Quality Feedback
Craig Stewart
Research Scientist, Unbabel
Marianna Buchicchio
Senior NLP Quality Analyst, Unbabel
Madalena Gonçalves
Junior NLP Quality Analyst, Unbabel
Alon Lavie
VP Language Technologies, Unbabel

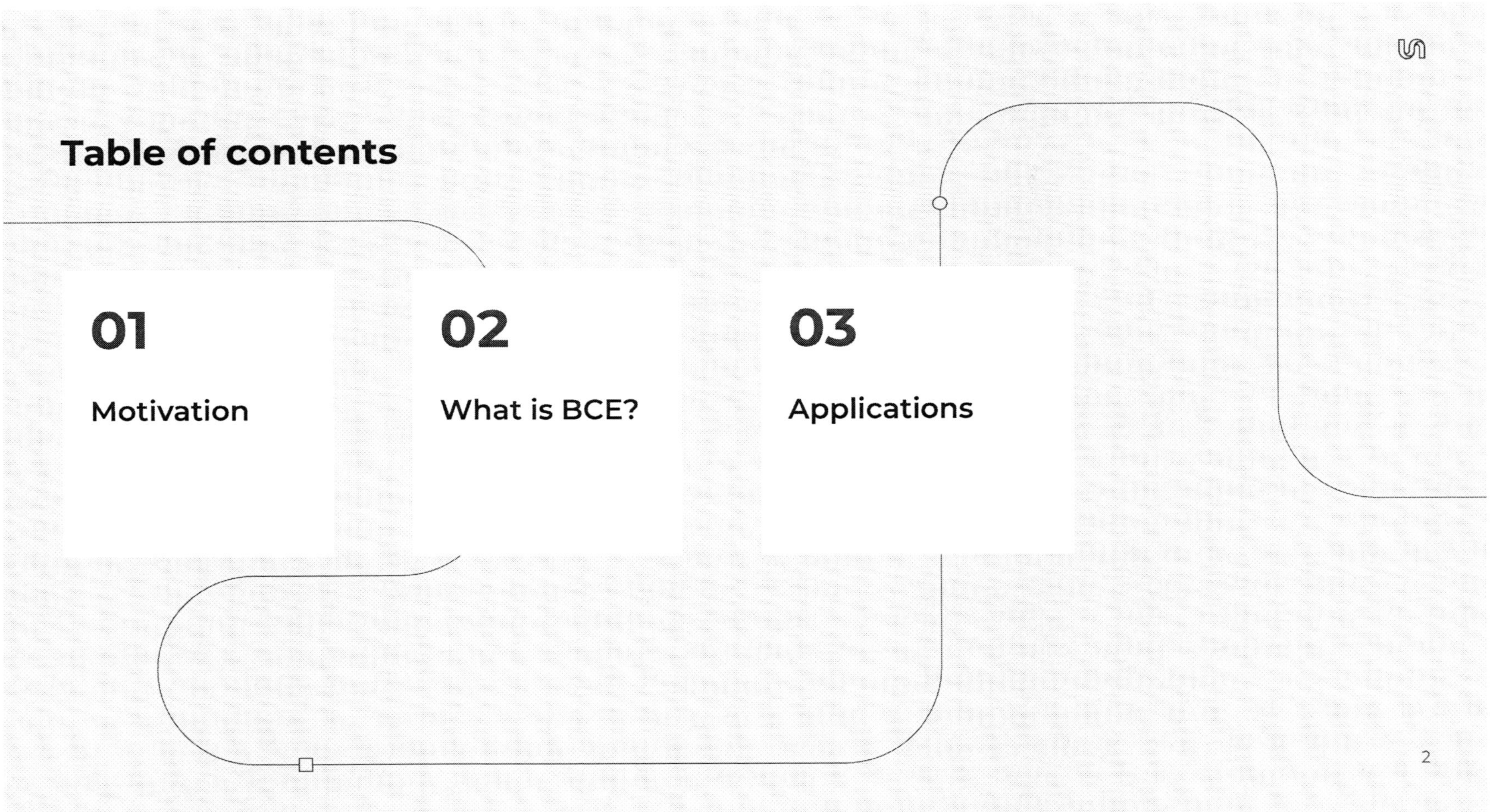
Table of contents
01
Motivation
02
What is BCE?
03
Applications
2

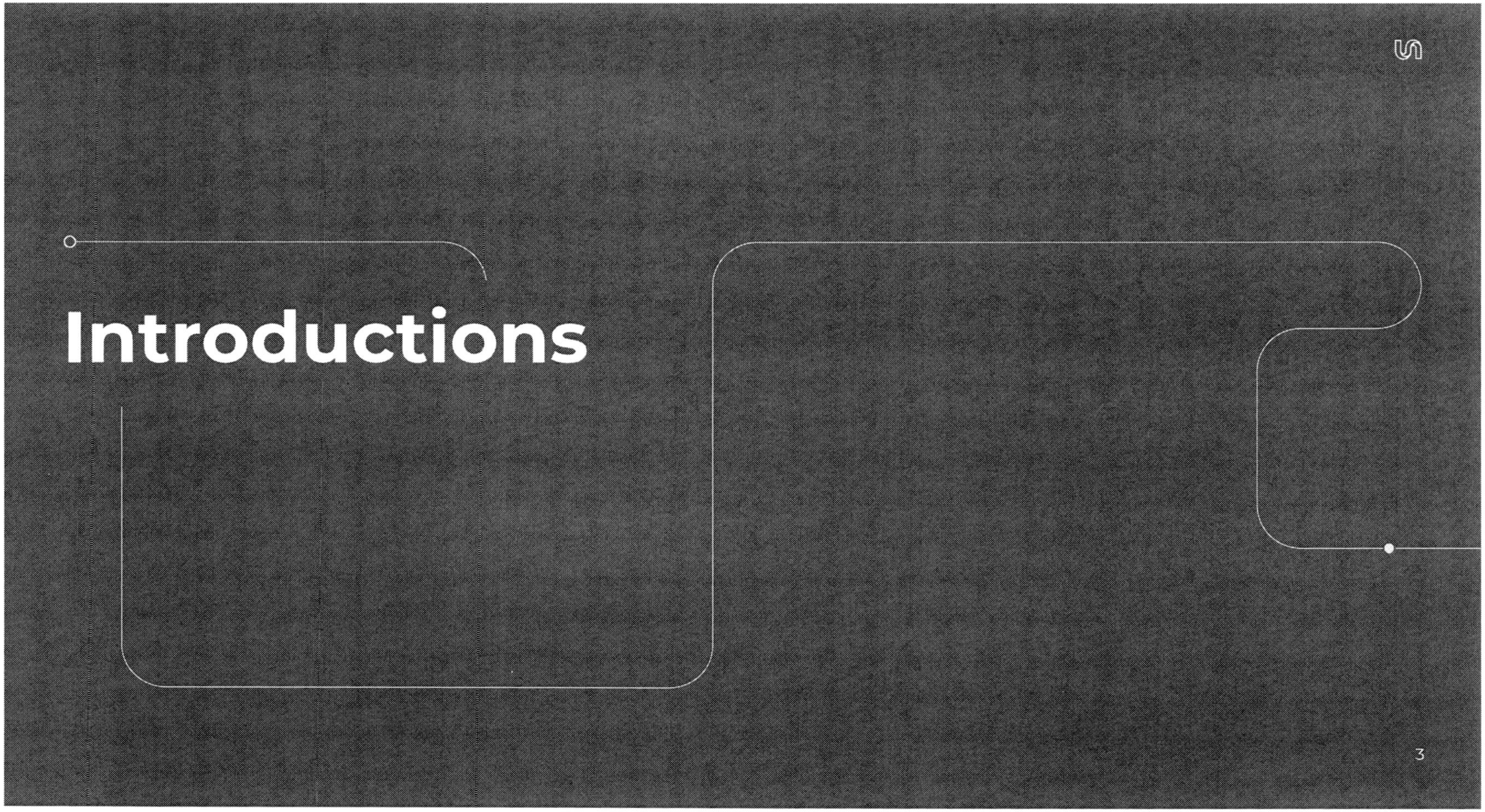
Introductions
3

Craig Stewart
Research Scientist

Marianna Buchicchio
Senior Quality Analyst

Madalena Gonçalves
Junior Quality Analyst

Alon Lavie
VP of Language Technologies

The Unbabel team

Roles & Responsibilities

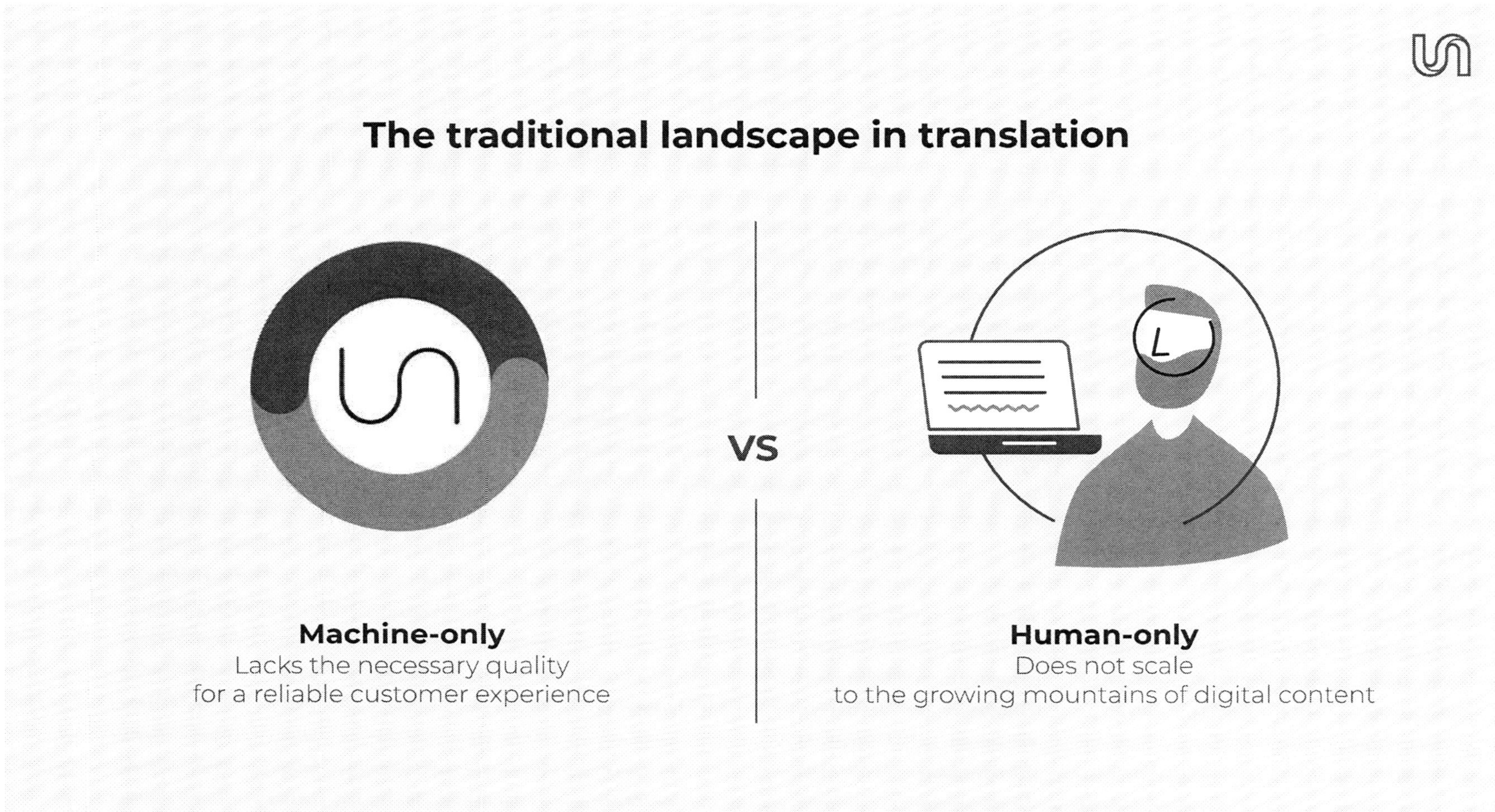
The traditional landscape in translation
VS
Machine-only
Lacks the necessary quality
for a reliable customer experience
Human-only
Does not scale
to the growing mountains of digital content

Unbabel's Translation Platform

AI Stack

Community

Proprietary data

Continuous learning

Seamless Integrations

6

Motivation

7

What is a ‘good’ translation?

In many cases, customer expectation can deviate from linguistic quality. Nuanced brand requirements, for example, can render perfectly sound translation ineffective for a specific use case:

What if a customer wants all of their content written in lower case?

What if they want to mix formal pronouns with a more informal discourse style?

Quality expectations can be both objective and subjective

What is a 'good' translation?

For this reason, at Unbabel we approach quality on **two dimensions**:

Linguistic Quality

To what extent is the translation linguistically accurate?

For us, at Unbabel, Multidimensional Quality Metrics* (MQM) is the most useful measure of linguistic accuracy.

We adapt the framework to align with our use cases.

*http://www.qt21.eu/mqm-definition/definition-2015-12-30.html

Utility

To what extent is the translation 'fit for purpose'?

MQM can capture some of this information and there are strategies for adapting MQM to customized requirements such as weighting systems on top of severity multipliers.

There is a growing need for leveraging MQM in different ways to accommodate variable expectations.

Unbabel is built on quality agility

We service the widest possible range of quality expectations from synchronous customer chat to on-brand marketing content.

We need a quality evaluation solution which can accommodate all expectations

MQM has been pivotal in allowing us to leverage an in-house community combined with a suite of AI evaluation tools which enable us to be highly adaptive. But we believe we can go further...

Proceedings of the 15th Biennial Conference of the Association for Machine Translation in the Americas, Orlando, USA, September 12-16, 2022. Volume 2: Users and Providers Track and Government Track

What is BCE?

11

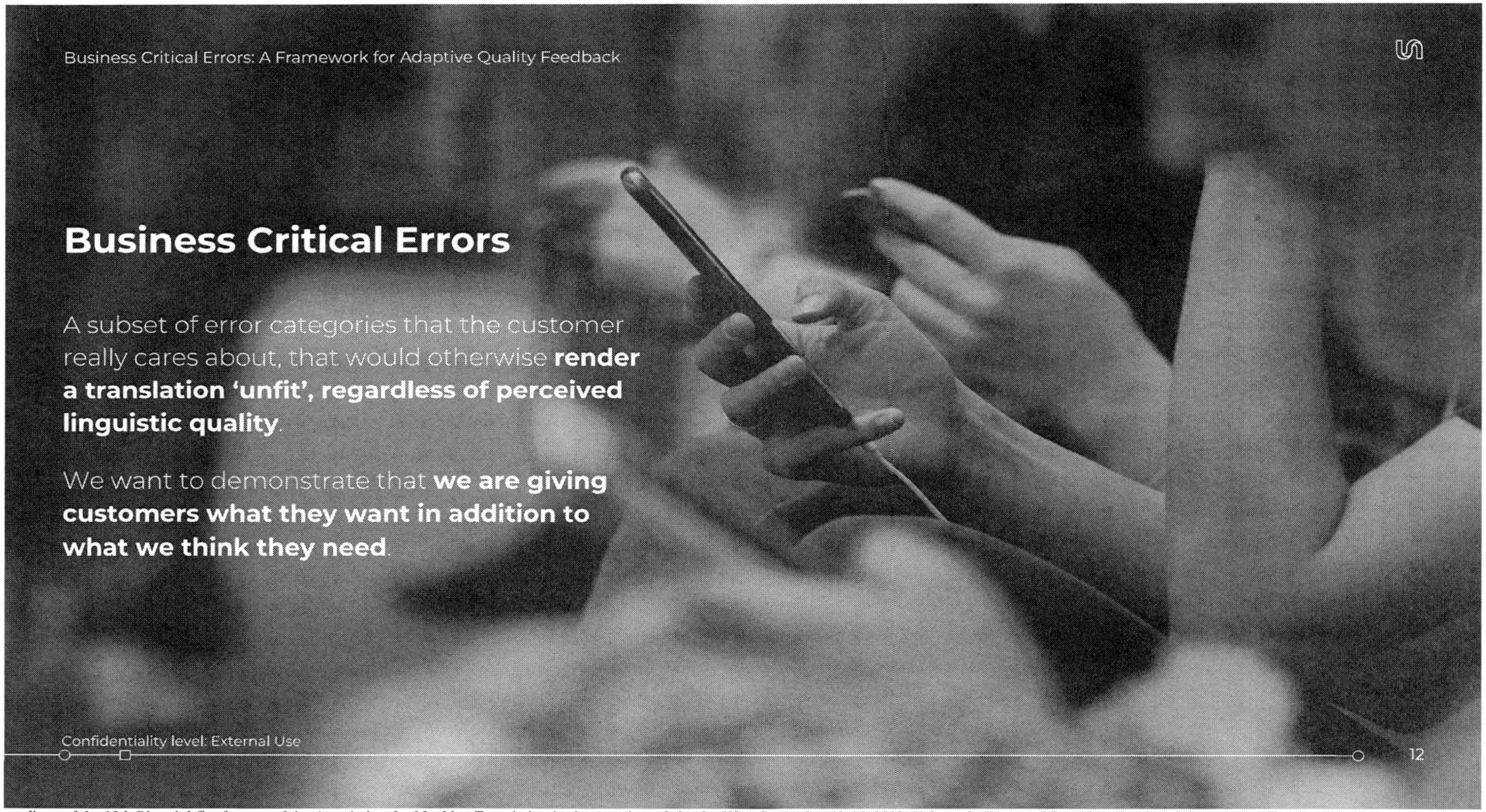
Business Critical Errors: A Framework for Adaptive Quality Feedback
Business Critical Errors
A subset of error categories that the customer really cares about, that would otherwise render a translation 'unfit', regardless of perceived linguistic quality.
We want to demonstrate that we are giving customers what they want in addition to what we think they need.
Confidentiality level: External Use
12

Business Critical Errors

Objectives

Expressivity

Articulating adherence:

We want the framework to adequately express how we are meeting expectations (or not!)

Efficiency

Minimize extra overhead:

Ideally we don't want to have to add any extra work for annotators or complicate and slow down the evaluation process

Simplicity

Minimize complexity:

Adding extra dimensions to MQM can make it difficult to interpret consistently.

Business Critical Errors

Approach

Expressivity

Figure out which error types the customer really cares about

Define priority error types that can be broadly applied and are impactful

Efficiency

Use the existing framework and ring fence a subset of errors

We only have to make a single pass of annotation with minimal special instructions to the annotator.

Simplicity

Define a minimalist set of error types

Report on counts of occurrences of BCE type errors and isolate that calculation from MQM.

Defining the framework

Data Collection	Ring fencing	Grouping	Implementation	Calibration
Gather feedback from customers, both from interview and existing complaints	Use distribution of collected data to establish the most critical error types	Establish a minimal set for groups of content relative to quality expectations	Develop tooling for pulling counts of BCE from annotations and for reporting	Working with customers to refine the categories, monitoring business impact

BCE as a Metric

How do we turn counts of these errors into a measurable metric?

We currently define our BCE metric as **the number of BCE errors per 1000 words**.

This is implemented such that **we can generate the metric once per quarter** in order to track progress over time and demonstrate improvement.

Why not just weight MQM scores?

We want this to be adaptive, so having different MQM values per customer would cause confusion

How has this been useful to us?

Allows us to prioritize

The biggest benefit is in **tightening our feedback loops** and allowing us to **focus on the issues that really matter**. Rather than sifting through all of the issues we can discover the issues that will have the greatest impact on the customer.

Quality Agility

With minimal overhead, we are now **able to customize quality feedback in meaningful ways** and show the customer that we really know and understand their expectations.

Improved processes and tooling

BCE generates an extra source of data that can complement our internal processes and tooling. We can **evaluate our MT models** specifically on BCE and **develop Quality Estimation models** focused on high impact error.

Applications
18

Applications of BCE at Unbabel

As we refine the framework we have found specific use cases in which we can use it to improve our tooling and processes:

Customer Utility Analysis

The primary intention for BCE is to **complement customer reporting**.

Our **Customer Utility Analysis Framework** allows us to clearly communicate the quality of translation.

We report **linguistic quality relative to distributions of bucketed MQM scores** which can be accompanied by our **BCE metric for translation utility**.

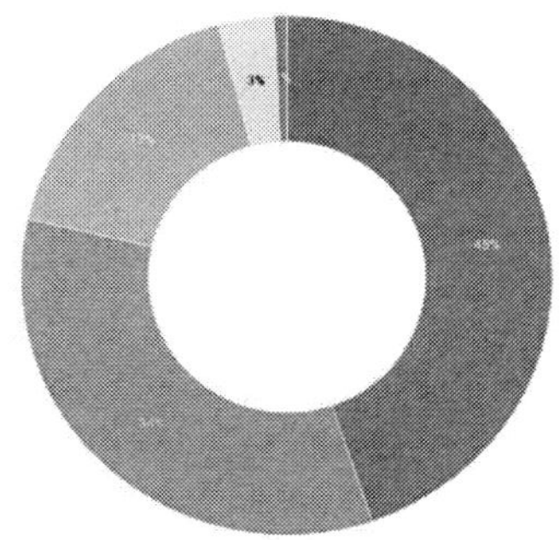

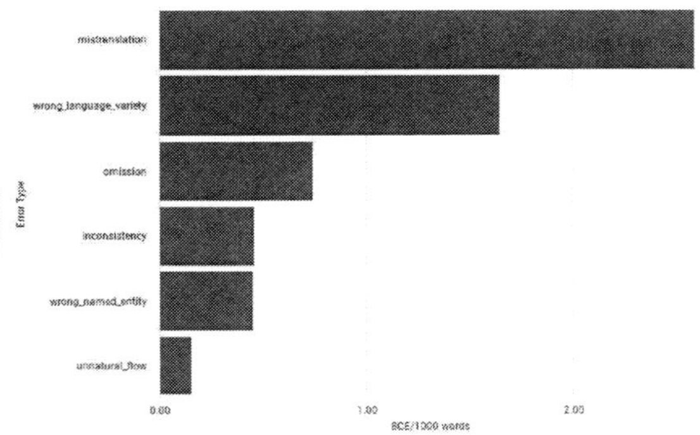

Applications of BCE at Unbabel

MT Model Evaluation

We have developed **BCE Test Suites**; benchmarking test sets by which we **evaluate the performance of our MT systems on specific phenomena**.

We put our **MT models through a gauntlet of specialized test sets** by which we established their ability to avoid certain BCE.

In this way we can **maximize translation quality downstream in meaningful ways**.

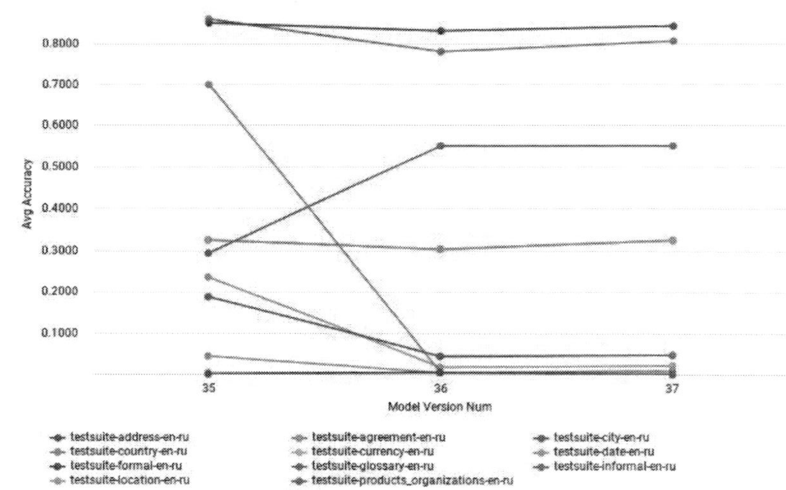

Applications of BCE at Unbabel

Automated Metric Evaluation

Our homegrown automated evaluation **metrics (COMET) are also tested for their ability to capture BCE**.

Similarly to MT systems, we have developed a gauntlet of test sets whereby **we ask our metrics to rank segments to ensure that the segment containing BCE receives a lower ranking**.

COMET

Proceedings of the 15th Biennial Conference of the Association for Machine Translation in the Americas, Orlando, USA, September 12-16, 2022. Volume 2: Users and Providers Track and Government Track

Applications of BCE at Unbabel

Quality Estimation

We have developed **specialized Quality Estimation systems that are trained on BCE data** and **predict the number of BCE errors per segment**.

We can use these systems as **a flagging mechanism to catch BCE before it goes out the door** and reroute it for human review.

OpenKiwi
By Unbabel

Summary
23

Key Takeaways

Quality expectations can be both **objective and subjective**

Business Critical Error (BCE)...

- is **focused on subjective expectation**
- allows us to **give customers what they want** vs **what we think they need**
- enables us to **prioritize issue resolution**
- can help us **design translation solutions that fit particular dimensions**
- provides **a rich source of high-impact data**

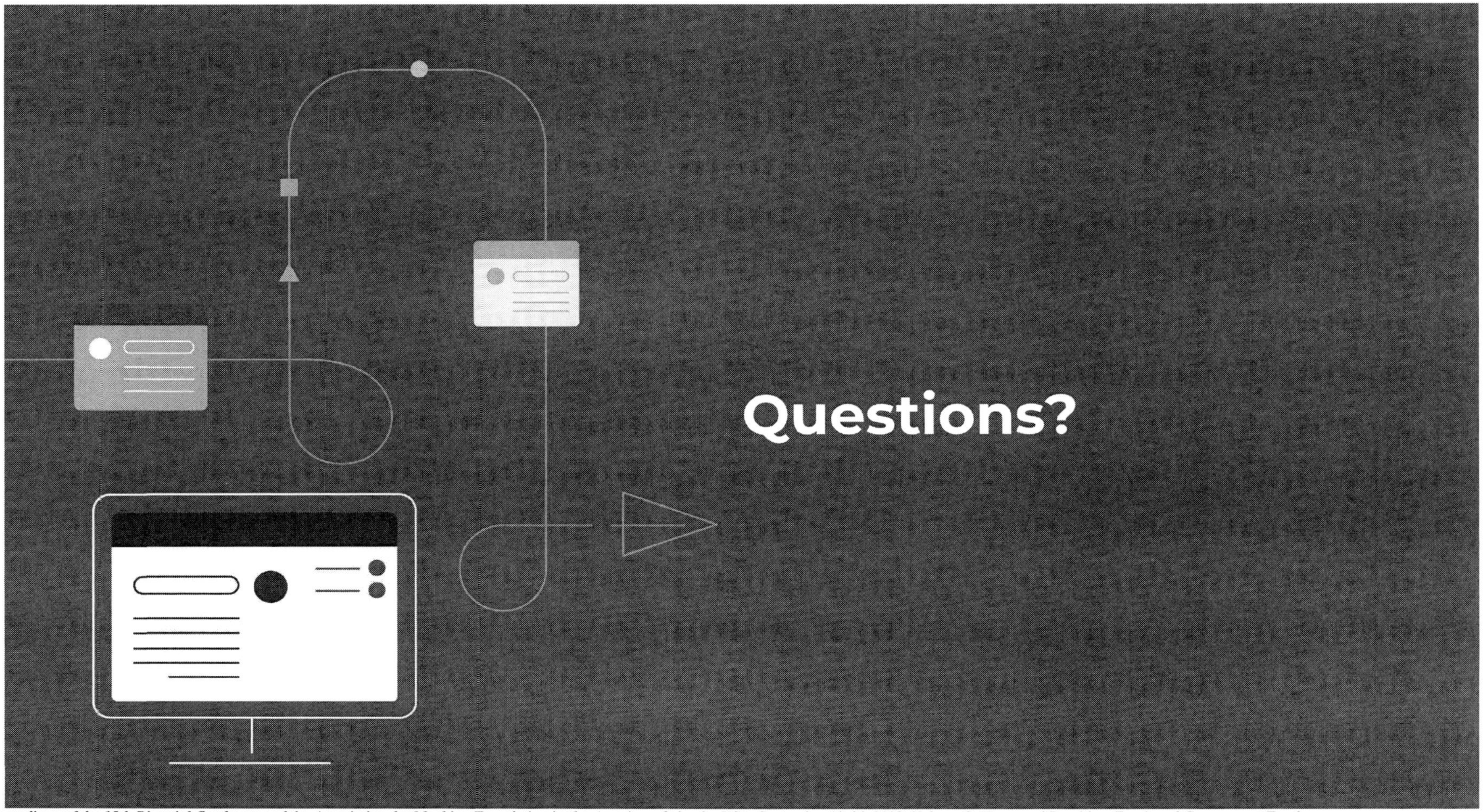
Questions?

Unbabel

A Snapshot into the Possibility of Video Game Machine Translation

Damien Hansen [1,2,3] damien.hansen@uliege.be
Pierre-Yves Houlmont [1,2] pyhoulmont@uliege.be
[1] University of Liège, CIRTI*, 4020 Liège, Belgium
[2] University of Liège, Liège Game Lab, 4000 Liège, Belgium
[3] Univ. Grenoble Alpes, CNRS, Grenoble INP**, LIG, 38000 Grenoble, France

Abstract

We present in this article what we believe to be one of the first attempts at video game machine translation. Our study shows that models trained only with limited in-domain data surpass publicly available systems by a significant margin, and a subsequent human evaluation reveals interesting findings in the final translation. The first part of the article introduces some of the challenges of video game translation, some of the existing literature, as well as the systems and data sets used in this experiment. The last sections discuss our analysis of the resulting translation and the potential benefits of such an automated system. One such finding highlights the model's ability to learn typical rules and patterns of video game translations from English into French. Our conclusions therefore indicate that the specific case of video game machine translation could prove very much useful given the encouraging results, the highly repetitive nature of the work, and the often poor working conditions that translators face in this field. As with other use cases of MT in cultural sectors, however, we believe this is heavily dependent on the proper implementation of the tool, which should be used interactively by human translators to stimulate creativity instead of raw post-editing for the sake of productivity.

1 Introduction

Since the apparition of recurrent neural networks with attention mechanisms (Bahdanau et al., 2014), neural machine translation (NMT) has improved to the point of becoming the default paradigm for this task. With new architectures such as the Transformer (Vaswani et al., 2017) and a similarly growing number of domain adaptation techniques (Chu and Wang, 2018), NMT has also started being used in increasingly more complex domains, and even tailored to the production of specific translators and companies.

The video game market similarly seems to have been ever growing in the last decades, becoming one of the fastest growing and highest grossing industries today within the cultural and entertainment sectors. The recent global health crisis further reinforced this trend and showed that games have an important role to play beyond just entertainment, as can be seen in a recent EU report on the cultural and creative sectors (CCS) in Europe (IDEA Consult et al., 2021): "Few winners can be found in the CCS during the COVID-19 global crisis. One of those, together with streaming platforms, is the video games sub-sector. With a turnover of EUR 21.6 billion and a 3% year-on-year growth from 2018, the gaming sub-sector has proven to be strong also in hard economic times."

*Centre Interdisciplinaire de Recherche en Traduction et en Interprétation.
**Institute of Engineering Univ. Grenoble Alpes.

As part of this success, it has now been expected for a while that video games be translated not just into the Western E-FIGS (English to French, Italian, German and Spanish), but into at least eight or ten languages in order to be considered a profitable and successful enterprise (Bernal-Merino, 2015). This creates, in turn, a huge demand for translation and a challenge in its own right, especially for smaller or newly formed studios.

It should furthermore be noted that, nowadays, video game localization is mainly considered from a market perspective. Indeed, the main purpose of this process is to make a given title available to a larger audience. To do so, several attempts have been made to produce game localization manifestos encouraging best practices (Chandler and Deming, 2012; Honeywood and Fung, 2012).

Those practices — and scientific studies in the field of video game localization in general — are said to be market-driven (O'Hagan, 2013). Even though video games represent an exceptional place of intercultural contact, cultural traces are quasi systematically neutralized in an attempt to ensure sales, to the point where they would be considered as localization errors were they to remain in the target version (Mandiberg, 2015), despite evidence from reception studies showing that current localization practices do not correspond to what players expect from a cultural point of view (Ellefsen and Bernal-Merino, 2018; Fernández Costales, 2016; Geurts, 2015).

On the other hand, the video game industry, as is the case with other digital productions[1], is characterized by a particularly high level of fan-made content (Barnabé, 2015; Hurel, in press), with undertakings varying from patches[2], mods[3], or even (re)creations that far outgrow the original games themselves. It is also very common for fans and volunteers to look into the original translations, sometimes correcting minor mistakes in these very large works, sometimes coming up with entirely new localization projects if the title was never translated or if the translation was not done by professionals and its quality deemed too poor (Díaz Montón, 2007; Muñoz Sánchez, 2009; Vazquez-Calvo et al., 2019).

Indeed, translation has traditionally been seen in the market as a trivial and disposable process that could be targeted to cut costs, leading up to the numerous examples of bad video game translations that careless uses of machine translation (MT) definitely did not help with (Mandelin and Kuchar, 2017). This brings several issues, not only for the players, but for the companies as well. As Bernal-Merino (2008) explains: "One of the most common complaints we can read about in internet forums is the lack of translation quality, and how sometimes they have to go back to the original version to find out what to do and how. In many cases, even though the game might have been translated and it is playable, fans fail to be impressed because the poor quality of the localisation defeats its own purpose: to thrill and engage the gamer. [...] Language and culture are ever-present elements in us and the things we do, players cannot help but notice continuous serious mistakes in the game, and it will erode their trust in some developer and publisher brands."

But what makes video game translation such an arduous task and how could machines play a role in it if it already proves challenging for humans? In addition to the common pitfalls of translation and creative works, translators in the field are typically presented with spreadsheets in which text segments are not ordered chronologically and do not offer any other kind of contextual information, concerning for instance the communication medium, the type of discourse,

[1] As the Web gave rise to the development of a "user-participatory culture" (Jenkins, 2006) and "user-generated content" (van Dijck, 2009), the translation sector similarly witnessed the emergence of "user" or "amateur" crowd-sourced translations (Lavault-Olléon, 2011; Gambier, 2016; Doherty, 2016).

[2] A patch, or fix, is a light modification made to a program in order to correct bugs, for example, to add a translation or to improve its usability.

[3] Mods affect the game more deeply and generally aim at customizing or expanding rather than fixing it. These modifications can affect its appearance, its story or even its gameplay (Barnabé, 2015).

the person speaking, etc. (Díaz Montón, 2007). What is more, a survey conducted with translators working in this sector found that only 30% of them had access to the game they were asked to translate (Theroine et al., 2021). The localization of video games, however, is dependent on more than just text, as it relies on a precise balancing of intersemiotic dynamics. Indeed, the different semiotic systems of a given game work together to provide a complete and coherent media experience, and may present "tensions" or a form of "interdependency" that can limit the spectrum of possibilities for the translator (Houlmont, 2022). This lack of audiovisual or contextual cues and text linearity is so prevalent that it has been theorized by Bernal-Merino (2015) as a double-blind process. In a sense, machines would therefore have as much (or rather as little) information at their disposal as humans do when translating video games. This observation thus makes us wonder what their performance would be in this scenario, but more importantly how useful they could be to translators.

2 State of the Art

As we mentioned, the advances in NMT architectures and domain adaptation techniques allowed for better performances in various domains. In the cultural sector, machine translation has mostly been used in the process of film subtitling, but a growing number of studies has focused on the challenges of its development, for instance, with literary texts (Sakamoto, 2020; Hansen, 2021).

Concerning video games, it is hard to find scientific sources that go further than acknowledging the existence of MT within this sector, as in O'Hagan and Mangiron (2013). This use of machine translation is further confirmed in various online posts and articles, but also in sessions dedicated to localization at the Game Developers Conference (Bartlet et al., 2014; IGDA, 2018). Some online translation service providers also put it forward, alongside with the traditional arguments of cost and time savings that typically accompany MT, and it would appear that some studios and translators are sometimes forced to turn to this technology in order to meet the strict and tight deadlines of the industry. It remains nevertheless agreed that MT would never be suitable for the translation of the more creative in-game contents, such as dialogues (O'Hagan and Mangiron, 2013). We can once again find confirmation for this observation in online interviews (Ruete, 2021), but also in the deployment and user feedback of open source tools like *RetroArch* (Libretro, 2019), that leverage Google's translation service to make retro games accessible to a larger public.

Machine translation, however, might benefit the video game localization industry, whether it is to cope with the heavy requirements of a simultaneous multilingual game delivery, to help fans make their content available to more people, or to assist professionals during this long-term and demanding task. Yet, we have found no evidence of MT tools being specifically adapted for the translation of video games, and the existing use of MT as well as the advances in NMT make it the perfect time to try and see how effective such a custom engine could be. To our knowledge, this is thus the first article to dive deeply into the possibility of video game machine translation, or, at the very least, that an MT system was specifically designed for such a task.

3 Methodology

Video game translation is an eminently difficult task that involves linguistic skills and cultural awareness from the two languages at hand, diegetic knowledge about the world in which the game takes place, as well as an understanding of how the game is to be played in real life and how the translation fits into its development. To have an idea of whether MT could be of help to professional translators, we built a first system tailored to the translation of video games for the English–French language pair.

This system was trained with the 2nd edition of the OpenNMT framework (Klein et al., 2017) on a custom-made corpus of video game translations. Our bespoke MT engine was then evaluated on two role-playing games (RPG), namely *The Elder Scrolls V: Skyrim* (Bethesda Game Studios, 2011) and *Fallout 4* (Bethesda Game Studios, 2015), taking place in a high fantasy and post-apocalyptic setting respectively.

3.1 Data set

For this task, we used a relatively small in-domain data set (of about 1 million sentences), that combines the official translations for 22 games, mainly from the fantasy and post-apocalyptic RPG genre.[4] The same corpus was used to train both models, but we extracted validation and test samples without replacement for each game being evaluated.

	Sentences	EN tokens	FR tokens
Training	951,373	16,942,551	18,008,101
Validation	4,785	70,576	74,189
Test	501	8,574	9,254

Table 1: Data sets for *The Elder Scrolls V: Skyrim* (Bethesda Game Studios, 2011).

	Sentences	EN tokens	FR tokens
Training	951,861	16,958,940	18,020,052
Validation	4,401	56,486	64,738
Test	397	6,275	6,754

Table 2: Data sets for *Fallout 4* (Bethesda Game Studios, 2015).

These titles were chosen not only for their wide popularity, but also because they are representative of the multiple difficulties professionals might have to face in this industry. One of them is the sheer volume of in-game content to be translated, which often results in multiple translators working on the same project (Díaz Montón, 2007). On top of this, both games make use of a very specific terminology that draws from their distinct fictional universe. This abundance of lexical creations, or *irrealia* (Loponen, 2009), is a challenge in its own right, especially if the work is collaborative in nature or if professionals are not familiar with it, but this aspect is all the more important as this terminology builds on previous titles.

The Elder Scrolls and the Fallout series have indeed distinguished themselves through their rich mythopoetic universe, which partly explains why fans have taken such an interest in creating content in and around the games. Proof of this is the breadth of the fictional literature found in *Skyrim* for instance. The number of these metadiegetic works and their size — several hundred pages for some — actually lead us to delete all books from the Elder Scrolls games in our corpus, as it would have needed an additional and separate alignment process, but they were the only material removed from the original files.

The acquisition method for this corpus was inspired by the work of hobbyist modders. This type of content is a useful way to foster player engagement and to extend the lifespan of a game, which is why developers and distributors facilitate the creation and sharing of content through the release of toolkits or dedicated interfaces such as the workshop section in *Steam* (Valve, 2003). Today, platforms such as the mod repository *Nexus Mods*[5] or the amateur French translation team *La Confrérie des Traducteurs*[6] serve as a testament to the dedication of some of the fans. Among these mods, a few pieces of software are built from scratch to help with the translation process.[7] They rely on custom translation memories (TMs) and allow the user to load translation files from existing games to help speed up and improve the quality of the translation.

[4] For a more detailed overview of the corpus, see appendix A.

[5] `https://www.nexusmods.com/`.

[6] `https://www.confrerie-des-traducteurs.fr/`.

[7] It might be important to keep in mind here that such practices are not at all intended to replace professional translators, but only to extend the reach of works that would never be translated otherwise.

And although most of these users are probably not even aware of this, the process is exactly similar to that of computer-assisted translation tools, which have long been used by professionals.[8]

In a similar fashion, we were able to retrieve the translation files for a number of games, convert them from their native format into spreadsheet files, and align each pair in a standard translation memory format though the *Heartsome TMX Editor 8.0* (Heartsome Technologies Ltd, 2014). The resulting bitexts were cleaned semi-manually with the same program and a few regex manipulations to discard duplicate, empty and untranslated segments, to normalize the extremely varied typographic conventions and to remove game-specific formatting — most tags and variables were still left as such. We then extracted and compiled the remaining 956,661 segments, many of which contain more than one sentence.

Since 1 million bilingual segments is scarce for NMT — 6 million is even considered "frugal" by today's standards (Blin, 2021) — we also built models which we fine-tuned on our gaming data set. The initial training was performed on common generic data sets for the same language pair: *Books*, *Europarl-v8*, *GlobalVoices-2018*, *News-Commentary-v16*, and *TED2020* (Tiedemann, 2012), for a total of 2,923,826 additional aligned sentences.[9]

3.2 Architecture

In each case, data sets were tokenized with Moses (Koehn et al., 2007) and further segmented with sentencepiece's unigram model (Kudo, 2018), using a vocabulary size of 32,000 tokens. We then trained two Transformer models for each scenario (fine-tuned and in-domain only) with OpenNMT's default parameters and the "base" architecture described in Vaswani et al. (2017): 6 encoder and decoder layers, 8 attention heads, a dimension of 512 and feed-forward layers of size 2048, with dropout 0.1. We stopped training models after convergence (200,000 steps) and translated all files with the default parameters of OpenNMT again, which uses a beam size of 5 at inference.

4 Results

For evaluation, we detokenized the output with the same Moses script and computed a BLEU score with sacreBLEU (Post, 2018). We first report in Table 3 the score obtained on *The Elder Scrolls V: Skyrim* and *Fallout 4*, two games for which we could compare the output with the official translation. These test sets contained mostly dialogues and, to a lesser extent, quest descriptions, action choices and instructions.

Our first comparison indicated that adding data did not necessarily increase performance. In the first case, the added 3 million segments resulted in a negligible increase in BLEU, whereas that score even decreased in the second case. For this reason, and since our aim was to evaluate systems trained on in-domain data, we discarded the tuned models. This decision was further motivated by our evaluation of the resulting translations, which showed that the in-domain models seemed to learn inherent rules of the domain which the fine-tuned models did not, such as the fact that gendered variables tend to disappear when translating into French:

	In-domain	**Fine-tuned**
Skyrim	37.14	37.38
Fallout 4	31.18	30.52

Table 3: Score given by sacreBLEU for the in-domain only and fine-tuned models on both games.

[8] Apart from in-house teams however, the use of TMs remains relatively uncommon in the video game industry.

[9] An experiment was also carried out with the dozens of millions of sentences from the WMT 2014 translation task (Bojar et al., 2014), but the final score dropped systematically due to the quality and dissimilarity of these data sets.

SRC: Is it true what they say? There was a dragon held captive in Whiterun, and you... you released it? **By the gods, woman, why?**

HYP (fine-tuned): C'est vrai ce qu'ils disent ? Il y avait un dragon captif à Blancherive, et vous... vous l'avez libéré ? **Par les dieux, femme, pourquoi ?**

HYP (in-domain): C'est vrai ce qu'on raconte ? Il y avait un dragon emprisonné à Blancherive et vous... vous l'avez libéré ? **Par les dieux, pourquoi ?**

REF: C'est vrai, ce qu'on raconte ? Qu'il y avait un dragon captif à Blancherive et que vous l'avez délivré ? **Mais pourquoi, par les dieux ?**

In doing so, we could assess more accurately the performance of systems trained only on data from the video game domain, which are already very encouraging considering that we used such a small training data set. To illustrate these results more clearly, we provide in Table 4 and Table 5 a comparison with publicly available systems using three measures provided by sacreBLEU. For each, an arrow indicates if the improvement is reflected by a higher or a lower score.[10]

	BLEU ⇑	chrF2++ ⇑	TER ⇓
Google Translate	27.75	48.25	66.75
DeepL	29.27	50.04	61.26
Custom	37.14	55.80	53.32

Table 4: Scores given by sacreBLEU for the custom and publicly available systems on *Skyrim*.

	BLEU ⇑	chrF2++ ⇑	TER ⇓
Google Translate	26.05	45.35	72.39
DeepL	27.60	47.04	67.94
Custom	31.18	48.80	62.96

Table 5: Scores given by sacreBLEU for the custom and publicly available systems on *Fallout 4*.

These automatic metrics are heavily dependent on form and processing, but this evolution gives an idea of the improvement, which according to Toral and Way (2015) should achieve at the very least a BLEU score of 20 to be useful in a post-editing workflow. To better describe the results, however, this last section offers a more qualitative analysis.

5 Analysis

As noted by Marie et al. (2021), MT evaluation has become less comprehensive and reliable over the last years, but one way to overcome this pitfall is to support automatic evaluation with human analysis. For this reason, we present two sets of evaluations. The first conveys the broad trends observed in our analysis of the two games presented previously, which we cannot publish for copyright reasons. We will further illustrate these remarks with a second set offering concrete examples from the translation of a fan-made mod. We believe the best way to transparently convey and judge the result of an automatically translated text is to provide a full and continuous example of this translation, so we have made it available online and we report here the index of the quoted sentence where appropriate.[11]

[10] Metric signatures for sacreBLEU (publicly available systems tested on 23/12/2020):
BLEU #:1|c:mixed|e:no|tok:13a|s:exp|v:2.0.0
chrF2++ #:1|c:mixed|e:yes|nc:6|nw:2|s:no|v:2.0.0
TER #:1|c:lc|t:tercom|nr:no|pn:yes|a:no|v:2.0.0.

[11] `https://gitlab.uliege.be/dhansen/VGMT-article/`.
We provide 323 segments, broken down into four illustrative excerpts. They are mainly made up of the dialogues that are often raised as criticism against MT and that were chosen because they formed mostly coherent pieces of conversation, with the exception of disrupting segments that are typical of video game files. The first excerpt is singular, as it contains segments from the 2002 game, which therefore also appear in our original training data. We included it nonetheless,

The mod, named *Beyond Skyrim*, comes from the fifth instalment of the Elder Scrolls series and has been in development for multiple years, with the aim of adding seven more provinces faithful to the game universe in addition to the only one featured in the original title. This includes a province featured in a former opus of the franchise, *The Elder Scrolls III: Morrowind* (Bethesda Softworks, 2002), on which we focused our attention. While there remains typical MT errors that require the intervention of a trained translator, the actual texts produced by our adapted engine for this mod made it also clear that such tools could be useful to the translation of games developed by studios and fan-made content.

5.1 General observations

As a note, we should clarify that these are not exhaustive analyses, but rather the main trends observed when assessing the resulting translations and subsequently using this material with students to initiate discussions about MT. We also provide a few examples, but we strongly invite readers to have their own look at the output. The main and somewhat expected observation is that although *Google Translate* and *DeepL* reach a respectable BLEU score and produce mostly understandable solutions, the concrete results seem hardly adapted to a video game translation, in particular when compared to an adapted system.

Indeed, both online systems have a hard time when it comes to **register**, for instance. Whereas our system was generally able to render the high register and medieval feel of *Skyrim*'s original French translation as well as the particularly colloquial, even crude register of *Fallout*, both were neutralized with the online tools (cf. in the provided translation to segments 7, 26). We noticed nonetheless that the training data from one game contaminated translations for the other, as crude language appeared on rare occasions in *Skyrim* and *Fallout*'s dialogues were sometimes too polite, or the French distinction between the informal/formal 2nd person singular/plural was not observed (97, 98, 115). This suggests that even with an in-domain data set, it could be useful to go beyond this simple video game adaptation and give different weights to the training data in order to further adapt the system on specific video games or franchises.

Another evident advantage of a custom system for which we do not even need to point to a given example is its ability to translate virtually all of the fictional content and terms from the games, be it names of people, institutions, places, spells, monsters, items, mythological concepts, expressions from constructed languages... This is all the more salient as terms such as "Dragonborn" (*Enfant de dragon*), "Greybeards" (*Grises-Barbes*) or "Skyrim" (*Bordeciel*) are at the very core of the story, and this **vocabulary** is always left untranslated by *Google Translate* or *DeepL*. A particularly representative example comes from *Fallout 4*, where "Dogmeat", the name of a dog companion, has been translated by *la viande de chien* in *DeepL* (literally "the canine flesh") instead of the meat brand for dogs (*Canigou*) that is used in the game. Closely related is the rules for the **capitalization** of words that are much more restrictive in French and observed by the personalized engine, whereas the online tools systematically copy the English case.

We have also noticed that our MT system has learned translation strategies used to anticipate **gender** variation. Indeed, players can often choose their gender in video games, but this is even more visible in *Skyrim*, where they can also choose between various fantasy races. While this is not a problem in English, many words referring to the player character change according to gender in French. As such, the common translation strategy is to neutralize the potential gender pitfall by deleting every direct mention of gender (as illustrated above), not using tenses that require a feminine or masculine form (cf. 28), omitting gendered words (218) or

as these intertextual references can be frequent and we will see that the system sometimes takes liberties with these. There follows three other excerpts for which the quality can be judged respectively as good, average or less adequate. For each of these, we also provide another machine translation suggested by the generic tool *DeepL* on 25/02/2022.

using generic terms/paraphrases in their stead (16). Our custom engine has applied this strategy systematically, interestingly showing that NMT can learn not only specific vocabulary but also translation strategies that can anticipate common sources of error in video game translations.

Lastly, the adapted MT engine offers surprising results as a whole with the translation of these **dialogues**. This if even true of khajiit and argonian languages, two races in the game speaking from a specific third-person point of view. There remains, however, notable difficulties, such as with characters speaking in a way that is depicted as drunk (250–252), with some — not all — idioms (208), colloquial speech (117, 212), or oral language that is ripe with pauses or incomplete sentences (128, 303) that the system tries to complete by itself.

A localization-related difficulty shared by all systems lies in the **ambiguities** between imperatives and infinitives, that take the same form in English but not in French. Paired with the lack of context, it is thus very hard for MT to differentiate between dialogue choices, orders given to the player or quest objectives and maintain a coherent translation. Hence, both French forms *-er* / *-ez* appear somewhat randomly. This is a challenge that human translators can face if they are not given any context, but that could be alleviated for both human and machine by using tags. A final obstacle faced by MT which makes human intervention imperative is its tendency to **translate literally** (61), especially when idioms are concerned (300), although we should perhaps remind that our model was trained with extremely limited data. More resources could improve this last point, as well as those that follow.

A last and interesting observation is that MT happens to correct human errors, which can be due to either time pressure or a lack of intersemiotic context, such as when the text describes a geographically situated object in the game and the translator cannot rely on any information. These scenarios reinforce our idea that MT could improve the quality of the final translation, by offering alternative solutions or encouraging translators to reflect on ambiguities.

5.2 Machine translation of fan-made content

Leaving behind questions of reference or comparison between generic and adapted models, we now want to delve into more a more language-specific analysis. For this, we focus exclusively on the translation of our mod and we continue to give references to specific examples.

The main observation, which is a known characteristic of NMT, is that while the system does not have many issues with form or fluency, there are many problems with meaning or adequacy. The most obvious and problematic are instances where the sentence is grammatically correct but has an **opposite meaning** (97, 112, 146, 263). In other cases, words are correctly translated but not in the given context, creating a **shift in meaning** (67, 114). On rarer occasions, words simply have a **wrong translation** (114, 132), or there is an **omission** (70) or **hallucination** (318) in the target text.

Our review has also highlighted other minor issues, for instance with **determiners**, especially if they are omitted in English (55, 75, 272). **Errors in the source text** can be problematic (289), even though this is not always the case (17). Finally, truecasing must be ignored seeing as case serves to distinguish most fantasy-related words, but terms in **all caps** usually confuse the machine (108, 244).

As a final note, we found that despite the presence of some segments in the training data for the first excerpt, the machine took some liberties with the translation. Some of these could arguably be said to work better than the original translation (36), but other dialogues show that the translation can simply vary while being equivalent to the reference (30), or introduce an error in the text (29). It is therefore necessary to remain mindful of these weaknesses. And while MT can bring more coherence between titles of the same franchise, these liberties can also be problematic, for instance with in-game books for which the translation should not be changed. With dialogues, however, these might lessen the feeling of *déjà vu* for players and rejuvenate the game experience through retranslation.

6 Discussion

As we have established in previous sections, we were able to achieve very encouraging results on a video game translation experiment by training an MT system on a surprisingly small in-domain data set. This was both expected and unexpected, in the sense that using relevant training data would logically boost performance and allow the system to assimilate specific terms or previously translated phrases, but we had not foreseen that this custom engine would learn abstract translation strategies that are particular to this domain, such as neutralizing variables when translating from a neutral into a gender-inflected language. We therefore think that, if implemented the right way, MT might be susceptible of helping with terminology and formal or standardized expressions, to offer relevant suggestions and maybe speed up the process, becoming a useful tool for either professional translators or amateurs working on fan translations.

This requires nevertheless that studios consider the translation process and resources as an integral part of the game development, which is not often the case and a source of problems even with human translation. Indeed, localization should be planned early in the development by rigorously following internationalization steps to accommodate translations into any language (Chandler and Deming, 2012). The use of MT further emphasizes this need, which could mean ensuring that texts are not hard-coded and mixed with lines of code, using tags that could be useful to human and machine to alleviate the ambiguities and lack of context, or refraining from imposing formal constraints to account for differences with languages other than English.

On the other hand, the video game industry benefits from a significant advantage, which is that all translations are already aligned and easily convertible into language resources. Yet, our study also highlighted the parallel between the decontextualized working conditions of the translator and the machine translation system. This lack of contextual information and resources is pointed as one of the main challenges translators have to face in the field (Bernal-Merino, 2008; Theroine et al., 2021), and one might wonder in these circumstances why translators so rarely have access to some kind of translation memory, or at least an official glossary. This alignment incidentally makes it easy to train MT systems tailored to the particular video game genre, or even specific works, which our study has shown to be able to effectively reproduce the expected terminology and offer relevant suggestions.

This might even come as a welcome change, if we consider that some professionals in the field (around 12%) already use MT in their workflow (Rivas Ginel and Theroine, 2021). With the convenience of a customized engine, we could even expect this number to rise, as such a tool help deliver faster translations, provide otherwise lacking information to translators and, most important of all, boost creativity. This last point might be the biggest asset of human translators in this domain, given that it is required to overcome the numerous technical and linguistic challenges that are typical of video game translation (Díaz Montón, 2007), without mentioning the very creative nature of the content itself. To this end, we plan to delve into a closer reading of these *ad hoc* MT solutions from the perspective of inter-semiotic dynamics (Houlmont, 2022).

In this respect, MT could free up time for creative thinking and particularly challenging segments or simply offer relevant suggestions, especially if it is used in combination with other tools and material such as TMs, reference corpora or termbases. However, we think this would happen if MT is used not as a first draft that may constrain the translation, but as a suggested translation akin to a TM match that would help correct points of interpretation in the source text, maintain stylistic and lexical cohesion, and even spot eventual mistakes in the target text.

On the amateur side, this technology could prove even more useful to fans for the translation of their user-generated content, thus expanding the success and replayability of their favourite games, or allowing games that were never intended to be translated to reach a wider audience. This, in turn, could promote cultural exchanges and sensitivity through a medium that otherwise tends to erase such influences against players' own expectations (Mandiberg, 2015).

All of these positive aspects of MT conversely depend on various ethical issues, the main one being the reason for its introduction. Relying on machine translation only for the sake of productivity, without human intervention, or blindly forcing its deployment even when it is not appropriate is sure to have a drastic impact on quality, creativity and the overall appeal of the game. Such habits evidently tie into much broader issues, some of which MT might even reinforce as in the case of amateur translations being used by companies seeking to cut costs. Finally, we should not forget that all of the resources used to train these systems depends on the quality of the material that is provided by human translators, whose rights seem to become less and less apparent as translation technologies progress (Bowker, 2021). We therefore hope that this exploratory article and its conclusions will hopefully start some discussions in the video game, or the cultural sector as a whole.

References

Bahdanau, Dzmitry, Kyunghyun Cho, and Yoshua Bengio (2014). Neural Machine Translation by Jointly Learning to Align and Translate. In *3rd International Conference on Learning Representations: Conference Track Proceedings*, pages 1–15, San Diego, CA.

Barnabé, Fanny (2015). Les détournements de jeux video par les joueurs. *Reset*, 4:1–42.

Bartlet, Michaela, Michel Buch Andersen, Beatrice Compagnon, Mike Dillinger, Declan Groves, and Kirti Vashee (2014). What is the Place of Machine Translation in Today's Gaming Industry? *2014 Game Developers Conference*. San Francisco, CA.

Bernal-Merino, Miguel (2008). Creativity in the Translation of Video Games. *Quaderns de Filologia: Estudis Literaris*, 13:57–70.

Bernal-Merino, Miguel (2015). *Translation and Localisation in Video Games: Making Entertainment Software Global*. Routledge, New York, NY.

Blin, Raoul (2021). Neural machine translation, corpus and frugality. *arXiv* preprint. arXiv:2101.10650.

Bojar, Ondřej, Christian Buck, Christian Federmann, Barry Haddow, Philipp Koehn, Johannes Leveling, Christof Monz, Pavel Pecina, Matt Post, Herve Saint-Amand, Radu Soricut, Lucia Specia, and Aleš Tamchyna (2014). Findings of the 2014 workshop on statistical machine translation. In *Proceedings of the Ninth Workshop on Statistical Machine Translation*, pages 12–58, Baltimore, MD. ACL.

Bowker, Lynne (2021). Translation technology and ethics. In Koskinen, Kaisa and Nike K. Pokorn, editors, *The Routledge Handbook of Translation and Ethics*, pages 187–221. Routledge, Abingdon, UK.

Chandler, Heather Maxwell and Stephanie O'Malley Deming (2012). *The Game Localization Handbook*. Jones & Bartlett Learning, Sudbury, MA, 2nd edition.

Chu, Chenhui and Rui Wang (2018). A Survey of Domain Adaptation for Neural Machine Translation. In *Proceedings of the 27th International Conference on Computational Linguistics*, pages 1304–1319, Santa Fe, NM. ACL.

Díaz Montón, Diana (2007). It's a Funny Game. *The Linguist*, 46(3):6–9.

Doherty, Stephen (2016). The Impact of Translation Technologies on the Process and Product of Translation. *International Journal of Communication*, 10:947–969.

Ellefsen, Ugo and Miguel Bernal-Merino (2018). Harnessing the Roar of the Crowd: A Quantitative Study of Language Preferences in Video Games of French Players of the Northern Hemisphere. *The Journal of Internationalization and Localization*, 5(1):21–48.

Fernández Costales, Alberto (2016). Analyzing Players' Perceptions on the Translation of Video Games: Assessing the Tension between the Local and the Global Concerning Language Use. In Esser, Andrea, Miguel Bernal-Merino, and Robert Smith, editors, *Media Across Borders Localizing TV, Film, and Video Games*, pages 182–201. Routledge, New York, NY.

Gambier, Yves (2016). Rapid and Radical Changes in Translation and Translation Studies. *International Journal of Communication*, 10:887–906.

Geurts, Francine (2015). What do you want to play? the desirability of video game translations from english into dutch according to dutch gamers and non-gamers. Master's thesis, Leiden University.

Hansen, Damien (2021). Les lettres et la machine : un état de l'art en traduction littéraire automatique. In *Actes de la 28e Conférence sur le Traitement Automatique des Langues Naturelles*, volume 2, pages 28–45, Lille, France. ATALA.

Honeywood, Richard and Jon Fung (2012). Best Practices for Game Localization. IGDA Localization SIG.

Houlmont, Pierre-Yves (2022). Traduire le jeu vidéo : un équilibrage des dynamiques intersémiotiques. *Sciences du jeu*, 17.

Hurel, Pierre-Yves (in press). L'amateurisme comme processus au cœur de la culture vidéoludique. In Krichane, Selim, Isaac Pante, and Yannick Rochat, editors, *Penser (avec) la culture vidéoludique : Discours, pratique, pédagogie*, pages 187–221. Presses universitaires de Liège, Liège, Belgium.

IDEA Consult, Goethe-Institut, Sylvia Amann, and Joost Heinsius (2021). Cultural and creative sectors in post-COVID-19 Europe: Crisis effects and policy recommendations. European Parliament.

IGDA (2018). Recap of our Roundtable at GDC. *Game Developer*, April 4.

Jenkins, Henry (2006). *Convergence Culture: Where Old and New Media Collide*. New York University Press, New York, NY.

Klein, Guillaume, Yoon Kim, Yuntian Deng, Jean Senellart, and Alexander Rush (2017). OpenNMT: Open-Source Toolkit for Neural Machine Translation. In *Proceedings of ACL 2017, System Demonstrations*, pages 67–72, Vancouver, Canada. ACL.

Koehn, Philipp, Hieu Hoang, Alexandra Birch, Chris Callison-Burch, Marcello Federico, Nicola Bertoldi, Brooke Cowan, Wade Shen, Christine Moran, Richard Zens, Chris Dyer, Ondřej Bojar, Alexandra Constantin, and Evan Herbst (2007). Moses: Open Source Toolkit for Statistical Machine Translation. In *Proceedings of the 45th Annual Meeting of the ACL on Interactive Poster and Demonstration Sessions*, pages 177–180, Prague, Czech Republic. ACL.

Kudo, Taku (2018). Subword Regularization: Improving Neural Network Translation Models with Multiple Subword Candidates. In *Proceedings of the 56th Annual Meeting of the Association for Computational Linguistics*, pages 66–75, Melbourne, Australia. ACL.

Lavault-Olléon, Elisabeth (2011). L'ergonomie, nouveau paradigme pour la traductologie. *ILCEA*, 14:1–17.

Loponen, Mika (2009). Translating Irrealia: Creating a Semiotic Framework for the Translation of Fictional Cultures. *Chinese semiotic studies*, 2(1):165–175.

Mandelin, Clyde and Tony Kuchar (2017). *This be book bad translation, video games!* Fangamer, Tucson, AZ.

Mandiberg, Stephen (2015). Playing (with) the Trace: Localized Culture in *Phoenix Wright*. *Kinephanos*, 5(1):111–141.

Marie, Benjamin, Atsushi Fujita, and Raphael Rubino (2021). Scientific Credibility of Machine Translation Research: A Meta-Evaluation of 769 Papers. In *Proceedings of the 59th Annual Meeting of the Association for Computational Linguistics and the 11th International Joint Conference on Natural Language Processing*, pages 7297–7306. ACL.

Muñoz Sánchez, Pablo (2009). Video Game Localisation for Fans by Fans: The Case of Romhacking. *The Journal of Internationalization and Localization*, 1(1):168–185.

O'Hagan, Minako (2013). *Game Localization: Translating for the Global Digital Entertainment Industry*. John Benjamins, Amsterdam, Netherlands.

O'Hagan, Minako and Carmen Mangiron (2013). *Game Localization: Translating for the global digital entertainment industry*. John Benjamins, Amsterdam, Netherlands.

Post, Matt (2018). A Call for Clarity in Reporting BLEU Scores. In *Proceedings of the Third Conference on Machine Translation: Research Papers*, pages 186–191, Brussels, Belgium. ACL.

Rivas Ginel, María Isabel and Sarah Theroine (2021). Machine Translation and Gender Biases in Video Game Localisation: A Corpus-Based Analysis. *Colloque interdisciplinaire "Vers une robotique du traduire ?"*. Strasbourg, France.

Ruete, Borja (2021). El Juego del Calamar usa posedición, ¿hay traducción automática en los videojuegos? *MeriStation*, November 24.

Sakamoto, Akiko (2020). The Value of Translation in the Era of Automation: An Examination of Threats. In Desjardins, Renée, Claire Larsonneur, and Philippe Lacour, editors, *When Translation Goes Digital: Case Studies and Critical Reflections*, pages 231–255. Palgrave Macmillan, Cham, Switzerland.

Theroine, Sarah, María Isabel Rivas Ginel, and Aurélie Perrin (2021). Au coeur de la terminologie du jeu vidéo. L'absence de ressources, frein majeur pour les traducteurs. *Traduire*, 244:27–40.

Tiedemann, Jörg (2012). Parallel Data, Tools and Interfaces in OPUS. In *Proceedings of the Eighth International Conference on Language Resources and Evaluation*, pages 2214–2218, Instanbul, Turkey. ELRA.

Toral, Antonio and Andy Way (2015). Machine-Assisted Translation of Literary Text: A Case Study. *Translation Spaces*, 4(2):240–267.

van Dijck, José (2009). Users like you? Theorizing agency in user-generated content. *Media, Culture & Society*, 31(1):41–58.

Vaswani, Ashish, Noam Shazeer, Niki Parmar, Jakob Uszkoreit, Llion Jones, Aidan N. Gomez, Łukasz Kaiser, and Illia Polosukhin (2017). Attention is All you Need. In *Proceedings of the 31st International Conference on Neural Information Processing Systems*, pages 6000–6010, Long Beach, CA. Curran Associates.

Vazquez-Calvo, Boris, Leticia Tian Zhang, Mariona Pascual, and Daniel Cassany (2019). Fan translation of games, anime, and fanfiction. *Language, Learning and Technology*, 23(1):49–71.

Appendix A. Corpus Specifications.

	Game	Developer	Size
1.	*Baldur's Gate*	BioWare, 1998	19 K segments
2.	*Baldur's Gate II: Shadows of Amn*	BioWare, 2000	62 K segments
3.	*Darkest Dungeon*	Red Hook Studios, 2016	8 K segments
4.	*Divinity: Original Sin II*	Larian Studios, 2017	85 K segments
5.	*Fallout*	Black Isle Studios, 1997	26 K segments
6.	*Fallout 2*	Black Isles Studios, 1998	56 K segments
7.	*Fallout 3*	Bethesda Game Studios, 2008	49 K segments
8.	*Fallout: New Vegas*	Obsidian Entertainment, 2010	64 K segments
9.	*Fallout 4*	Bethesda Game Studios, 2015	126 K segments
10.	*Planescape: Torment*	Black Isle Studios, 1999	39 K segments
11.	*Pillars of Eternity*	Obsidian Entertainment, 2015	48 K segments
12.	*Star Wars: Battlefront II*	Pandemic Studios, 2005	4 K segments
13.	*The Elder Scolls III: Morrowind*	Bethesda Softworks, 2002	37 K segments
14.	*The Elder Scrolls IV: Oblivion*	Bethesda Game Studios, 2006	40 K segments
15.	*The Elder Scrolls V: Skyrim*	Bethesda Game Studios, 2011	70 K segments
16.	*The Witcher 2: Assassins of Kings*	CD Projekt, 2011	32 K segments
17.	*The Witcher 3: Wild Hunt*	CD Projekt RED, 2015	78 K segments
18.	*Torment: Tides of Numenéra*	inXile Entertainment, 2017	49 K segments
19.	*Ultima VII: The Black Gate*	Origin Systems, 1992	12 K segments
20.	*Ultima VIII: Pagan*	Origin Systems, 1994	6 K segments
21.	*Ultima IX: Ascension*	Origin Systems, 1999	9 K segments
22.	*Wasteland 2*	inXile Entertainment, 2014	37 K segments
Total			956 K segments

Customization options for language pairs without English

Daniele Giulianelli
Leader Translations / POPM Newsroom @ Comparis

AMTA 2022

comparis.ch

Comparis

Online comparison

CONTENT AND SEO
Insurance, mortgages, consumer finance & more

1

IN SWITZERLAND

4

USER LANGUAGES

70%

NON-ENGLISH PAIRS

Translations at Comparis

Machine translation post-editing

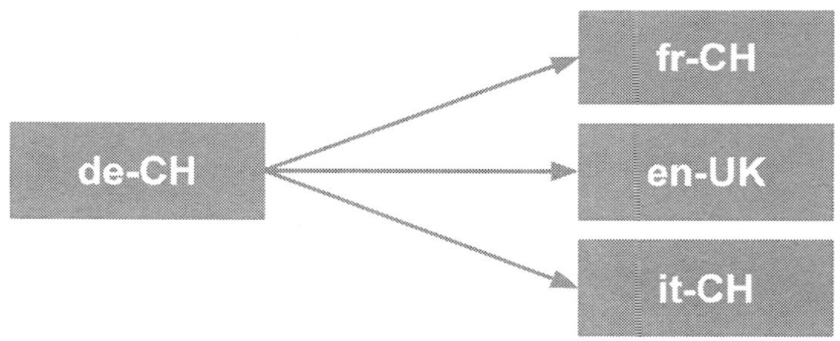

99% NOT FROM ENGLISH

70% NON-ENGLISH PAIRS

3

Translations at Comparis

Why does generic MT fail?

Comparis **domains**

Insurance, mortgages, consumer finance...

Swiss **target locales**

fr-CH, it-CH...

Terminology, price formatting, formality

4

Choosing the right MT engine

Custom Machine Translation is often not supported for non-English pairs

~~Google~~, ~~Microsoft~~, ~~DeepL~~...

Quality ⬇ Post-Editing Effort ⬆

5

Why ModernMT?

	Google	Microsoft	DeepL	ModernMT
Customizable with parallel data	✔	✔	✘	✔
Support for non-English language pairs	✘	✘	✘	✔
Adaptive + HITL	✘	✘	✘	✔
Easy to train	✘	✘	✔	✔

- also **cheaper** than DeepL and Google AutoML

6

1.Customization
2. Quality ↑
3. Post-editing effort ↓

Initial quality evaluation

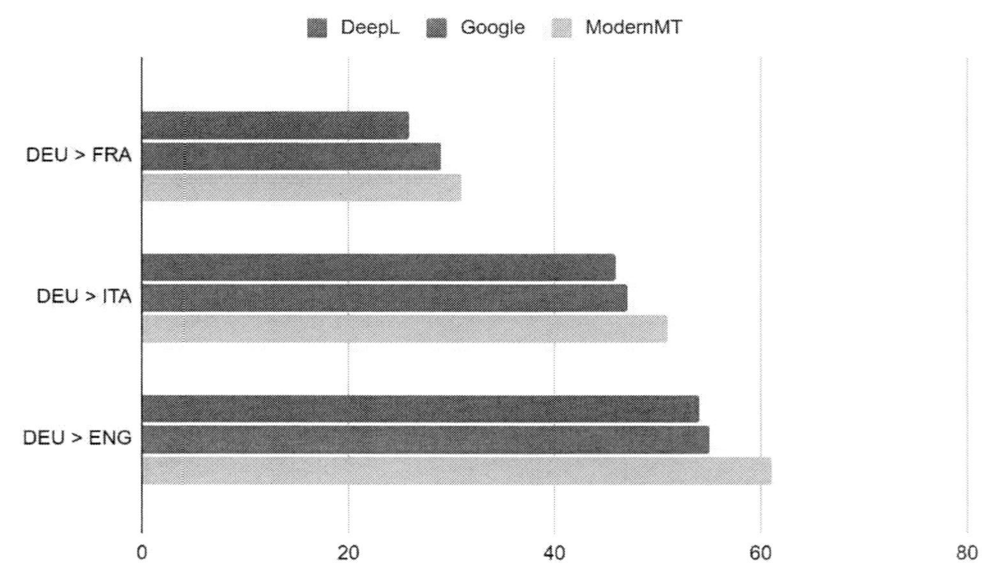

ModelFront analysis between generic DeepL, generic GT, customized ModernMT with one year of our in-house translations (2020)

8

TMS and integrations

	RWS	Lokalise	Crowdin	XTM
ModernMT integration	✔	*no custom MT at all*	✔	**via Intento**
Jira integration	✕	±	✔	✔
Terminology workflow	✕	✕	✕	✔
TM management	✔	✔	✔	✔

9

Initial results

We launched post-editing in February 2022.

4
SERVICE TIERS
Transcreation, HT, FPE, LPE

+30%
PRODUCTIVITY INCREASE

0
QUALITY CHANGE

Next challenges

- **Monitor final quality**
  - Human evaluation
- Monitor **post-editing effort**
  - By engine version, service tier
- **Predict post-editing effort**
  - Quality estimation for PI planning
- **Filter training data**
  - Adaptive - live customisation requires live filtering
  - High service tier to low service tier only
- **Improve TMS integration**
- Monitor value
  - **SEO signals** (engagement, conversion...) → Service tier

11

Danke vielmol
Merci
Grazie
Grazia fitsch
Thank you
Special thanks to:
- Laura Gianinazzi, PM Translations and "partner in crime"
- The Comparis Translations Team
- Elisabeth Rizzi & the whole Comparis Newsroom

Boosting Neural Machine Translation with Similar Translations

Jitao Xu[†‡], **Josep Crego**[†], **Jean Senellart**[†]

[†]SYSTRAN, 5 rue Feydeau, 75002 Paris, France
firstname.lastname@systrangroup.com
[‡]Université Paris-Saclay, CNRS, LIMSI, 91400, Orsay, France
jitao.xu@limsi.fr

Abstract

This paper explores data augmentation methods for training Neural Machine Translation to make use of similar translations, in a comparable way a human translator employs fuzzy matches. In particular, we show how we can simply feed the neural model with information on both source and target sides of the fuzzy matches, we also extend the similarity to include semantically related translations retrieved using distributed sentence representations. We show that translations based on fuzzy matching provide the model with "*copy*" information while translations based on embedding similarities tend to extend the translation "*context*". Results indicate that the effect from both similar sentences are adding up to further boost accuracy, are combining naturally with model fine-tuning and are providing dynamic adaptation for unseen translation pairs. Tests on multiple data sets and domains show consistent accuracy improvements. To foster research around these techniques, we also release an Open-Source toolkit with efficient and flexible fuzzy-match implementation.

1 Introduction

For decades, the localization industry has been proposing Fuzzy Matching technology in CAT tools allowing the human translator to visualize one or several fuzzy matches from translation memory when translating a sentence leading to higher productivity and consistency (Yamada, 2011). Hence, even though the concept of fuzzy match scores is not standardized and differs between CAT tools (Bloodgood and Strauss, 2014), translators generally accept discounted translation rate for sentences with "high" fuzzy matches[1]. With improving machine translation technology and training of models on translation memories, machine translated output has been progressively introduced as a substitute for fuzzy matches when no sufficiently "good" fuzzy match is found and proved to also increase translator productivity given appropriate post-editing environment (Plitt and Masselot, 2010).

These two technologies are entirely different in their finality - indeed, for a given source sentence, fuzzy matching is just a database retrieval and scoring technique always returning a pair of source and target segments, while machine translation is actually building an original translation. However, with Statistical Machine Translation, the two technologies are sharing the same simple idea about managing and retrieving optimal combination of longest translated n-grams and this property led to the development of several techniques like use of fuzzy matches in SMT decoding (Koehn and Senellart, 2010; Wang et al., 2013), adaptive machine translation (Zaretskaya et al., 2015) or "fuzzy match repairing" (Ortega et al., 2016).

With Neural Machine Translation (NMT), the integration of Fuzzy Matching is less obvious since NMT does not keep nor build a database of aligned sequences and does not explicitly use n-gram language models for decoding. The only obvious and important use of translation memory is to use them to train an NMT model from scratch or to adapt a generic translation model to a specific domain (fine-tuning) (Chu and Wang, 2018). While some works propose architecture changes (Zhang et al., 2018) or decoding constraints (Gu et al., 2018); a recent work (Bulté and Tezcan, 2019; Bulté et al., 2018) has proposed a simple and elegant framework where, like for human translation, translation of fuzzy matches are presented simultaneously with source sentence and the network learns to use this additional information. Even though this method has showed huge gains in quality, it also opens

[1]https://signsandsymptomsoftranslation.com/2015/03/06/fuzzy-matches/.

many questions.

In this work, we are pushing the concept further a) by proposing and evaluating new integration methods, b) by extending the notion of similarity and showing that fuzzy matches can be extended to embedding-based similarities, c) by analyzing how online fuzzy matching compares and combines with offline fine-tuning. Finally, our results also show that introducing similar sentence translation is helping NMT by providing sequences to copy (*copy effect*), but also providing additional context for the translation (*context effect*).

2 Translation Memories and NMT

A translation memory (TM) is a database that stores translated segments composed of a source and its corresponding translations. It is mostly used to match up previous translations to new content that is similar to content translated in the past.

Assuming that we translated the following English sentence into French: *[How long does the flight last?]* ⇝ *[Combien de temps dure le vol?]*. Both the English sentence and the corresponding French translation are saved to the TM. This way, if the same sentence appears in a future document (an *exact match*) the TM will suggest to reuse the translation that has just been saved. In addition to exact matches, TMs are also useful with *fuzzy matches*. These are useful when a new sentence is similar to a previously translated sentence, but not identical. For example, when translating the input sentence: *[How long does a cold last?]*, the TM may also suggest to reuse the previous translation since only two replacements (*a cold* by *the flight*) are needed to achieve a correct translation. TMs are used to reduce translation effort and to increase consistency over time.

2.1 Retrieving Similar Translations

More formally, we consider a TM as a set of K sentence pairs $\{(s_k, t_k) : k = 1, \ldots, K\}$ where s_k and t_k are mutual translations. A TM must be conveniently stored so as to allow fast access to the pair (s_k, t_k) that shows the highest similarity between s_k and any given new sentence. Many methods to compute sentence similarity have been explored, mainly falling into two broad categories: *lexical matches* (*i.e.* fuzzy match) and *distributional semantics*. The former relies on the number of overlaps between the sentences taken into account. The latter counts on the generalisation power of neural networks when building vector representations. Next, we describe the similarity measures employed in this work.

Fuzzy Matching Fuzzy matching is a lexicalised matching method aimed to identify non-exact matches of a given sentence. We define the fuzzy matching score $FM(s_i, s_j)$ between two sentences s_i and s_j as:

$$FM(s_i, s_j) = 1 - \frac{ED(s_i, s_j)}{max(|s_i|, |s_j|)}$$

where $ED(s_i, s_j)$ is the Edit Distance between s_i and s_j, and $|s|$ is the length of s. Many variants have been proposed to compute the edit distance, generally performed on normalized sentences (ignoring for instance case, number, punctuation, space or inline tags differences that are typically handled at a later stage). Also, IDF and stemming techniques are used to give more weight on significant words or less weight on morphological variants (Vanallemeersch and Vandeghinste, 2015; Bloodgood and Strauss, 2014).

Since we did not find an efficient TM fuzzy match library, we implemented an efficient and parameterizable algorithm in C++ based on suffix-array (Manber and Myers, 1993) that we open-sourced[2]. Fuzzy matching offers a great performance under large overlapping conditions. However, in some cases, sentences with large overlaps may receive low FM scores. Consider for instance the input: *[How long does the flight arriving in Paris from Barcelona last?]* and the TM entry of our previous example: *[How long does the flight last?]* ⇝ *[Combien de temps dure le vol?]*. Even though the TM entry may be of great help when translating the input sentence, it receives a low score ($1 - \frac{5}{12} = 0.583$) because of the multiple insertion/deletion operations needed. We thus introduce a second lexicalised similarity measure that focuses on finding the longest of n-gram overlap between sentences.

[2] https://github.com/systran/FuzzyMatch

N-gram Matching[3] We define the N-gram matching score $NM(s_i, s_j)$ between s_i and s_j:

$$NM(s_i, s_j) = \left| max\Big(\{\mathcal{N}(s_i) \cap \mathcal{N}(s_j)\}\Big) \right|$$

where $\mathcal{N}(s)$ denotes the set of n-grams in sentence s, $max(q)$ returns the longest n-gram in the set q and $|r|$ is the length of the n-gram r. For N-gram matching retrieval we also use our in-house open-sourced toolkit.

Distributed Representations The current research on sentence similarity measures has made tremendous advances thanks to distributed word representations computed by neural nets. In this work, we use `sent2vec`[4] (Pagliardini et al., 2018) to generate sentence embeddings. The network implements a simple but efficient unsupervised objective to train distributed representations of sentences. The authors claim that the algorithm performs state-of-the-art sentence representations on multiple benchmark tasks in particular for unsupervised similarity evaluation.

We define the similarity score $EM(s_i, s_j)$ between sentences s_i and s_j via cosine similarity of their distributed representations h_i and h_j:

$$EM(s_i, s_j) = \frac{h_i \cdot h_j}{||h_i|| \times ||h_j||}$$

where $||h||$ denotes the magnitude of vector h.

To implement fast retrieval between the input vector representation and the corresponding vector of sentences in the TM we use the `faiss`[5] toolkit (Johnson et al., 2019).

2.2 Related Words in TM Matches

Given an input sentence s, retrieving TM matches consists of identifying the TM entry (s_k, t_k) for which s_k shows the highest matching score. However, with the exception of perfect matches, not all words in s_k or s are present in the match. Considering the example in Section 2, the words *the flight* and *a cold* are not related to each other, from that follows that the TM target words *le vol* are irrelevant for the task at hand. In this section we discuss an algorithm capable of identifying the set of target words $\mathcal{T} \in t_k$ that are related to words of the input sentence s. Thus, we define the set $\mathcal{T}$ as:

$$\mathcal{T} = \left\{ \begin{array}{l} j \in t_k : \\ \quad \exists i \in \mathcal{LCS} \mid (i,j) \in \mathcal{A} \\ \wedge \quad \forall i \notin \mathcal{LCS} \mid (i,j) \notin \mathcal{A} \end{array} \right\}$$

where $\mathcal{A}$ is the set of word alignments between words in s_k and t_k, and $\mathcal{LCS}$ is the set of words in s_k which belong to the Longest Common Subsequence (LCS)[6] between s_k and s.

$\mathcal{LCS}$ is found as a sub-product of computing fuzzy or n-gram matches. Word alignments are performed by `fast_align`[7] (Dyer et al., 2013). Figure 1 illustrates the alignments and LCS between input sentences and their corresponding fuzzy (top) and N-gram (bottom) matches.

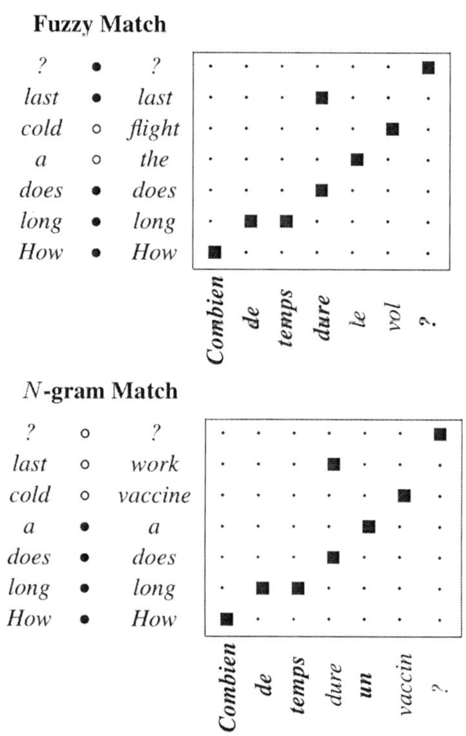

Figure 1: English-French TM entries with corresponding word alignments (right) and LCS of words with the input sentence (left). Matches are found following Fuzzy (top) and N-gram (bottom) techniques.

[3] Note that this practice is also called "subsequence" or "chunk" matching in CAT tools and is usually combined with source-target alignment in order to help human translators easily find translation fragments.

[4] `https://github.com/epfml/sent2vec`

[5] `https://github.com/facebookresearch/faiss`

[6] The LCS is computed as a by-product of the edit distance (Paterson and Dančík, 1994)

[7] `https://github.com/clab/fast_align`

The TM source sentence s_k of the fuzzy matching example has a $\mathcal{LCS}$ set of 5 words $\{How, long, does, last, ?\}$. The set of related target words $\mathcal{T}$ is also composed of 5 words $\{Combien, de, temps, dure, ?\}$, all aligned to at least one word in $\mathcal{S}$ and to no other word. The N-gram match example has a $\mathcal{LCS}$ set of 4 words $\{How, long, does, a\}$, while related target words $\mathcal{T}$ consists of $\{Combien, de, temps, un\}$. The target word *dure* is not part of $\mathcal{T}$ as it is aligned to *work* and *work* $\notin \mathcal{S}$. Notice that sets $\mathcal{S}$ and $\mathcal{T}$ consist of collections of indices (word positions in their corresponding sentences) while word strings are used in the previous examples to facilitate reading.

2.3 Integrating TM into NMT

We retrieve fuzzy, n-gram and sentence embedding matches as detailed in the previous section. We explore various ways to integrate matches in the NMT workflow. We follow the work by (Bulté and Tezcan, 2019) where the input sentence is augmented with the translation retrieved from the TM showing the highest matching score (FM, NM or EM). One special integration of fuzzy matching, denoted $\text{FM}_{\mathcal{T}}$, is rescoring fuzzy matches based on the *target edit distance*. This special integration, that is only performed on training data, is discussed in the **Target Fuzzy matches** section.

Figure 2 illustrates the main integration techniques considered in this work and detailed below. The input English sentence *[How long does the flight last?]* is differently augmented. For each alternative we show: the TM (English) sentence producing the match; the augmented input sentence with the corresponding TM (French) translation. Note that LCS words are displayed in boldface.

FM$^{\#}$ We implement the same format as detailed in (Bulté and Tezcan, 2019). The input English sentence is concatenated with the French translation with the (highest-scored) fuzzy match as computed by $FM(s_i, s_j)$. The token || is used to mark the boundary between both sentences.[8]

FM* We modify the previous format by masking the French words that are not related to the input sentence. Thus, sequences of unrelated tokens are replaced by the || token. The mechanism to identify relevant words is detailed in Section 2.2.

[8]The original paper uses '@@@' as break token. We made sure that || was not part of the vocabulary.

FM^{+} As a variant of FM*, we now mark target words which are not related to the input sentence in an attempt to help the network identify those target words that need to be copied in the hypothesis. However, we use an additional input stream (also called *factors*) to let the network access to the entire target sentence. Tokens used by this additional stream are: **S** for source words; **R** for unrelated target words and **T** for related target words.

NM^{+} In addition to fuzzy matches, we also consider arbitrary large n-gram matching. Thus, we use the same format as for FM^{+} but considering the highest scored n-gram match as computed by $NM(s_i, s_j)$.

EM^{+} Finally, we also retrieve the most similar TM sentences as computed by $EM(s_i, s_j)$. In this case, marking the words that are not related to the input sentence is not necessary since similar sentences retrieved following EM score do not necessarily present any lexical overlap. Note from the example in Table 2 that similar sentences retrieved with distributed representations may contain many word reorderings or synonyms (*i.e.*: *duration* – *last* or *flu* – *cold*) that makes it difficult to align both sentences. Hence, the same format employed for FM can be used here. However, since we plan to combine different kind of matches in a single model we adopt the format employed by NM^{+} and FM^{+} with a new factor label **E**.

FM$^{\#}$ — *How long does the flight last ?*

How long does** a cold **last ? || *Combien de temps dure le vol ?*

FM* — *How long does the flight last ?*

How long does** a cold **last ? || *Combien de temps dure || ?*

FM^{+} — *How long does the flight last ?*

How long does** a cold **last ? || *Combien de temps dure le vol ?*
S S S S S S S R T T T T R R T

NM^{+} — *How long does a vaccine work ?*

***How long does a** cold last ?* || *Combien de temps dure un vaccin ?*
S S S S S S S R T T T R T R R

EM^{+} — *What is the duration of flu symptoms ?*

How long does a cold last ? || *Quelle est la durée de la grippe ?*
S S S S S S S E E E E E E E E E

Figure 2: Input sentence augmented with different TM matches: FM$^{\#}$ (Bulté and Tezcan, 2019), FM*, FM^{+} and EM^{+}.

3 Experimental Framework

3.1 Corpora and Evaluation

We used the following corpora in this work[9] (Tiedemann, 2012): Proceedings of the European Parliament (EPPS); News Commentaries (NEWS); TED talk subtitles (TED); Parallel sentences extracted from Wikipedia (Wiki); Documentation from the European Central Bank (ECB); Documents from the European Medicines Agency (EMEA); Legislative texts of the European Union (JRC); Localisation files (GNOME, KDE4 and Ubuntu) and Manual texts (PHP). Detailed statistics about these are provided in Appendix A. We randomly split the corpora by keeping 500 sentences for validation, 1,000 sentences for testing and the rest for training. All data is preprocessed using the OpenNMT tokenizer[10] (conservative mode). We train a 32K joint byte-pair encoding (BPE) (Sennrich et al., 2016b) and use a joint vocabulary for both source and target.

Our NMT model follows the state-of-the-art Transformer base architecture (Vaswani et al., 2017) implemented in the `OpenNMT-tf`[11] toolkit (Klein et al., 2017). Further configuration details are given in Appendix B.

3.2 TM Retrieval

We perform fuzzy matching, ignoring exact matches, and keep the single best match if $FM(s_i, s_j) \geq 0.6$ with no approximation. Similarly, the largest N-gram match is used for each test sentence with a threshold $NM(s_i, s_j) \geq 5$. A similarity threshold $EM(s_i, s_j) \geq 0.8$ is also employed when retrieving similar sentences using distributed representations. The EM model is trained on the source training data with default *fasttext* params on 200 dimension, and 20 epochs.

Algorithm	Indexing (s)	Retrieval (word/s)
FM	546	607
NM	546	40,888
EM	181+342	4,142

Table 1: Indexing and retrieval time for the different matching algorithm run on single thread Intel Core i7, 2.8GHz. EM index time is the sum of embedding building for the 2M sentences and *faiss* index building.

[9] Freely available from `http://opus.nlpl.eu`

[10] `https://github.com/OpenNMT/Tokenizer`

[11] `https://github.com/OpenNMT/OpenNMT-tf`

The *faiss* search toolkit is used through python API with exact *FlatIP* index. Building and retrieval times for each algorithm on a 2M sentences translation memory (Europarl corpus) are provided in Table 1. Note that all retrieval algorithms are significantly faster than NMT Transformer decoding, thus, implying a very limited decoding overhead.

4 Results

We compare our baseline model, without augmenting input sentences, to different augmentation formats and retrieval methods. Our `base` model is built using the concatenation of all the original corpora. All other models extend the original corpora with sentences retrieved following various retrieval methods. It is worth to notice that extended bitexts share the target side with the original data.

Individual comparison of Matching algorithms and Augmentation methods In this experiment, all corpora are used to build the models while matches of a given domain are retrieved from the training data of this domain. Models are built using the original source and target training data (`base`), and after augmenting the source sentence as detailed in Section 2.3: $\text{FM}^{\#}$, $\text{FM}^{\#}_{T}$, FM^{*}, FM^{+}, NM^{+} and EM^{+}. Test sentences are augmented following the same technique as for training sentences[12]. Table 2 summarises the results that are divided in three blocks, showing results for the three types of matching studied in this work (FM, NM and EM).

Best scores are obtained by models using augmented inputs except for corpora not suited for translation memory usage: News, TED for which we observe no gains correlated to low matching rates. For the other corpora, large gains are achieved when evaluating test sentences with matches (up to +19 BLEU on GNOME corpus), while a very limited decrease in performance is observed for sentences that do not contain matches. This slight decrease is likely to come from the fact that we kept the corpus size and number of iterations identical while giving harder training tasks. Results are totally on par with the findings of (Bulté and Tezcan, 2019).

All types of matching indicate their suitability showing accuracy gains. In particular for fuzzy matching, which seems to be the best for our task. Among the different techniques used to insert fuzzy matching, FM^{+} obtains the best results, validating

[12] Except for $\text{FM}^{\#}_{T}$ for which we use $\text{FM}^{\#}$ test set

Model	News	TED	ECB	EMEA	JRC	GNOME	KDE4	PHP	Ubuntu	Avg
$\%FM$	*3.1%*	*10.3%*	*49.8%*	*69.8%*	*50.1%*	*59.7%*	*47.3%*	*41.0%*	*23.3%*	–
base	**37.16**	43.23	49.19	50.14	59.19	51.14	50.16	30.24	45.52	47.94
			57.69 - **41.95**	54.88 - 44.10	66.34 - 52.84	55.80 - **47.92**	53.05 - **48.77**	42.19 - 25.25	56.05 - 42.27	
$FM^{\#}$	36.68	42.93	55.15	61.16	66.35	61.82	54.37	33.10	48.26	54.32
			69.79 - 41.54	70.87 - 43.53	80.46 - 53.55	73.61 - 45.83	65.57 - 47.85	47.04 - 26.08	66.72 - 42.08	
$FM^{\#}_{T}$	36.79	43.14	55.41	60.32	66.41	62.01	53.65	33.22	**49.75**	54.40
			70.46 - 41.41	68.63 - **44.90**	80.57 - 53.57	74.05 - 45.58	64.77 - 47.20	46.31 - 26.30	**69.16** - **43.32**	
FM^{*}	36.44	**43.27**	54.52	59.49	65.24	59.54	53.30	32.77	48.74	53.37
			68.43 - 41.68	67.64 - 44.85	77.59 - **54.10**	70.16 - 45.19	62.63 - 48.00	44.50 - **26.31**	68.34 - 42.20	
FM^{+}	37.12	42.62	**56.18**	**61.97**	**66.91**	**62.68**	**54.59**	**33.81**	48.62	**54.97**
			72.26 - 41.25	**71.52** - 44.72	**81.58** - 53.62	**74.99** - 45.83	**65.95** - 48.01	**47.74** - 26.27	67.49 - 42.37	
$\%NM$	*45.5%*	*36.9%*	*69.9%*	*60.4%*	*69.6%*	*31.1%*	*22.9%*	*33.7%*	*14.1%*	–
base	**37.16**	**43.23**	49.19	50.14	59.19	51.14	50.16	30.24	45.52	47.94
			49.97 - **46.44**	50.94 - **47.43**	60.32 - **55.70**	53.86 - **46.59**	54.16 - **45.89**	34.64 - **26.88**	58.29 - **40.68**	
NM^{+}	36.74	43.07	**55.40**	**59.17**	**65.60**	**58.46**	**51.54**	**31.87**	**46.16**	**52.60**
			58.65 - 44.06	**62.69** - 46.60	**69.24** - 54.32	**70.05** - 42.21	**59.87** - 42.11	**39.35** - 26.10	**63.22** - 39.59	
base	**37.16**	**43.23**	49.19	50.14	59.19	51.14	50.16	30.24	45.52	47.94
			52.09 - 40.74	52.07 - 40.08	62.60 - 48.16	54.20 - **45.88**	51.62 - **48.60**	42.22 - **21.42**	52.20 - 41.82	
EM^{+}	36.50	42.89	**54.02**	**56.41**	**66.04**	**58.07**	**53.70**	**32.37**	**49.88**	**52.93**
			58.52 - **40.86**	**59.47** - **40.16**	**71.45** - **48.33**	**66.09** - 44.06	**59.43** - 47.43	**46.91** - 20.96	**62.04** - **43.20**	

Table 2: The first row in each block indicates the percentage of test sentences for which a match was found. Cells below contain the BLEU score over the entire test set (top number) and over the subset of test sentences augmented with matches (bottom left) and without matches (bottom right). Best scores of each column are outlined with bold fonts. Last column is the average of all corpus but News and TED.
For instance on KDE4: the base model obtains a BLEU score of 50.16 while FM^{+} obtains the highest score 54.59. Most of the gains are obtained over the test sentences having a fuzzy match (**65.95** vs. 53.05) while for sentences without fuzzy match the best score is obtained with the base system (**48.77** compared to 48.01).

Model	ECB	EMEA	JRC	GNOME	KDE4	PHP	Ubuntu	Avg
FM^{+}	56.18	61.97	66.91	62.68	54.59	33.81	48.62	54.97
$\ominus(FM^{+}, NM^{+})$	56.83	60.60	67.52	61.97	54.67	32.38	47.13	54.44
$\ominus(FM^{+}, EM^{+})$	56.71	61.61	67.64	62.71	54.82	**33.60**	**49.98**	55.30
$\ominus(FM^{+}, NM^{+}, EM^{+})$	56.20	61.30	67.43	62.14	55.05	32.33	48.96	54.77
$\oplus(FM^{+}, EM^{+})$	**57.08**	**62.27**	**68.06**	**63.30**	**55.48**	33.39	49.50	**55.58**
FT(base)	52.65	54.06	61.58	56.16	54.20	33.54	50.14	51.76
FT($\ominus(FM^{+}, EM^{+})$)	57.07	63.11	69.44	**65.97**	**59.30**	**36.26**	**52.77**	**57.70**
FT($\oplus(FM^{+}, EM^{+})$)	**57.44**	**63.41**	**69.82**	65.72	58.71	35.49	52.40	57.57

Table 3: BLEU scores of models combining several types of matches (2nd block) and over Fine-Tuned models (3rd block). We include again results of the FM^{+} model (1st block) to facilitate reading.

our hypothesis that marking related words is beneficial for the model. Masking sequences of unrelated words, FM^{*} under-performs showing that the neural network is more challenged when dealing with incomplete sentences than with sentences containing unrelated content.

Target fuzzy matches To evaluate if the fuzzy match quality is really the primary criterion for the observed improvements, we consider $\mathrm{FM}_T^{\#}$ where the fuzzy matches are rescored (on the training set only) with the edit distance between the reference translation and the target side of the fuzzy match. By doing so, we reduce the fuzzy match average FM source score by about 2%, but increase target edit distance from 61% to 69%.

The effect can be seen in Table 2 in the line $\mathrm{FM}_T^{\#}$ vs. $\mathrm{FM}^{\#}$. In average, this technique is performing better with large individual gains of +1.5 BLEU on the Ubuntu corpus. This shows that in this configuration where we do not differentiate related and unrelated words, the model mainly learns to copy fuzzy target words.

Unseen matches Note that in the previous experiments, matches were built over domain corpora that are already used to train the model. This is a common use case: the same translation memory used to train the system will be used in run time, but now we evaluate the ability of our model in a different context where a test set is to be translated for which we have a new TM that has never been seen when learning the original model. This use case corresponds to typical translation task where new entries will be added continuously to the TM and shall be used instantly for translation of following sentences. Hence, we only use EPPS, News, TED and Wiki data to build two models: the first employs only the original source and target sentences (base) the second learns to use fuzzy matches (FM^+). Table 4 shows results for this use case.

Model	ECB	EMEA	JRC	GNOME	KDE4	PHP	Ubuntu	Avg
$\%FM$	49.8	69.8	50.1	59.7	47.3	41.0	23.3	–
base	36.48	26.31	45.03	27.90	23.62	19.50	25.85	29.24
FM^+	**43.28**	**36.09**	**53.52**	**38.40**	**30.91**	**23.10**	**30.53**	**36.55**

Table 4: BLEU scores when models are only trained over EPPS, News, TED and Wiki datasets.

As it can be seen, the model using fuzzy matches shows clear accuracy gains. This confirms that gains obtained by FM^+ are not limited to remember an example previously "seen" during training. The model using fuzzy matches acquired the ability to actually copy or recycle words from the provided fuzzy matches and therefore is suitable for adaptive translation workflows. Note that all scores are lower than those showed in Table 2 as a result of discarding all in-domain data when training the models showing also that online use of translation memory is not a substitute for in-domain model fine-tuning as we will further investigate in **Fine Tuning**.

Combining matching algorithms Next, we evaluate the ability of our NMT models to combine different matching algorithms. First, we use $\ominus(M_1, M_2, ...)$ to denote the augmentation of an input sentence that considers first the match specified by M_1, if no match applies for the input sentence then it considers using the match specified by M_2, and so on. Note that at most one match is used. Sentences for which no match is found are kept without augmentation. Similar to Table 2, models are learned using all the available training data. Table 3 (2nd block) illustrates the results of this experiment. The first 3 lines show BLEU scores of models combining FM^+, NM^+ and EM^+. The last row illustrates the results of a model that learns to use two different matching algorithms. We use the best combination of matches obtained so far (FM^+ and EM^+) and augment input sentences with both matches. Figure 3 illustrates an example of an input sentence augmented with both a fuzzy match and an embedding match (FM^+ and EM^+). Notice that the model is able to distinguish between both types of augmented sequences by looking at the token used in the additional stream (*factor*). As it can be seen in Table 3 (2nd block), the best combination of matches is achieved by $\oplus(\mathrm{FM}^+, \mathrm{EM}^+)$ further boosting the performance of previous configurations. It is only surpassed by $\ominus(\mathrm{FM}^+, \mathrm{EM}^+)$ in two test sets by a slight margin.

Fine Tuning Results so far evaluate the ability of NMT models to integrate similar sentences. However, we have run our comparisons over a "generic" model built from a heterogeneous training data set while it is well known that these models do not achieve best performance on homogeneous test sets. Thus, we now assess the capability of our augmentation methods to enhance fine-tuned (Luong and Manning, 2015) models, a well known technique that is commonly used in domain adaptation scenarios obtaining state-of-the-art results. Table 3 illustrates the results of the model configurations previously described after fine-tuning the models towards each test set domain. Thus, building 7 fine-tuned models for each configuration. Note that similar sentences (matches) are retrieved from the same in-domain data sets used for fine tuning. As

$\oplus$(FM$^+$, EM$^+$)

How long does a cold last ? || Combien de temps dure le vol ? || Combien de temps dure un vaccin ?

S S S S S S S R T T T T R R T E E E E E E E E

Figure 3: Input sentence augmented with a fuzzy match FM$^+$ and an embedding match EM$^+$.

Token	base	FM$^\#$	FM$^+$	base	NM$^+$	base	EM$^+$	base	FT($\ominus$(FM$^+$, EM$^+$))
T	66.3%	79.9%	80.3%	68.9%	83.3%	–	–	66.3%	79.3%
R	31.3%	54.6%	49.3%	27.0%	34.4%	–	–	31.3%	46.2%
E	–	–	–	–	–	45.7%	58.6%	33.0%	37.7%

Table 5: Percentage of Tokens **T**, **R** and **E** effectively appearing in the translation.

shown in Table 3 (3rd block), models with FM/EM also increase performance of fine-tuned models gaining in average +6 BLEU on fine-tuned model baselines, and +2.5 compared to FM/EM on generic translation. This add-up effect is interesting since both approaches make use of the same data.

Copy Vs. Context We observe that models allowing for augmented input sentences effectively learn to output the target words used as augmented translations. Table 5 illustrates the rates of usage. We compute for each word added in the input sentence as **T** (part of a lexicalised match), **R** (not in the match) and **E** (from an embedding match), how often they appear in the translated sentence. Results show that **T** words increase their usage rate by more than 10% compared to the corresponding base models. Considering **R** words, models incorporating fuzzy matches increase their usage rate compared to base models, albeit with lower rates than for **T** words. Furthermore, the number of **R** words output by FM$^+$ is clearly lower than those output by FM$^\#$, demonstrating the effect of marking unrelated matching words. Thus, we can confirm the copy behaviour of the networks with lexicalised matches. Words marked as **E** (embedding matches) increase their usage rates when compared to base models but are far from the rates of **T** words. We hypothesize that these sentences are not copied by the translation model, rather they are used to further contextualise translations.

5 Related Work

Our work stems on the technique proposed by (Bulté and Tezcan, 2019) to train an NMT model to leverage fuzzy matches inserted in the source sentence. We extend the concept by experimenting with more general notions of similar sentences and techniques to inject fuzzy matches.

The use of similar sentences to improve translation models has been explored at scale in (Schwenk et al., 2019), where the authors use multilingual sentence embeddings to retrieve pairs of similar sentences and train models uniquely with such sentences. In (Niehues et al., 2016), input sentences are augmented with pre-translations performed by a phrase-based MT system. In our approach, similar sentence translations are provided dynamically to guide translation of a given sentence.

Similar to our work, (Farajian et al., 2017; Li et al., 2018) retrieve similar sentences from the training data to dynamically adapt individual input sentences. To compute similarity, the first work uses n-gram matches, the second includes dense vector representations. In (Xu et al., 2019) the same approach is followed but authors consider for adaptation a bunch of semantically related input sentences to reduce adaptation time.

Our approach combines source and target words within a same sentence - the same type of approach has also been proposed by (Dinu et al., 2019) for introduction of terminology translation.

Last, we can also compare the extra-tokens appended in augmented sentences as "side constraints" activating different translation paths on the same spirit than the work done by (Sennrich et al., 2016a; Kobus et al., 2017) for controlling translation.

6 Conclusions and Further Work

This paper explores augmentation methods for boosting Neural Machine Translation performance by using similar translations.

Based on "neural fuzzy repair" technique, we introduce tighter integration of fuzzy matches informing neural network of source and target and propose extension to similar translations retrieved from their distributed representations. We show that the different types of similar translations and model fine-tuning provide complementary information to the neural model outperforming consistently and significantly previous work. We perform data augmentation at inference time with negligible speed overhead and release an Open-Source toolkit with an efficient and flexible fuzzy-match implementation.

In our future work, we plan to optimise the thresholds used with the retrieval algorithms in order to more intelligently select those translations providing richest information to the NMT model and generalize the use of edit distance on the target side.

We would also like to explore better techniques to inject information of small-size n-grams with possible convergence with terminology injection techniques, unifying framework where target clues are mixed with source sentence during translation. As regards distributed representations, we plan to study alternative networks to more accurately model the identification and incorporation of additional context.

Acknowledgments

We would like to thank Professor François Yvon for his insightful comments as well as the anonymous reviewers for the useful suggestions.

References

Michael Bloodgood and Benjamin Strauss. 2014. Translation memory retrieval methods. In *Proceedings of the 14th Conference of the European Chapter of the Association for Computational Linguistics*, pages 202–210.

Bram Bulté and Arda Tezcan. 2019. Neural fuzzy repair: Integrating fuzzy matches into neural machine translation. In *Proceedings of the 57th Annual Meeting of the Association for Computational Linguistics*, pages 1800–1809, Florence, Italy. Association for Computational Linguistics.

Bram Bulté, Tom Vanallemeersch, and Vincent Vandeghinste. 2018. M3tra: integrating tm and mt for professional translators. pages 69–78. EAMT.

Chenhui Chu and Rui Wang. 2018. A survey of domain adaptation for neural machine translation. In *Proceedings of the 27th International Conference on Computational Linguistics*, pages 1304–1319, Santa Fe, New Mexico, USA. Association for Computational Linguistics.

Georgiana Dinu, Prashant Mathur, Marcello Federico, and Yaser Al-Onaizan. 2019. Training neural machine translation to apply terminology constraints. In *Proceedings of the 57th Annual Meeting of the Association for Computational Linguistics*, pages 3063–3068, Florence, Italy. Association for Computational Linguistics.

Chris Dyer, Victor Chahuneau, and Noah A. Smith. 2013. A simple, fast, and effective reparameterization of IBM model 2. In *Proceedings of the 2013 Conference of the North American Chapter of the Association for Computational Linguistics: Human Language Technologies*, pages 644–648, Atlanta, Georgia. Association for Computational Linguistics.

M. Amin Farajian, Marco Turchi, Matteo Negri, and Marcello Federico. 2017. Multi-domain neural machine translation through unsupervised adaptation. In *Proceedings of the Second Conference on Machine Translation*, pages 127–137, Copenhagen, Denmark. Association for Computational Linguistics.

Jiatao Gu, Yong Wang, Kyunghyun Cho, and Victor OK Li. 2018. Search engine guided neural machine translation. In *Thirty-Second AAAI Conference on Artificial Intelligence*.

Jeff Johnson, Matthijs Douze, and Hervé Jégou. 2019. Billion-scale similarity search with gpus. *IEEE Transactions on Big Data*.

Guillaume Klein, Yoon Kim, Yuntian Deng, Jean Senellart, and Alexander Rush. 2017. OpenNMT: Open-source toolkit for neural machine translation. In *Proceedings of ACL 2017, System Demonstrations*, pages 67–72, Vancouver, Canada. Association for Computational Linguistics.

Catherine Kobus, Josep Crego, and Jean Senellart. 2017. Domain control for neural machine translation. In *Proceedings of the International Conference Recent Advances in Natural Language Processing, RANLP 2017*, pages 372–378, Varna, Bulgaria. INCOMA Ltd.

Philipp Koehn and Jean Senellart. 2010. Convergence of Translation Memory and Statistical Machine Translation. In *Proceedings of AMTA Workshop on MT Research and the Translation Industry*, pages 21–31, Denver.

Xiaoqing Li, Jiajun Zhang, and Chengqing Zong. 2018. One sentence one model for neural machine translation. In *Proceedings of the 11th Language Resources and Evaluation Conference*, Miyazaki, Japan. European Language Resource Association.

Minh-Thang Luong and Christopher D. Manning. 2015. Stanford neural machine translation systems for spoken language domain. In *International Workshop on Spoken Language Translation*, Da Nang, Vietnam.

Udi Manber and Gene Myers. 1993. Suffix arrays: a new method for on-line string searches. *siam Journal on Computing*, 22(5):935–948.

Jan Niehues, Eunah Cho, Thanh-Le Ha, and Alex Waibel. 2016. Pre-translation for neural machine translation. *CoRR*, abs/1610.05243.

John E Ortega, Felipe Sánchez-Martınez, and Mikel L Forcada. 2016. Fuzzy-match repair using black-box machine translation systems: what can be expected. In *Proceedings of AMTA*, volume 1, pages 27–39.

Matteo Pagliardini, Prakhar Gupta, and Martin Jaggi. 2018. Unsupervised learning of sentence embeddings using compositional n-gram features. In *Proceedings of the 2018 Conference of the North American Chapter of the Association for Computational Linguistics: Human Language Technologies, Volume 1 (Long Papers)*, pages 528–540, New Orleans, Louisiana. Association for Computational Linguistics.

Mike Paterson and Vlado Dančík. 1994. Longest common subsequences. In *International Symposium on Mathematical Foundations of Computer Science*, pages 127–142. Springer.

Mirko Plitt and François Masselot. 2010. A productivity test of statistical machine translation post-editing in a typical localisation context. *The Prague bulletin of mathematical linguistics*, 93:7–16.

Holger Schwenk, Guillaume Wenzek, Sergey Edunov, Edouard Grave, and Armand Joulin. 2019. Ccmatrix: Mining billions of high-quality parallel sentences on the web. *arXiv preprint arXiv:1911.04944*.

Rico Sennrich, Barry Haddow, and Alexandra Birch. 2016a. Controlling politeness in neural machine translation via side constraints. In *Proceedings of the 2016 Conference of the North American Chapter of the Association for Computational Linguistics: Human Language Technologies*, pages 35–40, San Diego, California. Association for Computational Linguistics.

Rico Sennrich, Barry Haddow, and Alexandra Birch. 2016b. Neural machine translation of rare words with subword units. In *Proceedings of the 54th Annual Meeting of the Association for Computational Linguistics (Volume 1: Long Papers)*, pages 1715–1725, Berlin, Germany. Association for Computational Linguistics.

Jörg Tiedemann. 2012. Parallel data, tools and interfaces in OPUS. In *Proceedings of the Eighth International Conference on Language Resources and Evaluation (LREC'12)*, pages 2214–2218, Istanbul, Turkey. European Language Resources Association (ELRA).

Tom Vanallemeersch and Vincent Vandeghinste. 2015. Assessing linguistically aware fuzzy matching in translation memories. In *Proceedings of the 18th Annual Conference of the European Association for Machine Translation*, pages 153–160, Antalya, Turkey.

Ashish Vaswani, Noam Shazeer, Niki Parmar, Jakob Uszkoreit, Llion Jones, Aidan N. Gomez, Łukasz Kaiser, and Illia Polosukhin. 2017. Attention is all you need. In I. Guyon, U. V. Luxburg, S. Bengio, H. Wallach, R. Fergus, S. Vishwanathan, and R. Garnett, editors, *Advances in Neural Information Processing Systems 30*, pages 5998–6008. Curran Associates, Inc.

Kun Wang, Chengqing Zong, and Keh-Yih Su. 2013. Integrating translation memory into phrase-based machine translation during decoding. In *Proceedings of the 51st Annual Meeting of the Association for Computational Linguistics (Volume 1: Long Papers)*, pages 11–21, Sofia, Bulgaria. Association for Computational Linguistics.

Jitao Xu, Josep Crego, and Jean Senellart. 2019. Lexical micro-adaptation for neural machine translation. In *International Workshop on Spoken Language Translation*, Honk Kong, China.

Masaru Yamada. 2011. The effect of translation memory databases on productivity. *Translation research projects*, 3:63–73.

Anna Zaretskaya, Gloria Corpas Pastor, and Miriam Seghiri. 2015. Integration of machine translation in cat tools: State of the art, evaluation and user attitudes. *Skase Journal of Translation and Interpretation*, 8(1):76–89.

Jingyi Zhang, Masao Utiyama, Eiichro Sumita, Graham Neubig, and Satoshi Nakamura. 2018. Guiding neural machine translation with retrieved translation pieces. In *Proceedings of the 2018 Conference of the North American Chapter of the Association for Computational Linguistics: Human Language Technologies, Volume 1 (Long Papers)*, pages 1325–1335, New Orleans, Louisiana. Association for Computational Linguistics.

A Corpora Statistics

Corpus	#Sents (K)	L_{mean}		Vocab (K)	
		English	French	English	French
EPPS	1,992.8	27.7	32.0	129.5	149.2
News	315.3	25.3	31.7	90.5	96.7
TED	156.1	20.1	22.1	58.7	71.4
Wiki	749.0	25.9	23.5	527.5	506.6
ECB	174.1	28.6	33.8	45.3	53.5
EMEA	336.8	16.8	20.3	62.8	68.9
JRC	475.2	30.1	34.5	81.0	83.5
GNOME	51.9	9.6	11.6	19.0	21.6
KDE4	163.9	9.1	12.4	48.7	64.7
PHP	15.1	16.7	18.0	13.3	15.5
Ubuntu	7.1	6.7	8.3	7.5	7.9

Table 6: Corpora statistics. Note that K stands for thousands and L_{mean} is the average length in words.

B NMT Network Configuration

We use the next set of hyper-parameters: size of word embedding: 512; size of hidden layers: 512; size of inner feed forward layer: $2,048$; number of heads: 8; number of layers: 6; batch size: $4,096$ tokens. Note that when using factors ($\texttt{FM}^+$, $\texttt{NM}^+$ and $\texttt{EM}^+$) the final word embedding is built after concatenation of the word embedding (508 cells) and the additional factor embedding (4 cells).
We use the lazy Adam optimiser. We set warmup steps to $4,000$ and update learning rate for every 8 iterations. Models are optimised during $300K$ iterations. Fine-tuning is performed continuing Adam with the same learning rate decay schedule until convergence on the validation set. All models are trained using a single NVIDIA P100 GPU.
We limit the target sentence length to 100 tokens.The source sentence is limited to 100, 200 and 300 tokens depending on the number of sentences used to augment the input sentence. We use a joint vocabulary of 32K for both source and target sides. In inference we use a beam size of 5. For evaluation, we report BLEU scores computed by `multi-bleu.perl`.

C Example of Embedding Matching

The table below gives examples of retrieved EM with matching distance ≥ 0.8 and with Fuzzy Match distance lower than threshold 0.6.

Distance	Source Sentence	Matched Sentence
0.86	(i) supply of gas to power producers (CCGTs [10]);	(a) Gas supply to power producers (CCGTs)
0.87	The Commission shall provide the chairman and the secretariat for these working parties.	The Commission shall provide secretariat services for the Forum, the Bureau and the working parties.
0.93	Admission to a course of training as a pharmacist shall be contingent upon possession of a diploma or certificate giving access, in a Member State, to the studies in question, at universities or higher institutes of a level recognised as equivalent.	Admission to basic dental training presupposes possession of a diploma or certificate giving access, for the studies in question, to universities or higher institutes of a level recognised as equivalent, in a Member State.

tarjama
The impact of Quality, Quantity, or the Right Type of Nutrients
Feeding NMT a Healthy Diet
Abdallah Nasir – ML Tech Lead
Sara Alisis – AI Linguistic QA Lead
AMTA ORLANDO 2022
Try our NMT at:
https://translate.tarjama.com
amt

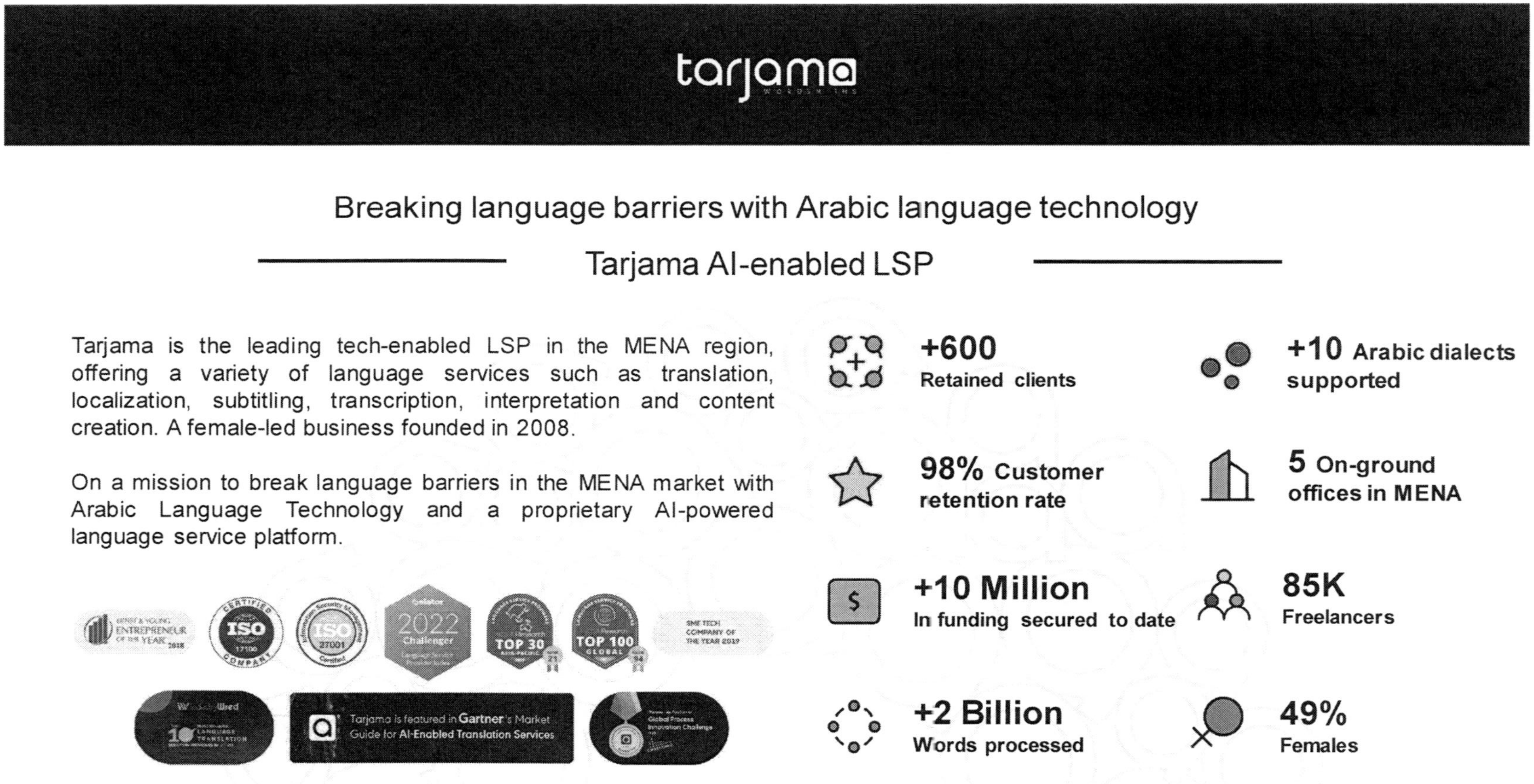
tarjama
Breaking language barriers with Arabic language technology
Tarjama AI-enabled LSP
Tarjama is the leading tech-enabled LSP in the MENA region, offering a variety of language services such as translation, localization, subtitling, transcription, interpretation and content creation. A female-led business founded in 2008.
On a mission to break language barriers in the MENA market with Arabic Language Technology and a proprietary AI-powered language service platform.
+600
Retained clients
+10 Arabic dialects supported
98% Customer retention rate
5 On-ground offices in MENA
+10 Million
In funding secured to date
85K
Freelancers
+2 Billion
Words processed
49%
Females
ENTREPRENEUR OF THE YEAR 2018
ISO
COMPANY
ISO
27001
2022
Challenger
TOP 30
TOP 100
GLOBAL
SME TECH COMPANY OF THE YEAR 2019
Tarjama is featured in Gartner's Market Guide for AI-Enabled Translation Services

The Impact of Healthy Data

Our NMT models are manually evaluated by our Linguistic QA team with Adapted MQM approach.

Manual Evaluation of 255 segments (5970 words).

84.9%→87.7%

Of translations considered OK, Good and Perfect

tarjama

NMT Results per Quality levels

MT Quality	Model 1 Good Data	Model 2 Good+Healthy Data
Perfect MT translation	46.2%	46.2%
Good MT translation (minor errors)	0.7%	1.9%
OK translation (few errors)	38%	39.6%
Bad translation	8.2%	6.2%
Nonsense translation	6.2%	5.8%

The Impact of Healthy Data

Our Healthy Data added to Model 2 was 18K parallel sentences only!

tarjama

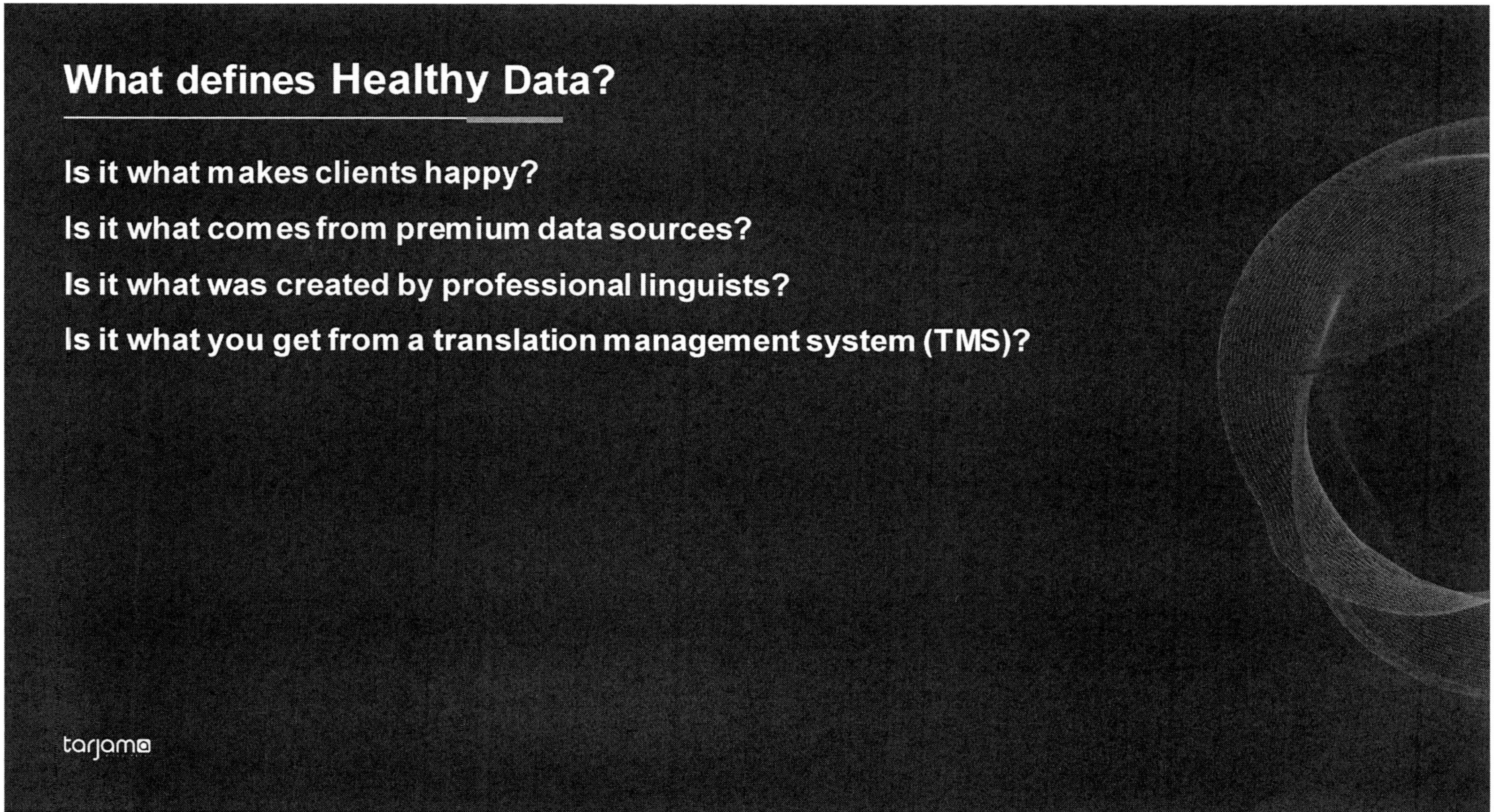
What defines Healthy Data?
Is it what makes clients happy?
Is it what comes from premium data sources?
Is it what was created by professional linguists?
Is it what you get from a translation management system (TMS)?
tarjama

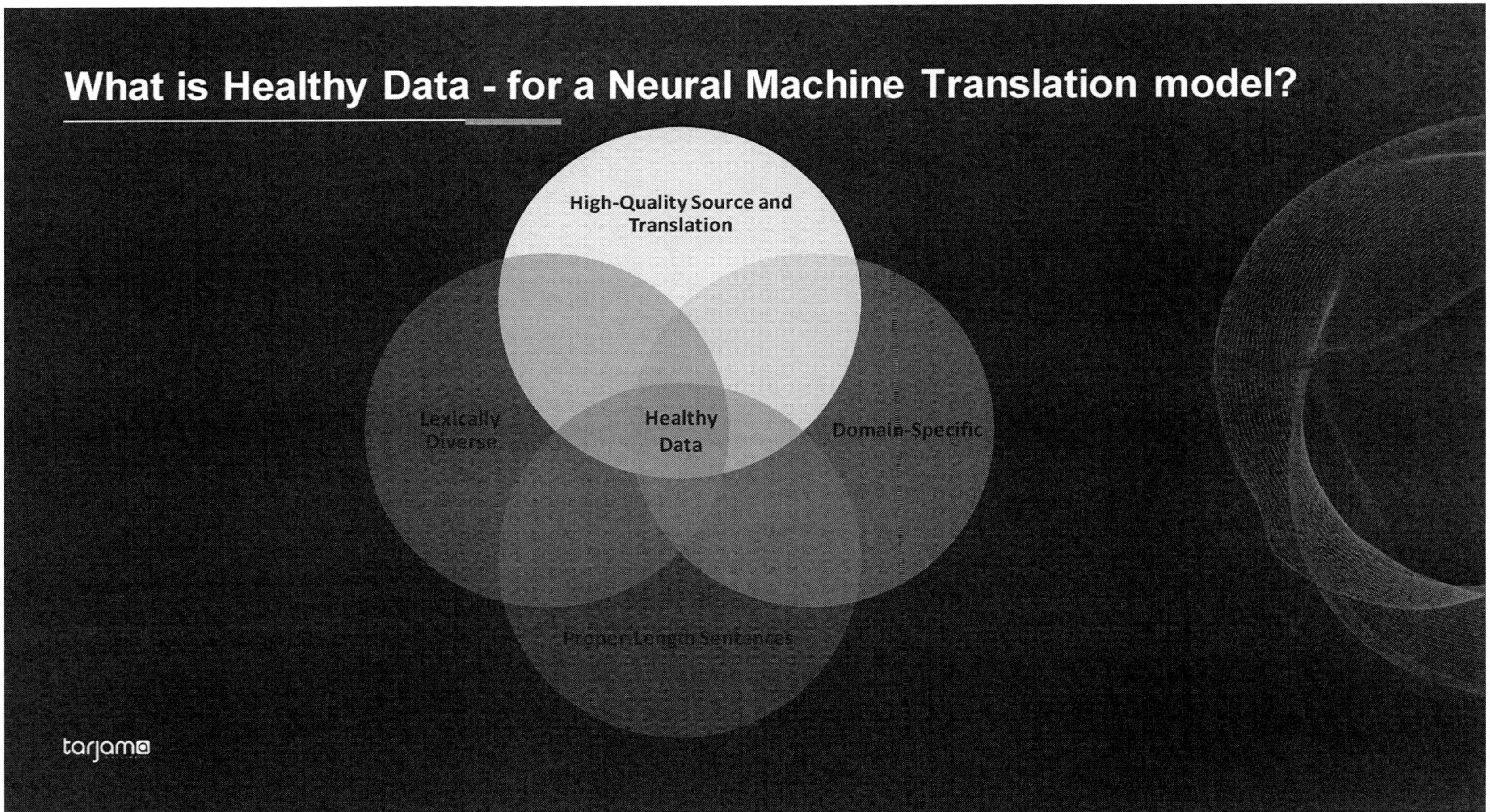
What is Healthy Data - for a Neural Machine Translation model?
High-Quality Source and Translation
Lexically Diverse
Healthy Data
Domain-Specific
Proper-Length Sentences
tarjama

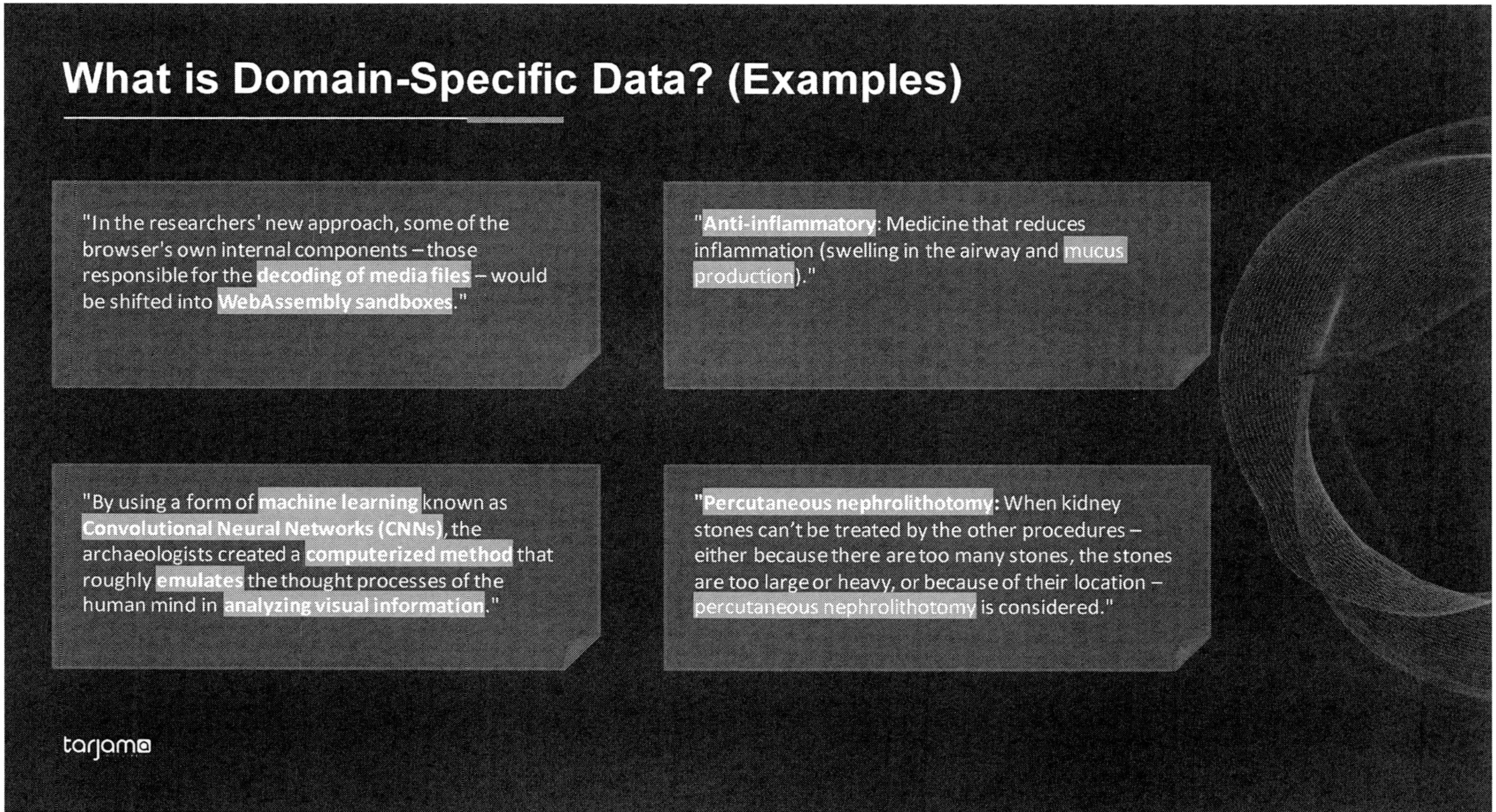
What is Domain-Specific Data? (Examples)
"In the researchers' new approach, some of the browser's own internal components – those responsible for the decoding of media files – would be shifted into WebAssembly sandboxes."
"Anti-inflammatory: Medicine that reduces inflammation (swelling in the airway and mucus production)."
"By using a form of machine learning known as Convolutional Neural Networks (CNNs), the archaeologists created a computerized method that roughly emulates the thought processes of the human mind in analyzing visual information."
"Percutaneous nephrolithotomy: When kidney stones can't be treated by the other procedures – either because there are too many stones, the stones are too large or heavy, or because of their location – percutaneous nephrolithotomy is considered."
tarjama

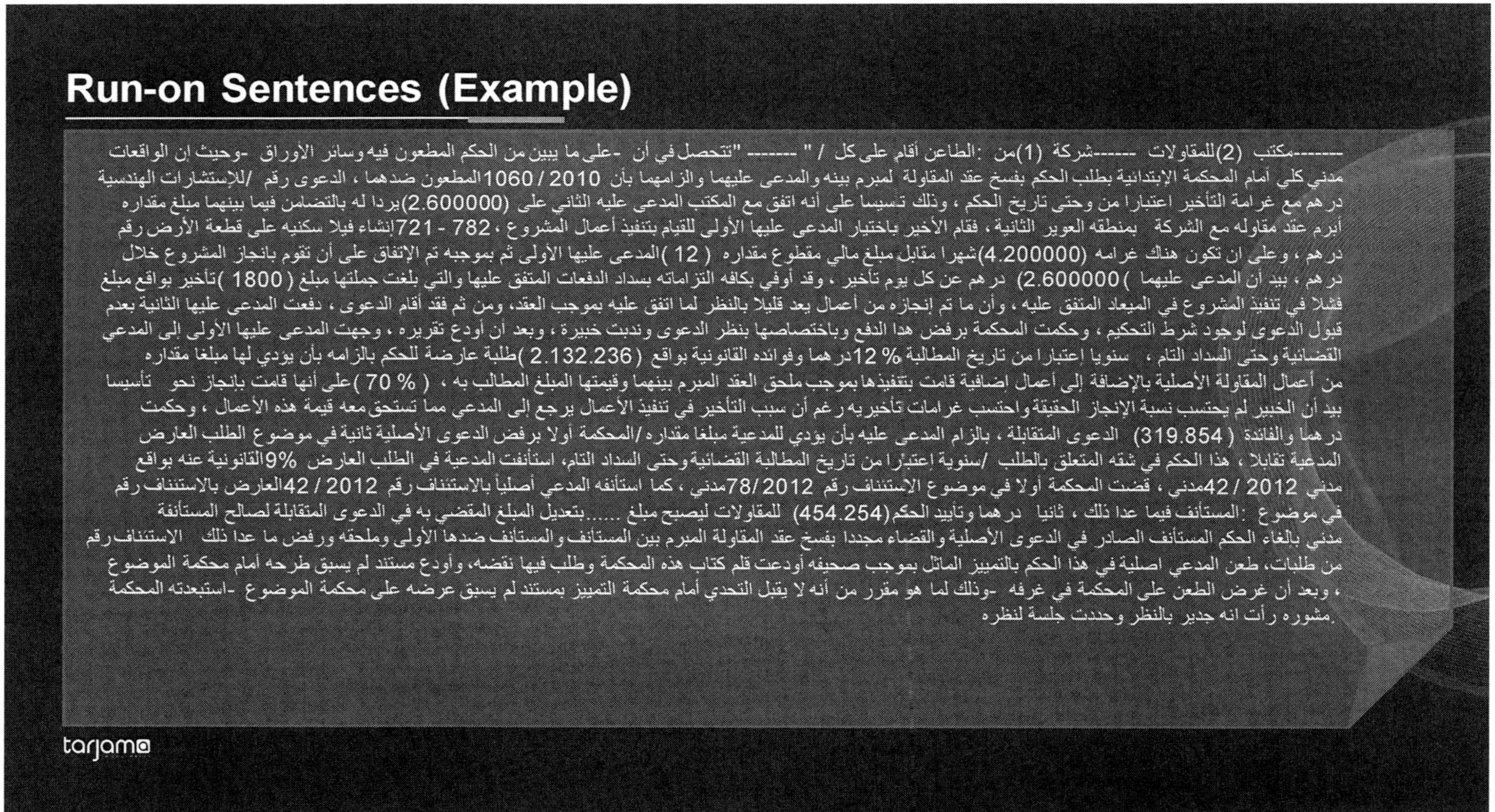
Run-on Sentences (Example)
-------مكتب (2)للمقاولات ------شركة (1)من :الطاعن أقام على كل / " ------- "تتحصل في أن -على ما يبين من الحكم المطعون فيه وسائر الأوراق -وحيث إن الواقعات
مدني كلي أمام المحكمة الإبتدائية بطلب الحكم بفسخ عقد المقاولة لمبرم بينه والمدعى عليهما والزامهما بأن 2010 / 1060 المطعون ضدهما ، الدعوى رقم /للإستشارات الهندسية
درهم مع غرامة التأخير اعتبارا من وحتى تاريخ الحكم ، وذلك تسيسا على أنه اتفق مع المكتب المدعى عليه الثاني على (2.600000)بردا له بالتضامن فيما بينهما مبلغ مقداره
أبرم عقد مقاوله مع الشركة بمنطقه العوير الثانية ، فقام الأخير باختيار المدعى عليها الأولى للقيام بتنفيذ أعمال المشروع ، 782 - 721إنشاء فيلا سكنيه على قطعة الأرض رقم
درهم ، وعلى ان تكون هناك غرامه (4.200000)شهرا مقابل مبلغ مالي مقطوع مقداره (12)المدعى عليها الاولى ثم بموجبه تم الإتفاق على أن تقوم بانجاز المشروع خلال
درهم ، بيد أن المدعى عليهما)2.600000) درهم عن كل يوم تأخير ، وقد أوفي بكافه التزاماته بسداد الدفعات المتفق عليها والتي بلغت جملتها مبلغ (1800)تأخير بواقع مبلغ
فشلا في تنفيذ المشروع في الميعاد المتفق عليه ، وأن ما تم إنجازه من أعمال يعد قليلا بالنظر لما اتفق عليه بموجب العقد، ومن ثم فقد أقام الدعوى ، دفعت المدعى عليها الثانية بعدم
قبول الدعوى لوجود شرط التحكيم ، وحكمت المحكمة برفض هذا الدفع وباختصاصها بنظر الدعوى وندبت خبيرة ، وبعد أن أودع تقريره ، وجهت المدعى عليها الأولى إلى المدعي
القضائية وحتى السداد التام ، سنويا إعتبارا من تاريخ المطالبة % 12درهما وفوائده القانونية بواقع (2.132.236)طلبة عارضة للحكم بالزامه بأن يؤدي لها مبلغا مقداره
من أعمال المقاولة الأصلية بالإضافة إلى أعمال إضافية قامت بتنفيذها بموجب ملحق العقد المبرم بينهما وقيمتها المبلغ المطالب به ، (% 70)على أنها قامت بإنجاز نحو تأسيسا
بيد أن الخبير لم يحتسب نسبة الإنجاز الحقيقة واحتسب غرامات تأخيريه رغم أن سبب التأخير في تنفيذ الأعمال يرجع إلى المدعي مما تستحق معه قيمة هذه الأعمال ، وحكمت
درهما والفائدة (319.854) الدعوى المتقابلة ، بالزام المدعى عليه بأن يؤدي للمدعية مبلغا مقداره /المحكمة أولا برفض الدعوى الأصلية ثانية في موضوع الطلب العارض
المدعية تقابلا ، هذا الحكم في شقه المتعلق بالطلب /سنوية إعتبارا من تاريخ المطالبة القضائية وحتى السداد التام، استأنفت المدعية في الطلب العارض %9القانونية عنه بواقع
مدني 2012 / 42مدني ، قضت المحكمة أولا في موضوع الاستئناف رقم 2012/78مدني ، كما استأنفه المدعي أصلياً بالاستئناف رقم 2012 / 42العارض بالاستئناف رقم
في موضوع :المستأنف فيما عدا ذلك ، ثانيا درهما وتأييد الحكم(454.254) للمقاولات ليصبح مبلغ ......بتعديل المبلغ المقضي به في الدعوى المتقابلة لصالح المستأنفة
مدني بالغاء الحكم المستأنف الصادر في الدعوى الأصلية والقضاء مجددا بفسخ عقد المقاولة المبرم بين المستأنف والمستأنف ضدها الأولى وملحقه ورفض ما عدا ذلك الاستئناف رقم
من طلبات، طعن المدعي اصلية في هذا الحكم بالتمييز الماثل بموجب صحيفه أودعت قلم كتاب هذه المحكمة وطلب فيها نقضه، وأودع مستند لم يسبق طرحه أمام محكمة الموضوع
، وبعد أن غرض الطعن على المحكمة في غرفه -وذلك لما هو مقرر من أنه لا يقبل التحدي أمام محكمة التمييز بمستند لم يسبق عرضه على محكمة الموضوع -استبعدته المحكمة
.مشوره رأت انه جدير بالنظر وحددت جلسة لنظره
tarjama

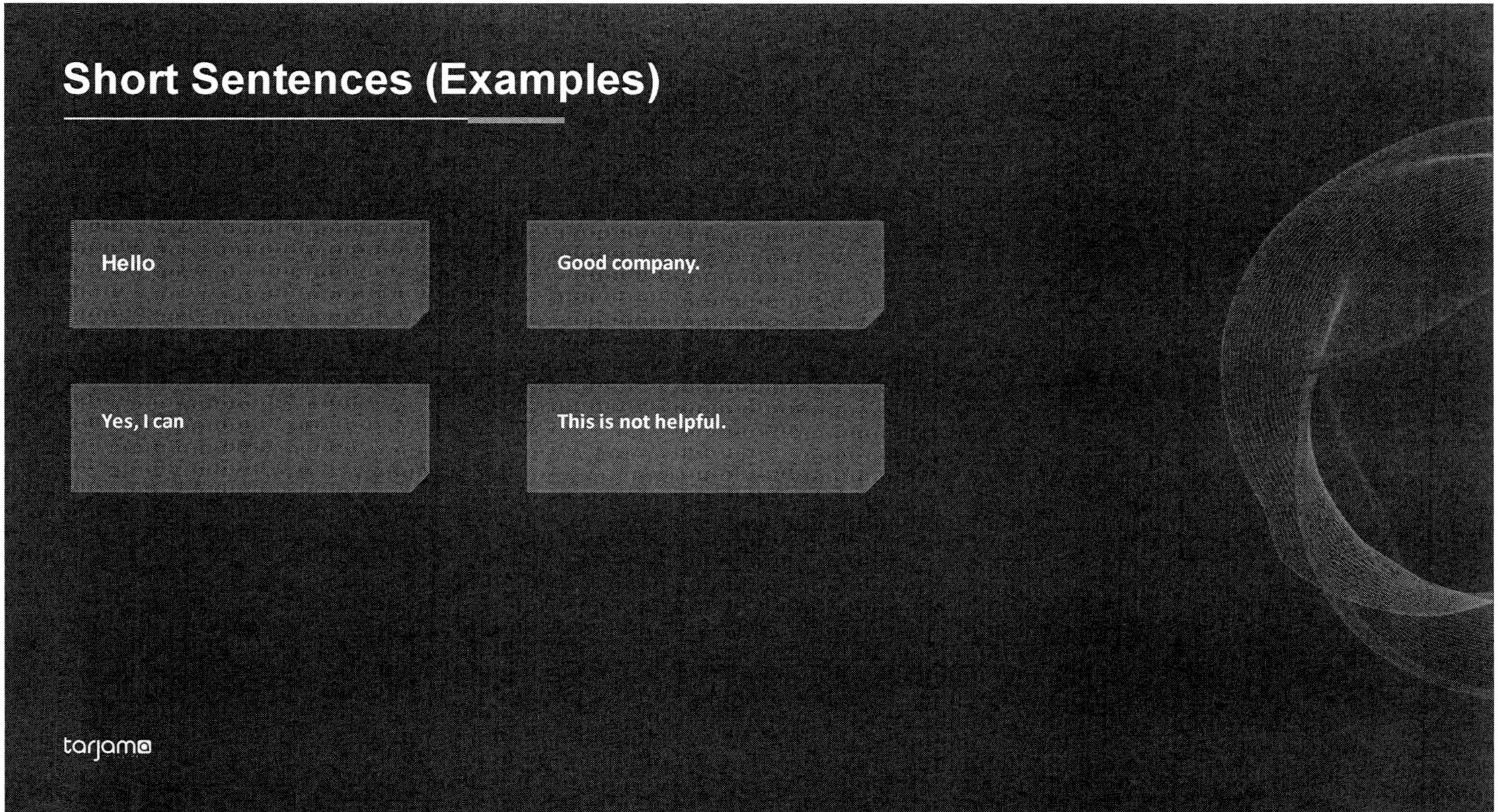
Short Sentences (Examples)
Hello
Good company.
Yes, I can
This is not helpful.
tarjama

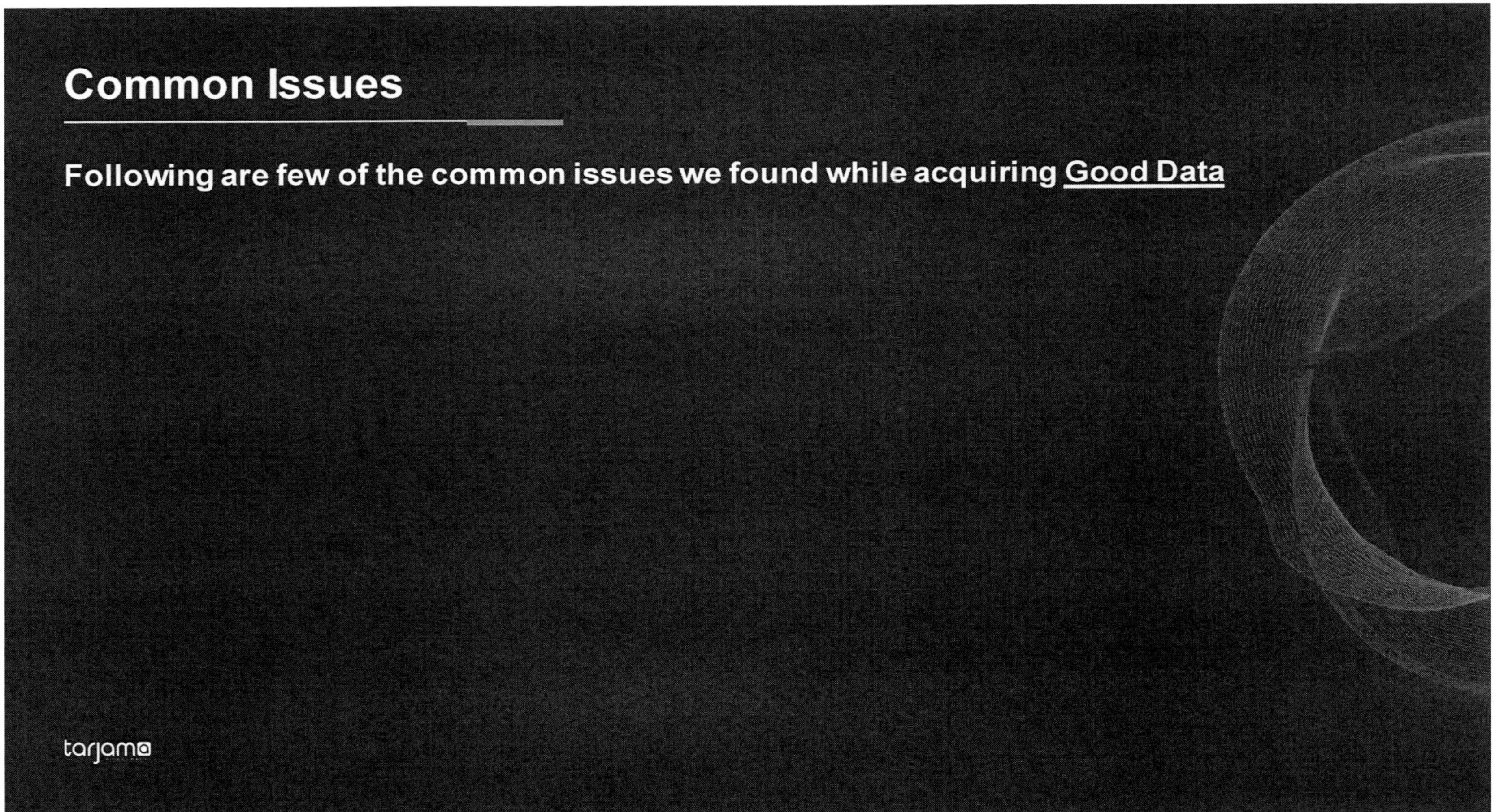
Common Issues
Following are few of the common issues we found while acquiring Good Data
tarjama

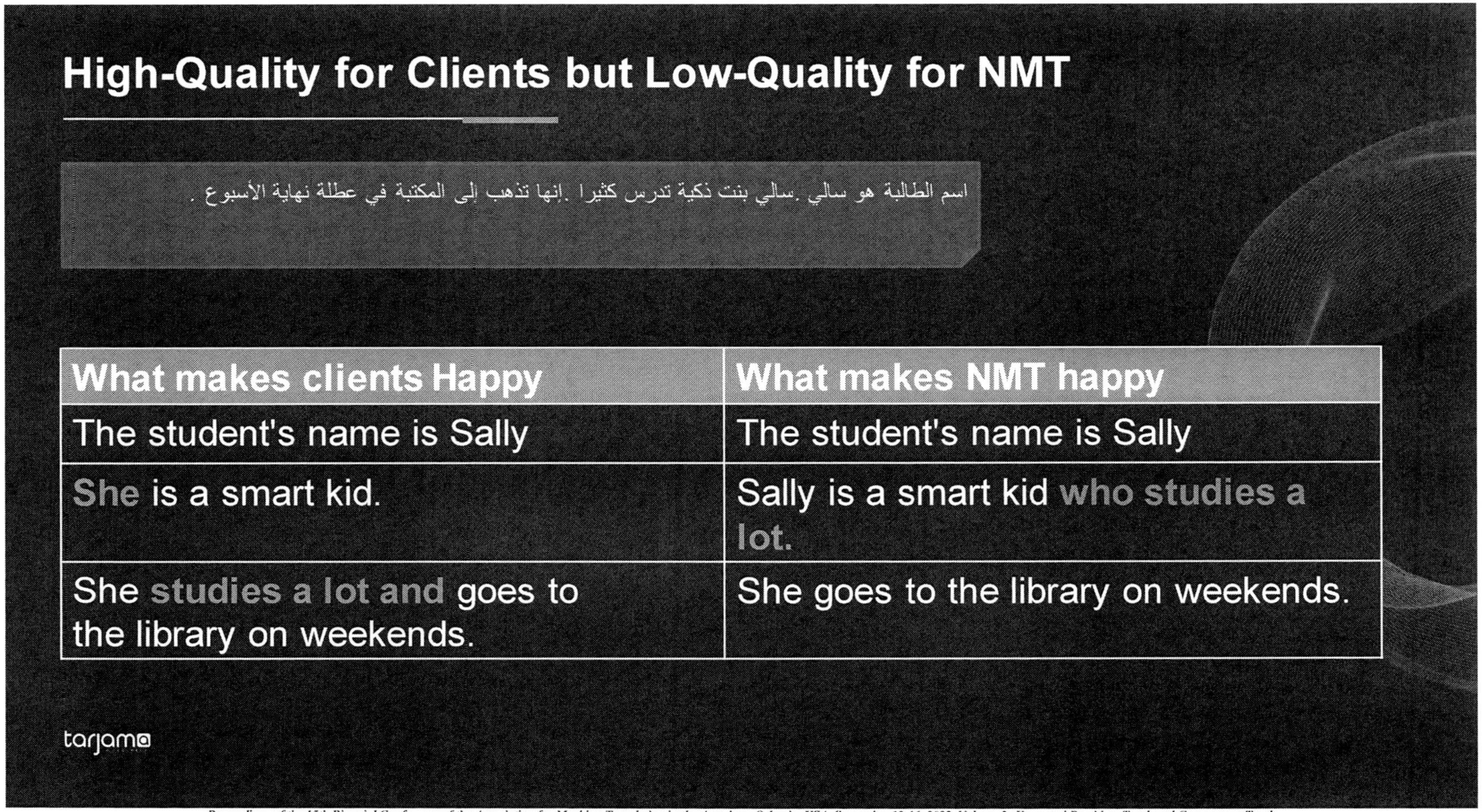
High-Quality for Clients but Low-Quality for NMT
اسم الطالبة هو سالي .سالي بنت ذكية تدرس كثيرا .إنها تذهب إلى المكتبة في عطلة نهاية الأسبوع .
What makes clients Happy
What makes NMT happy
The student's name is Sally
The student's name is Sally
She is a smart kid.
Sally is a smart kid who studies a lot.
She studies a lot and goes to the library on weekends.
She goes to the library on weekends.
tarjama

Transcreation (Examples)

Source	Human Transcreation	Literal Translation
أحد الأسئلة العميقة التي باتت ترتفع في سماوات العلاقات العربية - الأميركية عامة، والسعودية الأميركية خاصة	One of the biggest questions facing Arab-US relations in general, and Saudi-US ties in particular.	One of the deep questions that is rising in the heavens of Arab-American relations in general, and Saudi-US relations in particular.
يمكن القطع بأن المخاوف مشروعة ولا شك، ولا توجد عملية سي اسية تجري في فردوس للأطهار، بل على أرض الأشواك، حيث ال خير والشر يتلازمان منذ بداية الأيام إلى أن يرث الله الأرض ومن عليها	These fears are assuredly legitimate, as no political process is ideal and error-free in this world where good and evil have existed since the dawn of time.	There is no political process taking place in Ferdous, but on the land of the thorns, where good and evil have been in flux from the beginning of the days until God inherits the land and those on it.

tarjama

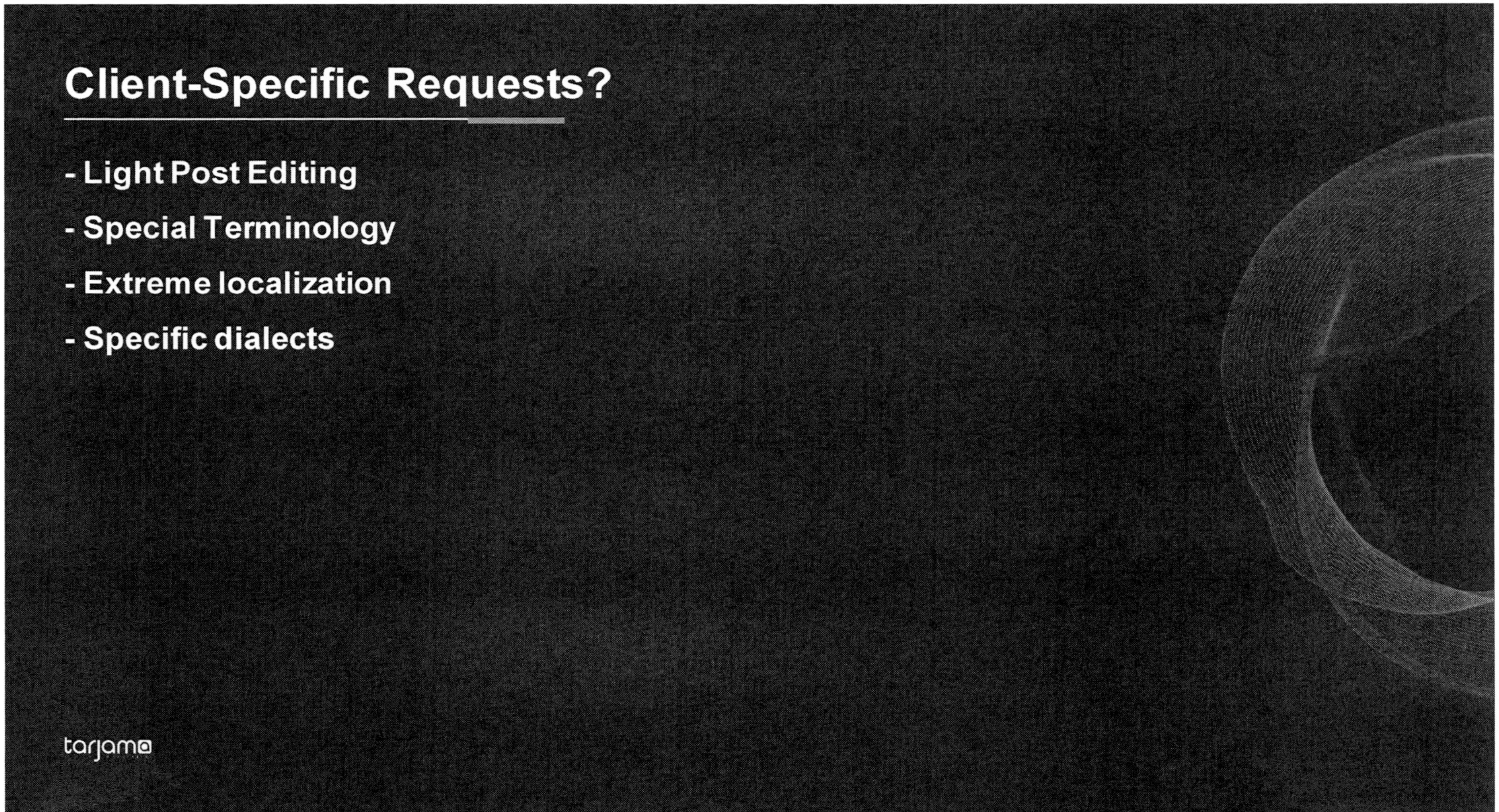
Client-Specific Requests?
- Light Post Editing
- Special Terminology
- Extreme localization
- Specific dialects
tarjama

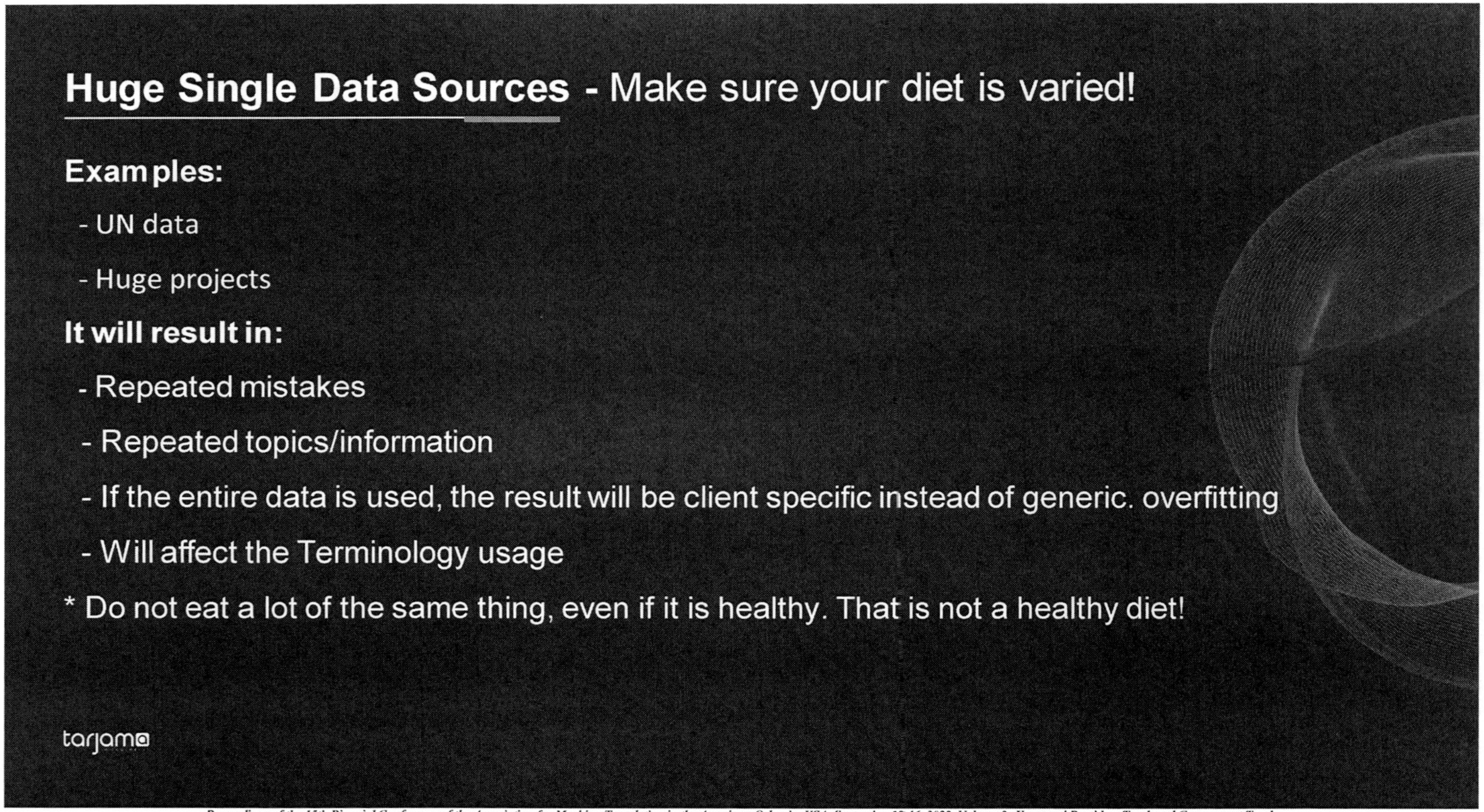
Huge Single Data Sources - Make sure your diet is varied!
Examples:
- UN data
- Huge projects
It will result in:
- Repeated mistakes
- Repeated topics/information
- If the entire data is used, the result will be client specific instead of generic. overfitting
- Will affect the Terminology usage
* Do not eat a lot of the same thing, even if it is healthy. That is not a healthy diet!
tarjama

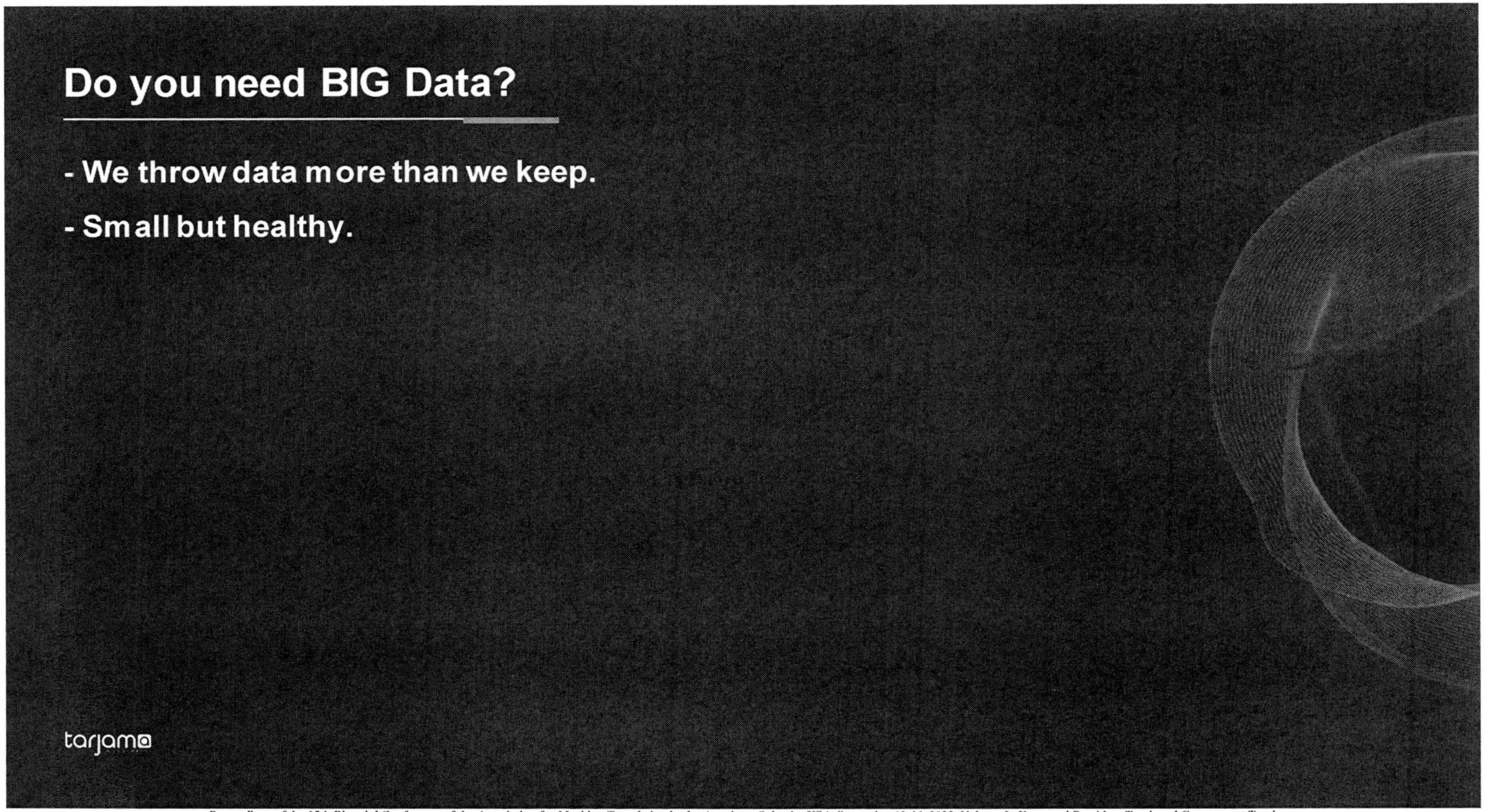
Do you need BIG Data?
- We throw data more than we keep.
- Small but healthy.
tarjama

Data Creation

* Happy customer ≠ Happy NMT

WHY not to consider NMT as our customer!

tarjama

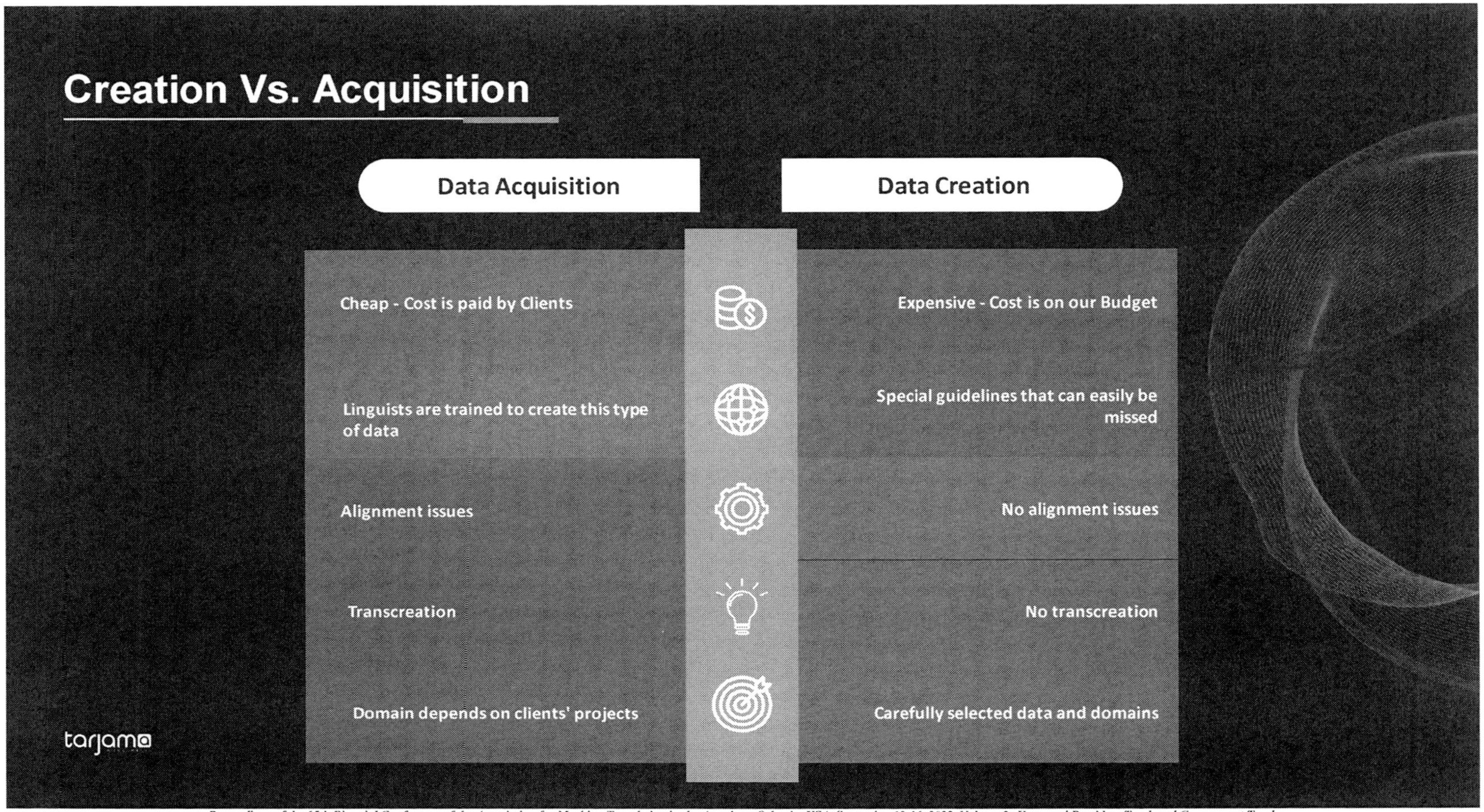
Creation Vs. Acquisition
Data Acquisition
Data Creation
Cheap - Cost is paid by Clients
Expensive - Cost is on our Budget
Linguists are trained to create this type of data
Special guidelines that can easily be missed
Alignment issues
No alignment issues
Transcreation
No transcreation
Domain depends on clients' projects
Carefully selected data and domains
tarjama

Guidelines for NMT Data Creation

- Select domains that you lack.
- Avoid generic articles. Aim for specialized ones for richer terminology.
- Educate linguists and PMs on how NMT learns.
- Explain common data issues: Like transcreation, alignment ...
- Ensure that the source is high quality. Proofread the source if needed.
- Do not use MT
- Iterate: Do not operate a big project with a huge budget for a specific domain. Start small.

tarjama

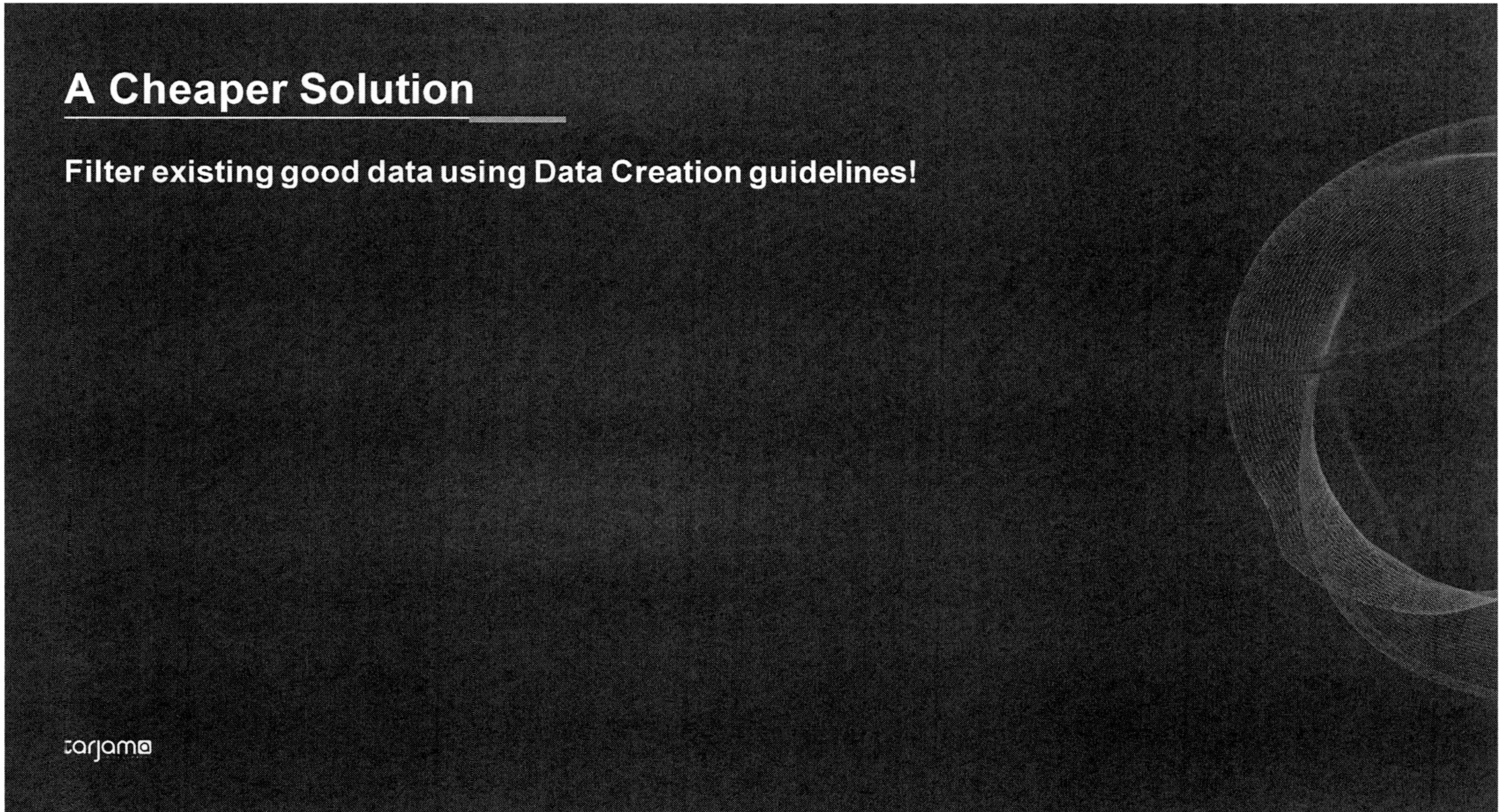
A Cheaper Solution
Filter existing good data using Data Creation guidelines!
tarjama

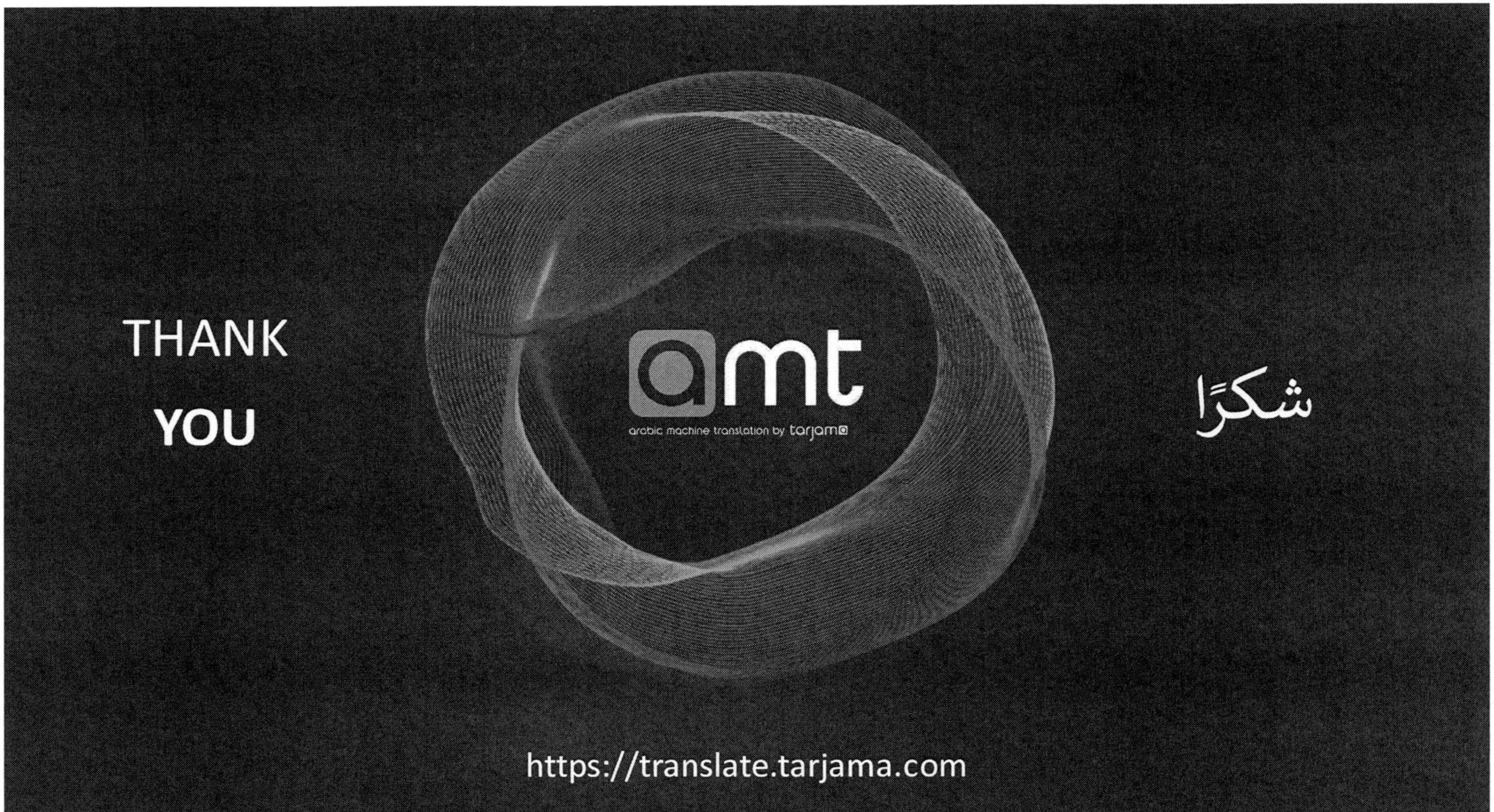
THANK
YOU
amt
arabic machine translation by tarjama
شكرًا
https://translate.tarjama.com

A Comparison of Data Filtering Methods for Neural Machine Translation

Fred Bane fbane@translations.com
Celia Soler Uguet csuguet@transperfect.com
Wiktor Stribiżew wstribizew@translations.com
Anna Zaretskaya azaretskaya@translations.com
Transperfect Translations, Barcelona, Spain

Abstract

With the increasing availability of large-scale parallel corpora derived from web crawling and bilingual text mining, data filtering is becoming an increasingly important step in neural machine translation (NMT) pipelines. This paper applies several available tools to the task of data filtration, and compares their performance in filtering out different types of noisy data. We also study the effect of filtration with each tool on model performance in the downstream task of NMT by creating a dataset containing a combination of clean and noisy data, filtering the data with each tool, and training NMT engines using the resulting filtered corpora. We evaluate the performance of each engine with a combination of MQM-based human evaluation and automated metrics. Our results show that cross-entropy filtering substantially outperforms the other tested methods for the types of noise we studied, and also leads to better NMT models. Our best results are obtained by training for a short time on all available data then filtering the corpus with cross-entropy filtering and training until convergence.

1 Introduction

Large-scale, publicly available bilingual corpora are an excellent resource for training neural machine translation (NMT) models. Performance in the NMT task improves as the size of the training data increases (Koehn and Knowles, 2017), and with datasets like CC Matrix (Schwenk et al., 2019), tens or even hundreds of millions of sentence pairs are freely available for many language pairs. However, these corpora are known to be noisy (Kreutzer et al., 2022), and NMT models are quite sensitive to noisy training data (Khayrallah and Koehn, 2018a). Thus, tools to filter noisy data are becoming an important step in NMT training pipelines.

In this paper, we compare the performance of several available tools in the task of data filtering, breaking down the results by different types of noise. We then train MT engines with different filtered versions of the same corpus to compare the effects of data filtering on the downstream task of translation.

2 Related Research

Cleaning noisy data with the purpose of using them for MT training has been a major topic in research. Since neural MT performance has shown to be highly dependent on the size of the training data (Koehn and Knowles, 2017) as well as their quality (Khayrallah and Koehn,

2018b), several large-scale initiatives for crawling and cleaning data from the web appeared, such as Paracrawl (Bañón et al., 2020) and CCMatrix (Schwenk et al., 2019).

For this reason, most works in this area focus on filtering this type of data, i.e. noisy data collected from the web. One of the earlier works proposed an unsupervised method, in particular using an outlier detection algorithm to filter a parallel corpus (Taghipour et al., 2011), which led to an increased performance of the SMT system trained on these cleaned data. Another unsupervised method consisted of a graph-based random walk algorithm and extracted phrase-pair scores to weigh the phrase translation probabilities to bias towards more trustworthy ones (Cui et al., 2013). The method is based on the observation that better sentence pairs often lead to better phrase extraction and vice versa.

Several subsequent works treated the data filtering task as a classification problem. An example of this is the method proposed in Xu and Koehn (2017), which is based on generating synthetic noisy data (inadequate and non-fluent translations) and using these data to train a classifier to identify good sentence pairs in a noisy corpus. Another classification approach was proposed within the 2020 task on parallel data filtering (Koehn et al., 2020). In this approach, the authors used an end-to-end classifier that learns to distinguish clean parallel data from misaligned sentence pairs. The system first uses a Transformer model to obtain sentence representations, followed either by a classifier (Siamese network) or additional layers that are fine-tuned (Açarçiçek et al., 2020).

Another popular approach is based on utilizing cross-entropy. In the 2018 edition of the shared task on data filtering, the winning system used neural MT models in both directions trained on clean data to score sentence pairs with dual cross-entropy (Junczys-Dowmunt, 2018). The divergent cross-entropies are penalized and the penalty is weighed by the average cross-entropy of the two NMT models. Another winning system in the 2020 shared task enhanced this approach by combining a dual cross-entropy from two NMT models with a number of other features: a bilingual GPT-2 model trained on source-target language pairs as well as a monolingual GPT-2 model for each of the languages, and statistical word translation model scores (Lu et al., 2020).

Recently, there has been a new direction in parallel data filtering research consisting of using multilingual language models, which create sentence representations in a multilingual vector space. Then, two parallel sentences are identified by taking the nearest neighbor of each source sentence in the target side according to cosine similarity, and filtering those below a fixed threshold (Schwenk, 2018). Another work improves on these results suggesting an alternative scoring method that uses the margin between the similarity of a given candidate and that of its k nearest neighbors (Artetxe and Schwenk, 2019).

As demonstrated in a recent work (Herold et al., 2021), the performance of a given parallel data cleaning method can vary significantly depending on the data conditions and the task definitions. In one attempt to clean mostly well-aligned bilingual data (Carpuat et al., 2017), the authors investigate the problem of filtering out semantically divergent sentences from a parallel corpus. Some sentence pairs considered "parallel" present source and target sentence that do not convey exactly the same meaning, which is quite a common phenomenon in curated parallel corpora originating from translation memories. In our experiment, we use several multilingual language models, a method based on cross-entropy and a pre-trained model for MT evaluation with the goal of identifying the methods that can be most successfully applied to our use case of filtering corpora to train MT systems.

3 Materials and Methods

For this study, we selected two language pairs: German>English (abbreviated below as 'DE>EN') and Japanese>English (abbreviated below as 'JA>EN'). These language pairs were chosen with consideration to their linguistic properties (diverse source languages with different scripts, differing levels of linguistic distance from English, and quite different linguistic characteristics), the demand for these language pairs in translation, and the availability of data and tools for the experiment.

3.1 Part I

In Part I of the study we created datasets for each language to be used in the experiments. We randomly sampled 5,000,000 sentence pairs for each language pair from the CC Matrix data set. Then, we synthesized 1,000,000 segments representing ten different types of noise and injected them into the CC Matrix data. We scored these 6 million sentences with each tool and retained the top 50% of sentences for each tool to be used as the training set for an NMT engine. We then trained engines with each data set and compared their performance after ten training epochs on a common test set sampled from the same distribution as the training data. We used the same arbitrary threshold for each tool and each language to minimize experimental complexity. The 50% threshold was chosen to account for the noise we introduced as well as the fact that we expect CC Matrix to contain significant amounts of native noise. Using the mean scores from the validation and test sets as the cutoff values was also considered, but the number of included segments was quite similar to using a fixed threshold, so we chose the simpler of the two options.

3.1.1 Collection and Synthesis of Noisy Data

With reference to Khayrallah and Koehn (2018a), we introduced 100,000 segments for each of the following types of noise:

1. **Word order permutations in target**: we introduced errors in an iterative way (i.e., starting from one error in the first 20,000 segments and adding one additional error every 20,000 segments until obtaining 100,000 segments);
2. **Spelling permutations in target**: in the same way as above, we added a number of spelling permutations which increased every 20,000 segments until we arrived at 100,000 segments;
3. **Untranslated segments**: to simulate untranslated segments, we copied the source segment and used it as the target;
4. **Third language in source**: we chose segments for each language pair that contained a different source language than German and Japanese. We tried to choose one language that was relatively close to the original and one that was linguistically distant from the original. For DE>EN we chose 50,000 segments with Dutch as source and 50,000 segments with Russian as source. In the case of JA>EN, we selected 50,000 segments with Chinese as source and 50,000 segments with German as source. In each case, the English target was a correct translation of the source;
5. **Third language in target**: in this case, we followed the same approach as the previous type of noise, but replacing the target instead of the source. In the case of DE>EN, we chose 50,000 segments with Dutch as a target language and 50,000 segments with Russian as target. For JA>EN, we chose 50,000 segments with Chinese as target and 50,000 segments with German as target.
6. **Missing content in source**: we deleted between 5%-50% of the words in source. The number of words deleted grew by 5% increments every 10,000 segments until we reached 100,000 segments. To create this type of noise, we used only sentences with more than 20 words in the source. We used Fugashi (McCann, 2020) to perform word segmentation in Japanese;

7. **Missing content in target**: we followed the same approach as in the previous type of noise, but this time we applied it to target segment;
8. **Mismatching numbers**: we searched for matching numbers in the source and target and increased the first number by a random integer between 1 and 1000. We changed numbers in 50,000 source segments and in 50,000 target segments, but we make no distinction in our analysis based on which number was modified;
9. **Complete misalignment**: we took a properly aligned corpus and intentionally moved several of the target segments from the head of the corpus to the end. In this way, we ended up with a misaligned corpus and sampled 100,000 random segments from it;
10. **Unbalanced [sic] tags**: This type of noise is possibly unique to our use case as a commercial translation provider with human translated data. But we find that unbalanced [sic] tags (i.e. which appear in only one of the source or target but not both) can introduce a systemic bias to the corpus and can cause hallucinations in an MT system if they are not removed prior to training. To create this type of segment, we searched for pairs of sentences that contained [sic] tags in the target but not in the source, but given that the CC Matrix corpus did not contain enough of these segments, we created them by inserting a [sic] tag after a random word in a total of 100,000 segments ;

3.1.2 Data Filtering

For the next step of the process, we concatenated the clean data with the noisy data and used the following tools to score each sentence pair in the combined dataset: XLM-R (Conneau et al., 2019), MUSE (Conneau et al., 2017) and LASER (Schwenk and Douze, 2017) - create sentence representations in an aligned multilingual vector space; COMET (Rei et al., 2020) - pre-trained model for MT evaluation; Marian-scorer (Junczys-Dowmunt et al., 2018) - part of the MarianNMT toolkit, computes cross-entropy.

For XLM-R, MUSE and LASER we used the open-source models available and computed cosine similarity between the resulting embeddings. For COMET, we used the wmt-20-qe-da model for Quality Estimation and Direct Assessment. And finally, for Marian-scorer, we used our company's existing Marian models (which were not trained using CC Matrix data) for the various language directions.

Having calculated scores for each sentence with each tool, we proceeded to filter the data to create datasets for each tool, retaining the top 50% of segments as scored by that tool (i.e., 3 million segments).

3.1.3 Engine Training

After filtering, we trained the following systems:

- One system for each of the training-sets generated by each scoring method;
- One system using the unfiltered dataset containing 5,000,000 clean segments and 1,000,000 noisy segments.

The engines were trained for 35,000 training steps each, and each training was repeated three times with different random seeds to control for the effects of random weight initialization. All other training parameters were held fixed across all runs, and used the base transformer configuration with tied embeddings and a shared sub-word vocabulary of 32,000.

3.1.4 Evaluation

For the engines in Part I, performance in the machine translation task was evaluated using the automated metrics BLEU, TER, and chrF2 obtained using the Sacrebleu package (Post,

2018). Statistical significance for automated metrics was calculated using the paired bootstrap comparison. We used common validation and test sets which were partitioned prior to noise injection and scoring. We report the scores from an ensemble translation with all three models for each tool.

3.2 Part II

3.2.1 Engine Training

In Part II of the study we continued training from some of the baseline models created in Part I using different conditions. For each language pair, we continued training the best performing individual model and one model trained on the unfiltered data set. To test if there are benefits to beginning training with all available data and continuing with a cleaner dataset after a small number of training epochs, we also continued training the best performing model trained on the full dataset using the dataset filtered by the best performing tool. We were also curious to see if a model trained on such data could be used to score and filter its own training data, so we used the best performing model trained on the unfiltered dataset to score and filter its training set, retaining the top 75% of sentences, and continued training using this newly filtered dataset. The engines were allowed to train for 170,000 training steps or until early stopping criteria were met (defined as no improvement in validation perplexity for 5 consecutive checkpoints, or 15,000 training steps).

3.2.2 Evaluation

Once these were trained, sample translations for an in-domain test set and an out-of-domain test set (WMT 2020) were obtained from each model. The translations were scored using the automated metrics BLEU, TER, and chrF2 (with statistical significance determined in the same way as in Part I), and a subset of the test set translations were sent for human annotation. We used an MQM-based annotation method, which, as demonstrated by Freitag et al. (2021a), is more accurate than the previously widely used direct assessment method, and is now the standard in the WMT shared tasks (Freitag et al., 2021b). We used the error types and severity levels, as well as the weights calculation described by Freitag et al. (2021a).

Sentences were selected for human review using different criteria: the most different translations (using Levenshtein distance), the five worst COMET scores from each engine, longest sentences, shortest sentences, and translations containing different numbers of brackets or whose numbers did not match. Out of the total of 200 source sentences per language, 100 were drawn from the in-domain test set, and the remaining 100 came from the out-of-domain test set.

4 Results

Below we present the results of the two parts of our study. The results of Part I show that cross-entropy filtering is significantly better for removing the types of noise we studied. The automated metrics from engine training reinforce this conclusion. The results from Part II are less clear cut, with filtering having a comparatively stronger beneficial effect for the JA>EN direction than the DE>EN direction.

4.1 Part I

4.1.1 Data Filtering Results

With few exceptions, marian-scorer was the clear winner in filtering out noisy data, allowing an order of magnitude fewer noisy segments than the next runner-up in multiple categories. The number of corrupt sentence pairs of each type included in the datasets for each tool are shown in Tables 1 and 2 below. A detailed breakdown of the performance of each tool on different types of noise is provided in Appendix A.

Examining the data in these tables, a few noteworthy observations present themselves:

- While third-language data is a common form of noise in parallel bilingual datasets, all of the tools we tested except marian-scorer are language-agnostic, and thus cannot be used for filtering this kind of noise;
- COMET was the only tool to fail to filter out all completely misaligned segments, but this tool excelled at filtering segments with word order or spelling permutations;
- COMET was much more sensitive to missing target content than to missing source content, while marian-scorer showed the opposite trend. In fact, the amount of missing text apparently made little difference in the scores from these tools (Figure 1). Other tools demonstrated more or less similar performance on these two types of noisy data;
- LASER and COMET did not do well in filtering out segments with mismatching numbers, while other tools generally did well.

4.1.2 First-Step Training Results

After filtration, the resulting datasets were used to train NMT engines. Each training was repeated three times with different random seeds to control for differences resulting from weight initialization. Translation of the common test set was obtained using an ensemble of the three models for each tool. After ten epochs, the models trained on data filtered by Marian performed the best for both languages, significantly outperforming the model trained with unfiltered data. Automated metrics for these translations are reported in Tables 3 and 4.

4.2 Part II

Given its superior performance in the initial training step, we selected Marian-scorer as the tool to use in the second part of the experiment. For each language pair, we trained three test models and one control model. The three test models included one trained to convergence using the dataset filtered by marian-scorer (referred to below as "Marian"), one which was trained on the unfiltered dataset for ten epochs then trained until convergence with the dataset filtered with Marian ("Marian from no filter"), and one which was trained on the unfiltered dataset for ten epochs then used to score and filter its own training data before training until convergence on

Table 1: Number of corrupt sentence pairs of each type included in each DE>EN data set.

Type of Corruption	MUSE	Marian-scorer	XLM-R	LASER	COMET
Word order permutations	39,369	**370**	15,876	7,072	873
Spelling permutations	9,435	**296**	5,073	8,008	1,270
Untranslated segments	100,000	**646**	100,000	99,972	86,588
Third language src	45,483	**375**	33,628	29,362	37,190
Third language tgt	29,930	**10**	55,091	52,279	58,280
Missing content src	8,102	**6,131**	13,126	12,574	33,549
Missing content tgt	9,908	11,056	10,155	**5,165**	9,569
Mismatching numbers	12,462	11,618	**4,797**	22,675	47,611
Complete misalignment	**0**	**0**	**0**	**0**	1,903
Unbalanced *sic* tags	43,009	**9,716**	48,468	20,117	31,116
TOTAL	297,968	**40,218**	286,412	257,224	307,994

Table 2: Number of corrupt sentence pairs of each type included in each JA>EN data set.

Type of Corruption	MUSE	Marian-scorer	XLM-R	LASER	COMET
Word order permutations	52,222	1,169	28,235	11,151	**367**
Spelling permutations	20,546	**503**	4,939	9,758	5,840
Untranslated segments	100,000	**269**	100,000	42,570	23,031
Third language src	79,446	**810**	38,550	34,708	24,898
Third language tgt	53,331	**30**	56,078	36,367	18,462
Missing content src	**24,948**	26,923	26,042	28,153	37,178
Missing content tgt	24,212	13,165	12,574	5,537	**4,837**
Mismatching numbers	32,241	20,410	**12,241**	27,737	25,532
Complete misalignment	**0**	**0**	**0**	**0**	21,914
Unbalanced *sic* tags	49,389	29,791	47,419	21,050	**13,826**
TOTAL	436,335	**93,070**	326,078	217,031	170,629

Table 3: Automated comparison of Ensemble translations for DE>EN.

System	BLEU ($\mu 95\% CI$)	chrF2 ($\mu 95\% CI$)	TER ($\mu 95\% CI$)
No filter (Baseline)	47.6 (47.6 ± 1.3)	70.0 (70.0 ± 0.9)	36.4 (36.4 ± 1.2)
COMET	46.7 (46.7 ± 1.3)	69.1 (69.1 ± 0.9)	37.3 (37.3 ± 1.2)
LASER	48.1 (48.1 ± 1.4)	**70.4** (70.4 ± 0.9)*	**36.0** (36.0 ± 1.2)
Marian	**48.2** (48.2 ± 1.3)*	**70.4** (70.4 ± 0.9)*	**36.0** (36.1 ± 1.2)
MUSE	46.1 (46.0 ± 1.4)*	68.7 (68.7 ± 0.9)*	37.8 (37.8 ± 1.2)*
XLMR	47.6 (47.6 ± 1.4)	69.7 (69.7 ± 0.9)	36.5 (36.5 ± 1.2)

* Indicates the result is a statistically significant ($p < 0.05$) improvement over the unfiltered baseline

Table 4: Automated comparison of Ensemble translations for JA>EN.

System	BLEU ($\mu 95\% CI$)	chrF2 ($\mu 95\% CI$)	TER ($\mu 95\% CI$)
No filter (Baseline)	25.1 (25.1 ± 1.9)	52.8 (52.8 ± 1.1)	63.4 (63.4 ± 2.4)
COMET	30.3 (30.3 ± 1.9)*	56.1 (56.1 ± 1.3)*	55.1 (55.1 ± 1.7)*
LASER	34.1 (34.0 ± 2.0)*	59.0 (58.9 ± 1.3)*	52.2 (52.2 ± 1.7)*
Marian	**35.2** (35.1 ± 1.9)*	**59.3** (59.3 ± 1.3)*	**51.8** (51.8 ± 1.8)*
MUSE	31.5 (31.5 ± 2.1)*	56.7 (56.7 ± 1.3)*	54.9 (54.9 ± 1.7)*
XLMR	32.7 (32.7 ± 2.0)*	57.5 (57.5 ± 1.3)*	53.7 (53.7 ± 1.8)*

* Indicates the result is a statistically significant ($p < 0.05$) improvement over the unfiltered baseline

Table 5: Automated comparison of DE>EN models on in-/out-of-domain test data.

System	BLEU	chrF2	TER
No filter (Baseline)	**51.4**/34.4	**72.2/62.9**	**33.4/52.2**
Marian	50.7/33.3	71.9/61.5	34.0/53.9
Marian from no filter	51.0/33.8	72.1/61.8	34.0/53.5
Train then filter	50.8/**34.6**	72.1/62.6	33.9/52.3

* Indicates the result is a statistically significant (p <0.05) improvement over the unfiltered baseline

Table 6: Automated comparison of JA>EN models on in-/out-of-domain test data.

System	BLEU	chrF2	TER
No filter (Baseline)	39.6/19.1	62.8/**50.6**	47.4/70.3
Marian	39.0/19.4	62.3/50.4	47.9/70.7
Marian from no filter	39.2/19.2	62.5/50.6	47.6/70.8
Train then filter	**40.5*/19.6***	**63.5***/49.9	**46.2*/70.1**

* Indicates the result is a statistically significant (p <0.05) improvement over the unfiltered baseline

the newly filtered data ("Train then filter"). The control model was trained on the unfiltered dataset ("No filter").

After training, we obtained translations of an in-domain test set and out-of-domain test set (WMT 2020) for each model and evaluated the translations with automated metrics and performed human evaluation.

4.2.1 Automated Metrics

For JA>EN, the "Train then filter" approach achieved results on the in-domain test set that were significantly better than any other model. It also achieved the best BLEU score on the out-of-domain test set. For the DE>EN language direction, the "No filter" baseline achieved the best scores for both test sets. Overall, scores were higher for the DE>EN models than for the JA>EN models. In Tables 5 and 6 below we report automated metrics for each system divided by language pair and domain.

4.2.2 Human Evaluation

Human evaluation results are mostly in line with the automatic metrics. Overall, judging by these results, we did not observe any statistically significant improvement over the "No filter" baseline thanks to data filtering (we used the Student t-test for statistical significance). In Table 7, we show the average scores for each model for both languages pairs. A score of 0 indicates a perfect translation, while 25 indicates the lowest possible quality. For the DE>EN language pair, the best result was achieved with the baseline method for out-of-domain data (which is is in line with most of the automatic metrics), while the "Train and then filter" method had the best score for the in-domain data set (although the difference was minimal). For the JA>EN language pair, we observed the best scores with the "Train and then filter" method, which, again, is in line with most of the automatic metrics.

5 Discussion

In this paper we explored the relative performance of different methods of filtering noise from natural language training data, and the effect of filtering on the downstream task of machine translation. We found that cross-entropy filtering using models trained for the translation task

Table 7: Average human MQM evaluation scores on in-/out-of-domain test data.

System	DE>EN	JA>EN
No filter (Baseline)	0.73/**1.32**	1.77/8.14
Marian	0.72/1.67	1.97/7.40
Marian from no filter	0.83/1.51	2.10/7.89
Train then filter	**0.71**/1.58	**1.67/7.00**

performed better than multilingual alternatives such as LASER or COMET at identifying the types of noise we introduced across almost all noise types in both the DE>EN and JA>EN language directions. Language agnostic models have another disadvantage, which is that they cannot be used to identify wrong language data, a common source of noise in bilingual corpora.

However, the clear superiority of cross-entropy filtering did not unambiguously extend to the downstream translation task, where a model trained on the unfiltered dataset performed the best in DE>EN translation, and no model achieved a statistically significant improvement over the baseline in the human evaluation. This suggests that in the regime of a few million sentences, the advantages of having more data volume or more diverse data can outweigh the costs incurred by significant noise present in the dataset.

Our results suggest that in situations where the quality of training data is uncertain, fair results can be obtained by training for a short time on all the available data, filtering the training data with LASER or cross-entropy scores, and then continuing to train on a cleaner subset of the data. Given that LASER is language-agnostic, an additional filtering step based on language-identification may be required when using this tool.

In this study we generally followed the noise taxonomy found in Khayrallah and Koehn (2018a), but other ways of categorizing noise also exist. We are also interested to investigate how these tools perform with noisy data categorized in linguistic terms, such as problems of fluency vs. adequacy. Does data filtration with these tools introduce systemic bias of some sort, such as by preferentially removing sentences with numerous acronyms, shorter sentences, or sentences with lots of punctuation marks? Would the same results be obtained with lower resource languages? We hope to pursue these questions in future research.

A Appendix A

In Figure 1 below, we provide a detailed breakdown of the number of sentences with different types of corruption included in the datasets for each engine, grouped by the degree of corruption. For word and spelling permutations, we included 20,000 sentences with 1 permutation, 20,000 sentences with 2 permutations, and so on up to 5 permutations. For missing source and missing target content, we removed 5% of the words in the first 10,000 sentences, 10% of the words in the second 10,000 sentences, and so on up to 50% of the words. For sentence pairs with a third-language source or target, for half the sentences we used a more similar language (Chinese for Japanese, Dutch for German), and for the other half we used a more distant language (German for Japanese, and Russian for German).

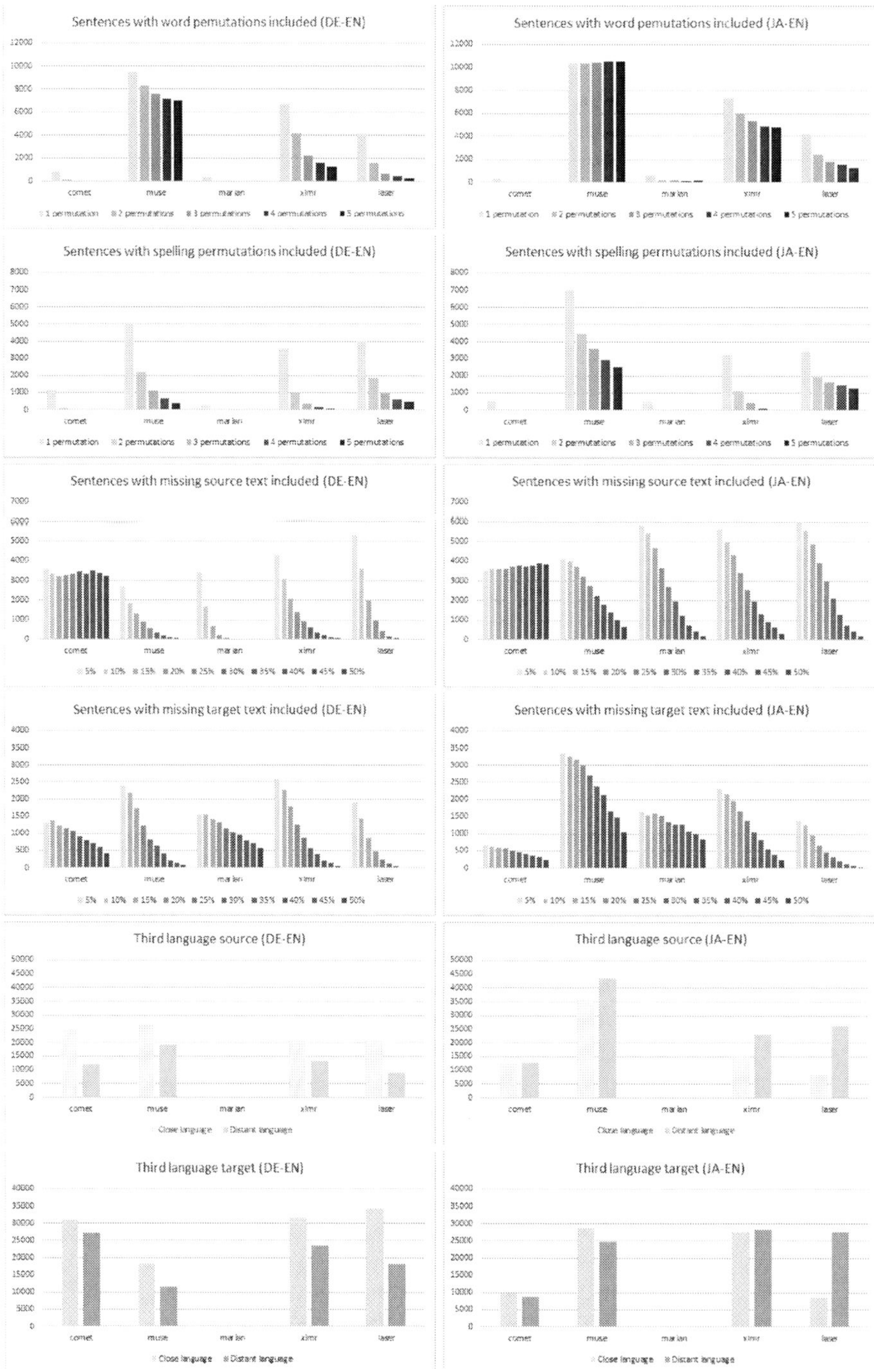

Figure 1: Comparison of filtering performance of different tools on different types of noise

References

Açarçiçek, H., Çolakoğlu, T., Aktan Hatipoğlu, P. E., Huang, C. H., and Peng, W. (2020). Filtering noisy parallel corpus using transformers with proxy task learning. In *Proceedings of the Fifth Conference on Machine Translation*, pages 940–946, Online. Association for Computational Linguistics.

Artetxe, M. and Schwenk, H. (2019). Margin-based parallel corpus mining with multilingual sentence embeddings. In *Proceedings of the 57th Annual Meeting of the Association for Computational Linguistics*, pages 3197–3203, Florence, Italy. Association for Computational Linguistics.

Bañón, M., Chen, P., Haddow, B., Heafield, K., Hoang, H., Esplà-Gomis, M., Forcada, M. L., Kamran, A., Kirefu, F., Koehn, P., Ortiz Rojas, S., Pla Sempere, L., Ramírez-Sánchez, G., Sarrías, E., Strelec, M., Thompson, B., Waites, W., Wiggins, D., and Zaragoza, J. (2020). ParaCrawl: Web-scale acquisition of parallel corpora. In *Proceedings of the 58th Annual Meeting of the Association for Computational Linguistics*, pages 4555–4567, Online. Association for Computational Linguistics.

Carpuat, M., Vyas, Y., and Niu, X. (2017). Detecting cross-lingual semantic divergence for neural machine translation. In *Proceedings of the First Workshop on Neural Machine Translation*, pages 69–79, Vancouver. Association for Computational Linguistics.

Conneau, A., Khandelwal, K., Goyal, N., Chaudhary, V., Wenzek, G., Guzmán, F., Grave, E., Ott, M., Zettlemoyer, L., and Stoyanov, V. (2019). Unsupervised cross-lingual representation learning at scale. *arXiv preprint arXiv:1911.02116*.

Conneau, A., Lample, G., Ranzato, M., Denoyer, L., and Jégou, H. (2017). Word translation without parallel data. *arXiv preprint arXiv:1710.04087*.

Cui, L., Zhang, D., Liu, S., Li, M., and Zhou, M. (2013). Bilingual data cleaning for SMT using graph-based random walk. In *Proceedings of the 51st Annual Meeting of the Association for Computational Linguistics (Volume 2: Short Papers)*, pages 340–345, Sofia, Bulgaria. Association for Computational Linguistics.

Freitag, M., Foster, G., Grangier, D., Ratnakar, V., Tan, Q., and Macherey, W. (2021a). Experts, errors, and context: A large-scale study of human evaluation for machine translation. *Transactions of the Association for Computational Linguistics*, 9:1460–1474.

Freitag, M., Rei, R., Mathur, N., Lo, C.-k., Stewart, C., Foster, G., Lavie, A., and Bojar, O. (2021b). Results of the WMT21 metrics shared task: Evaluating metrics with expert-based human evaluations on TED and news domain. In *Proceedings of the Sixth Conference on Machine Translation*, pages 733–774, Online. Association for Computational Linguistics.

Herold, C., Rosendahl, J., Vanvinckenroye, J., and Ney, H. (2021). Data filtering using cross-lingual word embeddings. In *Proceedings of the 2021 Conference of the North American Chapter of the Association for Computational Linguistics: Human Language Technologies*, pages 162–172, Online. Association for Computational Linguistics.

Junczys-Dowmunt, M. (2018). Dual conditional cross-entropy filtering of noisy parallel corpora. In *Proceedings of the Third Conference on Machine Translation: Shared Task Papers*, pages 888–895, Belgium, Brussels. Association for Computational Linguistics.

Junczys-Dowmunt, M., Grundkiewicz, R., Dwojak, T., Hoang, H., Heafield, K., Neckermann, T., Seide, F., Germann, U., Fikri Aji, A., Bogoychev, N., Martins, A. F. T., and Birch, A. (2018). Marian: Fast neural machine translation in C++. In *Proceedings of ACL 2018, System Demonstrations*, pages 116–121, Melbourne, Australia. Association for Computational Linguistics.

Khayrallah, H. and Koehn, P. (2018a). On the impact of various types of noise on neural machine translation. *arXiv preprint arXiv:1805.12282*.

Khayrallah, H. and Koehn, P. (2018b). On the impact of various types of noise on neural machine translation. In *Proceedings of the 2nd Workshop on Neural Machine Translation and Generation*, pages 74–83, Melbourne, Australia. Association for Computational Linguistics.

Koehn, P., Chaudhary, V., El-Kishky, A., Goyal, N., Chen, P.-J., and Guzmán, F. (2020). Findings of the WMT 2020 shared task on parallel corpus filtering and alignment. In *Proceedings of the Fifth Conference on Machine Translation*, pages 726–742, Online. Association for Computational Linguistics.

Koehn, P. and Knowles, R. (2017). Six challenges for neural machine translation. In *Proceedings of the First Workshop on Neural Machine Translation*, pages 28–39, Vancouver. Association for Computational Linguistics.

Kreutzer, J., Caswell, I., Wang, L., Wahab, A., van Esch, D., Ulzii-Orshikh, N., Tapo, A., Subramani, N., Sokolov, A., Sikasote, C., Setyawan, M., Sarin, S., Samb, S., Sagot, B., Rivera, C., Rios, A., Papadimitriou, I., Osei, S., Suarez, P. O., Orife, I., Ogueji, K., Rubungo, A. N., Nguyen, T. Q., Müller, M., Müller, A., Muhammad, S. H., Muhammad, N., Mnyakeni, A., Mirzakhalov, J., Matangira, T., Leong, C., Lawson, N., Kudugunta, S., Jernite, Y., Jenny, M., Firat, O., Dossou, B. F. P., Dlamini, S., de Silva, N., Ballı, S. Ç., Biderman, S., Battisti, A., Baruwa, A., Bapna, A., Baljekar, P., Azime, I. A., Awokoya, A., Ataman, D., Ahia, O., Ahia, O., Agrawal, S., and Adeyemi, M. (2022). Quality at a glance: An audit of web-crawled multilingual datasets. *Transactions of the Association for Computational Linguistics*, 10:50–72.

Lu, J., Ge, X., Shi, Y., and Zhang, Y. (2020). Alibaba submission to the WMT20 parallel corpus filtering task. In *Proceedings of the Fifth Conference on Machine Translation*, pages 979–984, Online. Association for Computational Linguistics.

McCann, P. (2020). fugashi, a tool for tokenizing Japanese in python. In *Proceedings of Second Workshop for NLP Open Source Software (NLP-OSS)*, pages 44–51, Online. Association for Computational Linguistics.

Post, M. (2018). A call for clarity in reporting BLEU scores. In *Proceedings of the Third Conference on Machine Translation: Research Papers*, pages 186–191, Belgium, Brussels. Association for Computational Linguistics.

Rei, R., Stewart, C., Farinha, A. C., and Lavie, A. (2020). COMET: A neural framework for MT evaluation. In *Proceedings of the 2020 Conference on Empirical Methods in Natural Language Processing (EMNLP)*, pages 2685–2702, Online. Association for Computational Linguistics.

Schwenk, H. (2018). Filtering and mining parallel data in a joint multilingual space. *CoRR*, abs/1805.09822.

Schwenk, H. and Douze, M. (2017). Learning joint multilingual sentence representations with neural machine translation. In *Proceedings of the 2nd Workshop on Representation Learning for NLP*, pages 157–167, Vancouver, Canada. Association for Computational Linguistics.

Schwenk, H., Wenzek, G., Edunov, S., Grave, E., and Joulin, A. (2019). Ccmatrix: Mining billions of high-quality parallel sentences on the web.

Taghipour, K., Khadivi, S., and Xu, J. (2011). Parallel corpus refinement as an outlier detection algorithm. In *MT Summit XIII. Machine Translation Summit (MT Summit-11), 13., September 19-23, Xiamen, China*. NA.

Xu, H. and Koehn, P. (2017). Zipporah: a fast and scalable data cleaning system for noisy web-crawled parallel corpora. In *Proceedings of the 2017 Conference on Empirical Methods in Natural Language Processing*, pages 2945–2950, Copenhagen, Denmark. Association for Computational Linguistics.

Machine Translate

Open resources and community

Cecilia OL Yalangozian, Vilém Zouhar and Adam Bittlingmayer

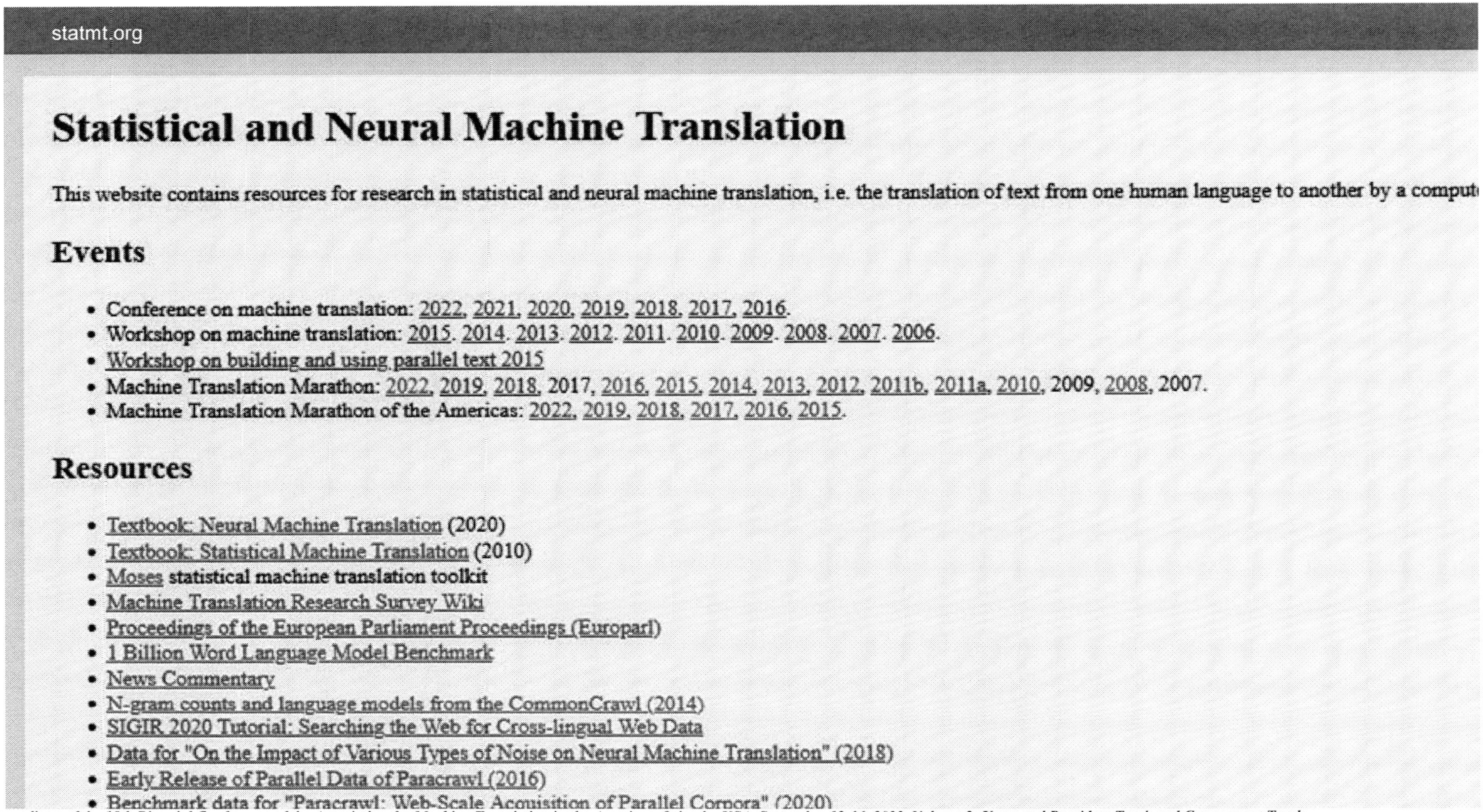
statmt.org

Statistical and Neural Machine Translation

This website contains resources for research in statistical and neural machine translation, i.e. the translation of text from one human language to another by a comput

Events

- Conference on machine translation: 2022, 2021, 2020, 2019, 2018, 2017, 2016.
- Workshop on machine translation: 2015. 2014. 2013. 2012. 2011. 2010. 2009. 2008. 2007. 2006.
- Workshop on building and using parallel text 2015
- Machine Translation Marathon: 2022, 2019, 2018, 2017, 2016, 2015, 2014, 2013, 2012, 2011b, 2011a, 2010, 2009, 2008, 2007.
- Machine Translation Marathon of the Americas: 2022, 2019, 2018, 2017, 2016, 2015.

Resources

- Textbook: Neural Machine Translation (2020)
- Textbook: Statistical Machine Translation (2010)
- Moses statistical machine translation toolkit
- Machine Translation Research Survey Wiki
- Proceedings of the European Parliament Proceedings (Europarl)
- 1 Billion Word Language Model Benchmark
- News Commentary
- N-gram counts and language models from the CommonCrawl (2014)
- SIGIR 2020 Tutorial: Searching the Web for Cross-lingual Web Data
- Data for "On the Impact of Various Types of Noise on Neural Machine Translation" (2018)
- Early Release of Parallel Data of Paracrawl (2016)
- Benchmark data for "Paracrawl: Web-Scale Acquisition of Parallel Corpora" (2020)

WAITING FOR UPDATES
TO STATMT.ORG

How can we do better?

How can we do better?

Open resources and community

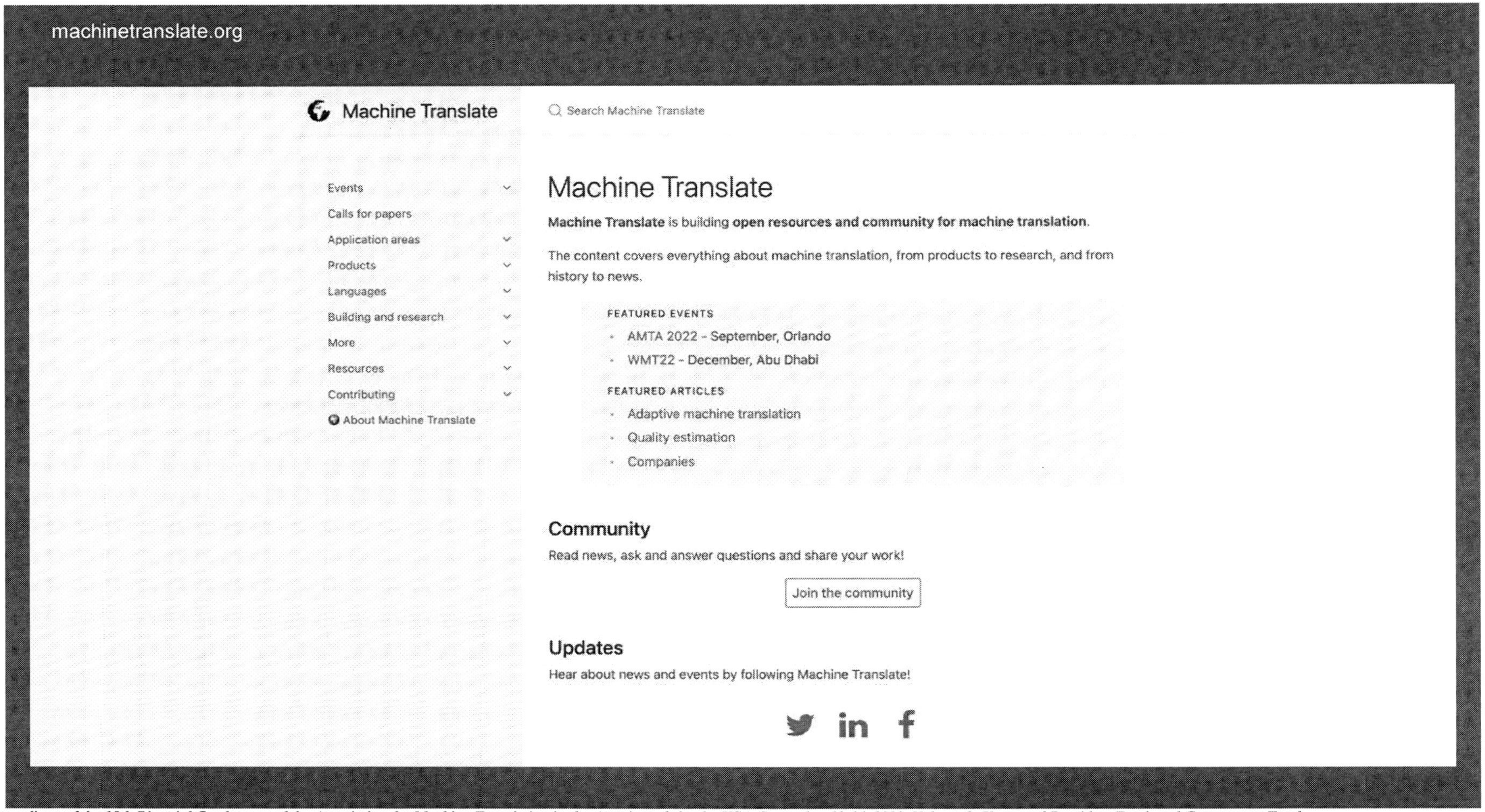
machinetranslate.org
Machine Translate
Search Machine Translate
Events
Calls for papers
Application areas
Products
Languages
Building and research
More
Resources
Contributing
About Machine Translate
Machine Translate
Machine Translate is building open resources and community for machine translation.
The content covers everything about machine translation, from products to research, and from history to news.
FEATURED EVENTS
AMTA 2022 - September, Orlando
WMT22 - December, Abu Dhabi
FEATURED ARTICLES
Adaptive machine translation
Quality estimation
Companies
Community
Read news, ask and answer questions and share your work!
Join the community
Updates
Hear about news and events by following Machine Translate!

“What engines support Armenian?”

Amazon Translate

AppTek

Google Translate

Language Weaver

LingvaNex

Microsoft Translator

ModernMT

Niutrans

PROMT

Rozetta T-400

Yandex Translate

Youdao Translate

"... or Canadian French?"

Alexa Translations A.I.
Amazon Translate
AppTek
Baidu Translate
KantanMT
Language Weaver
LingvaNex
Microsoft Translator
Mirai Translate

“Which TMSes support custom ModernMT?”

"What is back-translation?"

“What machine translation mailing lists exist?”

108
LANGUAGES

38
COMPANIES

45
ENGINES

52
EVENTS

165
INTEGRATIONS

17
CALLS FOR PAPERS

20+

CONTRIBUTORS

Lena Voita, Jörg Tiedemann…

1K+

EDITS

200+

ARTICLES

Create

Edit

Suggest topics

Join the community

machinetranslate.org

tarjama
Deep Learning segmentation and alignment for Arabic
Unlocking the value
of bilingual translated documents
Nour Al-Khdour – Applied ML Scientist
Dr. Rebecca Jonsson – Chief Product Officer
AMTA 2022 ORLANDO
Try our NMT at:
https://translate.tarjama.com
amt

tarjama

Breaking language barriers with Arabic language technology

AI-Enabled LSP

Tarjama is the leading AI-enabled LSP in the MENA region, offering a variety of language services such as translation, localization, subtitling, transcription, interpretation and content creation.
A female-led business founded in 2008.

On a mission to break language barriers in the MENA market with Arabic Language Technology and a proprietary AI-powered language service platform.

+600 Retained clients

+10 Arabic dialects supported

98% Customer retention rate

5 On-ground offices in MENA

+10 Million In funding secured to date

85K Freelancers

+2 Billion Words processed

49% Females

Tarjama is featured in Gartner's Market Guide for AI-Enabled Translation Services

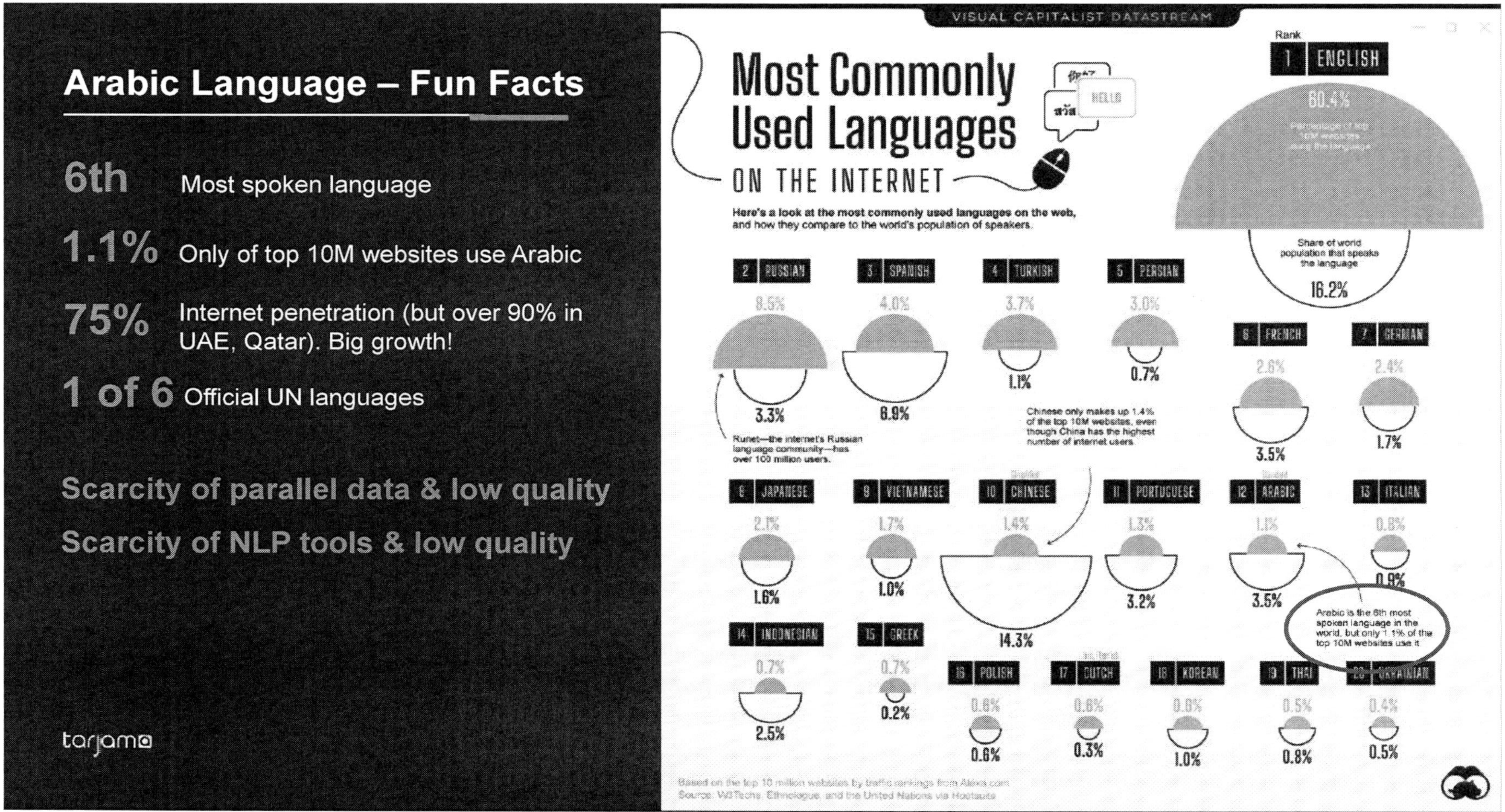
Arabic Language – Fun Facts
6th Most spoken language
1.1% Only of top 10M websites use Arabic
75% Internet penetration (but over 90% in UAE, Qatar). Big growth!
1 of 6 Official UN languages
Scarcity of parallel data & low quality
Scarcity of NLP tools & low quality
tarjama
VISUAL CAPITALIST DATASTREAM
Most Commonly Used Languages ON THE INTERNET
Here's a look at the most commonly used languages on the web, and how they compare to the world's population of speakers.
HELLO
Rank
1 ENGLISH
60.4%
Share of world population that speaks the language
16.2%
2 RUSSIAN
8.5%
3.3%
3 SPANISH
4.0%
6.9%
4 TURKISH
3.7%
1.1%
5 PERSIAN
3.0%
0.7%
6 FRENCH
2.6%
3.5%
7 GERMAN
2.4%
1.7%
Runet—the internet's Russian language community—has over 100 million users.
Chinese only makes up 1.4% of the top 10M websites, even though China has the highest number of internet users.
8 JAPANESE
2.1%
1.6%
9 VIETNAMESE
1.7%
1.0%
10 CHINESE
1.4%
14.3%
11 PORTUGUESE
1.3%
3.2%
12 ARABIC
1.1%
3.5%
13 ITALIAN
0.8%
0.9%
Arabic is the 6th most spoken language in the world, but only 1.1% of the top 10M websites use it
14 INDONESIAN
0.7%
2.5%
15 GREEK
0.7%
0.2%
16 POLISH
0.6%
0.6%
17 DUTCH
0.6%
0.3%
18 KOREAN
0.6%
1.0%
19 THAI
0.5%
0.8%
20 UKRAINIAN
0.4%
0.5%
Based on the top 10 million websites by traffic rankings from Alexa.com
Source: W3Techs, Ethnologue, and the United Nations via Hootsuite

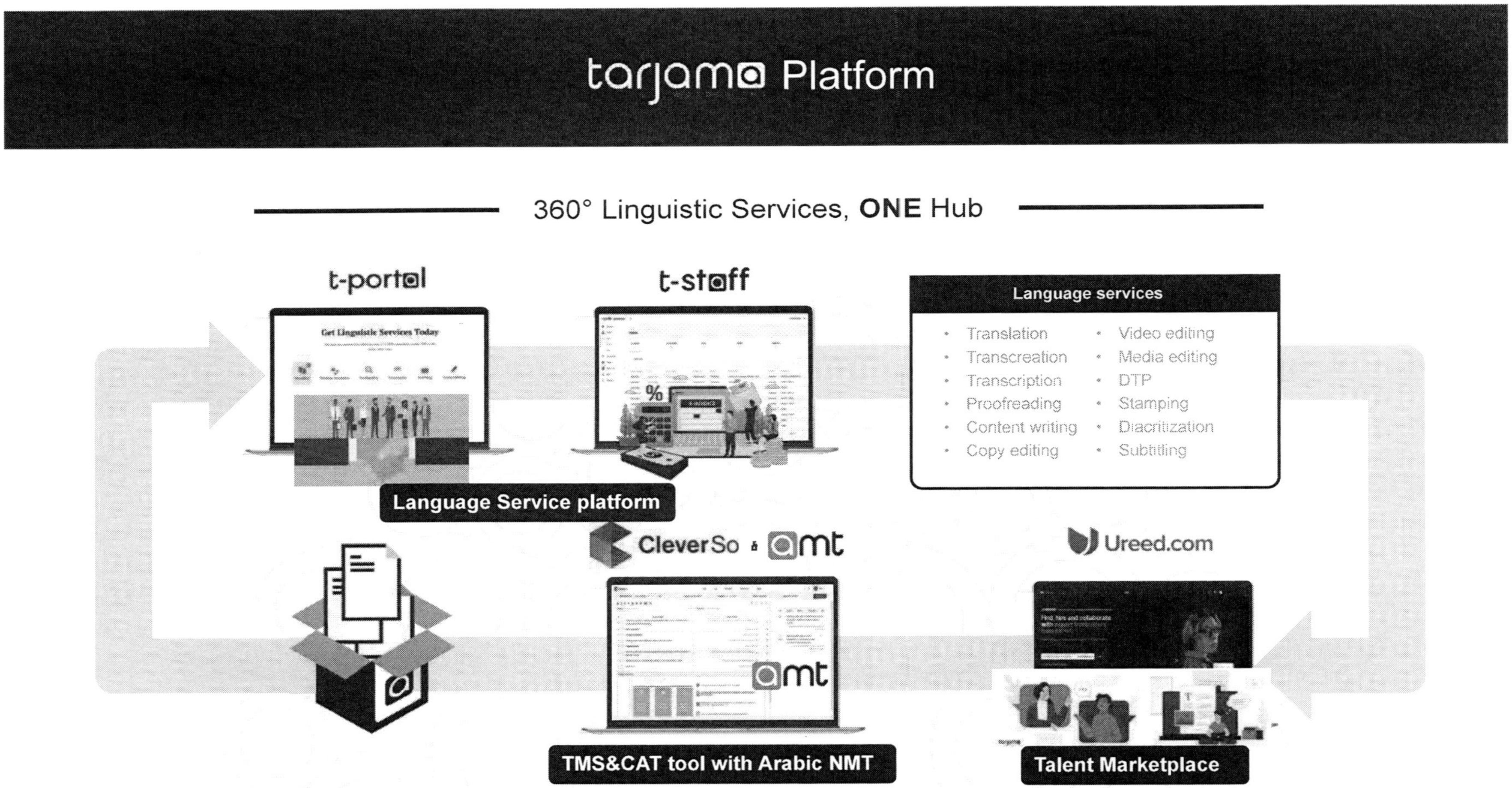

tarjama Platform
360° Linguistic Services, ONE Hub
t-portal
Get Linguistic Services Today
t-staff
Language Service platform
Language services
Translation
Transcreation
Transcription
Proofreading
Content writing
Copy editing
Video editing
Media editing
DTP
Stamping
Diacritization
Subtitling
CleverSo & amt
amt
TMS&CAT tool with Arabic NMT
Ureed.com
Talent Marketplace

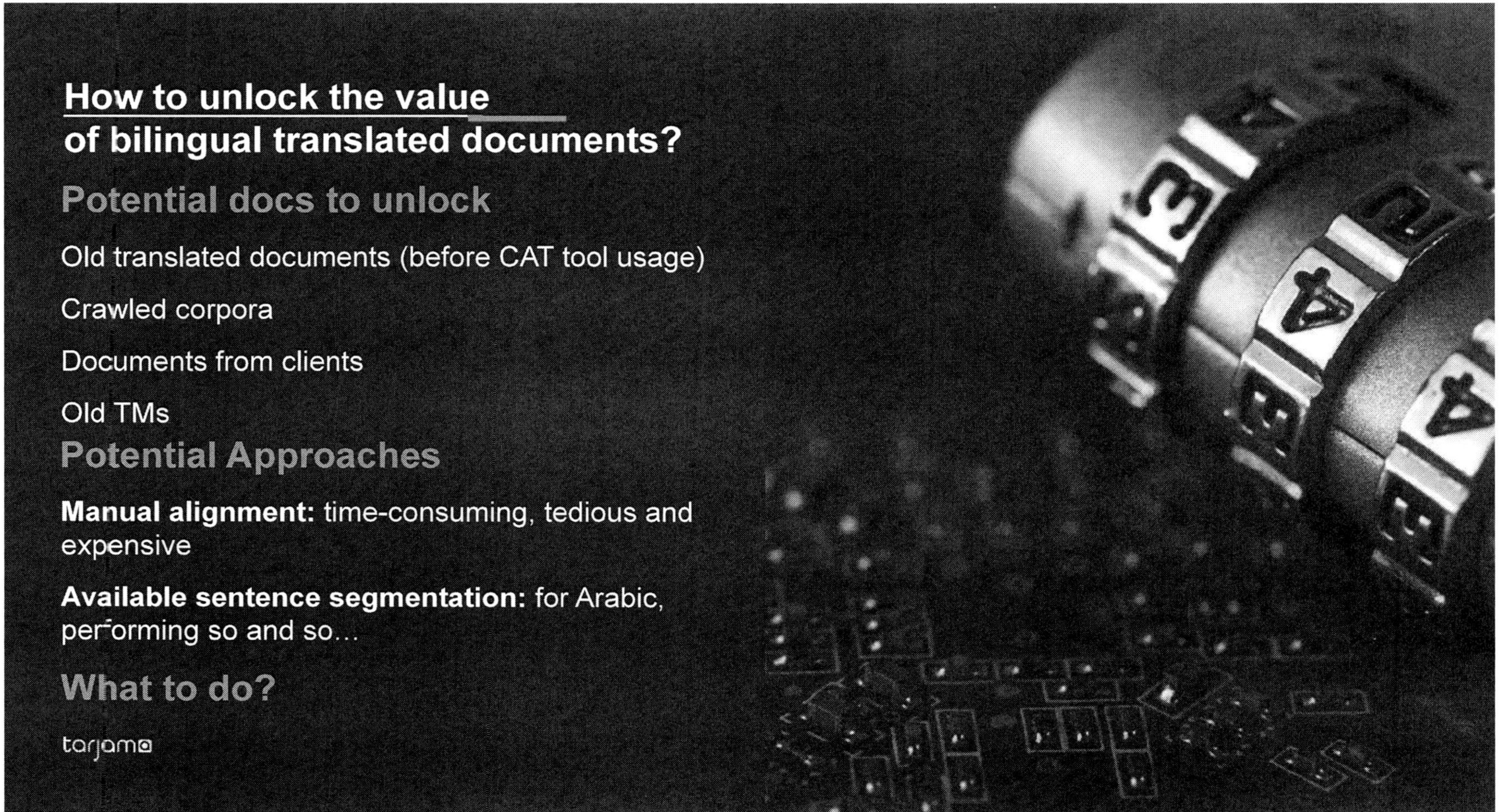
How to unlock the value
of bilingual translated documents?
Potential docs to unlock
Old translated documents (before CAT tool usage)
Crawled corpora
Documents from clients
Old TMs
Potential Approaches
Manual alignment: time-consuming, tedious and expensive
Available sentence segmentation: for Arabic, performing so and so...
What to do?
tarjama

Arabic Sentence Segmentation

Challenges

Detect the sentence boundary based on the context, not rule-based.

Ambiguity of full stops.

Arabic has no capital letters.

Arabic has different punctuation marks, such as (comma "،", and question mark "؟").

tarjama

Available Tools for Arabic Sentence Segmentation

Model	Approach	Support Arabic	Notes
AraNLP	ML	✔	
SAFAR	Rules-based + ML	✔	
pySBD	Rules-based	✔	
NLTK	unsupervised approach	✖	Modified to support the Arabic question mark.

Table 1: Information on Available Arabic Sentence Segmentation Tools

tarjama

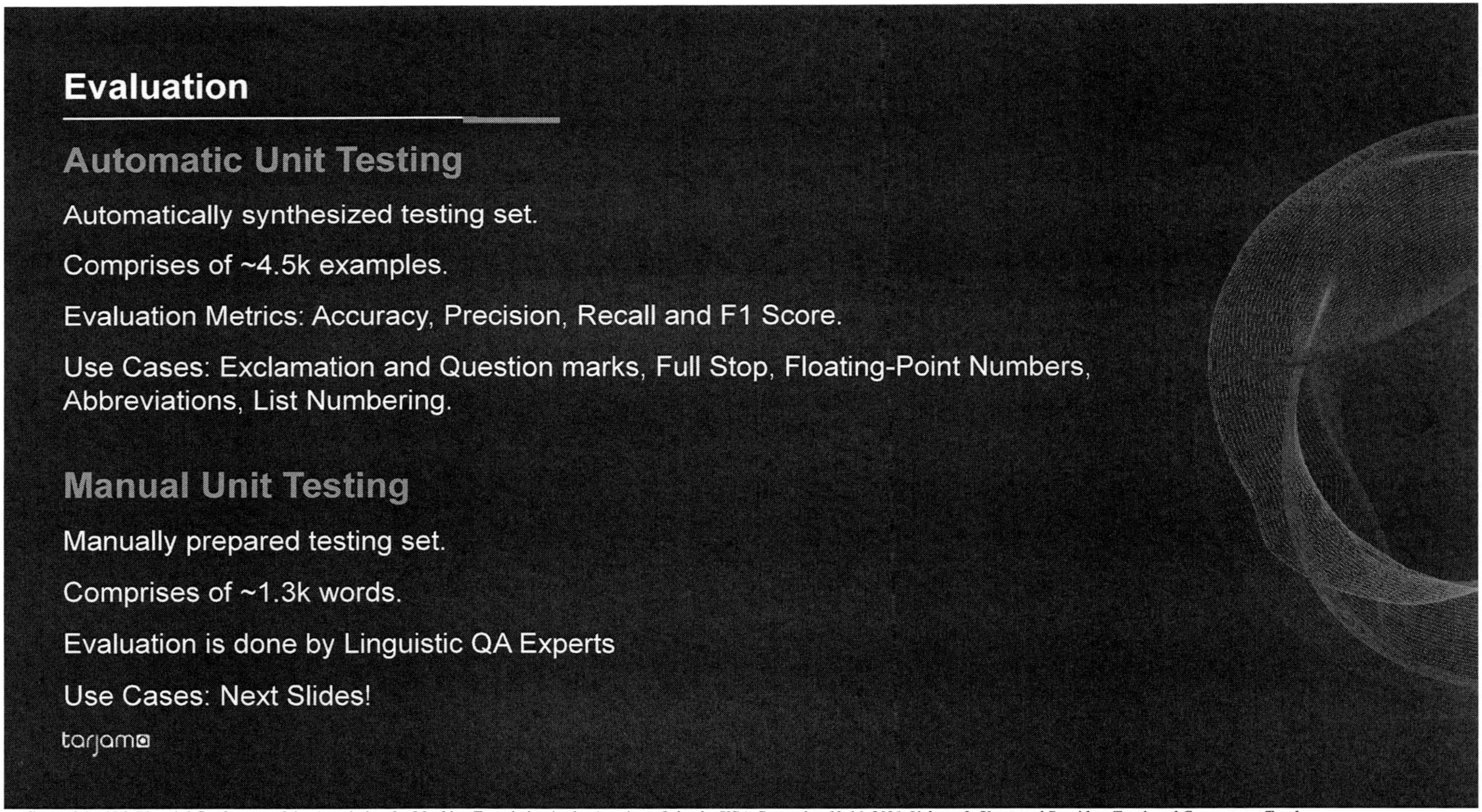
Evaluation
Automatic Unit Testing
Automatically synthesized testing set.
Comprises of ~4.5k examples.
Evaluation Metrics: Accuracy, Precision, Recall and F1 Score.
Use Cases: Exclamation and Question marks, Full Stop, Floating-Point Numbers, Abbreviations, List Numbering.
Manual Unit Testing
Manually prepared testing set.
Comprises of ~1.3k words.
Evaluation is done by Linguistic QA Experts
Use Cases: Next Slides!
tarjama

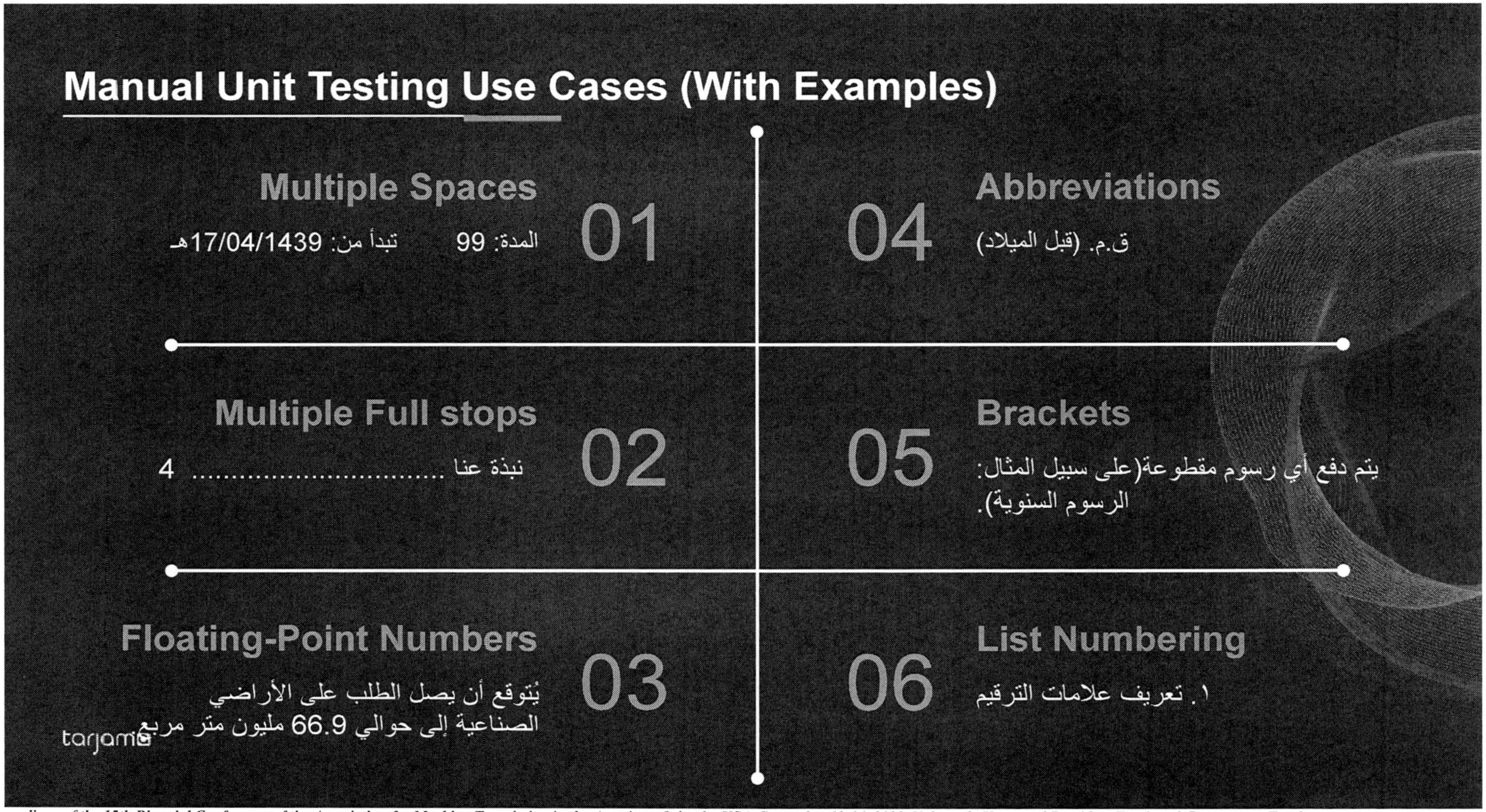
Manual Unit Testing Use Cases (With Examples)
01
Multiple Spaces
المدة: 99   تبدأ من: 17/04/1439هـ
02
Multiple Full stops
نبذة عنا 4
03
Floating-Point Numbers
يُتوقع أن يصل الطلب على الأراضي
الصناعية إلى حوالي 66.9 مليون متر مربع
04
Abbreviations
ق.م. (قبل الميلاد)
05
Brackets
يتم دفع أي رسوم مقطوعة(على سبيل المثال:
الرسوم السنوية).
06
List Numbering
١. تعريف علامات الترقيم
tarjama

Manual Unit Testing Use Cases (With Examples)

07 Paragraphs with Full Stops

تسبب الحطام المحترق ومخلفات النفط بأضرار جسيمة في الساحل السريلانكي المجاور. إن حجم الضرر جعل من هذا الحادث من أسوأ الكوارث البيئية في سيرلانكا. أنقذت البحرية السريلانكية 25 فردًا من أفراد طاقم سفينة الشحن بعد أن دمرت الانفجارات أجزاءً منها. كما ساعدت البحرية الهندية في السيطرة على الحريق.

08 Paragraphs without Full Stops

إن تعهدات أي من الطرفين بالتعويض مشروطة : (أ) بقيام الطرف الذي يمنح له التعويض بتزويد الطرف المانح للتعويض بإشعار خطي عاجل عن أي مطالبة (شريطة أن يعفي الإخفاق في تقديم الإشعار بصورة عاجلة الطرف المانح للتعويض من تعهده فقط بالقدر التي يستطيع فيه أن يبين الضرر المادي من مثل ذلك الإخفاق)، (ب) بحيازة الطرف الذي يمنح له التعويض للسيطرة والسلطة الحصرية فيما يتعلق بالدفاع والتسوية عن أي مطالبة من ذلك القبيل

09 Multiple Cases

السماعات.. كيف تكون؟ على موقع يوتيوب، بثت قناة مهتمة بالشأن التقني تسجيلا مصورا يُظهر لأول مرة ما يعتقد أنها سماعات الأذن التي تمتاز بأنها تأتي مع وصلة Lightning بدلا من موصل الصوت التقليدي 3.5 مم، وهي ما يشاع أنها ستأتي مع هاتف آبل المرتقب.

tarjama

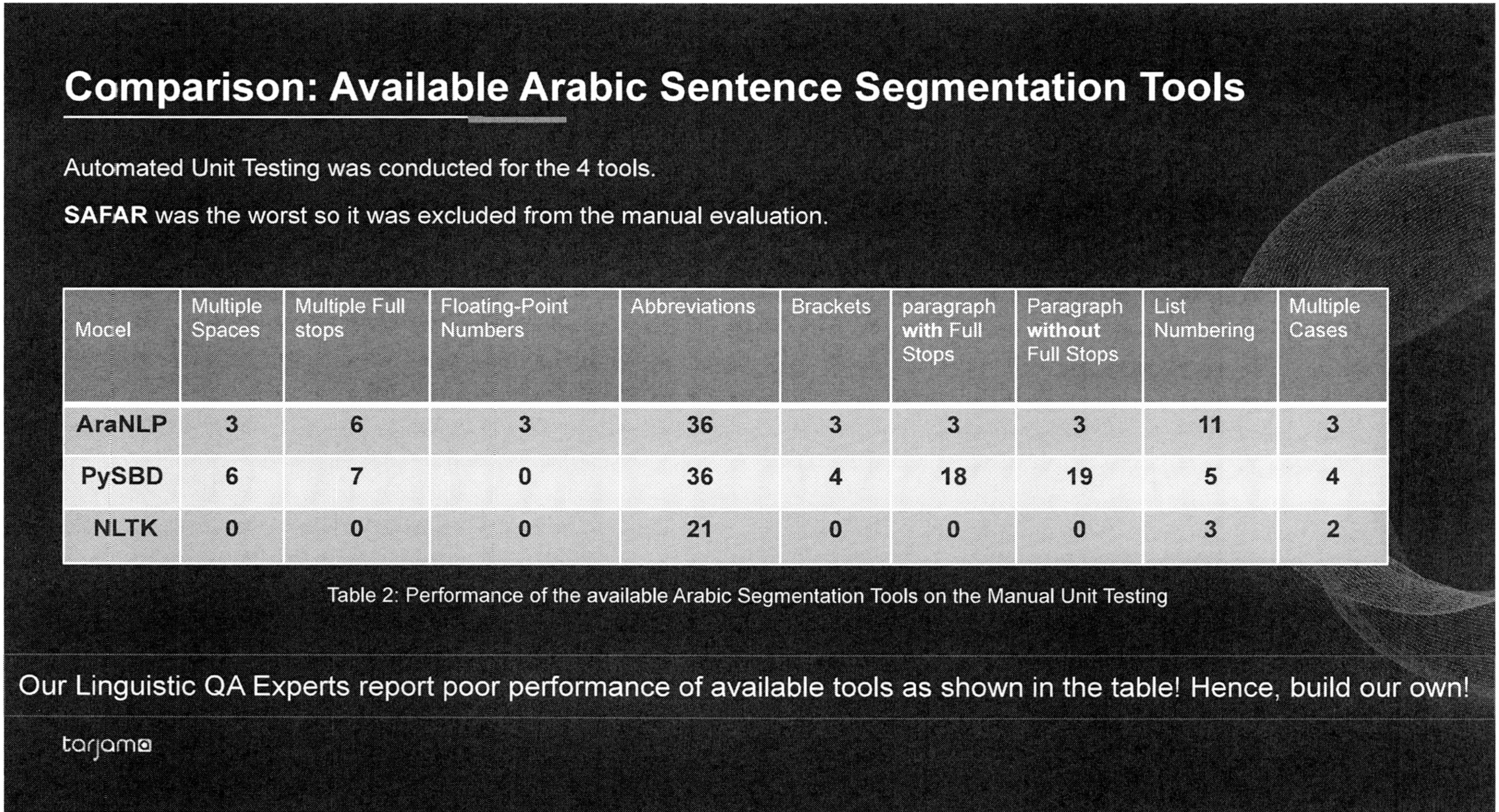

Comparison: Available Arabic Sentence Segmentation Tools

Automated Unit Testing was conducted for the 4 tools.

SAFAR was the worst so it was excluded from the manual evaluation.

Mocel	Multiple Spaces	Multiple Full stops	Floating-Point Numbers	Abbreviations	Brackets	paragraph **with** Full Stops	Paragraph **without** Full Stops	List Numbering	Multiple Cases
AraNLP	3	6	3	36	3	3	3	11	3
PySBD	6	7	0	36	4	18	19	5	4
NLTK	0	0	0	21	0	0	0	3	2

Table 2: Performance of the available Arabic Segmentation Tools on the Manual Unit Testing

Our Linguistic QA Experts report poor performance of available tools as shown in the table! Hence, build our own!

tarjama

Tarjama Arabic Sentence Segmentation Experiments

	Unsupervised Machine Learning (ML)	Deep Learning (DL)
Training Data Size	1477813	863821
Architecture	Punkt (Kiss & Strunk, 2006)	CNN bi-LSTM LSTM

Table 3: Information on Tarjama Arabic Sentence Segmentation Experiments

tarjama

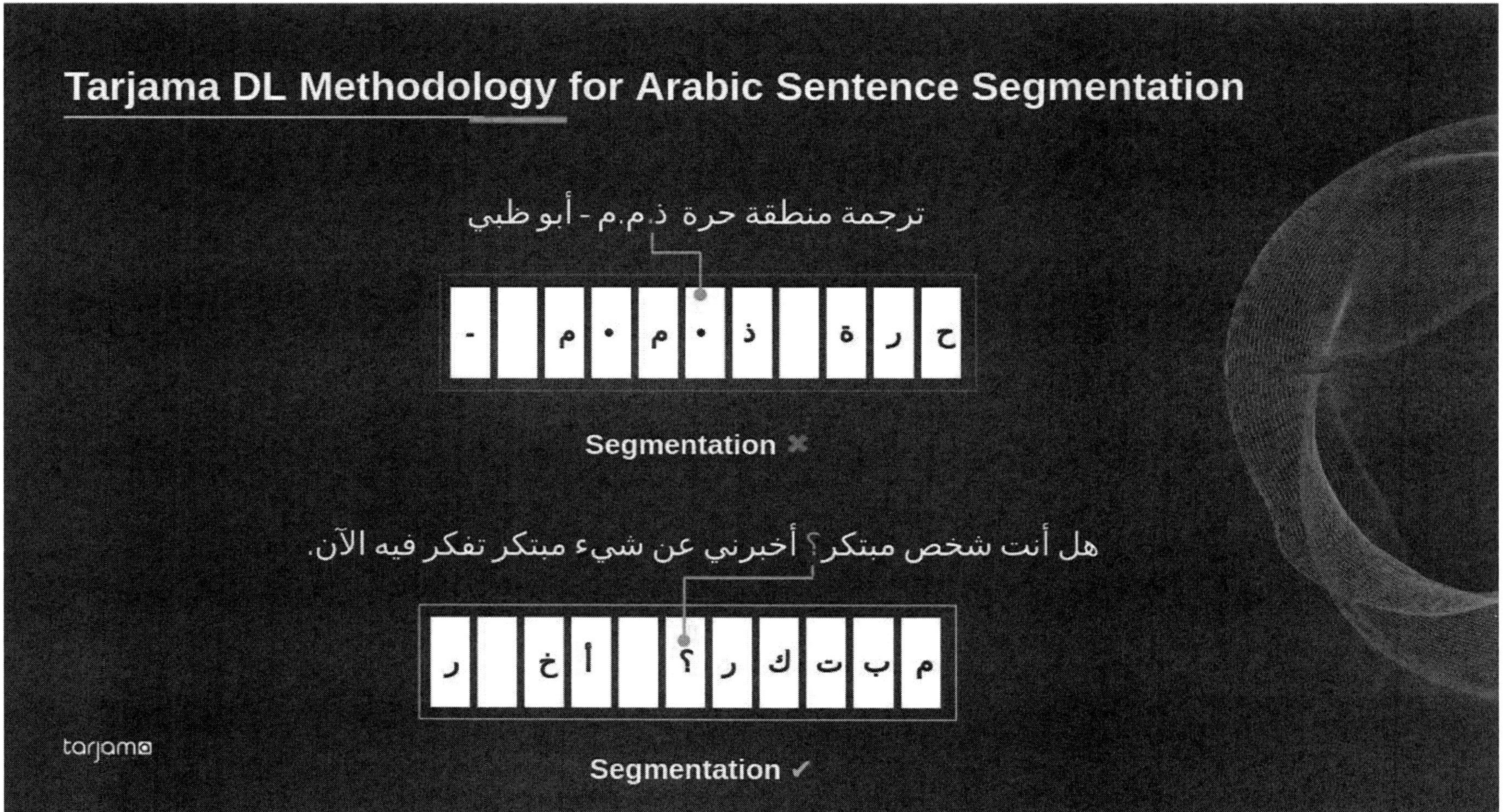
Tarjama DL Methodology for Arabic Sentence Segmentation
ترجمة منطقة حرة ذ.م.م - أبو ظبي
ح ر ة ذ • م • م -
Segmentation ✖
هل أنت شخص مبتكر؟ أخبرني عن شيء مبتكر تفكر فيه الآن.
م ب ت ك ر ؟ أ خ ر
Segmentation ✔
tarjama

Comparison: Available Tools Vs. Tarjama Models

Model	Multiple Spaces	Multiple Full stops	Floating-Point Numbers	Abbreviations	Brackets	paragraph **with** Full Stops	Paragraph **without** Full Stops	List Numbering	Multiple Cases
AraNLP	3	6	3	36	3	3	3	11	3
PySBD	6	7	0	36	4	18	19	5	4
NLTK	0	0	0	21	0	0	0	3	2
Unsupervised ML (Tarjama)	0	0	0	17	0	0	0	3	2
Deep Learning (Tarjama)	0	4	0	3	0	0	0	3	1

Table 4: Appending Tarjama Arabic Segmentation Models Results on the Manual Unit Testing

tarjama

Tarjama Deep Learning Model highly Outperforms available Arabic Segmentation Tools!

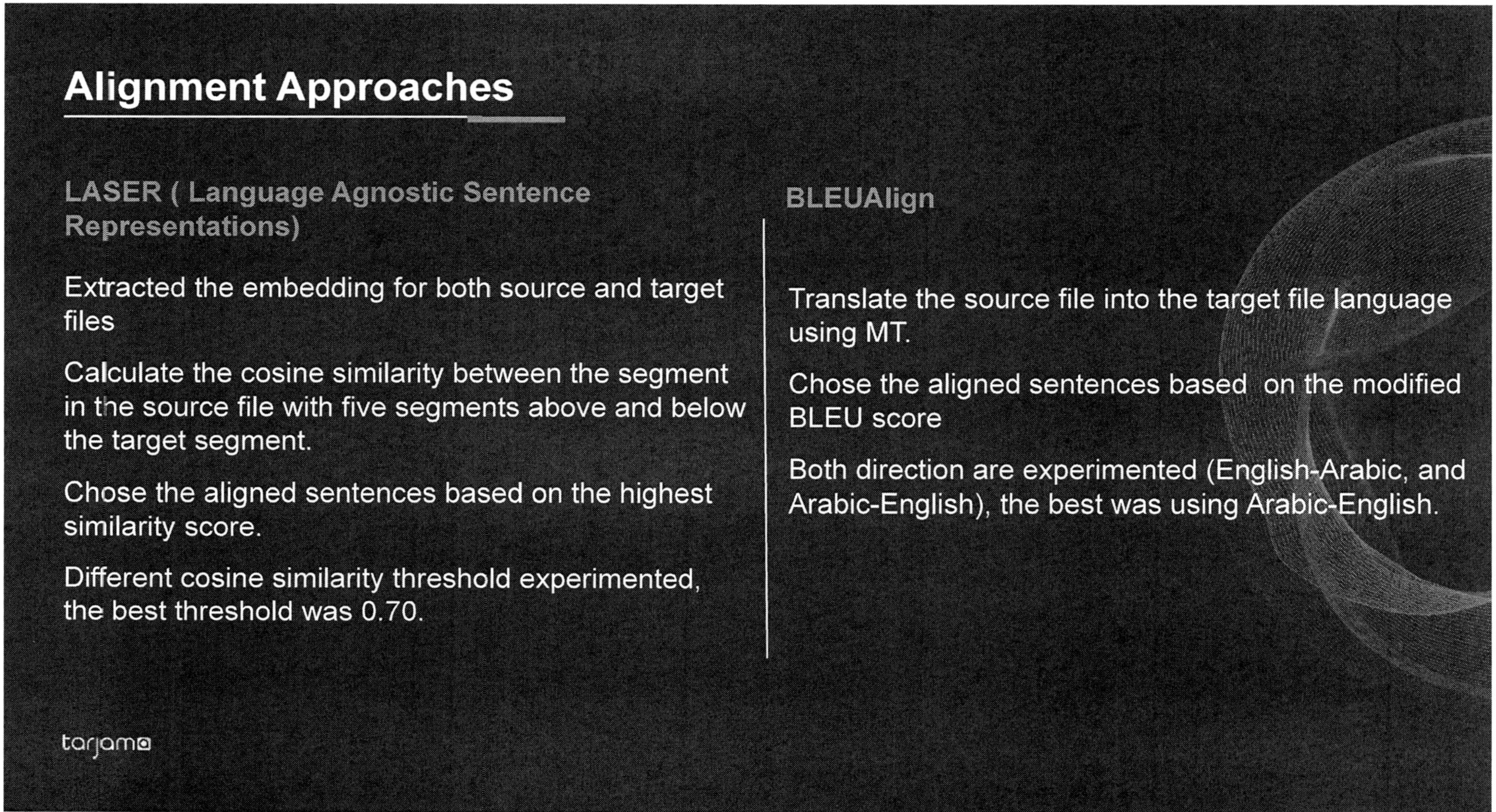
Alignment Approaches
LASER (Language Agnostic Sentence Representations)
Extracted the embedding for both source and target files
Calculate the cosine similarity between the segment in the source file with five segments above and below the target segment.
Chose the aligned sentences based on the highest similarity score.
Different cosine similarity threshold experimented, the best threshold was 0.70.
BLEUAlign
Translate the source file into the target file language using MT.
Chose the aligned sentences based on the modified BLEU score
Both direction are experimented (English-Arabic, and Arabic-English), the best was using Arabic-English.
tarjama

Alignment Scores

Model	No. of Aligned Segments	Precision	Recall	F1-Score
LASER	1643	94.21	88.25	91.13
BLEUALign	1649	94.60	88.93	91.68

Table 6: Results of Alignment Approaches on Automatic Evaluation Test Set

tarjama

Unlocking OLD Tarjama Data

Unlocking the value of ~60 GB of archived Bilingual documents translated by Tarjama before usage of CAT tools (2008-2016). Data was extracted, segmented and aligned by our Deep Learning model to produce TMs and Parallel Data.

	Sentences		Tokens			
	English	Arabic	English	%	Arabic	%
Original Data	1502878	1482443	7793757	100	7948912	100
BLEUAlign	1164634		6362165	81.6	6415418	80.7

Table 6: Coverage on English-Arabic Old Tarjama Data

tarjama

Value We Unlocked!

With Arabic Deep Learning Segmentation and Alignment

Old Tarjama data

Unlocking the value of ~60 GB of archived Bilingual documents translated by Tarjama before usage of CAT tools (2008-2016). Data was extracted, segmented and aligned by our Deep Learning model to produce TMs and Parallel Data.

Crawled Comparable corpora

Unlocked GlobalVoices and WorldBank crawled comparable corpora. Allowed us to feed our Generic NMT with this data for EN->AR

Creating TMs from Bilingual Docs

Allows us to create TMs from previous data that a client has translated outside CAT tools. Something quite common in the MENA region.

First automated TM for an e-commerce client

E-commerce client shared translated product descriptions which they wanted to be imported into our CAT tool as a TM. The problem: each entry was a large bulk of non-segmented text. In order to make use of this as a TM in our CAT tool, each entry had to be segmented and aligned into a new TM automatically.

With our new Arabic Deep Learning Segmentation and Alignment approach, we aligned these documents of over 300K words in one day. Would have taken weeks or even months to do manually! Happy client!

THANK YOU
amt
arabic machine translation by tarjama
شكرًا
https://translate.tarjama.com

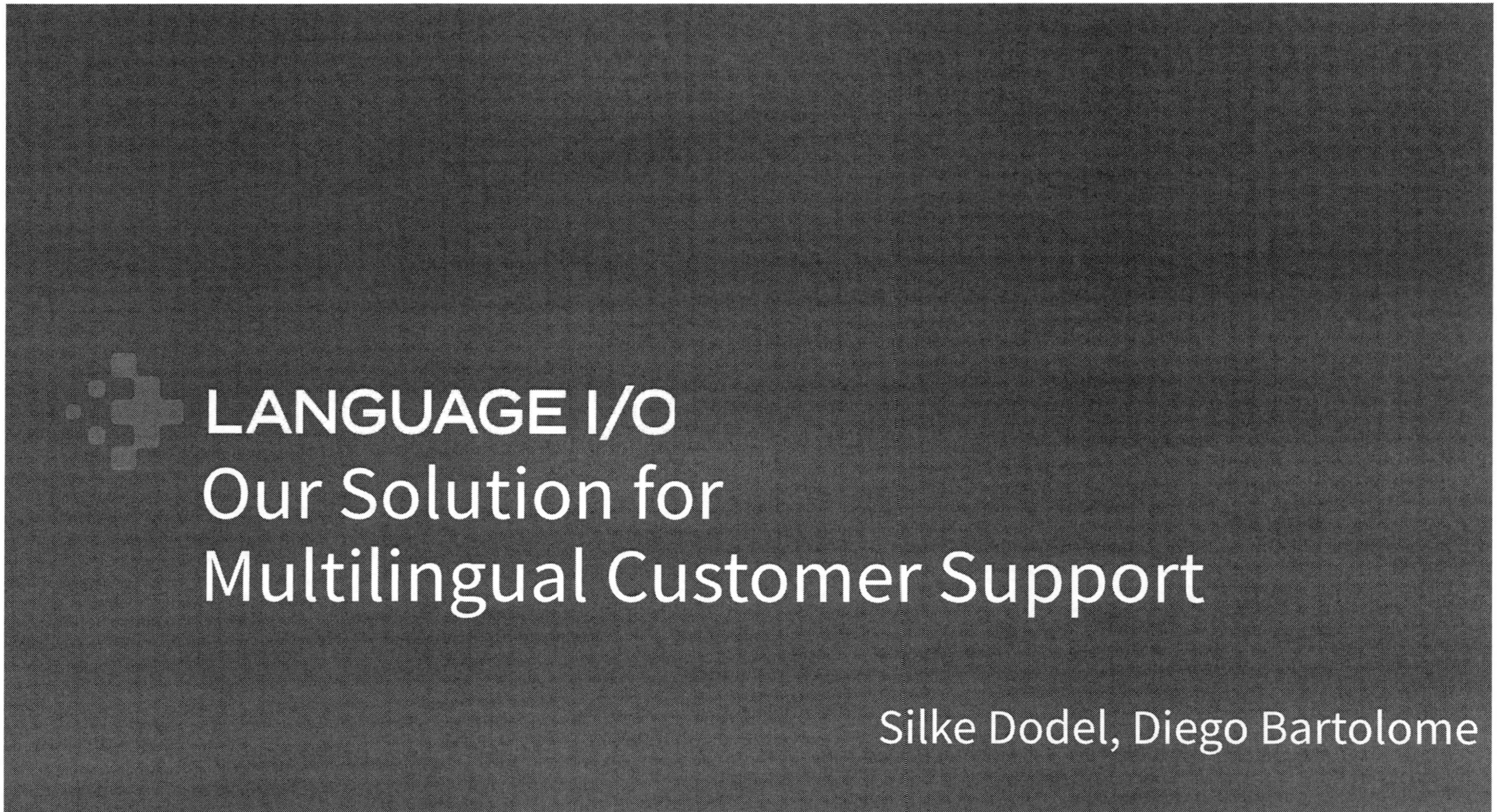
LANGUAGE I/O
Our Solution for
Multilingual Customer Support
Silke Dodel, Diego Bartolome

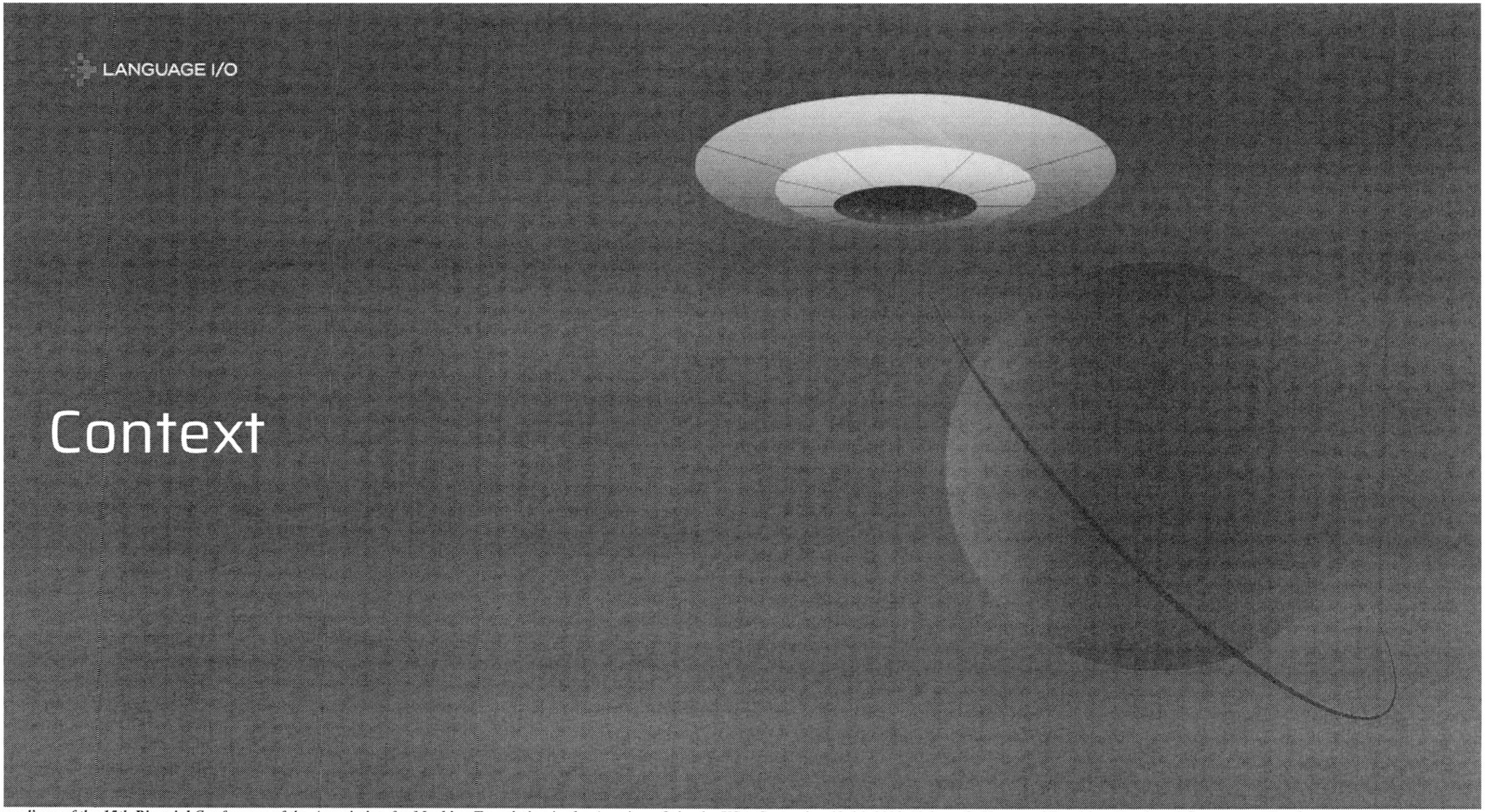
LANGUAGE I/O
Context

LANGUAGE I/O

Trends

1. Digital Customer Service

2. Knowledge Management for CS

3. Customer Service Analytics

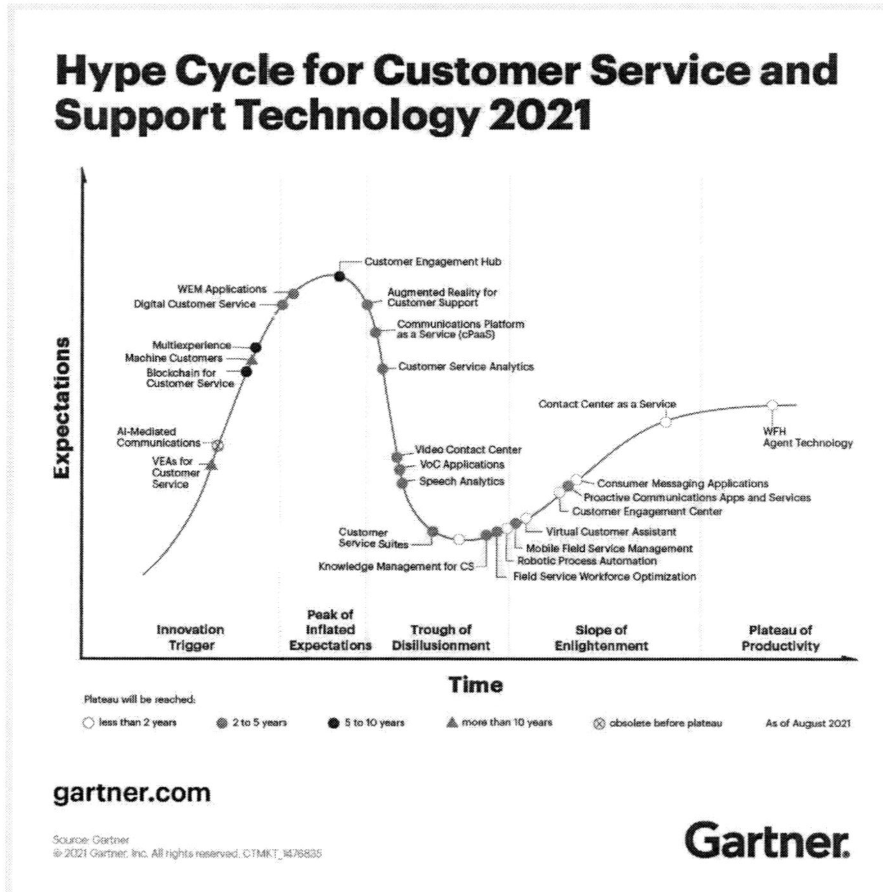

LANGUAGE I/O

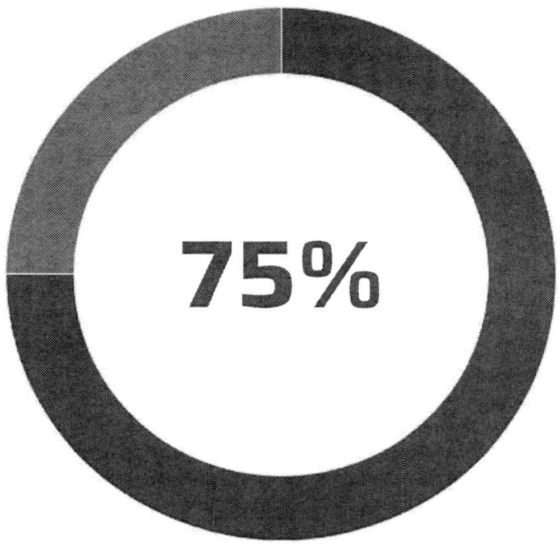

of B2B and B2C buyers surveyed agreed they would be more likely to repurchase from a brand if the after-sales care is in their native language.

-CSA Research

For European markets, **Nimdzi** found that having "no translated content" is the main customer service concern, and the second biggest concern for both the APAC and the Americas.

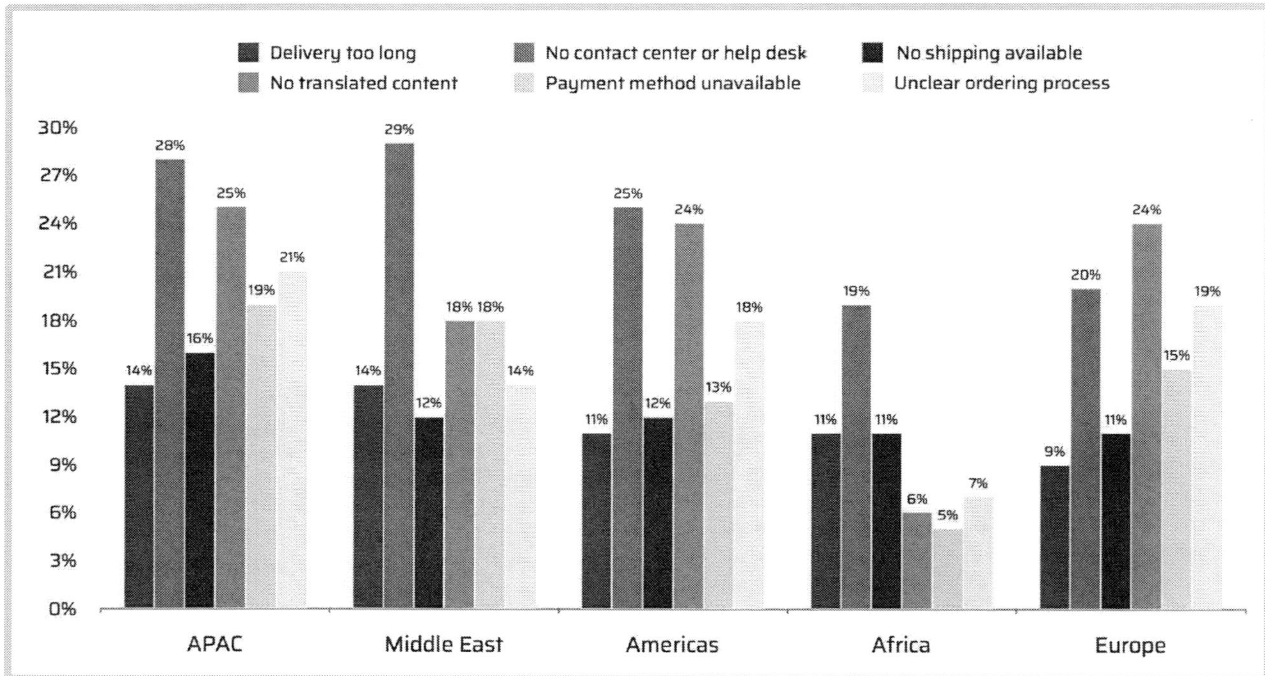

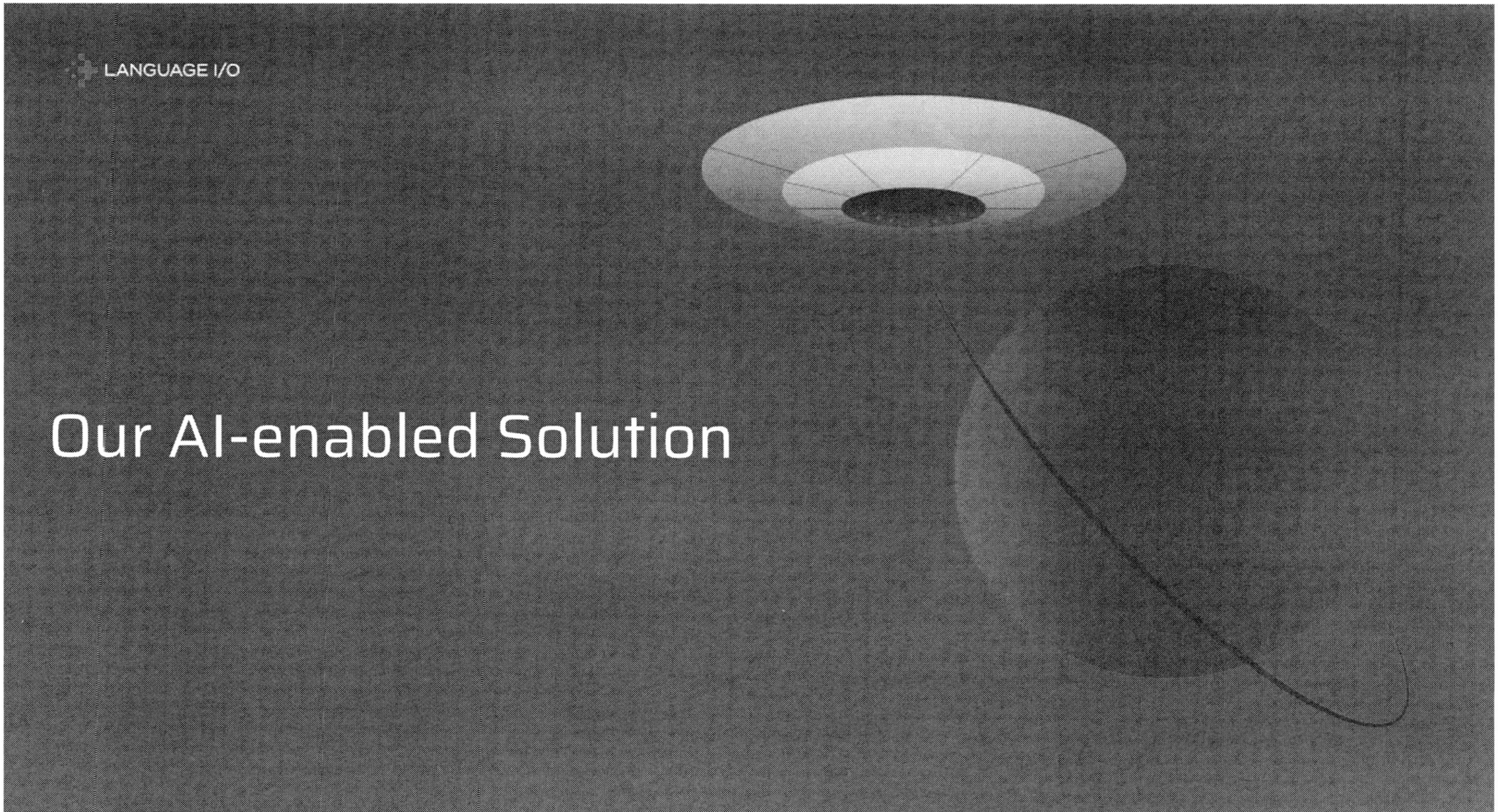
LANGUAGE I/O
Our AI-enabled Solution

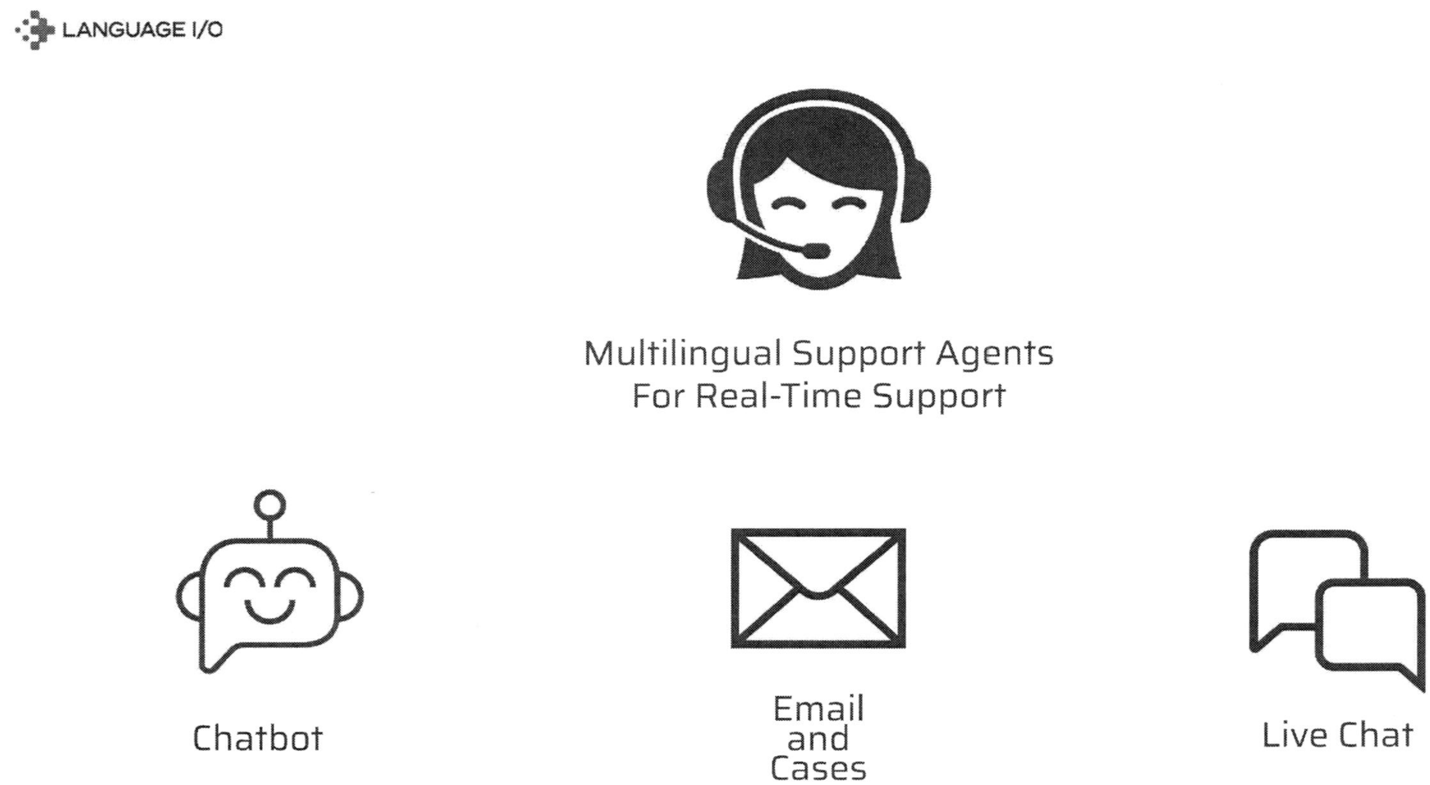
LANGUAGE I/O
Multilingual Support Agents
For Real-Time Support
Chatbot
Email
and
Cases
Live Chat

LANGUAGE I/O

Key Steps in Multilingual Customer Service

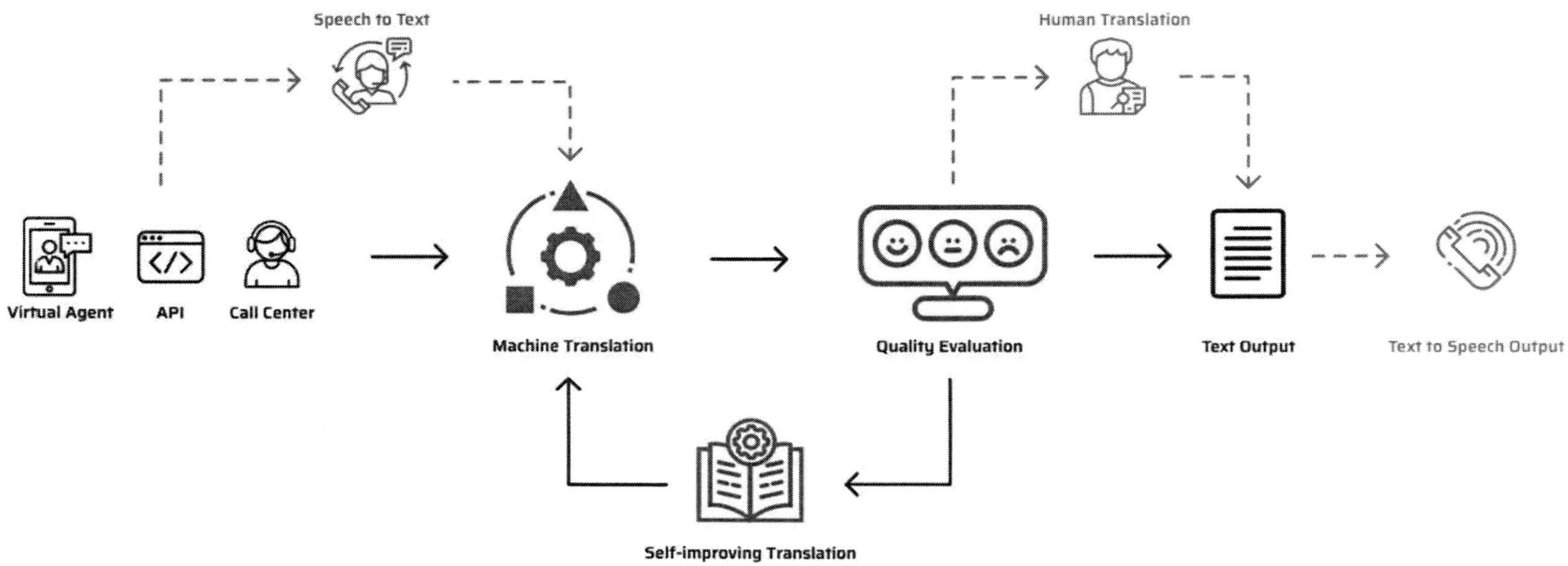

LANGUAGE I/O

Key components

- → CRM Integrations: Salesforce, Oracle, Zendesk, Service Now
- → Optimum MT selection per customer per content type
- → Self-Improving Glossary to handle terminology
- → Translation Quality Estimation and routing to human translation
- → Security: no data stored!
- → Setup in no time: less than 24 hours

LANGUAGE I/O

Details on Translation Quality Estimation

- ➔ Adaptive threshold per customer per language pair
- ➔ Continuously evolves with active learning technologies
- ➔ Using linguistic information as well as Language I/O's metadata
- ➔ Improves engine selection technology
- ➔ End goal is to minimize human processing

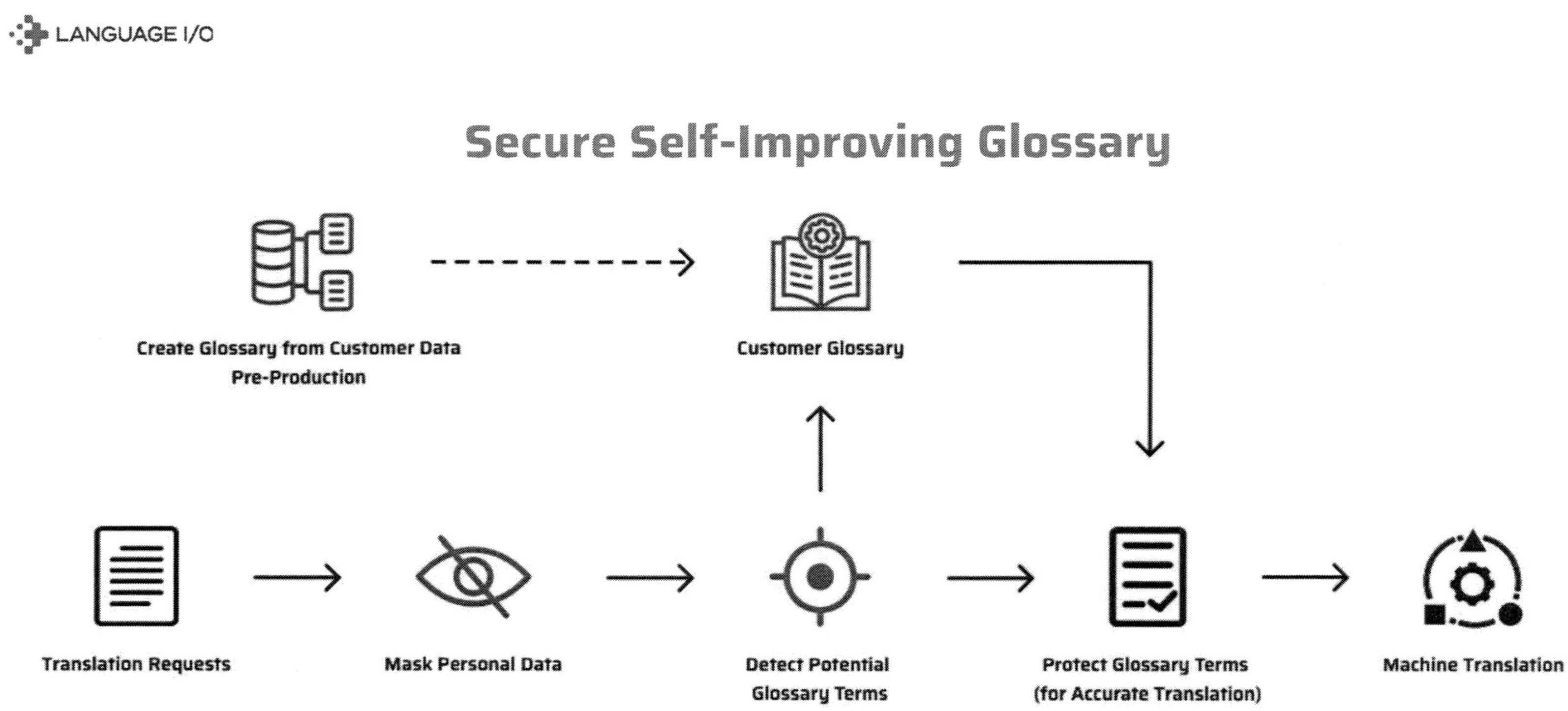
LANGUAGE I/O
Secure Self-Improving Glossary
Create Glossary from Customer Data
Pre-Production
Customer Glossary
Translation Requests
Mask Personal Data
Detect Potential
Glossary Terms
Protect Glossary Terms
(for Accurate Translation)
Machine Translation

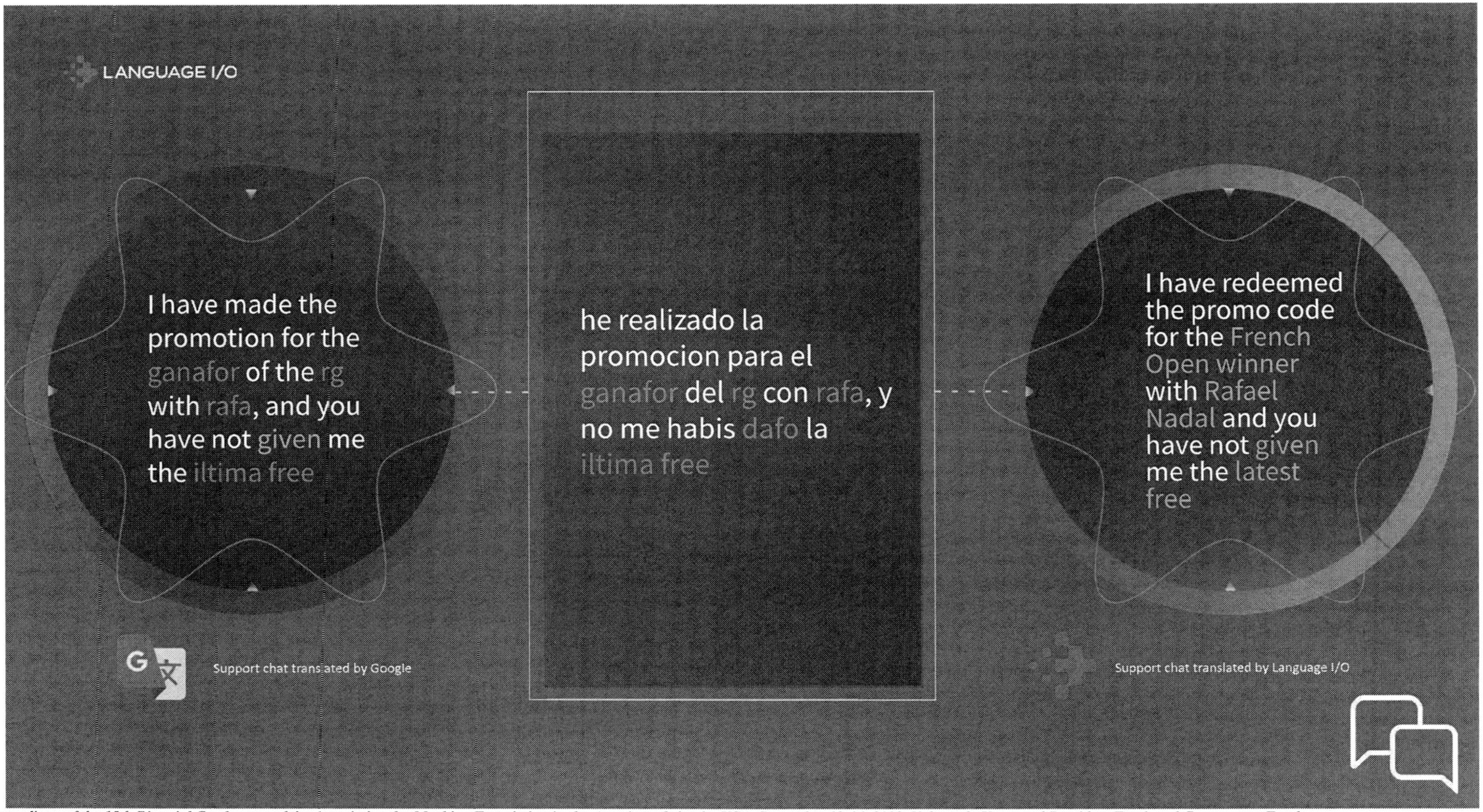
LANGUAGE I/O
I have made the promotion for the ganafor of the rg with rafa, and you have not given me the iltima free
he realizado la promocion para el ganafor del rg con rafa, y no me habis dafo la iltima free
I have redeemed the promo code for the French Open winner with Rafael Nadal and you have not given me the latest free
Support chat translated by Google
Support chat translated by Language I/O

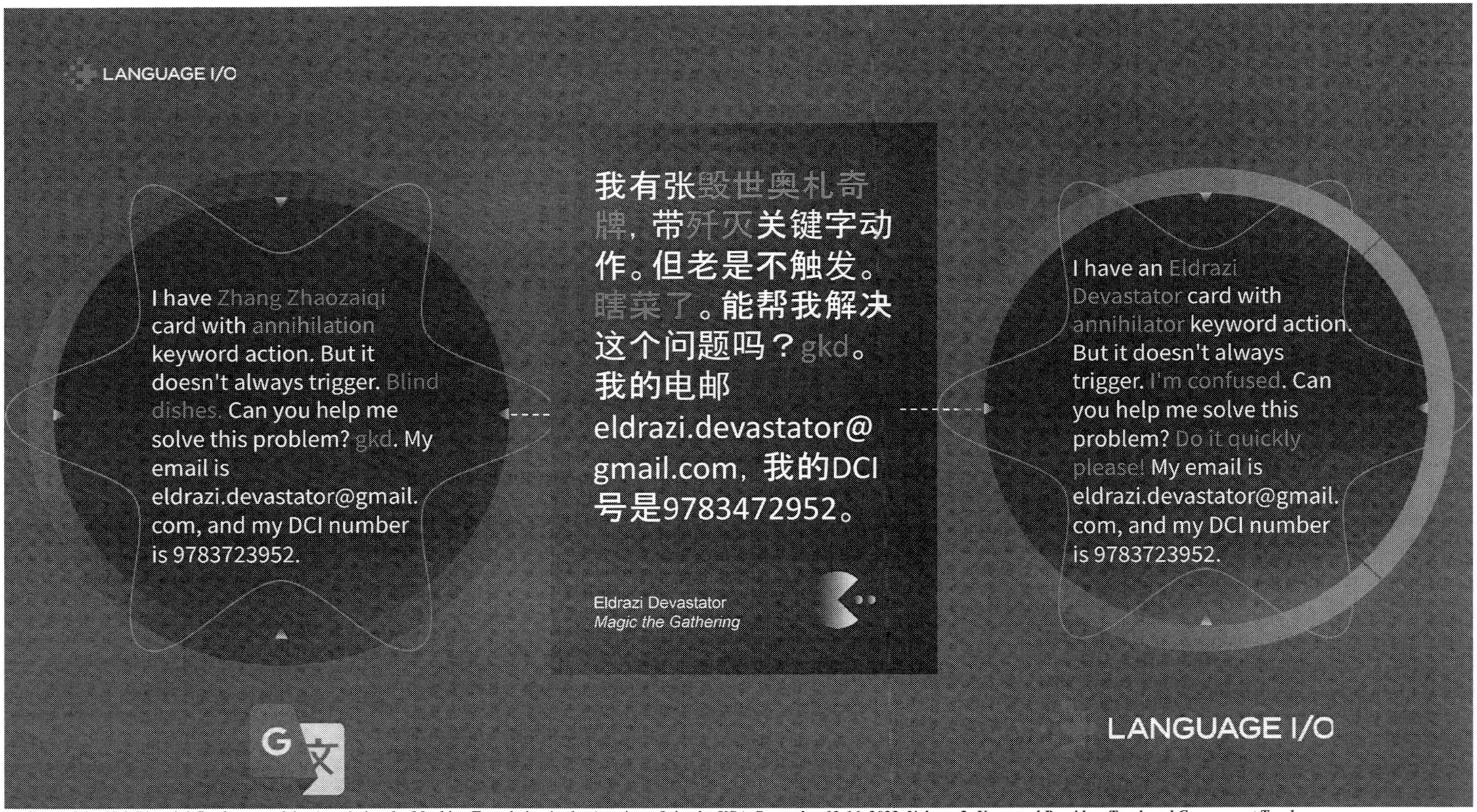
LANGUAGE I/O
I have Zhang Zhaozaiqi card with annihilation keyword action. But it doesn't always trigger. Blind dishes. Can you help me solve this problem? gkd. My email is eldrazi.devastator@gmail.com, and my DCI number is 9783723952.
我有张毁世奥札奇牌，带歼灭关键字动作。但老是不触发。瞎菜了。能帮我解决这个问题吗？gkd。我的电邮eldrazi.devastator@gmail.com，我的DCI号是9783472952。
Eldrazi Devastator
Magic the Gathering
I have an Eldrazi Devastator card with annihilator keyword action. But it doesn't always trigger. I'm confused. Can you help me solve this problem? Do it quickly please! My email is eldrazi.devastator@gmail.com, and my DCI number is 9783723952.
LANGUAGE I/O

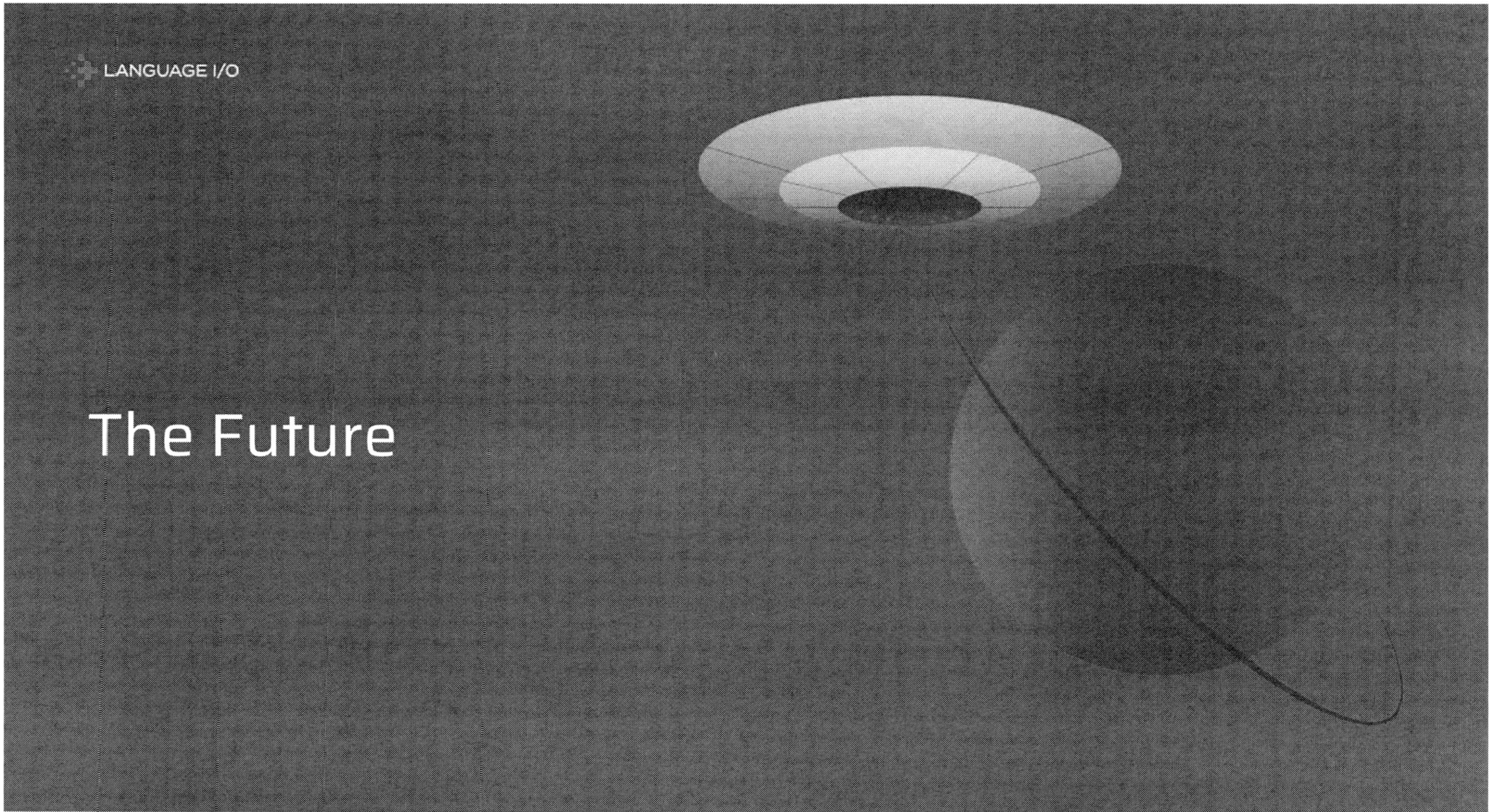
LANGUAGE I/O
The Future

LANGUAGE I/O

Chatbots

LANGUAGE I/O

Analytics

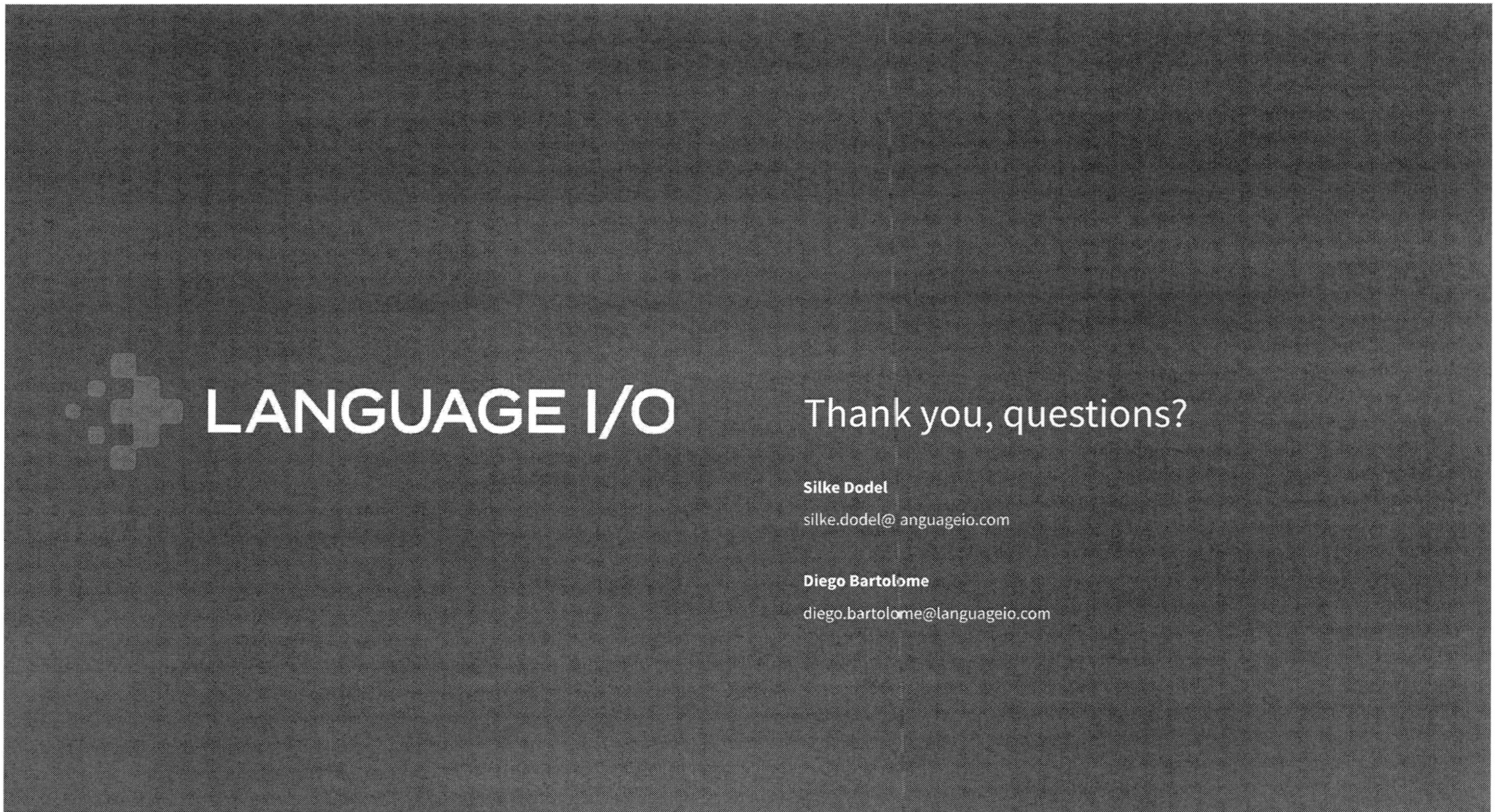
LANGUAGE I/O
Thank you, questions?
Silke Dodel
silke.dodel@ anguageio.com
Diego Bartolome
diego.bartolome@languageio.com

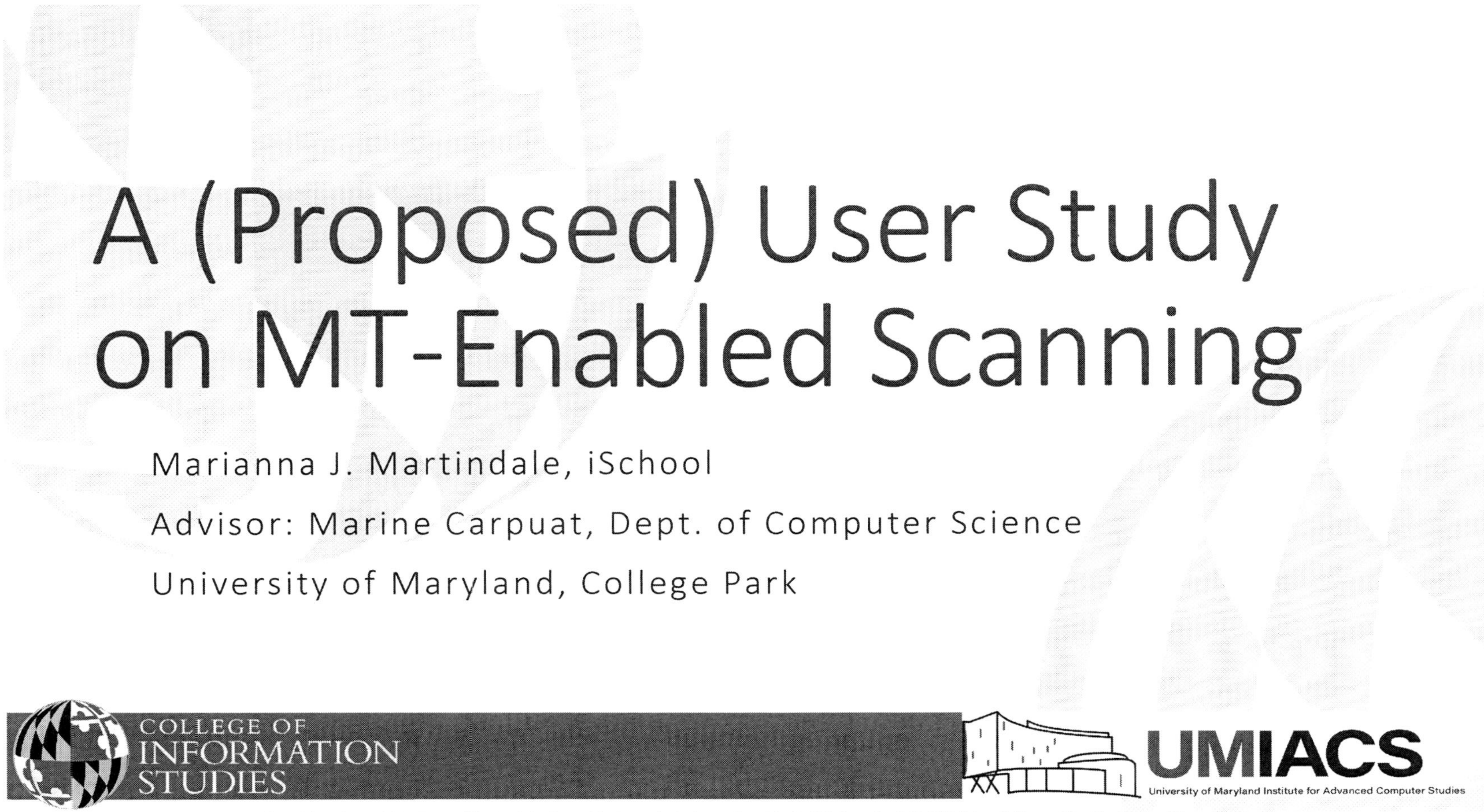
A (Proposed) User Study on MT-Enabled Scanning
Marianna J. Martindale, iSchool
Advisor: Marine Carpuat, Dept. of Computer Science
University of Maryland, College Park
COLLEGE OF INFORMATION STUDIES
UMIACS
University of Maryland Institute for Advanced Computer Studies

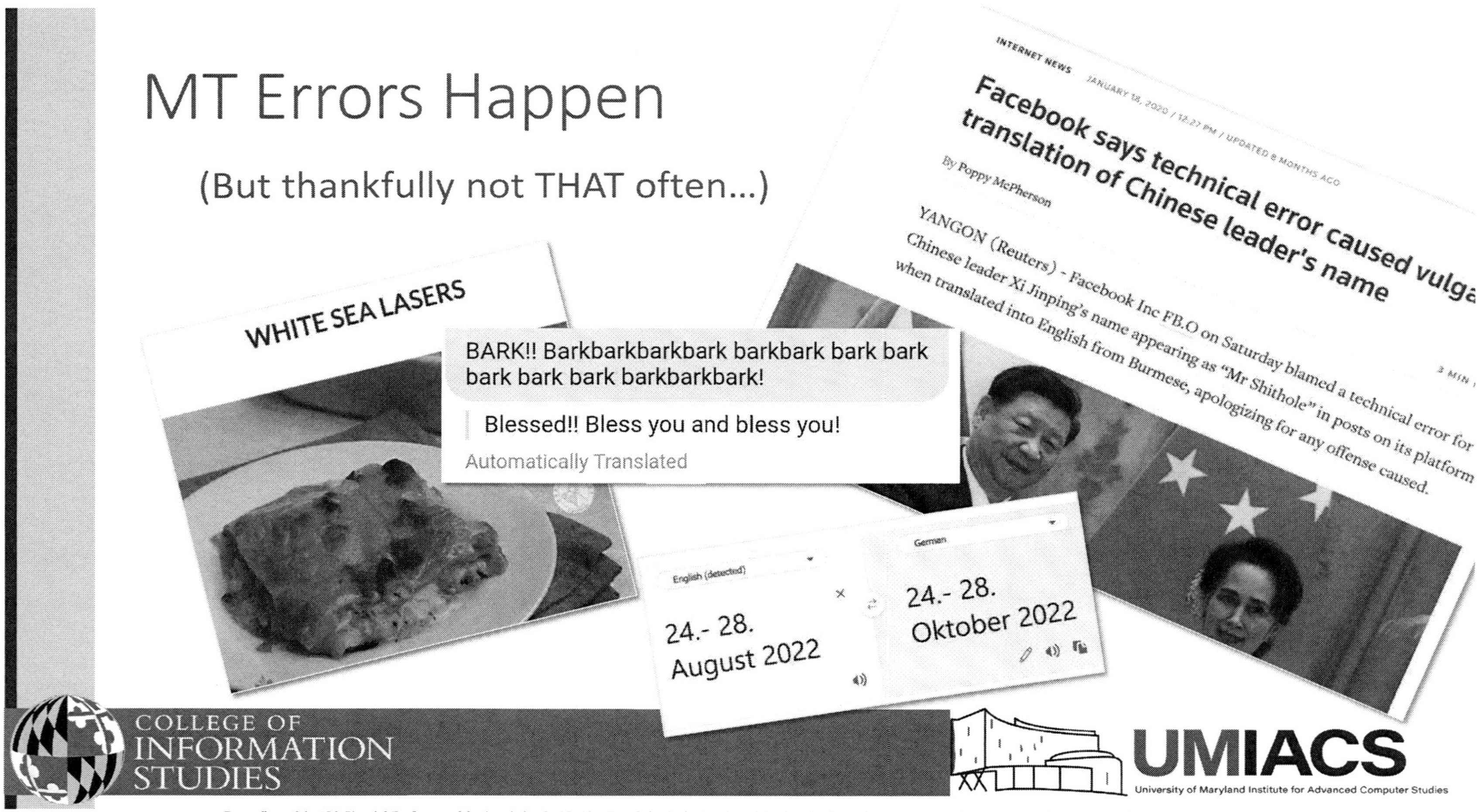
MT Errors Happen
(But thankfully not THAT often...)
WHITE SEA LASERS
BARK!! Barkbarkbarkbark barkbark bark bark bark bark bark barkbarkbark!
Blessed!! Bless you and bless you!
Automatically Translated
INTERNET NEWS
Facebook says technical error caused vulga
translation of Chinese leader's name
By Poppy McPherson
YANGON (Reuters) - Facebook Inc FB.O on Saturday blamed a technical error for Chinese leader Xi Jinping's name appearing as "Mr Shithole" in posts on its platform when translated into English from Burmese, apologizing for any offense caused.
English (detected)
24.- 28.
August 2022
German
24.- 28.
Oktober 2022
COLLEGE OF INFORMATION STUDIES
UMIACS
University of Maryland Institute for Advanced Computer Studies

MT Error Impact

Depends on:

- Severity
  - How wrong is it?
- Believability (in context)
  - Laughing? Confused? Convinced?
- **Actual use case**
  - Will users take action? What kind?

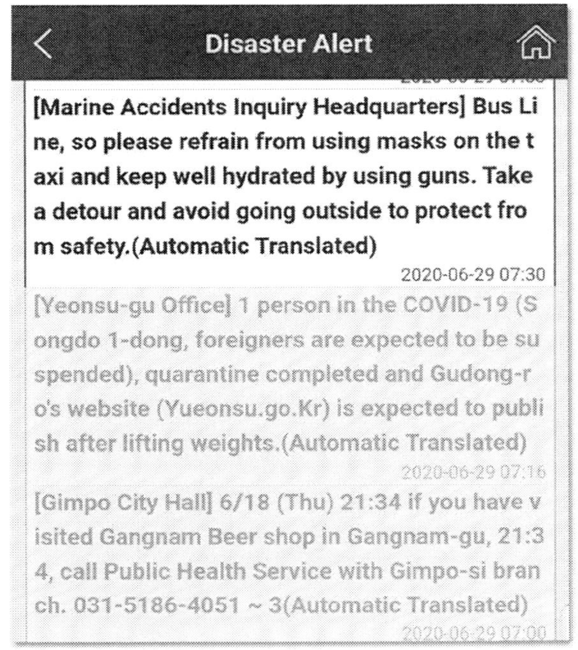

COLLEGE OF INFORMATION STUDIES

UMIACS
University of Maryland Institute for Advanced Computer Studies

Intelligence Analysis MT Use Cases

Like many assimilation use cases

- High volume of foreign language text
- Impractical to translate everything
- Monolingual domain experts use MT to triage

Unique risks and regulations

Personally relevant: 20 years USG MT experience

COLLEGE OF INFORMATION STUDIES

UMIACS University of Maryland Institute for Advanced Computer Studies

Use Case: Intelligence Analysis

High level workflow

Intelligence analysts receive trove of foreign language documents

1. Scanning: Identify relevant documents
   Assimilation use case
2. Produce official translation of relevant documents
   Dissemination use case
3. Reporting: Analyze and write report(s)
   (Problematic) Assimilation use case

COLLEGE OF INFORMATION STUDIES

UMIACS
University of Maryland Institute for Advanced Computer Studies

Scanning Use Case

MT-enabled analysts use MT to get the gist of foreign language documents

- Identify relevant documents and "NTR" (nothing to report) documents
  - Relevance judgment task
- Pass relevant documents to language analysts to translate
  - Often with a contextual note (e.g., "I believe this is a progress report on the HIGH NOON project")
    - Comprehension task
- **Currently acceptable use case and focus of my user study**

COLLEGE OF INFORMATION STUDIES

UMIACS
University of Maryland Institute for Advanced Computer Studies

Scanning Use Case

Types of error

- **False negative**: relevant document discarded
  - Omits or mistranslates critical information
  - Correct keywords not believable/recognizable in context
- **False positive**: irrelevant document sent for translation
  - Mistranslation or hallucination produces keywords believable in context

"I want to go to lunch at noon, but I generally have to"

"I want to go to lunch, but I have to brief HIGH NOON to the General"

"Want lunch but general high/very noon talk with/about"

COLLEGE OF INFORMATION STUDIES

UMIACS
University of Maryland Institute for Advanced Computer Studies

Reporting Use Case

Reporting directly off MT output requires deep comprehension

- Not simply a binary task = less room for error
  - Example: Errors in numbers or units
    - No effect on scanning
    - Big effect on reporting accuracy!

- **Not currently acceptable but tempting**
  - Process more foreign language material
  - Neural MT often looks good enough to use

Not focus of user study, but results may have implications

COLLEGE OF INFORMATION STUDIES

UMIACS
University of Maryland Institute for Advanced Computer Studies

User Study Research Questions

Goal: Establish a baseline

- **How accurately can analysts scan short documents w/ MT?**
  - Relevance judgment
  - Comprehension
- **How confident are they in those judgments?**
- **Is their confidence justified by their accuracy?**

Goal: Evaluate Interventions

- **Does intervention reduce how often analyst is misled?**
- **Does it help the analyst calibrate their confidence?**

COLLEGE OF INFORMATION STUDIES

UMIACS University of Maryland Institute for Advanced Computer Studies

Interventions

Goals

- Raise **prominence** of potential errors
- Help users **interpret** them more accurately
- Practical in USG environment today
  - Off-the-shelf technology

COLLEGE OF INFORMATION STUDIES

UMIACS University of Maryland Institute for Advanced Computer Studies

Intervention A: Two MT Outputs

Intuition:

- Users see and compare outputs
- Meaning differences ?= possible mistakes
- Common meaning despite disfluency ?= accurate
- Anecdotally, users like it!

Related Work:

- Shown to be effective in communication use cases
  (Xu et al., 2014; Gao et al., 2015)

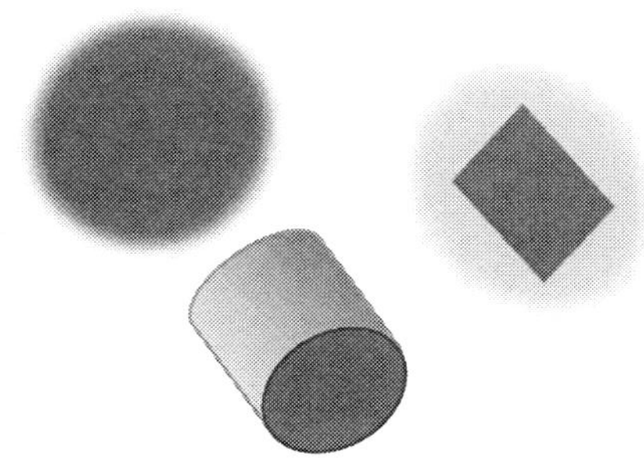

Caveat:

- Which will they pick when outputs disagree?

COLLEGE OF INFORMATION STUDIES

UMIACS University of Maryland Institute for Advanced Computer Studies

Intervention B: Rule-Based MT

Motrans rule-based MT (RBMT)

Intution:

- Scan for keywords and compare with NMT
  (like intervention A)
- Less fluent/comprehensible but more interpretable
- Freely available to USG through CyberTrans

Caveat:

- Users may ignore it due to lack of fluency/comprehensibility

It's not so ridiculous, I'm looking forward to it more.

MT1

It's not worth a lot of fun analysis. I'm going to make it more than that.

MT2

Analysis very ridiculous without value I don't want to criticize it more from this

RBMT*

*Not actual Motrans output

COLLEGE OF INFORMATION STUDIES

UMIACS
University of Maryland Institute for Advanced Computer Studies

User Study Scenario

Language: Persian/Farsi

Given chat conversations

- Comment threads from news articles related to the topic

Two different tasks/topics

1. In the context of the war in Ukraine, are participants in the conversations more sympathetic towards Russia or Ukraine?
2. Are participants in the conversations more supportive of Hezbollah or ISIS?

COLLEGE OF INFORMATION STUDIES

UMIACS
University of Maryland Institute for Advanced Computer Studies

User Study Scenario

For each comment

- Mark it as relevant to the topic or NTR
- If relevant, Use the pull-downs to "fill in the blanks" of a contextual note
- Provide a confidence rating
- Optional: any other important analyst comments

Not entirely realistic

- Analysts wouldn't work this granularly
- Necessary conceit to get enough data without overtaxing analysts

COLLEGE OF INFORMATION STUDIES

UMIACS University of Maryland Institute for Advanced Computer Studies

User Study Interface Mock-up

Pending pre-publication review

COLLEGE OF INFORMATION STUDIES

UMIACS

University of Maryland Institute for Advanced Computer Studies

User Study Interface Mock-up

Pending pre-publication review

COLLEGE OF INFORMATION STUDIES

UMIACS
University of Maryland Institute for Advanced Computer Studies

User Study Interface Mock-up

Pending pre-publication review

COLLEGE OF INFORMATION STUDIES

UMIACS
University of Maryland Institute for Advanced Computer Studies

You've translated it, now what?

Michael Maxwell mmaxwell@arlis.umd.edu
Shabnam Tafreshi stafreshi@arlis.umd.edu
Aquia Richburg arichbu1@umd.edu
Balaji Kodali bkodali@umd.edu
Kymani Brown krown001@terpmail.umd.edu

Abstract

Humans use document formatting to discover important phrases and document structure. But when machines process a paper–especially documents OCRed from images–these cues are often invisible to downstream processes: words in footnotes or body text are treated as just as important as words in titles. It would be better for indexing and summarization tools to be guided by implicit document structure.

In an ODNI-sponsored project, the Applied Research Laboratory for Intelligence and Security (ARLIS) looked at inferring document structure from the formatting in OCRed text. Most OCR engines output results as hOCR (an XML format), giving bounding boxes around characters. In theory, this also provides style information such as bolding and italicization, but in practice, this capability is limited. For example, the Tesseract OCR tool provides bounding boxes, but does not attempt to detect bold or italicized text (relevant to author emphasis and specialized fields in e.g. print dictionaries).

Our project inferred font size from hOCR bounding boxes, and using that and other cues (e.g. the fact that titles tend to be short) determined which text constituted section titles; from this, a document outline can be created. We also experimented with algorithms for detecting bold text. Our best algorithm has a much improved recall and precision, although the exact numbers are font-dependent.

The next step is to incorporate inferred structure into the output of machine translation. One method is to embed XML tags for inferred structure into the text extracted from the imaged document, and to either pass the strings enclosed by XML tags to the MT engine individually, or pass the tags through the MT engine without modification. This structural information can guide downstream bulk processing tasks such as summarization and search, and also enables building tables of contents for human users examining individual translated documents.

1 Introduction

As you decided whether to read this paper, you probably read the **title** first, then maybe the **abstract**. You might have looked at the **pictures** to see if they whetted your interest, and looked at the **title of this section** before starting to read the section itself.

You may also have noticed the bolding in the paragraph above, and thought that perhaps those were clues to what the paper is about—which of course would be *right*.

In short, you will undoubtedly made use of **the paper's formatting**, both to decide whether reading a paper is worth your time, and if so, to better understand what the paper is about.

Now suppose you have a PDF of a paper written in a language you don't know, or an image of a document that has to be OCRed, or a paper document. You extract the text and pass it through a machine translation system, and out comes translated text—and if you're lucky, the translation is both fluent and accurate. But where is the formatting that you found so helpful?

2 The Problem

Documents are often written using overt or covert markup, where the markup more or less explicitly defines the document structure. Overt structural markup is used in formats like the following:

- DocBook (Norman and Hamilton 2010), which defines structural tags for technical documentation, for example `<para>` (paragraph), `<qandaentry>` (a question-and-answer, or Q-and-A, entry), and `<guimenuitem>` (the name of a terminal menu item in a GUI).
- Text Encoding Initiative (TEI, `https://tei-c.org`), defining tags for texts of interest in the humanities context, for example `<front>` (front matter of a book), `<castList>` (a list of actors in a performance), tags for poetry, etc.
- TEXand LATEX, providing tags to format documents, such as `\textbf` (for bold font) or `\caption` (for the caption of a figure or table).

Other document formats, like Microsoft Word, use covert markup, i.e. markup that the user assigns but which then becomes more or less invisible, so that the document appears to the eye to be formatted without any markup.

Whether markup is overt or covert, the final document contains only a visual display which readers have come to understand: paragraphs are separated by spaces and possibly indented; Q-and-A lists are lists of paragraphs starting with a 'Q' or 'A'; lines of poetry use a ragged right margin; section titles are short lines, often in a larger font, and possibly preceded by a section number, and text which is bolded is represented by glyphs whose strokes are thicker.

In general terms, the task we are attempting is to reverse engineer the visual display of a document into an overt markup, by inferring a document's covert structure—the same thing a proficient human reader does when they read a document. We illustrate this problem with a few examples, before turning to some (in-progress) solutions.

Figure 1 shows a small snippet from a PDF document.[1] Two terms are italicized, indicating in this particular document that the terms are being defined. But the italicization shows up

[1]The image is taken from a pre-print of Bale and Reiss 2018.

neither in the plain text extracted by the Tesseract OCR program (figure 2), nor in Tesseract's more verbose hOCR output(figure 3).[2]

> and information relating to meaning. We call the information relevant to a morpheme's pronunciation its *phonological representation*, and we call the information relevant to its meaning its *semantic representation*.

Figure 1: Excerpt from PDF, showing italicization

> and information relating to meaning. We call the information relevant to a morpheme's pronunciation its phonological representation, and we call the information relevant to its meaning its semantic representation.

Figure 2: Excerpt of plain text OCR output from figure 1

Bold text is similarly not tagged as such in Tesseract's output.[3] The implication of this is that the fact that the original author has highlighted something as important, cannot be recovered; structural information has been lost.

Even more problematic is the situation where a textual document represents a highly structured database, and one wishes to reconstruct the structure of the data from the formatting. A common example of this is dictionaries, where lexical information is contained in fields delineated by the formatting. Figure 4 shows an example of this, here a Polish-English dictionary.[4] Notice that some of the fields within this entry are indicated by switching between bold and non-bold, such as the headword and its definition, or between the sub-entry '**z zapartym tchem**' and its definition "with bated breath"; other fields are indicated by switching between an italic font and a non-italic font, such as '*bez tchu*' and "out of breath."

At a higher level in the document, we also wish to infer things like chapters and sections with their titles, itemized lists, sidebars, footnotes, tables and their captions, and a host of other things that make a document structure apparent to the human reader.

Figure 5 (intentionally shown small to draw attention to the formatting) is a page from National Security Commission on Artificial Intelligence (NSCAI) 2021 (referred to later as the NSCAI report) shows many examples of this. The red text at the top highlights one of four 'Judgments' in the document; a list of these judgments appears in the blue side bar box to the right. A short paragraph of plain black text introduces a bulleted list, with each list item beginning with a bolded word, and using a dark blue font. More plain black text follows the list. A header and footer appear at the top and bottom of the page. Not readily visible in this image are several footnote numbers, indicated by a raised digit in a smaller font.

This document is about 750 pages. If one wanted to know the committee's judgments, a search for simply the word 'judgment' would pull up both the committee's judgments and

[2]Tesseract reports version `5.1.0-72-gb8b6`, with correspondingly updated libraries. It was installed as an Ubuntu-compatible binary from the Tesseract website on 22 July 2022.

[3]Tesseract version 3, used in M. Maxwell and Bills 2017 and M. Maxwell and Bills 2018, attempted to tag bold text, but its recall and precision were very poor in the documents we worked with. The ability to tag bold text was removed in Tesseract version 4.

[4]The dictionary shown is Oxford University Press 2010.

```
...
<span class='ocrx_word' id='word_1_15' title='bbox 178 23 194 33;
  x_wconf 96'>its</span>
<span class='ocrx_word' id='word_1_16' title='bbox 200 22 277 36;
  x_wconf 95'>phonological</span>
<span class='ocrx_word' id='word_1_17' title='bbox 284 23 376 36;
  x_wconf 96'>representation,</span>
<span class='ocrx_word' id='word_1_18' title='bbox 383 22 407 33;
  x_wconf 96'>and</span>
<span class='ocrx_word' id='word_1_19' title='bbox 413 26 430 33;
  x_wconf 96'>we</span>
<span class='ocrx_word' id='word_1_20' title='bbox 435 22 457 33;
  x_wconf 96'>call</span>
<span class='ocrx_word' id='word_1_21' title='bbox 463 22 484 33;
  x_wconf 93'>the</span>
<span class='ocrx_word' id='word_1_22' title='bbox 490 23 506 33;
  x_wconf 91'>in-</span>
</span>
<span class='ocr_line' id='line_1_3' title="bbox 2 40 396 54;
    baseline 0 -3; x_size 17.782608; x_descenders 3;
    x_ascenders 4.782609">
  <span class='ocrx_word' id='word_1_23' title='bbox 2 40 64 51;
    x_wconf 96'>formation</span>
  ...
```

Figure 3: Excerpt from hOCR output for figure 1

all other instances of the word 'judgment', of which there are about 30. Clearly it would be desirable to be able to restrict search to instance of that word in red text, and similarly for other pieces of structurally-delineated information in the report. Structural information based on formatting would also allow one to put together an outline of the document (there is a table of contents, but it includes only the chapter titles).

3 Previous Work

M. Maxwell and Bills (2017; 2018) describes parsing an OCRed Tzeltal-Spanish dictionary (Cruz, Gerdel, and Slocum 1999, similar to the Polish dictionary of figure 4 in its use of bolding)

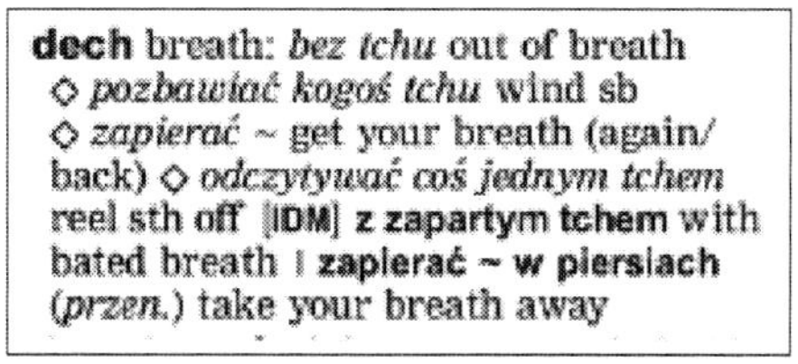
dech breath: *bez tchu* out of breath ◇ *pozbawiać kogoś tchu* wind sb ◇ *zapierać* ~ get your breath (again/back) ◇ *odczytywać coś jednym tchem* reel sth off [IDM] **z zapartym tchem** with bated breath | **zapierać ~ w piersiach** (*przen.*) take your breath away

Figure 4: Entry from Polish-English dictionary

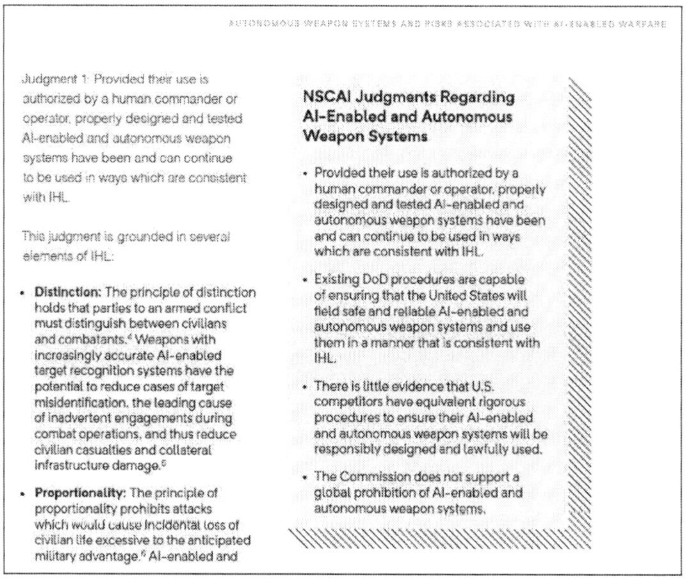

AUTONOMOUS WEAPON SYSTEMS AND RISKS ASSOCIATED WITH AI-ENABLED WARFARE

Judgment 1: Provided their use is authorized by a human commander or operator, properly designed and tested AI-enabled and autonomous weapon systems have been and can continue to be used in ways which are consistent with IHL.

This judgment is grounded in several elements of IHL:

- **Distinction:** The principle of distinction holds that parties to an armed conflict must distinguish between civilians and combatants.[4] Weapons with increasingly accurate AI-enabled target recognition systems have the potential to reduce cases of target misidentification, the leading cause of inadvertent engagements during combat operations, and thus reduce civilian casualties and collateral infrastructure damage.[5]
- **Proportionality:** The principle of proportionality prohibits attacks which would cause incidental loss of civilian life excessive to the anticipated military advantage.[6] AI-enabled and

NSCAI Judgments Regarding AI-Enabled and Autonomous Weapon Systems

- Provided their use is authorized by a human commander or operator, properly designed and tested AI-enabled and autonomous weapon systems have been and can continue to be used in ways which are consistent with IHL.
- Existing DoD procedures are capable of ensuring that the United States will field safe and reliable AI-enabled and autonomous weapon systems and use them in a manner that is consistent with IHL.
- There is little evidence that U.S. competitors have equivalent rigorous procedures to ensure their AI-enabled and autonomous weapon systems will be responsibly designed and lawfully used.
- The Commission does not support a global prohibition of AI-enabled and autonomous weapon systems.

Figure 5: Partial page from NSCAI report

to create an XML database with fields such as headwords, part of speech, definition, sub-entries etc. The failure to detect bold text marking the delineation between the Tzeltal and Spanish portions of subentries resulted in low parsing accuracy.

Document Image Analysis (DIA) tasks include document image classification and layout detection in images; the technology can be used to convert images of documents into structured data. Early work on DIA involved rule-based approaches, but deep learning (neural net) approaches are now more common.

Shen et al. 2021 describes Layout Parser, a trainable deep learning toolkit and model repository for DIA (see also their section on 'Related Work'). They use image processing and OCR to find rectangular boxes of text (and pictures) in document images being processed and label the function of each box; it also provides pre-trained structural models for certain types of documents. But since a given document can have a very different structure from the documents in Layout Parser's existing models, it is desireable to fine-tune a model that is similar to the target documents, or in the worst case to train a new model from scratch. In either case, a set of hand-labeled documents is required for the tuning or training.

Clausner, Pletschacher, and Antonacopoulos 2011 describes the University of Salford's Aletheia, a DIA system including tools for annotating document structure with the assistance of various semi-automated mechanisms. The university also maintains a dataset of annotated documents at `https://www.primaresearch.org/dataset/`.

In the next section, we describe on-going work in the evaluation and use of DIA tools (including the Layout Parser), while section 5 discusses experiments in improving the detection of bold text.

4 General Format Detection

We experimented with the Layout Parser on various documents, including the NSCAI report (a partial page of which was shown in figure 5). Our goal was to recognize significant text boxes, join boxes that were broken over page or column boundaries, and if possible label the boxes as to type (body text, footers and headers, section titles, etc.).

We selected a pre-trained model that worked reasonably well with our document's format, but even this best model showed some spurious or overlapping boxes in the output. However, we were able to eliminate most of these spurious boxes without losing valid boxes by ignoring boxes to which the program assigned a low confidence; this in turn eliminated most overlapping boxes. In addition, boxes frequently clipped off pieces of characters at the edges, but we addressed this by adding a small padding to increase the size of each box.

The model classified regions as (body) text, titles, lists, tables or figures; it was however confused by sidebar elements (like the one shown in the upper right-hand side of figure 5).

We experimented with the detection of titles by Layout Parser's PubLayNet dataset and its corresponding model (faster_rcnn_R_50_FPN_3x) [5] by running this over a set of test samples with 15 images. The aim of this experiment was to estimate the quality of the model performance, including a raw count of three categories:

1. 'Correct Bold Text' (34 instances): Boxes correctly tagged as titles, where the text was bold.
2. 'Incorrect Non-Bold Text' (16 instances): Boxes incorrectly tagged as titles, where the text was not bold.
3. 'Incorrect Bold Text' (7 instances): Boxes incorrectly not tagged as titles, where the text was bold.

Figure 6 shows some examples from the test set.

Notice that the raw number of incorrect bold text segments is relatively small compared to the number of bold text segments that are correctly classified. However the number of incorrectly classified non-bold texts is quite high, and another method should be used to lower this number. This model could perhaps be combined with other models or methods to decrease the number of incorrect non-bold text tags (ensemble models), but we did not have time to test this.

5 The Special Problem of Bold Font Detection

As mentioned, Tesseract does not currently attempt to distinguish between bold and non-bold (or italic) text. Since bolding is often used to emphasize important words, as well as distinguishing between fields in semi-structured data (like dictionary entries), we experimented with

[5] `https://layout-parser.readthedocs.io/en/latest/notes/modelzoo.html`, including the dataset `pubLayNet` and the model `faster_rcnn_R_50_FPN_3x`

A B C

Figure 6: Yellow boxes are marks for titles assigned by the Layout Parser (LP). Picture A shows two non-bold text segments that LP correctly tagged as titles. Picture B shows bold text that LP correctly boxed as titles (although it missed some bold text continued on to the next line). Picture C shows short bold texts at the beginning of the paragraphs that LP did not tag as titles, and red but non-bold text that is incorrectly tagged as a title.

methods for detecting bolded words, using for test data a Tzeltal-Spanish dictionary (Cruz, Gerdel, and Slocum 1999) and a Cubeo-Spanish dictionary (Morse and M. B. Maxwell 1999), as well as the previously mentioned NSCAI document.

The initial attempt used unsupervised clustering based on features such as bounding box dimensions, pixel counts and scaling by letter shape, but this unsupervised approach did not work well.

The best performing method used the OpenCV Python library, an open source library for image processing (`https://github.com/opencv/opencv-python`). We first converted the color image to gray scale, then 'thresholded' it to convert the gray scale into a black-and-white image (where gray turned into white), and finally used CV2's `dilation()` function to partially erode areas with black pixels. This had the effect of removing most of the pixels for non-bold characters, while leaving enough pixels in bold characters to enable approximate OCR of the bolded words. The result of applying this to the page shown in figure 5 is illustrated in figure 7; running this image through OCR gives the text shown in figure 8.

Clearly the OCR output from this degraded image is not good enough for downstream use by itself, however by using the bounding boxes in the hOCR output (not shown here), it was possible to pick out the spans in the original hOCR output that contained bold text in the original image.

The CV2 `dilation()` function has several adjustable parameters. The best settings are doubtless dependent on a number of factors (including the particular font and its size). For our experiments, we set these by hand, but for best results the parameter settings should be adjusted for particular documents or document classes based on a sampling of the outputs.

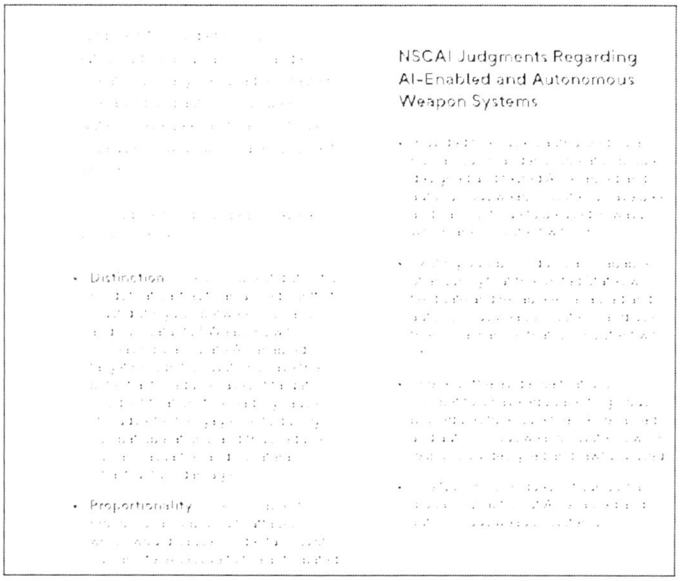

NSCAI Judgments Regarding
AI-Enabled and Autonomous
Weapon Systems

Distinction

Proportionality

Figure 7: Partial page from NSCAI report with bold detection enabled

NSCAI Judgments Regarding
Al-Enabled and Autonornous
Weapon Systems

Listing tign

Preaperticnvality . be at

Figure 8: Excerpt of plain text OCR output from figure 7

6 Passing Formatting through Machine Translation

The output of DIA has several potential uses:

1. Informing search processes as to which text is more important, which can be used to filter search results.
2. Informing summarization processes about important text strings.
3. Enabling translations to emulate the formatting of the original text, making the resulting documents more easily understood.

If search (1) or summarization (2) is done in the original document's language, and results are passed through Machine Translation (MT), then the inferred formatting tagging (likely in

XML or JSON) can be stripped before passing the outputs of these processes through MT. However, if search or summarization is instead done on the MT output, or if the MT output is to be formatted according to the input (3)[6], then the formatting needs to be passed transparently through the MT process.

How this would be done depends on the particular MT engine; one method would be to train the MT system to ignore such text. Much the same issue arises if named entity tagging is done in the source language, and must be transferred into the target language (cf. Hermjakob, Knight, and Daumé III 2008 for some observations on this problem, albeit in the context of statistical rather than neural net MT). Another method would be to only send blocks of text that are entirely inside a discovered box through translation, and to assemble the translated document using the boxes and their translated contents.

7 Future Work

Clearly much remains to be done before Document Image Analysis can be considered plug-and-play. Too much currently requires manual control. parameter setting (e.g. for the detection of bolding or the choice of confidence-based cutoffs in the boxing of document chunks), choosing pre-trained models, or deciding whether to use an existing pre-trained model as-is or to tune it.

We did not attempt to detect italicization (or underlining, which did not appear in the documents we experimented with). Font size detection is also relevant, e.g. for detecting section headers (which are often in a larger font) or captions or footnotes (often in a smaller font). Font size can probably be inferred from bounding boxes on OCRed text, provided one pays attention to capitalization, and ascenders and descenders.

Finally, some documents may be one-of-a-kind. Figure 9 shows a page from a hand-written Arabic book on Islamic rulings.[7] The page header includes a 'ruling' title on the left, a page number in the middle, and the 'book' (chapter) title on the right. Below the header is the section title, in red. A horizontal rule about a third of the way down the page separates the original text above from the commentary below. A red font has been used in the commentary to refer to words in bold characters above, as indicated by the orange lines I have drawn in. The words in the commentary circled in green are citations to sources from which the commentator drew, like '*Muraqi al-Falah: page 699*'. The words circled in brown are someone's explanation of the words they appear immediately under. Whether DIA is relevant for such unusual documents probably depends on the size and usefulness of the document in question, and in this case on whether OCR is even possible on this hand-written Arabic document.

In sum, while tools like the Layout Parser require substantial automated training material, for long documents (such as the NSCAI document) or for many documents of a single type (e.g. medical reports or other standardized documents), automating the Document Image Analysis (DIA) process would pay a return on investment by making it easier for users to make sense of Machine Translation output, enabling parsing of structured data such as dictionaries, and informing search by highlighting "hits" that occur in regions of higher importance.

[6]There may also need to be a mapping between input and output formats; for example, when translating italicized text into a script that does not use italicization would require some other form of emphasis.

[7]The image appears at `https://theislamshop.com/books/arabic-books/nur-al-idah-arabic`.

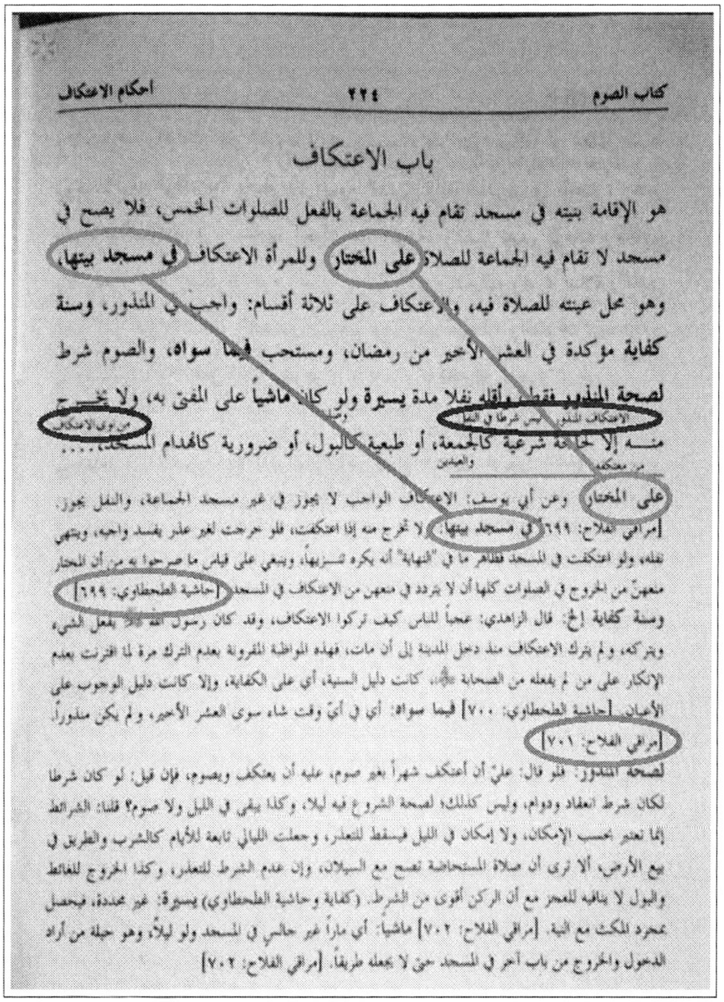

كتاب الصوم ٢٢٤ احكام الاعتكاف

باب الاعتكاف

هو الإقامة بنيته في مسجد تقام فيه الجماعة بالفعل للصلوات الخمس، فلا يصح في مسجد لا تقام فيه الجماعة للصلاة على المختار وللمرأة الاعتكاف في مسجد بيتها، وهو محل عينته للصلاة فيه، والاعتكاف على ثلاثة أقسام: واجب في المنذور، وسنة كفاية مؤكدة في العشر الأخير من رمضان، ومستحب فيما سواه، والصوم شرط لصحة المنذور فقط، وأقله نفلا مدة يسيرة ولو كان ماشياً على المفتى به، ولا يخرج منه إلا لحاجة شرعية كالجمعة، أو طبعية كالبول، أو ضرورية كانهدام المسجد، ....

على المختار: وعن أبي يوسف: الاعتكاف الواجب لا يجوز في غير مسجد الجماعة، والنفل يجوز. [مراقي الفلاح: ٦٩٩] في مسجد بيتها: لا تخرج منه إذا اعتكفت، فلو خرجت لغير عذر يفسد واجبه، وينتهي نفله، ولو اعتكفت في المسجد فظاهر ما في "النهاية" أنه يكره تنزيهاً، وينبغي على قياس ما صرحوا به من أن المختار منعهن من الخروج في الصلوات كلها أن لا يتردد في منعهن من الاعتكاف في المسجد. [حاشية الطحطاوي: ٦٩٩]
وسنة كفاية إلخ: قال الزاهدي: عجباً للناس كيف تركوا الاعتكاف، وقد كان رسول الله ﷺ يفعل الشيء ويتركه، ولم يترك الاعتكاف منذ دخل المدينة إلى أن مات، فهذه المواظبة المقرونة بعدم الترك مرة لما اقترنت بعدم الإنكار على من لم يفعله من الصحابة ﷺ، كانت دليل السنية، أي على الكفاية، وإلا كانت دليل الوجوب على الأعيان. [حاشية الطحطاوي: ٧٠٠] فيما سواه: أي في أيّ وقت شاء سوى العشر الأخير، ولم يكن منذوراً. [مراقي الفلاح: ٧٠١]
لصحة المنذور: فلو قال: عليّ أن أعتكف شهراً بغير صوم، عليه أن يعتكف ويصوم، فإن قيل: لو كان شرطا لكان شرط انعقاد ودوام، وليس كذلك؛ لصحة الشروع فيه ليلا، وكذا يبقى في الليل ولا صوم؟ قلنا: الشرائط إنما تعتبر بحسب الإمكان، ولا إمكان في الليل فيسقط للتعذر، وجعلت الليالي تابعة للأيام كالشرب والطريق في بيع الأرض، ألا ترى أن صلاة المستحاضة تصح مع السيلان، وإن عدم الشرط للتعذر، وكذا الخروج للغائط والبول لا ينافيه للعجز مع أن الركن أقوى من الشرط. (كفاية وحاشية الطحطاوي) يسيرة: غير محددة، فيحصل بمجرد المكث مع النية. [مراقي الفلاح: ٧٠٢] ماشياً: أي ماراً غير جالس في المسجد ولو ليلاً، وهو حيلة من أراد الدخول والخروج من باب آخر في المسجد حتى لا يجعله طريقاً. [مراقي الفلاح: ٧٠٢]

Figure 9: Excerpt from "Nur al-Adiyah"

References

Bale, A. and C. Reiss (2018). *Phonology: A Formal Introduction.* MIT Press. ISBN: 9780262348133. URL: https://books.google.com/books?id=t2V0DwAAQBAJ.

Clausner, C., S. Pletschacher, and A. Antonacopoulos (2011). "Aletheia - An Advanced Document Layout and Text Ground-Truthing System for Production Environments." In: *Proceedings of the 11th International Conference on Document Analysis and Recognition (ICDAR2011).* Beijing, China, pp. 48–52. URL: https://www.primaresearch.org/www/assets/papers/ICDAR2011_Clausner_Aletheia.pdf.

Cruz, Manuel A., Florence L. Gerdel, and Marianna C. Slocum (1999). *Diccionario tzeltal de Bachajón, Chiapas.* Serie de vocabularios y diccionarios indígenas "Mariano Silva y Aceves" 40. Coyoacán, D.F., Mexico: Instituto Lingüístico de Verano, A.C. URL: http://www.sil.org/system/files/reapdata/52/85/76/52857610164780871251544555610851968393/S040_DicTzeltalFacs_tzh.pdf.

Hermjakob, Ulf, Kevin Knight, and Hal Daumé III (2008). "Name Translation in Statistical Machine Translation — Learning When to Transliterate." In: *Proceedings of ACL-08: HLT.* Columbus, Ohio: Association for Computational Linguistics, pp. 389–397. URL: https://aclanthology.org/P08-1045.

Maxwell, Michael and Aric Bills (2017). "Endangered Data for Endangered Languages: Digitizing Print dictionaries." In: *Proceedings of the 2nd Workshop on the Use of Computational Methods in the Study of Endangered Languages.* Honolulu: Association for Computational Linguistics, pp. 85–91. URL: http://www.aclweb.org/anthology/W17-0112.

— (2018). "Giving Digital Life to a Print Dictionary." In: *6th International Conference on Language Documentation and Conservation (ICLDC).* Honolulu. URL: https://scholarspace.manoa.hawaii.edu/bitstreams/45151f4f-d3ba-4782-b5cc-5775f50e430f/download.

Morse, Nancy L. and Michael B. Maxwell (1999). *Cubeo Grammar.* Studies in the Languages of Colombia 5. Dallas: Summer Institute of Linguistics.

National Security Commission on Artificial Intelligence (NSCAI) (2021). *Final Report: National Security Commission on Artificial Intelligence.* Arlington, VA: National Security Commission on Artificial Intelligence.

Norman, Walsh and Richard L. Hamilton (2010). *DocBook 5: The Definitive Guide: The Official Documentation for DocBook.* 1st. Cambridge: O'Reilly.

Oxford University Press (2010). *Oxford Essential Polish Dictionary.* Oxford University Press.

Shen, Zejiang, Ruochen Zhang, Melissa Dell, Benjamin Charles Germain Lee, Jacob Carlson, and Weining Li (2021). "LayoutParser: A Unified Toolkit for Deep Learning Based Document Image Analysis." In: *arXiv preprint arXiv:2103.15348.* URL: https://arxiv.org/abs/2103.15348.

SG Translate Together - Uplifting Singapore's translation standards with the community through technology

Lee Siew Li LEE_Siew_Li@mci.gov.sg
Adeline Sim Adeline_SIM@mci.gov.sg
Gowri Kanagarajah Gowri_KANAGARAJAH@mci.gov.sg
Siti Amirah Siti_AMIRAH@mci.gov.sg
Foo Yong Xiang FOO_Yong_Xiang@mci.gov.sg
Gayathri Ayathorai Gayathri_AYATHORAI@mci.gov.sg
Sarina Mohamed Rasol Sarina_MOHAMED_RASOL@mci.gov.sg
Translation Department, Ministry of Communications and Information (MCI), Singapore
Aw Ai Ti aaiti@i2r.a-star.edu.sg
Wu Kui wuk@i2r.a-star.edu.sg
Zheng Weihua zhengw@i2r.a-star.edu.sg
Ding Yang ding_yang@i2r.a-star.edu.sg
Tarun Kumar Vangani vangani_tarun_kumar@i2r.a-star.edu.sg
Nabilah Binte Md Johan nabilah@i2r.a-star.edu.sg
Institute for Infocomm Research (I^{2}R), Agency for Science, Technology and Research (A*STAR), Singapore

Abstract

The Singapore's Ministry of Communications and Information (MCI) has officially launched the SG Translate Together (SGTT) web portal on 27 June 2022, with the aim of partnering its citizens to improve translation standards in Singapore.

This web portal houses the Singapore Government's first neural machine translation (MT) engine, known as SG Translate, which was jointly developed by MCI and the Institute for Infocomm Research (I^{2}R), Agency for Science, Technology and Research (A*STAR). Adapted using localised translation data, SG Translate is able to generate translations that are attuned to Singapore's context and supports Singapore's four (4) official languages – English (Singapore), Chinese (Singapore), Bahasa Melayu (Singapore) and Tamil (Singapore). Upon completion of development, MCI allowed all Government agencies to use SG Translate for their daily operations.

This presentation will briefly cover the methodologies adopted and showcase SG Translate's capability to translate content involving local culture, everyday life and government policies and schemes. This presentation will also showcase MCI's sustainable approach for the continual training of the SG Translate MT engine through citizenry participation.

1. Introduction

SG Translate is a customised Neural Machine Translation (MT) engine jointly developed by the Ministry of Communications and Information (MCI), Singapore and A*STAR's Institute for Infocomm Research (I^2R), Singapore. It was launched in July 2019 to Singapore's public service sectors via the Government intranet.

As SG Translate is trained with localised data such as government communications materials, it is able to produce first-cut translations that are suited to Singapore's context in Singapore's four (4) official languages – English (Singapore), Chinese (Singapore), Bahasa Melayu (Singapore) and Tamil (Singapore). The engine's performance has indicated its capability to translate localised content, especially local terms related to the Singapore Government's policies and operations, as well as those related to local culture, such as the names of local delicacies.

SG Translate was originally developed to help public officers in Singapore manage the increasing demand for government communications materials to be made available in all four official languages. The localised translations generated by SG Translate serve as drafts and reduce the need for translators to start from scratch, thereby improving work productivity and efficiency. In addition, the time saved can be channeled into post-editing and vetting to ensure that the translations are properly nuanced and are able to accurately convey the information to citizens. Response from public officers to the initial roll-out was positive and encouraging. Many lauded the quality of the machine's first-cut translation, and found the translation generated by SG Translate to be more accurate and suitable for the local audience than those produced by other translation engines in the market. During the height of the COVID-19 pandemic, MCI's Translation Department (MCI-TD) officers used SG Translate to generate first-cut translations before refining the text further. This shortened the time taken to translate relevant materials into the other three official languages, and allowed Singaporeans to receive timely updates on evolving situations.

After the successful delivery of SG Translate, the idea of a collaborative web portal was mooted in late 2019 to extend SG Translate to the public, as well as to create more opportunities to work with people in their translation journeys. This fosters partnership and strengthens communications with all segments of society. This led to the establishment of SG Translate Together (SGTT), an online web portal that allows members of the public to use the SG Translate MT engine on the internet.

The purpose of this paper is to highlight the technical aspects behind building SG Translate and the community engagement aspect of SG Translate Together. For the technical perspective, the paper seeks to showcase key methodology of how the translation engine was developed to cater specifically to Singapore's linguistic use. Additionally, the paper will also cover how the SG Translate Together Web Portal harnesses the benefits of community engagement by involving members of the public to contribute training data to SG Translate. Through this process of citizenry engagement and partnership, the Singapore Government hopes to co-create a better MT engine that belongs to Singaporeans and for all to use.

2. SG Translate Neural Machine Translation Engine

In recent years, Neural Machine Translation (NMT) has made remarkable progress in the field of natural language processing (Wu et al., 2016; Gehring et al., 2017; Vaswani et al., 2017; Chen et al., 2018). However, when the translation model is limited by the amount of data, developing an engine with good translation performance in a specific domain is a challenge. Whether the language pair is low- or high- resource, domain-specific training data are often rare, and it becomes a problem for data-hungry neural networks. This paper focuses on the development of SG Translate bi-directional translation engines for three language pairs (English-Chinese, English-Tamil, English-Malay) using NMT technology and the exploration of multi-stage domain adaptation and data augmentation methods to advance the engine's translation performance. Additionally, the placeholder-based fuzzy match mechanism for local terminology translation and data tagging strategy were employed to emphasise translation learning of Singapore-contextualised content. Experiments show that the present translation system generates more localised translations in Tamil, Malay and Chinese to English translations and vice versa as compared to commercially available solutions.

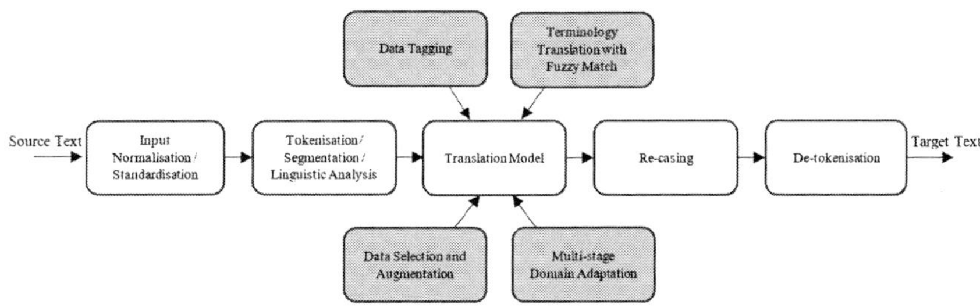

* The blue boxes are the methodologies applied to the translation model.

Figure 1. Overview of the translation system

Our translation system adopts standard sequence-to-sequence Transformer architecture (Vaswani et al., 2017). Figure 1 shows an overview of the translation system.

3. Methodology

SG Translate consists of three language pairs (English-Chinese, English-Malay, English-Tamil), of which English-Malay and English-Tamil are low-resource language pairs where both out-domain and domain-specific data are limited. This paper proposes strategies including data selection and augmentation, fuzzy terminology match, multi-stage domain adaptation and data tagging, which are proven to be effective for both low- and high-resource language pairs. The eventual product produces translation that suits the Singapore context, and is complemented by accurate translation of unique terminologies.

3.1. Data Selection and Augmentation

As deep learning requires large volumes of training data, the back translation (BT) method (Sennrich et al., 2015) was adopted to augment the training data. Back translation is proven to be effective under both low- and high-resource settings by exploiting monolingual data which is abundant and easily obtained. Firstly, an existing bilingual parallel corpus is used to construct a target-to-source NMT model, which is then used to translate target monolingual data into the source language. In doing so, a certain amount of pseudo bilingual parallel data is generated. This pseudo bilingual parallel data is used to augment the original bilingual dataset to train a new source-to-target model. For the selection of monolingual corpus to be used for back translation, the selection strategy targeting difficult words (Fadaee et al., 2018) is adopted. Word frequency counting is adopted for all words in the original training corpus. Sentences containing low-frequency words and out-of-vocabulary (OOV) words are allocated higher priority for selection. Through this method, the diversity of the training set is increased and the ability of the source-to-target translation model to process low-frequency words and OOV words is enhanced.

3.2. Terminology Translation with Fuzzy Match

Data augmentation helps the engine to gain translation knowledge of common words. However, it is challenging to source for a large amount of training data belonging to the domains of our interest. Therefore, the engine could not provide accurate translation for domain-specific terminologies as their occurrences were low and the model could not pick up the necessary translation knowledge. We then propose to leverage a terminology dictionary with placeholders to address this problem.

A terminology dictionary containing a list of terms and their corresponding reference translations, is first created. Terms in the terminology dictionary would need to be equivalent, specific and unique. The engines utilise the terminology dictionary and a placeholder-based mechanism to translate terms such as person and entity names more accurately. Since the NMT model is trained to translate placeholder tokens into themselves, the placeholder tokens in the translation output are substituted with pre-specified translations in the terminology dictionary.

This placeholder replacement works well when the sentence contains a small number of terms that need to be replaced (e.g. one to three) and there is sufficient contextual information left other than the placeholder tokens in the replaced sentence. However, when the number of replaced terms in a sentence increases (e.g. more than three) or the sentence after placeholder replacement has little contextual information left other than the placeholder tokens, translation errors may occur. Therefore, the information of the replaced words is kept together with the corresponding placeholder tokens in the source sentence to enable the translation model to learn the context of the source terms. (Wang T., 2019).

As shown in Figure 2, in the source sentence of the training data, both the replaced words and the placeholder tokens are kept in the replaced sentence, and separators such as "<s>, <m>, < e>" are introduced to identify the boundaries of the replaced part; in the replaced target sentence, only the placeholder and the boundary identifier exist, which are consistent with those in the source sentence.

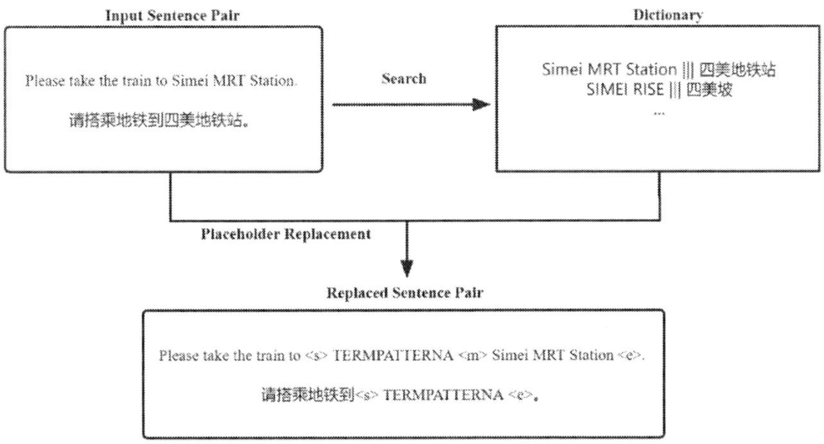

Figure 2. Example of retaining information of replaced terms in the source sentence

For terminology matching, if the match is only limited to an exact match between a term in the input sentence and the term in the terminology dictionary where only one form (usually root form) exists, variants of a term may be overlooked. For example, the term 'Community-in-Translation Events Grant' in the term dictionary will not be matched with 'Community in Translation Events Grant' (missing hyphens) or 'Community-in-Translation Event Grant (plural to singular form of 'event')' in an input sentence.

Therefore, fuzzy matching mechanism is deployed to resolve this issue in the term matching phase. Prior to term matching, the input sentence and the terms found in the terminology dictionary undergo a process known as de-punctuation. After term matching and replacement, the remaining punctuation in the sentence will be restored. At the same time, chained dictionaries and the stemming algorithm (Lovins J B., 1968) are introduced to rectify the issue of matching failures caused by tense differences or singular-plural form differences.

The principle of a chained dictionary is similar to that of a linked table, where a phrase is being split into words, with the preceding word in the phrase serving as the key to the following word, and the following word serving as the value of the preceding word. At each step of the chain dictionary query, if the word in the sentence or its stemmed form can match the key of the chain dictionary or the stemmed form of the key, the next query is performed. Otherwise, the query of the chain dictionary ends. The chained dictionary is also applicable to Tamil, Malay and Chinese.

Table 1. Comparison of model performance with and without fuzzy match

Language Pair	BLEU	
	With fuzzy match	Without fuzzy match
English to Tamil (EN2TA)	15.76	13.12
English to Chinese (EN2ZH)	16.55	13.7
English to Malay (EN2MS)	16.93	14.57
Tamil to English (TA2EN)	17.31	15.75

Chinese to English (ZH2EN)	19.77	18.82
Malay to English (MS2EN)	18.03	17.14

Table 1 shows that when fuzzy match is applied, the BLEU score for EN2TA, EN2ZH, EN2MS, TA2EN, ZH2EN and MS2EN improves by 2.64, 2.85, 2.36, 1.56, 0.95 and 0.89 respectively when translating 500 sentences containing input variants. The BLEU score improvement is remarkable in EN2TA, EN2ZH, EN2MS and TA2EN (more than 1 BLEU score). As only the de-punctuation operation was applied to the input sentences for ZH2EN and MS2EN translation engines, the performance of translation engines improved, but not significantly. Nonetheless, the results show that allowing the engine to recognise input variants via fuzzy match, improves the translation quality.

3.3. Multi-stage Domain Adaptation

To improve the translation performance of Singapore-contextualised content, adaptation (Chen et al., 2016) on domain-specific data related to Singapore content was carried out. Domain adaptation is performed in multiple stages. In the first stage, all domain bilingual data, including data not relevant to our domain and back-translation data, are used for building a base translation model which can acquire general translation knowledge. In the second stage, all high quality but non-domain specific training data are selected and used to further improve the translation quality of the model. In the final stage, high quality domain-specific data is used to further adapt the model finetuned in the second stage, thus emphasising translation learning of localised content.

3.4. Data Tagging

The training data sources for SGTT engine mainly include back-translation (BT) data, out-domain data and localised bilingual data. Among them, BT data and some out-domain data contain a certain degree of noise. Since the deep neural network is data-sensitive, when a translation system over-fits to certain features of noisy data, it will lead to the degradation of translation quality. Drawing on the approach mentioned by Marie B et al. (2020), we classify the data from different sources into two categories based on the quality of the data. A tag is added to the beginning of each sentence at the source side of each category of data to guide the model to gain data category information in the training process. We use "<BT>" for the data containing noise and "<PA>" for the data which is of good quality.

4. Illustrative Performance

This section illustrates SG Translate's capability to produce localised translations which are specific to Singapore's context.

4.1. Translation Related to Local Culture

SG Translate can translate sentences carrying local cultural context. In the example below, 'Hungry Ghost Festival' is a festival that is observed by many Chinese in the region and 'getai' is a live stage performance which usually takes place during the seventh month of the Chinese lunar calendar. The MT engine is able to recognise the cultural context and provide the translation suited for local audiences. Other MT engines may not be able to recognise this unique festival and this special genre of stage performance, which is seen only around this region.

Source (Chinese):	一提到**中元节**，人们一般上会想到**歌台**。
Target (English):	When it comes to **Hungry Ghost Festival**, people generally think of **getai**.

4.2. Translation Related to Everyday Life

'NRIC' is being used in Singaporeans' everyday life. It is a colloquial way of referring to one's identity card and stands for 'National Registration Identity Card'. The example below illustrates the positive outcome of domain adaptation where SG Translate is able to recognise 'NRIC' and provide an accurate translation of it in Tamil.

Source (English):	Bring your **NRIC** or valid passport, and poll card.
Target (Tamil):	*உங்கள் **அடையாள அட்டை** அல்லது செல்லுபடியாகும் கடவுச்சீட்டு மற்றும் வாக்கு அட்டை ஆகியவற்றைக் கொண்டு வாருங்கள்.*

4.3. Translation Related to the Government

The translation of government terms is standardised and has been included in terminology dictionaries to ensure that when the public translates local content related to government policies and schemes, the correct translation will be generated. As seen in the example below, the term 'Medishield Life' is a uniquely Singaporean term, as it is a healthcare insurance scheme administered by the Singapore Government. SG Translate is able to render the correct translation of 'Medishield Life' and its Malay equivalent, 'Medishield Hayat' as the term has been coined and added into the terminology dictionary of the MT Engine. Other MT engines may render it as 'Life Medishield' which is incorrect. Additionally, the Malay sentence is also a colloquial example of how Malay may be spoken in informal contexts in Singapore. SG Translate was able to render a satisfactory translation in English in spite of that, affirming the MT Engine's sensitivity to not only the local context but local linguistic patterns as well.

Source (Malay):	Awak tak tahu ke yang kita semua ada **MediShield Hayat?**
Target (English):	Don't you know we all have **MediShield Life?**

5. SG Translate Together Web Portal

Aligned with Singapore's Smart Nation initiatives, SG Translate was introduced to the public sphere via the SG Translate Together (SGTT) web portal (sgtranslatetogether.gov.sg). The portal aims to encourage more citizenry engagement to raise translation standards together. Besides performing translations via SG Translate, visitors can also access the one-stop repository of various translation events and translation-related resources on SGTT. Additionally, members of the public who are passionate about languages and translation can register for an account via Singapore's digital ID, Singpass, to take on translation tasks and contribute their post-edited translations to further train and improve the MT engine. The SGTT web portal was officially launched on 27 June 2022 and will be further enhanced with new features such as a community forum to promote interaction and collaboration between translation enthusiasts.

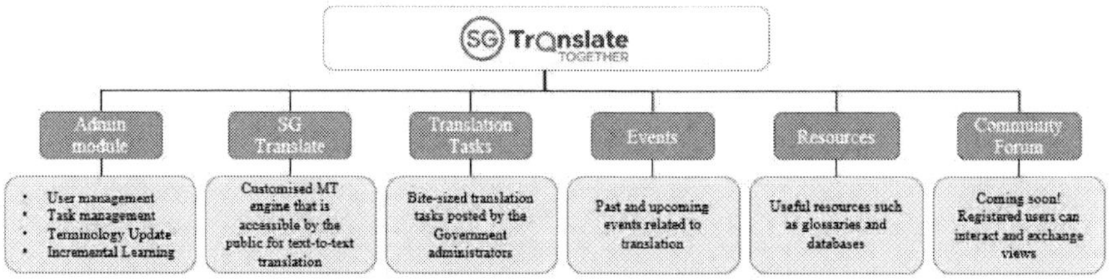

Figure 3. Overview of the SGTT web portal

5.1. Sustainable Approach

As continual training of the developed MT engine is paramount for improving its accuracy and ensuring its relevance in a rapidly-changing world, the incremental learning capability was developed to help the engine learn new knowledge and update the translation model when new data resources emerge. In addition, to overcome the problem of catastrophic forgetting caused by the introduction of new knowledge, the model ensemble technique (Garmash E et al., 2016) will be used in the final engine deployment phase.

As the Chinese, Malay and Tamil languages used in Singapore vary from those used in other regions, it is challenging to obtain new data to train the MT engine sustainably. Initially, MCI obtains quality bilingual data from Government agencies and partners from the private sector. With the establishment of the SGTT web portal, it has created an ecosystem that supports the sustainable training of SG Translate through the contribution of post-edited translations by registered users[1]. Many of them are volunteers called the Citizen Translators (CT) that MCI has recruited to work together to raise translation standards through a myriad of activities.

There are two types of registered users on the SGTT web portal: SGTT Translators and SGTT Proofreaders. Both types of users can take up translation tasks posted by the Singapore Government which includes a source text and the machine-generated translation, which is generated by SG Translate. They are required to post-edit the machine-generated translation and submit it for review. SGTT Proofreaders, who are registered users who are more experienced and well-versed with translations, will then review these translations by further editing them, and then providing ratings and feedback on the translation for the SGTT Translator. The reviewed translations are stored in the web portal and eventually extracted on a periodic basis to further train SG Translate via the incremental learning method designed by I^2R.

Through the abovementioned approach, the Singapore Government is able to sustainably obtain translation data through citizen engagement.

When registered users contribute their translations, their participation is recognised. Depending on their level of participation, they can receive e-certificates of recognition, e-vouchers or even being eligible to apply for training subsidies for translation-related courses. This mutually beneficial workflow allows the Singapore Government to obtain bilingual data by collaborating with citizens, consequently allowing them to hone their translation skills.

---

[1] Registered users are members of the public who have registered for a user account on SGTT via their digital ID, known as Singpass. Unlike non-registered users, this group of users are able to do more than just using the SG Translate MT engine to generate translations. They can contribute their own post-edited translation and/or give feedback to other translators on how to improve their translation. Registered users will also have access to the community forum which allows them to interact with one another and discuss translation matters.

5.2. Shaping Singapore's Translation Landscape and Nurturing the Next Generation of Translators

Translation is important in Singapore's multiracial and multilingual society. It not only bridges the communication gap between different communities, but also serves to strengthen mutual understanding. As we enter the digital era, there are more opportunities for the Singapore Government to harness technology to improve its work processes, as well as collaborate with the community. The SGTT web portal is one such opportunity.

By offering SG Translate to the public as a free-to-use tool, the Singapore Government hopes to lower the barriers in putting out content in the official languages to improve accessibility to information. Nonetheless, users are always reminded to check and edit the translation before disseminating the translated materials for public consumption. While technology can act as a catalyst, machines cannot replace human translators as communication is ultimately a connection between people, and translators are necessary to ensure that the content is best suited for the intended audience. Through the SGTT web portal, the Singapore Government hopes to encourage more people to adopt and develop translation technology to change the way translation is being done conventionally.

Prior to SGTT, there were numerous initiatives such as the Translation Talent Development Scheme (TTDS)[2] to support and nurture translation enthusiasts and practitioners. Complementing translation initiatives to date, the SGTT web portal is an addition to the suite of initiatives to uplift Singapore's translation standards. The web portal takes this a step further by providing interested individuals with a platform to learn from one another. As mentioned, SGTT Translators will receive feedback from SGTT Proofreaders on how to improve their translations. As users need not have prior experience to join SGTT as a Translator, anyone can join and hone their translation skills through the process. By gathering these passionate individuals - both inexperienced and experienced - "under one roof", it forms an active translation community in Singapore, fostering the spirit of sharing and learning, thereby nurturing the next generation of translators.

6. Summary

In this paper, we have presented the key methodology for the development of SG Translate – the Government customised MT engine. We also illustrated how SG Translate is able to translate content pertaining to local culture, everyday life and the Singapore Government. The results show that SG Translate has produced translations that are suited for Singapore's context. The paper also shared the conceptualisation and execution of SG Translate Together, and how it is used to obtain training data for SG Translate in a sustainable fashion.

Acknowledgement

This paper is co-tabled by the Translation Department from the Ministry of Communications and Information (Singapore), and the Institute for Infocomm Research (I^{2}R), Agency for Science, Technology and Research (Singapore). The SG Translate Customised Machine Translation Project is supported by the National Research Foundation, Singapore and Smart Nation and Digital Government Office, Singapore under its Translational R&D for Application

---

[2] The Translation Talent Development Scheme (TTDS) is a co-sponsorship grant set up by the National Translation Committee (NTC) to encourage Singaporean translation and interpretation (T&I) practitioners to further develop their capabilities and to attain mastery and deepening of their skills. The scheme also aims to nurture the next generation of translation talent in Singapore.

to Smart Nation (LOA No.: NRF2016IDM-TRANS001-062). Any opinions, findings and conclusions or recommendations expressed in this material are those of the author(s) and do not reflect the views of National Research Foundation, Singapore and Smart Nation and Digital Government Office, Singapore.

Our authors would like to express our gratitude to the aforementioned agencies for supporting the development of the SG Translate MT engine, as well as all Government agencies and private entities which have contributed their monolingual and bilingual data to develop and further train SG Translate. In addition, MCI would like to thank Government Technology Agency (GovTech), Singapore for their support in building the SG Translate Together Web Portal.

References

Chen, M. X., Firat, O., Bapna, A., Johnson, M., Macherey, W., Foster, G., ... & Hughes, M. (2018). The best of both worlds: Combining recent advances in neural machine translation. *arXiv preprint arXiv:1804.09849*.

Chen, B., Kuhn, R., Foster, G., Cherry, C., & Huang, F. (2016). Bilingual methods for adaptive training data selection for machine translation. *In Conferences of the Association for Machine Translation in the Americas: MT Researchers' Track (pp. 93-106).*

Fadaee, M., & Monz, C. (2018). Back-translation sampling by targeting difficult words in neural machine translation. *arXiv preprint arXiv:1808.09006.*

Gehring, J., Auli, M., Grangier, D., Yarats, D., & Dauphin, Y. N. (2017, July). Convolutional sequence to sequence learning. *In International conference on machine learning (pp. 1243-1252). PMLR.*

Garmash, E. & Monz, C. (2016). Ensemble Learning for Multi-Source Neural Machine Translation. *In Proceedings of the 26th International Conference on Computational Linguistics (COLING).*

Lovins, J. B. (1968). Development of a stemming algorithm. *Mech. Transl. Comput. Linguistics, 11(1-2), 22-31.*

Marie, B., Rubino, R., & Fujita, A. (2020, July). Tagged back-translation revisited: Why does it really work?. *In Proceedings of the 58th Annual Meeting of the Association for Computational Linguistics (pp. 5990-5997).*

Sennrich, R., Haddow, B., & Birch, A. (2015). Improving neural machine translation models with monolingual data. *arXiv preprint arXiv:1511.06709.*

Vaswani, A., Shazeer, N., Parmar, N., Uszkoreit, J., Jones, L., Gomez, A. N., ... & Polosukhin, I. (2017). Attention is all you need. *Advances in neural information processing systems, 30.*

Wu, Y., Schuster, M., Chen, Z., Le, Q. V., Norouzi, M., Macherey, W., ... & Dean, J. (2016). Google's neural machine translation system: Bridging the gap between human and machine translation. *arXiv preprint arXiv:1609.08144.*

Wang, T., Kuang, S., Xiong, D., & Branco, A. (2019). Merging external bilingual pairs into neural machine translation. *arXiv preprint arXiv:1912.00567.*

Multi-dimensional Consideration of Cognitive Effort in Translation and Interpreting Process Studies

(Deyan Zou, Dalian University of Foreign Languages, P. R. China)

Abstract: Cognitive effort is the core element of translation and interpreting process studies, but theoretical and practical issues such as the concept, the characteristics and the measurement of cognitive effort still need to be clarified. This paper firstly analyzes the concept and the research characteristics of cognitive effort in translation and interpreting process studies. Then, based on the cost concept (internal cost, opportunity cost) and the reward concept (need for cognition, learned industriousness) of cognitive effort, it carries out multi-dimensional analysis of the characteristics of cognitive effort. Finally, it points out the enlightenment of multi-dimensional consideration of cognitive effort to translation and interpreting process studies.

Key words: translation and interpreting process; cognitive effort; internal cost; opportunity cost; need for cognition; learned industriousness

I. Introduction

Many extraordinary human skills, such as reading, mastering a musical instrument, or writing complex software, require thousands of hours of practice and continuous cognitive effort. While cognitive effort is the most challenging to understand, studying this type of effort is key to gaining insights into the translation process (Lacruz, 2017: 387). Time constraints have increasingly become one of the common features of translation and interpreting. The cross-border integration of translation and interpreting has made time constraints more prominent in translation activities such as consecutive interpreting, simultaneous interpreting, sight translation, audiovisual translation, and translation under time pressure (Zou & Liu, 2020). The commonality of the above-mentioned time-limited translation activities is that translators need to adopt faster and greater information integration, simplified translation, literal translation, chunking and other decisions, which makes the trade-off between effort and effect in the translation process more important. On the one hand, people may voluntarily put in effort even without external rewards in everyday life, but popular scientific theory holds that effort is unpleasant and people avoid it as much as possible. On the other hand, some researchers have recently begun to critically question whether cognitive effort is always repulsive, instead arguing that challenging cognitive activities can be experienced as rewarding and valuable in certain situations. In other words, cognitive effort is both a cost and a reward, and its role in cognitive research of translation and interpreting still has huge room for exploration.

II. Cognitive effort and its research status in translation

2.1 Effort and Cognitive Effort

Effort is a purpose-based physical or mental activity, an explicit behavior that can be observed by oneself and others (de Morree & Marcora, 2010: 377). Cognitive effort is the proportion of limited-capacity central processing involved (Tyler et al., 1979: 607). There is a complex interaction between cognitive effort and task load, task performance, cognitive needs, learning motivation, cognitive competence, and other factors, which together play an important role in individuals' performance and competence development in complex tasks. This has become the focus of research in psychology, cognitive science, neuroscience, and other fields.

2.2 Research on Cognitive Effort during Translation and Interpreting

Cognitive research on translation and interpreting process began in the 1960s and 1970s and continued until the 1980s. Early researchers discussed cognitive resources (Gerver, 1969) and cognitive load (Kirchhoff, 1976) in the process of interpreting. Gutt (1991/2000) introduced the concept of cognitive processing effort into translation theory through Sperber and Wilson's Relevance Theory (1986). Gile (1995/2009) proposed a cognitive effort model for interpreting, which focuses on the cognitive effort and energy that interpreters actually allocate and coordinate in each subtask of the interpreting process and describes the cognitive limitations that interpreters may encounter during the interpreting process, which provides a cognitive explanation for the phenomenon of poor performance of interpreters (Su et al., 2021). Since the new century, with the continuous development of T&I cognitive research, the study of cognitive effort has become the focus of T&I process research.

However, the research on cognitive effort in T&I process still demonstrate the following deficiencies: 1) Definition and its understanding vague, cognitive effort is more of an adjunct to the task difficulty, cognitive load, and translator performance in T&I cognitive process. It brings challenges to the variable control and validity of related studies. 2) Discussion of subjects, conditions, limits, changes, development, and other traits of cognitive effort has been insufficient, which affects the cognitive research on traits and commonalities of related synchronic and diachronic factors in T&I process. 3) The measurement methods are limited, often mixed with the measurement methods of factors such as task load, and triangulation is insufficiently used, which affects the research design and the explanatory power of the results. 4) There is insufficient research space. Translation is a more complex language cognitive activity. Translation research is an indispensable field in human language research and cognitive development research. Therefore, translation research needs to draw on the latest methods and achievements in language and cognition research, to enpand the frontier and enhance the sustainability of its own research, and at the same time contribute to cognitive research of human language.

III. The Cost View of Cognitive Effort

Effort needs to consume resources, and individuals tend to avoid making effort, or obtain the maximum effect with the least effort, which reflects the characteristic of "effort is a cost", and contemporary theoretical and empirical studies in cognitive neuroscience and economics have confirmed and reinforced this view. The cost view of cognitive effort can be expounded from two aspects: the internal cost and the opportunity cost.

3.1 Internal Cost

Firstly, the internal cost of cognitive effort is reflected in the limited working memory of cognitive activity performers. Working memory capacity is a recognized determinant of human learning. The earliest research in this area proposed the magic number 7, which believed that the short-term memory span was 7 ± 2, that is, between 5-9, meaning in short-term memory tasks, people can remember about seven chunks of information (Miller, 1956). Subsequent research suggested that the magic number should be 4, and the short-term memory span should be 4 ± 1, or between 3-5; in young adults, it appears in blocks of three to five, and fewer in children and the elderly (Cowan, 2001). Recent research has pointed out that the magic number 4 is also overly optimistic, and it should be 2; the size of the chunks stored in short-term memory, not the number, enhances individual memory (Gobet & Clarkson, 2004). In conclusion, human cognitive resources are limited and must be allocated wisely. Cognitive effort is expensive, and humans are described as "cognitive misers", spending only the necessary effort to make satisfying decisions, not making the best decisions, but using shortcuts whenever possible.

Secondly, the internal cost of cognitive effort is reflected in the limited representational ability faced by the performers of cognitive activities. Individuals have a limited amount of representational information in a certain period of time (Musslick et al., 2016: 7), and face sharing, separation and distribution of representation, in multi-task cognitive activities, which will have an impact on the completion of specific cognitive tasks (Musslick & Cohen, 2021:757). The fuzzy-trace theory proposed by Brainerd & Reyna (1990) is widely used in many disciplines including linguistics. The theory holds that the relationship between precision and ambiguity is dialectically unified and contradictory, and there is no insurmountable gap between the two. In the process of extracting the meaning of information, individuals tend to use vague traces to represent information because it is more accessible and requires less cognitive effort; in contrast, precise traces are more likely to be disturbed and then forgotten. Most human cognitive activities are not accurate, but rely on vague representations (sensations, patterns, etc.). In addition, Good-enough Representation of language understanding also found that for a given task, the syntactic and semantic representations created by the language understanding system are only "good enough", not the speakers' accurate and detailed representations of utterances (Ferreira et al., 2002; Ferreira & Patson, 2007).

3.2 Opportunity Cost

Choosing one effort task often means losing the opportunity to complete other tasks, so cognitive effort is manifested as an opportunity cost (Kurzban et al., 2013: 665; Yi Wei et al., 2019: 1442). The opportunity cost of cognitive effort is mainly explained from the perspective of benefit and cost trade-off, which can be traced back to the "Least Effort Principle", that is, people perform the least labor-intensive behavior, complete a specific task, with the least amount of effort. necessary efforts to quantify (Zipf, 1949; Case, 2005). Since the "Least Effort Principle" was put forward, it has been studied, combined with language understanding and information processing. The researchers pointed out that the "Least Effort Principle" is a key concept to understand the true nature of language behavior (Martinet, 1960). Heuristics are not simply hobbled versions of optimal strategies; there are no optimal strategies in many real-world environments in the first place (Gigerenzer et al., 1999: 22). The search for the best solution for maximum benefit, reflected in translation, is that translators and interpreters pay the least effort to achieve the maximum effect (Levy, 1967: 1179).

The study found that both reading and listening comprehension processes involved in translation comprehension exhibit the effect of "least effort". On the one hand, eye-tracking technology-based reading research shows that readers' eyes are not reading word by word from left to right, it's just an illusion created by our brains. In fact, we only fix about 60% of the time we read (Rayner et al., 2011: 514), and the brain infers and obtains the entire information based on partial information and impressions, with the help of syntactic and semantic rules. The "Transposed Letter Effect" also verifies this. Randomizing letter positions in the middle of a word has little effect on the understanding of the text by skilled readers, as long as the first and last letters of the word are positioned correctly (Rawlinson, 1976). On the other hand, the study found that in the listening process, the listener's comprehension of the spoken sentence does not always stem from a comprehensive analysis of the words and syntax of the utterance; instead, listeners may instead conduct a superficial analysis, sampling some words and using presumed plausibility to arrive at an understanding of the sentence meaning (Ayasse et al., 2021: 1).

IV. The Reward View of Cognitive Effort

Effort is closely related to motivation and value. Effort can increase the result of effort and the value of effort itself, which can even play the role of a reinforcer to motivate effort, which reflects the characteristic of "Effort is a reward". The reward view of cognitive effort can be expounded from two aspects: Need for Cognition and Learned Industriousness.

4.1 Need for Cognition

Need for Cognition is defined as "a need to understand and make reasonable the experiential world" (Cohen et al., 1955: 291), "the tendency of individuals to engage in and enjoy thinking" (Cacioppo & Petty, 1982: 116). The latter has also developed Need for Cognition Scale, which can divide subjects into those with high Need for Cognition and those with low Need for Cognition, according to the scale scores, to study the individual differences in Need for Cognition and their effect and role in cognitive activities. The study found that cognitive needs affect the effort of individuals in information processing. Compared with people with low Need for Cognition, people with high Need for Cognition put more effort into cognitive activities, perform better in information recall, and complete cognitive tasks better (Xu & Zhou, 2010: 686). The reasons for individual differences in Need for Cognition are still unclear, but studies have found that individuals' learning experiences, tolerance for setbacks, and culturally related factors may have an impact on individuals' Need for Cognition (Cacioppo et al., 1996: 215; Inzlicht et al., 2018:

342). Need for Cognition has individual differences, and different individuals have different views and perceptions of effort and its rewards. In conclusion, Need for Cognition highlight the static individual differences in cognitive effort from the perspective of reward.

4.2 Learned Industriousness

If Need for Cognition highlights the static individual differences in cognitive effort from the perspective of reward, then Learned Industriousness shows more dynamic changes and development of cognitive effort from the perspective of reward. According to Learned Industriousness, "rewarded effort that contributes to durable individual differences in industriousness" (Eisenberger, 1992: 248). On the one hand, after individuals form a high-value experience of effort through conditional learning, they will tend to choose high-effort behaviors (Xu & Zhang, 1996: 188), and then increase the value of high-effort tasks (Yi et al., 2019: 1444; Clay et al., 2022). Cognitive load, on the other hand, is related to the amount of information that working memory can hold at one time (Sweller, 1988: 265); since working memory has a limited capacity, teaching methods should avoid overloading working memory with additional activities that do not directly contribute to learning, and avoid overloading, as both hinder the learning progress (Zhong & Sheng, 2017: 8). In conclusion, moderate cognitive load and cognitive effort contribute to Learned Industriousness, which shows the dynamic development of cognitive effort from the perspective of reward.

V. Implications for T&I Research

5.1 Cognitive Effort as a Cost

Firstly, we should be fully aware of the "dodging" of cognitive efforts. Behavioral research shows that the willingness of human beings to choose high effort will decrease with the increase of effort, which is expressed as "Effort Discounting"; when the incentive is low or the difficulty is too high, the individual's effort will not follow. As the difficulty of the task increases, the two can be separated (Kahneman, 1973; Brehm & Self, 1989; Richter, 2016). In T&I activities, cognitive effort is the "optimization" after weighing effort and effect; the phenomenon of Effort Discounting can help us optimize the research design of the T&I process and can also become a new research point. In short, we should pay full attention to the interaction between cognitive effort and other variables in T&I process research, and at the same time improve the reliability and validity of the research, we should pay attention to the multi-dimensional interpretation of the research process and results.

Secondly, on the basis of controlling variables, we should improve the reliability and validity of the research through triangulation. Task difficulty is considered an operational definition of effort (Wang, Zheng, & Meng, 2017). Generally speaking, the more difficult the task is, the more effort the individual has to put in; however, the effort is the active processing of the individual, and the difficulty is the attribute of the task itself (Cao et al., 2022: 877). In the translation activity, the subjects will reflect anxiety, stress, fatigue and other feelings while reporting their efforts, and these accompanying feelings are not conducive to the subjects' normal cognitive effort, which may be the trigger of Effort Discounting, which deserves sufficient attention and consideration from the researchers, in research design and process. Misuse of measures of cognitive effort and cognitive load should be avoided (Gile, 2021); in addition to subjective measures of the Need for Cognition Scale (NFC, Need for Cognition Scale), objective measures of Effort Expenditure for Rewards Task, Cognitive Effort Discounting Paradigm, Motivation for Cognition State Scale, etc. (Treadway et al., 2009; Westbrook et al., 2013; Westbrook & Braver, 2015; Blaise et al., 2021) can be used in research.

5.2 Cognitive Effort as a Reward

Firstly, we need to pay attention to individual differences in cognitive effort and take this into account in the research design and the interpretation of the findings. Effort is an active process that requires the participation of will. Based on this, in T&I process research, we need to pay attention to the group and individual differences in the cognitive effort of the translators and interpreters. According to individual differences in Need for Cognition and influencing factors, such as personal learning experience, tolerance for setbacks, cultural-related factors, etc., we can pay attention to the cognitive efforts of professional translators and student translators under different cognitive loads, or we can pay attention to the development of student translators' cognitive efforts at different stages. Translators and interpreters at different levels are different in competence, the input-output ratio between the input effort and the output effect is high among high-level translators, and the opposite for low-level translators. As research has found, learners increase this allocation of attentional resources when valuable information is encountered and perform better on tasks (Ariel & Castel, 2014: 344). It can also be said that whether cognitive effort can be used more efficiently is also part of a translator's competence.

Secondly, we need to pay attention to the changes and development of individual cognitive efforts, and to study their synergistic changes and development with cognitive and translation competence. Cognitive training in the past has not achieved a ubiquitous effect in improving cognitive skills. Relevant cognitive training such as Learned Industriousness may be a breakthrough for improving learning effect. By designing cognitive training tasks that can show the "optimized" cognitive load, mobilize cognitive efforts that conform to the general rules of skill acquisition and individualized development, maximize the added value of cognitive efforts, we can then expect to improve individual learning ability and learning effect through sustainable cognitive efforts. In this process, multiple or repeated measurements of cognitive effort in long-term tasks should be performed. This can effectively track the changes and development of cognitive effort and help further explore the role of cognitive effort in reflecting the complex interactive relationship between cognitive load and task performance.

Works Cited:

Ariel, R. & Castel, A. 2014. Eyes wide open: Enhanced pupil dilation when selectively studying important information [J]. *Experimental Brain Research*, 232 (1): 337-344.

Ayasse, N. D., Hodson, A. J., & Wingfield, A. 2021. The principle of least effort and comprehension of spoken sentences by younger and older adults [J]. *Frontiers in Psychology*, 12: 1-13.

Blaise, M., Marksteiner, T., Krispenz, A., & Bertrams, A. 2021. Measuring motivation for cognitive effort as state [J]. *Frontiers in Psychology*. 12:785094. doi: 10.3389/fpsyg.2021.785094

Brainerd, C. J. & Reyna, V. F. 1990. Gist is the grist: Fuzzy-trace theory and the new intuitionism [J]. *Developmental Review* (10): 3-47.

Brehm J. W. & Self, E. A. 1989. The intensity of motivation [J]. *Ann. Rev. Psychol*, 40: 109-131.

Cacioppo, J. T., Petty, R. E. 1982. The need for cognition [J]. *Journal of Personality and Social Psychology*, 42 (1): 116-131.

Cacioppo, J. T., Petty, R. E., Feinstein, J. A., & Jarvis, W. B. G. 1996. Dispositional differences in cognitive motivation: The life and times of individuals varying in need for cognition [J]. *Psychological Bulletin*, 119 (2): 197-253.

Case, D. O. 2005. Principle of least effort [C]. // K. E. Fisher, S. Erdelez & L. McKechnie (eds.). *Theories of Information Behavior*. Medford, N.J. : Information Today: 289-292.

Cao, S., Tang, C., Wu, H., & Liu, X. 2022. Value analysis determines when and how to strive [J]. *Advances in Psychological Science*, 30(4): 877-887. (in Chinese)

Clay, G., Mlynski, C., Korb, F. M., & Job, V. 2022. Rewarding cognitive effort increases the intrinsic value of mental labor [J]. *Psychological and Cognitive Sciences*, 119 (5): e2111785119.

Cohen, A. R., Stotland, E., & Wolfe, D. M. 1955. An experimental investigation of need for cognition [J]. *Journal of Abnormal Psychology*, 51 (2): 291-294.

Cowan, N. 2001. The magical number 4 in short-term memory: A reconsideration of mental storage capacity [J]. *Behavioral and Brain Sciences*, 24(1): 87-114.

de Morree, H. M. & Marcora, S. M. 2010. The face of effort: Frowning muscle activity reflects effort during a physical task [J]. *Biological Psychology*, 85 (3): 377-382.

Eisenberger, R. 1992. Learned Industriousness [J]. *Psychological Review*, 99 (2): 248-267.

Ferreira F., Bailey K G, & Ferraro V. 2002. Good enough representations in language comprehension[J]. *Current Directions in Psychological Science*, 11(1):11-15.

Ferreira, F., & Patson, N.D. 2007. The "good-enough" approach to language comprehension [J]. *Language and Linguistics Compass*, 1(1-2): 71-83.

Gerver, D. 1969. The effects of source language presentation rates on the performance of simultaneous conference interpreting [C]. // E. Foulke (eds.). *Proceedings of the Second Louisville Conference on Rate and / or Frequency-controlled Speech*. Louisville, Kentucky: Center for Rate-controlled Recordings, University of Louisville: 162-184.

Gigerenzer, G., Todd, P.M., & the ABC Group. 1999. *Simple heuristics that make us smart* [M]. New York: Oxford University Press.

Gile, D. 1995/2009. *Basic Concepts and Models for Interpreter and Translator Training* [M]. Amsterdam/Philadelphia: John Benjamins Publishing Company.

Gile, D. 2021. *Cognitive load and effort in translation and interpreting: Methodological issues*. Lecture at CRITT@kent Translation Colloquium.

Gobet, F. & G. Clarkson. 2004. Chunks in expert memory: Evidence for the magical number four…or is it two? [J]. *Memory*, 12(6): 732-747.

Gutt, E. 1991/2000. *Translation and Relevance: Cognition and Context* (2nd ed.) [M]. Manchester: St. Jerome.

Inzlicht, M., Shenhav, A., & Olivola, C. Y. 2018. The effort paradox: Effort is both costly and valued [J]. *Trends in Cognitive Sciences*, 22 (4): 337-349.

Kahneman, D. 1973. *Effort and Attention* [M]. Prentice-Hall.

Kirchhoff, H. 1976. Das Simultandolmetschen: Interdependenz der Variablen im Dolmetschprozess, Dolmetschmodelle und Dolmetschstrategien [C]. // H. W. Drescher, & S. Scheffzek (eds.). *Theorie und Praxis des Ubersetzens und Dolmetschen*. Frankfurt am Main: Peter Lang: 59-71.

Kurzban, R., Duckworth, A., Kable, J. W., & Myers, J. 2013. An opportunity cost model of subjective effort and task performance [J]. *Behavioral and Brain Sciences*, 36: 661-726.

Lacruz, I. 2017. Cognitive effort in translation, editing, and post-editing [C]. // J.W. Schiwieter & A. Ferreira (eds.). *The handbook of translation and cognition*. Wiley-Blackwell: 386-401.

Levy, J. 1967. Translation as a decision process [C]. // *To honor Roman Jakobson: Essays on the occasion of his seventieth birthday, vol. 2*. The Hague: Mouton: 1171-1182.

Martinet, A. 1960. *Elements of General Linguistics* [M]. London: Faber and Faber.

Miller, G. 1956. The magical number seven, plus or minus two: Some limits on our capacity for processing information [J]. *The Psychological Review*, 63: 81-97.

Musslick, S., Dey, B., Ozeimder, K., Patwary, M. M. A., Willke, T., & Cohen, J. D. 2016. Parallel processing capability versus efficiency of representation in neural networks [J]. *Network*, 8: 7.

Musslick, S. & Cohen, J. D. 2021. Rationalizing constraints on the capacity for cognitive control [J]. *Trends in Cognitive Science*, 25 (9): 757-775.

Rawlinson, G. E. 1976. *The Significance of Letter Position in Word Recognition* [D]. Unpublished PhD Thesis, Psychology Department, University of Nottingham, Nottingham UK.

Rayner, K., T.J. Slattery & D. Drieghe. 2011. Eye movements and word skipping during reading: Effects of word length and predictability [J]. *Journal of Experimental Psychology: Human Perception and Performance*, 37 (2): 514-528.

Richter, M, Gendolla, G. H. E., & Wright, R. A. 2016. Three decades of research on motivational intensity theory [C]. // A. J. Elliot (eds.). *Advances in Motivation Science*, Elsevier Inc.: 149-186.

Sperber, D., & Wilson, D. 1986. *Relevance: Communication and Cognition* [M]. Oxford: Blackwell.

Su, W., Li, D., & Cao, H. 2021. Eye-tracking studies of cognitive load in interpreting processes [J]. *Foreign Language Research* (3): 109-114. (in Chinese)

Sweller, J. 1988. Cognitive load during problem solving: Effects on learning [J]. *Cognitive Science*, 12 (2): 257–285.

Treadway, M. T., Buckholtz, J. W., Schwartzman, A. N., Lambert, W. E., & Zald, D. H. 2009. Worth the "EFFfRT"?

The effort expenditure for rewards task as an objective measure of motivation and anhedonia [J]. *PLoS One*, 4 (8), e6598.

Tyler, S. W., Hertel, P. T., McCallum, M. C., & Ellis, H. C. 1979. Cognitive effort and memory [J]. *Journal of Experimental Psychology: Human Learning and Memory*, 5: 607-617.

Wang, L., Zheng, J., & Meng, L. 2017. Effort provides its own reward: Endeavors reinforce subjective expectation and evaluation of task performance [J]. *Experimental Brain Research*, 235(4): 1107-1118.

Westbrook, A., & Braver, T. S. 2015. Cognitive effort: A neuroeconomic approach [J]. *Cognitive, Affective, & Behavioral Neuroscience*, 15 (2): 395-415.

Westbrook, A., Kester, D., & Braver, T. S. 2013. What is the subjective cost of cognitive effort? Load, trait, and aging effects revealed by economic preference [J]. *PloS One*, 8 (7), e68210.

Xu, G., & Zhang, Q. 1996. Experimental research and theoretical hypotheses of learned industriousness [J]. *Journal of Psychological Science*, (3): 187-189. (in Chinese)

Xu, H., & Zhou, N. 2010. The effects of need for cognition on the dispositional differences of individuals' information orocessing [J]. *Advances in Psychological Science*, 18(4): 685-690. (in Chinese)

Yi, W., Mei, S., & Zheng, Y. 2019. Effort: Cost or reward? [J]. *Advances in Psychological Science*, 27(8): 1439-1450. (in Chinese)

Zhong, L., & Sheng, Q. 2017. How to "optimize" the cognitive load: developing complex cognitive skills: An interview with the international famous cognitive expert Fred Paas [J]. *Research on Modern Distance Education*, 4: 3-10. (in Chinese)

Zipf, G. K. 1949. *Human Behavior and the Principle of Least Effort* [M]. Cambridge MA: Addison-Wesley.

Zou, D., & Liu, Z. 2020. Rethinking translation and interpreting from the perspective of cross-border integration [J]. *Foreign Language Studies*, (4): 68-74. (in Chinese)

History of Machine Translation in the United States

AMTA 2022

Dr. Jennifer DeCamp
MITRE

Background

- 2012 contacted by Routledge Publishing to write an article with Jost Zetzsche on "The History of Translation Technology in the United States" for the *Routledge Encyclopedia of Translation Technology,* published 2014
  - 2019 contacted to write an update, to be published in 2022
  - Discussed with AMTA and ATA leadership that this is a topic to cover as a community
- Like most people in this audience, I have:
  - Taught classes and workshops that included MT and NLP history
  - Provided conference presentations on the history
  - Been around for much of MT development
  - Always had a passion for MT anthropology
- In this presentation, I would like to describe:
  - The history of the history of MT
  - Reality Check: Xerox
  - Gaps
  - Recommendations

The History of the History of MT: W. John Hutchins

1939 – 2021

1960	Graduated with a bachelor's degree in French and German
1962	Obtained a diploma in librarianship
1962-1998	Worked as a librarian, publishing in translation and information retrieval
1978	Authored "Machine Translation and Machine-Aided Translation" in the *Journal of Documentation*
1986	Authored *Machine Translation: Past, Present, and Future*
1992:	Co-authored with Harold Somers: *An Introduction to Machine Translation*
2000:	Authored: *Early Years in Machine Translation* (author/editor)
2015:	Authored: "History of Research and Applications" in *The Routledge Encyclopedia of Translation Technology*
	Developed *MT Compendium of Translation Software*
	Ending in 2014? No prototypes or short-lived products

Donated his extensive library to the MT community (John W. Hutchins Machine Translation Archive)

Somers: "What perhaps many did not realize is that John's work on MT was entirely a labor of love, a kind of hobby, all completed in his own spare time: his job as a librarian did not include working on the MT Archive, nor I think did his employers properly realize and reward his fantastic contribution to the field. We were extremely fortunate to benefit from his skills: from a scientific viewpoint he was an informed observer free of any of the prejudices of the developer or researcher with his own theories and approaches to push."

Summary: Dedicated, detailed, objective librarianship
But ending around 2014; software compendium not covering prototypes and short-lived products; British focus

A Small Sample of Other Historians

- Harold Somers
  - 1915 - 2001
  - Hutchins, W. J., & Somer, H. L. (1992). An Introduction to Machine Translation
  - 1978 Retired
- Andy Way
- Chris Wendt
- Steve Richardson
- Mike Dillinger
- Jay Marciano
- Kathleen Egan (retired)
- DARPA and CAMT Program Managers
- Others in U.S. Government, but constrained in what they can say

Summary: More U.S. involvement
Many teaching courses and/or providing tutorials on Intro to MT
Little in U.S. Government operations

A Selection of Other Histories

- Timelines
  - Wikipedia
  - TAUS

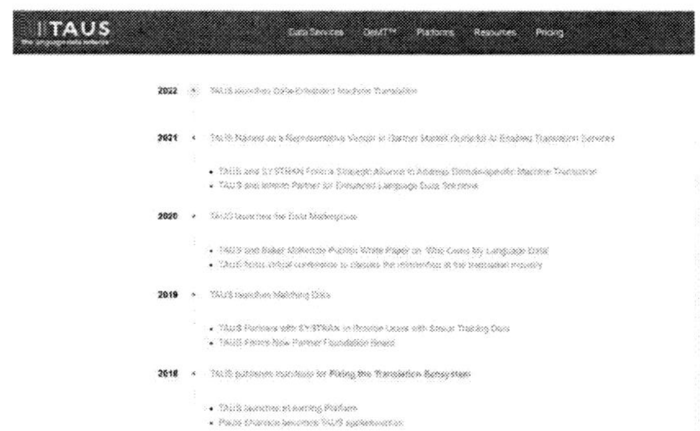

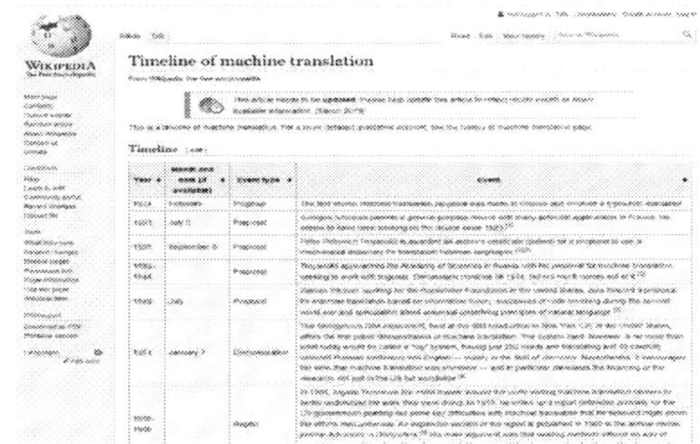

- Short histories
  - Wikipedia
  - IBM
  - Systran
  - AMTA
  - Many others

Summary: Documentation by companies (some—like IBM and SYSTRAN—focusing only on their own contributions), professional organizations, blogs, and Wikipedia

A Selection of Other Resources

- Publications (e.g., Routledge)
- Conference tutorials and presentations
- The W. John Hutchins MT Archive
- The EAMT Software Compendium
- AMTA Resources
- ACL Archives

Summary: Massive information but little curation, except in history-focused publications, tutorials and presentations

Reality Check: Xerox

- From: *An Introduction to Machine Translation* (Hutchins and Somers 1992)
  - Also checked Hutchins' *Machine Translation Past, Present, and Future (1986) and Early Years in Machine Translation (2000)*
- "Xerox installed Systran in 1982 for technical manuals," using "Multinational Customized English (MCE)," which had about 3000 words and "rules for unambiguous English"
- "At Xerox, texts for translation by Systran are composed in a controlled English vocabulary and syntax; and a major feature of the SMART systems is the pre-translation editor of English input."
  - **Not mentioned:**
    - Areas in source document would be highlighted for editing
    - Corresponding output would be highlighted to alert post-editors
- "The texts that their writers produce are clearer and more understandable"
  - **Not mentioned:**
    - The MT output had more consistent terminology
    - Some technical writers refused to use the pre-editor
- "Output from the system needs little or no post-editing"
  - **Not mentioned:**
    - The system reduced the highly valuable time at the end of the production cycle, when companies would start waiting on purchases until the new version came out
    - The system also reduced the time to produce last-minute revisions and post-shipment revisions.
- No discussion of Xerox DocuTrans
  - In 1989, Xerox provided MT from multiple engines with pre-editing and post editing, including confidence measures
    - Combination of SMART, SYSTRANn, and METAL (Mechanical Translation and Analysis of Languages, started by the Air Force)

Summary: No mention of key applications, confidence measures, post-editing tools, or multi-engine configurations
No mention of refusal by some technical writers to use pre-editor

Gaps

- **Time**, particularly before 1980 and after 2014
  - Due to lack of digitized resources and loss of key librarians
- **Efforts by the U.S. Government**, except for DARPA, IARPA, Wright Patterson Air Force Base, and occasionally a few general papers
  - Due to constraints on what could be publicly released
- **Efforts by LDS Church and other religious organizations**
  - Due to constraints on the quantity of data that could be handled
- **Lack of detail** (e.g., Xerox example)
  - Due to constraints on the quantity of data that could be handled
- **Lack of larger context** (e.g., histories of translation theory and practice, innovation, computer technology, popular culture, etc.)
  - Due to the constraints on the quantity of data that could be handled
- **Lack of information on how practices and decisions turned out** (e.g., Xerox pre-editing interface led to some groups not using the system)
  - Due to lack of time and/or focus
  - Maybe due to Hutchins waiting to see if the system had longevity

Why Try to Fill These Gaps and Provide Analysis?

- Identify best practices (e.g., responding to user feedback)
- Identify requirements and motivations that may have been forgotten (e.g., user interfaces)
- Analyze trends and identify areas of high potential
- Provide long term evaluation of processes and products (e.g., pre-translation editing)
- Improve planning through understanding the accuracy of past projections and forecasts
- Recognize outstanding work
- Protect and celebrate our remarkable history of MT, that helps to build our sense of community

Recommendations

- Address underrepresented areas (e.g., through AMTA panels)
  - Before 1980
  - After 2014
  - Efforts by the U.S. Government
  - Efforts by the LDS Church and other religious groups
  - Long-term results
- Plan AMTA panel on U.S. Government work in MT
  - Obtain more detail on work
  - Obtain official government disclosure and perhaps push the bar on what can be disclosed
- Plan cross-government panel at IAMT
  - Obtain more detail on work
  - Obtain more insights and ideas
- Encourage historical analysis as a field of research in MT/NLP
- Review and encourage expansion histories, timelines, and databases
  - AMTA site
  - EAMT site
  - Wikipedia
  - Publications
  - Company sites

References

Association for Machine Translation in the Americas (AMTA) (2022). "Machine Translation." AMTA Website. Available at: https://amtaweb.org/machine-translation/

AMTA (2022). "Resources." AMTA Website. Available: https://amtaweb.org/resources/#1506630470744-1df80718-e8a9

Baker, M. and Saldanha, G. (2021). *Routledge Encyclopedia of Translation Studies*, Third Edition. Routledge Publishing, London and New York.

Chan, S. W. (2022). *The Routledge Encyclopedia of Translation Technology.* Routledge Publishing Company, London and New York.

Chan, S. W. (2015). *The Routledge Encyclopedia of Translation Technology.* Routledge Publishing Company, London and New York.

DeCamp, J. (2022). "The History of Translation Technology in the United States." In *The Routledge Encyclopedia of Translation Technology*, Ed. Chan S. W. Routledge Publishing Company, London and New York.

DeCamp, J. (2015). "The History of Translation Technology in the United States." In *The Routledge Encyclopedia of Translation Technology*, Ed. Chan S. W. Routledge Publishing Company, London and New York.

Egan, K., Kubala, F., and Sears, A.(24 October 2008). "User-Centered Development and Implementation." Presentation at AMTA Government Users Presentation, AMTA Conference Waikiki. Available: https://aclanthology.org/2008.amta-govandcom.9.pdf

Hutchins, W.J. (2022). The W. John. Hutchins Machine Translation Archive. European Association for Machine Translation (EAMT) website. Available at https://mt-archive.net/

Hutchins, W.J. (2022). "Compendium of Translation Software." EAMT website. Available at: https://compendium.eamt.org/compendium/index.php

Hutchins (2015). "History of Research and Applications." In *The Routledge Encyclopedia of Translation Technology*, Ed. Chan S. W. Routledge Publishing Company, London and New York.

Hutchins (Ed.) (2000). *Early Years in Machine Translation*. John Benjamins Publishing Company, Amsterdam and Philadelphia.

Hutchins, W. J. (June 1978). "Machine Translation and Machine-Aided Translation" in the *Journal of Documentation,* Vol. 24, No. 2, pp. 119-159. Available at: https://mt-archive.net/70/JDoc-1978-Hutchins.pdf

Hutchins and H. Somers (1992). *An Introduction to Machine Translation*. Academic Press. Harcourt Brace Jovanovich Publishers, London.

IBM (2022). "701 Translator: IBM." IBM Archives website. Available: https://www.ibm.com/ibm/history/exhibits/701/701_translator.html

SYSTRAN (2022). "SYSTRAN: 50 Years of MT Innovation." SYSTRAN website. Available: https://www.systransoft.com/systran/translation-technology/systran-50-years-of-mt-innovation/

TAUS (2022). "Timeline." TAUS website. Available https://TAUS.net

Wikipedia (2022). "History of Machine Translation." Available at https://en.wikipedia.org/wiki/History_of_machine_translation

The
Translation
Bureau
HAND IN 01101000 01100001 01101110 01100100 WITH THE MACHINE:
A ROADMAP TO QUALITY
Caroline-Soledad Mallette, Director of Innovation,
Government of Canada's Translation Bureau
A-Z
Public Services and Procurement Canada
Services publics et Approvisionnement Canada
Canada

BACKGROUND

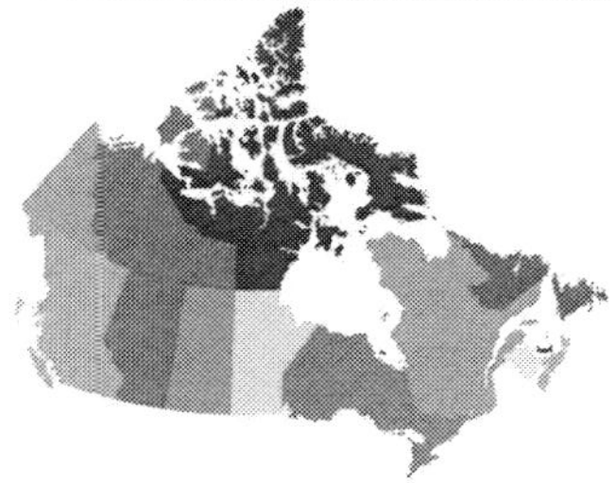

THE CANADIAN LANGUAGE INDUSTRY

- Has an estimated value of USD 1.2B.
- Employs an estimated 27,500 Canadians on a part-time, contract or as-needed basis.
- About 75% of its businesses have fewer than 10 employees; 1% have 100 employees or more.

THE TRANSLATION BUREAU: THE GC's CENTRE OF EXCELLENCE

- Provides optional translation, interpretation and terminology services in official, Indigenous, foreign and signed languages.
- Serves Parliament, the judiciary and federal departments and agencies, mostly on a cost-recovery basis.
- Is ranked 15th on CSA Research's Top 100 Language Service Providers list for 2022, with USD 154M in revenues.
- Outsources ~45% of its business volume.

BOASTING AN ORGANIZATIONAL INNOVATION TEAM: LICENSED TO TRY!

1,300 EMPLOYEES NATIONWIDE **28,000** HOURS OF INTERPRETATION IN 2021–2022 **360M** WORDS TRANSLATED IN 2021–2022

WHERE WE WERE A DOZEN YEARS AGO

Aging request management system

Data silos

Fractured TM (~600 textbases)

Inconsistent, human-intensive workflows

Lack of technological know-how and skillsets

A BRIGHT SPOT: MACHINE TRANSLATION OF WEATHER ALERTS

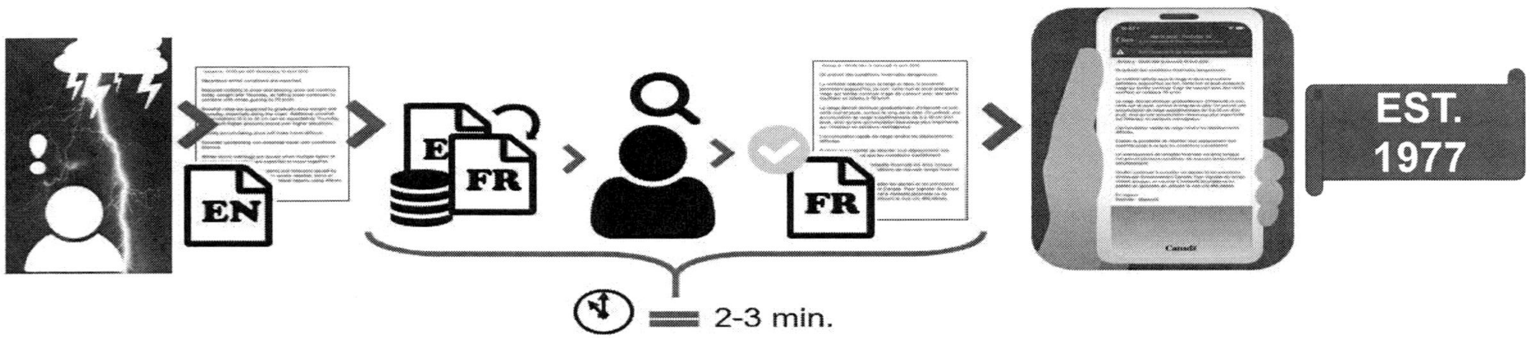

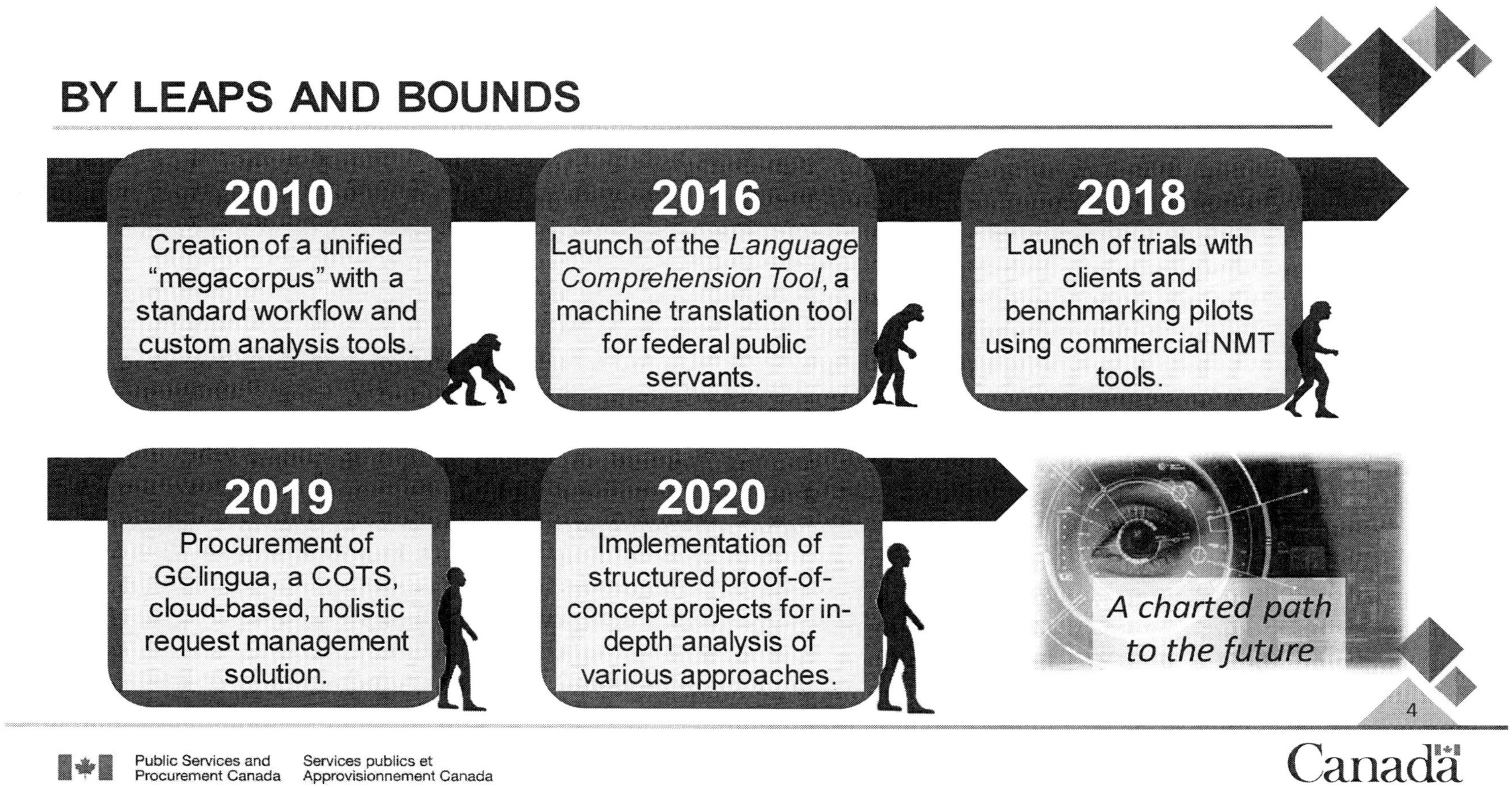
BY LEAPS AND BOUNDS
2010
Creation of a unified "megacorpus" with a standard workflow and custom analysis tools.
2016
Launch of the *Language Comprehension Tool*, a machine translation tool for federal public servants.
2018
Launch of trials with clients and benchmarking pilots using commercial NMT tools.
2019
Procurement of GClingua, a COTS, cloud-based, holistic request management solution.
2020
Implementation of structured proof-of-concept projects for in-depth analysis of various approaches.
A charted path to the future
4
Public Services and Procurement Canada
Services publics et Approvisionnement Canada
Canada

FRUITFUL PROOFS OF CONCEPT

King Kong (7M words)	▪ Manual processing—baseline
Turkish Delight (3M words) ↑70%	▪ Optimized processing, advanced analytics, automated packaging (daily workload) ▪ Traditional TM
Scientific abstracts (700 docs) ↑65%	▪ Intento NMT hub ▪ Custom-trained domain NMT only
1mill22 (1M words)	▪ Optimized processing, advanced analytics, automated packaging ▪ Domain TM, Intento NMT hub
Legal (700,000 words)	▪ Domain identification, metadata enrichment, content sectioning ▪ Custom TMs, MS Collab custom NMT and Intento NMT hub, with advanced analytics and processing, packaging, terminology extraction and Termium sync
Immigration and Refugee Board of Canada (10M classified words)	▪ Custom anonymization of training data to train MS Collab custom NMT

Public Services and Procurement Canada — Services publics et Approvisionnement Canada

Canada

LESSONS LEARNED: GOVERNMENTS HAVE SPECIFIC ADMINISTRATIVE HURDLES THAT MUST BE OVERCOME

- **Budget:** Strong advocacy is needed to put innovation at the forefront of the spending agenda.
- **Procurement:** An agile approach is needed to keep pace with progress (today's best-in-class is tomorrow's straggler).
- **Governance:** Working-level SMEs must be empowered to make decisions or supported by a nimble decision-making structure.
- **Security:** Specific safeguards must be put in place to protect the public and national interest without impeding innovation.
- **Workflows:** Processes must be aligned as closely as possible with the private sector to make the most of COTS solutions.
- **HR:** Public servants with the right skillset for AI innovation are scarce, and attracting the best and brightest is difficult.
- **Culture:** Strong change management is needed to ensure buy-in.

Public Services and Procurement Canada | Services publics et Approvisionnement Canada

Canada

LESSONS LEARNED: ONE SIZE DOES NOT FIT ALL

- Specialization is as much of an asset for MT as it is for translators.
- Generic MT systems show limited efficiencies in specialized domains.
- We need a responsive approach to MT.

Responsive MT Inputs and Capabilities

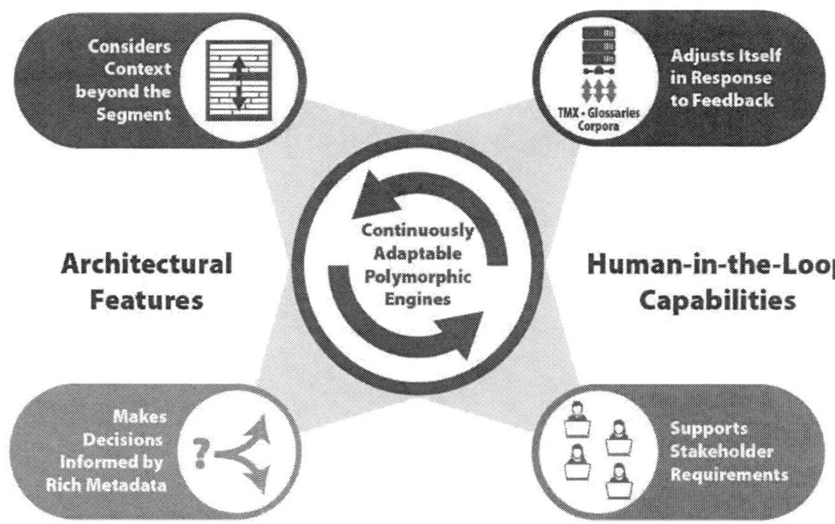

© CSA Research

Public Services and Procurement Canada | Services publics et Approvisionnement Canada

Canada

LESSONS LEARNED: KEEP HUMANS IN THE LOOP

- Equal content and quality in English and French is an obligation for the Government of Canada.
- Volumes far exceed human capacity, yet machines cannot provide sufficient quality
  → a hybrid model is required.
- Humans work with technology but remain in control of the process. They focus on the difficult aspects that machines cannot handle, rather than on low-value tasks.

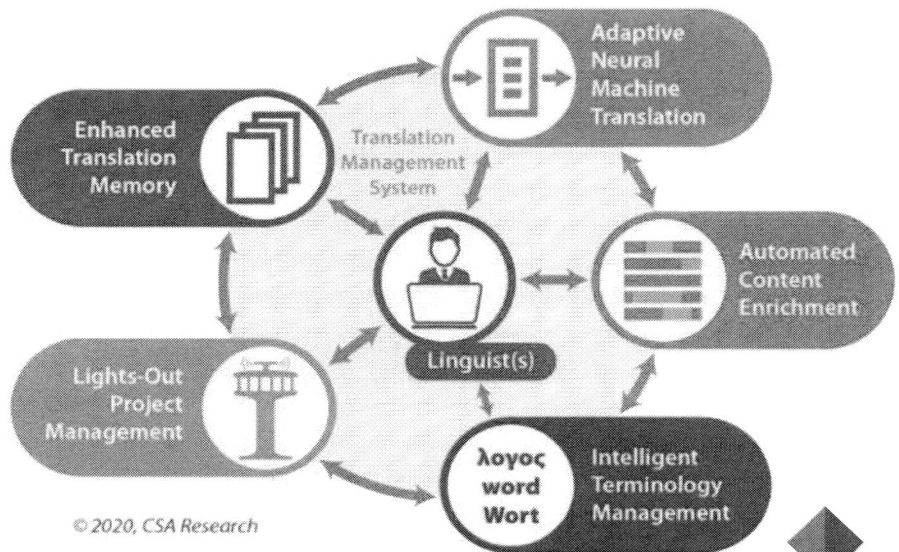

8

Public Services and Procurement Canada   Services publics et Approvisionnement Canada

Canada

LESSONS LEARNED: PROVIDE OUR PEOPLE WITH THE RIGHT TOOLS

PROJECT MANAGERS HAVE THE FEWEST TOOLS AVAILABLE TO THEM

The industry has focused on tools for language professionals...

...leaving PMs ill-equipped to make pivotal decisions at the start of a project.

PMS MUST BE PROVIDED WITH TOOLS TO SUPPORT...

- Clean import and segmentation
- Content identification
- Content distribution
- Workflow selection
- Lossless slicing and packaging
- Fluid timeline planning and adjustment
- Assignment of tasks to the most suitable resources (humans or machines)
- Real-time status updates
- Real-time communication
- Detailed reporting
- Improved efficiency

LESSONS LEARNED: PROVIDE OUR PEOPLE WITH THE RIGHT INFORMATION

FIRST: PROPERLY AND THOROUGHLY IDENTIFY THE SOURCE CONTENT

- By segment NOT by project
  - Domain and subdomains
  - Register and tone
  - Client or product-specific preferences

THEN: STOP THE DATA LOSS

- Properly tag and add metadata to the source content, and enrich as we go.
- Make sure all data remains in the target document
  - For information distribution
    → reusable metadata in source AND in target
  - For content searches and identification
  - For NMT training

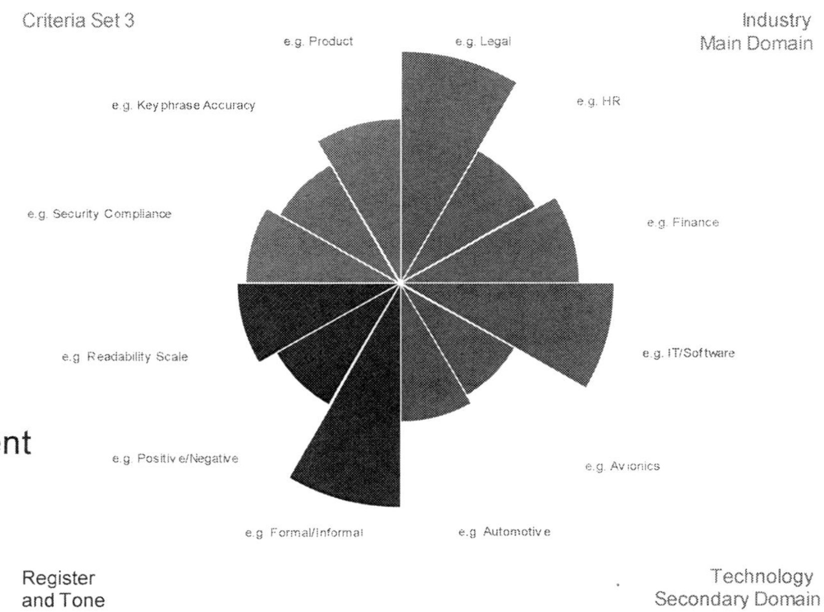

Public Services and Procurement Canada | Services publics et Approvisionnement Canada

Canada

LESSONS LEARNED: PROVIDE OUR PEOPLE WITH THE RIGHT TRAINING AND MINDSET

1) KNOWING ONE'S PLACE IN THE WORKFLOW

- What are the tasks assigned?
- What is my own role?
- What effect does my work have downstream?
- What can I do to make the next step easier?

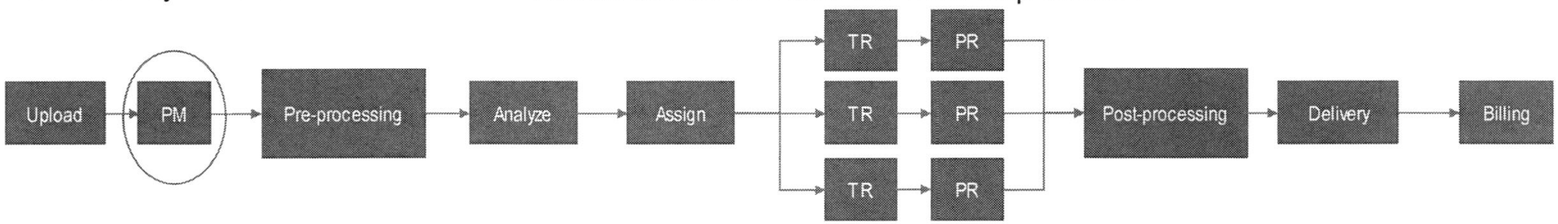

2) KNOWING **HOW** TO USE THE MACHINE

3) KNOWING **WHEN** TO USE THE MACHINE

- What type of text is it?
- What research will need to be done?
- What is the visibility/lifespan of the document?
- Could undetected errors have serious consequences?
- Is the source text well written? Is adaptation required?
- What is the deadline?

4) THINKING FORWARD, STAYING AGILE AND BROADENING ONE'S HORIZONS

LESSONS LEARNED: QUALITY IN, QUALITY OUT

- If we instruct post-editors to focus on “good enough” quality, how good will our training data for NMT be 5 years from now?
  → degraded NMT quality by design.
  - Overedit by design to have better quality for tomorrow.
  - Enhance data collection and stop the data loss (enrich metadata).
  - Optimize corpora to retain only data that will not mislead the AI (e.g. remove single-word segments).

What data do we need to generate today to ensure that AI tools are efficient tomorrow?

One overarching goal: QUALITY

Public Services and Procurement Canada | Services publics et Approvisionnement Canada

Canada

LESSONS LEARNED: NETWORKING IS KEY

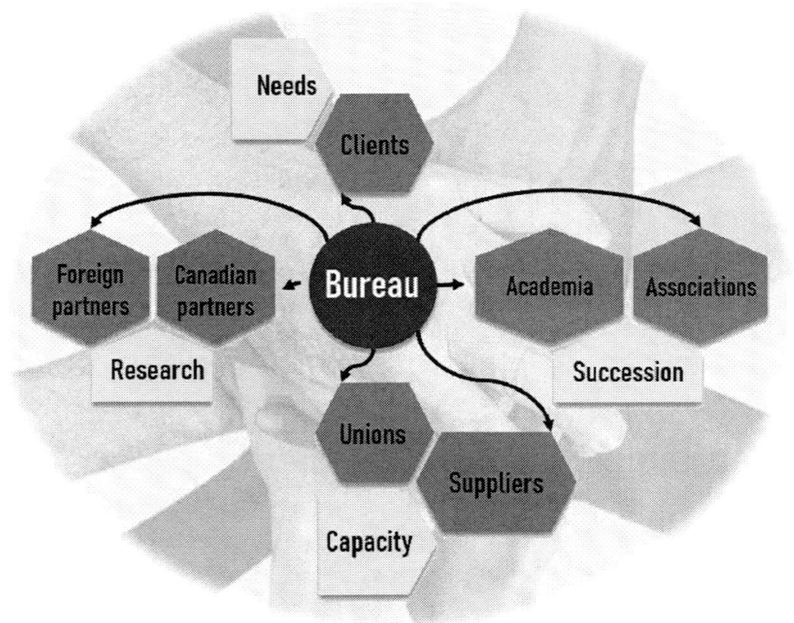

The Translation Bureau is applying a teamwork approach and actively reaching out to partners domestically and abroad to:

- Identify needs
- Share expertise
- Find innovative solutions to challenges
- Plan for the future

QUESTIONS OR COMMENTS?

Caroline-Soledad.Mallette@tpsgc-pwgsc.gc.ca

14

Public Services and Procurement Canada | Services publics et Approvisionnement Canada

Canada

APPENDIX | SOLID FOUNDATIONS: A COMPREHENSIVE AND FORWARD-LOOKING STRATEGY FOR AI

AMBITIOUS GOALS

Centre of excellence in leveraging AI for quality
Better, faster and cheaper services
Support for OGDs with AI projects
Creating trust throughout the continuum
Alignment with GC statutes, policies and priorities

GUIDING PRINCIPLES

Support (rather than replace) humans
Invest in people to create trust
Prepare our employees for the future of work
Start small: experiment and build
Partner with leaders in the field
Plan for bumps but don't wait for perfection

FOUR PILLARS

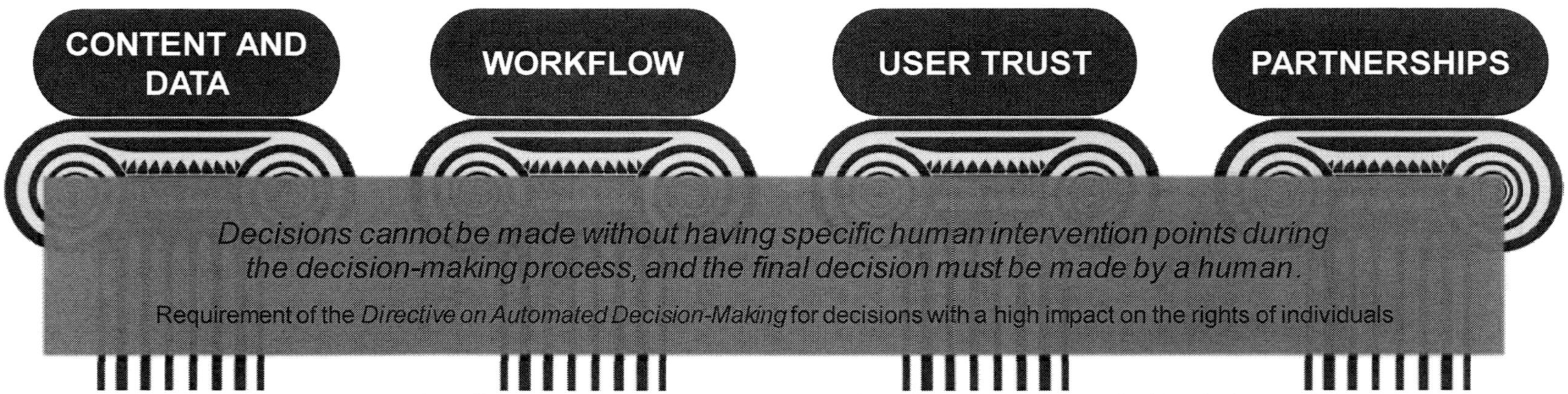

APPENDIX | SOLID FOUNDATIONS: A STRONG DATA MANAGEMENT STRATEGY

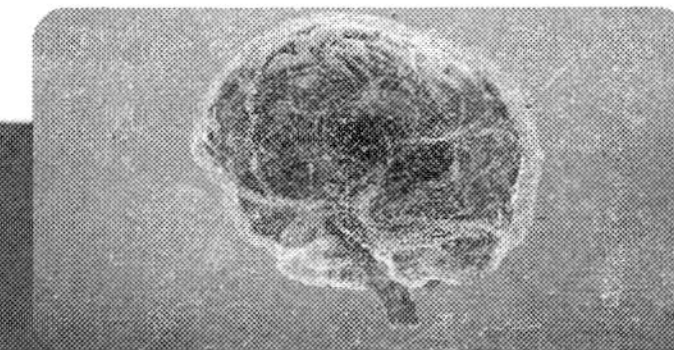

PEOPLE AND CULTURE

Identify the Bureau's data requirements

Establish a data governance committee

Form a network (hub) of data people

Assess data literacy and recommend training

ENVIRONMENT AND DIGITAL INFRASTRUCTURE

Assess the required data environment and digital infrastructure

Build a data warehouse

Develop a cloud-based infrastructure

Develop a modern analytics system for near-real-time reporting

DATA AS AN ASSET

Build a data analytics centre to support fast and confident decision-making

Develop and train AI tools for cost reduction

Generate new data for holistic reporting and quality improvement

APPENDIX | HOW TO DO BUSINESS WITH THE BUREAU

Translation services in Canada's official languages

- The Translation Bureau has a permanent Request for Supply Arrangements process posted on Buyandsell.gc.ca under which suppliers can apply at any time in order to qualify to fulfill requirements in official languages translation. Arrangements received over a calendar year are evaluated quarterly. Details are available at buyandsell.gc.ca/procurement-data/tender-notice/PW-ZF-526-40507.

Terminology services, translation services in Indigenous and foreign languages, and interpretation services in Canada's official languages, Indigenous languages, foreign languages and signed languages

- Visit the Translation Bureau Supplier Info website at https://www.tpsgc-pwgsc.gc.ca/bt-tb/services/accueil-home-eng.html for specific guidelines.

The Canadian Content Policy applies—see https://buyandsell.gc.ca/policy-and-guidelines/supply-manual/annex/3/6.

17

Public Services and Procurement Canada | Services publics et Approvisionnement Canada

Canada

Robust Translation of French Live Speech Transcripts

Elise Bertin-Lemée elise.bertinlemee@systrangroup.com
Guillaume Klein guillaume.klein@systrangroup.com
Josep Crego josep.crego@systrangroup.com
Jean Senellart jean.senellart@systrangroup.com
SYSTRAN, 5 rue Feydeau, 75002 Paris, France

Abstract

Despite a narrowed performance gap with direct approaches, cascade solutions, involving automatic speech recognition (ASR) and machine translation (MT) are still largely employed in speech translation (ST). Direct approaches employing a single model to translate the input speech signal suffer from the critical bottleneck of data scarcity. In addition, multiple industry applications display speech transcripts alongside translations, making cascade approaches more realistic and practical. In the context of cascaded simultaneous ST, we propose several solutions to adapt a neural MT network to take as input the transcripts output by an ASR system. Adaptation is achieved by enriching speech transcripts and MT data sets so that they more closely resemble each other, thereby improving the system robustness to error propagation and enhancing result legibility for humans. We address aspects such as sentence boundaries, capitalisation, punctuation, hesitations, repetitions, homophones, *etc.* while taking into account the low latency requirement of simultaneous ST systems.

1 Introduction

Speech translation is the task of converting speech utterances given in a source language into text written in a different, target language. Conventional ST systems employ a two-step cascaded pipeline composed of ASR and MT modules Casacuberta et al. (2004); Waibel and Fugen (2008). One of the main drawbacks of these systems is error propagation, a problem that has received considerable attention in the last years Ruiz and Federico (2014); Sperber et al. (2017b). Multiple research efforts have tried to tightly integrate both modules by using N-best lists or word lattices Matusov et al. (2006); Dyer et al. (2008); Sperber et al. (2017a). These systems are nowadays strongly challenged by direct approaches employing a single model to translate the input speech signal, where all network components are jointly trained to maximize translation performance without the need for an intermediate readable representation Berard et al. (2016); Bansal et al. (2017); Weiss et al. (2017). Despite their architectural simplicity, reduced information loss and minimal error propagation of direct systems, cascaded solutions are still not widely used, mainly because of the data scarcity problem. Moreover, industry applications usually display speech transcripts alongside translations, making cascade approaches more realistic and practical.

Within the standard cascaded framework, researchers have encountered many challenges, mainly based on the fact that ASR transcripts exhibit very different features from those of the texts used to train neural machine translation (NMT) networks. While NMT models are often trained with clean and well-structured text, spoken utterances contain multiple disfluencies and recognition errors which are not well modeled by NMT systems. In addition, ASR systems do not usually predict sentence boundaries or capital letters correctly, as they are not reliably accessible as acoustic cues Makhija et al. (2019); Nguyen et al. (2019). While ASR output is sufficient for many applications, where speech segments are usually short, it is difficult to use in applications that transcribe long speech segments Li et al. (2021). Typical ASR systems segment the input speech using only acoustic information, i.e., pauses in speaking, which greatly differ from the units expected by conventional MT systems. At the other end of the spectrum, systems using longer segments may span multiple sentences. This causes important translation delays, which harms the reading experience. Limited translation delays are typically achieved via starting translation before the entire audio input is received, a practice that introduces important challenges Matusov et al. (2007); Niehues et al. (2016); Arivazhagan et al. (2020).

In this work, we consider live speech-to-text translation, a task closely resembling simultaneous interpreting, that performs multilingual translations in real time and that has recently been in increasing demand in a variety of settings (radio and television broadcasts, movies, podcasts, online meetings, conferences and lectures, live events, *etc.*). We propose a simple but efficient ST system following a cascaded ASR-MT pipeline for live translation of French speeches into English with focus on the political discourse domain. Figure 1 shows a screenshot of our live ST system interface. Inspired by Martucci et al. (2021); Ruiz et al. (2015), we propose several data augmentation techniques to simulate errors generated by an ASR system, thus allowing the MT system to recover from ASR errors.

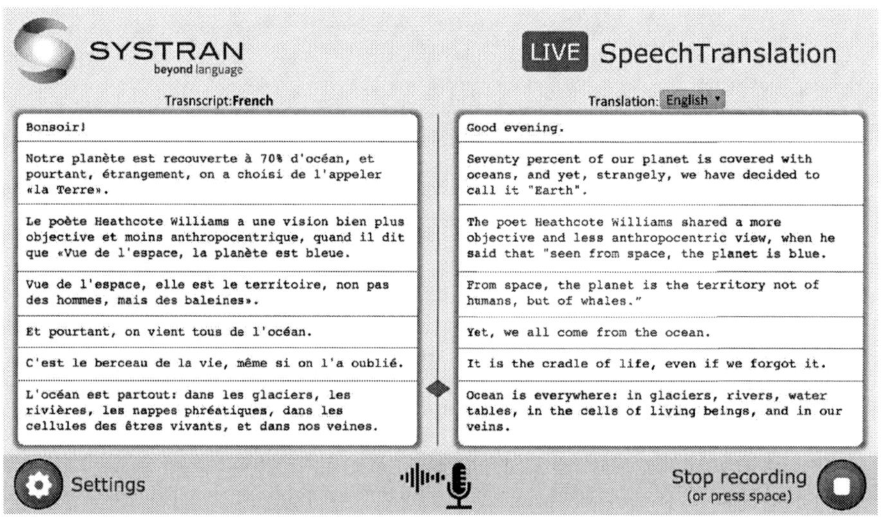

Figure 1: Speech translation system in action. French transcriptions and English translations are shown in real-time as they are decoded from the ASR transcripts.

Our contributions are summarised as follows:

- We detail our framework for multilingual live speech translation in the discourse domain.
- We identify discrepancies between written texts, commonly used in MT training data sets, and ASR outputs.

- To strengthen MT robustness, we propose several data augmentation methods to corrupt clean texts so as to emulate ill-formed transcripts. Notice that our approach is ASR-independent, noise introduced in the MT training can be successfully applied to errors made by other ASR systems.

- We conduct an empirical evaluation of our proposed workflows for a French-English multilingual translation task.

After introducing and presenting related work, we outline the particularities of the used speech transcripts in section 2. Details of the presented framework for live multilingual ST are given in section 3. Section 4 describes our experimental framework. Results are presented in section 5. Finally, section 6 concludes this work.

2 Speech Transcripts

A vast amount of audio sources are nowadays being produced on a daily basis. ASR systems enable such speech content to be used in multiple applications (*i.e.* indexing, cataloging, subtitling, translation, multimedia content production, *etc*). Details depend of individual ASR systems but their output, commonly called transcripts, typically consist of plain text enriched with time codes. Figure 2 (top) illustrates the transcript resulting from a French utterance. Notice time codes and confidence scores for each record. Latency records indicate pauses.

<Word stime="0.34" dur="0.34" conf="0.984"> **madame** </Word>
<Word stime="0.76" dur="0.06" conf="0.994"> **la** </Word>
<Word stime="0.82" dur="0.54" conf="0.986"> **présidente** </Word>
<Word stime="1.41" dur="0.15" conf="0.958"> **chers** </Word>
<Word stime="1.60" dur="0.48" conf="0.958"> **collègues** </Word>
<Latency stime="0.00" etime="2.19" seg="-0.7" avg="-0.7"/>
<Word stime="2.19" dur="0.52" conf="0.989"> **depuis** </Word>
<Word stime="2.75" dur="0.17" conf="0.989"> **2** </Word>
<Word stime="2.97" dur="0.19" conf="0.989"> **1000** </Word>
<Word stime="3.19" dur="0.27" conf="0.966"> **1** </Word>

en complément des tests **ça l' hiver** la grande nouveauté de la reprise
olivier veran **on** y reviendra sera le déploiement des auto- tests

depuis nous avons **euh** cherch**er** une solution qui puisse être accept**é**
par les groups politiqu**e** à propos de la 3ème partie de cet amendement

Figure 2: Examples of ASR transcripts: analysing the French utterance **Madame la présidente, chers collègues, depuis 2001**; showing an homophone (**ça l' hiver** → salivaires) and a wrongly inserted word (**on**); containing 3 inflection changes (cherch**er** → cherché; accept**é** → acceptée; politiqu**e** → politiques) and a hesitation (**euh**).

This paper focuses on French discourses, *i.e.* speeches delivered in reasonably good acoustic conditions and by speakers used to addressing large audiences. Under these particular conditions, we next identify the most challenging features of this kind of speeches that need to be tackled for better human or machine processing:

Sentence boundaries Speech units contained in transcripts do not always correspond to sentences as they are established in written text. Sentence boundaries provide a basis for further processing of natural language.

Punctuation Partially due to absence of sentence boundaries, no punctuation marks are produced by ASR systems in real time mode, a key feature for the legibility of speech transcriptions.

Capitalisation Transcriptions do not include correct capitalisation. A truecasing task is needed to assign each word its corresponding case information, usually depending on context.

Number representation Numbers provide a challenge for transcription, in particular number segmentation. See for instance the example of Figure 2 (top) where the uttered number 2001 is wrongly transcribed as a sequence of three numbers: 2, 1000 and 1. Both transcriptions may be possible, only the use of context can help to pick the right one.

Disfluencies Speech disfluencies such as hesitations, filled pauses, lengthened syllables, within-phrase silent pauses, repetitions are among the most frequent markers of spontaneity. Disfluencies are the most important source of discrepancies between spontaneous speech and text. Figure 2 (middle and bottom) shows transcripts with speech disfluencies.

Recognition errors ASR systems are error-prone. Multiple misrecognition types exist. For this work, we mainly consider errors due to homophones, missed utterances, wrongly inserted words and inflection changes. Figure 2 (middle and bottom) illustrates a transcript containing some of such errors.

3 Live Speech Translation

Our ST system is a standard cascading ASR-MT pipeline, where ASR outputs a French single-best hypothesis without punctuation, lower-cased, non segmented and containing multiple recognition disfluencies. To alleviate the ASR-MT mismatch we employ neural models that: (1) transform noisy ASR hypotheses into clean data (`FR2fr`) prior to translation (`fr2en`); (2) translate noisy ASR outputs (`FR2en`) and (3) performs both tasks at the same time, cleaning the ASR output and translation (`FR2fr:en`). Figure 3 illustrates the three translation pipelines implemented in this work that perform translation into English of French utterances. We use `FR` to indicate French transcripts while `fr` indicate French clean sentences.

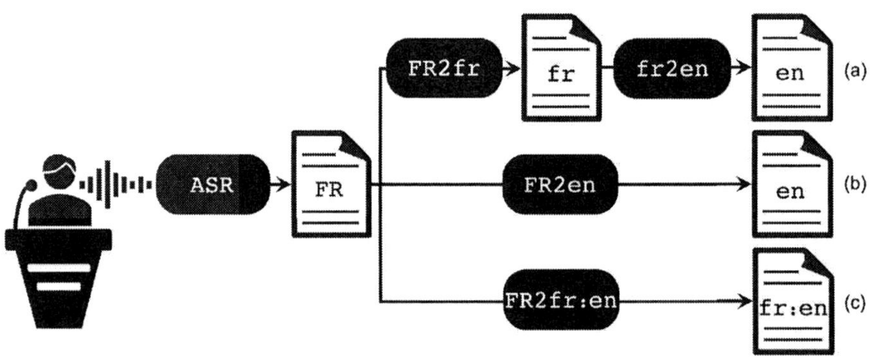

Figure 3: Speech translation pipelines.

High quality neural models can only be learned when feeded with large amounts of parallel data. Since there are scarce parallel noisy/clean resources for French, we decide to generate synthetic ASR noise from clean French texts for which English translations exist, thereby making the triplets noisy French/clean French/clean English available. In the next lines we detail the generation of different types of noise injected into clean French speeches to make them similar

t	FR	fr	en	fr:en
1	le	Le	The	Le
2	le palais	Le palais	The palace	Le palais
3	le palais est	Le palais est	The palace is	Le palais est
4	le palais est vite	Le palais est vide	The palace is empty	Le palais est vide
5	le palais est vite (pause)	Le palais est vide . (eos)	The palace is empty . (eos)	Le palais est vide . (eos) (en) The palace is empty . (eos)
6	le palais est vite (pause) le	Le palais est vide . (eos) le	The palace is empty . (eos) le	Le palais est vide . (eos) (en) The palace is empty . (eos) le
7	le palais est vite (pause) le roi	Le palais est vide . (eos) le roi	The palace is empty . (eos) le roi	Le palais est vide . (eos) (en) The palace is empty . (eos) le roi
8	. (eos) le roi et	Le roi est	The king is	Le roi est
9	. (eos) le roi et parti	Le roi est parti : (eos)	The king is gone : (eos)	Le roi est parti : (eos) (en) The king is gone : (eos)
10	. (eos) le roi et parti il	Le roi est parti : (eos) il	The king is gone : (eos) il	Le roi est parti : (eos) (en) The king is gone : (eos) il
11	. (eos) le roi et parti il reviens	Le roi est parti : (eos) il reviens	The king is gone : (eos) il reviens	Le roi est parti : (eos) (en) The king is gone : (eos) il reviens
12	: (eos) il reviens demain	il revient demain . (eos)	he returns tomorrow . (eos)	il revient demain . (eos) (en) he returns tomorrow . (eos)

Figure 4: Inference is performed for each new token output by the ASR. The first column indicates input streams feeded to our models at each time step t. The rest of columns show respectively the output produced by our **FR2fr**, **FR2en** and **FR2fr:en** networks. We use blue color to identify cleaned segmented French and green for cleaned segmented English translations.

to ASR transcripts. Notice that we consider a speech an arbitrary long and ordered sequence of sentences uttered by a speaker. Since ASR hypotheses do not segment speech into smaller units (sentences), we also delete such boundaries from our clean texts. The boundaries must therefore be predicted by our models.

Some noise options are tuned to generate in the training data natural discrepancies observed between text and real-time non-punctuated ASR output:

Repetitions Inserts 1 to 3 repetitions of a word with probability inversely proportional to word length, and decreasing probability according to the number of repetition (84% chance to repeat once, 13% to repeat twice, 3% to repeat 3 times).

Deletions Deletes a word with probability inversely proportional to word length.

Homophones Replaces a word with a word of different orthography but similar pronunciation, according to this homophone frequency in the language, with tolerance for frequent variation in French pronunciation ([e]/[ϵ]).

Numbers Replaces a string representing a number with a phonetically plausible decomposition of it (e.g. *2001* $\rightarrow$ *2 1000 1*).

Speechify Lower-cases words and strips punctuation.

Other options teach the model the ability to handle special tokens representing information available in ASR transcripts:

OOVs In train replaces random words with *(oov)*, in inference corresponds to genuine out of vocabulary words for the model.

Pauses In train replaces random punctuation signs with *(pause)*, in inference corresponds to pauses detected by the ASR.

Breaks In train replaces random final marks with *(break)*, in inference corresponds to a configurable pause in speaker's speech.

While current MT systems provide reasonable translation quality, users of live ST systems have to wait for the translation to be delivered. This greatly reduces the system's usefulness in practice. Limited translation delays are typically achieved via starting translation before the entire audio input is received, a practice that introduces important processing challenges Arivazhagan et al. (2020).

We tackle this problem by decoding the ASR output whenever new words become available. Figure 4 illustrates the inference steps performed by our networks when decoding the French ASR transcript *le palais est vite (pause) le roi et parti il reviens demain*[1]. Column **FR** indicates, in red color, words output by the ASR at each time step t. Columns **fr**, **en** and **fr:en** indicate the corresponding output of our models (respectively **FR2fr**, **FR2en** and **FR2fr:en**) for the input (**FR**) at time step t. Notice that input streams remove previous sentences when an end of sentence *(eos)* is predicted by our model followed by N words[2]. This strikes a fair balance between flexibility and stability for segmentation choices, allowing the model to reconsider its initial prediction while ensuring consistent choices to be retained. Notice also that after predicting *(eos)*, words output by our models consist of the same words output by the ASR, This allow us to identify the prefix to use when building new inputs (underlined strings). The prefix also contains the last token predicted for the previous sentence followed by *(eos)* to predict the case of the initial word of each sentence.

4 Experimental setup

pronounced	Ces alignements-là pour que le système d'intelligence artificielle fonctionne, il faut le faire sur beaucoup beaucoup de données.
transcript	ces alignements la pour que le système d'Intelligence artificielle fonctionne il faut le faire sur beaucoup beaucoup de données
FR2fr	Ces alignements là pour que le système d'intelligence artificielle fonctionne, il faut le faire sur beaucoup de données.
FR2fr+fr2en	These alignments there for the artificial intelligence system to work, it must be done on a lot of data.
Pronounced	J'en, on voit quand même qu'il y avait des choses qui fonctionnent pas mal.
Transcript	Jean on voit quand même qu'il y avait des choses qui fonctionne pas mal
FR2fr	Jean, on voit quand même qu'il y avait des choses qui ne fonctionnent pas mal.
FR2fr+fr2en	Jean, we can still see that there were some things that did not work badly.

Figure 5: Examples where **FR2fr** model segments and punctuates the ASR output, correcting homophones, repetition and missing words. We observe that further work could tackle multi-word homophones or quasi-homophones and written rewording of speech-specific structures.

Transcript	et c'est ici que s'est produite la faillite fondamental de l' homme (pause) si fondamental que toutes les autres en découle merci
fr2en	And here's the fundamental bankruptcy of the human, if all the others are thank.
FR2fr	Et c'est ici que s'est produite la faillite fondamentale de l'homme, si fondamentale que toutes les autres en découlent. merci
FR2fr+fr2en	And here's the fundamental bankruptcy of man, so fundamental that all others derive from it. thank you.
FR2en	And this is where the fundamental human failure has taken place. So fundamental. Thank you for all the other things
FR2fr:en	And this is where the fundamental human failure has taken place. So fundamental. Thank you for all the other things.
Reference	[...] And here occurred man's fundamental failure, so fundamental that all other failures ensue it ..." Thank you.

Figure 6: Example where **FR2fr+fr2en** achieves the best translation by correcting homophones and meaningfully segmenting (in red incorrect segmentations incurred by other models).

4.1 Datasets

Table 1 provides some statistics on the parallel French-English corpora employed for in this work. Statistics are computed after a light tokenization (splitting off punctuation). We employ for training available corpora close to the political discourse domain consisting on: EPPS Tiedemann (2012) (proceedings of the European Parliament), TEDX Reimers and Gurevych (2020) (subtitles of TED talks), and UNPC Ziemski et al. (2016) (official records and documents of the United Nations Parliament). For testing we use the testsets from two multilingual ST corpus,

[1]The transcript contains a pause indication *(pause)* and 3 ASR recognition errors: *vite* instead of *vide*, *et* instead of *est* and *reviens* instead of *revient*.

[2]In the example we use $N = 2$

EPST Iranzo-Sánchez et al. (2020)(Europarl ST) and MTEDXSalesky et al. (2021) (Multilingual TEDx). All data is pre-processed using the OpenNMT tokenizer[3].

Corpus	Sentences	Words		Vocab	
		En	Fr	En	Fr
Train					
EPPS	2.1M	57.7M	66.7M	97.7k	126.9k
TEDX	0.4M	8.4M	9.1M	79.3k	101.7k
UNPC	30.3M	792.5M	1016.3M	945.5k	1007.4k
Test					
EPST	1804	50k	55k	5.4k	6.4k
MTEDX	1059	18k	21k	3.1k	3.4k

Table 1: Statistics of parallel corpora used for train and test sets.

4.2 Network and Training Details

All our models follow the Transformer architecture Vaswani et al. (2017) implemented by the `OpenNMT-tf`[4] toolkit. More precisely, our **fr2en**, **FR2fr**, **FR2en** and **FR2fr:en** models use: Word embedding size: 1024; Number of layers: 6; Number of heads in multi-head self-attention layer: 16; Inner dimension of feedforward layer: 4096; Dropout rate: 0.1. Our **FR2fr** model uses a smaller version of the same architecture with: Word embedding size: 512; Number of layers: 4; Number of heads in multi-head self-attention layer: 8; Inner dimension of feedforward layer: 1024; In all cases, we use shared embeddings for both the input and output layers. The encoder and decoder use the same BPE units learned from source and target corpora with $16,000$ merge operations. Learning is performed over 1 GPU during $300K$ steps with a batch size of $64K$ tokens per step. We applied label smoothing to the cross-entropy loss with a rate of 0.1. Resulting models are built after averaging the last five checkpoints of the training process.

In order to build our **FR2xx** models we need parallel speeches rather than parallel sentences: to simulate consecutive sentences we join lists of 5 to 25 random sentences of the corpora. Note that inter-sentence context is only employed by our models to predict the case of the initial word of each sentence. All our experiments use ASR transcripts produced by VoxSigma web service API by Vocapia Research[5], a state-of-the-art neural ASR system for French language.

5 Experimental Results

Table 2 indicates BLEU[6] accuracy results of our three different pipelines as detailed in Figure 3 as well as the **fr2en** system that is trained on clean parallel texts.

As it can be seen, the **fr2en** model, trained on clean parallel data, exhibits the worst results. Differences in training and inference data sets significantly impact performance. Concerning models learned using noisy source data, best BLEU performance is achieved by the **FR2en** model. We hypothesize that **FR2fr+fr2en** suffers from error propagation, which means errors introduced in the first module **FR2fr** can not be recovered by the **fr2en** module. Results by **FR2fr:en** are very similar to those obtained by **FR2fr+fr2en**. Despite its

[3]`https://github.com/OpenNMT/Tokenizer`
[4]`https://github.com/OpenNMT/OpenNMT-tf`
[5]`https://www.vocapia.com/voxsigma-speech-to-text.html`
[6]`https://github.com/mjpost/sacrebleu`

lower BLEU score, the model **`FR2fr+fr2en`** outputs clean **`fr`** transcripts, which is an important asset for some industry applications, and can impact segmentation and translation, as can be seen in Figure 6.

System	Europarl ST	MTEDX
`fr2en`	28.56	23.20
`FR2fr+fr2en`	32.65	29.53
`FR2en`	**35.21**	**32.86**
`FR2fr:en`	31.80	29.87

Table 2: BLEU score on Europarl ST and Multilingual TEDx testset

The presented framework delivers translations with very low delay rates. Each new word supplied by the ASR produces a new translation hypothesis which is immediately displayed to the user. Even though the segment being decoded can fluctuate (translation changes when including additional words), as soon as an end of segment *(eos)* followed by a fixed number of words is predicted, the segment remains unchanged. We encountered very limited fluctuations, impacting the last words of the hypotheses being decoded.

6 Conclusions

We presented a framework for live speech translation based on the cascaded approach. We proposed several techniques to automatically enrich clean parallel corpora with several noise types typically present in speech transcripts, thereby improving the system robustness to error propagation. We pay special attention to translation delay rates to enhance legibility for humans. Results indicate the suitability of the framework presented showing important accuracy gains when compared to a baseline system and attaining very low delay rates. We plan to extend this work using a transformer with dual decoder: a system that uses a single encoder for the ASR transcripts and two parallel decoders to produce a clean version of the transcript in the same language and its corresponding translation, with the ability to attend to each other. This way, we expect to obtain similar delay rates with improved translation accuracy than our best performing model, and to additionally produce clean transcripts.

Acknowledgements

The work presented in this paper was partially supported by the European Commission under contract H2020-787061 ANITA.

References

Arivazhagan, N., Cherry, C., Te, I., Macherey, W., Baljekar, P., and Foster, G. (2020). Re-translation strategies for long form, simultaneous, spoken language translation. In *ICASSP 2020-2020 IEEE International Conference on Acoustics, Speech and Signal Processing (ICASSP)*, pages 7919–7923. IEEE.

Bansal, S., Kamper, H., Lopez, A., and Goldwater, S. (2017). Towards speech-to-text translation without speech recognition. *CoRR*, abs/1702.03856.

Berard, A., Pietquin, O., Servan, C., and Besacier, L. (2016). Listen and translate: A proof of concept for end-to-end speech-to-text translation. *ArXiv*, abs/1612.01744.

Casacuberta, F., Ney, H., Och, F., Vidal, E., Vilar, J., Barrachina, S., García-Varea, I., Llorens, D., Martínez, C., Molau, S., Nevado, F., Pastor, M., Picó, D., Sanchis, A., and Tillmann, C. (2004). Some approaches to statistical and finite-state speech-to-speech translation. *Computer Speech & Language*, 18(1):25–47.

Dyer, C., Muresan, S., and Resnik, P. (2008). Generalizing word lattice translation. In *Proceedings of ACL-08: HLT*, pages 1012–1020, Columbus, Ohio. Association for Computational Linguistics.

Iranzo-Sánchez, J., Silvestre-Cerdà, J. A., Jorge, J., Roselló, N., Giménez, A., Sanchis, A., Civera, J., and Juan, A. (2020). Europarl-st: A multilingual corpus for speech translation of parliamentary debates. In *ICASSP 2020 - 2020 IEEE International Conference on Acoustics, Speech and Signal Processing (ICASSP)*, pages 8229–8233.

Li, D., Te, I., Arivazhagan, N., Cherry, C., and Padfield, D. (2021). Sentence boundary augmentation for neural machine translation robustness. In *ICASSP 2021-2021 IEEE International Conference on Acoustics, Speech and Signal Processing (ICASSP)*, pages 7553–7557. IEEE.

Makhija, K., Ho, T.-N., and Chng, E.-S. (2019). Transfer learning for punctuation prediction. In *2019 Asia-Pacific Signal and Information Processing Association Annual Summit and Conference (APSIPA ASC)*, pages 268–273.

Martucci, G., Cettolo, M., Negri, M., and Turchi, M. (2021). Lexical Modeling of ASR Errors for Robust Speech Translation. In *Proc. Interspeech 2021*, pages 2282–2286.

Matusov, E., Hillard, D., Magimai-Doss, M., Hakkani-Tur, D., Ostendorf, M., and Ney, H. (2007). Improving speech translation with automatic boundary prediction. In *8th Annual Conference of the International Speech Communication Association (INTERSPEECH 2007)*, pages 2449–2452.

Matusov, E., Kanthak, S., and Ney, H. (2006). Integrating speech recognition and machine translation: Where do we stand? In *2006 IEEE International Conference on Acoustics Speech and Signal Processing Proceedings*, volume 5, pages V–V.

Nguyen, B., Nguyen, V. B. H., Nguyen, H., Phuong, P. N., Nguyen, T., Do, Q. T., and Mai, L. C. (2019). Fast and accurate capitalization and punctuation for automatic speech recognition using transformer and chunk merging. *CoRR*, abs/1908.02404.

Niehues, J., Nguyen, T. S., Cho, E., Ha, T.-L., Kilgour, K., Müller, M., Sperber, M., Stüker, S., and Waibel, A. H. (2016). Dynamic transcription for low-latency speech translation. In *INTERSPEECH*.

Reimers, N. and Gurevych, I. (2020). Making monolingual sentence embeddings multilingual using knowledge distillation. In *Proceedings of the 2020 Conference on Empirical Methods in Natural Language Processing*. Association for Computational Linguistics.

Ruiz, N. and Federico, M. (2014). Assessing the impact of speech recognition errors on machine translation quality. In *Proceedings of the 11th Conference of the Association for Machine Translation in the Americas: MT Researchers Track*, pages 261–274, Vancouver, Canada. Association for Machine Translation in the Americas.

Ruiz, N., Gao, Q., Lewis, W., and Federico, M. (2015). Adapting machine translation models toward misrecognized speech with text-to-speech pronunciation rules and acoustic confusability. In *Proceedings of Interspeech 2015*.

Salesky, E., Wiesner, M., Bremerman, J., Cattoni, R., Negri, M., Turchi, M., Oard, D. W., and Post, M. (2021). Multilingual tedx corpus for speech recognition and translation.

Sperber, M., Neubig, G., Niehues, J., and Waibel, A. (2017a). Neural lattice-to-sequence models for uncertain inputs. In *Proceedings of the 2017 Conference on Empirical Methods in Natural Language Processing*, pages 1380–1389, Copenhagen, Denmark. Association for Computational Linguistics.

Sperber, M., Niehues, J., and Waibel, A. H. (2017b). Toward robust neural machine translation for noisy input sequences. In *Proceedings of the 15th Conference of the European Chapter of the Association for Computational Linguistics: Volume 2, Short Papers*.

Tiedemann, J. (2012). Parallel data, tools and interfaces in opus. In Chair), N. C. C., Choukri, K., Declerck, T., Dogan, M. U., Maegaard, B., Mariani, J., Odijk, J., and Piperidis, S., editors, *Proceedings of the Eight International Conference on Language Resources and Evaluation (LREC'12)*, Istanbul, Turkey. European Language Resources Association (ELRA).

Vaswani, A., Shazeer, N., Parmar, N., Uszkoreit, J., Jones, L., Gomez, A. N., Kaiser, L., and Polosukhin, I. (2017). Attention is all you need. In Guyon, I., Luxburg, U. V., Bengio, S., Wallach, H., Fergus, R., Vishwanathan, S., and Garnett, R., editors, *Advances in Neural Information Processing Systems 30*, pages 5998–6008. Curran Associates, Inc.

Waibel, A. and Fugen, C. (2008). Spoken language translation. *IEEE Signal Processing Magazine*, 25(3):70–79.

Weiss, R. J., Chorowski, J., Jaitly, N., Wu, Y., and Chen, Z. (2017). Sequence-to-sequence models can directly translate foreign speech.

Ziemski, M., Junczys-Dowmunt, M., and Pouliquen, B. (2016). The United Nations parallel corpus v1.0. In *Proceedings of the Tenth International Conference on Language Resources and Evaluation (LREC'16)*, pages 3530–3534, Portorož, Slovenia. European Language Resources Association (ELRA).

Speech-to-Text and Evaluation of Multiple Machine Translation Systems

Evelyne Tzoukermann evelyne.tzoukermann@nvtc.gov
Steven Van Guilder sevanguilder@nvtc.gov
Jennifer Doyon jennifer.doyon@nvtc.gov
Ekaterina Harke eharke@nvtc.gov
National Virtual Translation Center, Washington, DC, USA

Abstract

The National Virtual Translation Center (NVTC) and the larger Federal Bureau of Investigation (FBI) seek to acquire tools that will facilitate its mission to provide English translations of non-English language audio and video files. In the text domain, NVTC has been using translation memory (TM) for some time and has reported on the incorporation of machine translation (MT) into that workflow. While we have explored the use of speech-to-text (STT) and speech translation (ST) in the past, we have now invested in the creation of a substantial human-created corpus to thoroughly evaluate alternatives in three languages: French, Russian, and Persian. We report on the results of multiple STT systems combined with four MT systems for these languages. We evaluated and scored the different systems in combination and analyzed results. This points the way to the most successful tool combination to deploy in this workflow.

1. Introduction

We report on the evaluation of multiple speech-to-text (STT) systems combined with four machine translation (MT) systems in order to perform comparisons on each combination. The goal of this project was to determine which combination of STT and MT systems would be optimal for a given language. That way, translators can benefit from this evaluation and use the optimal combination for any of these three languages. By combining and testing different configurations of STT and MT in a novel way, we have been able to determine strengths and weaknesses of these different workflows. In 2021, we reported on STT performance comparison and evaluation (see Miller et al. 2021). This year, we are presenting the results of the performance of multiple MT systems combined with the STT systems from last year. More specifically, we report on the evaluation of three to seven speech-to-text systems with four machine translation (MT) systems in order to perform comparisons for each combination. For French, we also compared the results with a speech translation system (all-in-one). The paper presents results and analysis of combinations for French, Russian, and Persian.

2. Evaluation Corpus

The corpus for this evaluation was comprised of two hours of audio for each language, which corresponded roughly to 2,000 sentences for each of these languages. French was based on a conversational document where a set of experts gathered in a panel, in person and virtually, to discuss state-of-the art in technological innovations in the space domain. Russian data collected was also conversational speech discussing technical innovations in the additive manufacturing and 3D printing domain. The Persian data was a broadcast interview on cybersecurity, cyber attacks and strategies for defense. Prior work (Miller et al. 2021) provides more detail on the data selected, and the processes put in place for manual transcription, manual translation, as well as descriptions of the different STT systems that were used.

3. Systems and Scoring

We provide results for a multi-system comparison of French, Russian, and Persian. Table 1 lists all of the STT systems that were used[1]. STT-COTS are commercial-off-the-shelf STTs whereas STT-GOTS are government-off-the-shelf STT systems. As shown on the table, Russian is the only language on which seven STT systems were available to be run and analyzed. French was run on five available systems, which includes STT-COTS1 for European French and STT-COTS1-1 for Canadian French. Persian was run on the only three systems that were able to process Persian. For French only, we had access to a commercial, all-in-one speech system and the results are presented in the French Results section.

STT Systems	FRENCH	RUSSIAN	PERSIAN
STT-COTS1	FRE √	√	√
STT-COTS1-1	CAN √		
STT-COTS2	√	√	√
STT-COTS3	√	√	
STT-COTS4	√	√	
STT-COTS5		√	√
STT-GOTS1		√	
STT-GOTS2		√	

Table 1. Speech-to-text systems run with each of the three languages.

All but one of the four MT systems used in this project were commercial products. All three COTS products were multilingual, neural-based engines. The fourth system was a government product. This product was an integration of several, multilingual MT engines that employ a number of approaches for performing automatic translation, including direct and statistical methods[2]. This GOTS system is only available to government users. Table 2 lists the machine translation systems that were used in the combination.

MT Systems	FRENCH	RUSSIAN	PERSIAN
MT-COTS1	√	√	√
MT-COTS2	√	√	√
MT-COTS3	√	√	√
MT-GOTS1	√	√	√

Table 2. Machine translation systems used for the three languages.

Naturally, this yielded a very rich combination of STT systems and MT systems. The numbers of systems that were compared were as follows:

- 20 combinations for French
- 28 combinations for Russian
- 12 combinations for Persian

[1] For the sake of anonymity, we renamed all the systems by a number, differentiating them only by their commercial or government source.

[2] Direct machine translation systems are generally rule-based, whereas statistical machine translation systems learn how to translate by analyzing existing human translations based on bilingual text corpora.

This is the first time that we had the privilege of using such a large number of automatic tools in one of our evaluations. As a result, it generated a rich and comprehensive evaluation of multiple systems.

The BLEU (BiLingual Evaluation Understudy) metric was used to score the output of all the MT systems. BLEU is the commonly used metric for automatically evaluating machine-translated text (see Papineni et al. 2002 and NLTK[3]). The BLEU score is a number between zero and one that measures the similarity of the machine-translated text to a set of high-quality reference translations produced by human translators. It has been shown that BLEU scores tend to correlate with human judgment of translation quality (see Chen and Cherry 2014 and Banerjee and Lavie 2005)[4].

For the evaluation performed during this project, we had access to one human-produced reference translation available against which all the STT/MT workflow outputs were scored. The all-in-one pipeline was scored using this single human reference for comparison as well as using the output translations of all the STT/MT combinations to see if additional translation would yield different results when used as reference.

4. Speech-To-Text and Machine Translation Results

The following sections present the results of the different combinations for each of the four languages; the results are analyzed and discussed.

4.1. French Results

Table 3 shows the 20 system workflows along with the MT BLEU scores for each combination from the STT standpoint as opposed to Table 4 which shows results from the MT standpoint. The middle column displays the STT and MT specific workflow, and the numbers in the right column indicate the score for each. The higher the number, the better the score; red cells show lower scores than orange, yellow, and green cells. The green cells show the highest scores. The highest performing system pairs are STT-COTS2 + MT-COTS2 (line 19) followed by STT-COTS1-1 + MT-COTS2 (line 7), closely followed by STT-COTS2 + MT-COTS3 (line 20). The lowest performing system pair is STT-COTS3 + MT-GOTS1 (line 1), which is significantly lower. Although at first glance, the scores in Table 2 might look low, it is important to remember that these reflect a challenging pipeline from STT to MT.

[3] NLTK: nltk.translate.nist_score https://www.nltk.org/_modules/nltk/translate/nist_score.html

[4] Note that even human translators do not achieve a perfect BLEU score of 1.0. Several smoothing functions have been put forward for BLEU to deal with n-gram results of zero which often occur in higher-level n-grams. Since the overall BLEU score is the geometric mean of the different n-gram levels, a single n-gram result of zero would cause the overall score to be zero. The smoothing method used in this evaluation was a simple one put forward in the NIST Toolkit 'mteval-v13a.pl', where the first zero value encountered was assigned a value of ½, the second was assigned a value of ¼, the third a value of 1/8, and so on (See Papineni et al. 2002).

	French STT/MT Combinations	BLEU Scores
1	STT-COTS3 + MT-GOTS1	0.07779377
2	STT-COTS3 + MT-COTS1	0.12499899
3	STT-COTS3 + MT-COTS2	0.13734244
4	STT-COTS3 + MT-COTS3	0.12797222
5	STT-COTS1-1 + MT-GOTS1	0.15692103
6	STT-COTS1-1 + MT-COTS1	0.26834392
7	STT-COTS1-1 + MT-COTS2	0.30656324
8	STT-COTS1-1 + MT-COTS3	0.2770375
9	STT-COTS1 + MT-GOTS1	0.14525775
10	STT-COTS1 + MT-COTS1	0.25602079
11	STT-COTS1 + MT-COTS2	0.29186129
12	STT-COTS1 + MT-COTS3	0.26635345
13	STT-COTS4 + MT-GOTS1	0.1488969
14	STT-COTS4 + MT-COTS1	0.2354315
15	STT-COTS4 + MT-COTS2	0.26638751
16	STT-COTS4 + MT-COTS3	0.24955649
17	STT-COTS2 + MT-GOTS1	0.15188625
18	STT-COTS2 + MT-COTS1	0.27867294
19	STT-COTS2 + MT-COTS2	0.31683667
20	STT-COTS2 + MT-COTS3	0.29572112

Table 3. Twenty (20) STT and MT system combinations with BLEU scores for French

Table 4 synthesizes the system combinations showing the results from the MT system standpoint. Again, colors are very helpful to visualize the results. STT-COTS3 is clearly a low STT performer, and MT-GOTS1 is a low MT performer. In contrast, STT-COTS2 and MT-COTS2 show the highest performance, and MT-COTS2 remains a high performing system when paired with the other STT systems as well.

MT Systems	STT Systems				
	STT-COTS3	STT-COTS1-1	STT-COTS1	STT-COTS4	STT-COTS2
MT-GOTS1	0.077793768	0.156921027	0.145257748	0.148896898	0.151886249
MT-COTS1	0.124998991	0.268343922	0.25602079	0.235431496	0.278672936
MT-COTS2	0.137342442	0.306563239	0.291861286	0.266387507	0.316836666
MT-COTS3	0.127972218	0.277037504	0.266353446	0.249556491	0.295721118

Table 4. The 20 STT and MT systems from the MT standpoint for French

French was also evaluated on an all-in-one system consisting of integrated STT and MT to produce an English text translation of the French audio source. Note that we evaluated and compared two different versions for ST-COTS2[5], a January and February version, which returned slightly different results. Table 5 shows three sets of results. The results in A show the

[5] ST-COTS2 is based on STT-COTS2 and MT-COTS2, both high performing systems.

system scores after ingesting the audio, getting the English text, and scoring the results using the human translation as a reference. The B section results show the same process, but this time using the four machine translation outputs as reference translations, and not the human translation. Section C results show the same operation again, this time using the human translation as well as the other four machine translations as reference translations, for a total of five reference translations. For the BLEU score, the more reference translations, the better the system scores, because the addition of translation variants increases the system translation. The resulting scores in Table 5 clearly demonstrates this effect, and the five reference translations in C exhibit the highest translation scores. It is important to note that the results in sections B and C ranging from .78 to .85 are several orders of magnitude higher than the STT-MT combinations in Tables 3 and 4, varying from 0.316836666 to 0.316836666.

	All-in-One Speech Translation	Bleu Scores
A	ST-COTS2 January (1 human reference translation)	0.32152296
	ST-COTS2 February (1 human reference translation)	0.321454151
B	ST-COTS2 January (4 MT translations)	0.779563801
	ST-COTS2 February (4 MT translations)	0.797920901
C	ST-COTS2 January (1 human + 4 MT translations)	0.876123775
	ST-COTS2 February (1 human + 4 MT translations)	0.846498433

Table 5. Three ST systems with variable number of reference translations.

4.2. Russian Results

Russian, as mentioned earlier, was processed with the highest number of STT systems, that is seven (7). Table 6 shows the STT/MT combinations with BLEU scores. This time, the three dominant systems are STT-GOTS2 + MT-COTS2, as shown in line 27 of Table 6, STT-GOTS1 + MT-COTS2 in line 23, and STT-GOTS2 + MT-COTS3 (in line 28). Interestingly, these 3 combinations both have used a version of STT-GOTS, the government created systems. The 3 worst performing combinations are STT-COTS4 + MT-GOTS1 (line 13), STT-COTS1 + MT-COTS3 (line 4), and STT-COTS2 + MT-GOTS1 in line 5.

	Russian STT/MT Combinations	BLEU Scores
1	STT-COTS1 + MT-GOTS1	0.071936558
2	STT-COTS1 + MT-COTS1	0.128206719
3	STT-COTS1 + MT-COTS2	0.153879991
4	STT-COTS1 + MT-COTS3	0.064070521
5	STT-COTS2 + MT-GOTS1	0.064070521
6	STT-COTS2 + MT-COTS1	0.162268592
7	STT-COTS2 + MT-COTS2	0.148891882
8	STT-COTS2 + MT-COTS3	0.140978788
9	STT-COTS3 + MT-GOTS1	0.068786887
10	STT-COTS3 + MT-COTS1	0.107556239
11	STT-COTS3 + MT-COTS2	0.143115371
12	STT-COTS3 + MT-COTS3	0.131434129

13	STT-COTS4 + MT-GOTS1	0.045528381
14	STT-COTS4 + MT-COTS1	0.065932173
15	STT-COTS4 + MT-COTS2	0.093096203
16	STT-COTS4 + MT-COTS3	0.083497782
17	STT-COTS5 + MT-GOTS1	0.068218524
18	STT-COTS5 + MT-COTS1	0.101121023
19	STT-COTS5 + MT-COTS2	0.140348315
20	STT-COTS5 + MT-COTS3	0.129364632
21	STT-GOTS1 + MT-GOTS1	0.082513608
22	STT-GOTS1 + MT-COTS1	0.144663213
23	STT-GOTS1 + MT-COTS2	0.174511147
24	STT-GOTS1 + MT-COTS3	0.153340608
25	STT-GOTS2 + MT-GOTS1	0.089778715
26	STT-GOTS2 + MT-COTS1	0.157261373
27	STT-GOTS2 + MT-COTS2	0.190733115
28	STT-GOTS2 + MT-COTS3	0.168950871

Table 6. Twenty-eight (28) STT and MT system combinations with BLEU scores from the STT standpoint for Russian

Table 7 outlines MT scores. Indeed, MT-GOTS1 performs significantly lower than the other systems. The table shows how the combination with STT-COTS4 generates poor results. On the other hand, MT-COTS2 is the highest performing MT system except when in combination with STT-COTS4. This demonstrates how strong MT-COTS2 performs but that its performance is negatively impacted with the weaker STT-COTS4.

STT systems	STT systems			
	MT-GOTS1	MT-COTS1	MT-COTS2	MT-COTS3
STT-COTS1	0.071936558	0.128206719	0.153879991	0.064070521
STT-COTS2	0.064070521	0.162268592	0.148891882	0.140978788
STT-COTS3	0.068786887	0.107556239	0.143115371	0.131434129
STT-COTS4	0.045528381	0.065932173	0.093096203	0.083497782
STT-COTS5	0.068218524	0.101121023	0.140348315	0.129364632
STT-GOTS1	0.082513608	0.144663213	0.174511147	0.153340608
STT-GOTS2	0.089778715	0.157261373	0.190733115	0.168950871

Table 7. The twenty-eight (28) STT and MT systems from the MT standpoint for Russian

4.3. Persian Results

The Persian data was run on three STT systems and three MT systems. STT-COTS1 and STT-COTS2 performed well (see lines 2, 3, 4, and 6, 7, 8) except when combined with MT-GOTS1 (see lines 1 and 5). In contrast, STT-COTS5 did not perform well with any of the MT systems and shows the lowest results when associated with MT-GOTS1 (see line 9).

	Persian STT/MT Combinations	Bleu Scores
1	STT-COTS1 + MT-GOTS1	0.076480559
2	STT-COTS1 + MT-COTS1	0.155602641
3	STT-COTS1 + MT-COTS2	0.139287289
4	STT-COTS1 + MT-COTS3	0.131836115
5	STT-COTS2 + MT-GOTS1	0.092067026
6	STT-COTS2 + MT-COTS1	0.186981095
7	STT-COTS2 + MT-COTS2	0.186434702
8	STT-COTS2 + MT-COTS3	0.168386801
9	STT-COTS5 + MT-GOTS1	0.047054087
10	STT-COTS5 + MT-COTS1	0.095733738
11	STT-COTS5 + MT-COTS2	0.099165053
12	STT-COTS5 + MT-COTS3	0.081293357

Table 8. The twelve (12) STT and MT system combinations with BLEU scores from the STT standpoint for Persian

In Table 9, we clearly see that the combinations between STT-COTS1, STT-COTS2 and all of the MT-COTS systems is superior to the combinations with MT-GOTS1.

STT Systems	STT Systems			
	MT-GOTS1	MT-COTS1	MT-COTS2	MT-COTS3
STT-COTS1	0.076480559	0.155602641	0.13928729	0.131836115
STT-COTS2	0.092067026	0.186981095	0.1864347	0.168386801
STT-COTS5	0.047054087	0.095733738	0.09916505	0.081293357

Table 9. The twelve (12) STT and MT systems from the MT standpoint for Persian

4.4. Summary of Results across Languages

We compare here the highest combinations for the four languages in order to gain a deeper understanding of why each combination might be more (or less) effective. The first observation, as mentioned in the French results section, is that the scores of French ST (line 1 in Table 10) is several orders of magnitude higher than the French STT-MT combination. Our initial conjecture is that STT and MT working in tandem allow for the optimal translation. The system appears to be selecting the optimal hypothesis in the joint language models of French and English (see Matusov et al. 2005 and Lamel et al. 2011). These ideas will be further explored. The second observation is that the results of French STT-MT are almost two times better than the other languages. We believe that this may be due to the fact that French STT-MT pairs are more mature, thus more robust than they are for the other languages.

	Languages	STT/MT combinations	Bleu scores
1	French	ST-COTS2 with 1 human + 4 MT translation references	0.876123775
2	French	STT-COTS2 + MT-COTS2	0.31683667
3	Russian	STT-GOTS2 + MT-COTS2	0.190733115
4	Persian	STT-COTS2 + MT-COTS1	0.186981095

Table 10. Highest performing STT-MT Combinations

5. Conclusion[6]

The goal of this project is to determine which combination of STT and MT systems would be optimal for a given language in order to optimize an audio to translation workflow. We had access to STTs and MTs systems and analyzed 60 combinations. The results provided in the paper demonstrate very clearly the strong and poor STT and MT combinations. Our evaluation results show that for French, the speech translation (all-in-one system) along with multiple reference translations appears to be the best selection for integration into the NVTC workflow. Of course, this depends on the maturity of the systems, and we have observed these results since the selected French ST-COTS2 very robust. We are planning on exploring the use of ST-COTS2 on other languages to see if the conclusions appear to be the same as for French.

References

Banerjee, S., & Lavie, A. (2005, June). METEOR: An automatic metric for MT evaluation with improved correlation with human judgments. In Proceedings of the ACL workshop on intrinsic and extrinsic evaluation measures for machine translation and/or summarization (pp. 65-72).

Chen, B., & Cherry, C. (2014, June). A systematic comparison of smoothing techniques for sentence-level bleu. In Proceedings of the ninth workshop on statistical machine translation (pp. 362-367).

Lamel, L., Courcinous, S., Despres, J., Gauvain, J. L., Josse, Y., Kilgour, K., ... & Woehrling, C. (2011). Speech recognition for machine translation in Quaero. In *Proceedings of the 8th International Workshop on Spoken Language Translation: Evaluation Campaign*.

Matusov, E., Kanthak, S., & Ney, H. (2005). On the integration of speech recognition and statistical machine translation. In *Ninth European Conference on Speech Communication and Technology*.

Miller, C., Tzoukermann, E., Doyon, J., & Mallard, E. (2021, August). Corpus Creation and Evaluation for Speech-to-Text and Speech Translation. In Proceedings of Machine Translation Summit XVIII: Users and Providers Track (pp. 44-53).

Papineni, K., Roukos, S., Ward, T., & Zhu, W. J. (2002, July). Bleu: a method for automatic evaluation of machine translation. In Proceedings of the 40th annual meeting of the Association for Computational Linguistics (pp. 311-318).

Reiter, E. (2018). A structured review of the validity of BLEU. Computational Linguistics, 44(3), 393-401.

Tzoukermann, E. and Miller, C. (2018). Evaluating Automatic Speech Recognition in Translation. In *Proceedings of AMTA 2018*, vol. 2, pages 294-302, Boston.

[6] The authors would like to thank Dr. Corey Miller for his contributions.

Association for Computational Linguistics
209 N. Eighth Street
Stroudsburg, Pennsylvania 18360

ISBN 978-1-7138-6758-6

CURRAN ASSOCIATES INC.
proceedings.com